Get the eBooks FREE!

(PDF, ePub, and Kindle all included)

We believe that once you buy a book from us, you should be able to read it in any format we have available. To get electronic versions of this book at no additional cost to you, purchase and then register this book at the Manning website following the instructions inside this insert.

That's it!
Thanks from Manning!

To register this book and download your free ebook:
1. Go to http://www.manning.com/ebookoffer
2. Enter the codes from this table when prompted
3. Download ebook using link emailed to you

	A	B	C	D	E	F	G	H	I
1	VW 730 7595	BG 345 7196	BG 841 3290	EE 138 2362	OA 734 2679	CD 428 5257	QN 376 2671	OF 349 1567	BH 365 6269
2	JH 682 6230	KK 347 0182	GD 533 7442	MT 125 0749	QJ 244 3771	TF 722 4944	GX 231 6346	BI 510 8696	JU 900 7373
3	SB 966 2463	GB 335 1971	FA 870 1161	WG 971 3631	AU 292 9476	ER 530 6581	RE 430 6666	RJ 153 8718	JC 486 7158
4	II 290 5690	CT 608 3811	GW 631 7016	MO 265 4344	FU 908 7363	YI 706 2916	US 906 2952	SX 815 2995	YO 830 8390
5	NW 694 9190	CN 474 0096	XU 329 3932	RW 246 9239	FC 586 2708	SB 176 1485	WO 379 5122	UT 674 5942	FV 196 1530
6	OI 646 3573	LX 600 9095	UK 563 6122	WA 612 5320	QD 606 6935	PE 231 6140	BG 472 3756	XP 136 0084	HS 637 0506

	A	B	C	D	E	F	G	H	I
7	**LY 451 6958**	JF 659 9062	TR 401 9803	RD 901 2695	**MM 916 7156**	**XP 655 6035**	**UO 850 5305**	**RA 648 7519**	BG 907 0808
8	QV 701 7684	CA 141 6028	YK 391 4152	TK 413 4921	OD 585 4302	VM 742 8018	BS 899 7668	NH 420 7452	IC 681 0111
9	IF 979 8511	AJ 329 9113	LB 331 1706	KW 224 5519	**KD 667 7628**	QS 131 1614	VI 849 2172	CM 286 8173	YL 886 9044
10	**LF 568 0899**	NJ 771 4819	CV 323 6804	DE 343 3785	UT 793 8534	DC 349 9776	FJ 628 6865	PV 231 3831	**OG 286 1832**
11	**PM 352 0701**	QD 696 2169	**UH 701 1601**	JA 433 1338	RB 571 0764	**QD 591 0643**	**US 899 4387**	MK 271 1738	MM 416 1241
12	YF 296 2631	**AQ 638 0290**	BD 417 9291	JV 831 3803	**VK 762 5983**	**EQ 812 4491**	RD 702 8658	HA 679 4159	**QV 514 2917**
13	**JV 416 8318**	MQ 742 5637	**FI 992 3015**	LG 862 5635	RN 864 1497	YC 249 3310	BV 226 9501	SJ 142 6769	**GC 665 3750**
14	KL 651 9998	VN 152 1424	WE 226 7837	QU 391 3757	LS 455 0411	CJ 413 0830	**OQ 236 1456**	UA 598 5620	QV 989 7262
15	**BG 746 7407**	TX 105 0869	UG 584 6510	**RI 672 0155**	**EY 311 1549**	IO 655 2155	**PO 266 1818**	EO 857 6859	KR 504 7696
16	GQ 923 4031	**MW 350 3087**	**WW 773 8659**	AT 407 2344	WU 577 6252	PX 759 1602	HW 768 9421	**OJ 223 7194**	**MM 856 3998**
17	**CQ 578 3555**	OC 436 2067	MN 380 1384	ST 834 6995	OA 270 6904	**EK 213 4708**	TC 743 9959	YW 495 6870	**NP 931 4690**
18	TU 540 5317	**ML 138 9685**	PA 870 4911	WI 499 2017	DS 412 9330	MD 877 4317	RL 126 2645	**FB 373 6017**	LE 392 4422
19	**KL 351 7534**	**UJ 286 6109**	FH 872 0019	QE 438 4306	BG 165 3807	XQ 773 6477	HI 541 5794	QB 131 7095	MS 587 4094
20	CU 730 6235	YP 839 4114	RV 449 9202	**DM 170 6917**	**FH 507 8731**	FN 714 9798	OM 354 0181	BQ 971 8415	**DT 749 7497**

Praise for the Second Edition

A masterpiece about C#.

—Kirill Osenkov, Microsoft C# Team

If you are looking to master C# then this book is a must-read.

—Tyson S. Maxwell
Sr. Software Engineer, Raytheon

We're betting that this will be the best C# 4.0 book out there.

—Nikander Bruggeman and Margriet Bruggeman
.NET consultants, Lois & Clark IT Services

A useful and engaging insight into the evolution of C# 4.

—Joe Albahari
Author of *LINQPad* and *C# 4.0 in a Nutshell*

One of the best C# books I have ever read.

—Aleksey Nudelman
CEO, C# Computing, LLC

This book should be required reading for all professional C# developers.

—Stuart Caborn
Senior Developer, BNP Paribas

A highly focused, master-level resource on language updates across all major C# releases. This book is a must-have for the expert developer wanting to stay current with new features of the C# language.

—Sean Reilly, Programmer/Analyst
Point2 Technologies

Why read the basics over and over again? Jon focuses on the chewy, new stuff!

—Keith Hill, Software Architect
Agilent Technologies

Everything you didn't realize you needed to know about C#.

—Jared Parsons
Senior Software Development Engineer
Microsoft

Praise for the First Edition

Simply put, C# in Depth is perhaps the best computer book I've read.
—Craig Pelkie, Author, *System iNetwork*

I have been developing in C# from the very beginning and this book had some nice surprises even for me. I was especially impressed with the excellent coverage of delegates, anonymous methods, covariance and contravariance. Even if you are a seasoned developer, C# in Depth will teach you something new about the C# language... This book truly has depth that no other C# language book can touch.
—Adam J. Wolf
Southeast Valley .NET User Group

I enjoyed reading the whole book; it is well-written—the samples are easy to understand. I actually found it very easy to engage into the whole lambda expressions topic and really liked the chapter about lambda expressions.
—Jose Rolando Guay Paz
Web Developer, CSW Solutions

This book wraps up the author's great knowledge of the inner workings of C# and hands it over to readers in a well-written, concise, usable book.
—Jim Holmes
Author of *Windows Developer Power Tools*

Every term is used appropriately and in the right context, every example is spot-on and contains the least amount of code that shows the full extent of the feature...this is a rare treat.
—Franck Jeannin, Amazon UK reviewer

If you have developed using C# for several years now, and would like to know the internals, this book is absolutely right for you.
—Golo Roden
Author, Speaker, and Trainer for .NET
and related technologies

The best C# book I've ever read.
—Chris Mullins, C# MVP

C# in Depth

THIRD EDITION

JON SKEET

MANNING
SHELTER ISLAND

For online information and ordering of this and other Manning books, please visit
www.manning.com. The publisher offers discounts on this book when ordered in quantity.
For more information, please contact

> Special Sales Department
> Manning Publications Co.
> 20 Baldwin Road
> PO Box 261
> Shelter Island, NY 11964.

 Manning Publications Co.   Development editor   Jeff Bleiel
20 Baldwin Road   Copyeditor: Andy Carroll
PO Box 261   Proofreader: Katie Tennant
Shelter Island, NY 11964   Typesetter: Dottie Marsico
                                 Cover designer: Marija Tudor

ISBN 9781617291340
Printed in the United States of America
3 4 5 6 7 8 9 10 – MAL – 18 17 16 15 14

To my boys, Tom, Robin, and William

brief contents

         13   ▪   Minor changes to simplify code   371
         14   ▪   Dynamic binding in a static language   409

PART 5   C# 5: ASYNCHRONY MADE SIMPLE 461

         15   ▪   Asynchrony with async/await   463
         16   ▪   C# 5 bonus features and closing thoughts   519

contents

ix

foreword

There are two kinds of pianists.

There are some pianists who play, not because they enjoy it, but because their parents force them to take lessons. Then there are those who play the piano because it pleases them to create music. They don't need to be forced; on the contrary, they sometimes don't know when to stop.

Of the latter kind, there are some who play the piano as a hobby. Then there are those who play for a living. That requires a higher level of dedication, skill, and talent. They may have some degree of freedom about what genre of music they play and the stylistic choices they make in playing it, but fundamentally those choices are driven by the needs of the employer or the tastes of the audience.

Of the latter kind, there are some who do it primarily for the money. Then there are those professionals who would want to play the piano in public even if they weren't being paid. They enjoy using their skills and talents to make music for others. That they can have fun and get paid for it is so much the better.

Of the latter kind, there are some who are self-taught, who play by ear, who might have great talent and ability, but can't communicate that intuitive understanding to others except through the music itself. Then there are those who have formal training in both theory and practice. They can explain what techniques the composer used to achieve the intended emotional effect, and use that knowledge to shape their interpretation of the piece.

Of the latter kind, there are some who have never looked inside their pianos. Then there are those who are fascinated by the clever escapements that lift the damper felts a fraction of a second before the hammers strike the strings. They own key levelers and capstan wrenches. They take delight and pride in being able to understand the mechanisms of an instrument that has 5–10,000 moving parts.

Of the latter kind, there are some who are content to master their craft and exercise their talents for the pleasure and profit it brings. Then there are those who are not just artists, theorists, and technicians; somehow they find the time to pass that knowledge on to others as mentors.

I have no idea if Jon Skeet is a pianist or musician of any sort. But from my email conversations with him as one of the C# team's Most Valuable Professionals over the years, from reading his blog, and from reading every word of each of his books at least three times, it has become clear to me that Jon is that latter kind of software developer: enthusiastic, knowledgeable, talented, curious, analytical—and a teacher of others.

C# is a highly pragmatic and rapidly evolving language. Through the addition of query comprehensions, richer type inference, a compact syntax for anonymous functions, and so on, I hope that we have enabled a whole new style of programming while still staying true to the statically typed, component-oriented approach that has made C# a success.

Many of these new stylistic elements have the paradoxical quality of feeling very old (lambda expressions go back to the foundations of computer science in the first half of the twentieth century) and yet at the same time feeling new and unfamiliar to developers used to a more modern object-oriented approach.

Jon gets all that. This book is ideal for professional developers who have a need to understand the *what* and *how* of the latest revision to C#. But it is also for those developers whose understanding is enriched by exploring the *why* of the language's design principles.

Being able to take advantage of all that new power requires new ways of thinking about data, functions, and the relationship between them. It's not unlike trying to play jazz after years of classical training—or vice versa. Either way, I'm looking forward to finding out what sorts of functional compositions the next generation of C# programmers come up with. Happy composing, and thanks for choosing the key of C# to do it in.

ERIC LIPPERT
C# ANALYSIS ARCHITECT
COVERITY

Oh boy. When writing this preface, I started off with the preface to the second edition, which began by saying how long it felt since writing the preface to the first edition. The second edition is now a distant memory, and the first edition seems like a whole different life. I'm not sure whether that says more about the pace of modern life or my memory, but it's a sobering thought either way.

The development landscape has changed enormously since the first edition, and even since the second. This has been driven by many factors, with the rise of mobile devices probably being the most obvious. But many challenges have remained the same. It's still hard to write properly internationalized applications. It's still hard to handle errors gracefully in all situations. It's still fairly hard to write correct multi-threaded applications, although this task has been made significantly simpler by both language and library improvements over the years.

Most importantly in the context of this preface, I believe developers still need to know the language they're using at a level where they're confident in how it will behave. They may not know the fine details of every API call they're using, or even some of the obscure corner cases of the language that they don't happen to use,[1] but the core of the language should feel like a solid friend that the developer can rely on to behave predictably.

In addition to the letter of the language you're developing in, I believe there's great benefit in understanding its spirit. While you may occasionally find you have a fight on your hands however hard you try, if you attempt to make your code work in the way the language designers intended, your experience will be a much more pleasant one.

---

[1] I have a confession to make: I know very little about unsafe code and pointers in C#. I've simply never needed to find out about them.

acknowledgments

You might expect that putting together a third edition—and one where the main change consists of two new chapters—would be straightforward. Indeed, writing the "green field" content of chapters 15 and 16 was the easy part. But there's a lot more to it than that—tweaking little bits of language throughout the rest of the book, checking for any aspects which were fine a few years ago but don't quite make sense now, and generally making sure the whole book is up to the high standards I expect readers to hold it to. Fortunately, I have been lucky enough to have a great set of people supporting me and keeping the book on the straight and narrow.

Most importantly, my family have been as wonderful as ever. My wife Holly is a children's author herself, so our kids are used to us having to lock ourselves away for a while to meet editorial deadlines, but they've remained cheerfully encouraging throughout. Holly herself takes all of this in stride, and I'm grateful that she's never reminded me just how many books she's started from scratch and completed in the time I've been working on this third edition.

The formal peer reviewers are listed later on, but I'd like to add a note of personal thanks to all those who ordered early access copies of this third edition, finding typos and suggesting changes...also constantly asking when the book was coming out. The very fact that I had readers who were eager to get their hands on the finished book was a huge source of encouragement.

I always get on well with the team at Manning, and it's been a pleasure to work with some familiar friends from the first edition as well as newcomers. Mike Stephens and Jeff Bleiel have guided the whole process smoothly, as we decided what to change from the earlier editions and what to keep. They've generally put the whole thing into the right shape. Andy Carroll and Katie Tennant provided expert copyediting and proofreading, respectively, never once expressing irritation with my Englishness, pickiness, or general bewilderment. The production team has worked its magic in the background, as ever, but I'm grateful to them nonetheless: Dottie Marsico, Janet Vail, Marija Tudor, and Mary Piergies. Finally, I'd like to thank the publisher, Marjan Bace, for allowing me a third edition and exploring some interesting future options.

Peer review is immensely important, not only for getting the technical details of the book right, but also the balance and tone. Sometimes the comments we received have merely shaped the overall book; in other cases I've made very specific changes in response. Either way, all feedback has been welcome. So thanks to the following reviewers for making the book better for all of us: Andy Kirsch, Bas Pennings, Bret Colloff, Charles M. Gross, Dror Helper, Dustin Laine, Ivan Todorović, Jon Parish, Sebastian Martín Aguilar, Tiaan Geldenhuys, and Timo Bredenoort.

I'd particularly like to thank Stephen Toub and Stephen Cleary, whose early reviews of chapter 15 were invaluable. Asynchrony is a particularly tricky topic to write about clearly but accurately, and their expert advice made a very significant difference to the chapter.

Without the C# team, this book would have no cause to exist, of course. Their dedication to the language in design, implementation and testing is exemplary, and I look forward to seeing what they come up with next. Since the second edition was published, Eric Lippert has left the C# team for a new fabulous adventure, but I'm enormously grateful that he was still able to act as the tech reviewer for this third edition. I also thank him for the foreword that he originally wrote to the first edition and that is included again this time. I refer to Eric's thoughts on various matters throughout the book, and if you aren't already reading his blog (http://ericlippert.com), you really should be.

about this book

This is a book about C# from version 2 onward—it's as simple as that. I barely cover C# 1 and only cover the .NET Framework libraries and Common Language Runtime (CLR) when they're related to the language. This is a deliberate decision, and the result is a book quite different from most of the C# and .NET books I've seen.

By assuming a reasonable amount of knowledge of C# 1, I avoid spending hundreds of pages covering material that I think most people already understand. This gives me room to expand on the details of later versions of C#, which is what I hope you're reading the book for. When I wrote the first edition of this book, even C# 2 was relatively unknown to some readers. By now, almost all C# developers have some experience with the features introduced in C# 2, but I've still kept that material in this edition, as it's so fundamental to what comes later.

Who should read this book?

This book is squarely aimed at developers who already know some C#. For absolute maximum value, you'd know C# 1 well but know very little about later versions. There aren't many readers in that sweet spot any more, but I believe there are still lots of developers who can benefit from digging deeper into C# 2 and 3, even if they've already been using them for a while...and many developers haven't yet used C# 4 or 5 to any extent.

If you don't know any C# at all, this probably isn't the book for you. You could struggle through, looking up aspects you're not familiar with, but it wouldn't be a very efficient way of learning. You'd be better off starting with a different book, and then gradually adding *C# in Depth* to the mix. There's a wide variety of books that cover C#

from scratch, in many different styles. The *C# in a Nutshell* series (O'Reilly) has always been good in this respect, and *Essential C# 5.0* (Addison-Wesley Professional) is also a good introduction.

I'm not going to claim that reading this book will make you a fabulous coder. There's so much more to software engineering than knowing the syntax of the language you happen to be using. I give some words of guidance, but ultimately there's a lot more gut instinct in development than most of us would like to admit. What I will claim is that if you read and understand this book, you should feel comfortable with C# and free to follow your instincts without too much apprehension. It's not about being able to write code that no one else will understand because it uses unknown corners of the language; it's about being confident that you know the options available to you, and know which path the C# idioms are encouraging you to follow.

Roadmap

The book's structure is simple. There are five parts and three appendixes. The first part serves as an introduction, including a refresher on topics in C# 1 that are important for understanding later versions of the language, and that are often misunderstood. The second part covers the new features introduced in C# 2, the third part covers C# 3, and so on.

There are occasions when organizing the material this way means we'll come back to a topic a couple of times—in particular, delegates are improved in C# 2 and then again in C# 3—but there is method in my madness. I anticipate that a number of readers will be using different versions for different projects; for example, you may be using C# 4 at work, but experimenting with C# 5 at home. That means it's useful to clarify what is in which version. It also provides a feeling of context and evolution—it shows how the language has developed over time.

Chapter 1 sets the scene by taking a simple piece of C# 1 code and evolving it, seeing how later versions allow the source to become more readable and powerful. We'll look at the historical context in which C# has grown, and the technical context in which it operates as part of a complete platform; C# as a language builds on framework libraries and a powerful runtime to turn abstraction into reality.

Chapter 2 looks back at C# 1, and at three specific aspects: delegates, the type system characteristics, and the differences between value types and reference types. These topics are often understood "just well enough" by C# 1 developers, but as C# has evolved and developed them significantly, a solid grounding is required in order to make the most of the new features.

Chapter 3 tackles the biggest feature of C# 2, and potentially the hardest to grasp: generics. Methods and types can be written generically, with type parameters standing in for real types that are specified in the calling code. Initially it's as confusing as this description makes it sound, but once you understand generics, you'll wonder how you survived without them.

If you've ever wanted to represent a null integer, chapter 4 is for you. It introduces nullable types: a feature, built on generics, that takes advantage of support in the language, runtime, and framework.

Chapter 5 shows the improvements to delegates in C# 2. Until now, you may have only used delegates for handling events such as button clicks. C# 2 makes it easier to create delegates, and library support makes them more useful for situations other than events.

In chapter 6 we'll examine iterators, and the easy way to implement them in C# 2. Few developers use iterator blocks, but as LINQ to Objects is built on iterators, they'll become more and more important. The lazy nature of their execution is also a key part of LINQ.

Chapter 7 shows a number of smaller features introduced in C# 2, each making life a little more pleasant. The language designers have smoothed over a few rough places in C# 1, allowing more flexible interaction with code generators, better support for utility classes, more granular access to properties, and more.

Chapter 8 once again looks at a few relatively simple features—but this time in C# 3. Almost all the new syntax is geared toward the common goal of LINQ, but the building blocks are also useful in their own right. With anonymous types, automatically implemented properties, implicitly typed local variables, and greatly enhanced initialization support, C# 3 gives a far richer language with which your code can express its behavior.

Chapter 9 looks at the first major topic of C# 3—lambda expressions. Not content with the reasonably concise syntax discussed in chapter 5, the language designers have made delegates even easier to create than in C# 2. Lambdas are capable of more— they can be converted into expression trees, a powerful way of representing code as data.

In chapter 10 we'll examine extension methods, which provide a way of fooling the compiler into believing that methods declared in one type actually belong to another. At first glance this appears to be a readability nightmare, but with careful consideration it can be an extremely powerful feature—and one that's vital to LINQ.

Chapter 11 combines the previous three chapters in the form of query expressions, a concise but powerful way of querying data. Initially we'll concentrate on LINQ to Objects, but you'll see how the query expression pattern is applied in a way that allows other data providers to plug in seamlessly.

Chapter 12 is a quick tour of various different uses of LINQ. First we'll look at the benefits of query expressions combined with expression trees—how LINQ to SQL is able to convert what appears to be normal C# into SQL statements. We'll then move on to see how libraries can be designed to mesh well with LINQ, taking LINQ to XML as an example. Parallel LINQ and Reactive Extensions show two alternative approaches to in-process querying, and the chapter closes with a discussion of how you can extend LINQ to Objects with your own LINQ operators.

Coverage of C# 4 begins in chapter 13, where we'll look at named arguments and optional parameters, COM interop improvements, and generic variance. In some ways these are very separate features, but named arguments and optional parameters contribute to COM interop as well as the more specific abilities that are only available when working with COM objects.

Chapter 14 describes the single biggest feature in C# 4: dynamic typing. The ability to bind members dynamically at execution time instead of statically at compile time is a huge departure for C#, but it's applied selectively—only code that involves a dynamic value will be executed dynamically.

Chapter 15 is all about asynchrony. C# 5 only contains one major feature—the ability to write asynchronous functions. This single feature is simultaneously brain-bustingly complicated to understand thoroughly and awe-inspiringly elegant to use. At long last, we can write asynchronous code that doesn't read like spaghetti.

We'll wind down in chapter 16 with the remaining features of C# 5 (both of which are tiny) and some thoughts about the future.

The appendixes are all reference material. In appendix A, I cover the LINQ standard query operators, with some examples. Appendix B looks at the core generic collection classes and interfaces. Appendix C provides a brief look at the different versions of .NET, including the different flavors such as the Compact Framework and Silverlight.

Terminology, typography, and downloads

Most of the terminology of the book is explained as it goes along, but there are a few definitions that are worth highlighting here. I use C# 1, C# 2, C# 3, C# 4, and C# 5 in a reasonably obvious manner—but you may see other books and websites referring to C# 1.0, C# 2.0, C# 3.0, C# 4.0, and C# 5.0. The extra ".0" seems redundant to me, which is why I've omitted it—I hope the meaning is clear.

I've appropriated a pair of terms from a C# book by Mark Michaelis. To avoid the confusion between *runtime* being an execution environment (as in "the Common Language Runtime") and a point in time (as in "overriding occurs at runtime"), Mark uses *execution time* for the latter concept, usually in comparison with *compile time*. This seems to me to be a thoroughly sensible idea, and one that I hope catches on in the wider community. I'm doing my bit by following his example in this book.

I frequently refer to "the language specification" or just "the specification"—unless I indicate otherwise, this means the C# language specification. However, multiple versions of the specification are available, partly due to different versions of the language itself and partly due to the standardization process. Any section numbers provided are from the C# 5.0 language specification from Microsoft.

This book contains numerous pieces of code, which appear in a `fixed-width font like this`; output from the listings appears in the same way. Code annotations accompany some listings, and at other times particular sections of the code are shown in bold to highlight a change, improvement, or addition. Almost all of the code appears in snippet form, allowing it to stay compact but still runnable—within the right environment. That environment is Snippy, a custom tool that is introduced in section 1.8. Snippy is available for download, along with all of the code from the book (in the form of snippets, full Visual Studio solutions, or more often both) from the book's website at csharpindepth.com, as well as from the publisher's website at manning.com/CSharpinDepthThirdEdition.

Author Online and the C# in Depth website

Purchase of *C# in Depth, Third Edition* includes free access to a private web forum run by Manning Publications where you can make comments about the book, ask technical questions, and receive help from the author and other users. To access the forum and subscribe to it, point your web browser to www.manning.com/CSharpinDepth-ThirdEdition. This page provides information on how to get on the forum once you are registered, what kind of help is available, and the rules of conduct on the forum.

The Author Online forum and the archives of previous discussions will be accessible from the publisher's website as long as the book is in print.

In addition to Manning's own website, I have set up a companion website for the book at csharpindepth.com, containing information that didn't quite fit into the book, downloadable source code for all the listings in the book, and links to other resources.

about the author

I'm not a typical C# developer, I think it's fair to say. For the last five years, almost all of my time working with C# has been for fun—effectively as a somewhat obsessive hobby. At work, I've been writing server-side Java in Google London, and I can safely claim that few things help you to appreciate new language features more than having to code in a language that doesn't have them, but is similar enough to remind you of their absence.

I've tried to keep in touch with what other developers find hard about C# by keeping a careful eye on Stack Overflow, posting oddities to my blog, and occasionally talking about C# and related topics just about anywhere that will provide people to listen to me. Additionally, I'm actively developing an open source .NET date and time API called Noda Time (see http://nodatime.org). In short, C# is still coursing through my veins as strongly as ever.

For all these oddities—and despite my ever-surprising micro-celebrity status due to Stack Overflow—I'm a very ordinary developer in many other ways. I write plenty of code that makes me grimace when I come back to it. My unit tests don't always come first...and sometimes they don't even exist. I make off-by-one errors every so often. The type inference section of the C# specification still confuses me, and there are some uses of Java wildcards that make me want to have a little lie-down. I'm a deeply flawed programmer.

That's the way it should be. For the next few hundred pages, I'll try to pretend otherwise: I'll espouse best practices as if I always followed them myself, and frown on dirty shortcuts as if I'd never dream of taking them. Don't believe a word of it. The truth of the matter is, I'm probably just like you. I happen to know a bit more about how C# works, that's all...and even that state of affairs will only last until you've finished the book.

about the cover illustration

The caption for the illustration on the cover of *C# in Depth, Third Edition* is "Musician." The illustration is taken from a collection of costumes of the Ottoman Empire published on January 1, 1802, by William Miller of Old Bond Street, London. The title page is missing from the collection and we have been unable to track it down to date. The book's table of contents identifies the figures in both English and French, and each illustration bears the names of two artists who worked on it, both of whom would no doubt be surprised to find their art gracing the front cover of a computer programming book...two hundred years later.

The collection was purchased by a Manning editor at an antiquarian flea market in the "Garage" on West 26th Street in Manhattan. The seller was an American based in Ankara, Turkey, and the transaction took place just as he was packing up his stand for the day. The Manning editor didn't have on his person the substantial amount of cash that was required for the purchase and a credit card and check were both politely turned down. With the seller flying back to Ankara that evening, the situation was getting hopeless. What was the solution? It turned out to be nothing more than an old-fashioned verbal agreement sealed with a handshake. The seller simply proposed that the money be transferred to him by wire and the editor walked out with the bank information on a piece of paper and the portfolio of images under his arm. Needless to say, we transferred the funds the next day, and we remain grateful and impressed by this unknown person's trust in one of us. It recalls something that might have happened a long time ago.

We at Manning celebrate the inventiveness, the initiative, and, yes, the fun of the computer business with book covers based on the rich diversity of regional life of two centuries ago, brought back to life by the pictures from this collection.

Part 1

Preparing for the journey

Every reader will come to this book with a different set of expectations and a different level of experience. Are you an expert looking to fill some holes, however small, in your present knowledge? Perhaps you consider yourself an average developer, with a bit of experience in using generics and lambda expressions, but a desire to better understand how they work. Maybe you're reasonably confident with C# 2 and 3 but have no experience with C# 4 or 5.

As an author, I can't make every reader the same—and I wouldn't want to, even if I could. But I hope that all readers have two things in common: the desire for a deeper relationship with C# as a language, and at least a basic knowledge of C# 1. If you can bring those elements to the party, I'll provide the rest.

The potentially huge range of skill levels is the main reason why this part of the book exists. You may already know what to expect from later versions of C#—or it could all be brand new to you. You could have a rock-solid understanding of C# 1, or you might be rusty on some of the details—some of which will become increasingly important as you learn about the later versions. By the end of part 1, I won't have leveled the playing field entirely, but you should be able to approach the rest of the book with confidence and an idea of what's coming later.

In the first two chapters, we'll look both forward and back. One of the key themes of the book is evolution. Before introducing any feature into the language, the C# design team carefully considers that feature in the context of what's already present and the general goals for the future. This brings a feeling of consistency to the language even in the midst of change. To understand how and why the language is evolving, you need to see where it's come from and where it's going.

Chapter 1 presents a bird's-eye view of the rest of the book, taking a brief look at some of the biggest features of C# beyond version 1. I'll show a progression of code from C# 1 onward, applying new features one by one until the code is almost unrecognizable from its humble beginnings. We'll also look at some of the terminology I'll use in the rest of the book, as well as the format for the sample code.

Chapter 2 is heavily focused on C# 1. If you're an expert in C# 1, you can skip this chapter, but it does tackle some of the areas of C# 1 that tend to be misunderstood. Rather than try to explain the whole of the language, the chapter concentrates on features that are fundamental to the later versions of C#. From this solid base, you can move on and look at C# 2 in part 2 of the book.

The changing face of C# development

This chapter covers

- An evolving example
- The composition of .NET
- Using the code in this book
- The C# language specification

Do you know what I really like about dynamic languages such as Python, Ruby, and Groovy? They suck away fluff from your code, leaving just the essence of it—the bits that really *do* something. Tedious formality gives way to features such as generators, lambda expressions, and list comprehensions.

The interesting thing is that few of the features that tend to give dynamic languages their lightweight feel have anything to do with being dynamic. Some do, of course—duck typing and some of the magic used in Active Record, for example—but statically typed languages don't *have* to be clumsy and heavyweight.

Enter C#. In some ways, C# 1 could have been seen as a nicer version of the Java language, circa 2001. The similarities were all too clear, but C# had a few extras: properties as a first-class feature in the language, delegates and events, foreach

3

loops, using statements, explicit method overriding, operator overloading, and custom value types, to name a few. Obviously, language preference is a personal issue, but C# 1 definitely felt like a step up from Java when I first started using it.

Since then, things have only gotten better. Each new version of C# has added significant features to reduce developer angst, but always in a carefully considered way, and with little backward incompatibility. Even before C# 4 gained the ability to use dynamic typing where it's genuinely useful, many features traditionally associated with dynamic and functional languages had made it into C#, leading to code that's easier to write and maintain. Similarly, while the features around asynchrony in C# 5 aren't exactly the same as those in F#, it feels to me like there's a definite influence.

In this book, I'll take you through those changes one by one, in enough detail to make you feel comfortable with some of the miracles the C# compiler is now prepared to perform on your behalf. All that comes later, though—in this chapter I'll whiz through as many features as I can, barely taking a breath. I'll define what I mean when I talk about C# as a language compared with .NET as a platform, and I'll offer a few important notes about the sample code for the rest of the book. Then we can dive into the details.

We won't be looking at *all* the changes made to C# in this single chapter, but you'll see generics, properties with different access modifiers, nullable types, anonymous methods, automatically implemented properties, enhanced collection initializers, enhanced object initializers, lambda expressions, extension methods, implicit typing, LINQ query expressions, named arguments, optional parameters, simpler COM interop, dynamic typing, and asynchronous functions. These will carry us from C# 1 all the way up to the latest release, C# 5. Obviously that's a lot to get through, so let's get started.

1.1   *Starting with a simple data type*

In this chapter I'll let the C# compiler do amazing things without telling you how and barely mentioning the what or the why. This is the only time that I won't explain how things work or try to go one step at a time. Quite the opposite, in fact—the plan is to impress rather than educate. If you read this entire section without getting at least a little excited about what C# can do, maybe this book isn't for you. With any luck, though, you'll be eager to get to the details of how these magic tricks work, and that's what the rest of the book is for.

The example I'll use is contrived—it's designed to pack as many new features into as short a piece of code as possible. It's also clichéd, but at least that makes it familiar. Yes, it's a product/name/price example, the e-commerce alternative to "hello, world." We'll look at how various tasks can be achieved, and how, as we move forward in versions of C#, you can accomplish them more simply and elegantly than before. You won't see any of the benefits of C# 5 until right at the end, but don't worry—that doesn't make it any less important.

1.1.1 The Product type in C# 1

We'll start off with a type representing a product, and then manipulate it. You won't see anything particularly impressive yet—just the encapsulation of a couple of properties. To make life simpler for demonstration purposes, this is also where we'll create a list of predefined products.

Listing 1.1 shows the type as it might be written in C# 1. We'll then move on to see how the code might be rewritten for each later version. This is the pattern we'll follow for each of the other pieces of code. Given that I'm writing this in 2013, it's likely that you're already familiar with code that uses some of the features I'll introduce, but it's worth looking back so you can see how far the language has come.

Listing 1.1 The Product type (C# 1)

```
using System.Collections;
public class Product
{
    string name;
    public string Name { get { return name; } }

    decimal price;
    public decimal Price { get { return price; } }

    public Product(string name, decimal price)
    {
        this.name = name;
        this.price = price;
    }

    public static ArrayList GetSampleProducts()
    {
        ArrayList list = new ArrayList();
        list.Add(new Product("West Side Story", 9.99m));
        list.Add(new Product("Assassins", 14.99m));
        list.Add(new Product("Frogs", 13.99m));
        list.Add(new Product("Sweeney Todd", 10.99m));
        return list;
    }

    public override string ToString()
    {
        return string.Format("{0}: {1}", name, price);
    }
}
```

Nothing in listing 1.1 should be hard to understand—it's just C# 1 code, after all. There are three limitations that it demonstrates, though:

- An `ArrayList` has no compile-time information about what's in it. You could accidentally add a string to the list created in `GetSampleProducts`, and the compiler wouldn't bat an eyelid.
- You've provided public getter properties, which means that if you wanted matching setters, they'd have to be public, too.

- There's a lot of fluff involved in creating the properties and variables—code that complicates the simple task of encapsulating a string and a decimal.

Let's see what C# 2 can do to improve matters.

1.1.2   *Strongly typed collections in C# 2*

Our first set of changes (shown in the following listing) tackles the first two items listed previously, including the most important change in C# 2: generics. The parts that are new are in bold.

> **Listing 1.2   Strongly typed collections and private setters (C# 2)**

```
public class Product
{
    string name;
    public string Name
    {
        get { return name; }
        private set { name = value; }
    }

    decimal price;
    public decimal Price
    {
        get { return price; }
        private set { price = value; }
    }

    public Product(string name, decimal price)
    {
        Name = name;
        Price = price;
    }

    public static List<Product> GetSampleProducts()
    {
        List<Product> list = new List<Product>();
        list.Add(new Product("West Side Story", 9.99m));
        list.Add(new Product("Assassins", 14.99m));
        list.Add(new Product("Frogs", 13.99m));
        list.Add(new Product("Sweeney Todd", 10.99m));
        return list;
    }

    public override string ToString()
    {
        return string.Format("{0}: {1}", name, price);
    }
}
```

You now have properties with private setters (which you use in the constructor), and it doesn't take a genius to guess that List<Product> is telling the compiler that the list contains products. Attempting to add a different type to the list would result in a compiler error, and you also don't need to cast the results when you fetch them from the list.

The changes in C# 2 leave only one of the original three difficulties unanswered, and C# 3 helps out there.

1.1.3 *Automatically implemented properties in C# 3*

We're starting off with some fairly tame features from C# 3. The automatically implemented properties and simplified initialization shown in the following listing are relatively trivial compared with lambda expressions and the like, but they can make code a lot simpler.

Listing 1.3 Automatically implemented properties and simpler initialization (C# 3)

```
using System.Collections.Generic;

class Product
{
    public string Name { get; private set; }
    public decimal Price { get; private set; }

    public Product(string name, decimal price)
    {
        Name = name;
        Price = price;
    }

    Product() {}

    public static List<Product> GetSampleProducts()
    {
        return new List<Product>
        {
            new Product { Name="West Side Story", Price = 9.99m },
            new Product { Name="Assassins", Price=14.99m },
            new Product { Name="Frogs", Price=13.99m },
            new Product { Name="Sweeney Todd", Price=10.99m}
        };
    }

    public override string ToString()
    {
        return string.Format("{0}: {1}", Name, Price);
    }
}
```

Now the properties don't have any code (or visible variables!) associated with them, and you're building the hardcoded list in a very different way. With no name and price variables to access, you're forced to use the properties everywhere in the class, improving consistency. You now have a private parameterless constructor for the sake of the new property-based initialization. (This constructor is called for each item before the properties are set.)

In this example, you could've removed the public constructor completely, but then no outside code could've created other product instances.

1.1.4   *Named arguments in C# 4*

For C# 4, we'll go back to the original code when it comes to the properties and constructor, so that it's fully immutable again. A type with only private setters can't be *publicly* mutated, but it can be clearer if it's not privately mutable either.[1] There's no shortcut for read-only properties, unfortunately, but C# 4 lets you specify argument names for the constructor call, as shown in the following listing, which gives you the clarity of C# 3 initializers without the mutability.

Listing 1.4   Named arguments for clear initialization code (C# 4)

```csharp
using System.Collections.Generic;
public class Product
{
    readonly string name;
    public string Name { get { return name; } }

    readonly decimal price;
    public decimal Price { get { return price; } }

    public Product(string name, decimal price)
    {
        this.name = name;
        this.price = price;
    }

    public static List<Product> GetSampleProducts()
    {
        return new List<Product>
        {
            new Product( name: "West Side Story", price: 9.99m),
            new Product( name: "Assassins", price: 14.99m),
            new Product( name: "Frogs", price: 13.99m),
            new Product( name: "Sweeney Todd", price: 10.99m)
        };
    }

    public override string ToString()
    {
        return string.Format("{0}: {1}", name, price);
    }
}
```

The benefits of specifying the argument names explicitly are relatively minimal in this particular example, but when a method or constructor has several parameters, it can make the meaning of the code much clearer—particularly if they're of the same type, or if you're passing in null for some arguments. You can choose when to use this feature, of course, only specifying the names for arguments when it makes the code easier to understand.

Figure 1.1 summarizes how the Product type has evolved so far. I'll include a similar diagram after each task, so you can see the pattern of how the evolution of C#

---

[1] The C# 1 code could've been immutable too—I only left it mutable to simplify the changes for C# 2 and 3.

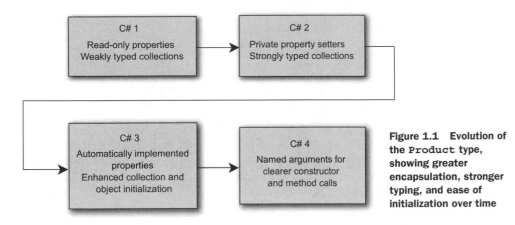

Figure 1.1 Evolution of the Product type, showing greater encapsulation, stronger typing, and ease of initialization over time

improves the code. You'll notice that C# 5 is missing from all of the block diagrams; that's because the main feature of C# 5 (asynchronous functions) is aimed at an area that really hasn't evolved much in terms of language support. We'll take a peek at it before too long, though.

So far, the changes are relatively minimal. In fact, the addition of generics (the List<Product> syntax) is probably the most important part of C# 2, but you've only seen part of its usefulness so far. There's nothing to get the heart racing yet, but we've only just started. Our next task is to print out the list of products in alphabetical order.

1.2 Sorting and filtering

In this section, we won't change the Product type at all—instead, we'll take the sample products and sort them by name, and then find the expensive ones. Neither of these tasks is exactly *difficult*, but you'll see how much simpler they become over time.

1.2.1 Sorting products by name

The easiest way to display a list in a particular order is to sort the list and then run through it, displaying items. In .NET 1.1, this involved using ArrayList.Sort, and optionally providing an IComparer implementation to specify a particular comparison. You could make the Product type implement IComparable, but that would only allow you to define one sort order, and it's not a stretch to imagine that you might want to sort by price at some stage, as well as by name.

The following listing implements IComparer, and then sorts the list and displays it.

Listing 1.5 Sorting an ArrayList using IComparer (C# 1)

```
class ProductNameComparer : IComparer
{
    public int Compare(object x, object y)
    {
        Product first = (Product)x;
        Product second = (Product)y;
        return first.Name.CompareTo(second.Name);
```

```
    }
}
...
ArrayList products = Product.GetSampleProducts();
products.Sort(new ProductNameComparer());
foreach (Product product in products)
{
    Console.WriteLine (product);
}
```

The first thing to spot in listing 1.5 is that you had to introduce an extra type to help with the sorting. That's not a disaster, but it's a lot of code if you only want to sort by name in one place. Next, look at the casts in the Compare method. Casts are a way of telling the compiler that you know more information than it does, and that usually means there's a chance you're wrong. If the ArrayList you returned from Get-SampleProducts *did* contain a string, that's where the code would go bang—where the comparison tries to cast the string to a Product.

You also have a cast in the code that displays the sorted list. It's not obvious, because the compiler puts it in automatically, but the foreach loop implicitly casts each element of the list to Product. Again, that cast could fail at execution time, and once more generics come to the rescue in C# 2. The following listing shows the previous code with the use of generics as the *only* change.

Listing 1.6   Sorting a List<Product> using IComparer<Product> (C# 2)

```
class ProductNameComparer : IComparer<Product>
{
    public int Compare(Product x, Product y)
    {
        return x.Name.CompareTo(y.Name);
    }
}
...
List<Product> products = Product.GetSampleProducts();
products.Sort(new ProductNameComparer());
foreach (Product product in products)
{
    Console.WriteLine(product);
}
```

The code for the comparer in listing 1.6 is simpler because you're given products to start with. No casting is necessary. Similarly, the invisible cast in the foreach loop is effectively gone now. The compiler still has to consider the conversion from the source type of the sequence to the target type of the variable, but it knows that in this case both types are Product, so it doesn't need to emit any code for the conversion.

That's an improvement, but it'd be nice if you could sort the products by simply specifying the comparison to make, without needing to implement an interface to do so. The following listing shows how to do precisely this, telling the Sort method how to compare two products using a delegate.

Listing 1.7 Sorting a `List<Product>` using `Comparison<Product>` (C# 2)

```
List<Product> products = Product.GetSampleProducts();

products.Sort(delegate(Product x, Product y)
   { return x.Name.CompareTo(y.Name); }
);
foreach (Product product in products)
{
    Console.WriteLine(product);
}
```

Behold the lack of the `ProductNameComparer` type. The statement in bold font creates a delegate instance, which you provide to the `Sort` method in order to perform the comparisons. You'll learn more about this feature (*anonymous methods*) in chapter 5.

You've now fixed all the problems identified in the C# 1 version. That doesn't mean that C# 3 can't do better, though. First, you'll replace the anonymous method with an even more compact way of creating a delegate instance, as shown in the following listing.

Listing 1.8 Sorting using `Comparison<Product>` from a lambda expression (C# 3)

```
List<Product> products = Product.GetSampleProducts();
products.Sort((x, y) => x.Name.CompareTo(y.Name));
foreach (Product product in products)
{
    Console.WriteLine(product);
}
```

You've gained even more strange syntax (a *lambda expression*), which still creates a `Comparison<Product>` delegate, just as listing 1.7 did, but this time with less fuss. You didn't have to use the `delegate` keyword to introduce it, or even specify the types of the parameters.

There's more, though: with C# 3, you can easily print out the names in order without modifying the original list of products. The next listing shows this using the `OrderBy` method.

Listing 1.9 Ordering a `List<Product>` using an extension method (C# 3)

```
List<Product> products = Product.GetSampleProducts();
foreach (Product product in products.OrderBy(p => p.Name) )
{
    Console.WriteLine (product);
}
```

In this listing, you appear to be calling an `OrderBy` method on the list, but if you look in MSDN, you'll see that it doesn't even exist in `List<Product>`. You're able to call it due to the presence of an *extension method*, which you'll see in more detail in chapter 10. You're not actually sorting the list "in place" anymore, just retrieving the contents

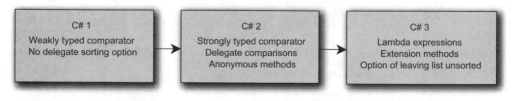

Figure 1.2   Features involved in making sorting easier in C# 2 and 3

of the list in a particular order. Sometimes you'll need to change the actual list; sometimes an ordering without any other side effects is better.

The important point is that this code is much more compact and readable (once you understand the syntax, of course). We wanted the list ordered by name, and that's exactly what the code says. It doesn't say to sort by comparing the name of one product with the name of another, like the C# 2 code did, or to sort by using an instance of another type that knows how to compare one product with another. It just says to order by name. This simplicity of expression is one of the key benefits of C# 3. When the individual pieces of data querying and manipulation are so simple, larger transformations can remain compact and readable in one piece of code. That, in turn, encourages a more data-centric way of looking at the world.

You've seen more of the power of C# 2 and 3 in this section, with a lot of (as yet) unexplained syntax, but even without understanding the details you can see the progress toward clearer, simpler code. Figure 1.2 shows that evolution.

That's it for sorting.[2] Let's do a different form of data manipulation now—querying.

1.2.2   Querying collections

Your next task is to find all the elements of the list that match a certain criterion—in particular, those with a price greater than $10. The following listing shows how, in C# 1, you need to loop around, testing each element and printing it out when appropriate.

Listing 1.10   Looping, testing, printing out (C# 1)

```
ArrayList products = Product.GetSampleProducts();
foreach (Product product in products)
{
    if (product.Price > 10m)
    {
        Console.WriteLine(product);
    }
}
```

This code is *not* difficult to understand. But it's worth bearing in mind how intertwined the three tasks are—looping with foreach, testing the criterion with if, and

---

[2]   C# 4 does provide one feature that can be relevant when sorting, called *generic variance*, but giving an example here would require too much explanation. You can find the details near the end of chapter 13.

then displaying the product with `Console.WriteLine`. The dependency is obvious because of the nesting.

The following listing demonstrates how C# 2 lets you flatten things out a bit.

Listing 1.11   Separating testing from printing (C# 2)

```
List<Product> products = Product.GetSampleProducts();

Predicate<Product> test = delegate(Product p) { return p.Price > 10m; };
List<Product> matches = products.FindAll(test);

Action<Product> print = Console.WriteLine;
matches.ForEach(print);
```

The `test` variable is initialized using the anonymous method feature you saw in the previous section. The `print` variable initialization uses another new C# 2 feature called *method group conversions* that makes it easier to create delegates from existing methods.

I'm not going to claim that this code is simpler than the C# 1 code, but it *is* a lot more powerful.[3]

In particular, the technique of separating the two concerns like this makes it *very* easy to change the condition you're testing for and the action you take on each of the matches independently. The delegate variables involved (`test` and `print`) could be passed into a method, and that same method could end up testing radically different conditions and taking radically different actions. Of course, you could put all the testing and printing into one statement, as shown in the following listing.

Listing 1.12   Separating testing from printing redux (C# 2)

```
List<Product> products = Product.GetSampleProducts();
products.FindAll(delegate(Product p) { return p.Price > 10;})
        .ForEach(Console.WriteLine);
```

In some ways, this version is better, but the `delegate(Product p)` is getting in the way, as are the braces. They're adding noise to the code, which hurts readability. I still prefer the C# 1 version in cases where I only ever want to use the same test and perform the same action. (It may sound obvious, but it's worth remembering that there's nothing stopping you from using the C# 1 code with a later compiler version. You wouldn't use a bulldozer to plant tulip bulbs, which is the kind of overkill used in the last listing.)

The next listing shows how C# 3 improves matters dramatically by removing a lot of the fluff surrounding the actual *logic* of the delegate.

---

[3]   In some ways, this is cheating. You could've defined appropriate delegates in C# 1 and called them within the loop. The `FindAll` and `ForEach` methods in .NET 2.0 just encourage you to consider separation of concerns.

```
List<Product> products = Product.GetSampleProducts();
foreach (Product product in products.Where(p => p.Price > 10))
{
    Console.WriteLine(product);
}
```

The combination of the lambda expression putting the test in just the right place and a well-named method means you can *almost* read the code out loud and understand it without thinking. You still have the flexibility of C# 2—the argument to `Where` could come from a variable, and you could use an `Action<Product>` instead of the hard-coded `Console.WriteLine` call if you wanted to.

This task has emphasized what you already knew from sorting—anonymous methods make writing a delegate simple, and lambda expressions are even more concise. In both cases, that brevity means that you can include the query or sort operation inside the first part of the `foreach` loop without losing clarity.

Figure 1.3 summarizes the changes we've just looked at. C# 4 doesn't offer anything to simplify this task any further.

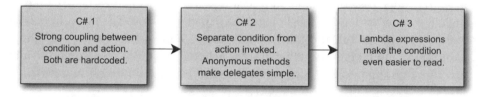

Figure 1.3   Anonymous methods and lambda expressions in C# 2 and 3 aid separation of concerns and readability.

Now that you've displayed the filtered list, let's consider a change to your initial assumptions about the data. What happens if you don't always know the price of a product? How can you cope with that within the `Product` class?

1.3   *Handling an absence of data*

We'll look at two different forms of missing data. First we'll deal with the scenario where you genuinely don't have the information, and then see how you can actively *remove* information from method calls, using default values.

1.3.1   *Representing an unknown price*

I won't present much code this time, but I'm sure it'll be a familiar problem to you, especially if you've done a lot of work with databases. Imagine your list of products contains not just products on sale right now, but ones that aren't available yet. In some cases, you may not know the price. If `decimal` were a reference type, you could just use `null` to represent the unknown price, but since it's a value type, you can't. How would you represent this in C# 1?

There are three common alternatives:

- Create a reference type wrapper around decimal.
- Maintain a separate Boolean flag indicating whether the price is known.
- Use a "magic value" (decimal.MinValue, for example) to represent the unknown price.

I hope you'll agree that none of these holds much appeal. Time for a little magic: you can solve the problem by adding a single character in the variable and property declarations. .NET 2.0 makes matters a lot simpler by introducing the Nullable<T> structure, and C# 2 provides some additional syntactic sugar that lets you change the property declaration to this block of code:

```
decimal? price;
public decimal? Price
{
    get { return price; }
    private set { price = value; }
}
```

The constructor parameter changes to decimal?, and then you can pass in null as the argument, or say Price = null; within the class. The meaning of the null changes from "a special reference that doesn't refer to any object" to "a special value of any nullable type representing the absence of other data," where all reference types and all Nullable<T>-based types count as *nullable types*.

That's a lot more expressive than any of the other solutions. The rest of the code works as is—a product with an unknown price will be considered to be less expensive than $10, due to the way nullable values are handled in greater-than comparisons. To check whether a price is known, you can compare it with null or use the HasValue property, so to show all the products with unknown prices in C# 3, you'd write the following code.

Listing 1.14 Displaying products with an unknown price (C# 3)

```
List<Product> products = Product.GetSampleProducts();
foreach (Product product in products.Where(p => p.Price == null))
{
    Console.WriteLine(product.Name);
}
```

The C# 2 code would be similar to that in listing 1.12, but you'd need to check for null in the anonymous method:

```
List<Product> products = Product.GetSampleProducts();
products.FindAll(delegate(Product p) { return p.Price == null; })
        .ForEach(Console.WriteLine);
```

C# 3 doesn't offer any changes here, but C# 4 has a feature that's at least tangentially related.

1.3.2   *Optional parameters and default values*

Sometimes you don't want to tell a method everything it needs to know, such as when you almost always use the same value for a particular parameter. Traditionally the solution has been to overload the method in question, but C# 4 introduced *optional parameters* to make this simpler.

In the C# 4 version of the `Product` type, you have a constructor that takes the name and the price. You can make the price a nullable decimal, just as in C# 2 and 3, but let's suppose that *most* of the products don't have prices. It would be nice to be able to initialize a product like this:

```
Product p = new Product("Unreleased product");
```

Prior to C# 4, you would've had to introduce a new overload in the `Product` constructor for this purpose. C# 4 allows you to declare a default value (in this case, `null`) for the `price` parameter:

```
public Product(string name, decimal? price = null)
{
    this.name = name;
    this.price = price;
}
```

You always have to specify a constant value when you declare an optional parameter. It doesn't have to be `null`; that just happens to be the appropriate default in this situation. The requirement that the default value is a constant applies to any type of parameter, although for reference types other than strings you *are* limited to `null` as the only constant value available.

Figure 1.4 summarizes the evolution we've looked at across different versions of C#.

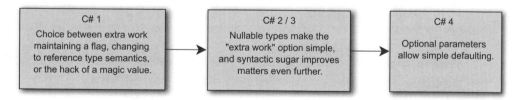

Figure 1.4   Options for working with missing data

So far the features have been useful, but perhaps nothing to write home about. Next we'll look at something rather more exciting: LINQ.

1.4   *Introducing LINQ*

LINQ (Language-Integrated Query) is at the heart of the changes in C# 3. As its name suggests, LINQ is all about queries—the aim is to make it easy to write queries against multiple data sources with consistent syntax and features, in a readable and composable fashion.

Whereas the features in C# 2 are arguably more about fixing annoyances in C# 1 than setting the world on fire, almost everything in C# 3 builds toward LINQ, and the result is rather special. I've seen features in other languages that tackle *some* of the same areas as LINQ, but nothing quite so well-rounded and flexible.

1.4.1 Query expressions and in-process queries

If you've seen any LINQ code before, you've probably seen *query expressions* that allow you to use a declarative style to create queries on various data sources. The reason none of this chapter's examples have used query expressions so far is that the examples have all been simpler *without* using the extra syntax. That's not to say you couldn't use it anyway—the following listing, for example, is equivalent to listing 1.13.

Listing 1.15 First steps with query expressions: filtering a collection

```
List<Product> products = Product.GetSampleProducts();
var filtered = from Product p in products
               where p.Price > 10
               select p;
foreach (Product product in filtered)
{
    Console.WriteLine(product);
}
```

Personally, I find the earlier listing easier to read—the only benefit to this query expression version is that the where clause is simpler. I've snuck in one extra feature here—*implicitly typed local variables*, which are declared using the var contextual keyword. These allow the compiler to infer the type of a variable from the value that it's initially assigned—in this case, the type of filtered is IEnumerable<Product>. I'll use var fairly extensively in the rest of the examples in this chapter; it's particularly useful in books, where space in listings is at a premium.

But if query expressions are no good, why does everyone make such a fuss about them, and about LINQ in general? The first answer is that although query expressions aren't particularly beneficial for simple tasks, they're *very* good for more complicated situations that would be hard to read if written out in the equivalent method calls (and would be fiendish in C# 1 or 2). Let's make things a little harder by introducing another type—Supplier.

Each supplier has a Name (string) and a SupplierID (int). I've also added SupplierID as a property in Product and adapted the sample data appropriately. Admittedly that's not a very object-oriented way of giving each product a supplier—it's much closer to how the data would be represented in a database. It does make this particular feature easier to demonstrate for now, but you'll see in chapter 12 that LINQ allows you to use a more natural model too.

Now let's look at the code (listing 1.16) that joins the sample products with the sample suppliers (obviously based on the supplier ID), applies the same price filter as before to the products, sorts by supplier name and then product name, and prints out the name of both the supplier and the product for each match. That was a mouthful, and in earlier versions of C# it would've been a nightmare to implement. In LINQ, it's almost trivial.

Listing 1.16   Joining, filtering, ordering, and projecting (C# 3)

```
List<Product> products = Product.GetSampleProducts();
List<Supplier> suppliers = Supplier.GetSampleSuppliers();
var filtered = from p in products
               join s in suppliers
                  on p.SupplierID equals s.SupplierID
               where p.Price > 10
               orderby s.Name, p.Name
               select new { SupplierName = s.Name, ProductName = p.Name };
foreach (var v in filtered)
{
    Console.WriteLine("Supplier={0}; Product={1}",
                      v.SupplierName, v.ProductName);
}
```

You might have noticed that this looks remarkably like SQL. Indeed, the reaction of many people on first hearing about LINQ (but before examining it closely) is to reject it as merely trying to put SQL into the language for the sake of talking to databases. Fortunately, LINQ has borrowed the syntax and some ideas from SQL, but as you've seen, you needn't be anywhere near a database in order to use it. None of the code you've seen so far has touched a database at all. Indeed, you could be getting data from any number of sources: XML, for example.

1.4.2   *Querying XML*

Suppose that instead of hardcoding your suppliers and products, you'd used the following XML file:

```xml
<?xml version="1.0"?>
<Data>
  <Products>
    <Product Name="West Side Story" Price="9.99" SupplierID="1" />
    <Product Name="Assassins" Price="14.99" SupplierID="2" />
    <Product Name="Frogs" Price="13.99" SupplierID="1" />
    <Product Name="Sweeney Todd" Price="10.99" SupplierID="3" />
  </Products>

  <Suppliers>
    <Supplier Name="Solely Sondheim" SupplierID="1" />
    <Supplier Name="CD-by-CD-by-Sondheim" SupplierID="2" />
    <Supplier Name="Barbershop CDs" SupplierID="3" />
  </Suppliers>
</Data>
```

The file is simple enough, but what's the best way of extracting the data from it? How do you query it? Join on it? Surely it's going to be somewhat harder than what you did in listing 1.16, right? The following listing shows how much work you have to do in LINQ to XML.

Listing 1.17 Complex processing of an XML file with LINQ to XML (C# 3)

```
XDocument doc = XDocument.Load("data.xml");
var filtered = from p in doc.Descendants("Product")
               join s in doc.Descendants("Supplier")
                   on (int)p.Attribute("SupplierID")
                   equals (int)s.Attribute("SupplierID")
               where (decimal)p.Attribute("Price") > 10
               orderby (string)s.Attribute("Name"),
                       (string)p.Attribute("Name")
               select new
               {
                   SupplierName = (string)s.Attribute("Name"),
                   ProductName = (string)p.Attribute("Name")
               };
foreach (var v in filtered)
{
    Console.WriteLine("Supplier={0}; Product={1}",
                 v.SupplierName, v.ProductName);
}
```

This approach isn't quite as straightforward, because you need to tell the system how it should understand the data (in terms of what attributes should be used as what types), but it's not far off. In particular, there's an obvious relationship between each part of the two listings. If it weren't for the line-length limitations of books, you'd see an exact line-by-line correspondence between the two queries.

Impressed yet? Not quite convinced? Let's put the data where it's much more likely to be—in a database.

1.4.3 LINQ to SQL

There's some work involved in letting LINQ to SQL know what to expect in what table, but it's all fairly straightforward and much of it can be automated. We'll skip straight to the querying code, which is shown in the following listing. If you want to see the details of LinqDemoDataContext, they're all in the downloadable source code.

Listing 1.18 Applying a query expression to a SQL database (C# 3)

```
using (LinqDemoDataContext db = new LinqDemoDataContext())
{
var filtered = from p in db.Products
               join s in db.Suppliers
                   on p.SupplierID equals s.SupplierID
               where p.Price > 10
               orderby s.Name, p.Name
               select new { SupplierName = s.Name, ProductName = p.Name };
foreach (var v in filtered)
{
    Console.WriteLine("Supplier={0}; Product={1}",
                 v.SupplierName, v.ProductName);
    }
}
```

By now, this should be looking incredibly familiar. Everything below the `join` line is cut and pasted directly from listing 1.16 with no changes.

That's impressive enough, but if you're performance-conscious, you may be wondering why you'd want to pull down all the data from the database and then apply these .NET queries and orderings. Why not get the database to do it? That's what it's good at, isn't it? Well, indeed—and that's exactly what LINQ to SQL does. The code in listing 1.18 issues a database request, which is basically the query translated into SQL. Even though you've *expressed* the query in C# code, it's been *executed* as SQL.

You'll see later that there's a more relation-oriented way of approaching this kind of join when the schema and the entities know about the relationship between suppliers and products. The result is the same, though, and it shows just how similar LINQ to Objects (the in-memory LINQ operating on collections) and LINQ to SQL can be.

LINQ is extremely flexible—you can write your own provider to talk to a web service or translate a query into your own specific representation. In chapter 13, we'll look at how broad the term *LINQ* really is, and how it can go beyond what you might expect in terms of querying collections.

1.5   COM and dynamic typing

Next, I'd like to demonstrate some features that are specific to C# 4. Whereas LINQ was the major focus of C# 3, interoperability was the biggest theme in C# 4. This includes working with both the old technology of COM and also the brave new world of dynamic languages executing on the *Dynamic Language Runtime* (DLR). We'll start by exporting the product list to an Excel spreadsheet.

1.5.1   Simplifying COM interoperability

There are various ways of making data available to Excel, but using COM to control it gives you the most power and flexibility. Unfortunately, previous incarnations of C# made it quite difficult to work with COM; VB had much better support. C# 4 largely rectifies that situation.

The following listing shows some code to save your data to a new spreadsheet.

Listing 1.19   Saving data to Excel using COM (C# 4)

```
var app = new Application { Visible = false };
Workbook workbook = app.Workbooks.Add();
Worksheet worksheet = app.ActiveSheet;
int row = 1;
foreach (var product in Product.GetSampleProducts()
                               .Where(p => p.Price != null))
{
    worksheet.Cells[row, 1].Value = product.Name;
    worksheet.Cells[row, 2].Value = product.Price;
    row++;
}
workbook.SaveAs(Filename: "demo.xls",
            FileFormat: XlFileFormat.xlWorkbookNormal);
app.Application.Quit();
```

This may not be quite as nice as you'd like, but it's a *lot* better than it would've been using earlier versions of C#. In fact, you already know about some of the C# 4 features shown here—but there are a couple of others that aren't so obvious. Here's the full list:

- The SaveAs call uses named arguments.
- Various calls omit arguments for optional parameters—in particular, SaveAs would normally have an extra 10 arguments!
- C# 4 can embed the relevant parts of the *primary interop assembly* (PIA) into the calling code, so you no longer need to deploy the PIA separately.
- In C# 3, the assignment to worksheet would fail without a cast, because the type of the ActiveSheet property is represented as object. When using the embedded PIA feature, the type of ActiveSheet becomes dynamic, which leads to an entirely different feature.

Additionally, C# 4 supports named indexers when working with COM—a feature not demonstrated in this example.

I've already mentioned the final feature: dynamic typing in C# using the dynamic type.

1.5.2 Interoperating with a dynamic language

Dynamic typing is such a big topic that the entirety of chapter 14 is dedicated to it. I'll just show you one small example of what it can do here.

Suppose your products aren't stored in a database, or in XML, or in memory. They're accessible via a web service of sorts, but you only have Python code to access it, and that code uses the dynamic nature of Python to build results without declaring a type containing all the properties you need to access on each result. Instead, the results let you ask for any property, and try to work out what you mean at execution time. In a language like Python, there's nothing unusual about that. But how can you access your results from C#?

The answer comes in the form of dynamic—a new type[4] that the C# compiler allows you to use dynamically. If an expression is of type dynamic, you can call methods on it, access properties, pass it around as a method argument, and so on—and most of the normal binding process happens at execution time instead of compile time. You can implicitly convert a value from dynamic to any other type (which is why the worksheet cast in listing 1.19 worked) and do all kinds of other fun stuff.

This behavior can also be useful even within pure C# code, with no interop involved, but it's fun to see it working with other languages. The following listing shows how you can get the list of products from IronPython and print it out. This includes all the setup code to run the Python code in the same process.

---

[4] Sort of, anyway. It's a type as far as the C# compiler is concerned, but the CLR doesn't know anything about it.

Listing 1.20   Running IronPython and extracting properties dynamically (C# 4)

```
ScriptEngine engine = Python.CreateEngine();
ScriptScope scope = engine.ExecuteFile("FindProducts.py");
dynamic products = scope.GetVariable("products");
foreach (dynamic product in products)
{
    Console.WriteLine("{0}: {1}", product.ProductName, product.Price);
}
```

Both products and product are declared to be dynamic, so the compiler is happy to let you iterate over the list of products and print out the properties, even though it doesn't know whether it'll work. If you make a typo, using product.Name instead of product.ProductName, for example, that would only show up at execution time.

This is completely contrary to the rest of C#, which is statically typed. But dynamic typing only comes into play when expressions with a type of dynamic are involved; most C# code is likely to remain statically typed throughout.

1.6   *Writing asynchronous code without the heartache*

Finally you get to see C# 5's big feature: asynchronous functions, which allow you to pause code execution without blocking a thread.

This topic is big—really big—but I'll give you just a snippet for now. As I'm sure you're aware, there are two golden rules when it comes to threading in Windows Forms: you mustn't block the UI thread, and you mustn't access UI elements on any other thread, except in a few well-specified ways. The following listing shows a single method that handles a button click in a Windows Forms application and displays information about a product, given its ID.

Listing 1.21   Displaying products in Windows Forms using an asynchronous function

```
private async void CheckProduct(object sender, EventArgs e)
{
    try
    {
        productCheckButton.Enabled = false;
        string id = idInput.Text;

        Task<Product> productLookup = directory.LookupProductAsync(id);
        Task<int> stockLookup = warehouse.LookupStockLevelAsync(id);
        Product product = await productLookup;
        if (product == null)
        {
            return;
        }
        nameValue.Text = product.Name;
        priceValue.Text = product.Price.ToString("c");

        int stock = await stockLookup;
        stockValue.Text = stock.ToString();
    }
```

```
    finally
    {
    productCheckButton.Enabled = true;
    }
}
```

The full method is a little longer than the one shown in listing 1.22, displaying status messages and clearing the results at the start, but this listing contains all the important parts. The new parts of syntax are in bold—the method has the new `async` modifier, and there are two `await` expressions.

If you squint and ignore those for the moment, you can probably understand the general flow of the code. It starts off performing lookups on both the product directory and warehouse to find out the product details and current stock. The method then waits until it has the product information, and quits if the directory has no entry for the given ID. Otherwise, it fills in the UI elements for the name and price, and then waits to get the stock information, and displays that too.

Both the product and stock lookups are asynchronous—they could be database operations or web service calls. It doesn't matter—when you await the results, you're not actually blocking the UI thread, even though all the code in the method *runs* on that thread. When the results come back, the method continues from where it left off. The example also demonstrates that normal flow control (`try/finally`) operates exactly as you'd expect it to. The really surprising thing about this method is that it has managed to achieve exactly the kind of asynchrony you want without any of the normal messing around starting other threads or `BackgroundWorkers`, calling `Control.BeginInvoke`, or attaching callbacks to asynchronous events. Of course you still need to think—asynchrony doesn't become *easy* using async/await, but it becomes less tedious, with far less boilerplate code to distract you from the inherent complexity you're trying to control.

Are you dizzy yet? Relax, I'll slow down considerably for the rest of the book. In particular, I'll explain some of the corner cases, going into more detail about *why* various features were introduced, and giving some guidance as to when it's appropriate to use them.

So far I've been showing you features of C#. Some of these features require library assistance, and some of them require runtime assistance. I'll say this sort of thing a lot, so let's clear up what I mean.

1.7 Dissecting the .NET platform

When it was originally introduced, *.NET* was used as a catchall term for a vast range of technologies coming from Microsoft. For instance, Windows Live ID was called *.NET Passport*, despite there being no clear relationship between that and what you currently know as .NET. Fortunately, things have calmed down somewhat since then. In this section, we'll look at the various parts of .NET.

In several places in this book, I'll refer to three different kinds of features: features of C# as a *language*, features of the *runtime* that provides the "engine," if you will, and features of the .NET *framework libraries*. This book is heavily focused on the language of C#, and I'll generally only discuss runtime and framework features when they relate to features of C# itself. Often features will overlap, but it's important to understand where the boundaries lie.

1.7.1   C#, the language

The language of C# is defined by its specification, which describes the format of C# source code, including both syntax and behavior. It doesn't describe the platform that the compiler output will run on, beyond a few key points where the two interact. For instance, the C# language requires a type called System.IDisposable, which contains a method called Dispose. These are required in order to define the using statement. Likewise, the platform needs to be able to support (in one form or another) both value types and reference types, along with garbage collection.

In theory, any platform that supports the required features could have a C# compiler targeting it. For example, a C# compiler could legitimately produce output in a form other than the *Intermediate Language* (*IL*), which is the typical output at the time of this writing. A runtime could interpret the output of a C# compiler, or convert it all to native code in one step rather than JIT-compiling it. Though these options are relatively uncommon, they do exist in the wild; for example, the Micro Framework uses an interpreter, as can Mono (http://mono-project.net). At the other end of the spectrum, ahead-of-time compilation is used by NGen and by Xamarin.iOS (http://xamarin .com/ios)—a platform for building applications for the iPhone and other iOS devices.

1.7.2   Runtime

The runtime aspect of the .NET platform is the relatively small amount of code that's responsible for making sure that programs written in IL execute according to the *Common Language Infrastructure* (CLI) specification (ECMA-335 and ISO/IEC 23271), partitions I to III. The runtime part of the CLI is called the *Common Language Runtime* (CLR). When I refer to *the CLR* in the rest of the book, I mean Microsoft's implementation.

Some elements of the C# language never appear at the runtime level, but others cross the divide. For instance, enumerators aren't defined at a runtime level, and neither is any particular meaning attached to the IDisposable interface, but arrays and delegates are important to the runtime.

1.7.3   Framework libraries

Libraries provide code that's available to your programs. The framework libraries in .NET are largely built as IL themselves, with native code used only where necessary. This is a mark of the strength of the runtime: your own code isn't expected to be a second-class citizen—it can provide the same kind of power and performance as the libraries it utilizes. The amount of code in the libraries is much greater than that of the runtime, in the same way that there's much more to a car than the engine.

The framework libraries are partially standardized. Partition IV of the CLI specification provides a number of different profiles (*compact* and *kernel*) and libraries. Partition IV comes in two parts—a general textual description of the libraries identifying, among other things, which libraries are required within which profiles, and another part containing the details of the libraries themselves in XML format. This is the same form of documentation produced when you use XML comments within C#.

There's much within .NET that's *not* within the base libraries. If you write a program that *only* uses libraries from the specification, and uses them correctly, you should find that your code works flawlessly on any implementation—Mono, .NET, or anything else. But in practice, almost any program of any size will use libraries that aren't standardized—Windows Forms or ASP.NET, for instance. The Mono project has its own libraries that aren't part of .NET, such as GTK#, and it implements many of the nonstandardized libraries.

The term *.NET* refers to the combination of the runtime and libraries provided by Microsoft, and it also includes compilers for C# and VB.NET. It can be seen as a whole *development platform* built on top of Windows. Each aspect of .NET is versioned separately, which can be a source of confusion. Appendix C gives a quick rundown of which version of what came out when and with what features.

If that's all clear, I have one last bit of housekeeping to go through before we really start diving into C#.

1.8 Making your code super awesome

I apologize for the misleading heading. This section (in itself) will *not* make your code super awesome. It won't even make it refreshingly minty. It will help you make the most of this book, though—and that's why I wanted to make sure you actually read it. There's more of this sort of thing in the front matter (the bit before page 1), but I know that many readers skip over that, heading straight for the meat of the book. I can understand that, so I'll make this as quick as possible.

1.8.1 Presenting full programs as snippets

One of the challenges when writing a book about a computer language (other than scripting languages) is that complete programs—ones that the reader can compile and run with no source code other than what's presented—get long pretty quickly. I wanted to get around this, to provide you with code that you could easily type in and experiment with. I believe that actually *trying* something is a much better way of learning than just reading about it.

With the right assembly references and the right `using` directives, you can accomplish a lot with a fairly short amount of C# code, but the killer is the fluff involved in writing those `using` directives, declaring a class, and declaring a `Main` method before you've written the first line of *useful* code. My examples are mostly in the form of *snippets*, which ignore the fluff that gets in the way of simple programs, concentrating on the important parts. The snippets can be run directly in a small tool I've built, called *Snippy*.

If a snippet doesn't contain an ellipsis (...), then all of the code should be considered to be the body of the Main method of a program. If there *is* an ellipsis, then everything before it is treated as declarations of methods and nested types, and everything after the ellipsis goes in the Main method. For example, consider this snippet:

```
static string Reverse(string input)
{
    char[] chars = input.ToCharArray();
    Array.Reverse(chars);
    return new string(chars);
}
...
Console.WriteLine(Reverse("dlrow olleH"));
```

This is expanded by Snippy into the following:

```
using System;
public class Snippet
{
    static string Reverse(string input)
    {
        char[] chars = input.ToCharArray();
        Array.Reverse(chars);
        return new string(chars);
    }

    [STAThread]
    static void Main()
    {
        Console.WriteLine(Reverse("dlrow olleH"));
    }
}
```

In reality, Snippy includes far more using directives, but the expanded version was already getting long. Note that the containing class will always be called Snippet, and any types declared within the snippet will be nested within that class.

There are more details about how to use Snippy on the book's website (http://mng.bz/Lh82), along with all the examples as both snippets and expanded versions in Visual Studio solutions. Additionally, there's support for LINQPad (http://www.linqpad.net)—a similar tool developed by Joe Albahari, with particularly helpful features for exploring LINQ.

Next, let's look at what's wrong with the code we've just seen.

1.8.2 *Didactic code isn't production code*

It'd be lovely if you could take all the examples from this book and use them directly in your own applications with no further thought involved...but I strongly suggest you don't. Most examples are presented to demonstrate a specific point—and that's usually the limit of the intent. Most snippets don't include argument validation, access modifiers, unit tests, or documentation. They may also fail when used outside their intended context.

For example, let's consider the body of the method previously shown for reversing a string. I use this code several times in the course of the book:

```
char[] chars = input.ToCharArray();
Array.Reverse(chars);
return new string(chars);
```

Leaving aside argument validation, this succeeds in reversing the sequence of UTF-16 code points within a string, but in some cases that's not good enough. For example, if a single displayed glyph is composed of an *e* followed by a combining character representing an acute accent, you don't want to switch the sequence of the code points; the accent will end up on the wrong character. Or suppose your string contains a character outside the basic multilingual plane, formed from a surrogate pair—reordering the code points will lead to a string that's effectively invalid UTF-16. Fixing these problems would lead to much more complicated code, distracting from the point it's meant to be demonstrating.

You're welcome to use the code from the book, but please bear this section in mind if you do so—it'd be much better to take inspiration from it than to copy it verbatim and assume it'll meet your particular requirements.

Finally, there's another book you should download in order to make the absolute most of this one.

1.8.3 *Your new best friend: the language specification*

I've tried extremely hard to be accurate in this book, but I'd be amazed if there were no errors at all—indeed, you'll find a list of known errors on the book's website (http://mng.bz/m1Hh). If you think you've found a mistake, I'd be grateful if you could email me (skeet@pobox.com) or add a note on the author forum (http://mng.bz/TQmF). But you may not want to wait for me to get back to you, or you may have a question that isn't covered in the book. Ultimately, the definitive source for the intended behavior of C# is the language specification.

There are two important forms of the spec—the international standard from ECMA, and the Microsoft specification. As I write this, the ECMA specification (ECMA-334 and ISO/IEC 23270) only covers C# 2, despite being the fourth edition. It's unclear whether or when this will be updated, but the Microsoft version is complete and freely available. This book's website has links to all the available versions of both specification flavors (http://mng.bz/8s38), and Visual Studio ships with a copy too.[5] When I refer to sections of the specification within this book, I'll use numbering from

---

[5] The exact location of the specification will depend on your system, but on my Visual Studio 2012 Professional installation, it's in C:\Program Files (x86)\Microsoft Visual Studio 11.0\VC#\Specifications\1033.

the Microsoft C# 5 specification, even when I'm talking about earlier versions of the language. I strongly recommend that you download this version and have it on hand whenever you find yourself eager to check out a weird corner case.

One of my aims is to make the spec *mostly* redundant for developers—to provide a more developer-oriented form covering everything you're likely to see in everyday code, without the huge level of detail required by compiler authors. Having said that, it's extremely readable as specifications go, and you shouldn't be daunted by it. If you find the spec interesting, there are annotated versions available for C# 3 and C# 4. Both contain fascinating comments from the C# team and other contributors. (Disclaimer: I'm one of the "other contributors" for the C# 4 edition…but all the *other* comments are great!)

1.9   *Summary*

In this chapter, I've shown (but not explained) some of the features that are tackled in depth in the rest of the book. There are plenty more that I haven't shown here, and many of the features you've seen so far have further subfeatures associated with them. Hopefully what you've seen here has whetted your appetite for the rest of the book.

Although features have taken up most of the chapter, we've also looked at some areas that should help you get the most out of the book. I've clarified what I mean when I refer to the language, runtime, and libraries, and I've also explained how code will be laid out in the book.

There's one more area we need to cover before we dive into the features of C# 2, and that's C# 1. Obviously, as an author I have no idea how knowledgeable you are about C# 1, but I *do* have some understanding of which areas of C# often cause conceptual problems. Some of these areas are critical to getting the most out of the later versions of C#, so in the next chapter I'll go over them in some detail.

Core foundations: building on C# 1

This chapter covers

- Delegates
- Type system characteristics
- Value/reference types

This isn't a refresher on the whole of C# 1. Let's get that out of the way immediately. I couldn't do justice to *any* topic in C# if I had to cover the whole of the first version in a single chapter. I've written this book assuming that you're at least reasonably competent in C# 1. What counts as "reasonably competent" is, of course, somewhat subjective, but I'll assume you'd *at least* be happy to walk into an interview for a junior C# developer role and answer technical questions appropriate to that job. You may well have more experience, but that's the level of knowledge I'm assuming.

In this chapter, we'll focus on three areas of C# 1 that are particularly important in order to understand the features of later versions. This should raise the lowest common denominator a little, so that I can make slightly greater assumptions later in the book. Given that it *is* a lowest common denominator, you may find you already have a perfect understanding of all the concepts in this chapter. If you believe that's the case without even reading the chapter, then feel free to skip it.

You can always come back later if it turns out something isn't as simple as you thought. If you're not certain you know everything in this chapter, you might want to look at the summary at the end of each section, which highlights the important points—if any of those sound unfamiliar, it's worth reading that section in detail.

We'll start off by looking at delegates, then consider how the C# type system compares with some other possibilities, and finally look at the differences between value types and reference types. For each topic, I'll describe the ideas and behavior, as well as take the opportunity to define terms so that I can use them later on. After we've looked at how C# 1 works, I'll show you a quick preview of how many of the new features in later versions relate to the topics examined in this chapter.

2.1   Delegates

I'm sure you already have an instinctive idea about what a delegate is, even though it can be hard to articulate. If you're familiar with C and had to describe delegates to another C programmer, the term *function pointer* would no doubt crop up. Essentially, delegates provide a level of indirection: instead of specifying behavior to be executed immediately, the behavior can somehow be "contained" in an object. That object can then be used like any other, and one operation you can perform with it is to execute the encapsulated action. Alternatively, you can think of a delegate type as a single-method interface, and a delegate instance as an object implementing that interface.

If that's just gobbledygook to you, maybe an example will help. It's slightly morbid, but it does capture what delegates are all about. Consider your will—your last will and testament. It's a set of instructions: "pay the bills, make a donation to charity, leave the rest of my estate to the cat," for instance. You write it *before* your death, and leave it in an appropriately safe place. *After* your death, your attorney will (you hope!) act on those instructions.

A delegate in C# acts like your will does in the real world—it allows you to specify a sequence of actions to be executed at the appropriate time. Delegates are typically used when the code that wants to execute the actions doesn't know the details of what those actions should be. For instance, the only reason why the `Thread` class knows what to run in a new thread when you start it is because you provide the constructor with a `ThreadStart` or `ParameterizedThreadStart` delegate instance.

We'll start our tour of delegates with the four absolute basics, without which none of the rest would make sense.

2.1.1   A recipe for simple delegates

In order for a delegate to do anything, four things need to happen:

- The *delegate type* needs to be declared.
- The code to be executed must be contained in a method.
- A *delegate instance* must be created.
- The delegate instance must be *invoked*.

Let's take each step of this recipe in turn.

DECLARING THE DELEGATE TYPE

A *delegate type* is effectively a list of parameter types and a return type. It specifies what kind of action can be represented by instances of the type.

For instance, consider a delegate type declared like this:

```
delegate void StringProcessor(string input);
```

The code says that if you want to create an instance of `StringProcessor`, you'll need a method with one parameter (a `string`) and a `void` return type (the method doesn't return anything).

It's important to understand that `StringProcessor` really is a type, deriving from `System.MulticastDelegate`, which in turn derives from `System.Delegate`. It has methods, you can create instances of it and pass around references to instances, the whole works. There are obviously a few special features, but if you're ever stuck wondering what'll happen in a particular situation, first think about what would happen if you were using a normal reference type.

> **SOURCE OF CONFUSION: THE AMBIGUOUS TERM DELEGATE**   Delegates can be misunderstood because the word *delegate* is often used to describe both a *delegate type* and a *delegate instance*. The distinction between these two is exactly the same as between any other type and instances of that type—the `string` type itself is different from a particular sequence of characters, for example. I've used the terms *delegate type* and *delegate instance* throughout this chapter to try to keep clear exactly what I'm talking about at any point.

We'll use the `StringProcessor` delegate type when we consider the next ingredient.

FINDING AN APPROPRIATE METHOD FOR THE DELEGATE INSTANCE'S ACTION

The next ingredient is to find (or write) a method that does what you want and has the same signature as the delegate type you're using. The idea is to make sure that when you try to invoke a delegate instance, the parameters you use will all match up, and you'll be able to use the return value (if any) in the way you expect—just like a normal method call.

Consider these five method signatures as candidates to be used for a `String-Processor` instance:

```
void PrintString(string x)
void PrintInteger(int x)
void PrintTwoStrings(string x, string y)
int GetStringLength(string x)
void PrintObject(object x)
```

The first method has everything right, so you can use it to create a delegate instance. The second method has one parameter, but it's not `string`, so it's incompatible with `StringProcessor`. The third method has the correct first parameter type, but it has another parameter as well, so it's still incompatible. The fourth method has the right parameter list but a nonvoid return type. (If your delegate type had a return type, the return type of the method would have to match that too.)

The fifth method is interesting—any time you invoke a `StringProcessor` instance, you could call the `PrintObject` method with the same arguments, because `string` derives from `object`. It would make sense to be able to use it for an instance of `StringProcessor`, but in C# 1 the delegate must have *exactly* the same parameter types.[1] C# 2 changes this situation—see chapter 5 for more details. In some ways, the fourth method is similar, since you could always ignore the unwanted return value. But void and nonvoid return types are currently always deemed to be incompatible. This is partly because other aspects of the system (particularly the JIT) need to know whether a value will be left on the stack as a return value when a method is executed.[2]

Let's assume you have a method body for the compatible signature (`PrintString`) and move on to the next ingredient—the delegate instance itself.

CREATING A DELEGATE INSTANCE

Now that you have a delegate type and a method with the right signature, you can create an instance of that delegate type, specifying that this method be executed when the delegate instance is invoked. No official terminology has been defined for this, but for this book I'll call it the *action* of the delegate instance.

The exact form of the expression used to create the delegate instance depends on whether the action uses an instance method or a static method. Suppose `PrintString` is a static method in a type called `StaticMethods` and an instance method in a type called `InstanceMethods`. Here are two examples of creating an instance of `String-Processor`:

```
StringProcessor proc1, proc2;
proc1 = new StringProcessor(StaticMethods.PrintString);
InstanceMethods instance = new InstanceMethods();
proc2 = new StringProcessor(instance.PrintString);
```

When the action is a static method, you only need to specify the type name. When the action is an instance method, you need an instance of the type (or a derived type), as you normally would. This object is called the *target* of the action, and when the delegate instance is invoked, the method will be called on that object. If the action is within the same class (as it often is, particularly when you're writing event handlers in UI code), you don't need to qualify it either way—the `this` reference is used implicitly for instance methods.[3] Again, these rules act just as if you were calling the method directly.

> **UTTER GARBAGE! (OR NOT, AS THE CASE MAY BE)** It's worth being aware that a delegate instance will prevent its target from being garbage collected if the delegate instance itself can't be collected. This can result in apparent

---

[1] In addition to the parameter types, you have to match whether the parameter is `in` (the default), `out`, or `ref`. It's reasonably rare to use `out` and `ref` parameters with delegates, though.

[2] This is a deliberately vague use of the word *stack* to avoid going into too much irrelevant detail. See Eric Lippert's blog post "The void is invariant" for more information (http://mng.bz/4g58).

[3] Of course, if the action is an instance method and you're trying to create a delegate instance from within a static method, you'll still need to provide a reference to be the target.

memory leaks, particularly when a short-lived object subscribes to an event in a long-lived object, using itself as the target. The long-lived object indirectly holds a reference to the short-lived one, prolonging its lifetime.

There's not much point in creating a delegate instance if it doesn't get invoked at some point. Let's look at the last step—the invocation.

INVOKING A DELEGATE INSTANCE

Invoking a delegate instance is the really easy bit:[4] it's just a matter of calling a method on the delegate instance. The method itself is called `Invoke`, and it's always present in a delegate type with the same list of parameters and return type that the delegate type declaration specifies. In our continuing example, there's a method like this:

```
void Invoke(string input)
```

Calling `Invoke` will execute the action of the delegate instance, passing on whatever arguments you've specified in the call to `Invoke`, and (if the return type isn't `void`) returning the return value of the action.

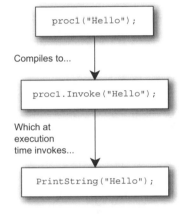

Compiles to...

Which at execution time invokes...

As simple as this is, C# makes it even easier; if you have a variable[5] whose type is a delegate type, you can treat it as if it were a method itself. It's easiest to see this happening as a chain of events occurring at different times, as shown in figure 2.1.

As you can see, that's simple too. All the ingredients are now in place, so you can preheat your CLR to 200°C, stir everything together, and see what happens.

Figure 2.1   Processing a call to a delegate instance that uses the C# shorthand syntax

A COMPLETE EXAMPLE AND SOME MOTIVATION

It's easiest to see all this in action in a complete example—finally, something you can actually run! As there are lots of bits and pieces involved, I've included the whole source code this time rather than using snippets. There's nothing mind-blowing in the following listing, so don't expect to be amazed—it's just useful to have concrete code to discuss.

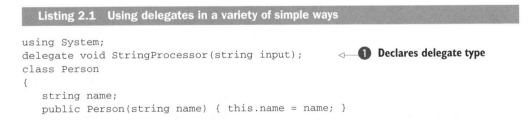

Listing 2.1   Using delegates in a variety of simple ways

```
using System;
delegate void StringProcessor(string input);                    ← ❶ Declares delegate type
class Person
{
    string name;
    public Person(string name) { this.name = name; }
```

---

[4] For synchronous invocation, anyway. You can use `BeginInvoke` and `EndInvoke` to invoke a delegate instance asynchronously, but that's beyond the scope of this chapter.

[5] Or any other kind of expression—but it's usually a variable.

```
    public void Say(string message)
    {
        Console.WriteLine("{0} says: {1}", name, message);
    }
}
class Background
{
    public static void Note(string note)
    {
        Console.WriteLine("({0})", note);
    }
}
class SimpleDelegateUse
{
    static void Main()
    {
        Person jon = new Person("Jon");
        Person tom = new Person("Tom");
        StringProcessor jonsVoice, tomsVoice, background;
        jonsVoice = new StringProcessor(jon.Say);
        tomsVoice = new StringProcessor(tom.Say);
        background = new StringProcessor(Background.Note);
        jonsVoice("Hello, son.");
        tomsVoice.Invoke("Hello, Daddy!");
        background("An airplane flies past.");
    }
}
```

⊲ ❷ Declares compatible instance method

❸ Declares compatible static method ⊲

❹ Creates three delegate instances

❺ Invokes delegate instances

To start with, you declare the delegate type ❶. Next, you create two methods (❷ and ❸) that are both compatible with the delegate type. You have one instance method (Person.Say) and one static method (Background.Note), so you'll see how they're used differently when you create the delegate instances ❹. Listing 2.1 includes two instances of the Person class, so you can see the difference that the target of a delegate makes.

When jonsVoice is invoked ❺, it calls the Say method on the Person object with the name Jon; likewise, when tomsVoice is invoked, it uses the object with the name Tom. This code includes both ways of invoking delegate instances that you've seen—calling Invoke explicitly and using the C# shorthand—just for interest's sake. Normally you'd use the shorthand.

The output of listing 2.1 is fairly obvious:

```
Jon says: Hello, son.
Tom says: Hello, Daddy!
(An airplane flies past.)
```

Frankly, there's an awful lot of code in listing 2.1 to display three lines of output. Even if you wanted to use the Person class and the Background class, there's no real need to use delegates here. So what's the point? Why not just call the methods directly? The answer lies in our original example of an attorney executing a will—just because you want something to happen doesn't mean you're always there at the right time and place to make it happen. Sometimes you need to give instructions—to *delegate* responsibility, as it were.

I should stress that back in the world of software, this isn't a matter of objects leaving dying wishes. Often the object that first creates a delegate instance is still alive and well when the delegate instance is invoked. Instead, it's about specifying some code to be executed at a particular time, when you may not be able (or may not want) to change the code that's running at that point. If I want something to happen when a button is clicked, I don't want to have to change the code of the *button*—I just want to tell the button to call one of my methods, which will take the appropriate action. It's a matter of adding a level of *indirection*, as so much of object-oriented programming is. As you've seen, this adds complexity (look at how many lines of code it took to produce so little output!) but also flexibility.

Now that you understand more about simple delegates, we'll take a brief look at combining delegates together to execute a whole bunch of actions instead of just one.

2.1.2 Combining and removing delegates

So far, all the delegate instances we've looked at have had a single action. In reality, life is a bit more complicated: a delegate instance actually has a list of actions associated with it called the *invocation list*. The static `Combine` and `Remove` methods of the `System.Delegate` type are responsible for creating new delegate instances by respectively splicing together the invocation lists of two delegate instances or removing the invocation list of one delegate instance from another.

> **DELEGATES ARE IMMUTABLE** Once you've created a delegate instance, nothing about it can be changed. This makes it safe to pass around references to delegate instances and combine them with others without worrying about consistency, thread safety, or anyone trying to change their actions. This is like strings, which are also immutable, and `Delegate.Combine` is just like `String.Concat`—they both combine existing instances together to form a new one without changing the original objects at all. In the case of delegate instances, the original invocation lists are concatenated together. Note that if you ever try to combine `null` with a delegate instance, the `null` is treated as if it were a delegate instance with an empty invocation list.

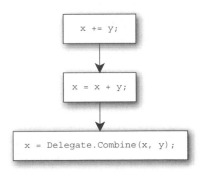

You'll rarely see an explicit call to `Delegate.Combine` in C# code—usually the + and += operators are used. Figure 2.2 shows the translation process, where x and y are both variables of the same (or compatible) delegate types. All of this is done by the C# compiler.

Figure 2.2 The transformation process used for the C# shorthand syntax for combining delegate instances

As you can see, it's a straightforward transformation, but it makes the code a lot neater. Just as you can combine delegate instances, you can remove one from another with the `Delegate.Remove` method, and C# uses the shorthand of the - and -= operators in the obvious way. `Delegate.Remove(source, value)` creates a new delegate whose invocation list is the one from `source`, with the list from `value` having been removed. If the result would have an empty invocation list, `null` is returned.

When a delegate instance is invoked, all its actions are executed in order. If the delegate's signature has a nonvoid return type, the value returned by `Invoke` is the value returned by the *last* action executed. It's rare to see a nonvoid delegate instance with more than one action in its invocation list because it means the return values of all the other actions are never seen unless the invoking code explicitly executes the actions one at a time, using `Delegate.GetInvocationList` to fetch the list of actions.

If any of the actions in the invocation list throws an exception, that prevents any of the subsequent actions from being executed. For example, if a delegate instance with an invocation list [a, b, c] is invoked, and action b throws an exception, the exception will be propagated immediately and action c won't be executed.

Combining and removing delegate instances is particularly useful when it comes to events. Now that you understand what combining and removing involves, we can talk about events.

2.1.3   *A brief diversion into events*

You probably have an instinctive idea about the overall *point* of events, particularly if you've written any UIs. The idea is that an event allows code to react when something happens—saving a file when the appropriate button is clicked, for example. In this case, the event is the clicking of the button, and the action is the saving of the file. Understanding the reason for the concept isn't the same as understanding how C# defines events in language terms, though.

Developers often confuse events and delegate instances, or events and fields declared with delegate types. The difference is important: *events aren't fields*. The reason for the confusion is that C# provides a shorthand in the form of *field-like events*. We'll come to those in a minute, but first let's consider what events consist of as far as the C# compiler is concerned.

It's helpful to think of events as being similar to properties. To start with, both of them are declared to be of a certain type—an event is forced to be a delegate type.

When you use properties, it *looks* like you're fetching or assigning values directly to fields, but you're actually calling methods (getters and setters). The property implementation can do what it likes within those methods—it just happens that most properties are implemented with simple fields backing them, sometimes with some validation in the setter and sometimes with some thread safety thrown in for good measure.

Likewise, when you subscribe to or unsubscribe from an event, it *looks* like you're using a field whose type is a delegate type, with the += and -= operators. Again, though, you're actually calling methods (add and remove).[6] That's all you can do with an event—subscribe to it (add an event handler) or unsubscribe from it (remove an event handler). It's up to the event methods to do something useful, such as taking notice of the event handlers you're trying to add and remove, and making them available elsewhere within the class.

The reason for having events in the first place is much like the reason for having properties—they add a layer of encapsulation, implementing the publish/subscribe pattern (see my article, "Delegates and Events," here: http://mng.bz/HPx6). Just as you don't want other code to be able to set field values without the owner at least having the option of validating the new value, you often don't want code outside a class to be able to arbitrarily change (or call) the handlers for an event. Of course, a class *can* add methods to give extra access—for instance, to reset the list of handlers for an event, or to raise the event (in other words, to call its event handlers). For example, `BackgroundWorker.OnProgressChanged` just calls the `ProgressChanged` event handlers. But if you only expose the event itself, code outside the class only has the ability to add and remove handlers.

Field-like events make the implementation of all of this much simpler to look at—a single declaration and you're done. The compiler turns the declaration into both an event with default add/remove implementations and a private field of the same type. Code inside the class sees the field; code outside the class only sees the event. This makes it *look* as if you can invoke an event, but what you actually do to call the event handlers is invoke the delegate instance stored in the field.

The details of events are outside the scope of this chapter—events themselves haven't changed much in later versions of C#,[7] but I wanted to draw attention to the difference between delegate instances and events now, to prevent confusion later on.

2.1.4 *Summary of delegates*

Let's summarize what we've covered on delegates:

- Delegates encapsulate behavior with a particular return type and set of parameters, similar to a single-method interface.
- The type signature described by a delegate type declaration determines which methods can be used to create delegate instances, and the signature for invocation.
- Creating a delegate instance requires a method and (for instance methods) a target to call the method on.
- Delegate instances are immutable.
- Delegate instances each contain an invocation list—a list of actions.

---

[6] These aren't their names in the compiled code; otherwise you could only have one event per type. The compiler creates two methods with names that aren't used elsewhere, and includes a special piece of metadata to let other types know that there's an event with the given name, and what its add/remove methods are called.

[7] There are very small changes to field-like events in C# 4. See section 4.2 for details.

- Delegate instances can be combined with and removed from each other.
- Events aren't delegate instances—they're just add/remove method pairs (think property getters/setters).

Delegates are one specific feature of C# and .NET—a detail in the grand scheme of things. Both of the other reminder sections in this chapter deal with much broader topics. First, we'll consider what it means to talk about C# being a *statically typed* language and the implications that has.

2.2   *Type system characteristics*

Almost every programming language has a type system of some kind. Over time, these have been classified as strong/weak, safe/unsafe, static/dynamic, and no doubt some more esoteric variations. It's obviously important to understand the type system you're working with, and it's reasonable to expect that knowing the categories into which a language falls would give you a lot of information on that front. But because the terms are used by different people to mean somewhat different things, miscommunication is almost inevitable. I'll try to explain *exactly* what I mean by each term to minimize confusion.

One important thing to note is that this section is only applicable to *safe* code, which means all C# code that isn't explicitly within an unsafe context. As you might judge from the name, code within an unsafe context can do various things that safe code can't, and that may violate some aspects of normal type safety, although the type system is still safe in many other ways. Most developers are unlikely ever to need to write unsafe code, and the characteristics of the type system are far simpler to describe and understand when only safe code is considered.

This section shows what restrictions are and aren't enforced in C# 1 while defining some terms to describe that behavior. We'll then look at a few things you can't do with C# 1—first from the point of view of what you *can't* tell the compiler, and then from the point of view of what you might wish you didn't *have* to tell the compiler.

Let's start off with what C# 1 does, and with the terminology that's usually used to describe that kind of behavior.

2.2.1   *C#'s place in the world of type systems*

It's easiest to begin by making a statement and then clarifying what it means and what the alternatives might be:

> *C# 1's type system is static, explicit, and safe.*

You might have expected the word *strong* to appear in the list, and I had half a mind to include it. But although most people can reasonably agree on whether a language has the characteristics I listed, deciding whether a language is *strongly typed* can cause heated debate because the definitions vary so wildly. Some meanings (those preventing any conversions, explicit or implicit) would clearly rule C# out, whereas others are quite close to (or even the same as) *statically typed*, which would include C# 1. Most of the articles and books I've read that describe C# as a strongly typed language are effectively using "strongly typed" to mean statically typed.

Let's take the terms in the definition one at a time and shed some light on them.

STATIC TYPING VERSUS DYNAMIC TYPING

C# 1 is *statically typed*: each variable is of a particular type, and that type is known at compile time.[8] Only operations that are known for that type are allowed, and this is enforced by the compiler. Consider this example of enforcement:

```
object o = "hello";
Console.WriteLine(o.Length);
```

As you look at the code, it's obvious that the value of o refers to a string, and that the string type has a Length property, but the compiler only thinks of o as being of type object. If you want to get to the Length property, you have to tell the compiler that the value of o refers to a string:

```
object o = "hello";
Console.WriteLine(((string)o).Length);
```

The compiler is then able to find the Length property of System.String. It uses this to validate that the call is correct, emit the appropriate IL, and work out the type of the larger expression. The compile-time type of an expression is also known as its static type—so you might say, "The static type of o is System.Object."

> **WHY IS IT CALLED STATIC TYPING?** The word *static* is used to describe this kind of typing because the analysis of what operations are available is performed using *unchanging* data: the compile-time types of expressions. Suppose a variable is declared to be of type Stream; the type of the variable doesn't change even if the value of the variable varies from a reference to a MemoryStream, a FileStream, or no stream at all (with a null reference). Even within static type systems, there can be some dynamic behavior; the actual *implementation* executed by a virtual method call will depend on the value it's called on. The idea of unchanging information is also the motivation behind the static modifier, but it's generally simpler to think of a static member as one belonging to the type itself rather than to any particular instance of the type. For most practical purposes, you can think of the two uses of the word as unrelated.

The alternative to static typing is *dynamic typing*, which can take a variety of guises. The essence of dynamic typing is that variables just have values—they aren't restricted to particular types, so the compiler can't perform the same sort of checks. Instead, the execution environment attempts to understand expressions in an appropriate manner for the values involved. For example, if C# 1 *were* dynamically typed, you could do this:

---

[8] This applies to most expressions too, but not quite all of them. Certain expressions don't have a type, such as void method invocations, but this doesn't affect C# 1's status of being statically typed. I've used the word *variable* throughout this section to avoid unnecessary brain strain.

WHAT IF?

```
o = "hello";
Console.WriteLine(o.Length);
o = new string[] {"hi", "there"};
Console.WriteLine(o.Length);
```

This would invoke two completely unrelated `Length` properties—`String.Length` and `Array.Length`—by examining the types dynamically at execution time. Like many aspects of type systems, there are different levels of dynamic typing. Some languages allow you to specify types where you want to—possibly still treating them dynamically apart from assignment—but let you use untyped variables elsewhere.

Although I've specified C# 1 repeatedly in this description, C# was entirely statically typed up to and including C# 3. You'll see later that C# 4 introduced some dynamic typing, although the vast majority of code in most C# 4 applications will still use static typing.

EXPLICIT TYPING VERSUS IMPLICIT TYPING

The distinction between *explicit typing* and *implicit typing* is only relevant in statically typed languages. With explicit typing, the type of every variable must be explicitly stated in the declaration. Implicit typing allows the compiler to infer the type of the variable based on its use. For example, the language could dictate that the type of the variable is the type of the expression used to assign the initial value.

Consider a hypothetical language that uses the keyword `var` to indicate type inference.[9] Table 2.1 shows how code in such a language could be written in C# 1. The code in the left column is *not* allowed in C# 1, but the code in the right column is the equivalent valid code.

Table 2.1   An example showing the differences between implicit and explicit typing

Invalid C# 1—implicit typing	Valid C# 1—explicit typing
`var s = "hello";`	`string s = "hello";`
`var x = s.Length;`	`int x = s.Length;`
`var twiceX = x * 2;`	`int twiceX = x * 2;`

Hopefully it's clear why this is only relevant for statically typed situations: for both implicit and explicit typing, the type of the variable is *known* at compile time, even if it's not explicitly stated. In a dynamic context, the variable doesn't even *have* a compile-time type to state or infer.

TYPE-SAFE VERSUS TYPE-UNSAFE

The easiest way of describing a type-safe system is to describe its opposite. Some languages (I'm thinking particularly of C and C++) allow you to do some really devious things. They're potentially powerful in the right situations, but with great power comes a free box of donuts, or however the expression goes, and the right situations

---

[9]   Okay, not so hypothetical. See section 8.2 for C# 3's implicitly typed local variable capabilities.

are relatively rare. Some of these devious things can shoot you in the foot if you get them wrong. Abusing the type system is one of them.

With the right voodoo rituals, you can persuade these languages to treat a value of one type as if it were a value of a *completely* different type without applying any conversions. I don't just mean calling a method that happens to have the same name, as in the dynamic typing example earlier. I mean code that looks at the raw bytes within a value and interprets them in the "wrong" way. The following listing gives a simple C example of what I mean.

Listing 2.2 Demonstrating a type-unsafe system with C code

```
#include <stdio.h>
int main(int argc, char**argv)
{
    char *first_arg = argv[1];
    int *first_arg_as_int = (int *)first_arg;
    printf ("%d", *first_arg_as_int);
}
```

If you compile listing 2.2 and run it with a simple argument of "hello", you'll see a value of 1819043176—at least on a little-endian architecture with a compiler treating int as 32 bits and char as 8 bits, and where text is represented in ASCII or UTF-8. The code is treating the char pointer as an int pointer, so dereferencing it returns the first 4 bytes of text, treating them as a number.

In fact, this tiny example is tame compared with other potential abuses—casting between completely unrelated structs can easily result in total mayhem. It's not that this happens in real life very often, but some elements of the C typing system often require you to tell the compiler what to do, leaving it no option but to trust you even at execution time.

Fortunately, none of this occurs in C#. Yes, there are plenty of conversions available, but you can't pretend that data for one particular type of object is actually data for a different type. You can *try* by adding a cast to give the compiler this extra (and incorrect) information, but if the compiler spots that it's actually *impossible* for that cast to work, it'll trigger a compilation error—and if it's theoretically allowed but actually incorrect at execution time, the CLR will throw an exception.

Now that you know a little about how C# 1 fits into the bigger picture of type systems, I'd like to mention a few downsides of its choices. That's not to say the choices are *wrong*—they're just limiting in some ways. Often language designers have to choose between different paths that add different limitations or have other undesirable consequences. I'll start with the case where you *want* to give the compiler more information, but there's no way of doing so.

2.2.2 When is C# 1's type system not rich enough?

There are two common situations where you might want to expose more information to the caller of a method, or perhaps force the caller to limit what it provides in its arguments. The first involves collections, and the second involves inheritance and overriding methods or implementing interfaces. We'll examine each in turn.

COLLECTIONS, STRONG AND WEAK

Having avoided the terms *strong* and *weak* for the C# type system in general, I'll use them when talking about collections. The terms are used almost everywhere in this context, with little room for ambiguity. Broadly speaking, three kinds of collection types are built into .NET 1.1:

- Arrays—strongly typed—in both the language and the runtime
- Weakly typed collections in the `System.Collections` namespace
- Strongly typed collections in the `System.Collections.Specialized` namespace

Arrays are strongly typed,[10] so at compile time you can't set an element of a `string[]` to be a `FileStream`, for instance. But reference type arrays also support *covariance*, which provides an implicit conversion from one type of array to another, as long as there's a conversion between the element types. Checks occur at execution time to make sure that the wrong type of reference isn't being stored, as shown in the following listing.

Listing 2.3   Demonstration of array covariance and execution-time checking

```
string[] strings = new string[5];          ❶ Applies covariant conversion
object[] objects = strings;
objects[0] = new Button();

                                           ❷ Attempts to store a Button
```

If you run listing 2.3, you'll see that an `ArrayTypeMismatchException` is thrown ❷. This is because the conversion from `string[]` to `object[]` ❶ returns the original reference—both `strings` and `objects` refer to the same array. The array itself knows it's a string array and will reject attempts to store references to nonstrings. Array covariance is occasionally useful, but it comes at the cost of implementing some of the type safety at execution time instead of compile time.

Let's compare this with the situation that weakly typed collections, such as `Array-List` and `Hashtable`, put you in. The API of these collections uses `object` as the type of keys and values. When you write a method that takes an `ArrayList`, for example, there's no way of making sure at compile time that the caller will pass in a list of strings. You can document it, and the type safety of the runtime will enforce it if you cast each element of the list to `string`, but you don't get compile-time type safety. Likewise, if you return an `ArrayList`, you can indicate in the documentation that it'll just contain strings, but callers will have to trust that you're telling the truth, and they'll have to insert casts when they access the elements of the list.

---

[10] At least, the language allows them to be. You can use the `Array` type for weakly typed access to arrays, though.

Finally, consider strongly typed collections, such as `StringCollection`. These provide a strongly typed API, so you can be confident that when you receive a `String-Collection` as a parameter or return value, it'll only contain strings, and you don't need to cast when fetching elements of the collection. It sounds ideal, but there are two problems. First, it implements `IList`, so you can still *try* to add nonstrings to it (although you'll fail at execution time). Second, it only deals with strings. There are other specialized collections, but all told they don't cover much ground. There's the `CollectionBase` type, which can be used to build your own strongly typed collections, but that means creating a new collection type for each element type, which is also not ideal.

Now that you've seen the problem with collections, let's consider the issue that can occur when you're overriding methods and implementing interfaces. It's related to the idea of covariance, which we've already seen with arrays.

Lack of covariant return types

`ICloneable` is one of the simplest interfaces in the framework. It has a single method, `Clone`, which should return a copy of the object that the method is called on. Now, leaving aside the issue of whether this should be a deep or shallow copy, let's look at the signature of the `Clone` method:

```
object Clone()
```

It's a straightforward signature, certainly—but as I said, the method should return a copy of the object it's called on. That means it needs to return an object of the same type, or at least a compatible one (where that meaning will vary depending on the type).

It would make sense to be able to override the method with a signature that gives a more accurate description of what the method actually returns. For example, in a `Person` class it'd be nice to be able to implement `ICloneable` with

```
public Person Clone()
```

That wouldn't break anything—code expecting any old object would still work fine. This feature is called *return type covariance* but, unfortunately, interface implementation and method overriding don't support it. Instead, the normal workaround for interfaces is to use *explicit interface implementation* to achieve the desired effect:

```
public Person Clone()
{
    [Implementation goes here]
}
object ICloneable.Clone()          ◁── Implements interface explicitly
{
    return Clone();                ◁── Calls noninterface method
}
```

Any code that calls `Clone()` on an expression with a static type of `Person` will call the top method; if the type of the expression is `ICloneable`, it'll call the bottom method. This works, but it's really ugly. The mirror image of this situation also occurs with parameters, where if you had an interface or virtual method with a signature of, say, `void Process(string x)`, it'd seem logical to be able to implement or override the method with a less demanding signature, such as `void Process(object x)`. This is called *parameter type contravariance*; it's just as unsupported as return type covariance, and you have to use the same workaround for interfaces and normal overloading for virtual methods. It's not a showstopper, but it's irritating.

Of course, C# 1 developers put up with all of these issues for a long time, and Java developers had a similar situation for far longer. Although compile-time type safety is a great feature in general, I can't remember seeing many bugs where people actually put the wrong type of element in a collection. I can live with the workaround for the lack of covariance and contravariance. But there's such a thing as elegance and making your code clearly express what you mean, preferably *without* needing explanatory comments. Even if bugs don't strike, enforcing the documented contract that a collection *must* only contain strings (for example) can be expensive and fragile in the face of mutable collections. This is the sort of contract you really want the type system itself to enforce.

You'll see later that C# 2 isn't flawless either, but it makes large improvements. There are more changes in C# 4, but even so, return type covariance and parameter contravariance are missing.[11]

2.2.3   *Summary of type system characteristics*

In this section, you've learned some of the differences between type systems, and in particular which characteristics apply to C# 1:

- C# 1 is statically typed—the compiler knows what members to let you use.
- C# 1 is explicit—you have to state the type of every variable.
- C# 1 is safe—you can't treat one type as if it were another unless there's a genuine conversion available.
- Static typing doesn't allow a single collection to be a strongly typed list of strings or list of integers without a lot of code duplication for different element types.
- Method overriding and interface implementation don't allow covariance or contravariance.

The next section covers one of the most fundamental aspects of C#'s type system beyond its high-level characteristics—the differences between structs and classes.

2.3   *Value types and reference types*

It would be hard to overstate how important the subject of this section is. Everything you do in .NET will deal with either a value type or a reference type, and yet it's curiously possible to develop for a long time with only a vague idea of what the difference is. Worse yet, there are plenty of myths to confuse things further. The unfortunate fact is that it's easy to make a short but incorrect statement that's close enough to the truth

---

[11] C# 4 introduced limited *generic* covariance and contravariance, but that's not quite the same thing.

to be plausible but inaccurate enough to be misleading—but it's relatively tricky to come up with a concise but accurate description.

This section isn't a complete breakdown of how types are handled, marshaling between application domains, interoperability with native code, and the like. Instead, it's a brief look at the absolute basics of the topic (as applied to C# 1) that are crucial in order to come to grips with later versions of C#.

We'll start off by seeing how the fundamental differences between value types and reference types appear naturally in the real world, as well as in .NET.

2.3.1 Values and references in the real world

Suppose you're reading something fantastic, and you want a friend to read it too. Let's further suppose that it's a document in the public domain, just to avoid any accusations of supporting copyright violation. What do you need to give your friend so that he can read it too? It depends entirely on what you're reading.

First we'll deal with the case where you have real paper in your hands. To give your friend a copy, you'd need to photocopy all the pages and then give it to him. At that point, he has his own complete copy of the document. In this situation, you're dealing with *value type* behavior. All the information is directly in your hands—you don't need to go anywhere else to get it. Your copy of the information is also independent of your friend's after you've made the copy. You could add some notes to your pages, and his pages wouldn't be changed at all.

Compare that with the situation where you're reading a web page. This time, all you have to give your friend is the URL of the web page. This is *reference type* behavior, with the URL taking the place of the reference. In order to read the document, you have to navigate the reference by putting the URL in your browser and asking it to load the page. If the web page changes for some reason (imagine it's a wiki page and you've added your notes to the page), both you and your friend will see that change the next time each of you loads the page.

These differences in the real world illustrate the heart of the distinction between value types and reference types in C# and .NET. Most types in .NET are reference types, and you're likely to create *far* more reference than value types. The most common cases are classes (declared using `class`), which are reference types, and structures (declared using `struct`), which are value types. The other situations are as follows:

- Array types are reference types, even if the element type is a value type (so `int[]` is still a reference type, even though `int` is a value type).
- Enumerations (declared using `enum`) are value types.
- Delegate types (declared using `delegate`) are reference types.
- Interface types (declared using `interface`) are reference types, but they can be implemented by value types.

Now that you have a basic idea of what reference types and value types are about, we'll look at a few of the most important details.

2.3.2   *Value and reference type fundamentals*

The key concept to grasp when it comes to value types and reference types is what the value of a particular expression is. To keep things concrete, I'll use variables as the most common examples of expressions, but the same thing applies to properties, method calls, indexers, and other expressions.

As we discussed in section 2.2.1, most expressions have a static type associated with them. The value of a value type expression is the value, plain and simple. For instance, the value of the expression "2 + 3" is 5. The value of a *reference* type expression, though, is a reference—it's *not* the object that the reference refers to. The value of the expression String.Empty is *not* an empty string—it's a reference to an empty string. In everyday discussions and even in documentation, we tend to blur this distinction. For instance, I might describe String.Concat as returning "a string that's the concatenation of all the parameters." Using precise terminology here would be time consuming and distracting, and there's no problem as long as everyone involved understands that only a *reference* is returned.

To demonstrate this further, consider a Point type that stores two integers, x and y. It could have a constructor that takes the two values. This type could be implemented as either a struct or a class. Figure 2.3 shows the result of executing the following lines of code:

```
Point p1 = new Point(10, 20);
Point p2 = p1;
```

The left side of figure 2.3 indicates the values involved when Point is a class (a reference type), and the right side shows the situation when Point is a struct (a value type). In both cases, p1 and p2 have the same value after the assignment. But in the case where Point is a reference type, that value is a reference: both p1 and p2 refer to the same object. When Point is a value type, the value of p1 is the whole of the data for a point—the x and y values. Assigning the value of p1 to p2 copies all of that data.

The values of variables are stored wherever they're declared. Local variable values are always stored on the stack,[12] and instance variable values are always stored

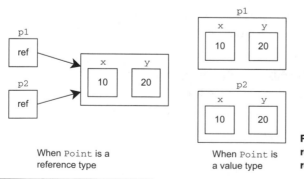

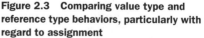

When Point is a reference type

When Point is a value type

Figure 2.3   Comparing value type and reference type behaviors, particularly with regard to assignment

---

[12] This is only totally true for C# 1. You'll see later that local variables can end up on the heap in certain situations in later versions.

wherever the instance itself is stored. Reference type instances (objects) are always stored on the heap, as are static variables.

Another difference between the two kinds of type is that value types can't be derived from. One consequence of this is that the value doesn't need any extra information about what type that value *actually* is. Compare that with reference types, where each object contains a block of data at the start identifying the type of the object, along with some other information. You can never change the type of an object—when you perform a simple cast, the runtime just takes a reference, checks whether the object it refers to is a valid object of the desired type, and returns the reference if it's valid or throws an exception otherwise. The reference itself doesn't know the type of the object, so the same reference value can be used for multiple variables of different types. For instance, consider the following code:

```
Stream stream = new MemoryStream();
MemoryStream memoryStream = (MemoryStream) stream;
```

The first line creates a new `MemoryStream` object and sets the value of the `stream` variable to be a reference to that new object. The second line checks whether the value of `stream` refers to a `MemoryStream` (or derived type) object and sets the value of `memoryStream` to be the same as `stream`.

Once you understand these basic points, you can apply them when thinking about some of the falsehoods that are often stated about value types and reference types.

2.3.3 Dispelling myths

Various myths do the rounds on a regular basis. I'm sure the misinformation is almost always passed on with no malice and with no idea of the inaccuracies involved, but it's unhelpful nonetheless. In this section, I'll tackle the most prominent myths, explaining the true situation as I go.

MYTH #1: STRUCTS ARE LIGHTWEIGHT CLASSES

This myth comes in a variety of forms. Some people believe that value types can't or shouldn't have methods or other significant behavior—they should be used as simple data transfer types, with just public fields or simple properties. The `DateTime` type is a good counterexample to this: it makes sense for it to be a value type, in terms of being a fundamental unit like a number or a character, and it *also* makes sense for it to be able to perform calculations based on its value. Looking at things from the other direction, data transfer types should often be reference types anyway—the decision should be based on the desired value or reference type semantics, not the simplicity of the type.

Other people believe that value types are "lighter" than reference types in terms of performance. The truth is that in *some* cases value types are more performant— they don't require garbage collection unless they're boxed, don't have the type identification overhead, and don't require dereferencing, for example. But in other ways, reference types are more performant— parameter passing, assigning values to variables, returning values, and similar operations only require 4 or 8 bytes to be copied (depending on whether you're running the 32-bit or 64-bit CLR) rather than copying *all* the data. Imagine if `ArrayList` were somehow a "pure" value type, and passing an `ArrayList` expression to a method involved copying all its data! In almost all cases, performance isn't really determined by this sort of decision anyway. Bottlenecks are almost never where you think they'll be, and before you make a design decision based on performance, you should measure the different options.

It's worth noting that the combination of the two beliefs doesn't work either. It doesn't matter how many methods a type has (whether it's a class or a struct)—the memory taken per instance isn't affected. (There's a cost in terms of the memory taken up for the code itself, but that's incurred once rather than for each instance.)

MYTH #2: REFERENCE TYPES LIVE ON THE HEAP; VALUE TYPES LIVE ON THE STACK

This one is often caused by laziness on the part of the person repeating it. The first part is correct—an instance of a reference type is always created on the heap. It's the second part that causes problems. As I've already noted, a variable's value lives wherever it's declared, so if you have a class with an instance variable of type `int`, that variable's value for any given object will always be where the rest of the data for the object is—on the heap. Only local variables (variables declared within methods) and method parameters live on the stack. In C# 2 and later, even some local variables don't really live on the stack, as you'll see when we look at anonymous methods in chapter 5.

> **ARE THESE CONCEPTS RELEVANT NOW?**   It's arguable that if you're writing managed code, you should let the runtime worry about how memory is best used. Indeed, the language specification makes no guarantees about what lives where; a future runtime may be able to create some objects on the stack if it knows it can get away with it, or the C# compiler could generate code that hardly uses the stack at all.

The next myth is usually just a terminology issue.

MYTH #3: OBJECTS ARE PASSED BY REFERENCE IN C# BY DEFAULT

This is probably the most widely propagated myth. Again, the people who make this claim often (though not always) know how C# actually behaves, but they don't know what "pass by reference" really means. Unfortunately, this is confusing for people who *do* know what it means.

The formal definition of *pass by reference* is relatively complicated, involving *l-values* and similar computer-science terminology, but the important thing is that if you pass a variable by reference, the method you're calling can change the *value of the caller's variable* by changing its parameter value. Now, remember that the value of a reference type variable is the *reference*, not the object itself. You can change the *contents* of the object that a parameter refers to without the parameter itself being passed by reference. For instance, the following method changes the contents of the `StringBuilder` object in question, but the caller's expression will still refer to the same object as before:

```
void AppendHello(StringBuilder builder)
{
    builder.Append("hello");
}
```

When this method is called, the parameter value (a reference to a `StringBuilder`) is passed by value. If you were to change the value of the `builder` variable within the method—for example, with the statement `builder = null;`—*that* change wouldn't be seen by the caller, contrary to the myth.

It's interesting to note that not only is the "by reference" bit of the myth inaccurate, but so is the "objects are passed" bit. Objects themselves are *never* passed, either by reference or by value. When a reference type is involved, either the variable is passed by reference or the value of the argument (the reference) is passed by value. Aside from anything else, this answers the question of what happens when `null` is used as a by-value argument—if objects were being passed around, that would cause issues, as there wouldn't be an object to pass! Instead, the `null` reference is passed by value in the same way as any other reference would be.

If this quick explanation has left you bewildered, you might want to look at my article, "Parameter passing in C#," (http://mng.bz/otVt), which goes into much more detail.

These myths aren't the only ones around. Boxing and unboxing come in for their fair share of misunderstanding, which I'll try to clear up next.

2.3.4 Boxing and unboxing

Sometimes, you just don't want a value type value. You want a reference. There are various reasons why this can happen, and fortunately C# and .NET provide a mechanism called *boxing* that lets you create an object from a value type value and use a reference to that new object. Before we leap into an example, let's start off by reviewing two important facts:

- The value of a reference type variable is always a reference.
- The value of a value type variable is always a value of that type.

Given those two facts, the following three lines of code don't seem to make much sense at first glance:

```
int i = 5;
object o = i;
int j = (int) o;
```

You have two variables: `i` is a value type variable, and `o` is a reference type variable. How does it make sense to assign the value of `i` to `o`? The value of `o` has to be a reference, and the number 5 isn't a reference—it's an integer value. What's actually happening is boxing: the runtime creates an object (on the heap—it's a normal object) that contains the value (5). The value of `o` is then a reference to that new object. The value in the object is a *copy* of the original value—changing the value of `i` won't change the value in the box at all.

The third line performs the reverse operation—*unboxing*. You have to tell the compiler which type to unbox the object as, and if you use the wrong type (if it's a boxed `uint` or `long`, for example, or not a boxed value at all), an `InvalidCastException` is thrown. Again, unboxing copies the value that was in the box; after the assignment, there's no further association between j and the object.

That's boxing and unboxing in a nutshell. The only remaining problem is knowing when boxing and unboxing occur. Unboxing is usually obvious, because the cast is present in the code. Boxing can be more subtle. You've seen the simple version, but it can also occur if you call the `ToString`, `Equals`, or `GetHashCode` methods on the value of a type that doesn't override them,[13] or if you use the value as an interface expression—assigning it to a variable whose type is an interface type or passing it as the value for a parameter with an interface type. For example, the statement `IComparable x = 5;` would box the number 5.

It's worth being aware of boxing and unboxing because of the potential performance penalty involved. A single box or unbox operation is cheap, but if you perform hundreds of thousands of them, you not only have the cost of the operations, but you're also creating a *lot* of objects, which gives the garbage collector more work to do. This performance hit isn't usually an issue, but it's worth being aware of so you can measure the effect if you're concerned.

2.3.5   *Summary of value types and reference types*

In this section, we've looked at the differences between value types and reference types and at some of the myths surrounding them. Here are the key points:

- The value of a reference type expression (a variable, for example) is a reference, not an object.
- References are like URLs—they're small pieces of data that let you access the real information.
- The value of a value type expression is the actual data.
- There are times when value types are more efficient than reference types, and vice versa.
- Reference type objects are always on the heap, but value type values can be on either the stack or the heap, depending on context.
- When a reference type is used as a method parameter, by default the argument is passed *by value*, but the value itself is a reference.
- Value type values are boxed when reference type behavior is needed; unboxing is the reverse process.

Now that we've had a look at all the bits of C# 1 that you need to be comfortable with, it's time to take a quick look forward and see where each of the features are enhanced by the later versions of C#.

---

[13] Boxing will *always* occur when you call `GetType()` on a value type variable, because it can't be overridden. You should already know the exact type if you're dealing with the unboxed form, so you can just use `typeof` instead.

2.4 Beyond C# 1: new features on a solid base

The three topics covered in this chapter are vital to all versions of C#. Almost all the new features relate to at least one of them, and they change the balance of how the language is used. Before we wrap up the chapter, let's explore how the new features relate to the old ones. I won't give many details (for some reason the publisher didn't want a 600-page section), but it's helpful to have an idea of where we're going before we get to the nitty-gritty. We'll look at them in the same order as we covered them earlier, starting with delegates.

2.4.1 Features related to delegates

Delegates of all kinds get a boost in C# 2, and then they're given even more special treatment in C# 3. Most of the features aren't new to the CLR but are clever compiler tricks to make delegates work more smoothly within the language. The changes affect not just the syntax you *can* use, but the appearance and feeling of idiomatic C# code. Over time, C# is gaining a more functional approach.

C# 1 has pretty clumsy syntax when it comes to creating a delegate instance. For one thing, even if you need to accomplish something straightforward, you have to write a whole separate method to create a delegate instance for it. C# 2 fixed this with anonymous methods and introduced a simpler syntax for the cases where you still want to use a normal method to provide the action for the delegate. You can also create delegate instances using methods with *compatible* signatures—the method signature no longer has to be exactly the same as the delegate's declaration.

The following listing demonstrates all these improvements.

Listing 2.4 Improvements in delegate instantiation brought in by C# 2

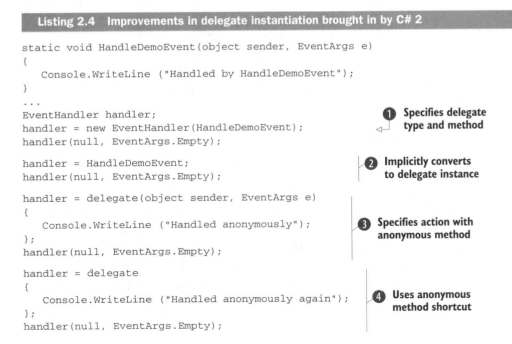

```
static void HandleDemoEvent(object sender, EventArgs e)
{
    Console.WriteLine ("Handled by HandleDemoEvent");
}
...
EventHandler handler;
handler = new EventHandler(HandleDemoEvent);          ❶ Specifies delegate
handler(null, EventArgs.Empty);                           type and method

handler = HandleDemoEvent;                            ❷ Implicitly converts
handler(null, EventArgs.Empty);                          to delegate instance

handler = delegate(object sender, EventArgs e)
{
    Console.WriteLine ("Handled anonymously");        ❸ Specifies action with
};                                                       anonymous method
handler(null, EventArgs.Empty);

handler = delegate
{
    Console.WriteLine ("Handled anonymously again");  ❹ Uses anonymous
};                                                       method shortcut
handler(null, EventArgs.Empty);
```

```
MouseEventHandler mouseHandler = HandleDemoEvent;
mouseHandler(null, new MouseEventArgs(MouseButtons.None,
                                       0, 0, 0, 0));
```

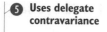 **Uses delegate contravariance**

The first part of the main code ❶ is just C# 1 code, kept for comparison. The remaining delegates all use new features of C# 2. Method group conversions ❷ make event subscription code read a lot more pleasantly—lines such as saveButton.Click += SaveDocument; are straightforward, with no extra fluff to distract the eye. The anonymous method syntax ❸ is a little cumbersome, but it does allow the action to be clear at the point of creation, rather than being another method to look at before you understand what's going on. A shortcut is available when using anonymous methods ❹, but this form can only be used when you don't need the parameters. Anonymous methods have other powerful features as well, but we'll see those later.

The final delegate instance created ❺ is an instance of MouseEventHandler rather than just EventHandler, but the HandleDemoEvent method can still be used due to *contravariance*, which specifies parameter compatibility. *Covariance* specifies return type compatibility. We'll look at both of these in more detail in chapter 5. Event handlers are probably the biggest beneficiaries of this, because suddenly the Microsoft guideline to make all delegate types used in events follow the same convention makes a lot more sense. In C# 1, it didn't matter whether two different event handlers looked quite similar—you had to have a method with an *exactly* matching signature in order to create a delegate instance. In C# 2, you may find yourself able to use the same method to handle many different kinds of events, particularly if the purpose of the method is fairly event independent, such as logging.

C# 3 provides special syntax for instantiating delegate types, using *lambda expressions*. To demonstrate these, we'll use a new delegate type. When the CLR gained generics in .NET 2.0, generic delegate types became available and were used in a number of API calls in generic collections. .NET 3.5 takes things a step further, introducing a group of generic delegate types called Func that all take parameters of specified types and return a value of another specified type. The following listing shows the use of a Func delegate type as well as lambda expressions.

Listing 2.5   Lambda expressions—like improved anonymous methods

```
Func<int,int,string> func = (x, y) => (x * y).ToString();
Console.WriteLine(func(5, 20));
```

Func<int,int,string> is a delegate type that takes two integers and returns a string. The lambda expression in listing 2.5 specifies that the delegate instance (held in func) should multiply the two integers together and call ToString(). The syntax is much more straightforward than that of anonymous methods, and there are other benefits in terms of the amount of type inference the compiler is prepared to perform for you. Lambda expressions are absolutely crucial to LINQ, and you should get ready to make them a core part of your language toolkit. They're not restricted to working with LINQ, though—any use of anonymous methods from C# 2 can use lambda expressions in C# 3, and that will almost always lead to shorter code.

To summarize, the new features related to delegates are as follows:

- *Generics (generic delegate types)*—C# 2
- *Delegate instance creation expressions*—C# 2
- *Anonymous methods*—C# 2
- *Delegate covariance/contravariance*—C# 2
- *Lambda expression*—C# 3

Additionally, C# 4 allows *generic* covariance and contravariance for delegates, which goes beyond what you've just seen. Indeed, generics form one of the principal enhancements to the type system, which we'll look at next.

2.4.2 *Features related to the type system*

The primary new feature in C# 2 regarding the type system is the inclusion of generics. It largely addresses the issues I raised in section 2.2.2 about strongly typed collections, although generic types are useful in a number of other situations too. As a feature, it's elegant, it solves a real problem, and despite a few wrinkles it generally works well. You've seen examples of this in quite a few places already, and it's described fully in the next chapter, so I won't go into any more detail here. Generics form probably the most important feature in C# 2 with respect to the type system, and you'll see generic types throughout the rest of the book.

C# 2 doesn't tackle the issues of return type covariance and parameter contravariance for overriding members or implementing interfaces. But it *does* improve the situation for creating delegate instances in certain situations, as you saw in section 2.4.1.

C# 3 introduced a wealth of new concepts in the type system, most notably *anonymous types*, *implicitly typed local variables*, and *extension methods*. Anonymous types themselves are mostly present for the sake of LINQ, where it's useful to be able to effectively create a data transfer type with a bunch of read-only properties without having to actually write the code for them. There's nothing to stop them from being used outside LINQ, though, which makes life easier for demonstrations. Listing 2.6 shows both features in action.

Listing 2.6 Demonstration of anonymous types and implicit typing

```
var jon = new { Name = "Jon", Age = 31 };
var tom = new { Name = "Tom", Age = 4 };
Console.WriteLine ("{0} is {1}", jon.Name, jon.Age);
Console.WriteLine ("{0} is {1}", tom.Name, tom.Age);
```

The first two lines each show implicit typing (the use of var) and anonymous object initializers (the new {...} bit), which create instances of anonymous types.

There are two things worth noting at this stage, long before we get into the details—points that have caused people to worry needlessly before. The first is that C# 3 is still statically typed. The C# compiler has declared jon and tom to be of a particular type, just as normal, and when you use the properties of the objects, they're normal properties—no dynamic lookup is going on. It's just that you (as a source code author) can't tell the compiler what type to use in the variable declaration because the compiler will be generating the type itself. The properties are also statically typed—here the Age property is of type int, and the Name property is of type string.

The second point is that we haven't created two different anonymous types here. The variables jon and tom both have the same type because the compiler uses the property names, types, and order to work out that it can generate just one type and use it for both statements. This is done on a per-assembly basis, and makes life a lot simpler in terms of being able to assign the value of one variable to another (for example, jon = tom; would be permitted in the previous code) and similar operations.

Extension methods are also there for the sake of LINQ but can be useful outside it. Think of all the times you've wished that a framework type had a certain method, and you've had to write a static utility method to implement it. For instance, to create a new string by reversing an existing one, you might write a static StringUtil.Reverse method. Well, the extension method feature effectively lets you call that static method as if it existed on the string type itself, so you could write

```
string x = "dlrow olleH".Reverse();
```

Extension methods also let you appear to add methods with implementations to interfaces, and LINQ relies on this heavily, allowing calls to all kinds of methods on IEnumerable<T> that have never previously existed.

C# 4 has two features related to the type system. A relatively minor feature is covariance and contravariance for generic delegates and interfaces. This has been present in the CLR since .NET 2.0 came out, but only with the introduction of C# 4 and updates to the generic types in the *Base Class Library* (BCL) has it become usable for C# developers. A far bigger feature—although one many coders may never need—is dynamic typing in C#.

Remember the introduction I gave to static typing, where I tried to use the Length property of an array and a string via the same variable? Well, in C# 4 it works—when you want it to. The following listing shows the same code except for the variable declaration, but working as valid C# 4 code.

Listing 2.7   Dynamic typing in C# 4

```
dynamic o = "hello";
Console.WriteLine(o.Length);
o = new string[] {"hi", "there"};
Console.WriteLine(o.Length);
```

By declaring the variable o as having a static type of dynamic (yes, you read that right), the compiler handles almost everything to do with o differently, leaving all the binding decisions (such as what Length means) until execution time.

Obviously we're going to look at dynamic typing in greater depth, but I want to stress now that C# 4 is still a statically typed language for the most part. Unless you're using the dynamic type (which acts as a static type denoting a dynamic value), every-thing works exactly the same way as before. Most C# developers will only rarely need dynamic typing, and for the rest of the time they can ignore it. When dynamic typing *is* handy, it can be really slick—and it lets you play nicely with code written in dynamic languages running on the *Dynamic Language Runtime* (DLR). I'd just advise you not to start using C# as a primarily dynamic language. If that's what you want, use Iron-Python or something similar; languages that are designed to support dynamic typing from the ground up are likely to have fewer unexpected gotchas.

Here's the quick-view list of these features, along with which version of C# they're introduced in:

- *Generics*—C# 2
- *Limited delegate covariance/contravariance*—C# 2
- *Anonymous types*—C# 3
- *Implicit typing*—C# 3
- *Extension methods*—C# 3
- *Limited generic covariance/contravariance*—C# 4
- *Dynamic typing*—C# 4

After that fairly diverse set of features on the type system, let's look at the features added to one specific part of typing in .NET—value types.

2.4.3 *Features related to value types*

There are only two features to talk about here, both introduced in C# 2. The first goes back to generics yet again, and in particular to collections. One common complaint about using value types in collections with .NET 1.1 was that due to all of the general-purpose APIs being specified in terms of the object type, every operation that added a struct value to a collection would involve boxing it, and you'd have to unbox it when retrieving it. While boxing is pretty cheap for an individual call, it can cause a signifi-cant performance hit if it's used every time with frequently accessed collections. It also takes more memory than it needs to, due to the per-object overhead. Generics fix both the speed and memory deficiencies by using the *real* type involved rather than a general-purpose object. For example, it would've been madness to read a file and store each byte as an element in an ArrayList in .NET 1.1, but in .NET 2.0 it wouldn't be crazy to do the same with a List<byte>.

The second feature addresses another common cause of complaint, particularly when talking to databases—the fact that you can't assign null to a value type variable. There's no such concept as an int value of null, for instance, even though a *database* integer field may well be nullable. That makes it hard to model the database table within a statically typed class without ugliness of some form or another. Nullable types are part of .NET 2.0, and C# 2 includes extra syntax to make them easy to use. The fol-lowing listing gives a brief example of this.

Listing 2.8   Demonstration of a variety of nullable type features

```
int? x = null;                              ◁── Declares, sets nullable variable
x = 5;
if (x != null)                              ◁── Tests for presence of real value
{
  int y = x.Value;                          ◁── Obtains real value
  Console.WriteLine (y);
}
int z = x ?? 10;                            ◁── Uses null-coalescing operator
```

Listing 2.8 shows a number of the features of nullable types and the shorthand that C# provides for working with them. We'll get around to the details of each feature in chapter 4, but the important point here is how much easier and cleaner all of this is than any of the workarounds used in the past.

The list of enhancements is smaller this time, but they're important features in terms of both performance and elegance of expression:

- *Generics—C# 2*
- *Nullable types—C# 2*

2.5   Summary

This chapter has mostly been a revision exercise for C# 1. The aim wasn't to cover any one topic in its entirety, but merely to get everyone on the same page so that I can describe the later features without worrying about the ground that I'm building on.

All of the topics we've covered are core to C# and .NET, but I've seen a lot of misunderstandings around them within community discussions. Although this chapter hasn't gone into much depth about any one point, it'll hopefully have cleared up any confusion that would've made the rest of the book harder to understand.

The three core topics we briefly covered in this chapter have all been significantly enhanced since C# 1, and some features touch on more than one topic. In particular, the addition of generics has an impact on almost every area we've covered in this chapter—it's probably the most widely used and important feature in C# 2. Now that we've finished all our preparations, we can start looking at generics properly in the next chapter.

Part 2

C# 2: Solving the issues of C# 1

In part 1 we took a quick look at a few of the features of C# 2. Now it's time to do the job properly. You'll see how C# 2 fixes various problems that developers ran into when using C# 1, and how C# 2 makes existing features more useful by streamlining them. This is no mean feat, and life with C# 2 is much more pleasant than with C# 1.

The new features in C# 2 have a certain amount of independence. That's not to say they're not related at all; many of the features are based on—or at least interact with—the massive contribution that generics make to the language. But the different topics we'll look at in the next five chapters don't combine into one super-feature.

The first four chapters of this part cover the biggest new features. We'll look at the following:

- *Generics*—The most important new feature in C# 2 (and indeed in the CLR for .NET 2.0), generics allow type and method parameterization in terms of the types they interact with.
- *Nullable types*—Value types such as int and DateTime don't have any concept of "no value present"; nullable types allow you to represent the absence of a meaningful value.
- *Delegates*—Although delegates haven't changed at the CLR level, C# 2 makes them a lot easier to work with. In addition to a few simple shortcuts, the introduction of anonymous methods begins the movement toward a more functional style of programming—a trend that continues in C# 3.

- *Iterators*—Although using iterators has always been simple in C# with the `foreach` statement, it's a pain to implement them in C# 1. The C# 2 compiler is happy to build a state machine for you behind the scenes, hiding a lot of the complexity involved.

Once we've covered the major, complex new features of C# 2 with a chapter dedicated to each one, chapter 7 rounds off the coverage by introducing several simpler features. Simpler doesn't necessarily mean less useful; partial types, in particular, are crucial for better designer support in versions of Visual Studio from 2005 onward. The same feature is beneficial for other generated code, too. Likewise, many C# developers take the ability to write a property with a public getter and a private setter for granted these days, but it was only introduced in C# 2.

When the first edition of this book was published, many developers still hadn't used C# 2 at all. My impression in 2013 is that it's rare to find someone who's currently using C#, but who hasn't at least dabbled with C# 2, probably 3, and quite often 4. The topics covered here are fundamental to how later versions of C# work; in particular, attempting to learn about LINQ without understanding generics and iterators would be tricky. The chapter on iterators is also related to C# 5's asynchronous methods; the two features are very different on the face of it, but both involve state machines built by the compiler to change the conventional flow of execution.

If you've been using C# 2 and upward for a while, you may find a lot of this part covers familiar ground, but I suspect you'll still benefit from a deeper knowledge of the details presented.

Parameterized typing
with generics

This chapter covers

- Type inference for generic methods
- Type constraints
- Reflection and generics
- CLR behavior
- Limitations of generics
- Comparisons with other languages

True story:[1] The other day my wife and I went out to do our weekly grocery shopping. Just before we left, she asked me if I had the list. I confirmed that I *did* have the list, and off we went. It was only when we got to the grocery store that our mistake became obvious. My wife had been asking about the *shopping* list, whereas I'd brought the list of neat features in C# 2. When we asked an assistant whether we could buy any anonymous methods, we received a strange look.

---

[1] By which I mean "convenient for the purposes of introducing the chapter"—not necessarily *accurate*.

If only we could've expressed ourselves more clearly! If only she'd had some way of saying that she wanted me to bring the list of items we wanted to buy! If only we'd had generics…

For most developers, generics are the most important new feature of C# 2. They enhance performance, make your code more expressive, and move a lot of safety checks from execution time to compile time. Essentially, they allow you to *parameterize* types and methods. Just as normal method calls often have parameters to tell them what *values* to use, generic types and methods have type parameters to tell them what *types* to use. It all sounds confusing to start with—and if you're completely new to generics, you can expect a certain amount of head scratching—but once you get the basic idea, you'll come to love them.

In this chapter, we'll look at how to use generic types and methods that others have provided (whether in the framework or as third-party libraries), and how to write your own. Along the way, we'll look at how generics work with the reflection calls in the API, and at a bit of detail around how the CLR handles generics. To conclude the chapter, I'll present some of the most frequently encountered limitations of generics, along with possible workarounds, and compare generics in C# with similar features in other languages.

First, though, you need to understand the problems that led to generics being devised in the first place.

3.1   *Why generics are necessary*

If you still have any C# 1 code available, look at it and count the casts—particularly in code that uses collections extensively. Don't forget that almost every use of foreach contains an implicit cast. When you use types that are designed to work with many different types of data, that naturally leads to casting, quietly telling the compiler not to worry, that everything's fine; just treat the expression over there as if it had *this* particular type. Using almost any API that has object as either a parameter type or a return type will probably involve casts at some point. Having a single-class hierarchy with object as the root makes some things more straightforward, but the object type in itself is extremely dull, and to do anything genuinely useful with an object you almost always need to cast it.

Casts are bad, m'kay? Not bad in an *almost never do this* kind of way (like mutable structs and nonprivate fields) but bad in a *necessary evil* kind of way. They're an indication that you ought to give the compiler more information somehow, and that you're choosing to ask the compiler to trust you at compile time and to generate a check that will run at execution time to keep you honest.

If you need to tell the compiler the information somehow, chances are that anyone *reading* your code is also going to need the same information. They can see it where you're casting, of course, but that's not terribly useful. The ideal place to keep such information is usually at the point where you declare a variable or method. This is even more important if you're providing a type or method that other people will call *without access to your code.* Generics allow library providers to prevent their users from compiling code that calls the library with bad arguments.

In C# 1, you had to rely on manually written documentation, which can easily become incomplete or inaccurate, as duplicate information so often is. When the extra information can be declared in code as part of a method or type declaration, everyone can work more productively. The compiler can do more checking; the IDE can present IntelliSense options based on the extra information (for instance, offering the members of `string` as the next step when you access an element within a list of strings); callers of methods can be more confident that arguments passed in and values returned are correct; and anyone maintaining your code can better understand what was running through your head when you originally wrote it.

> **WILL GENERICS REDUCE YOUR BUG COUNT?** Every description of generics I've read (including my own) emphasizes the importance of compile-time type checking over execution-time type checking. I'll let you in on a secret: I can't remember ever fixing a bug in released code that was directly due to the lack of type checking. In other words, the casts we put in C# 1 code always worked, in my experience. Those casts were like warning signs, forcing us to think about the type safety explicitly rather than it flowing naturally in the code we wrote. But although generics may not radically reduce the number of type safety bugs you encounter, the greater readability they afford can reduce the number of bugs across the board. Code that's simple to understand is simple to get right. Likewise, code that has to be robust in the face of malicious callers is much simpler to write correctly when the type system can provide appropriate guarantees.

All of this would be enough to make generics worthwhile, but there are performance improvements, too. First, because the compiler can perform more enforcement, that leaves less to be checked at execution time. Second, the JIT can treat value types in a particularly clever way that manages to eliminate boxing and unboxing in many situations. In some cases, this can make a huge difference in performance in terms of both speed and memory consumption.

Many of the benefits of generics may strike you as being similar to the benefits of statically typed languages over dynamic ones: better compile-time checking, more information expressed directly in the code, more IDE support, better performance. The reason for this is fairly simple: when you're using a general API (such as `Array-List`) that can't differentiate between the different types, you effectively *are* in a dynamic situation in terms of access to that API. The reverse isn't generally true, by the way—the benefits that dynamic languages provide rarely apply to the choice between generic and nongeneric APIs. When you *can* reasonably use generics, the decision to do so is usually a no-brainer.

So, those are the goodies awaiting you in C# 2—now it's time to start using generics.

3.2   *Simple generics for everyday use*

The topic of generics has a lot of dark corners if you want to know *everything* about it. The C# language specification goes into a great deal of detail in order to make sure that the behavior is specified in pretty much every conceivable case. But you don't need to understand most of those corner cases in order to be productive. (The same is true in other areas, in fact. For example, you don't need to know all the exact rules about definite assignment—you just fix the code appropriately when the compiler complains.)

This section will cover most of what you'll need in your day-to-day use of generics, both for consuming generic APIs that other people have created and for creating your own. If you get stuck while reading this chapter but want to keep making progress, I suggest you concentrate on what you need to know in order to use generic types and methods within the framework and other libraries; writing your own generic types and methods crops up a lot less often than using the framework ones.

We'll start by looking at one of the collection classes introduced in .NET 2.0—
Dictionary<TKey,TValue>.

3.2.1   *Learning by example: a generic dictionary*

Using generic types can be straightforward if you don't happen to hit some of the limitations and start wondering what's wrong. You don't even need to know any of the terminology to make a pretty good guess as to what a piece of code will do, and with a bit of trial and error you could experiment your way to writing your own working code. (One of the benefits of generics is that more checking is done at compile time, so you're more likely to have working code when it all compiles—this makes the experimentation simpler.) Of course, the aim of this chapter is to build your knowledge so that you *won't* be using guesswork—you'll know what's going on at every stage.

For now, let's look at some code that's straightforward, even if the syntax is unfamiliar. The following listing uses a Dictionary<TKey,TValue> (roughly the generic equivalent of the nongeneric Hashtable class) to count the frequencies of words in a given piece of text.

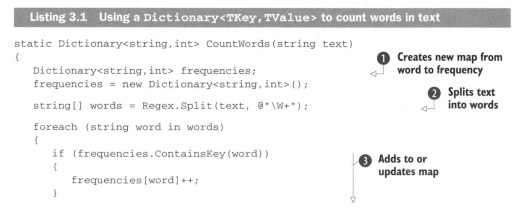

Listing 3.1   Using a `Dictionary<TKey,TValue>` to count words in text

```
static Dictionary<string,int> CountWords(string text)
{
   Dictionary<string,int> frequencies;
   frequencies = new Dictionary<string,int>();

   string[] words = Regex.Split(text, @"\W+");

   foreach (string word in words)
   {
      if (frequencies.ContainsKey(word))
      {
         frequencies[word]++;
      }
```

❶ Creates new map from word to frequency

❷ Splits text into words

❸ Adds to or updates map

```
        else
        {
            frequencies[word] = 1;
        }
    }
    return frequencies;
}
...
string text = @"Do you like green eggs and ham?
                I do not like them, Sam-I-am.
                I do not like green eggs and ham.";

Dictionary<string,int> frequencies = CountWords(text);
foreach (KeyValuePair<string,int> entry in frequencies)
{
    string word = entry.Key;
    int frequency = entry.Value;
    Console.WriteLine ("{0}: {1}", word, frequency);
}
```

❸ **Adds to or updates map**

❹ **Prints each key/value pair from map**

The CountWords method first creates an empty map from string to int ❶. This will effectively count how often each word is used within the given text. You then use a regular expression ❷ to split the text into words. It's crude—you end up with an empty string due to the period at the end of the text, and *do* and *Do* are counted separately. These issues are easily fixable, but I wanted to keep the code as simple as possible for this example.

For each word, you check whether it's already in the map. If it is, you increment the existing count; otherwise, you give the word an initial count of 1 ❸. Note how the incrementing code doesn't need to do a cast to int in order to perform the addition; the value you retrieve is known to be an int at compile time. The step incrementing the count is actually performing a get on the indexer for the map, then incrementing, and then performing a set on the indexer. You may find it easier to keep this explicit, using frequencies[word] = frequencies[word] + 1; instead.

The final part of the listing is familiar: enumerating through a Hashtable gives a similar (nongeneric) DictionaryEntry with Key and Value properties for each entry ❹. But in C# 1, you would've needed to cast both the word and the frequency, because the key and value would've been returned as just object. That also means that the frequency would've been boxed. Admittedly you don't *have* to put the word and the frequency into variables—you could've had a single call to Console.Write-Line and passed entry.Key and entry.Value as arguments. I included the variables here to ram home the point that no casting is necessary.

Now that you've seen an example, let's look at what it means to talk about Dictionary<TKey,TValue> in the first place. What are TKey and TValue, and why do they have angle brackets around them?

3.2.2 *Generic types and type parameters*

There are two forms of generics in C#: *generic types* (including classes, interfaces, delegates, and structures—there are no generic enums) and *generic methods*. Both are essentially ways of expressing an API (whether it's for a single generic method or a whole generic type) such that in some places where you'd expect to see a normal type, you'll see a *type parameter* instead.

A type parameter is a placeholder for a real type. Type parameters appear in angle brackets within a generic declaration, using commas to separate them. So in `Dictionary<TKey,TValue>`, the type parameters are `TKey` and `TValue`. When you use a generic type or method, you specify the *real* types you want to use. These are called the *type arguments*—for example, in listing 3.1 the type arguments were `string` (for `TKey`) and `int` (for `TValue`).

> **JARGON ALERT!** A lot of detailed terminology is involved in generics. I've included it for reference—and because occasionally it makes it easier to talk about topics precisely. It could also be useful if you ever need to consult the language specification, but you're unlikely to need this terminology in day-to-day life. Just grin and bear it for the moment. A lot of this terminology is defined in section 4.4 of the C# 5 specification ("Constructed Types")—look there for further details.

The form of a generic type where none of the type parameters have been provided with type arguments is called an *unbound generic type*. When type arguments are specified, the type is said to be a *constructed type*. Unbound generic types are effectively blueprints for constructed types, much like how types (generic or not) can be regarded as blueprints for objects. It's a sort of extra layer of abstraction. Figure 3.1 shows this graphically.

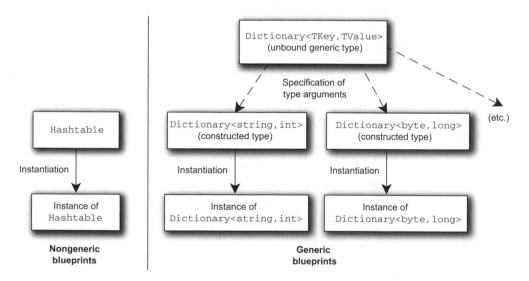

Figure 3.1 Unbound generic types act as blueprints for constructed types, which then act as blueprints for actual objects, just as nongeneric types do.

As a further complication, types can be open or closed. An *open type* is one that still involves a type parameter (as one of the type arguments, or as the array element type, for example), whereas a *closed type* is one that isn't open; every aspect of the type is known precisely. All code actually *executes* in the context of a closed constructed type. The only time you'll see an unbound generic type within C# code (other than as a declaration) is within the typeof operator, which you'll meet in section 3.4.4.

The idea of a type parameter "receiving" information and a type argument "providing" the information—the dashed lines in figure 3.1—is exactly the same as with method parameters and arguments, although type arguments have to be types rather than just arbitrary values. The type argument has to be known at compile time, but it can be (or can involve) a type parameter from the relevant context.

You can think of a closed type as having the API of the open type but with the type parameters being replaced with their corresponding type arguments.[2] Table 3.1 shows some public method and property declarations from the open type Dictionary <TKey,TValue> and the equivalent member in the closed type you built from it— Dictionary<string,int>.

Table 3.1 Examples of how method signatures in generic types contain placeholders, which are replaced when the type arguments are specified

Method signature in generic type	Method signature after type parameter substitution
void Add(TKey key, TValue value)	void Add(string key, int value)
TValue this[TKey key] { get; set; }	int this[string key] { get; set; }
bool ContainsValue(TValue value)	bool ContainsValue(int value)
bool ContainsKey(TKey key)	bool ContainsKey(string key)

One important thing to note is that none of the methods in table 3.1 are actually generic methods. They're normal methods within a generic type, and they happen to use the type parameters declared as part of the type. We'll look at generic methods in the next section.

Now that you know what TKey and TValue mean, and what the angle brackets are for, you can see what the declarations in table 3.1 would look like within the class declaration. Here's what the code for Dictionary<TKey,TValue> might look like, although the actual method implementations are all missing, and there are more members in reality:

```
namespace System.Collections.Generic
{
    public class Dictionary<TKey,TValue>           Declares
                                                   generic
                                                   class
        : IEnumerable<KeyValuePair<TKey,TValue>>
                                                   Implements
                                                   generic
                                                   interface
```

---

[2] It doesn't always work *exactly* that way—there are corner cases that break when you apply that simple rule—but it's an easy way of thinking about generics that works in the vast majority of situations.

```
    {
        public Dictionary() { ... }
        public void Add(TKey key, TValue value) { ... }
        public TValue this[TKey key]
        {
            get { ... }
            set { ... }
        }

        public bool ContainsValue(TValue value) { ... }

        public bool ContainsKey(TKey key) { ... }

        [... other members ...]
    }
}
```

Declares method using type parameters (points to `public void Add(TKey key, TValue value) { ... }`)

Declares parameterless constructor (points to `public Dictionary() { ... }`)

Note how `Dictionary<TKey,TValue>` implements the generic interface `IEnumerable<KeyValuePair<TKey,TValue>>` (and many other interfaces in real life). Whatever type arguments you specify for the class are applied to the interface where the same type parameters are used, so in this example, `Dictionary<string,int>` implements `IEnumerable<KeyValuePair<string,int>>`. That's sort of a doubly generic interface—it's the `IEnumerable<T>` interface with the structure `KeyValuePair<string,int>` as the type argument. It's because it implements that interface that listing 3.1 was able to enumerate the keys and values as it did.

It's also worth pointing out that the constructor doesn't list the type parameters in angle brackets. The type parameters belong to the *type* rather than to the particular constructor, so that's where they're declared. Members only declare type parameters when they're introducing new ones—and only methods can do that.

> **PRONOUNCING GENERICS**   If you ever need to describe a generic type to a colleague, it's conventional to use "of" to introduce the type parameters or arguments—so `List<T>` is pronounced "list of T," for example. In VB, this is part of the language: the type itself would be written as `List(Of T)`. When there are multiple type parameters, I find it makes sense to separate them with a word appropriate to the meaning of the overall type, so I'd talk about a "dictionary of string *to* int" in order to emphasize the mapping aspect, but a "tuple of string *and* int."

Generic types can effectively be overloaded on the number of type parameters, so you could define `MyType`, `MyType<T>`, `MyType<T,U>`, `MyType<T,U,V>`, and so forth, all within the same namespace. The names of the type parameters aren't used when considering this—just how many there are. These types are unrelated except in name—there's no default conversion from one to another, for instance. The same is true for generic methods: two methods can be exactly the same in signature other than the number of type parameters. Although this may sound like a recipe for disaster, it can be useful if you want to take advantage of *generic type inference* where the compiler can work out some of the type arguments for you. We'll come back to that in section 3.3.2.

NAMING CONVENTIONS FOR TYPE PARAMETERS Although you *could* have a type with type parameters T, U, and V, it wouldn't give much indication of what they actually meant or how they should be used. Compare this with Dictionary <TKey,TValue>, where it's obvious that TKey represents the type of the keys and TValue represents the type of the values. Where you have a single type parameter and its meaning is clear, T is conventionally used (List<T> is a good example of this). Multiple type parameters should usually be named according to meaning, using the prefix T to indicate a type parameter. Every so often, you may run into a type with multiple single-letter type parameters (SynchronizedKeyedCollection<K,T>, for example), but you should try to avoid creating the same situation yourself.

Now that you have an idea of what generic types do, let's look at generic methods.

3.2.3 *Generic methods and reading generic declarations*

I've mentioned generic methods a few times, but we haven't actually met one yet. You may find the overall idea of generic methods more confusing than generic types—they're somehow less natural for the brain—but it's the same basic principle. You're used to the parameters and return value of a method having firmly specified types, and you've seen how a generic type can use its type parameters in method declarations. Generic methods go one step further: even if you know exactly which constructed type you're dealing with, an individual method can have type parameters too. Don't worry if you're still none the wiser—the concept is likely to click at some point, after you've seen enough examples.

Dictionary<TKey,TValue> doesn't have any generic methods, but its close neighbor List<T> does. As you can imagine, List<T> is just a list of items of whatever type is specified—List<string> is a list of strings, for instance. Remembering that T is the type parameter for the whole *class*, let's dissect a generic method declaration. Figure 3.2 identifies the different parts of the declaration of the ConvertAll method.

When you look at a generic declaration—whether it's for a generic type or a generic method—trying to work out what it means can be daunting, particularly if you have to deal with generic types of generic types, as you did when you saw the interface implemented by the dictionary. The key is to not panic—just take things calmly and pick an example situation. Use a different type for each type parameter, and apply them all consistently.

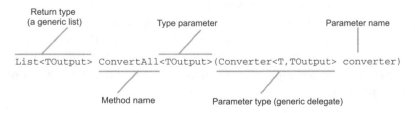

Figure 3.2   The anatomy of a generic method declaration

In this case, let's start by replacing the type parameter of the type containing the method (the <T> part of List<T>). We'll stick with the concept of a list of strings and replace T with string everywhere in the method declaration:

```
List<TOutput> ConvertAll<TOutput>(Converter<string,TOutput> converter)
```

That looks a bit better, but you've still got TOutput to deal with. You can tell that it's a method's type parameter (apologies for the confusing terminology) because it's in angle brackets directly after the name of the method, so let's try another familiar type—Guid—as the type argument for TOutput. Again you replace the type parameter with the type argument everywhere. You can now think of the method as if it were nongeneric, removing the type parameter part of the declaration:

```
List<Guid> ConvertAll(Converter<string,Guid> converter)
```

Now everything is expressed in terms of a concrete type, so it's easier to think about. Even though the real method is generic, we'll treat it as if it weren't for the sake of understanding it better. Let's go through the elements of this declaration from left to right:

- The method returns a List<Guid>.
- The method's name is ConvertAll.
- The method has a single parameter: a Converter<string,Guid> called converter.

Now you just need to know what Converter<string,Guid> is and you're all done. Not surprisingly, Converter<string,Guid> is a constructed *generic delegate type* (the unbound type is Converter<TInput,TOutput>), which is used to convert a string to a GUID.

So you have a method that can operate on a list of strings, using a converter to produce a list of GUIDs. Now that you understand the method's signature, it's easier to understand the documentation, which confirms that this method does the obvious thing and creates a new List<Guid>, converts each element in the original list into the target type, adding it to the new list, and then returns that list. Thinking about the signature in concrete terms gives you a clearer mental model, and makes it simpler to think about what the method might do. Although this technique may sound somewhat simplistic, I find it useful for complicated methods even now. Some of the LINQ method signatures with four type parameters are fearsome beasts, but putting them into concrete terms tames them significantly.

Just to prove I haven't been leading you down the garden path, let's take a look at the ConvertAll method in action. The following listing shows the conversion of a list of integers into a list of floating-point numbers, where each element of the second list is the square root of the corresponding element in the first list. After the conversion, the results are printed.

Listing 3.2 The `List<T>.ConvertAll<TOutput>` method in action

```
static double TakeSquareRoot(int x)
{
    return Math.Sqrt(x);
}
...
List<int> integers = new List<int>();
integers.Add(1);
integers.Add(2);
integers.Add(3);
integers.Add(4);
Converter<int,double> converter = TakeSquareRoot;
List<double> doubles;
doubles = integers.ConvertAll<double>(converter);
foreach (double d in doubles)
{
    Console.WriteLine(d);
}
```

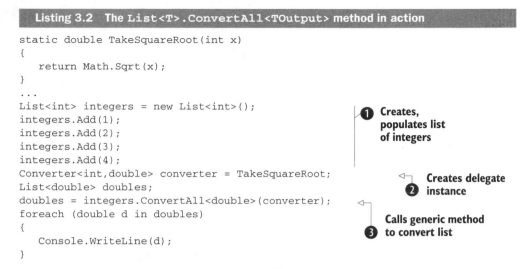

❶ Creates, populates list of integers

❷ Creates delegate instance

❸ Calls generic method to convert list

The creation and population of the list ❶ is straightforward enough—it's just a strongly typed list of integers. The assignment to `converter` ❷ uses a feature of delegates (method group conversions) which is new to C# 2 and which we'll discuss in more detail in section 5.2. Although I don't like using a feature before describing it fully, the line would've been too long to fit on the page with the C# 1 delegate syntax. It does what you expect it to, though. At ❸ you call the generic method, specifying the type argument for the method in the same way you've seen for generic types. This is one situation where you could've used type inference to avoid explicitly specifying the type argument, but I wanted to take it one step at a time. Writing out the list that has been returned is simple, and when you run the code you'll see it print 1, 1.414…, 1.732…, and 2, as expected.

What's the point of all of this? We could've just used a `foreach` loop to go through the integers and printed out the square root immediately, of course, but it's not uncommon to want to convert a list of one type to a list of another by performing some logic on it. The code to do it manually is simple, but it's easier to read a version that does it in a single method call. That's often the way with generic methods—they often do things that previously you'd have happily done "longhand" but that are simpler with a method call. Before generics, there could've been a similar operation to `ConvertAll` on `ArrayList` converting from `object` to `object`, but it would've been a lot less satisfactory. Anonymous methods (see section 5.4) also help here—if you hadn't wanted to introduce an extra method, you could've specified the conversion inline. LINQ and lambda expressions take this pattern much further, as you'll see in part 3 of the book.

Note that generic methods can be part of nongeneric types as well. The following listing shows a generic method being declared and used within a normal nongeneric type.

Listing 3.3   Implementing a generic method in a nongeneric type

```
static List<T> MakeList<T>(T first, T second)
{
    List<T> list = new List<T>();
    list.Add(first);
    list.Add(second);
    return list;
}
...
List<string> list = MakeList<string>("Line 1", "Line 2");
foreach (string x in list)
{
    Console.WriteLine (x);
}
```

The `MakeList<T>` generic method only needs one type parameter (`T`). All it does is build a list containing the two parameters. It's worth noting that you can use `T` as a type argument when you create the `List<T>` in the method. Just as when we were looking at generic declarations, you can think of the implementation as (roughly speaking) replacing all of the mentions of `T` with `string`. When you call the method, you use the same syntax you've seen before to specify the type arguments.

All okay so far? You should now have the hang of simple generics. There's a bit more complexity to come, I'm afraid, but if you're happy with the fundamental idea of generics, you've jumped the biggest hurdle. Don't worry if it's still a bit hazy (particularly when it comes to the open/closed/unbound/constructed terminology), but now would be a good time to do some experimentation so you can see generics in action before you go any further. If you haven't used the generic collections before, you might want to quickly look at appendix B, which describes what's available. The collection types give you a simple starting point for playing with generics, and they're widely used in almost every nontrivial .NET program.

One thing you may find when you experiment is that it's hard to go only part of the way. Once you make one part of an API generic, you'll often find that you need to rework other code, either making that generic too or putting in the casts required by the new, more strongly typed method calls. An alternative would be to have a strongly typed implementation, using generic classes under the covers, but leaving a weakly typed API for the moment. As time goes on, you'll become more confident about when it's appropriate to use generics.

3.3   *Beyond the basics*

The relatively simple uses of generics we've looked at so far can get you a long way, but there are some more features that can help you go further.

We'll start by examining *type constraints*, which give you more control over which type arguments can be specified. They're useful when creating your own generic types and methods, and you'll need to understand them in order to know what options are available when using the framework, too.

We'll then examine *type inference*—a handy compiler trick that allows you to not explicitly state the type arguments when you're using generic methods. You don't have to use it, but it can make your code a lot easier to read when used appropriately. You'll see in part 3 of the book that the C# compiler is gradually being allowed to infer a lot more information from your code, while still keeping the language safe and statically typed.[3]

The last part of this section deals with obtaining the default value of a type parameter and the comparisons that are available when you're writing generic code. We'll wrap up with an example that demonstrates most of the features we've covered and that's a useful class in itself.

Although this section delves a bit deeper into generics, there's nothing *really* hard about it. There's plenty to remember, but all the features serve a purpose, and you'll be grateful for them when you need them. Let's get started.

3.3.1 *Type constraints*

So far, all the type parameters we've looked at can be applied to any type at all—they're *unconstrained*. You can have a List<int>, a Dictionary<object,FileMode>, anything. That's fine when you're dealing with collections that don't have to interact with what they store, but not all uses of generics are like that. Often you want to call methods on instances of the type parameter, or create new instances, or make sure you only accept reference types (or only accept value types). In other words, you want to specify rules that say which type arguments are considered valid for your generic type or method. In C# 2, you do this with *constraints*.

Four kinds of constraints are available, and the general syntax is the same for all of them. Constraints come at the end of the declaration of a generic method or type and are introduced by the contextual keyword where. They can be combined together in sensible ways, as you'll see later. First, though, we'll explore each kind of constraint in turn.

REFERENCE TYPE CONSTRAINTS

The first kind of constraint ensures that the type argument used is a reference type. It's expressed as T : class and must be the first constraint specified for that type parameter. The type argument can be any class, interface, array, delegate, or another type parameter that's already known to be a reference type. For example, consider the following declaration:

```
struct RefSample<T> where T : class
```

Valid closed types using this declaration include

- RefSample<IDisposable>
- RefSample<string>
- RefSample<int[]>

---

[3] Well, aside from any C# 4 code that *explicitly* uses dynamic typing, anyway.

Invalid closed types include

- `RefSample<Guid>`
- `RefSample<int>`

I deliberately made `RefSample` a `struct` (and therefore a value type) to emphasize the difference between the constrained type parameter and the type itself. `RefSample<string>` is still a value type with value semantics everywhere—it just happens to use the `string` type wherever `T` is specified in the code.

When a type parameter is constrained this way, you can compare references (including `null`) with `==` and `!=`, but be aware that unless there are any other constraints, only references will be compared, even if the type in question overloads those operators (as `string` does, for example). With a conversion type constraint (described shortly), you can end up with *compiler guaranteed* overloads of `==` and `!=`, in which case those overloads are used—but that's relatively rare.

VALUE TYPE CONSTRAINTS

The value type constraint, expressed as `T : struct`, ensures that the type argument used is a value type, including enums. It excludes nullable types (as described in chapter 4), though. Let's look at an example declaration:

```
class ValSample<T> where T : struct
```

Valid closed types include

- `ValSample<int>`
- `ValSample<FileMode>`

Invalid closed types include

- `ValSample<object>`
- `ValSample<StringBuilder>`

This time `ValSample` is a reference type, despite `T` being constrained to be a value type. Note that `System.Enum` and `System.ValueType` are both reference types in themselves, so they aren't allowed as valid type arguments for `ValSample`. When a type parameter is constrained to be a value type, comparisons using `==` and `!=` are prohibited.

I rarely find myself using value or reference type constraints, although you'll see in the next chapter that nullable value types rely on value type constraints. The remaining two constraints are likely to prove more useful when you're writing your own generic types.

CONSTRUCTOR TYPE CONSTRAINTS

The constructor type constraint is expressed as `T : new()` and must be the *last* constraint for any particular type parameter. It simply checks that the type argument used has a parameterless constructor that can be used to create an instance. This is the case for any value type; for any nonstatic, nonabstract class without any explicitly declared constructors; and for any nonabstract class with an explicit public parameterless constructor.

C# VERSUS CLI STANDARDS   There's a discrepancy between the C# and CLI standards when it comes to value types and constructors. The C# specification states that all value types have a default parameterless constructor, and the language uses the same syntax to call both explicitly declared constructors and the parameterless one, relying on the compiler to do the right thing underneath. The CLI specification has no such requirement but provides a special instruction to create a default value without specifying any parameters. You can see this discrepancy at work when you use reflection to find the constructors of a value type—you won't see a parameterless one.

Again, let's look at a quick example, this time for a method. Just to show how it's useful, I'll give the implementation of the method too:

```
public T CreateInstance<T>() where T : new()
{
    return new T();
}
```

This method returns a new instance of whatever type you specify, provided that it has a parameterless constructor. That means calls to `CreateInstance<int>()` and `CreateInstance<object>()` are okay, but `CreateInstance<string>()` isn't, because `string` doesn't have a parameterless constructor.

There's no way of constraining type parameters to force other constructor signatures. For instance, you can't specify that there has to be a constructor taking a single string parameter. It can be frustrating, but that's unfortunately just the way it is. We'll look at this issue in more detail when we consider the various restrictions of .NET generics in section 3.5.

Constructor type constraints can be useful when you need to use factory-like patterns, where one object will create another one as and when it needs to. Factories often need to produce objects that are compatible with a certain interface, of course, and that's where our last type of constraint comes in.

CONVERSION TYPE CONSTRAINTS

The final (and most complicated) kind of constraint lets you specify another type that the type argument must be implicitly convertible to via an identity, reference, or boxing conversion. You can specify that one type argument be convertible to another type argument, too—this is called a *type parameter* constraint. These constraints make it harder to understand the declaration, but they can be handy every so often. Table 3.2 shows some examples of generic type declarations with conversion type constraints, along with valid and invalid examples of corresponding constructed types.

The third constraint in table 3.2, `T : IComparable<T>`, is just one example of using a generic type as the constraint. Other variations, such as `T : List<U>` (where `U` is another type parameter) and `T : IList<string>`, are also fine.

Table 3.2   Examples of conversion type constraints

Declaration	Constructed type examples
`class Sample<T> where T : Stream`	*Valid:* `Sample<Stream>` (identity conversion) *Invalid:* `Sample<string>`
`struct Sample<T> where T : IDisposable`	*Valid:* `Sample<SqlConnection>` (reference conversion) *Invalid:* `Sample<StringBuilder>`
`class Sample<T> where T : IComparable<T>`	*Valid:* `Sample<int>` (boxing conversion) *Invalid:* `Sample<FileInfo>`
`class Sample<T,U> where T : U`	*Valid:* `Sample<Stream,IDisposable>` (reference conversion) *Invalid:* `Sample<string,IDisposable>`

You can specify multiple interfaces, but only one class. For instance, this is fine (if hard to satisfy):

```
class Sample<T> where T : Stream,
                         IEnumerable<string>,
                         IComparable<int>
```

But this isn't:

```
class Sample<T> where T : Stream,
                         ArrayList,
                         IComparable<int>
```

No type can derive directly from more than one class anyway, so such a constraint would usually either be impossible (like the preceding one) or part of it would be redundant (specifying that the type had to derive from both `Stream` and `Memory-Stream`, for example).

There's one more set of restrictions: the type you specify can't be a value type, a sealed class (such as `string`), or any of the following "special" types:

- `System.Object`
- `System.Enum`
- `System.ValueType`
- `System.Delegate`

WORKING AROUND THE LACK OF ENUM AND DELEGATE CONSTRAINTS   The inability to specify the preceding types in conversion type constraints sounds like it's due to a CLR restriction—but it's not. That may have been true historically (at some point when generics were still being designed), but if you construct the appropriate code in IL, it works fine. The CLI specification even lists enum and delegate constraints as examples and explains what would be valid and what wouldn't. This is frustrating, and there are plenty of generic methods that would be useful when restricted to delegates or enums. I have an open source project called Unconstrained Melody (http://code.google.com/ p/unconstrained-melody/), which performs some hackery to build a class library that *does* have these constraints on various utility methods. Although the C# compiler won't let you declare such constraints, it's happy to apply them when you call the methods in the library. Perhaps the prohibition will be lifted in a future version of C#.

Conversion type constraints are probably the most useful kind, as they mean you can use members of the specified type on instances of the type parameter. One particularly handy example of this is T : IComparable<T>, which enables you to compare two instances of T meaningfully and directly. We'll look at an example of this (and discuss other forms of comparison) in section 3.3.3.

COMBINING CONSTRAINTS

I've mentioned the possibility of having multiple constraints, and you've seen them in action for conversion type constraints, but I haven't shown the different kinds being combined together. Obviously no type can be both a reference type and a value type, so that combination is forbidden. Likewise, *every* value type has a parameterless constructor, so you can't specify the construction constraint when you already have a value type constraint (although you can still use new T() within methods if T is constrained to be a value type). If you have multiple conversion type constraints and one of them is a class, that has to come before the interfaces—and you can't specify the same interface more than once. Different type parameters can have different constraints, and they're each introduced with a separate where.

Let's look at some valid and invalid examples:

Valid:
```
class Sample<T> where T : class, IDisposable, new()
class Sample<T> where T : struct, IDisposable
class Sample<T,U> where T : class where U : struct, T
class Sample<T,U> where T : Stream where U : IDisposable
```

Invalid:
```
class Sample<T> where T : class, struct
class Sample<T> where T : Stream, class
class Sample<T> where T : new(), Stream
class Sample<T> where T : IDisposable, Stream
class Sample<T> where T : XmlReader, IComparable, IComparable
class Sample<T,U> where T : struct where U : class, T
class Sample<T,U> where T : Stream, U : IDisposable
```

I included the last example in each list because it's so easy to try the invalid one instead of the valid version, and the compiler error isn't at all helpful. Just remember that each list of type parameter constraints needs its own introductory where. The third valid example is interesting—if U is a value type, how can it derive from T, which is a reference type? The answer is that T could be an object or an interface that U implements. It's a pretty nasty constraint, though.

SPECIFICATION TERMINOLOGY The specification categorizes constraints slightly differently—into *primary* constraints, *secondary* constraints, and *constructor* constraints. A primary constraint is a reference type constraint, a value type constraint, or a conversion type constraint using a class. A secondary constraint is a conversion type constraint using an interface or another type parameter. I don't find these particularly useful categories, but they make it easier to define the grammar of constraints: the primary constraint is optional but you can only have one; you can have as many secondary constraints as you like; the constructor constraint is optional (unless you have a value type constraint, in which case it's forbidden).

Now that you know all you need to read generic type declarations, let's look at the type argument inference that I mentioned earlier. In listing 3.2 you explicitly stated the type arguments to List<T>.ConvertAll, and you did the same in listing 3.3 for the MakeList method—now let's ask the compiler to work them out when it can, making it simpler to call generic methods.

3.3.2   *Type inference for type arguments of generic methods*

Specifying type arguments when you're calling a generic method can often seem pretty redundant. Usually it's obvious what the type arguments should be, based on the method arguments themselves. To make life easier, from C# 2 onward, the compiler is allowed to be smart in tightly defined ways, so you can call the method without explicitly stating the type arguments. But before we go any further, I should stress that this is only true for generic *methods*. It doesn't apply to generic *types*.

Let's look at the relevant lines from listing 3.3 and see how things can be simplified. Here are the lines declaring and invoking the method:

```
static List<T> MakeList<T>(T first, T second)
...
List<string> list = MakeList<string>("Line 1", "Line 2");
```

Look at the arguments—they're both strings. Each of the parameters in the method is declared to be of type T. Even if you didn't have the <string> part of the method invocation expression, it would be fairly obvious that you meant to call the method using string as the type argument for T. The compiler allows you to omit it, leaving this:

```
List<string> list = MakeList("Line 1", "Line 2");
```

That's a bit neater, isn't it? At least, it's shorter. That doesn't always mean it's more readable, of course. In some cases it'll be harder for the reader to work out what type arguments you're trying to use, even if the compiler can do it easily. I recommend that you judge each case on its merits. My personal preference is to let the compiler infer the type arguments in *most* cases where it works.

Note how the compiler definitely knows that you're using string as the type argument, because the assignment to list works too, and that still *does* specify the type argument (and has to). The assignment has no influence on the type argument inference process, though. It just means that if the compiler works out what type arguments it thinks you want to use but gets it wrong, you're still likely to get a compile-time error.

How could the compiler get it wrong? Suppose you actually want to use object as the type argument. The method parameters are still valid, but the compiler thinks you meant to use string, as they're both strings. Changing one of the parameters to explicitly be cast to object makes type inference fail, as one of the method arguments would suggest that T should be string, and the other suggests that T should be object. The compiler *could* look at this and say that setting T to object would satisfy everything but setting T to string wouldn't, but the specification only has a limited number of steps to follow. This subject is fairly complicated in C# 2, and C# 3 takes things even further. I won't try to cover all the nuts and bolts of the C# 2 rules here, but the basic steps are as follows:

1 For each method argument (the bits in normal parentheses, not angle brackets), try to infer some of the type arguments of the generic method, using some fairly simple techniques.

2 Check that all the results from the first step are consistent. In other words, if one argument implied one type argument for a particular type parameter, and another implied a different type argument for the same type parameter, then inference fails for the method call.

3 Check that all the type parameters needed for the generic method have been inferred. You can't let the compiler infer some while you specify others explicitly—it's all or nothing.

To avoid learning all the rules (and I wouldn't recommend it unless you're particularly interested in the fine details), there's one simple thing to do: try it and see what happens. If you think the compiler *might* be able to infer all the type arguments, try calling the method without specifying any. If it fails, stick the type arguments in explicitly. You lose nothing more than the time it takes to compile the code once, and you don't need to have all the extra language-lawyer garbage in your head.

To make it easier to use generic types, type inference can be combined with the idea of overloading type names based on the number of type parameters. We'll look at an example of this in a while, when we put everything together.

3.3.3 *Implementing generics*

You're likely to spend more time using generic types and methods than writing them yourself. Even when you're providing the implementation, you can usually just pretend that T (or whatever your type parameter is called) is the name of a type and get on with writing code as if you weren't using generics at all. But there are a few extra things you should know.

DEFAULT VALUE EXPRESSIONS

When you know exactly what type you're working with, you know its default value— the value an otherwise uninitialized field would have, for instance. When you don't know what type you're referring to, though, you can't specify that default value directly. You can't use `null` because it might not be a reference type. You can't use 0 because it might not be a numeric type.

It's fairly rare to need the default value, but it can be useful on occasion. `Dictionary <TKey,TValue>` is a good example—it has a `TryGetValue` method that works a bit like the `TryParse` methods on the numeric types: it uses an output parameter for the value you're trying to fetch and a Boolean return value to indicate whether it succeeded. This means that the method *has* to have some value of type `TValue` to populate the output parameter with. (Remember that output parameters must be assigned before the method returns normally.)

> **THE TRYXXX PATTERN**   A few patterns in .NET are easily identifiable by the names of the methods involved—`BeginXXX` and `EndXXX` suggest an asynchronous operation, for example. The `TryXXX` pattern is one that has had its use expanded from .NET 1.1 to 2.0. It's designed for situations that might normally be considered to be errors (in that the method can't perform its primary duty), but where failure could well occur without indicating a serious issue, and shouldn't be deemed exceptional. For instance, users often fail to type in numbers correctly, so being able to *try* to parse some text without having to catch an exception and swallow it is useful. Not only does it improve performance in the failure case, but more importantly, it saves exceptions for genuine error cases where something is wrong in the *system* (however widely you wish to interpret that). It's a useful pattern to have up your sleeve as a library designer, when applied appropriately.

C# 2 provides the *default value expression* to care for just this need. The specification doesn't refer to it as an operator, but you can think of it as being similar to the `typeof` operator, just returning a different value. The following listing shows this in a generic method, and also gives an example of type inference and a conversion type constraint in action.

Listing 3.4   Comparing a given value to the default in a generic way

```
static int CompareToDefault<T>(T value)
    where T : IComparable<T>
{
    return value.CompareTo(default(T));
}
...
Console.WriteLine(CompareToDefault("x"));
Console.WriteLine(CompareToDefault(10));
Console.WriteLine(CompareToDefault(0));
Console.WriteLine(CompareToDefault(-10));
Console.WriteLine(CompareToDefault(DateTime.MinValue));
```

Listing 3.4 shows a generic method being used with three different types: `string`, `int`, and `DateTime`. The `CompareToDefault` method dictates that it can only be used with types implementing the `IComparable<T>` interface, which allows you to call

CompareTo(T) on the value passed in. The other value you use for the comparison is the default value for the type. As string is a reference type, the default value is null, and the documentation for CompareTo states that for reference types, everything should be greater than null, so the first result is 1. The next three lines show comparisons with the default value of int, demonstrating that the default value is 0. The output of the last line is 0, showing that DateTime.MinValue is the default value for DateTime.

Of course, the method in listing 3.4 will fail if you pass it null as the argument—the line calling CompareTo will throw NullReferenceException in the normal way. Don't worry about that for the moment—there's an alternative using IComparer<T>, as you'll see soon.

DIRECT COMPARISONS

Although listing 3.4 showed how a comparison is possible, you won't always want to constrain your types to implement IComparable<T> or its sister interface, IEquatable<T>, which provides a strongly typed Equals(T) method to complement the Equals (object) method that all types have. Without the extra information these interfaces give you access to, there's little you can do in terms of comparisons, other than calling Equals(object), which will result in boxing the value you want to compare with when it's a value type. (There are a couple of types to help you in some situations—we'll come to them in a minute.)

When a type parameter is unconstrained (no constraints are applied to it), you can use the == and != operators, but *only* to compare a value of that type with null; you can't compare two values of type T with each other. When the type argument is a reference type, the normal reference comparison will be used. In the case where the type argument provided for T is a non-nullable value type, a comparison with null will always decide that they're unequal (so the comparison can be removed by the JIT compiler). When the type argument is a nullable value type, the comparison will behave in the natural way, making the comparison against the null value of the type.[4] (Don't worry if this last bit doesn't make sense yet—it will when you've read the next chapter. Some features are too intertwined to allow me to describe either of them completely without referring to the other, unfortunately.)

When a type parameter is constrained to be a value type, == and != can't be used with it at all. When it's constrained to be a reference type, the kind of comparison performed depends on how the type parameter is constrained. If the only constraint is that it's a reference type, simple reference comparisons are performed. If it's further constrained to derive from a particular type that overloads the == and != operators, those overloads are used. Beware, though—extra overloads that happen to be made available by the type argument specified by the caller are *not* used. The next

---

[4] At the time of this writing (testing with .NET 4.5 and earlier), the code generated by the JIT compiler for comparing unconstrained type parameter values against null is extremely slow for nullable value types. If you constrain a type parameter T to be non-nullable and then compare a value of type T? against null, that comparison is much faster. This shows some scope for future JIT optimization.

listing demonstrates this with a simple reference type constraint and a type argument of `string`.

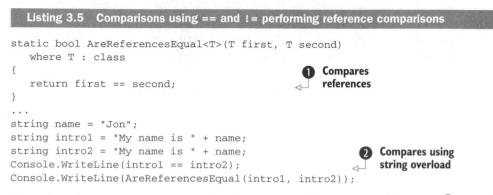

Listing 3.5   Comparisons using == and != performing reference comparisons

```
static bool AreReferencesEqual<T>(T first, T second)
   where T : class
{                                              ❶ Compares
   return first == second;                        references
}
...
string name = "Jon";
string intro1 = "My name is " + name;
string intro2 = "My name is " + name;          ❷ Compares using
Console.WriteLine(intro1 == intro2);              string overload
Console.WriteLine(AreReferencesEqual(intro1, intro2));
```

Even though `string` overloads `==` (as demonstrated by the comparison at ❷ printing True), this overload isn't used by the comparison at ❶. Basically, when `AreReferences-Equal<T>` is compiled, the compiler doesn't know what overloads will be available—it's as if the parameters passed in were of type `object`.

This isn't specific to operators—on encountering a generic type, the compiler resolves all the method overloads when compiling the unbound generic type, rather than reconsidering each possible method call for more specific overloads at execution time. For instance, a statement of `Console.WriteLine(default(T));` will always resolve to a call to `Console.WriteLine(object value)`—it doesn't call `Console.WriteLine(string value)` when `T` happens to be `string`. This is similar to the normal situation of overloads being chosen at compile time rather than execution time, but readers familiar with templates in C++ may be surprised nonetheless.[5]

Two classes that are *extremely* useful when it comes to comparing values are `EqualityComparer<T>` and `Comparer<T>`, both in the `System.Collections.Generic` namespace. They implement `IEqualityComparer<T>` and `IComparer<T>`, respectively, and the `Default` property returns an implementation that generally does the right thing for the appropriate type.

> **THE GENERIC COMPARISON INTERFACES**   There are four main generic interfaces for comparisons. Two of them—`IComparer<T>` and `IComparable<T>`—are about comparing values for *ordering* (is one value less than, equal to, or greater than the other?), and the other two—`IEqualityComparer<T>` and `IEquatable<T>`—are for comparing two items for *equality* according to some criteria and for finding the hash of an item (in a manner compatible with the same notion of equality).
>
> Splitting the four another way, `IComparer<T>` and `IEqualityComparer<T>` are implemented by types that are capable of comparing two different values, whereas an instance of `IComparable<T>` or `IEquatable<T>` is capable of comparing *itself* with another value.

---

[5] You'll see in chapter 14 that dynamic typing provides the ability to resolve overloads at execution time.

See the documentation for more details, and consider using these (and similar types such as `StringComparer`) when performing comparisons. We'll use `Equality-Comparer<T>` in the next example.

FULL COMPARISON EXAMPLE: REPRESENTING A PAIR OF VALUES

To finish off our section on implementing generics, here's a complete example. It implements a useful generic type—a `Pair<T1,T2>` that holds two values together, like a key/value pair, but with no expectations as to the relationship between the two values.

> **.NET 4 AND TUPLES**   .NET 4 provides a lot of this functionality out of the box—and for many different numbers of type parameters, too. Look for `Tuple<T1>`, `Tuple<T1,T2>`, and so on in the `System` namespace.

In addition to providing properties to access the values themselves, you'll override `Equals` and `GetHashCode` to allow instances of your type to play nicely when used as keys in a dictionary. The following listing gives the complete code.

Listing 3.6   Generic class representing a pair of values

```
using System;
using System.Collections.Generic;

public sealed class Pair<T1, T2> : IEquatable<Pair<T1, T2>>
{
    private static readonly IEqualityComparer<T1> FirstComparer =
        EqualityComparer<T1>.Default;
    private static readonly IEqualityComparer<T2> SecondComparer =
        EqualityComparer<T2>.Default;

    private readonly T1 first;
    private readonly T2 second;

    public Pair(T1 first, T2 second)
    {
        this.first = first;
        this.second = second;
    }

    public T1 First { get { return first; } }

    public T2 Second { get { return second; } }

    public bool Equals(Pair<T1, T2> other)
    {
        return other != null &&
            FirstComparer.Equals(this.First, other.First) &&
            SecondComparer.Equals(this.Second, other.Second);
    }

    public override bool Equals(object o)
    {
        return Equals(o as Pair<T1, T2>);
    }
```

```
public override int GetHashCode()
{
   return FirstComparer.GetHashCode(first) * 37 +
      SecondComparer.GetHashCode(second);
}
}
```

Listing 3.6 is straightforward. The constituent values are stored in appropriately typed member variables, and access is provided by simple read-only properties. You implement IEquatable<Pair<T1,T2>> to give a strongly typed API that'll avoid unnecessary execution-time checks. The equality and hash-code computations both use the default equality comparer for the two type parameters—these handle nulls automatically, which makes the code somewhat simpler. The static variables used to store the equality comparers for T1 and T2 are mostly there for the sake of formatting the code for the printed page, but they'll also be useful as a reference point in the next section.

> **CALCULATING HASH CODES** The formula used for calculating the hash code based on the two "part" results comes from *Effective Java*, 2nd edition (Addison-Wesley, 2008), by Joshua Bloch. It certainly doesn't guarantee a good distribution of hash codes, but in my opinion it's better than using a bitwise exclusive OR. See *Effective Java* for more details, and for many other useful tips and design insights.

Now that you have your Pair class, how do you construct an instance of it? At the moment, you'd need to use something like this:

```
Pair<int,string> pair = new Pair<int,string>(10, "value");
```

That's not terribly nice. It would be good to use type inference, but that only works for generic methods, and you don't have any of those. If you put a generic method in the generic type, you'd still need to specify the type arguments for the type before you could call a method on it, which would defeat the purpose. The solution is to use a nongeneric helper class with a generic method in it, as shown in the following listing.

Listing 3.7   Using a nongeneric type with a generic method to enable type inference

```
public static class Pair
{
   public static Pair<T1,T2> Of<T1,T2>(T1 first, T2 second)
   {
      return new Pair<T1,T2>(first, second);
   }
}
```

If this is your first time reading this book, ignore the fact that the class is declared to be static—we'll come to that in chapter 7. The important point is that you have a nongeneric class with a generic method. That means you can turn the previous example into this far-more-pleasant version:

```
Pair<int,string> pair = Pair.Of(10, "value");
```

In C# 3 you could even dispense with the explicit typing of the pair variable, but let's not get ahead of ourselves. This use of nongeneric helper classes (or *partially* generic helper classes, if you have two or more type parameters and want to infer some of them but leave others explicit) is a handy trick.

We've finished looking at the intermediate features now. I realize it can all seem complicated at first, but don't be put off; the benefits of generics far outweigh the added complexity. Over time, they become second nature. Now that you have the Pair class as an example, it might be worth looking over your own code base to see whether there are some patterns that you keep reimplementing solely to use different types.

In any large topic there's always more to learn. The next section will take you through the most important advanced topics in generics. If you're feeling overwhelmed at this point, you might want to skip to the relative comfort of section 3.5, where we'll explore some of the limitations of generics. It's worth understanding the topics in the next section *eventually*, but if everything so far has been new to you, it won't hurt to skip it for the moment.

3.4 *Advanced generics*

You may expect me to claim that in the rest of this chapter we'll cover every aspect of generics that we haven't looked at so far. But there are *so many* little nooks and crannies involving generics that it's simply not possible—and I certainly wouldn't want to read about all the details, let alone write about them. Fortunately, the nice people at Microsoft and ECMA have written down all the details in the language specification, so if you ever want to check some obscure situation that isn't covered here, that should be your next port of call. Unfortunately I can't point to one particular area of the specification that covers generics: they pop up almost everywhere. Arguably, if your code ends up in a corner case so complicated that you need to consult the specification to work out what it should do, you should refactor it into a more obvious form anyway; you don't want each maintenance engineer from now until eternity to have to read the gory details.

My aim with this section is to cover everything you're *likely* to want to know about generics. I'll talk more about the CLR and the framework side of things than the particular syntax of the C# 2 language, although it's all relevant when developing in C#. We'll start by considering static members of generic types, including type initialization. From there, it's a natural step to wonder how all this is implemented under the covers, but we'll keep it fairly light on detail, concentrating on the important effects of the implementation decisions. We'll look at what happens when you enumerate a generic collection using foreach in C# 2, and round off the section by seeing how reflection in the .NET Framework is affected by generics.

3.4.1 Static fields and static constructors

Just as instance fields belong to an instance, static fields belong to the type they're declared in. If you declare a static field x in class SomeClass, there's exactly one Some-Class.x field, no matter how many instances of SomeClass you create, and no matter how many types derive from SomeClass.[6] That's the familiar scenario from C# 1—so how does it map across to generics?

The answer is that each *closed* type has its own set of static fields. You saw this in listing 3.6 when you stored the default equality comparers for T1 and T2 in static fields, but let's look at it in more detail with another example. The following listing creates a generic type including a static field. You set the field's value for different closed types and then print out the values to show that they're separate.

Listing 3.8   Proof that different closed types have different static fields

```
class TypeWithField<T>
{
    public static string field;
    public static void PrintField()
    {
        Console.WriteLine(field + ": " + typeof(T).Name);
    }
}
...
TypeWithField<int>.field = "First";
TypeWithField<string>.field = "Second";
TypeWithField<DateTime>.field = "Third";

TypeWithField<int>.PrintField();
TypeWithField<string>.PrintField();
TypeWithField<DateTime>.PrintField();
```

You set the value of each field to a different value and then print out each field along with the name of the type argument used for that closed type. Here's the output from listing 3.8:

```
First: Int32
Second: String
Third: DateTime
```

The basic rule is one static field per closed type. The same applies for static initializers and static constructors. But it's possible to have one generic type nested within another, and types with multiple generic parameters. This *sounds* a lot more complicated, but it works as you probably think it should. The following listing shows this in action, this time using static constructors to show just how many types there are.

---

[6] Well, there's one per application domain. For the purposes of this section, we'll assume we're only dealing with one application domain. The concepts for different application domains work the same with generics as with nongeneric types. Variables decorated with [ThreadStatic] violate this rule, too.

Listing 3.9 Static constructors with nested generic types

```
public class Outer<T>
{
    public class Inner<U,V>
    {
        static Inner()
        {
            Console.WriteLine("Outer<{0}>.Inner<{1},{2}>",
                              typeof(T).Name,
                              typeof(U).Name,
                              typeof(V).Name);
        }
        public static void DummyMethod() {}
    }
}
...
Outer<int>.Inner<string,DateTime>.DummyMethod();
Outer<string>.Inner<int,int>.DummyMethod();
Outer<object>.Inner<string,object>.DummyMethod();
Outer<string>.Inner<string,object>.DummyMethod();
Outer<object>.Inner<object,string>.DummyMethod();
Outer<string>.Inner<int,int>.DummyMethod();
```

The first call to `DummyMethod()` for any type will cause the type to be initialized, at which point the static constructor prints out some diagnostics. Each different list of type arguments counts as a different closed type, so the output of listing 3.9 looks like this:

```
Outer<Int32>.Inner<String,DateTime>
Outer<String>.Inner<Int32,Int32>
Outer<Object>.Inner<String,Object>
Outer<String>.Inner<String,Object>
Outer<Object>.Inner<Object,String>
```

Just as with nongeneric types, the static constructor for any closed type is only executed once, which is why the last line of listing 3.9 doesn't create a sixth line of output—the static constructor for `Outer<string>.Inner<int,int>` executed earlier, producing the second line of output.

To clear up any doubts, if you had a nongeneric `PlainInner` class inside `Outer`, there still would've been one possible `Outer<T>.PlainInner` type per closed `Outer` type, so `Outer<int>.PlainInner` would be separate from `Outer<long>.PlainInner`, with a separate set of static fields, as seen earlier.

Now that you've seen what constitutes a different type, we should look at what the effects of that might be in terms of the amount of native code generated. And no, it's not as bad as you might think...

3.4.2 *How the JIT compiler handles generics*

Given that we have all of these different closed types, the JIT's job is to convert the IL of the generic type into native code so it can actually be run. In some ways, you shouldn't care exactly how it does that—beyond keeping a close eye on memory and CPU time, you wouldn't see much difference if the JIT took the simplest possible approach and generated native code for each closed type separately, as if each one had nothing to do with any other type. But the JIT authors are clever enough that it's worth looking at what they've done.

Let's start with a simple situation first, with a single type parameter—we'll use List<T> for the sake of convenience. The JIT creates different code for each closed type with a type argument that's a value type—int, long, Guid, and the like. But it shares the native code generated for all the closed types that use a reference type as the type argument, such as string, Stream, and StringBuilder. It can do this because all references are the same size (the size varies between a 32-bit CLR and a 64-bit CLR, but within any one CLR all references are the same size). An array of references will always be the same size, whatever the references happen to be. The space required on the stack for a reference will always be the same. The JIT can use the same optimizations to store references in registers regardless of the type—the List<Reason> goes on.

Each of the types still has its own static fields, as described in section 3.4.1, but the executable code itself is reused. Of course, the JIT does all of this lazily—it won't generate the code for List<int> before it needs to, and it'll cache that code for all future uses of List<int>.

In theory, it's possible to share code for at least *some* value types. The JIT would have to be careful, not just due to size, but also for garbage collection reasons—it would have to be able to quickly identify areas of a struct value that are live references. But value types that are the same size and have the same in-memory footprint as far as the garbage collector is concerned *could* share code. At the time of this writing, that's been of sufficiently low priority that it hasn't been implemented, and it may well stay that way.

This level of detail is primarily of academic interest, but it does have a slight performance impact in terms of more code being JIT compiled. The performance benefits of generics can be huge, though, and again that comes down to having the opportunity to compile to different code for different types. Consider a List<byte>, for instance. In .NET 1.1, adding individual bytes to an ArrayList would've meant boxing each one of them and storing a reference to each boxed value. Using List<byte> has no such impact—List<T> has a member of type T[] to replace the object[] within ArrayList, and that array is of the appropriate type, taking the appropriate space. List<byte> has a straight byte[] within it used to store the elements of the array. (In many ways, this makes a List<byte> behave like a MemoryStream.)

Figure 3.3 shows an ArrayList and a List<byte>, each with the same six values. The arrays themselves have more than six elements, to allow for growth. Both List<T> and ArrayList have a buffer, and they create a larger buffer when they need to.

The difference in efficiency here is incredible. Let's look at the ArrayList first, considering a 32-bit CLR.[7] Each of the boxed bytes will take up 8 bytes of object overhead,

---

[7] When running on a 64-bit CLR, the overheads are bigger.

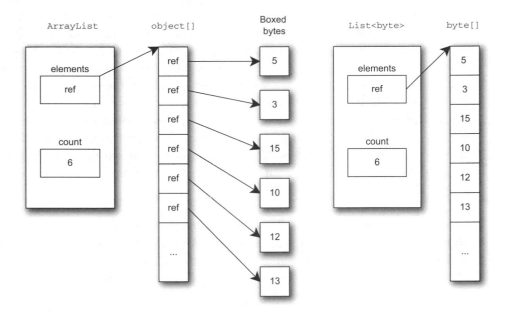

Figure 3.3 Visual demonstration of why List<T> takes up a lot less space than ArrayList when storing value types

plus 4 bytes (1 byte, rounded up to a word boundary) for the data itself. On top of that, you have all the references themselves, each of which takes up 4 bytes. So for each byte of useful data, you're paying at least 16 bytes—and then there's the extra unused space for references in the buffer.

Compare this with the List<byte>. Each byte in the list takes up a single byte within the elements array. There's still wasted space in the buffer, waiting to be used by new items, but at least you're only wasting a single byte per unused element there.

You don't just gain space, you gain execution speed, too. You save the time taken to allocate the box, to perform the type checking involved in unboxing the bytes in order to get at them, and to garbage collect the boxes when they're no longer referenced.

You don't have to go down to the CLR level to find things happening transparently on your behalf, though. C# has always made life easier with syntactic shortcuts, and the next section looks at a familiar example but with a generic twist: iterating with foreach.

3.4.3 *Generic iteration*

One of the most common operations you'll want to perform on a collection is to iterate through all its elements. Usually, the simplest way of doing that is to use the foreach statement. In C# 1, this relied on the collection either implementing the System.Collections.IEnumerable interface or having a similar GetEnumerator() method that returned a type with a suitable MoveNext() method and a Current property. The Current property didn't have to be of type object, and that was the whole point of having these extra rules, which look odd at first sight. Yes, even in C# 1 you could avoid boxing and unboxing during iteration if you had a custom iteration type.

C# 2 makes this somewhat easier, as the rules for the foreach statement have been extended to also use the System.Collections.Generic.IEnumerable<T> interface along with its partner, IEnumerator<T>. These are simply the generic equivalents of the old iteration interfaces, and they're used in preference to the nongeneric versions. This means that if you iterate through a generic collection of value type elements—List<int>, for example—then no boxing is performed at all. If the old interface had been used instead, you wouldn't have incurred the boxing cost while *storing* the elements of the list, but you'd still have ended up boxing them when you retrieved them using foreach.

All of this is done for you under the covers—all you need to do is use the foreach statement in the normal way, using an appropriate type for the iteration variable, and all will be well. That's not the end of the story, though. In the relatively rare situation where you need to implement iteration over one of your own types, you'll find that IEnumerable<T> extends the old IEnumerable interface, which means you have to implement two different methods:

```
IEnumerator<T> GetEnumerator();
IEnumerator GetEnumerator();
```

Can you see the problem? The methods differ only in return type, and the overloading rules of C# prevent you from writing two such methods normally. Back in section 2.2.2, you saw a similar situation, and you can use the same workaround here. If you implement IEnumerable using explicit interface implementation, you can implement IEnumerable<T> with a "normal" method. Fortunately, because IEnumerator<T> extends IEnumerator, you can use the same return value for both methods and implement the nongeneric method by just calling the generic version. Of course, now you need to implement IEnumerator<T> and you quickly run into similar problems, this time with the Current property.

The following listing gives a full example, implementing an enumerable class that always enumerates the integers 0 to 9.

Listing 3.10   A full generic iterator—of the numbers 0 to 9

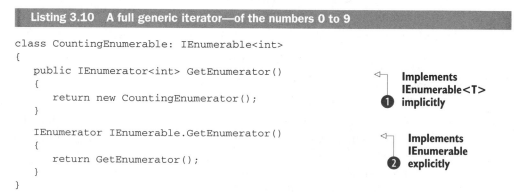

```
class CountingEnumerable: IEnumerable<int>
{
    public IEnumerator<int> GetEnumerator()          ◁─┐  Implements
    {                                                   │  IEnumerable<T>
        return new CountingEnumerator();              ❶ implicitly
    }

    IEnumerator IEnumerable.GetEnumerator()          ◁─┐  Implements
    {                                                   │  IEnumerable
        return GetEnumerator();                       ❷ explicitly
    }
}
```

```
class CountingEnumerator : IEnumerator<int>
{
    int current = -1;

    public bool MoveNext()
    {
        current++;
        return current < 10;
    }
    public int Current { get { return current; } }

    object IEnumerator.Current { get { return Current; } }

    public void Reset()
    {
        current = -1;
    }
    public void Dispose() {}
}
...
CountingEnumerable counter = new CountingEnumerable();
foreach (int x in counter)
{
    Console.WriteLine(x);
}
```

❸ Implements IEnumerator<T>.Current implicitly

Implements IEnumerator.Current explicitly ❹

❺ Proves that enumerable type works

Clearly these results aren't particularly useful, but the code shows the little hoops you have to go through in order to implement generic iteration appropriately—at least if you're doing it all longhand. (And that's without making an effort to throw exceptions if Current is accessed at an inappropriate time.) If you think that listing 3.10 looks like a lot of work just to print out the numbers 0 to 9, I can't help but agree with you, and there'd be even more code if you wanted to iterate over anything useful. Fortunately, you'll see in chapter 6 that C# 2 takes a large amount of the work away from iterators in many cases. I've shown the full version here so you can appreciate the slight wrinkles that have been introduced by the design decision for IEnumerable<T> to extend IEnumerable. I'm not suggesting it was the wrong decision, though; it allows you to pass any IEnumerable<T> into a method written in C# 1 with an IEnumerable parameter. That's not as important now as it was back in 2005, but it's still a useful transition path.

You only need the trick of using explicit interface implementation twice—once for IEnumerable.GetEnumerator ❷ and once for IEnumerator.Current ❹. Both of these call their generic equivalents (❶ and ❸, respectively). Another addition to IEnumerator<T> is that it extends IDisposable, so you have to provide a Dispose method. The foreach statement in C# 1 already called Dispose on an iterator if it implemented IDisposable, but in C# 2 no execution-time testing is required—if the compiler finds that you've implemented IEnumerable<T>, it creates an unconditional call to Dispose at the end of the loop (in a finally block). Many iterators won't actually need to dispose of anything, but it's nice to know that when it *is* required, the most common way of working through an iterator (the foreach statement ❺) handles the calling side automatically. This is most commonly used to release resources when you've finished iterating. For example, you might have an iterator that reads lines from a file and needs to close the file handle when the calling code has finished looping.

We'll now go from compile-time efficiency to execution-time flexibility: our final advanced topic is reflection. Even in .NET 1.0/1.1, reflection could be tricky, but generic types and methods introduce an extra level of complexity. The framework provides everything you need (with a bit of helpful syntax from C# 2 as a language), and although the additional considerations can be daunting, it's not too bad if you take it one step at a time.

3.4.4   *Reflection and generics*

Reflection is used by different people for all sorts of things. You might use it for execution-time introspection of objects to perform a simple form of data binding. You might use it to inspect a directory full of assemblies to find implementations of a plug-in interface. You might write a file for an inversion of control framework (see www.martinfowler.com/articles/injection.html) to load and dynamically configure your application's components. As the uses of reflection are so diverse, I won't focus on any particular one but will instead give you more general guidance on performing common tasks. We'll start by looking at the extensions to the typeof operator.

USING TYPEOF WITH GENERIC TYPES

Reflection is all about examining objects and their types. As such, one of the most important things you need to be able to do is obtain a reference to a particular System.Type object, which allows access to all the information about that type. C# uses the typeof operator to obtain such a reference for types known at compile time, and this has been extended to encompass generic types.

There are two ways of using typeof with generic types—one retrieves the *generic type definition* (in other words, the unbound generic type) and one retrieves a particular constructed type. To obtain the generic type definition—the type with none of the type arguments specified—you simply take the name of the type as it would've been declared and remove the type parameter names, keeping any commas. To retrieve constructed types, you specify the type arguments in the same way as you would to declare a variable of the generic type. The next listing gives an example of both uses. It uses a generic method so we can revisit how typeof can be used with a type parameter, which we previously saw in 3.8.

> **Listing 3.11   Using the `typeof` operator with type parameters**

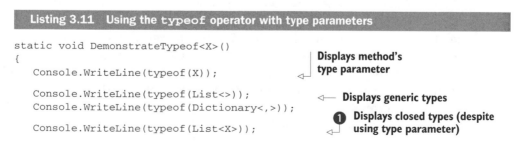

```
static void DemonstrateTypeof<X>()
{
    Console.WriteLine(typeof(X));                       Displays method's
                                                        type parameter

    Console.WriteLine(typeof(List<>));              Displays generic types
    Console.WriteLine(typeof(Dictionary<,>));
                                                    ❶ Displays closed types (despite
    Console.WriteLine(typeof(List<X>));               using type parameter)
```

```
    Console.WriteLine(typeof(Dictionary<string,X>));

    Console.WriteLine(typeof(List<long>));                    ⟵ Displays closed types
    Console.WriteLine(typeof(Dictionary<long,Guid>));
}
...
DemonstrateTypeof<int>();
```

Most of listing 3.11 works as you might naturally expect, but it's worth pointing out two things. First, look at the syntax for obtaining the generic type definition of `Dictionary <TKey,TValue>`. The comma in the angle brackets is required to tell the compiler to look for the type with two type parameters; remember that there can be several generic types with the same name, as long as they vary by the number of type parameters they have. Similarly, you'd retrieve the generic type definition for `MyClass <T1,T2,T3,T4>` using `typeof(MyClass<,,,>)`. The number of type parameters is specified in IL (and in full type names as far as the framework is concerned) by putting a back tick after the first part of the type name and then the number. The type parameters are then indicated in square brackets instead of the angle brackets we're used to. For instance, the second line printed ends with `List`1[T]`, showing that there's one type parameter, and the third line includes `Dictionary`2[TKey,TValue]`.

Second, note that wherever the method's type parameter (X) is used, the actual value of the type argument is used at execution time. So this line ❶ prints `List`1[System.Int32]` rather than `List`1[X]`, which you might have expected.[8] In other words, a type that's open at compile time may be closed at execution time. *This is very confusing. You should be aware of it in case you don't get the results you expect, but otherwise, don't worry.* To retrieve a truly open constructed type at execution time, you need to work a bit harder. See the MSDN documentation for `Type.IsGenericType` for a suitably convoluted example (http://mng.bz/9W6O).

For reference, here's the output of listing 3.11:

```
System.Int32
System.Collections.Generic.List`1[T]
System.Collections.Generic.Dictionary`2[TKey,TValue]
System.Collections.Generic.List`1[System.Int32]
System.Collections.Generic.Dictionary`2[System.String,System.Int32]
System.Collections.Generic.List`1[System.Int64]
System.Collections.Generic.Dictionary`2[System.Int64,System.Guid]
```

Having retrieved an object representing a generic type, there are many next steps you can take. All the previously available ones (finding the members of the type, creating an instance, and so on) are still present—although some aren't applicable for generic type definitions—and there are new ones as well that let you inquire about the generic nature of the type.

---

[8] I deliberately bucked the convention of using a type parameter named T, precisely so that we could tell the difference between the T in the `List<T>` declaration and the X in our method declaration.

METHODS AND PROPERTIES OF SYSTEM.TYPE

There are far too many new methods and properties to look at them all in detail, but there are two particularly important ones: `GetGenericTypeDefinition` and `Make-GenericType`. They're effectively opposites—the first acts on a constructed type, retrieving the generic type definition; the second acts on a generic type definition and returns a constructed type. Arguably it would've been clearer if this method had been called `ConstructType`, `MakeConstructedType`, or some other name with *construct* or *constructed* in it, but we're stuck with what we've got.

Just like normal types, there's only one `Type` object for any particular type—so calling `MakeGenericType` twice with the same types as arguments will return the same reference twice. Similarly, calling `GetGenericTypeDefinition` on two types constructed from the same generic type definition will give the same result for both calls, even if the constructed types are different (such as `List<int>` and `List<string>`).

Two other methods worth exploring—this time methods that already existed in .NET 1.1—are `Type.GetType(string)` and its related `Assembly.GetType(string)` method, both of which provide a dynamic equivalent to `typeof`. You might expect to be able to feed each line of the output of listing 3.11 to the `GetType` method called on an appropriate assembly, but unfortunately life isn't quite that straightforward. It's fine for closed constructed types—the type arguments just go in square brackets. For generic type definitions, though, you need to remove the square brackets entirely—otherwise `GetType` thinks you mean an array type. The following listing shows all of these methods in action.

Listing 3.12 Various ways of retrieving generic and constructed Type objects

```
string listTypeName = "System.Collections.Generic.List`1";

Type defByName = Type.GetType(listTypeName);

Type closedByName = Type.GetType(listTypeName + "[System.String]");
Type closedByMethod = defByName.MakeGenericType(typeof(string));
Type closedByTypeof = typeof(List<string>);

Console.WriteLine(closedByMethod == closedByName);
Console.WriteLine(closedByName == closedByTypeof);

Type defByTypeof = typeof(List<>);
Type defByMethod = closedByName.GetGenericTypeDefinition();

Console.WriteLine(defByMethod == defByName);
Console.WriteLine(defByName == defByTypeof);
```

The output of listing 3.12 is just `True` four times, validating that however you obtain a reference to a particular type object, only one such object is involved.

As I mentioned earlier, there are many new methods and properties on `Type`, such as `GetGenericArguments`, `IsGenericTypeDefinition`, and `IsGenericType`. Again, the documentation for `IsGenericType` is probably the best starting point for further exploration.

REFLECTING GENERIC METHODS

Generic methods have a similar (though smaller) set of additional properties and methods. The following listing gives a brief demonstration of this, calling a generic method by reflection.

> **Listing 3.13 Retrieving and invoking a generic method with reflection**

```
public static void PrintTypeParameter<T>()
{
    Console.WriteLine(typeof(T));
}
...
Type type = typeof(Snippet);
MethodInfo definition = type.GetMethod("PrintTypeParameter");
MethodInfo constructed = definition.MakeGenericMethod(typeof(string));
constructed.Invoke(null, null);
```

First you retrieve the generic method definition, and then you make a constructed generic method using `MakeGenericMethod`. As with types, you could go the other way if you wanted to, but unlike `Type.GetType`, there's no way of specifying a constructed method in the `GetMethod` call. The framework also has a problem if methods are overloaded purely by number of type parameters—there are no methods in `Type` that allow you to specify the number of type parameters, so instead you'd have to call `Type.GetMethods` and find the right one by looking through *all* the methods.

After retrieving the constructed method, you invoke it. The arguments in this example are both `null`, as you're invoking a static method that doesn't have any normal parameters. The output is `System.String`, as you'd expect. Note that the methods retrieved from generic type definitions can't be invoked directly—instead, you must get the methods from a constructed type. This applies to both generic and nongeneric methods.

> **SAVED BY C# 4** If all of this looks messy to you, I agree. Fortunately, in many cases C#'s dynamic typing can come to the rescue, taking a lot of the work out of generic reflection. It doesn't help in all situations, so it's worth being aware of the general flow of the preceding code, but where it *does* apply it's great. We'll look at dynamic typing in detail in chapter 14.

Again, more methods and properties are available on `MethodInfo`, and `IsGeneric-Method` is a good starting point in MSDN (http://mng.bz/P36u). Hopefully the information in this section will have been enough to get you going, and to point out some of the added complexities you might not have otherwise anticipated when first starting to access generic types and methods with reflection.

That's all we'll cover in the way of advanced features. Just to reiterate, this chapter isn't meant to be a complete guide to generics by any means, but most developers are unlikely to need to know the more obscure details. I hope for your sake that you fall into this camp, as specifications tend to get harder to read the deeper you go into them. Remember that unless you're developing alone and just for yourself, you're unlikely to be the only one to work on your code. If you need features that are more complex than the ones demonstrated here, you should assume that anyone reading your code will need help to understand it. On the other hand, if you find that your co-workers don't know about some of the topics we've covered so far, please feel free to direct them to the nearest bookshop…

Our final main section of the chapter looks at some of the limitations of generics in C# and considers similar features in other languages.

3.5   *Limitations of generics in C# and other languages*

There's no doubt that generics contribute a great deal to C# in terms of expressiveness, type safety, and performance. The feature has been carefully designed to cope with most of the tasks that C++ programmers typically used templates for, but without some of the accompanying disadvantages. But this isn't to say limitations don't exist. There are some problems that C++ templates solve with ease but that C# generics can't help with. Similarly, though generics in Java are generally less powerful than in C#, there are some concepts that can be expressed in Java but that don't have a C# equivalent. This section will take you through some of the most commonly encountered weaknesses, and I'll briefly compare the C#/.NET implementation of generics with C++ templates and Java generics.

It's important to stress that pointing out these snags doesn't imply that they should've been avoided in the first place. In particular, I'm in no way saying that I could've done a better job! The language and platform designers have had to balance power with complexity (and the small matter of achieving both design and implementation within a reasonable time scale). Most likely, you won't encounter problems, and if you do, you'll be able to work around them with the guidance given here.

We'll start with the answer to a question that almost everyone raises sooner or later: Why can't I convert a `List<string>` to a `List<object>`?

3.5.1   *Lack of generic variance*

In section 2.2.2, we looked at the *covariance* of arrays—the fact that an array of a reference type can be viewed as an array of its base type, or an array of any of the interfaces it implements. There are actually two forms of this idea, called *covariance* and *contravariance*, or collectively just *variance*. Generics don't support this—they're *invariant*. This is for the sake of type safety, as you'll see, but it can be annoying.

One thing I'd like to make clear to start with: C# 4 improves the generic variance situation somewhat. Many of the restrictions listed here *do* still apply though, and this section serves as a useful introduction to the idea of variance. We'll see how C# 4 helps in chapter 13, but many of the clearest examples of generic variance rely on other new features from C# 3, including LINQ. Variance is also quite a complicated topic in itself, so it's worth waiting until you're comfortable with the rest of C# 2 and 3 before you tackle it. For the sake of readability, I won't point out every place in this section that's slightly different in C# 4…it'll all become clear in chapter 13.

WHY DON'T GENERICS SUPPORT COVARIANCE?

Suppose you have two classes, `Turtle` and `Cat`, both of which derive from an abstract `Animal` class. In the code that follows, the array code (first block) is valid C# 2; the generic code (second block) isn't.

Valid (at compile time)	Invalid
`Animal[] animals = new Cat[5];` `animals[0] = new Turtle();`	`List<Animal> animals = new List<Cat>();` `animals.Add(new Turtle());`

The compiler has no problem with the second line in either case, but the first line under *Invalid* causes the following error:

```
error CS0029: Cannot implicitly convert type
    'System.Collections.Generic.List<Cat>' to
    'System.Collections.Generic.List<Animal>'
```

This was a deliberate choice on the part of the framework and language designers. The obvious question to ask is *why* this is prohibited, and the answer lies in the second line.

There's nothing about the second line that should raise any suspicion. After all, `List<Animal>` effectively has a method with the signature `void Add(Animal value)`—you should be able to put a `Turtle` into any list of animals, for instance. But the *actual* object referred to by `animals` is a `Cat[]` (in the code under *Valid*) or a `List<Cat>` (under *Invalid*), both of which require that only references to instances of `Cat` (or further subclasses) are stored in them. Although the array version will compile, it'll fail at execution time. This was deemed by the designers of generics to be worse than failing at compile time, which is reasonable—the whole point of static typing is to find out about errors before the code ever gets run.

> **WHY ARE ARRAYS COVARIANT?** Having answered the question about why generics are invariant, the *next* obvious step is to question why arrays are covariant. According to the *Common Language Infrastructure Annotated Standard* (Miller and Ragsdale, Addison-Wesley Professional, 2003), for the first version of .NET the designers wanted to reach as broad an audience as possible, which included being able to run code compiled from Java source. In other words, .NET has covariant arrays because Java has covariant arrays—despite this being a known wart in Java.

So, that's why things are the way they are—but why should you care, and how can you get around the restriction?

WHERE COVARIANCE WOULD BE USEFUL

The example I've given with a list is clearly problematic. You can add items to the list, which is where you lose the type safety in this case, and an add operation is an example of a value being used as an *input* into the API: the caller is supplying the value. What would happen if you limited yourself to getting values out?

The obvious examples of this are IEnumerator<T> and (by association) IEnumerable<T>. In fact, these are almost the *canonical* examples for generic covariance. Together they describe a sequence of values—all you know about the values you see is that each one will be compatible with T, such that you can always write

```
T currentValue = iterator.Current;
```

This uses the normal idea of compatibility—it would be fine for an IEnumerator<Animal> to yield references to instances of Cat or Turtle, for example. There's no way you can push values that are inappropriate for the actual sequence type, so you'd like to be able to treat an IEnumerator<Cat> as an IEnumerator<Animal>. Let's consider an example of where that might be useful.

Suppose you take the customary shape example for inheritance, but using an interface (IShape). Now consider another interface, IDrawing, that represents a drawing made up of shapes. You'll have two concrete types of drawing—a MondrianDrawing (made of rectangles) and a SeuratDrawing (made of circles).[9] Figure 3.4 shows the class hierarchies involved.

Both drawing types need to implement the IDrawing interface, so they need to expose a property with this signature:

```
IEnumerable<IShape> Shapes { get; }
```

But each drawing type would probably find it easier to maintain a more strongly typed list internally. For example, a Seurat drawing may include a field of type List<Circle>. It's useful for it to have this rather than a List<IShape> so that if it needs to manipulate the circles in a circle-specific way, it can do so without casting. If you had a List<IShape>, you could either return it directly or at least wrap it in a ReadOnlyCollection<IShape> to prevent callers from messing with it via casting—the property implementation would be cheap and simple either way. But you can't do that when your types don't match up. You can't convert from an IEnumerable<Circle> to an IEnumerable<IShape>. So what *can* you do?

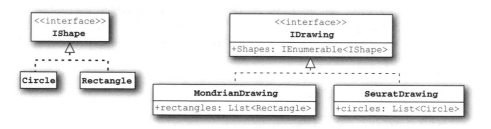

Figure 3.4   Interfaces for shapes and drawings, and two implementations of each

---

9   If these names mean nothing to you, check out the artists' Wikipedia entries (http://en.wikipedia.org/wiki/Piet_Mondrian and http://en.wikipedia.org/wiki/Georges-Pierre_Seurat). They have special meanings to me for different reasons: Mondrian is also the name of a code review tool we used at Google, and Seurat is the eponymous George of *Sunday in the Park with George*—a wonderful musical by Stephen Sondheim.

There are a few options here:

- Change the field type to `List<IShape>` and just live with the casts. This isn't pleasant, and it pretty much defeats the point of using generics.
- Use the new features provided by C# 2 for implementing iterators, as you'll see in chapter 6. This is a reasonable solution for this particular case, but *only* this case (where you're dealing with `IEnumerable<T>`).
- Make each `Shapes` property implementation create a new copy of the list, possibly using `List<T>.ConvertAll` for simplicity. Creating an independent copy of a collection is often the right thing to do in an API anyway, but it causes a lot of copying, which can be unnecessarily inefficient in many cases.
- Make `IDrawing` generic, indicating the type of shapes in the drawing. Thus, `MondrianDrawing` would implement `IDrawing<Rectangle>`, and `SeuratDrawing` would implement `IDrawing<Circle>`. This is only viable when you own the interface.
- Create a helper class to adapt one kind of `IEnumerable<T>` into another:

```
class EnumerableWrapper<TOriginal, TWrapper> : IEnumerable<TWrapper>
    where TOriginal : TWrapper
```

Again, as this particular situation (`IEnumerable<T>`) is special, you could get away with just a utility method. In fact, .NET 3.5 ships with two useful methods like this: `Enumerable.Cast<T>` and `Enumerable.OfType<T>`. They're part of LINQ, and we'll look at them in chapter 11. Although this is a special case, it's probably the most common form of generic covariance you'll come across.

When you run into covariance issues, you may need to consider all of these options and anything else you can think of. It depends heavily on the exact nature of the situation. Unfortunately, covariance isn't the only problem you have to deal with. There's also the matter of *contravariance*, which is like covariance in reverse.

WHERE CONTRAVARIANCE WOULD BE USEFUL

Contravariance feels slightly less intuitive than covariance, but it does make sense. With covariance, you were trying to convert from `SomeType<Circle>` to `SomeType<IShape>` (using `IEnumerable<T>` for `SomeType` in the previous example). Contravariance is about converting the other way—from `SomeType<IShape>` to `SomeType<Circle>`. How can that be safe? Well, covariance is safe when `SomeType` only describes operations that *return* the type parameter—and contravariance is safe when `SomeType` only describes operations that *accept* the type parameter.[10]

The simplest example of a type that only uses its type parameter in an input position is `IComparer<T>`, which is commonly used to sort collections. Let's expand the `IShape` interface (which has been empty so far) to include an `Area` property. It's now easy to write an implementation of `IComparer<IShape>` that compares any two shapes by area. You'd then *like* to be able to write the following code:

---

[10] You'll see in chapter 13 that there's slightly more to it than that, but that's the general principle.

```
IComparer<IShape> areaComparer = new AreaComparer();
List<Circle> circles = new List<Circle>();
circles.Add(new Circle(Point.Empty, 20));
circles.Add(new Circle(Point.Empty, 10));
circles.Sort(areaComparer);
```

INVALID

That won't work, though, because the Sort method on List<Circle> effectively takes an IComparer<Circle>. The fact that AreaComparer can compare *any* shape rather than just circles doesn't impress the compiler at all. It considers IComparer <Circle> and IComparer<IShape> to be completely different types. Maddening, isn't it? It would be nice if the Sort method had this signature instead:

```
void Sort<S>(IComparer<S> comparer) where T : S
```

Unfortunately, not only is that *not* the signature of Sort, but it *can't* be—the constraint is invalid, because it's a constraint on T instead of S. You want a conversion type constraint but in the other direction, constraining the S to be somewhere *up* the inheritance tree of T instead of *down*.

Given that this isn't possible, what *can* you do? There are fewer options this time. First, you could revisit the idea of creating a generic helper class, as follows.

Listing 3.14 Working around the lack of contravariance with a helper

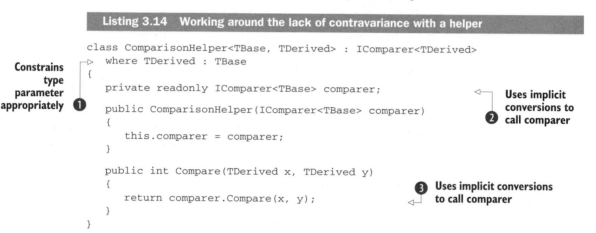

Constrains type parameter appropriately ❶

Uses implicit conversions to call comparer ❷

Uses implicit conversions to call comparer ❸

```
class ComparisonHelper<TBase, TDerived> : IComparer<TDerived>
    where TDerived : TBase
{
    private readonly IComparer<TBase> comparer;
    public ComparisonHelper(IComparer<TBase> comparer)
    {
        this.comparer = comparer;
    }
    public int Compare(TDerived x, TDerived y)
    {
        return comparer.Compare(x, y);
    }
}
```

This is an example of the adapter pattern at work, although instead of adapting one interface to a completely different one, you're just adapting from IComparer<TBase> to IComparer<TDerived>. You just remember the original comparer providing the real logic to compare items of the base type ❷ and then call it when you're asked to compare items of the derived type ❸. The fact that no casts are involved (not even hidden ones) should give you some confidence: this helper is completely type-safe. You're able to call the base comparer due to an implicit conversion being available from TDerived to TBase, which you required with a type constraint ❶.

The second option is to make the area-comparison class generic with a conversion type constraint, so it can compare any two values of the same type, as long as that type implements IShape. For the sake of simplicity in the situation where you really don't need this functionality, you could keep the nongeneric class by just making it derive from the generic one:

```
class AreaComparer<T> : IComparer<T> where T : IShape

class AreaComparer : AreaComparer<IShape>
```

Of course, you can only do this when you're able to change the comparison class. This can be an effective solution, but it still feels unnatural—why should you have to construct the comparer in various ways for different types when it's not going to behave any differently? Why should you have to derive from the class to simplify things when you're not actually specializing the behavior?

Note that the various options for both covariance and contravariance use more generics and constraints to express the interface in a more general manner, or to provide generic helper classes. I know that adding a constraint makes it sound *less* general, but the generality is added by first making the type or method generic. When you run into a problem like this, adding a level of genericity somewhere with an appropriate constraint should be the first option to consider. Generic *methods* (rather than generic types) are often helpful here, as type inference can make the lack of variance invisible to the naked eye. This is particularly true in C# 3, which has stronger type inference capabilities than C# 2.

This limitation is a *very* common cause of questions on C# discussion sites. The remaining issues are either relatively academic or affect only a moderate subset of the development community. The next one mostly affects those who do a lot of calculations (usually scientific or financial) in their work.

3.5.2 *Lack of operator constraints or a "numeric" constraint*

C# isn't without its downsides when it comes to heavily mathematical code. The need to explicitly use the Math class for every operation beyond the simplest arithmetic and the lack of C-style typedefs to allow the data representation used throughout a program to be easily changed have always been raised by the scientific community as barriers to C#'s adoption. Generics weren't likely to fully solve either of those issues, but there's a common problem that stops generics from helping as much as they could have.

Consider this (illegal) generic method:

```
public T FindMean<T>(IEnumerable<T> data)
{
    T sum = default(T);
    int count = 0;
    foreach (T datum in data)
    {
        sum += datum;
        count++;
    }
    return sum / count;
}
```

INVALID ▷

Obviously that could never work for *all* types of data—what could it mean to add one Exception to another, for instance? Clearly a constraint of some kind is called for... something that can express what you need to be able to do: add two instances of T together, and divide a T by an integer. If that were available, even if it were limited to built-in types, you could write generic algorithms that wouldn't care whether they were working on an int, a long, a double, a decimal, and so forth.

Limiting it to the built-in types would've been disappointing, but better than nothing. The ideal solution would have to also allow user-defined types to act in a numeric capacity, so you could define a Complex type to handle complex numbers, for instance.[11] That complex number could then store each of its components in a generic way as well, so you could have a Complex<float>, a Complex<double>, and so on.

Two related (but hypothetical) solutions present themselves. One would be to allow constraints on operators, so you could write a set of constraints such as these (currently invalid) ones:

```
where T : T operator+ (T, T), T operator/ (T, int)
```

This would require that T have the operations you need in the earlier code. The other solution would be to define a few operators and perhaps conversions that must be supported in order for a type to meet the extra constraint—you could make it the "numeric constraint" written where T : numeric.

One problem with both of these options is that they can't be expressed as normal interfaces, because operator overloading is performed with *static* members, which can't be used to implement interfaces. I find the idea of *static interfaces* appealing: interfaces that only declare static members, including methods, operators, and constructors. Such static interfaces would only be useful within type constraints, but they'd present a type-safe generic way of accessing static members. This is just blue sky thinking, though (see my blog post on the topic for more details: http://mng.bz/ 3Rk3). I don't know of any plans to include this in a future version of C#.

The two neatest workarounds for this problem to date require later versions of .NET: one designed by Marc Gravell (http://mng.bz/9m8i) uses expression trees (which you'll meet in chapter 9) to build dynamic methods; the other uses the dynamic features of C# 4. You'll see an example of the latter in chapter 14. But, as you can tell by the descriptions, both of these are dynamic—you have to wait until execution time to see whether your code will work with a particular type. There are a few workarounds that still use static typing, but they have other disadvantages (surprisingly enough, they can sometimes be slower than the dynamic code).

The two limitations we've looked at so far have been quite practical—they've been issues you may well run into during actual development. But if you're generally curious like I am, you may also be asking yourself about other limitations that don't necessarily slow down development but are intellectual curiosities. In particular, why are generics limited to types and methods?

[11] This is assuming you're not using .NET 4 or higher, of course, because then you could use System .Numerics.Complex.

3.5.3 Lack of generic properties, indexers, and other member types

We've looked at generic types (classes, structs, delegates, and interfaces) and generic methods. There are plenty of other members that *could* be parameterized, but there are no generic properties, indexers, operators, constructors, finalizers, or events.

First, let's be precise about what we mean here: clearly an indexer can have a return type that's a type parameter—List<T> is an obvious example. KeyValue-Pair<TKey,TValue> provides similar examples for properties. What you *can't* have is an indexer or property (or any of the other members in that list) with *extra* type parameters.

Leaving the possible syntax of declaration aside for the minute, let's look at how these members might have to be called:

```
SomeClass<string> instance = new SomeClass<string><Guid>("x");
int x = instance.SomeProperty<int>;
byte y = instance.SomeIndexer<byte>["key"];
instance.Click<byte> += ByteHandler;
instance = instance +<int> instance;
```

INVALID ▷

I hope you'll agree that all of those look somewhat silly. Finalizers can't even be called explicitly from C# code, which is why there isn't a line for them. The fact that you can't do any of these isn't going to cause significant problems anywhere, as far as I can see—it's just worth being aware of this as an academic limitation.

The member where this restriction is most irritating is probably the constructor. A static generic method in the class is a good workaround for this, though, and the sample generic constructor syntax shown previously with two lists of type arguments is horrific.

These are by no means the *only* limitations of C# generics, but I believe they're the ones that you're most likely to run up against, either in your daily work, in community conversations, or when idly considering the feature as a whole. In the next two sections, we'll look at how some aspects of these aren't issues in the two other languages whose features are most commonly compared with C#'s generics: C++ (with templates) and Java (with generics, as of Java 5). We'll tackle C++ first.

3.5.4 Comparison with C++ templates

C++ templates are a bit like macros taken to an extreme level. They're incredibly powerful, but there are costs associated with them both in terms of code bloat and ease of understanding.

When a template is used in C++, the code is compiled for that particular set of template arguments, as if the template arguments were in the source code. This means that there's not as much need for constraints, because the compiler will check what you're allowed to do with the type while it's compiling the code for this particular set of template arguments. The C++ standards committee has recognized that constraints are still useful, though. Constraints were included and then removed from C++11 (the latest version of C++) but they may yet see the light of day, under the name of *concepts*.

The C++ compiler is smart enough to compile the code only once for any given set of template arguments, but it isn't able to share code in the way that the CLR does with reference types. That lack of sharing does have its benefits, though—it allows type-specific optimizations, such as inlining method calls for some type parameters but not others, from the same template. It also means that overload resolution can be performed separately for each set of type parameters, rather than just once based solely on the limited knowledge the C# compiler has due to any constraints present.

Don't forget that with normal C++ there's only one compilation involved, rather than the "compile to IL" and then "JIT compile to native code" model of .NET. A program using a standard template in 10 different ways will include the code 10 times in a C++ program. A similar program in C# using a generic type from the framework in 10 different ways won't include the code for the generic type at all—it'll refer to it, and the JIT will compile as many different versions as required (as described in section 3.4.2) at execution time.

One significant feature that C++ templates have over C# generics is that the template arguments don't have to be type names. Variable names, function names, and constant expressions can be used as well. A common example of this is a buffer type that has the size of the buffer as one of the template arguments—a `buffer <int,20>` will always be a buffer of 20 integers, and a `buffer<double,35>` will always be a buffer of 35 doubles. This ability is crucial to template metaprogramming (see the Wikipedia article, http://en.wikipedia.org/wiki/Template_metaprogramming), which is an advanced C++ technique, the very idea of which scares me but that can be powerful in the hands of experts.

C++ templates are more flexible in other ways too. They don't suffer from the lack of operator constraints described in section 3.5.2, and there are a few other restrictions that don't exist in C++: you can derive a class from one of its type parameters, and you can specialize a template for a particular set of type arguments. The latter ability allows the template author to write general code to be used when there's no more knowledge available, and specific (often highly optimized) code for particular types.

The same variance issues of .NET generics exist in C++ templates as well. An example given by Bjarne Stroustrup (the inventor of C++) is that there are no implicit conversions between `vector<shape*>` and `vector<circle*>` with similar reasoning—in this case, it might allow you to put a square peg in a round hole.

For further details on C++ templates, I recommend Stroustrup's *The C++ Programming Language,* 3rd edition (Addison-Wesley Professional, 1997). It's not always the easiest book to follow, but the templates chapter is fairly clear (once you get your mind around C++ terminology and syntax). For more comparisons with .NET generics, look at the blog post by the Visual C++ team on this topic (http://mng.bz/En13).

The other obvious language to compare with C# in terms of generics is Java, which introduced the feature into the mainstream language for the 1.5 release[12] several years after other projects had created Java-like languages that supported generics.

---

[12] Or 5.0, depending on which numbering system you use. Don't get me started.

3.5.5 Comparison with Java generics

Where C++ includes *more* of the template in the generated code than C# does, Java includes *less*. In fact, the Java runtime doesn't know about generics at all. The Java byte-code (roughly equivalent to IL) for a generic type includes some extra metadata to say that it's generic, but after compilation the calling code doesn't have much to indicate that generics were involved at all, and an instance of a generic type only knows about the nongeneric side of itself. For example, an instance of HashSet<E> doesn't know whether it was created as a HashSet<String> or a HashSet<Object>. The compiler effectively adds casts where necessary and performs more sanity checking.

Here's an example—first the generic Java code:

```
ArrayList<String> strings = new ArrayList<String>();
strings.add("hello");
String entry = strings.get(0);
strings.add(new Object());
```

And here's the equivalent nongeneric code:

```
ArrayList strings = new ArrayList();
strings.add("hello");
String entry = (String) strings.get(0);
strings.add(new Object());
```

They would generate the same Java bytecode, except for the last line, which is valid in the nongeneric case but will be caught by the compiler as an error in the generic version. You can use a generic type as a raw type, which is similar to using java.lang.Object for each of the type arguments. This rewriting—and loss of information—is called *type erasure*. Java doesn't have user-defined value types, but you can't even use the built-in ones as type arguments. Instead, you have to use the boxed versions—ArrayList<Integer> for a list of integers, for example.

You'll be forgiven for thinking this is all a bit disappointing compared with generics in C#, but there are some nice features of Java generics too:

- The virtual machine doesn't know anything about generics, so you can use code compiled using generics on an older version, as long as you don't use any classes or methods that aren't present on the old version. Versioning in .NET is much stricter in general—for each assembly you reference, you can specify whether the version number has to match exactly. In addition, code built to run on the 2.0 CLR won't run on .NET 1.1.

- You don't need to learn a new set of classes to use Java generics—where a nongeneric developer would use ArrayList, a generic developer just uses ArrayList<E>. Existing classes can be upgraded to generic versions reasonably easily.

- The previous feature has been utilized quite effectively with the reflection system—java.lang.Class (the equivalent of System.Type) is generic, which allows compile-time type safety to be extended to cover many situations involving reflection. In some other situations it's a pain, though.

- Java has support for generic variance using wildcards. For instance, `ArrayList <? extends Base>` can be read as "this is an `ArrayList` of some type that derives from `Base`, but we don't know which exact type." When we discuss C# 4's support for generic variance in chapter 13, we'll revisit this with a short example.

My personal opinion is that .NET generics are superior in almost every respect, although when I run into covariance/contravariance issues, I often wish I had wildcards. C# 4's limited generic variance improves this somewhat, but there are still times when the variance Java model works better. Java with generics is still much better than Java without generics, but there are no performance benefits and the safety only applies at compile time.

3.6   Summary

Phew! It's a good thing generics are simpler to use in reality than they are to describe. Although they *can* get complicated, they're widely regarded as the most important addition to C# 2 and they're incredibly useful. The worst thing about writing code using generics is that if you ever have to go back to C# 1, you'll miss them terribly. (Fortunately that's becoming increasingly unlikely, of course.)

In this chapter, I haven't tried to cover every detail of what is and isn't allowed when using generics—that's the job of the language specification, and it makes for dry reading. Instead, I've aimed for a practical approach, providing the information you'll need in everyday use, with a smattering of theory for the sake of academic interest.

We've looked at the three main benefits of generics: compile-time type safety, performance, and code expressiveness. Being able to get the IDE and compiler to validate your code early is certainly a good thing, but it's arguable that more is to be gained from tools providing intelligent options based on the types involved than from the actual safety aspect.

Performance is improved most radically when it comes to value types, which no longer need to be boxed and unboxed when they're used in strongly typed generic APIs, particularly the generic collection types provided in .NET 2.0. Performance with reference types is usually improved but only slightly.

Your code is able to express its intention more clearly using generics—instead of a comment or a long variable name being required to describe exactly what types are involved, the details of the type itself can do the work. Comments and variable names can often become inaccurate over time, as they can be forgotten when the code is changed, but the type information is correct by definition.

Generics aren't capable of doing *everything* you might sometimes like them to do, and I've covered some of their limitations in the chapter, but if you truly embrace C# 2 and the generic types within the .NET 2.0 Framework, you'll come across good uses for them incredibly frequently in your code.

This topic will come up time and time again in future chapters, as other new features build on this key one. Indeed, the subject of the next chapter would be very different without generics—we'll look at nullable types, as implemented by `Nullable<T>`.

Saying nothing
with nullable types

Nullity is a concept that has provoked debate over the years. Is a null reference a value, or the absence of a value? Is "nothing" a "something"? Should languages support the concept of nullity at all, or should it be represented in other patterns?

In this chapter, I'll try to stay more practical than philosophical. First we'll look at why there's a problem at all—why you can't set a value type variable to null in C# 1 and what the traditional alternatives have been. After that, I'll introduce you to our knight in shining armor—System.Nullable<T>—and then we'll look at how C# 2 makes working with nullable types simple and compact. Like generics, nullable types sometimes have uses beyond what you might expect, and we'll look at a few examples of these at the end of the chapter.

So, when is a value not a value? Let's find out.

4.1   *What do you do when you just don't have a value?*

The C# and .NET designers don't add features just for kicks. There has to be a real, significant problem that needs fixing before they'll go as far as changing C# as a language or .NET at the platform level. In this case, the problem is best summed up in one of the most frequently asked questions in C# and .NET discussion groups:

> *I need to set my* DateTime *variable to* null, *but the compiler won't let me. What should I do?[1]*

It's a question that comes up fairly naturally—an example might be in an e-commerce application where users are looking at their account history. If an order has been placed but not delivered, there may be a purchase date but no dispatch date, so how would you represent that in a type that's meant to provide the order details?

Before C# 2, the answer to the question usually came in two parts: an explanation of why you couldn't use null in the first place, and a list of which options were available. Nowadays the answer would usually explain nullable types instead, but it's worth looking at the C# 1 options to understand where the problem comes from.

4.1.1   *Why value type variables can't be null*

As you saw in chapter 2, the value of a reference type variable is a reference, and the value of a value type variable is the real data itself. A non-null reference is a way of getting at an object, but null acts as a special value that means *I don't refer to any object*.

If you want to think of references as being like URLs, null is (*very* roughly speaking) the reference equivalent of about:blank. It's represented as all zeroes in memory (which is why it's the default value for all reference types—clearing a whole block of memory is cheap, so that's the way objects are initialized), but it's still basically stored in the same way as other references. There's no extra bit hidden somewhere for each reference type variable. That means you can't use the "all zeroes" value for a real reference, but that's okay—your memory is going to run out long before you have that many live objects anyway. This is the key to why null isn't a valid *value* type value.

Let's consider the byte type as a familiar one that's easy to think about. The value of a variable of type byte is stored in a single byte—it may be padded for alignment purposes, but the value itself is conceptually only made up of one byte. You've *got* to be able to store the values 0–255 in that variable; otherwise it's useless for reading arbitrary binary data. With the 256 normal values and one null value, you'd have to cope with a total of 257 values, and there's no way of squeezing that many values into a single byte. The designers could've decided that every value type would have an extra flag bit somewhere determining whether a value was null or contained real data, but the memory usage implications are horrible, not to mention the fact that you'd have to check the flag every time you wanted to use the value. In a nutshell, with value types you often care about having the whole range of possible bit patterns available as real

---

[1]   It's almost always DateTime rather than any other value type. I'm not entirely sure why—it's as if developers inherently understand why a byte shouldn't be null, but feel that dates are more inherently nullable.

values, whereas with reference types it's okay to lose one potential value in order to gain the benefits of making the `null` reference available.

That's the usual situation. Now why would you *want* to be able to represent `null` for a value type anyway? The most common reason is simply because databases typically support `NULL` as a value for every type (unless you specifically make the field non-nullable), so you can have nullable character data, nullable integers, nullable Booleans—the whole works. When you fetch data from a database, it's generally not a good idea to lose information, so you want to be able to represent the nullity of whatever you read, somehow.

That just moves the question one step further on, though. Why do databases allow null values for dates, integers, and the like? Null values are typically used for unknown or missing values, such as the dispatch date in the earlier e-commerce example. Nullity represents an absence of definite information, which can be important in many situations. Indeed, there doesn't have to be a database involved for nullable value types to be useful; that's just the scenario where developers typically encounter the problem first.

That brings us to options for representing null values in C# 1.

4.1.2 *Patterns for representing null values in C# 1*

There are three basic patterns commonly used to get around the lack of nullable value types in C# 1. Each has its pros and cons—mostly cons—and all of them are fairly unsatisfying. But they're worth knowing, partly to more fully appreciate the benefits of the integrated solution in C# 2.

PATTERN 1: THE MAGIC VALUE

The first pattern is to sacrifice one value to represent a null value. This tends to be used as the solution for `DateTime`; few people expect their databases to *actually* contain dates in AD 1, so `DateTime.MinValue` can be used as a convenient magic value without losing any useful data. In other words, it goes against the line of reasoning I gave earlier, which assumes that every possible value needs to be available for normal purposes. The *semantic* meaning of such a null value will vary from application to application—it may mean that the user hasn't entered the value into a form yet, or that it's not required for that record, for example.

The good news is that using a magic value doesn't waste any memory or require any new types. But it does rely on you picking an appropriate value that you'll never want to use for real data. Also, it's basically inelegant. It just doesn't feel right. If you ever find yourself needing to go down this path, you should at least use a constant (or static read-only value for types that can't be expressed as constants) to represent the magic value—comparisons with `DateTime.MinValue` everywhere, for instance, don't express the meaning of the magic value. Additionally, it's easy to accidentally use the magic value as if it were a normal, meaningful value—neither the compiler nor the runtime will help you spot the error. In contrast, most of the other solutions presented here (including the one in C# 2) would result in either a compilation error or an exception at execution time, depending on the exact situation.

The magic value pattern is deeply embedded in computing in the form of IEEE-754 binary floating-point types such as `float` and `double`. These go further than the idea of a single value representing *this isn't really a number*—there are *many* bit patterns that are classified as not-a-number (NaN), as well as values for positive and negative infinity. I suspect few programmers (myself included) are as cautious around these values as we should be, which is another indication of the pattern's shortcomings.

ADO.NET has a variation on this pattern where the same magic value—`DBNull.Value`—is used for *all* null values, regardless of the type. In this case, an extra value and indeed an extra type have been introduced to indicate when a database has returned `null`. But it's only applicable where compile-time type safety isn't important (in other words, when you're happy to use `object` and cast after testing for nullity), and again it doesn't feel quite right. In fact, it's a mixture of the magic value pattern and the reference type wrapper pattern, which we'll look at next.

PATTERN 2: A REFERENCE TYPE WRAPPER

The second solution can take two forms. The simpler one is to use `object` as the variable type, boxing and unboxing values as necessary. The more complex (and more appealing) form is to have a reference type for each value type you need in a nullable form, containing a single instance variable of that value type, and with implicit conversion operators to and from the value type. With generics, you *could* do this in one generic type, but if you're using C# 2 anyway, you might as well use the nullable types described in this chapter instead. If you're stuck in C# 1, you have to create extra source code for each type you want to wrap. This isn't hard to put in the form of a template for automatic code generation, but it's still a burden that's best avoided if possible.

Both of these forms have the problem that though they allow you to use `null` directly, they require objects to be created on the heap, which can lead to garbage collection pressure if you need to use this approach frequently and adds memory use due to the overhead associated with objects. For the more complex solution, you could make the reference type mutable, which may reduce the number of instances you need to create, but it could also make for some unintuitive code.

PATTERN 3: AN EXTRA BOOLEAN FLAG

The final pattern involves a normal value type value and another value—a Boolean flag—indicating whether the value is "real" or whether it should be disregarded. Again, there are two ways of implementing this solution. Either you could maintain two separate variables in the code that uses the value, or you could encapsulate the value-plus-flag into another value type.

This latter solution is quite similar to the more complicated reference type idea described earlier, except that you avoid the garbage collection issue by using a value type and indicate nullity within the encapsulated value rather than with a null reference. The downside of having to create a new one of these types for every value type you wish to handle is the same, though. Also, if the value is ever boxed for some reason, it'll be boxed in the normal way whether it's considered to be null or not.

The last pattern (in the more encapsulated form) is effectively how nullable types work in C# 2, although the new features of the framework, CLR, and language all combine to provide a solution that's significantly neater than anything that was possible in C# 1. The next section deals with the support provided by the framework and the CLR in .NET 2: if C# 2 *only* supported generics, most of section 4.2 would still be relevant and the feature would still work and be useful. But C# 2 provides extra syntactic sugar to make it even better—that's the subject of section 4.3.

4.2 System.Nullable<T> and System.Nullable

The core structure at the heart of nullable types is the System.Nullable<T> struct. In addition, the System.Nullable static class provides utility methods that occasionally make nullable types easier to work with. (From now on I'll leave out the namespace, to make life simpler.) We'll look at both of these types in turn, and for this section I'll avoid any extra features provided by the language, so you'll be able to understand what's going on in the IL code when we *do* look at the shorthand provided by C# 2.

4.2.1 Introducing Nullable<T>

As you can tell by its name, Nullable<T> is a generic type. The type parameter T has a value type constraint, so you can't use Nullable<Stream>, for example. As I mentioned in section 3.3.1 this also means you can't use another nullable type as the argument, so Nullable<Nullable<int>> is forbidden, even though Nullable<T> is a value type in every other way. The type of T for any particular nullable type is called the *underlying type* of that nullable type. For example, the underlying type of Nullable<int> is int.

The most important parts of Nullable<T> are its properties, HasValue and Value. They do the obvious: Value represents the non-nullable value (the *real* one, if you will), when there is one, and throws an InvalidOperationException if (conceptually) there's no real value. HasValue is a Boolean property indicating whether there's a real value or whether the instance should be regarded as null. For now, I'll talk about an "instance with a value" or an "instance without a value," which mean an instance where the HasValue property returns true or false, respectively.

These properties are backed by simple fields in the obvious way. Figure 4.1 shows instances of Nullable<int> representing (from left to right) no value, 0, and 5. Remember that Nullable<T> is still a value type, so if you have a variable of type Nullable<int>, the variable's value will directly contain a bool and an int—it won't be a reference to a separate object.

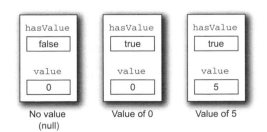

Figure 4.1 Sample values of Nullable<int>

Now that you know what the properties should achieve, let's look at how you can create an instance of the type. `Nullable<T>` has two constructors: the default one (creating an instance without a value) and one taking an instance of `T` as the value. Once an instance has been constructed, it's immutable.

Value types and mutability

A type is said to be *immutable* if it's designed so that an instance can't be changed after it's been constructed. Immutable types often lead to a cleaner design than you'd get if you had to keep track of what *might* be changing shared values—particularly among different threads.

Immutability is particularly important for value types; they should almost always be immutable. Most value types in the framework are immutable, but there are some commonly used exceptions—in particular, the `Point` structures for both Windows Forms and Windows Presentation Foundation are mutable.

If you need a way of basing one value on another, follow the lead of `DateTime` and `TimeSpan`—provide methods and operators that return a new value rather than modifying an existing one. This avoids all kinds of subtle bugs, including situations where you may *appear* to be changing something, but you're actually changing a copy. Just say *No* to mutable value types.

`Nullable<T>` introduces a single new method, `GetValueOrDefault`, which has two overloads. Both return the value of the instance if there is one, or a default value otherwise. One overload doesn't have any parameters (in which case the default value of the underlying type is used), and the other allows you to specify the default value to return if necessary.

The other methods implemented by `Nullable<T>` all override existing methods: `GetHashCode`, `ToString`, and `Equals`. `GetHashCode` returns 0 if the instance doesn't have a value, or the result of calling `GetHashCode` on the value if there is one. `ToString` returns an empty string if there isn't a value, or the result of calling `ToString` on the value if there is. `Equals` is slightly more complicated—we'll come back to it when we've discussed boxing.

Finally, two conversions are provided by the framework. First, there's an *implicit* conversion from `T` to `Nullable<T>`. This always results in an instance where `HasValue` returns `true`. Likewise, there's an *explicit* conversion from `Nullable<T>` to `T`, which behaves exactly the same as the `Value` property, including throwing an exception when there's no real value to return.

WRAPPING AND UNWRAPPING The C# specification names the process of converting an instance of `T` to an instance of `Nullable<T>` *wrapping*, with the obvious opposite process being called *unwrapping*. The specification defines these terms with reference to the constructor taking a parameter and the `Value` property, respectively. Indeed, these calls are generated by the C# code even when it otherwise *looks* as if you're using the conversions provided by the framework. The results are the same either way, though. For the rest of this chapter, I won't distinguish between the two implementations available.

Before we go any further, let's see all this in action. The following listing shows everything you can do with `Nullable<T>` directly, leaving `Equals` aside for the moment.

Listing 4.1 Using various members of `Nullable<T>`

```
static void Display(Nullable<int> x)                          ◁┐ ❶ Displays
{                                                                    diagnostics
   Console.WriteLine("HasValue: {0}", x.HasValue);
   if (x.HasValue)
   {
      Console.WriteLine("Value: {0}", x.Value);
      Console.WriteLine("Explicit conversion: {0}", (int)x);
   }
   Console.WriteLine("GetValueOrDefault(): {0}",
                     x.GetValueOrDefault());
   Console.WriteLine("GetValueOrDefault(10): {0}",
                     x.GetValueOrDefault(10));
   Console.WriteLine("ToString(): \"{0}\"", x.ToString());
   Console.WriteLine("GetHashCode(): {0}", x.GetHashCode());
   Console.WriteLine();
}
...
Nullable<int> x = 5;                                          ┌ ❷ Wraps
x = new Nullable<int>(5);                                     │   value of 5
Console.WriteLine("Instance with value:");
Display(x);

x = new Nullable<int>();                                      ◁┐ Constructs instance
Console.WriteLine("Instance without value:");                     ❸ without value
Display(x);
```

In listing 4.1, you first use the two different ways (in terms of C# source code) of wrapping a value of the underlying type ❷, and then you use various different members on the instance ❶. Next, you create an instance that *doesn't* have a value ❸ and use the same members in the same order, just omitting the `Value` property and the explicit conversion to `int`, because these would throw exceptions.

The output of listing 4.1 is as follows:

```
Instance with value:
HasValue: True
Value: 5
Explicit conversion: 5
GetValueOrDefault(): 5
GetValueOrDefault(10): 5
ToString(): "5"
GetHashCode(): 5

Instance without value:
HasValue: False
GetValueOrDefault(): 0
GetValueOrDefault(10): 10
```

```
ToString(): ""
GetHashCode(): 0
```

So far, you could probably have predicted all of the results by looking at the members provided by `Nullable<T>`. When it comes to boxing and unboxing, though, there's special behavior to make nullable types behave how you'd really *like* them to behave, rather than how they'd behave if you slavishly followed the normal boxing rules.

4.2.2 *Boxing Nullable<T> and unboxing*

It's important to remember that `Nullable<T>` is a struct—a value type. This means that if you want to convert it to a reference type (`object` is the most obvious example), you'll need to box it. It's only with respect to boxing and unboxing that the CLR has any special behavior regarding nullable types—the rest is standard generics, conversions, method calls, and so forth. In fact, the behavior was only changed shortly before the release of .NET 2.0, as the result of community requests. In the preview releases, nullable value types were boxed just like any other value types.

An instance of `Nullable<T>` is boxed to either a null reference (if it doesn't have a value) or a boxed value of `T` (if it does), as shown in figure 4.2. It never boxes to a "boxed nullable `int`"—there's no such type.

You can unbox from a boxed value either to its normal type or to the corresponding nullable type. Unboxing a null reference will throw a `NullReference-Exception` if you unbox to the normal type, but will unbox to an instance without a value if you unbox to the appropriate nullable type. This behavior is shown in the following listing.

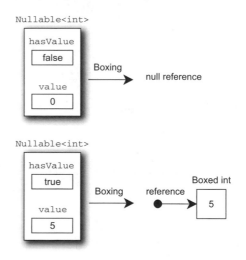

Figure 4.2 Results of boxing an instance without a value (top) and with a value (bottom)

Listing 4.2   Boxing and unboxing behavior of nullable types

```
Nullable<int> nullable = 5;

object boxed = nullable;                    Boxes nullable
Console.WriteLine(boxed.GetType());         with value

int normal = (int)boxed;                    Unboxes to non-
Console.WriteLine(normal);                  nullable variable

nullable = (Nullable<int>)boxed;            Unboxes to
Console.WriteLine(nullable);                nullable variable

nullable = new Nullable<int>();             Boxes nullable
boxed = nullable;                           without value
```

```
Console.WriteLine(boxed == null);

nullable = (Nullable<int>)boxed;              ←— Unboxes to nullable variable
Console.WriteLine(nullable.HasValue);
```

The output of listing 4.2 shows the type of the boxed value as `System.Int32` (not `System.Nullable<System.Int32>`). This confirms that you can retrieve the value by unboxing to either `int` or to `Nullable<int>`. Finally, the output demonstrates that you can box from a nullable instance without a value to a null reference and successfully unbox again to another valueless nullable instance. If you'd tried unboxing the last value of `boxed` to a non-nullable `int`, the program would've blown up with a `NullReferenceException`.

Now that you understand the behavior of boxing and unboxing, we can begin to tackle the behavior of `Nullable<T>.Equals`.

4.2.3 *Equality of Nullable<T> instances*

`Nullable<T>` overrides `object.Equals(object)` but doesn't introduce any equality operators or provide an `Equals(Nullable<T>)` method. Because the framework has supplied the basic building blocks, languages can add extra functionality on top, including making existing operators work as you'd expect them to. You'll see the details of that in section 4.3.3, but the basic equality, as defined by the vanilla `Equals` method, follows these rules for a call to `first.Equals(second)`:

- If `first` has no value and `second` is `null`, they're equal.
- If `first` has no value and `second` isn't `null`, they aren't equal.
- If `first` has a value and `second` is `null`, they aren't equal.
- Otherwise, they're equal if `first`'s value is equal to `second`.

Note that you don't have to consider the case where `second` is another `Nullable<T>` because the rules of boxing prohibit that situation. The type of `second` is `object`, so in order to be a `Nullable<T>`, it would have to be boxed, and as you've just seen, boxing a nullable instance creates a box of the non-nullable type or returns a null reference. Initially, the first rule may appear to be breaking the contract for `object.Equals(object)`, which insists that `x.Equals(null)` returns `false`—but that's only when x is a non-null reference. Again, due to the boxing behavior, `Nullable<T>`'s implementation will never be called via a reference.

The rules are mostly consistent with the rules of equality elsewhere in .NET, so you can use nullable instances as keys for dictionaries and any other situations where you need equality. Just don't expect equality to differentiate between a non-nullable instance and a nullable instance with a value—it's been carefully set up so that those two cases *are* treated the same way as each other.

That covers the `Nullable<T>` structure itself, but it has a shadowy partner: the `Nullable` class.

4.2.4 *Support from the nongeneric Nullable class*

The `System.Nullable<T>` struct does almost everything you want it to, but it gets help from the `System.Nullable` class. This is a static class—it only contains static methods, and you can't create an instance of it.[2] In fact, everything it does could've been done equally well by other types, and if Microsoft had shown more foresight, the `Nullable` class might not have even existed—which would've saved some confusion over what the two types are there for. But this accident of history has three methods to its name, and they're still useful.

The first two are comparison methods:

```
public static int Compare<T>(Nullable<T> n1, Nullable<T> n2)
public static bool Equals<T>(Nullable<T> n1, Nullable<T> n2)
```

`Compare` uses `Comparer<T>.Default` to compare the two underlying values (if they exist), and `Equals` uses `EqualityComparer<T>.Default`. When presented with instances with no values, the results returned from each method comply with the .NET conventions of nulls comparing equal to each other and less than anything else.

Both of these methods could happily be part of `Nullable<T>` as static but nongeneric methods. The one small advantage of having them as generic methods in a nongeneric type is that generic type inference can be applied, so you'll rarely need to explicitly specify the type parameter.

The final method of `System.Nullable` isn't generic—it couldn't be. Its signature is as follows:

```
public static Type GetUnderlyingType(Type nullableType)
```

If the parameter is a nullable type, the method returns its underlying type; otherwise it returns `null`. The reason this couldn't be a generic method is that if you knew the underlying type to start with, you wouldn't have to call it.

You've now seen what the framework and the CLR provide to support nullable types—but C# 2 adds language features to make life a lot more pleasant.

4.3 *C# 2's syntactic sugar for nullable types*

So far you've seen nullable types doing their jobs, but the examples haven't been particularly pretty to look at. Admittedly it's clear that you're using nullable types when you have to type `Nullable<>` around the name of the type you're interested in, but that makes the nullability more prominent than the underlying type, which is usually not a good idea.

In addition, the very name *nullable* suggests that you should be able to assign `null` to a variable of a nullable type, and you haven't seen that—you've always used the default constructor of the type. In this section, we'll look at how C# 2 deals with these issues and others.

---

[2] You'll learn more about static classes in chapter 7.

Before we get into the details of what C# 2 provides as a language, there's one definition I can finally introduce. The *null value* of a nullable value type is the value where `HasValue` returns `false`—or an "instance without a value," as I referred to it in section 4.2. I didn't use the term before because it's specific to C#. The CLI specification doesn't mention it, and the documentation for `Nullable<T>` itself doesn't mention it. I've honored that difference by waiting until we're specifically talking about C# 2 before introducing the term. The term also applies to reference types: the null value of a reference type is simply the null reference you're familiar with from C# 1.

> **NULLABLE TYPE VERSUS NULLABLE VALUE TYPE**   In the C# language specification, *nullable type* is used to mean any type with a null value—so any reference type, or any `Nullable<T>`. You may have noticed that I've been using this term as if it were synonymous with *nullable value type* (which obviously doesn't include reference types). Although I'm usually a huge pedant when it comes to terminology, if I'd used "nullable value type" everywhere in this chapter, it would've been horrible to read. You should also expect "nullable type" to be used ambiguously in the real world: it's probably more common to use it when describing `Nullable<T>` than in the sense described in the specification.

With that out of the way, let's see what features C# 2 gives us, starting by reducing the clutter in our code.

4.3.1   The ? modifier

There are some elements of syntax that may be unfamiliar at first but that have an appropriate *feel* to them. The conditional operator (a ? b : c) is one of them for me—it asks a question and then has two corresponding answers. In the same way, the ? modifier for nullable types just feels right.

The ? modifier is a shorthand way of specifying a nullable type, so instead of using `Nullable <byte>`, you can use `byte?` throughout your code. The two are interchangeable and compile to exactly the same IL, so you can mix and match them if you want to—but on behalf of whoever reads your code next, I urge you to pick one way or the other and use it consistently. The following listing is exactly equivalent to listing 4.2 but uses the ? modifier, as shown in bold.

Listing 4.3   The same code as 4.2 but using the ? modifier

```
int? nullable = 5;

object boxed = nullable;
Console.WriteLine(boxed.GetType());

int normal = (int)boxed;
Console.WriteLine(normal);

nullable = (int?)boxed;
Console.WriteLine(nullable);

nullable = new int?();
```

```
boxed = nullable;
Console.WriteLine(boxed == null);

nullable = (int?)boxed;
Console.WriteLine(nullable.HasValue);
```

I won't go through what the code does or how it does it, because the result is exactly the same as in listing 4.2. The two listings compile down to the same IL—they simply use different syntax, just as `int` is interchangeable with `System.Int32`. You can use the shorthand version everywhere, including in method signatures, `typeof` expressions, casts, and the like.

The reason I feel the modifier is well chosen is that it adds an air of uncertainty to the nature of the variable. Does the variable `nullable` in listing 4.3 have an integer value? Well, at any particular time it might, or it might be the null value.

From now on, I'll use the ? modifier in all the examples—it's neater, and it's arguably the idiomatic way to use nullable types in C#. But you may feel that it's too easy to miss when reading the code, in which case there's nothing to stop you from using the longer syntax. You might want to compare the listings in this and the previous section to see which you find more clear.

Given that the C# 2 specification defines the null value, it would be odd if we couldn't use the `null` literal that's already in the language to represent it. Fortunately we can...

4.3.2   *Assigning and comparing with null*

A concise author could cover this whole section in a single sentence: "The C# compiler allows the use of `null` to represent the null value of a nullable type in both comparisons and assignments." I prefer to show you what it means in real code and to consider *why* the language has been given this feature.

You may have felt uncomfortable every time you used the default constructor of `Nullable<T>`. It achieves the desired behavior, but it doesn't express the *reason* why you want to do it—it doesn't leave the right impression with the reader. It should ideally give the same sort of feeling that using `null` does with reference types.

If it seems odd to you that I've talked about feelings in both this section and the previous one, just think about who writes code and who reads it. Sure, the compiler has to understand the code, and it couldn't care less about the subtle nuances of style, but few pieces of code used in production systems are written and then never read again. Anything you can do to get the reader into the mental process you were going through when you originally wrote the code is good, and using the familiar `null` literal helps to achieve that.

With that in mind, we'll switch from using an example that just shows syntax and behavior to one that gives an impression of how nullable types might be used. We'll model a `Person` class where you need to know a person's name, date of birth, and date of death. We'll only keep track of people who have definitely been born, but some of those people may still be alive—in which case the date of death will be represented by

null. The following listing shows some of the possible code. A real class would have
more operations available—we'll just look at the calculation of age for this example.

Listing 4.4   Part of a `Person` class including calculation of age

```
class Person
{
    DateTime birth;
    DateTime? death;
    string name;

    public TimeSpan Age
    {
        get
        {
            if (death == null)                              ◁—❶ Checks HasValue
            {
                return DateTime.Now - birth;
            }
            else
            {
                return death.Value - birth;                 ◁—❷ Unwraps for calculation
            }
        }
    }

    public Person(string name,
                  DateTime birth,
                  DateTime? death)
    {
        this.birth = birth;
        this.death = death;
        this.name = name;
    }
}
...
Person turing = new Person("Alan Turing ",
                           new DateTime(1912, 6, 23),
                           new DateTime(1954, 6, 7));        ❸ Wraps DateTime
                                                               as nullable
Person knuth = new Person("Donald Knuth ",
                          new DateTime(1938, 1, 10),
                          null);                             ❹ Specifies null
                                                               date of death
```

Listing 4.4 doesn't produce any output, but the fact that it compiles might have surprised you before reading this chapter. Apart from the use of the ? modifier causing
confusion, you might have found it odd that you could compare a DateTime? with
null or pass null as the argument for a DateTime? parameter.

   Hopefully by now the meaning is intuitive—when you compare the death variable
with null, you're asking whether its value is the null value or not. Likewise when you use
null as a DateTime? instance, you're really creating the null value for the type by calling
the default constructor. Indeed, you can see in the generated IL that the code the compiler spits out for listing 4.4 really does just call the death.HasValue property ❶ and
create a new instance of DateTime? ❹ using the default constructor (represented in IL

as the `initobj` instruction). The date of Alan Turing's death ❸ is created by calling the normal `DateTime` constructor and then passing the result into the `Nullable <Date-Time>` constructor that takes a parameter.

I mention looking at the IL because that can be a useful way of finding out what your code is actually doing, particularly if something compiles when you don't expect it to. You can use the ildasm tool that comes with the .NET SDK, or one of the many decompilers now available, such as .NET Reflector, ILSpy, dotPeek, or JustDecompile. (Whenever I refer to Reflector in this book, it's solely because that's the tool I use out of habit. The others are perfectly fine too, I'm sure.)

You've seen how C# provides shorthand syntax for the concept of a null value, making the code more expressive once nullable types are understood in the first place. But one part of listing 4.4 took a bit more work than you might have hoped—the subtraction at ❷. Why did you have to unwrap the value? Why couldn't you just return `death - birth` directly? What would you want that expression to mean if `death` had been `null` (excluded in this code by the earlier test)? These questions—and more—are answered in the next section.

4.3.3 *Nullable conversions and operators*

You've seen that you can compare instances of nullable types with `null`, but there are other comparisons that can be made and other operators that can be used in some cases. Likewise you've seen wrapping and unwrapping, but other conversions can be used with some types. This section explains what's available. I'm afraid it's pretty much impossible to make this kind of topic genuinely exciting, but carefully designed features like these are what make C# a pleasant language to work with in the long run. Don't worry if not all of it sinks in the first time through: just remember that the details are here if you need to refer to them in the middle of a coding session.

The executive summary is that if there's an operator or conversion available on a non-nullable value type, and that operator or conversion only involves other non-nullable value types, then the nullable value type also has the same operator or conversion available, usually converting the non-nullable value types into their nullable equivalents. To give a more concrete example, there's an implicit conversion from `int` to `long`, and that means there's also an implicit conversion from `int?` to `long?` that behaves in the obvious manner.

Unfortunately, although that broad description gives the right general idea, the exact rules are slightly more complicated. Each rule is simple, but there are quite a few of them. It's worth knowing about them because otherwise you might end up staring at a compiler error or warning for a while, wondering why it believes you're trying to make a conversion that you never intended in the first place. We'll start with the conversions and then look at the operators.

CONVERSIONS INVOLVING NULLABLE TYPES

For completeness, let's start with the conversions you already know about:

- An implicit conversion from the `null` literal to `T?`
- An implicit conversion from `T` to `T?`
- An explicit conversion from `T?` to `T`

Now consider the predefined and user-defined conversions available on types. For instance, there's a predefined conversion from `int` to `long`. For any conversion like this, from one non-nullable value type (`S`) to another (`T`), the following conversions are also available:

- `S?` to `T?` (explicit or implicit depending on original conversion)
- `S` to `T?` (explicit or implicit depending on original conversion)
- `S?` to `T` (always explicit)

To carry the example forward, this means that you can convert implicitly from `int?` to `long?` and from `int` to `long?` as well as explicitly from `int?` to `long`. The conversions behave in the natural way, with null values of `S?` converting to null values of `T?`, and non-null values using the original conversion. As before, the explicit conversion from `S?` to `T` will throw an `InvalidOperationException` when converting from a null value of `S?`. For user-defined conversions, these extra conversions involving nullable types are known as *lifted conversions*.

So far, so relatively simple. Now let's consider the operators, where things are slightly more tricky.

OPERATORS INVOLVING NULLABLE TYPES

C# allows the following operators to be overloaded:[3]

- Unary: `+ ++ - -- ! ~ truefalse`
- Binary: `+ - * / % & | ^ << >>`
- Equality: `== !=`
- Relational: `< > <= >=`

When these operators are overloaded for a non-nullable value type `T`, the nullable type `T?` has the same operators, with slightly different operand and result types. These are called *lifted operators*, whether they're predefined operators such as addition on numeric types or user-defined operators such as adding a `TimeSpan` to a `DateTime`. There are a few restrictions as to when they apply:

- The `true` and `false` operators are never lifted. They're incredibly rare in the first place, though, so it's no great loss.
- Only operators with non-nullable value types for the operands are lifted.

---

[3] The equality and relational operators are also binary operators, but they behave slightly differently than the others; hence their separation in this list.

- For the unary and binary operators (other than equality and relational operators), the return type has to be a non-nullable value type.
- For the equality and relational operators, the return type has to be `bool`.
- The `&` and `|` operators on `bool?` have separately defined behavior, which you'll see in section 4.3.4.

For all the operators, the operand types become their nullable equivalents. For the unary and binary operators, the return type also becomes nullable, and a null value is returned if any of the operands is a null value. The equality and relational operators keep their non-nullable Boolean return types. For equality, two null values are considered equal, and a null value and any non-null value are considered different, which is consistent with the behavior you saw in section 4.2.3. The relational operators always return `false` if either operand is a null value. When none of the operands is a null value, the operator of the non-nullable type is invoked in the obvious way.

All these rules sound more complicated than they really are—for the most part, everything works as you probably expect it to. It's easiest to see what happens with a few examples, and as `int` has so many predefined operators (and integers can be so easily expressed), it's the natural demonstration type. Table 4.1 shows a number of expressions, the lifted operator signature, and the result. It's assumed that there are variables `four`, `five`, and `nullInt`, each with type `int?` and with the obvious values.

Table 4.1 Examples of lifted operators applied to nullable integers

Expression	Lifted operator	Result
`-nullInt`	`int? -(int? x)`	`null`
`-five`	`int? -(int? x)`	`-5`
`five + nullInt`	`int? +(int? x, int? y)`	`null`
`five + five`	`int? +(int? x, int? y)`	`10`
`nullInt == nullInt`	`bool ==(int? x, int? y)`	`true`
`five == five`	`bool ==(int? x, int? y)`	`true`
`five == nullInt`	`bool ==(int? x, int? y)`	`false`
`five == four`	`bool ==(int? x, int? y)`	`false`
`four < five`	`bool <(int? x, int? y)`	`true`
`nullInt < five`	`bool <(int? x, int? y)`	`false`
`five < nullInt`	`bool <(int? x, int? y)`	`false`
`nullInt < nullInt`	`bool <(int? x, int? y)`	`false`
`nullInt <= nullInt`	`bool <=(int? x, int? y)`	`false`

Possibly the most surprising line of the table is the last one—that a null value isn't deemed less than or equal to another null value, even though they *are* deemed to be equal to each other (as per the fifth row)! Very odd, but unlikely to cause problems in real life, in my experience.

One aspect of lifted operators and nullable conversion that has caused some confusion is unintended comparisons with `null` when using a non-nullable value type. The code that follows is legal, but not useful:

```
int i = 5;
if (i == null)
{
   Console.WriteLine ("Never going to happen");
}
```

The C# compiler raises warnings on this code, but you may consider it surprising that it's allowed at all. What's happening is that the compiler sees the `int` expression on the left side of the `==`, sees `null` on the right side, and knows that there's an implicit conversion to `int?` from each of them. Because a comparison between two `int?` values is perfectly valid, the code doesn't generate an error—just the warning. As a further complication, this *isn't* allowed in the case where, instead of `int`, you're dealing with a generic type parameter that has been constrained to be a value type—the rules on generics prohibit the comparison with `null` in that situation.

Either way, there'll be an error or a warning, so as long as you look closely at warnings, you shouldn't end up with deficient code due to this quirk, and hopefully my pointing it out to you now will save you from getting a headache trying to work out exactly what's going on.

Now you can answer the question at the end of the previous section—why we used `death.Value - birth` in listing 4.4 instead of just `death - birth`. Applying the previous rules, you *could* have used the latter expression, but the result would've been a `TimeSpan?` instead of a `TimeSpan`. This would've left you with the options of casting the result to `TimeSpan` using its `Value` property, or changing the `Age` property to return a `TimeSpan?`, which just pushes the issue onto the caller. It's still a bit ugly, but you'll see a nicer implementation of the `Age` property in section 4.3.6.

In the list of restrictions regarding operator lifting, I mentioned that `bool?` works slightly differently than the other types. The next section explains this and pulls the lens back to see the bigger picture of why all these operators work the way they do.

4.3.4 Nullable logic

I vividly remember my early electronics lessons at school. They always seemed to revolve around either working out the voltage across different parts of a circuit using the V=IxR formula, or applying *truth tables*—the reference charts for explaining the difference between NAND gates and NOR gates and so on. The idea is simple—a truth table maps out every possible combination of inputs into whatever piece of logic you're interested in and tells you the output.

The truth tables we drew for simple, two-input logic gates always had four rows—each input had two possible values, which means there were four possible combinations. Boolean logic is simple like that, but what happens when you have a tristate logical type? Well, `bool?` is just such a type—the value can be `true`, `false`, or `null`. That means that your truth tables now need nine rows for binary operators as there are nine combinations. The specification only highlights the logical AND and inclusive OR operators (`&` and `|`, respectively) because the other operators—unary logical negation (`!`) and exclusive OR (`^`)—follow the same rules as other lifted operators. There are no conditional logical operators (the short-circuiting `&&` and `||` operators) defined for `bool?`, which makes life simpler.

For the sake of completeness, table 4.2 gives the truth table for all four valid `bool?` logical operators.

Table 4.2   Truth table for the logical operators AND, inclusive OR, exclusive OR, and logical negation, applied to the `bool?` type

x	y	x & y	x | y	x ^ y	!x
true	true	true	true	false	false
true	false	false	true	true	false
true	null	null	true	null	false
false	true	false	true	true	true
false	false	false	false	false	true
false	null	false	null	null	true
null	true	null	true	null	null
null	false	false	null	null	null
null	null	null	null	null	null

If you find reasoning about rules easier to understand than looking up values in tables, the idea is that a null `bool?` value is in some senses a "maybe." If you imagine that each null entry in the input side of the table is a variable instead, you'll always get a null value on the output side of the table if the result depends on the value of that variable. For instance, looking at the third line of the table, the expression `true & y` will only be `true` if y is `true`, but the expression `true | y` will always be `true` whatever the value of y is, so the nullable results are `null` and `true`, respectively.

When considering the lifted operators and particularly how nullable logic works, the language designers had two slightly contradictory sets of existing behavior—C# 1 null references and SQL NULL values. In many cases, these don't conflict at all—C# 1 had no concept of applying logical operators to null references, so there was no problem in using the SQL-like results given earlier. The definitions you've seen may surprise some SQL developers, though, when it comes to comparisons. In standard SQL, the result of comparing two values (in terms of equality or greater than/less than) is always unknown if either value is NULL. The result in C# 2 is *never* null, and in particular two null values are considered to be equal to each other.

> **REMINDER: THIS IS C# SPECIFIC!**   It's worth remembering that the lifted operators and conversions, along with the `bool?` logic described in this section, are all provided by the C# compiler and *not* by the CLR or the framework itself. If you use ildasm on code that evaluates any of these nullable operators, you'll find that the compiler has created all the appropriate IL to test for null values and dealt with them accordingly. This means that different languages can behave differently on these matters—definitely something to look out for if you need to port code between different .NET-based languages. For example, VB treats lifted operators far more like SQL, so the result of x < y is Nothing if x or y is Nothing.

Another familiar operator is now available with nullable value types, and it behaves exactly as you'd expect it to if you consider your existing knowledge of null references and just tweak it to be in terms of *null values*.

4.3.5 *Using the as operator with nullable types*

Prior to C# 2, the as operator was only available for reference types. As of C# 2, it can now be applied to nullable value types as well. The result is a value of that nullable type—either the null value if the original reference was the wrong type or null, or a meaningful value otherwise. Here's a short example:

```
static void PrintValueAsInt32(object o)
{
   int? nullable = o as int?;
   Console.WriteLine(nullable.HasValue ?
                     nullable.Value.ToString() : "null");
}
...
PrintValueAsInt32(5);                    ⟵── Yields 5
PrintValueAsInt32("some string");             ⟵── Yields null
```

This allows you to safely convert from an arbitrary reference to a value in a single step—although you'd normally check. In C# 1, you'd have had to use the is operator followed by a cast, which is inelegant: it's essentially asking the CLR to perform the same type check twice.

> **SURPRISING PERFORMANCE TRAP** I'd always assumed that doing one check would be faster than two, but it appears that's not the case—at least with the versions of .NET I've tested with (up to and including .NET 4.5). When writing a quick benchmark that summed all the integers within an array of type object[], where only a third of the values were actually boxed integers, using is and then a cast ended up being *20 times faster* than using the as operator. The details are beyond the scope of this book, and as always you should test performance with your actual code and data before deciding on the best course of action for your specific situation, but it's worth being aware of.

You now know enough to use nullable types and predict how they'll behave, but C# 2 has a sort of "bonus track" when it comes to syntax enhancements: the null coalescing operator.

4.3.6 *The null coalescing operator*

Aside from the ? modifier, all of the rest of the C# compiler's tricks relating to nullable types so far have worked with the existing syntax. But C# 2 introduces a new operator that can occasionally make code shorter and sweeter. It's called the *null coalescing operator* and appears in code as ?? between its two operands. It's like the conditional operator but specially tweaked for nulls.

It's a binary operator that evaluates first ?? second by going through the following steps (roughly speaking):

1 Evaluate `first`.

2 If the result is non-null, that's the result of the whole expression.

3 Otherwise, evaluate `second`; the result then becomes the result of the whole expression.

I say "roughly speaking" because the formal rules in the specification have to deal with situations involving conversions between the types of `first` and `second`. As ever, these aren't important in most uses of the operator, and I don't intend to go through them—consult section 7.13 of the specification ("The Null Coalescing Operator") if you need the details.

Importantly, if the type of the second operand is the underlying type of the first operand (and therefore non-nullable), the overall result is that underlying type. For example, this code is perfectly valid:

```
int? a = 5;
int b = 10;
int c = a ?? b;
```

Note that you're assigning directly to c even though its type is the non-nullable int type. You can only do this because b is non-nullable, so you know that you'll get a non-nullable result eventually.

Obviously that's a pretty simplistic example; let's find a more practical use for this operator by revisiting the Age property from listing 4.4. As a reminder, here's how it was implemented back then, along with the relevant variable declarations:

```
DateTime birth;
DateTime? death;

public TimeSpan Age
{
    get
    {
        if (death == null)
        {
            return DateTime.Now - birth;
        }
        else
        {
            return death.Value - birth;
        }
    }
}
```

Note how both branches of the if statement subtract the value of birth from some non-null DateTime value. The value you're interested in is the latest time the person was alive—the time of the person's death if they have already died, or now otherwise. To make progress in little steps, let's try using the normal conditional operator first:

```
DateTime lastAlive = (death == null ? DateTime.Now : death.Value);
return lastAlive - birth;
```

That's progress of a sort, but arguably the conditional operator has made it harder to read rather than easier, even though the new code is shorter. The conditional operator is often like that—how much you use it is a matter of personal preference, although it's worth consulting the rest of your team before using it extensively. Let's see how the null coalescing operator improves things. You want to use the value of death if it's non-null, and DateTime.Now otherwise. You can change the implementation to the following:

```
DateTime lastAlive = death ?? DateTime.Now;
return lastAlive - birth;
```

Note how the type of the result is DateTime rather than DateTime? because you've used DateTime.Now as the second operand. You *could* shorten the whole thing to one expression:

```
return (death ?? DateTime.Now) - birth;
```

But this is more obscure—in particular, in the two-line version the name of the last-Alive variable helps the reader to see why you're applying the null coalescing operator. I hope you agree that the two-line version is simpler and more readable than either the original version using the if statement or the version using the normal conditional operator from C# 1. Of course, it relies on the reader understanding what the null coalescing operator does. In my experience, this is one of the least-known aspects of C# 2, but it's useful enough to make it worth trying to enlighten your co-workers rather than avoiding it.

There are two further aspects that increase the operator's usefulness. First, it doesn't just apply to nullable value types—it works with reference types too; you just can't use a non-nullable value type for the first operand, as that would be pointless. Also, it's *right associative*, which means an expression of the form first ?? second ?? third is evaluated as first ?? (second ?? third)—and so it continues for more operands. You can have any number of expressions, and they'll be evaluated in order, stopping with the first non-null result. If all of the expressions evaluate to null, the result will be null too.

As a concrete example of this, suppose you have an online ordering system with the concepts of a billing address, contact address, and shipping address. The business rules declare that any user *must* have a billing address, but the contact address is optional. The shipping address for a particular order is also optional, defaulting to the billing address. These optional addresses are easily represented as null references in the code. To determine who should be contacted in the case of a problem with a shipment, the code in C# 1 might look something like this:

```
Address contact = user.ContactAddress;
if (contact == null)
{
    contact = order.ShippingAddress;
    if (contact == null)
    {
```

```
            contact = user.BillingAddress;
        }
    }
```

Using the conditional operator in this case is even more horrible. But using the null coalescing operator makes the code very straightforward:

```
Address contact = user.ContactAddress ??
                  order.ShippingAddress ??
                  user.BillingAddress;
```

If the business rules changed to use the shipping address by default instead of the user's contact address, the change here would be extremely obvious. It wouldn't be *particularly* taxing with the if/else version, but I know I'd have to stop and think twice, and verify the code mentally. I'd also be relying on unit tests, so there'd be little chance of actually getting it wrong, but I'd prefer not to think about things like this unless I absolutely have to.

> **EVERYTHING IN MODERATION**   Just in case you're thinking that my code is littered with uses of the null coalescing operator, it's really not. I tend to consider it when I see defaulting mechanisms involving nulls and possibly the conditional operator, but it doesn't come up often. When its use is natural, though, it can be a powerful tool in the battle for readability.

You've seen how nullable types can be used for ordinary properties of objects—cases where you naturally might not have a value for some particular aspect that's still best expressed with a value type. Those are the more obvious uses for nullable types and indeed the most common ones. A few other patterns aren't as obvious, but can still be powerful when you're used to them. We'll explore two of these patterns in the next section. This is more for the sake of interest than as part of learning about the behavior of nullable types themselves—you now have all the tools you need to use them in your own code. If you're interested in quirky ideas and perhaps trying something new, read on…

4.4   *Novel uses of nullable types*

Before nullable types became a reality, I saw lots of people effectively asking for them, usually in relation to database access. That's not the only use they can be put to, though. The patterns presented in this section are unconventional but can make code simpler. If you always stick to normal idioms of C#, that's fine—this section might not be for you, and I have a lot of sympathy for that point of view. I usually prefer simple code over code that's clever, but if a whole *pattern* provides benefits, that sometimes makes the pattern worth learning. Whether you use these techniques is entirely up to you—you may find that they suggest other ideas to use elsewhere in your code.

Without further ado, let's start with an alternative to the TryXXX pattern mentioned in section 3.3.3.

4.4.1 *Trying an operation without using output parameters*

The pattern of using a return value to say whether an operation worked and using an output parameter to return the real result is becoming increasingly common in the .NET Framework. I have no issues with the aims—the idea that some methods are *likely* to fail to perform their primary purpose in non-exceptional circumstances is common sense. My one problem with it is that I'm not a huge fan of output parameters. There's something slightly clumsy about the syntax of declaring a variable on one line, and then immediately using it as an output parameter.

Methods returning reference types have often used a pattern of returning `null` on failure and non-null on success, but that doesn't work so well when `null` is a valid return value in the success case. `Hashtable` is an example of both of these statements, in a slightly ambivalent way: `null` is a theoretically valid value in a `Hashtable`, but in my experience most *uses* of `Hashtable` never use null values, which makes it perfectly acceptable to have code that assumes that a null value means a missing key.

One common scenario is to have each value of the `Hashtable` as a list: the first time an item is added for a particular key, a new list is created and the item is added to it. Thereafter, adding another item for the same key involves adding the item to the existing list. Here's the code in C# 1:

```
ArrayList list = hash[key];
if (list == null)
{
    list = new ArrayList();
    hash[key] = list;
}
list.Add(newItem);
```

Hopefully you'd use variable names more specific to your situation, but I'm sure you get the idea and you may well have used the pattern yourself.[4] With nullable types, this pattern can be extended to value types, and it's *safer* with value types, because if the natural result type is a value type, then a null value could *only* be returned as a result of failure. Nullable types add that extra Boolean piece of information in a nice general way with language support, so why not use them?

To demonstrate this pattern in practice and in a context other than dictionary lookups, I'll use the classic example of the `TryXXX` pattern—parsing an integer. The implementation of the `TryParse` method in the following listing shows the version of the pattern using an output parameter, but then you see the version using nullable types in the main part at the bottom.

---

[4] Wouldn't it be great if `Hashtable` and `Dictionary<TKey, TValue>` could take a delegate to call whenever a new value was required due to looking up a missing key? Situations like this would be a lot simpler.

Listing 4.5   An alternative implementation of the `TryXXX` pattern

```
static int? TryParse(string text)
{
    int ret;
    if (int.TryParse(text, out ret))       Classic call with
    {                                       output parameter
        return ret;
    }
    else
    {
        return null;
    }
}
...
int? parsed = TryParse("Not valid");       ◁──── Nullable call
if (parsed != null)
{
    Console.WriteLine ("Parsed to {0}", parsed.Value);
}
else
{
    Console.WriteLine ("Couldn't parse");
}
```

You may think there's little to distinguish the two versions here—they're the same number of lines, after all. But I believe there's a difference in emphasis. The nullable version encapsulates the natural return value and the success or failure into a single variable. It also separates the *doing* from the *testing*, which puts the emphasis in the right place, in my opinion. Usually, if I call a method in the condition part of an `if` statement, that method's primary purpose is to return a Boolean value. Here, the return value is in some ways less important than the output parameter. When you're reading code, it's easy to miss an output parameter in a method call and be left wondering what's actually doing all the work and magically giving the answer. With the nullable version, this is more explicit—the result of the method has all the information you're interested in. I've used this technique in a number of places (often with more method parameters, at which point output parameters become even harder to spot), and I believe it has improved the general feel of the code. Of course, this only works for value types.

Another advantage of this pattern is that it can be used in conjunction with the null coalescing operator—you can try to understand several pieces of input, stopping at the first valid one. The normal `TryXXX` pattern allows this using the short-circuiting operators, but the meaning isn't nearly as clear when you use the same variable for two different output parameters in the same statement.

ALTERNATIVELY, USE A TUPLE...   Another alternative to using a nullable result is to use a return type with two very clearly separate members, one of which is responsible for indicating success or failure and another of which is responsible for indicating the value on success. `Nullable<T>` is convenient because it gives you a Boolean property and another of type T, but the *meaning* of the return value could perhaps be more explicit. .NET 4 includes the Tuple family of types: arguably a Tuple<int, bool> might be cleaner than int? here. Even cleaner would be a custom type to represent the result of a parse operation: ParseResult<T>, for example. In this case, you could hand the value around to other code without any fear that its meaning will be confused, and you can add extra information such as the *cause* of any parsing failure.

The next pattern is an answer to a specific pain point—the irritation and fluff that can be present when writing multitiered comparisons.

4.4.2 Painless comparisons with the null coalescing operator

I suspect you dislike writing the same code over and over again as much as I do. Refactoring can often get rid of duplication, but some cases resist refactoring surprisingly effectively. Code for Equals and Compare often falls firmly into this category.

Suppose you're writing an e-commerce site and have a list of products. You might want to sort them by popularity (descending), then price, then name—so that the five-star-rated products come first, but the cheapest five-star products come before the more expensive ones. If there are multiple products with the same price, products beginning with *A* are listed before products beginning with *B*. This isn't a problem specific to e-commerce sites—sorting data by multiple criteria is a fairly common requirement in computing.

Assuming you have a suitable Product type, you could write the comparison with code like this in C# 1:

```
public int Compare(Product first, Product second)
{
    // Reverse comparison of popularity to sort descending
    int ret = second.Popularity.CompareTo(first.Popularity);
    if (ret != 0)
    {
        return ret;
    }
    ret = first.Price.CompareTo(second.Price);
    if (ret != 0)
    {
        return ret;
    }
    return first.Name.CompareTo(second.Name);
}
```

This assumes that you won't be asked to compare null references and that all of the properties will return non-null references too. You could use some up-front null comparisons and Comparer<T>.Default to handle those cases, but that would make the code even longer and more involved. The code could be shorter (and avoid returning from the middle of the method) if you rearranged it slightly, but the fundamental "compare, check, compare, check" pattern would still be present, and it wouldn't be as obvious that once you have a nonzero answer you're done.

Ah…that last sentence is reminiscent of something else: the null coalescing operator. As you saw in section 4.3, if you have a lot of expressions separated by ??, then the operator will be repeatedly applied until it hits a non-null expression. Now all you have to do is work out a way of returning null instead of zero from a comparison. This is easy to do in a separate method that can also encapsulate the use of the default comparer. You can even have an overload to use a specific comparer if you want. You can also deal with the case where either of the Product references you're passed is null.

First, let's look at the class implementing the helper methods, as shown in the following listing.

Listing 4.6   Helper class for providing partial comparisons

```
public static class PartialComparer
{
    public static int? Compare<T>(T first, T second)
    {
        return Compare(Comparer<T>.Default, first, second);
    }

    public static int? Compare<T>(IComparer<T> comparer,
                                  T first, T second)
    {
        int ret = comparer.Compare(first, second);
        return ret == 0 ? new int?() : ret;
    }

    public static int? ReferenceCompare<T>(T first, T second)
        where T : class
    {
        return first == second ? 0
             : first == null ? -1
             : second == null ? 1
             : new int?();
    }
}
```

The Compare methods in listing 4.6 are almost pathetically simple—when a comparer isn't specified, the default comparer for the type is used, and all that happens to the comparison's return value is that zero is translated to the null value.

NULL VALUES AND THE CONDITIONAL OPERATOR   You may have been surprised to see me use new int?() rather than null to return the null value in the second Compare method. The conditional operator requires that its second and third operands either be of the same type, or that there be an implicit conversion from one to the other, and that wouldn't be the case with null, because the compiler wouldn't know what type the value was meant to be. The language rules don't take the overall aim of the statement (returning from a method with a return type of int?) into account when examining subexpressions. Other options include casting either operand to int? explicitly or using default(int?) for the null value. Basically, the important thing is to make sure that one of the operands is known to be an int? value.

The `ReferenceCompare` method uses another conditional operator—three of them, in fact. You may find this less readable than the (rather longer) equivalent code using `if/else` blocks—it depends on how comfortable you are with the conditional operator. I like it because it makes the order of the comparisons clear. Also, this could easily have been a nongeneric method with two `object` parameters, but this form prevents you from accidentally using the method to compare value types via boxing. The method really is only useful with reference types, which is indicated by the type parameter constraint.

Even though this class is simple, it's remarkably useful. You can now replace the previous product comparison with a neater implementation:

```
public int Compare(Product first, Product second)
{
    return PC.ReferenceCompare(first, second) ??
            // Reverse comparison of popularity to sort descending
            PC.Compare(second.Popularity, first.Popularity) ??
            PC.Compare(first.Price, second.Price) ??
            PC.Compare(first.Name, second.Name) ??
            0;
}
```

As you may have noticed, I've used `PC` rather than `PartialComparer`—this is solely for the sake of being able to fit the lines on the printed page. In real code, I'd use the full type name and still have one comparison per line. Of course, if you wanted short lines for some reason, you could specify a `using` directive to make `PC` an alias for `Partial-Comparer`—I just wouldn't recommend it.

The final `0` indicates that if all of the earlier comparisons have passed, the two `Product` instances are equal. You *could* just use `Comparer<string>.Default.Compare (first.Name, second.Name)` as the final comparison, but that would hurt the symmetry of the method.

This comparison plays nicely with nulls, it's easy to modify, it forms an easy pattern to use for other comparisons, and it only compares as far as it needs to—if the prices are different, the names won't be compared.

You may be wondering whether the same technique could be applied to equality tests, which often have similar patterns. There's much less point in the case of equality, because after the nullity and reference equality tests, you can just use `&&` to provide the desired short-circuiting functionality for Booleans. A method returning a `bool?` can be used to obtain an initial *definitely equal*, *definitely not equal*, or *unknown* result based on the references, though. The complete code of `PartialComparer` on this book's website contains the appropriate utility method and examples of its use.

4.5 Summary

When faced with a problem, developers tend to take the easiest short-term solution, even if it's not particularly elegant. That's often the right decision—you don't want to be guilty of overengineering, after all. But it's always nice when a *good* solution is also the *easiest* solution.

Nullable types solve a specific problem that only had somewhat ugly solutions before C# 2. The features provided are a better-supported version of a solution that was feasible but time consuming in C# 1. The combination of generics (to avoid code duplication), CLR support (to provide suitable boxing and unboxing behavior), and language support (to provide concise syntax along with convenient conversions and operators) makes the solution far more compelling than it was previously.

It just so happens that in providing nullable types, the C# and framework designers have made some other patterns available that weren't worth the effort before. We've looked at some of them in this chapter, and I wouldn't be surprised to see more of them appearing over time.

So far generics and nullable types have addressed areas where in C# 1 you occasionally had to hold your nose due to unpleasant code smells. This pattern continues in the next chapter, where we'll discuss the enhancements to delegates. These form an important part of the subtle change of direction of both the C# language and the .NET Framework toward a slightly more functional viewpoint. This emphasis is made even clearer in C# 3, so although we're not looking at those features *quite* yet, the delegate enhancements in C# 2 act as a bridge between the familiarity of C# 1 and the style of idiomatic C# 3, which can often be radically different from earlier versions.

Fast-tracked delegates 5

This chapter covers

- Long-winded C# 1 syntax
- Simplified delegate construction
- Covariance and contravariance
- Anonymous methods
- Captured variables

The journey of delegates in C# and .NET has been an interesting one, showing remarkable foresight (or really good luck) on the part of the designers. The conventions suggested for event handlers in .NET 1.0/1.1 didn't make a lot of sense—until C# 2 showed up. Likewise, the effort put into delegates for C# 2 seems in some ways out of proportion to how widely used they are—until you see how pervasive they are in idiomatic C# 3 code. In other words, it's as if the language and platform designers had a vision of at least the rough direction they'd be taking, years before the destination itself became clear.

Of course, C# 3 isn't a final destination in itself—generic delegates get a bit more flexibility in C# 4, C# 5 makes it easy to write asynchronous delegates, and we may see even more advances in the future—but the differences between C# 1 and

C# 3 in this area are the most startling ones. (The primary change in C# 3 supporting delegates is in lambda expressions, which you'll meet in chapter 9.)

C# 2 is a sort of stepping stone in terms of delegates. Its new features pave the way for the dramatic changes of C# 3, keeping developers *reasonably* comfortable while still providing useful benefits. I'm reliably informed that language designers were aware that the combined feature set of C# 2 would open up whole new ways of looking at code, but they didn't necessarily know where those paths would lead. So far, their instincts have proved remarkably beneficial in the area of delegates.

Delegates play a more prominent part in .NET 2.0 than in earlier versions, although they're not as common as they are in .NET 3.5. In chapter 3 you saw how they can be used to convert from one type of list to another, and way back in chapter 1 you sorted a list of products using the Comparison delegate instead of the IComparer interface. Although the framework and C# keep a respectful distance from each other where possible, I believe that the language and platform drove each other in this case: the inclusion of more delegate-based API calls supports the improved syntax available in C# 2, and vice versa.

In this chapter, we'll look at how C# 2 includes two small changes that make life easier when creating delegate instances from normal methods, and then we'll look at the biggest change: anonymous methods, which allow you to specify a delegate instance's action inline at the point of its creation. The largest section of the chapter is devoted to the most complicated part of anonymous methods—captured variables—which provide delegate instances with a richer environment to play in. We'll cover the topic in significant detail due to its importance and complexity. Once you've come to grips with anonymous methods, lambda expressions are easy to understand.

First, though, let's review the pain points of C# 1's delegate facilities.

5.1   *Saying goodbye to awkward delegate syntax*

The syntax for delegates in C# 1 doesn't *sound* too bad—the language already has syntactic sugar around Delegate.Combine, Delegate.Remove, and the invocation of delegate instances. It makes sense to specify the delegate type when creating a delegate instance; after all, it's the same syntax used to create instances of other types.

This is all true, but for some reason it also sucks. It's hard to say exactly why the delegate creation expressions of C# 1 raise hackles, but they do—at least for me. When hooking up a bunch of event handlers, it just looks ugly to have to write new Event-Handler (or whatever is required) all over the place, when the event itself has specified which delegate type it'll use. Beauty is in the eye of the beholder, of course, and you could argue that there's less call for guesswork when reading event handler wiring code in the C# 1 style, but the extra text just gets in the way and distracts from the important part of the code: the method you want to handle the event.

Life becomes more black and white when you consider covariance and contravariance as applied to delegates. Suppose you have an event handling method that saves the current document, or logs that it's been called, or performs any number of other actions that may not need to know details of the event. The event itself shouldn't mind that your method is capable of working with only the information provided by the EventHandler signature, even though the event is declared to pass in mouse event details. Unfortunately, in C# 1 you need to have a different method for each different event handler signature.

Likewise it's undeniably ugly to write methods that are so simple that their implementation is shorter than their signature, solely because delegates need to have an action to execute in the form of a method. It adds an extra layer of indirection between the code *creating* the delegate instance and the code that should execute when it's invoked. Extra layers of indirection are often welcome—that option hasn't been removed in C# 2—but at the same time it frequently makes the code harder to read and pollutes the class with a bunch of methods that are only used for delegates.

Unsurprisingly, all of these issues are improved greatly in C# 2. The syntax can still be wordier than you might like (until you get lambda expressions in C# 3), but the difference is significant. To illustrate the pain, we'll start with some code in C# 1 and improve it in the next couple of sections. The following listing builds a (very) simple form with a button and then subscribes to three of the button's events.

Listing 5.1 Subscribing to three of a button's events

```
static void LogPlainEvent(object sender, EventArgs e)
{
    Console.WriteLine("LogPlain");
}

static void LogKeyEvent(object sender, KeyPressEventArgs e)
{
    Console.WriteLine("LogKey");
}

static void LogMouseEvent(object sender, MouseEventArgs e)
{
    Console.WriteLine("LogMouse");
}
...
Button button = new Button();
button.Text = "Click me";
button.Click      += new EventHandler(LogPlainEvent);
button.KeyPress   += new KeyPressEventHandler(LogKeyEvent);
button.MouseClick += new MouseEventHandler(LogMouseEvent);

Form form = new Form();
form.AutoSize = true;
form.Controls.Add(button);
Application.Run(form);
```

The output lines in the three event handling methods are there to prove that the code is working: if you press the spacebar with the button highlighted, you'll see that the Click and KeyPress events are both raised. Pressing Enter just raises the Click event;

clicking on the button raises the `Click` and `MouseClick` events. In the following sections, we'll improve this code using some of the C# 2 features.

Let's start by asking the compiler to make a pretty obvious deduction—which delegate type you want to use when subscribing to an event.

5.2   *Method group conversions*

In C# 1, if you want to create a delegate instance, you need to specify both the delegate type and the action. Chapter 2 defined the *action* as the method to call and (for instance methods) the *target* as the object it's called on.

For example, in listing 5.1, this expression was used to create a `KeyPressEvent-Handler`:

```
new KeyPressEventHandler(LogKeyEvent)
```

As a standalone expression, it doesn't look too bad. Even used in a simple event subscription it's tolerable. It becomes uglier when used as part of a longer expression, though. A common example of this is starting a new thread:

```
Thread t = new Thread(new ThreadStart(MyMethod));
```

What you want to do is start a new thread that'll execute `MyMethod`. As ever, you want to express yourself as simply as possible, and C# 2 allows you to do this by means of an implicit conversion from a *method group* to a compatible delegate type. A method group is simply the name of a method, optionally with a target—exactly the same kind of expression you used in C# 1 to create delegate instances. (Indeed, the expression was called a method group back then—it's just that the conversion wasn't available.) If the method is generic, the method group may also specify type arguments—although this is rarely used, in my experience. The new implicit conversion allows you to turn your event subscription into

```
button.KeyPress += LogKeyEvent;
```

Likewise, the thread-creation code becomes simply

```
Thread t = new Thread(MyMethod);
```

The readability differences between the original and the streamlined versions aren't huge for a single line, but in the context of a significant amount of code, they can reduce the clutter considerably. To make it seem less like magic, let's briefly look at what this conversion is doing.

First, let's consider the expressions `LogKeyEvent` and `MyMethod` as they appear in the examples. The reason they're classified as method *groups* is because more than one method may be available, due to overloading. The implicit conversions available will convert a method group to any delegate type with a compatible signature. So, if you had two method signatures like these,

```
void MyMethod()
void MyMethod(object sender, EventArgs e)
```

you could use `MyMethod` as the method group in an assignment to either a `Thread-Start` or an `EventHandler`, as follows:

```
ThreadStart x = MyMethod;
EventHandler y = MyMethod;
```

But you *couldn't* use it as the parameter to a method that itself was overloaded to take either a `ThreadStart` or an `EventHandler`—the compiler would complain that the call was ambiguous. Likewise, you unfortunately can't use an implicit method group conversion to convert to the plain `System.Delegate` type, because the compiler doesn't know which specific delegate type to create an instance of. This is a pain, but you *can* still be slightly briefer than in C# 1 by making the conversion explicit. Here's an example:

```
Delegate invalid = SomeMethod;
Delegate valid = (ThreadStart)SomeMethod;
```

For local variables this usually isn't a problem, but it's somewhat more annoying when you're using an API that has a parameter of type `Delegate`, such as `Control.Invoke`. There are a few solutions here: using a helper method, casting, or using an intermediate variable. Here's an example using the `MethodInvoker` delegate type, which takes no parameters and doesn't return anything:

```
static void SimpleInvoke(Control control,
                         MethodInvoker invoker)
{
    control.Invoke(invoker);
}
...
SimpleInvoke(form, UpdateUI);                    Invokes with a helper method
form.Invoke((MethodInvoker)UpdateUI);        ◁——— Invokes with a cast
MethodInvoker invoker = UpdateUI;                Invokes with a local variable
form.Invoke(invoker);
```

Different situations will encourage different solutions; none of these is particularly appealing, but they're not awful either.[1]

As with generics, the precise rules of conversion validity are slightly complicated, and the just-try-it approach works well; if the compiler complains that it doesn't have enough information, just tell it what conversion to use, and all should be well. If it doesn't complain, you should be fine. For the exact details, consult the language specification, section 6.6 ("Method group conversions"). Speaking of possible conversions, there may be more than you expect, as you'll see in the next section.

5.3 *Covariance and contravariance*

We've already talked a lot about the concepts of covariance and contravariance in different contexts, usually bemoaning their absence, but delegate construction is the one area in which they're available in C# prior to version 4. If you want to refresh

---

[1] Extension methods (discussed in chapter 10) make the helper method approach somewhat more appealing if you're using C# 3.

yourself about the meaning of the terms at a relatively detailed level, refer back to section 2.2.2, but the gist of the topic with respect to delegates is that if it would be valid (in a static typing sense) to call a method and use its return value everywhere that you could invoke an instance of a particular delegate type and use *its* return value, then that method can be used to create an instance of that delegate type. That's wordy—it's a lot simpler with examples.

> **DIFFERENT TYPES OF VARIANCE IN DIFFERENT VERSIONS** You may already be aware that C# 4 offers *generic* covariance and contravariance for delegates and interfaces. This is entirely different from the variance we're looking at here—we're only dealing with creating *new* instances of delegates at the moment. The generic variance in C# 4 uses *reference conversions*, which don't create new objects—they just view the existing object as a different type.

We'll look at contravariance first, and then covariance.

5.3.1 *Contravariance for delegate parameters*

Let's consider the event handlers in the little Windows Forms application in listing 5.1. The signatures of the three delegate types are as follows:[2]

```
void EventHandler(object sender, EventArgs e)
void KeyPressEventHandler(object sender, KeyPressEventArgs e)
void MouseEventHandler(object sender, MouseEventArgs e)
```

Consider that `KeyPressEventArgs` and `MouseEventArgs` both derive from `EventArgs` (as do a lot of other types—MSDN lists 403 types that derive directly from `EventArgs` in .NET 4). If you have a method with an `EventArgs` parameter, you could always call it with a `KeyPressEventArgs` argument instead. It therefore makes sense to be able to use a method with the same signature as `EventHandler` to create an instance of `Key-PressEventHandler`, and that's exactly what C# 2 does. This is an example of contravariance of parameter types.

To see that in action, think back to listing 5.1 and suppose that you don't need to know which event was firing—you just want to write out the fact that an event has happened. Using method group conversions and contravariance, the code becomes a lot simpler, as shown in the following listing.

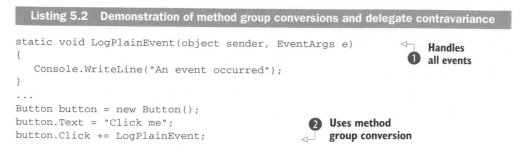

Listing 5.2 Demonstration of method group conversions and delegate contravariance

```
static void LogPlainEvent(object sender, EventArgs e)          ◁  Handles
{                                                              ❶  all events
    Console.WriteLine("An event occurred");
}
...
Button button = new Button();
button.Text = "Click me";                        ❷  Uses method
button.Click += LogPlainEvent;                   ◁  group conversion
```

---

[2] I've removed the *public delegate* part for reasons of space.

```
button.KeyPress += LogPlainEvent;
button.MouseClick += LogPlainEvent;

Form form = new Form();
form.AutoSize = true;
form.Controls.Add(button);
Application.Run(form);
```

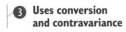
❸ Uses conversion and contravariance

The two handler methods that dealt specifically with key and mouse events have been completely removed, and you're now using one event handling method for everything ❶. Of course, this isn't terribly useful if you want to do different things for different types of events, but sometimes all you need to know is that an event occurred and, potentially, the source of the event. The subscription to the `Click` event ❷ only uses the implicit conversion we discussed in the previous section because it has a simple `EventArgs` parameter, but the other event subscriptions ❸ involve the conversion and contravariance due to their different parameter types.

I mentioned earlier that the .NET 1.0/1.1 event handler convention didn't make much sense when it was first introduced. This example shows exactly why the guidelines are more useful with C# 2. The convention dictates that event handlers should have a signature with two parameters, the first of which is of type `object` and is the origin of the event, and the second of which carries any extra information about the event in a type deriving from `EventArgs`. Before contravariance became available, this wasn't useful—there was no benefit to making the informational parameter derive from `EventArgs`, and sometimes there wasn't much use for the origin of the event. It was often more sensible to pass the relevant information directly in the form of normal parameters with appropriate types, just like any other method. Now you can use a method with the `EventHandler` signature as the action for *any* delegate type that honors the convention.

So far we've looked at the values entering a method or delegate—what about the value coming out?

5.3.2 *Covariance of delegate return types*

Demonstrating covariance is harder, as relatively few of the delegates available in .NET 2.0 are declared with a nonvoid return type, and those that are tend to return value types. There are some available, but it's easier to declare your own delegate type that uses `Stream` as its return type. For simplicity, we'll make it parameterless:[3]

```
delegate Stream StreamFactory();
```

You can now use this with a method that's declared to return a specific type of stream, as shown in the following listing. You declare a method that always returns a `Memory-Stream` with some sequential data (bytes 0, 1, 2, and so on up to 15), and then use that method as the action for a `StreamFactory` delegate instance.

---

[3] Return type covariance and parameter type contravariance can be used at the same time, but you're unlikely to come across situations where that would be useful.

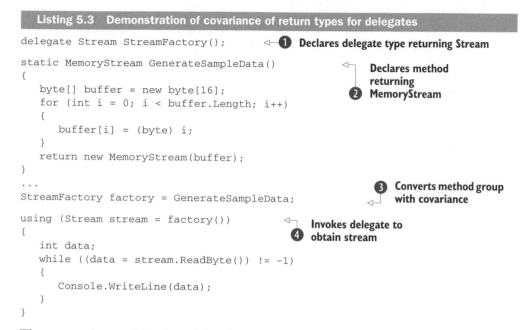

Listing 5.3   Demonstration of covariance of return types for delegates

```
delegate Stream StreamFactory();          ←① Declares delegate type returning Stream

static MemoryStream GenerateSampleData()     ←
{                                              │  Declares method
   byte[] buffer = new byte[16];            ② returning
   for (int i = 0; i < buffer.Length; i++)     MemoryStream
   {
      buffer[i] = (byte) i;
   }
   return new MemoryStream(buffer);
}
...
StreamFactory factory = GenerateSampleData;  ③ Converts method group
                                                with covariance

using (Stream stream = factory())       ←  ④ Invokes delegate to
{                                              obtain stream
   int data;
   while ((data = stream.ReadByte()) != -1)
   {
      Console.WriteLine(data);
   }
}
```

The generation and display of the data in listing 5.3 is only present to give the code something to do. The important points are the annotated lines. You declare that the delegate type has a return type of Stream ①, but the GenerateSampleData method has a return type of MemoryStream ②. The line creating the delegate instance ③ performs the conversion you saw earlier and uses covariance of return types to allow GenerateSampleData to be used as the action for StreamFactory. By the time you invoke the delegate instance ④, the compiler no longer knows that a MemoryStream will be returned—if you changed the type of the stream variable to MemoryStream, you'd get a compilation error.

Covariance and contravariance can also be used to construct one delegate instance from another. For instance, consider these two lines of code (which assume an appropriate HandleEvent method):

```
EventHandler general = new EventHandler(HandleEvent);
KeyPressEventHandler key = new KeyPressEventHandler(general);
```

The first line is valid in C# 1, but the second isn't—in order to construct one delegate from another in C# 1, the signatures of the two delegate types involved have to match. For instance, you could create a MethodInvoker from a ThreadStart, but you couldn't create a KeyPressEventHandler from an EventHandler as shown in the second line. You're using contravariance to create a new delegate instance from an existing one with a *compatible* delegate type signature, where compatibility is defined in a less restrictive manner in C# 2 than in C# 1.

All of this is positive, except for one small fly in the ointment.

5.3.3   *A small risk of incompatibility*

This new flexibility in C# 2 creates one of the few cases where existing valid C# 1 code may produce different results when compiled under C# 2. Suppose a derived class overloads a method declared in its base class, and you try to create an instance of a delegate using a method group conversion. A conversion that previously only matched the base class method could match the derived class method due to covariance or contravariance in C# 2, in which case that derived class method would be chosen by the compiler. The following listing gives an example of this.

Listing 5.4   Demonstration of breaking change between C# 1 and C# 2

```
delegate void SampleDelegate(string x);

public void CandidateAction(string x)
{
    Console.WriteLine("Snippet.CandidateAction");
}

public class Derived : Snippet
{
    public void CandidateAction(object o)
    {
        Console.WriteLine("Derived.CandidateAction");
    }
}
...
Derived x = new Derived();
SampleDelegate factory = new SampleDelegate(x.CandidateAction);
factory("test");
```

Remember that Snippy[4] will be generating all of this code within a class called `Snippet`, which the nested type derives from. Under C# 1, listing 5.4 would print `Snippet.CandidateAction` because the method taking an `object` parameter wasn't compatible with `SampleDelegate`. Under C# 2, the method *is* compatible, and it's the method chosen due to being declared in a more derived type, so the result is that `Derived.CandidateAction` is printed.

Fortunately, the C# 2 compiler knows that this is a breaking change and issues an appropriate warning. I've included this section because you ought to be aware of the possibility of such a problem, but I'm sure it's rarely encountered in real life.

Enough doom and gloom about potential breakage. We've still got to see the most important new feature regarding delegates: anonymous methods. They're a bit more complicated than the topics we've covered so far, but they're also *very* powerful—and a large step toward C# 3.

---

[4]   In case you skipped the first chapter, Snippy is a tool I've built to create short but complete code samples. See section 1.8.1 for more details.

5.4   *Inline delegate actions with anonymous methods*

Back in C# 1, it was common to implement a delegate with a particular signature, even though you already had a method with exactly the right behavior but a slightly different set of parameters. Likewise, you'd often want a delegate to do just one teeny, tiny thing—but that meant you needed a whole extra method. The new method would represent behavior that was only relevant within the original method, but it was now exposed to the whole class, creating noise in IntelliSense and generally getting in the way.

All this was intensely frustrating. The covariance and contravariance features we've just talked about can *sometimes* help with the first problem, but often they don't. *Anonymous methods*, which are also new in C# 2, can pretty much *always* help with these issues.

Informally, anonymous methods allow you to specify the action for a delegate instance inline as part of the delegate instance creation expression. They also provide some far more powerful behavior in the form of *closures*, but we'll come to those in section 5.5. For the moment, let's stick with relatively simple stuff.

First we'll look at examples of anonymous methods that take parameters but don't return any values; then we'll explore the syntax involved in providing return values and a shortcut available when you don't need to use the parameter values passed to you.

5.4.1   *Starting simply: acting on a parameter*

.NET 2.0 introduced a generic delegate type called Action<T>, which we'll use for our examples. Its signature is simple (aside from the fact that it's generic):

```
public delegate void Action<T>(T obj)
```

In other words, an Action<T> does something with a value of type T; for example, an Action<string> could reverse the string and print it out, an Action<int> could print out the square root of the number passed to it, and an Action<IList<double>> could find the average of all the numbers given to it and print that out. By complete coincidence, these examples are all implemented using anonymous methods in the following listing.

> **Listing 5.5   Anonymous methods used with the Action<T> delegate type**

```
Action<string> printReverse = delegate(string text)          ❶ Uses anonymous
{                                                               method to create
    char[] chars = text.ToCharArray();                         Action<string>
    Array.Reverse(chars);
    Console.WriteLine(new string(chars));
};

Action<int> printRoot = delegate(int number)
{
    Console.WriteLine(Math.Sqrt(number));
};
```

```
Action<IList<double>> printMean = delegate(IList<double> numbers)
{
    double total = 0;
    foreach (double value in numbers)
    {
        total += value;
    }
    Console.WriteLine(total / numbers.Count);
};

printReverse("Hello world");
printRoot(2);
printMean(new double[] { 1.5, 2.5, 3, 4.5 });
```

❷ **Uses loop in anonymous method**

❸ **Invokes delegates as normal**

Listing 5.5 shows a few of the different features of anonymous methods. First, there's the syntax of anonymous methods: use the `delegate` keyword, followed by the parameters (if there are any), followed by the code for the action of the delegate instance, in a block. The string-reversal code ❶ shows that the block can contain local variable declarations, and the list-averaging code ❷ demonstrates looping within the block. Basically, you can do (almost) anything in an anonymous method that you can do in a normal method body. Likewise, the result of an anonymous method is a delegate instance that can be used like any other one ❸. But be warned that contravariance doesn't apply to anonymous methods; you have to specify the parameter types that match the delegate type exactly.

> **A COUPLE OF RESTRICTIONS...** One slight oddity is that if you're writing an anonymous method in a value type, you can't reference `this` from within it. There's no such restriction within a reference type. Additionally, in the Microsoft C# 2 and 3 compiler implementations, accessing a base member within an anonymous method via the `base` keyword resulted in a warning that the resulting code was unverifiable. This has been fixed in the C# 4 compiler.

In terms of implementation, you're still creating a method in IL for each anonymous method in the source code. The compiler will generate a method within the existing class and use that as the action when it creates the delegate instance, just as if it were a normal method.[5] The CLR neither knows nor cares that an anonymous method was used. You can see the extra methods within the compiled code using ildasm or Reflector. (Reflector knows how to interpret the IL to display anonymous methods in the method that uses them, but the extra methods are still visible.) These methods have *unspeakable names*—ones that are valid in IL, but invalid in C#. This stops you from attempting to refer to them directly in your C# code and avoids the possibility of naming collisions. Many of the features of C# 2 and later versions are implemented in a similar way; one easy way to spot them is that they usually contain angle brackets. For example, an anonymous method in a `Main` method *might* cause a method called `<Main>b__0` to be created. It's entirely implementation-specific, though. Microsoft

---

[5] You'll see in section 5.5.4 that although there's always a new method, it's not always created where you might expect.

could change its private conventions in a future version, for example. This shouldn't break anything, as nothing should be relying on these names.

It's worth pointing out at this stage that listing 5.5 is exploded compared with how anonymous methods normally look in real code. You'll often see them used as arguments to another method (rather than assigned to a variable of the delegate type) and with few line breaks—compactness is part of the reason for using them, after all. To demonstrate this, we'll use the `List<T>.ForEach` method that takes an `Action<T>` as a parameter and performs that action on each element. The following listing shows an extreme example, applying the same square-rooting action you used in listing 5.5, but in a compact form.

Listing 5.6   Extreme example of code compactness. Warning: unreadable code ahead!

```
List<int> x = new List<int>();
x.Add(5);
x.Add(10);
x.Add(15);
x.Add(20);
x.Add(25);

x.ForEach(delegate(int n){Console.WriteLine(Math.Sqrt(n));});
```

That's pretty horrendous—especially when the last six characters appear to be ordered almost at random. There's a happy medium, of course. I tend to break my usual "braces on a line on their own" rule for anonymous methods (as I do for trivial properties), but I still allow a decent amount of whitespace. I might well write the last line of listing 5.6 in one of these two forms:

```
x.ForEach(delegate(int n)
    { Console.WriteLine(Math.Sqrt(n)); }
);

x.ForEach(delegate(int n) {
    Console.WriteLine(Math.Sqrt(n));
});
```

Even just adding spaces to listing 5.6 would've helped. In each of these formats, the parentheses and braces are now less confusing, and the what-it-does part stands out appropriately. Of course, how you space out your code is entirely your own business, but I encourage you to actively think about where you want to strike the balance, and talk about it with your teammates to try to achieve some consistency. Consistency doesn't *always* lead to the most readable code, though—sometimes keeping everything on one line is the most straightforward format.

So far the only interaction you've had with the calling code is through parameters. What about return values?

5.4.2   *Returning values from anonymous methods*

The Action<T> delegate has a void return type, so you haven't had to return anything from your anonymous methods yet. To demonstrate how you can do so when you need to, we'll use the Predicate<T> delegate type from .NET 2.0, which has this signature:

```
public delegate bool Predicate<T>(T obj)
```

The following listing shows an anonymous method creating an instance of Predicate<T> to return whether the argument passed in is odd or even. Predicates are usually used in filtering and matching—you could use the code in this listing to filter a list for just the even elements, for instance.

Listing 5.7   Returning a value from an anonymous method

```
Predicate<int> isEven = delegate(int x) { return x % 2 == 0; };

Console.WriteLine(isEven(1));
Console.WriteLine(isEven(4));
```

The new syntax is almost certainly what you'd have expected—you return the appropriate value as if the anonymous method were a normal method. You may have expected to see a return type declared near the delegate keyword, but there's no need. The compiler checks that all the possible return values are compatible with the declared return type of the delegate type it's trying to convert the anonymous method into.

> **JUST WHAT ARE YOU RETURNING FROM?**   When you return a value from an anonymous method, it really is only returning from the anonymous method—it's not returning from the method creating the delegate instance. It's easy to look down some code, see the return keyword, and think that it's an exit point from the current method, so be careful.

As I mentioned before, relatively few delegates in .NET 2.0 return values, although as you'll see in part 3 of this book, .NET 3.5 uses this idea *much* more often, particularly with LINQ. There's another reasonably common delegate type in .NET 2.0 though: Comparison<T>, which can be used when sorting collections. It's the delegate equivalent of the IComparer<T> interface. Often you only need a particular sort order in one situation, so it makes sense to be able to specify that order inline, rather than exposing it as a method within the rest of the class. The following listing demonstrates this, printing out the files within the C:\ directory, ordering them first by name and then (separately) by size.

Listing 5.8   Using anonymous methods to sort files simply

```
static void SortAndShowFiles(string title, Comparison<FileInfo> sortOrder)
{
    FileInfo[] files = newDirectoryInfo(@"C:\").GetFiles();

    Array.Sort(files, sortOrder);
```

```
    Console.WriteLine(title);
    foreach (FileInfo file in files)
    {
        Console.WriteLine (" {0} ({1} bytes)", file.Name, file.Length);
    }
}
...
SortAndShowFiles("Sorted by name:", delegate(FileInfo f1, FileInfo f2)
    { return f1.Name.CompareTo(f2.Name); }
);

SortAndShowFiles("Sorted by length:", delegate(FileInfo f1, FileInfo f2)
    { return f1.Length.CompareTo(f2.Length); }
);
```

If you weren't using anonymous methods, you'd need a separate method for each sort order. Instead, listing 5.8 makes it clear what you'll sort by in each case right where you call SortAndShowFiles. (Sometimes you'll be calling Sort directly at the point where the anonymous method is called for. In listing 5.8, you're performing the same fetch/sort/display sequence twice, just with different sort orders, so I encapsulated those steps in their own method.)

One special syntactic shortcut is sometimes applicable. If you don't care about the parameters of a delegate, you don't have to declare them at all. Let's see how that works.

5.4.3 *Ignoring delegate parameters*

Occasionally, you want to implement a delegate that doesn't depend on its parameter values. You might want to write an event handler whose behavior is only appropriate for one event and doesn't depend on the event arguments—saving the user's work, for instance. The event handlers from the example in listing 5.1 fit this criterion perfectly. In this case, you can leave out the parameter list entirely, just using the delegate keyword and then a block of code as the action for the method. The following listing is equivalent to listing 5.1 but uses the shorter syntax.

Listing 5.9 Subscribing to events with anonymous methods that ignore parameters

```
Button button = new Button();
button.Text = "Click me";
button.Click      += delegate { Console.WriteLine("LogPlain"); };
button.KeyPress   += delegate { Console.WriteLine("LogKey"); };
button.MouseClick += delegate { Console.WriteLine("LogMouse"); };

Form form = new Form();
form.AutoSize = true;
form.Controls.Add(button);
Application.Run(form);
```

Normally you'd have to write each subscription as something like this:

```
button.Click += delegate(object sender, EventArgs e) { ... };
```

That wastes a lot of space for little reason—you don't need the values of the parameters, so the compiler lets you get away with not specifying them at all.

I've found this shortcut most useful when it comes to implementing my own events. For example, I get sick of having to perform a nullity check before raising an event. One way of getting around this is to make sure that the event starts off with a handler, which is then never removed. As long as the handler doesn't do anything, all you lose is a tiny bit of performance. Before C# 2, you had to explicitly create a method with the right signature, which usually wasn't worth the benefit, but now you can write code like this:

```
public event EventHandler Click = delegate {};
```

From then on, you can just call `Click` without any nullity tests.

You should be aware of one trap related to this parameter wildcarding feature—if the anonymous method could be converted to multiple delegate types (for example, to call different method overloads), the compiler needs more help. To show you what I mean, let's take the same troublesome example we looked at with method group conversions: starting a new thread. There are four thread constructors in .NET 2.0:

```
public Thread(ParameterizedThreadStart start)
public Thread(ThreadStart start)
public Thread(ParameterizedThreadStart start, int maxStackSize)
public Thread(ThreadStart start, int maxStackSize)
```

These are the two delegate types involved:

```
public delegate void ThreadStart()
public delegate void ParameterizedThreadStart(object obj)
```

Now, consider the following three attempts to create a new thread:

```
new Thread(delegate()         { Console.WriteLine("t1"); } );
new Thread(delegate(object o) { Console.WriteLine("t2"); } );
new Thread(delegate          { Console.WriteLine("t3"); } );
```

The first and second lines contain parameter lists—the compiler knows that it can't convert the anonymous method in the first line into a `ParameterizedThreadStart` or convert the anonymous method in the second line into a `ThreadStart`. Those lines compile because there's only one applicable constructor overload in each case. The third line, though, is ambiguous—the anonymous method can be converted into either delegate type, so both of the single parameter constructor overloads are applicable. In this situation, the compiler throws its hands up and issues an error. You can solve this either by specifying the parameter list explicitly or casting the anonymous method to the right delegate type.

Hopefully what you've seen of anonymous methods so far will have provoked some thought about your own code and made you consider where you could use these techniques to good effect. Indeed, even if anonymous methods could *only* do what you've already seen, they'd be very useful. But there's more to anonymous methods than just avoiding the inclusion of an extra method in your code. Anonymous methods are

C# 2's implementation of a feature known elsewhere as *closures* by way of *captured variables*. The next section explains both of these terms and shows how anonymous methods can be extremely powerful—and confusing if you're not careful.

5.5   Capturing variables in anonymous methods

I don't like having to give warnings, but I think it makes sense to include one here: if this topic is new to you, then don't start this section until you're feeling reasonably awake and have a bit of time to spend on it. I don't want to alarm you unnecessarily, and you should feel confident that there's nothing here so insanely complicated that you won't be able to understand it with a little effort. It's just that captured variables can be somewhat confusing to start with, partly because they overturn some of your existing knowledge and intuition.

Stick with it, though! The payback can be *massive* in terms of code simplicity and readability. This topic will also be crucial when we look at lambda expressions and LINQ in C# 3, so it's worth the investment.

Let's start with a few definitions.

5.5.1   Defining closures and different types of variables

The concept of *closures* is an old one, first implemented in Scheme, but it's been gaining more prominence in recent years as more mainstream languages have taken it on board. The basic idea is that a function[6] is able to interact with an environment beyond the parameters provided to it. That's all there is to it in abstract terms, but to understand how it applies to C# 2, we need a couple more terms:

- An *outer variable* is a local variable or parameter (excluding `ref` and `out` parameters) whose scope includes an anonymous method. The `this` reference also counts as an outer variable of any anonymous method within an instance member of a class.

- A *captured outer variable* (usually shortened to *captured variable*) is an outer variable that's used within an anonymous method. To go back to closures, the function part is the anonymous method, and the environment it can interact with is the set of variables captured by it.

That's all very dry and may be hard to imagine, but the main thrust is that an anonymous method can use local variables defined in the same method that declares it. This may not sound like a big deal, but in many situations it's enormously handy—you can use contextual information that you have on hand rather than having to set up extra types just to store data you already know. We'll look at some *useful* concrete examples soon, I promise—but first it's worth looking at some code to clarify these definitions.

Listing 5.10 provides an example with a number of local variables, and it's a single method, so it can't be run on its own. I'm not going to explain how it would work or

---

[6]   This is general computer science terminology, not C# terminology.

what it would do yet; I just want to discuss how the different variables are classified. Again, we'll use the MethodInvoker delegate type for simplicity.

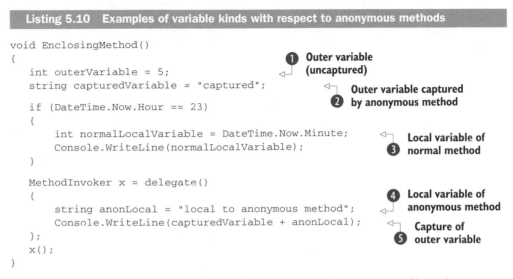

Listing 5.10 Examples of variable kinds with respect to anonymous methods

```
void EnclosingMethod()
{
    int outerVariable = 5;                                    ① Outer variable
                                                                 (uncaptured)
    string capturedVariable = "captured";                     ② Outer variable captured
                                                                 by anonymous method
    if (DateTime.Now.Hour == 23)
    {
        int normalLocalVariable = DateTime.Now.Minute;        ③ Local variable of
        Console.WriteLine(normalLocalVariable);                  normal method
    }

    MethodInvoker x = delegate()
    {                                                         ④ Local variable of
                                                                 anonymous method
        string anonLocal = "local to anonymous method";
        Console.WriteLine(capturedVariable + anonLocal);      ⑤ Capture of
    };                                                           outer variable
    x();
}
```

Let's go through all the variables from the simplest to the most complicated:

- normalLocalVariable ③ isn't an outer variable because there are no anonymous methods within its scope. It behaves exactly the way that local variables always have.

- anonLocal ④ isn't an outer variable either, but it's local to the anonymous method, not to EnclosingMethod. It'll only exist (in terms of being present in an executing stack frame) when the delegate instance is invoked.

- outerVariable ① is an outer variable because the anonymous method is declared within its scope. But the anonymous method doesn't refer to it, so it's not captured.

- capturedVariable ② is an outer variable because the anonymous method is declared within its scope, and it's *captured* by virtue of being used at ⑤.

Okay, you now understand the terminology, but we're not a lot closer to seeing what captured variables do. I suspect you could guess the output if you ran the method from listing 5.10, but there are some other cases that would probably surprise you. We'll start off with a simple example and build up to more complex ones.

5.5.2 *Examining the behavior of captured variables*

When a variable is captured, it really is the *variable* that's captured by the anonymous method, not its value at the time the delegate instance was created. You'll see later that this has far-reaching consequences, but first you need to understand what that means for a relatively straightforward situation.

The following listing has a captured variable and an anonymous method that both prints out and changes the variable. You'll see that changes to the variable from outside the anonymous method are visible within the anonymous method, and vice versa.

Listing 5.11   Accessing a variable both inside and outside an anonymous method

```
string captured = "before x is created";

MethodInvoker x = delegate
{
    Console.WriteLine(captured);
    captured = "changed by x";
};

captured = "directly before x is invoked";
x();

Console.WriteLine(captured);

captured = "before second invocation";
x();
```

The output of listing 5.11 is as follows:

```
directly before x is invoked
changed by x
before second invocation
```

Let's look at how this happens. First, you declare the variable captured and set its value with a perfectly normal string literal. So far, there's nothing special about the variable. You then declare x and set its value using an anonymous method that captures captured. The delegate instance will always print out the current value of captured and then set it to "changed by x." Don't forget that creating this delegate instance *doesn't execute it.*

To make it absolutely clear that just creating the delegate instance doesn't read the variable and stash its value away somewhere, you now change the value of captured to "directly before x is invoked." You then invoke x for the first time. It reads the value of captured and prints it out—the first line of output. It sets the value of captured to "changed by x" and returns. When the delegate instance returns, the normal method continues in the usual way. It prints out the current value of captured, giving the second line of output.

The normal method then changes the value of captured yet again (this time to "before second invocation") and invokes x for the second time. The current value of captured is printed out, giving the last line of output. The delegate instance changes the value of captured to "changed by x" and returns, at which point the normal method has run out of code and it's done.

That's a lot of detail about how a short piece of code works, but there's really only one crucial idea in it: *the captured variable is the same one that the rest of the method uses.* For some people, that's hard to grasp; for others it comes naturally. Don't worry if it's tricky to start with—it'll get easier over time.

Even if you've understood everything easily so far, you may be wondering why you'd want to do any of this. It's about time we had an example that was actually useful.

5.5.3 *What's the point of captured variables?*

To put it simply, captured variables eliminate the need to write extra classes just to store the information a delegate needs to act on, beyond what it's passed via parameters. Before `ParameterizedThreadStart` existed, if you wanted to start a new (non-threadpool) thread and give it some information—the URL of a page to fetch, for instance—you had to create an extra type to hold the URL and put the action of the `ThreadStart` delegate instance in that type. Even with `ParameterizedThreadStart`, your method had to accept a parameter of type `object` and cast it to the type you really wanted. It was an ugly way of achieving something that should've been simple.

As another example, suppose you had a list of people and wanted to write a method that would return a second list containing all the people who were under a given age. `List<T>` has a method called `FindAll` that returns another list of everything matching the specified predicate. Before anonymous methods and captured variables, it wouldn't have made much sense for `List<T>.FindAll` to exist, because of all the hoops you'd have to go through in order to create the right delegate to start with. It would've been simpler to do all the iteration and copying manually. With C# 2, though, you can do it all very easily:

```
List<Person> FindAllYoungerThan(List<Person> people, int limit)
{
    return people.FindAll(delegate (Person person)
        { return person.Age < limit; }
    );
}
```

Here you're capturing the `limit` parameter within the delegate instance—if you'd had anonymous methods but not captured variables, you could've performed a test against a hardcoded limit, but not one that was passed into the method as a parameter. I hope you'll agree that this approach is neat: it expresses exactly *what* you want to do with much less fuss about exactly *how* it should happen than you'd have seen in a C# 1 version. (It's even neater in C# 3, admittedly...)[7] It's relatively rare that you come across a situation where you need to *write* to a captured variable, but again that can have its uses.

Still with me? Good. So far, you've only used the delegate instance within the method that creates it. That doesn't raise many questions about the lifetime of the captured variables—but what would happen if the delegate instance escaped into the big bad world? How would it cope after the method that created it had finished?

---

[7] In case you're wondering: `return people.Where(person => person.Age < limit);`

5.5.4 *The extended lifetime of captured variables*

The simplest way of tackling this topic is to state a rule, give an example, and then think about what would happen if the rule weren't in place. Here we go:

A captured variable lives for at least as long as any delegate instance referring to it.

Don't worry if it doesn't make a lot of sense yet—that's what the example is for. The following listing shows a method that *returns* a delegate instance. That delegate instance is created using an anonymous method that captures an outer variable. So, what'll happen when the delegate is invoked after the method has returned?

Listing 5.12   Demonstration of a captured variable having its lifetime extended

```
static MethodInvoker CreateDelegateInstance()
{
    int counter = 5;

    MethodInvoker ret = delegate
    {
        Console.WriteLine(counter);
        counter++;
    };
    ret();
    return ret;
}
...
MethodInvoker x = CreateDelegateInstance();
x();
x();
```

The output of listing 5.12 consists of the numbers 5, 6, and 7 on separate lines. The first line of output comes from the invocation of the delegate instance within `Create-DelegateInstance`, so it makes sense that the value of `counter` is available at that point. But what about after the method has returned? Normally you'd consider `counter` to be on the stack, so when the stack frame for `CreateDelegateInstance` is destroyed, you'd expect `counter` to effectively vanish…and yet subsequent invocations of the returned delegate instance seem to keep using it.

The secret is to challenge the assumption that `counter` is on the stack in the first place. It isn't. The compiler has actually created an extra class to hold the variable. The `CreateDelegateInstance` method has a reference to an instance of that class so it can use `counter`, and the delegate has a reference to the same instance, which lives on the heap in the normal way. That instance isn't eligible for garbage collection until the delegate is ready to be collected.

Some aspects of anonymous methods are very compiler-specific (different compilers could achieve the same semantics in different ways), but it's hard to see how the specified behavior could be achieved *without* using an extra class to hold the captured variable. Note that if you only capture `this`, no extra types are required—the compiler just creates an instance method to act as the delegate's action. As I mentioned before, you probably shouldn't worry about the stack and heap details too much, but it's worth knowing what the compiler is capable of doing, just in case you get confused as to how the specified behavior is even possible.

Okay, so local variables can live on even after a method has returned. You may be wondering what I could possibly throw at you next—how about multiple delegates capturing different instances of the same variable? It sounds crazy, so it's just the kind of thing you should be expecting by now.

5.5.5 *Local variable instantiations*

On a good day, captured variables act exactly the way I expect them to at a glance. On a bad day, I'm still surprised when I'm not careful. When there are problems, it's almost always due to my forgetting how many "instances" of local variables I'm actually creating. A local variable is said to be *instantiated* each time execution enters the scope where it's declared.

Here's a simple example comparing two very similar bits of code:

```
int single;                              for (int i = 0; i < 10; i++)
for (int i = 0; i < 10; i++)             {
{                                            int multiple = 5;
    single = 5;                              Console.WriteLine(multiple + i);
    Console.WriteLine(single + i);       }
}
```

In the good old days, it was reasonable to say that pieces of code like this were semantically identical. Indeed, they'd usually compile to the same IL—and they still will, if there aren't any anonymous methods involved. All the space for local variables is allocated on the stack at the start of the method, so there's no cost to redeclaring the variable for each iteration of the loop.[8] In our new terminology, the single variable will be instantiated only once, but the multiple variable will be instantiated 10 times—it's as if there were 10 local variables, all called multiple, which were created one after another.

I'm sure you can see where I'm going—when a variable is captured, it's the relevant "instance" of the variable that's captured. If you captured multiple inside the loop, the variable captured in the first iteration would be different from the variable captured the second time round, and so on. The following listing shows exactly this effect.

Listing 5.13   Capturing multiple variable instantiations with multiple delegates

```
List<MethodInvoker> list = new List<MethodInvoker>();

for (int index = 0; index < 5; index++)
{
    int counter = index * 10;              ◁——❶ Instantiates counter
```

---

[8]   In my view, it's also cleaner to redeclare the variable unless you explicitly need to maintain its value between iterations.

```
    list.Add(delegate
    {
        Console.WriteLine(counter);
        counter++;
    });
}

foreach (MethodInvoker t in list)
{
    t();
}
list[0]();
list[0]();
list[0]();

list[1]();
```

② Prints and increments captured variable

③ Executes all five delegate instances

④ Executes first one three more times

⑤ Executes second one again

Listing 5.13 creates five different delegate instances **②**—one for each time you go around the loop. Invoking the delegate will print out the value of counter and then increment it. Because counter is declared *inside* the loop, it's instantiated for each iteration **①**, and each delegate captures a different variable. When you go through and invoke each delegate **③**, you see the different values initially assigned to counter: 0, 10, 20, 30, 40. Just to hammer the point home, when you then go back to the first delegate instance and execute it three more times **④**, it keeps going from where that instance's counter variable had left off: 1, 2, 3. Finally you execute the second delegate instance **⑤**, and that keeps going from where *that* instance's counter variable had left off: 11.

As you can see, each of the delegate instances has captured a different variable. Before we leave this example, I should point out what would've happened if you'd captured index—the variable declared by the for loop—instead of counter. In this case, all the delegates would have shared the same variable. The output would've been the numbers 5 to 13; 5 first because the last assignment to index before the loop terminates would've set it to 5, and then incrementing the same variable regardless of which delegate was involved. You'd see the same behavior with a foreach loop (in C# 2–4): the variable declared by the initial part of the loop is only instantiated once. It's easy to get this wrong! If you want to capture the value of a loop variable for that particular iteration of the loop, introduce another variable within the loop, copy the loop variable's value into it, and capture that new variable—effectively what you did in listing 5.13 with the counter variable.

THIS CHANGES IN C# 5...   Though the behavior in a for loop is reasonable— the variable does appear to be declared just once, after all—it's more surprising in the foreach case. In fact, it's *almost always* wrong to capture a foreach iteration variable in an anonymous method that's going to exist beyond the immediate iteration. (It's fine if the delegate instance is only used within that iteration.) This has caused problems for so many developers that the C# team has changed the semantics of foreach for C# 5 to make it act more naturally—as if each iteration had its own separate variable. See section 16.1 for more details.

For our final example, let's look at something really nasty—sharing some captured variables but not others.

5.5.6 *Mixtures of shared and distinct variables*

Let me say before I show you this next example that it's *not* code I'd recommend. In fact, the whole point of presenting it is to show how if you try to use captured variables in too complicated a fashion, things can get tricky really fast. The following listing creates two delegate instances that each capture "the same" two variables. But the story gets more convoluted when you look at what's actually captured.

Listing 5.14 Capturing variables in different scopes. Warning: nasty code ahead!

```
MethodInvoker[] delegates = new MethodInvoker[2];

int outside = 0;                              ◁── ❶ Instantiates variable once

for (int i = 0; i < 2; i++)
{
    int inside = 0;                           ◁── ❷ Instantiates variable multiple times

    delegates[i] = delegate                              ◁┐ Captures
    {                                                      │  variables with
        Console.WriteLine ("({0},{1})", outside, inside);  │  anonymous
        outside++;                                         │  method
        inside++;                                        ❸ ┘
    };
}

MethodInvoker first = delegates[0];
MethodInvoker second = delegates[1];

first();
first();
first();

second();
second();
```

How long would it take you to predict the output from listing 5.14 (even with the annotations)? Frankly, it would take me a while—longer than I like to spend understanding code. Just as an exercise, though, let's look at what happens.

First consider the `outside` variable ❶. The scope it's declared in is only entered once, so it's a straightforward case—there's only ever one of it, effectively. The `inside` variable ❷ is a different matter—each loop iteration instantiates a new one. That means that when you create the delegate instance ❸, the `outside` variable is shared between the two delegate instances, but each of them has its own `inside` variable.

After the loop has ended, you call the first delegate instance you created three times. Because it's incrementing both of its captured variables each time, and both of them started off as 0, you see (0,0), then (1,1), and then (2,2). The difference between the two variables in terms of scope becomes apparent when you execute the second delegate instance. It has a different `inside` variable, so that still has its initial value of 0, but the `outside` variable is the one you've already incremented three times. The output from calling the second delegate twice is therefore (3,0), and then (4,1).

Just for the sake of interest, let's think about how this is implemented—at least with Microsoft's C# 2 compiler. What happens is that one extra class is generated to hold the `outside` variable, and another one is generated to hold an `inside` variable *and a reference to the first extra class.* Essentially, each scope that contains a captured variable gets its own type, with a reference to the next scope out that contains a captured variable. In this example, there were two instances of the type holding `inside`, and they both referred to the same instance of the type holding `outside`. Other implementations may vary, but this is the most obvious way of doing things. Figure 5.1 shows the values after listing 5.14 has executed. (The names in the figure aren't the ones that the compiler would generate, but they're close enough. Note that the delegate instances would also have other members in reality—only the target is interesting here, though.)

Even after you understand this code fully, it's still a good template for experimenting with other elements of captured variables. As I noted earlier, certain elements of variable capture are implementation-specific, and it's often useful to refer to the specification to see what's guaranteed. But it's also important to *play* with code to see what happens.

It's possible that there are situations where code like listing 5.14 would be the simplest and clearest way of expressing the desired behavior, but I'd have to see it to believe it, and I'd certainly want comments in the code to explain what would happen. So, when is it appropriate to use captured variables, and what do you need to look out for?

5.5.7   *Captured variable guidelines and summary*

Hopefully this section has convinced you to be *very* careful with captured variables. They make good logical sense (and almost any change to make them simpler would

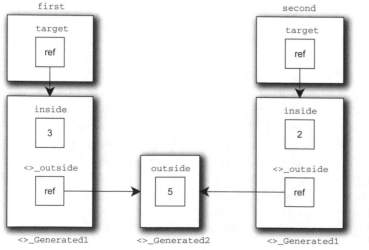

Figure 5.1   Snapshot of multiple captured variable scopes in memory

probably make them either less useful or less logical), but they also make it easy to produce horribly complicated code.

Don't let that discourage you from using them sensibly, though—they can save you masses of tedious code, and when they're used appropriately they can be the most readable way of getting the job done. But what counts as *sensible?*

Here are some suggestions for using captured variables:

- If code that doesn't use captured variables is just as simple as code that does, don't use them.
- Before capturing a variable declared by a `for` or `foreach` statement, consider whether your delegate is going to live beyond the loop iteration, and whether you want it to see the subsequent values of that variable. If not, create another variable inside the loop that just copies the value you *do* want. (In C# 5 you don't need to worry about `foreach` statements, but you still need to take care in `for` statements.)
- If you create multiple delegate instances (whether in a loop or explicitly) that capture variables, put thought into whether you want them to capture the same variable.
- If you capture a variable that doesn't actually change (either in the anonymous method or the enclosing method body), you don't need to worry as much.
- If the delegate instances you create never escape from the method—in other words, they're never stored anywhere else, or returned, or used for starting threads—life is a lot simpler.
- Consider the extended lifetime of any captured variables in terms of garbage collection. This is normally not an issue, but if you capture an object that's expensive in terms of memory, it may be significant.

The first point is the golden rule. Simplicity is a good thing, so any time the use of a captured variable makes your code simpler after you've factored in the additional inherent complexity of forcing your code's maintainers to understand what the captured variable does, use it. You need to include that extra complexity in your considerations, that's all—don't just go for minimal line count.

We've covered a lot of ground in this section, and I'm aware that it can be hard to take in. I've listed the most important things to remember next, so that if you need to come back to this section later, you can jog your memory without having to read through the whole thing again:

- The *variable* is captured—not its value at the point of delegate instance creation.
- Captured variables have lifetimes extended to at least that of the capturing delegate.
- Multiple delegates can capture the same variable…
- …but within loops, the same variable declaration can effectively refer to different variable "instances."

- `for` loop declarations create variables that live for the duration of the loop—they're not instantiated on each iteration. The same is true for `foreach` statements before C# 5.
- Extra types are created, where necessary, to hold captured variables.
- Be careful! Simple is almost always better than clever.

You'll see more variables being captured when we look at C# 3 and its lambda expressions, but for now you may be relieved to hear that we've finished our rundown of the new C# 2 delegate features.

5.6   *Summary*

C# 2 has radically changed the ways in which delegates can be created, and in doing so it's opened up the framework to a more functional style of programming. There are more methods in .NET 2.0 that take delegates as parameters than there were in .NET 1.0/1.1, and this trend continues in .NET 3.5. The `List<T>` type is the best example of this, and it's a good test bed for checking your skills with using anonymous methods and captured variables. Programming in this way requires a slightly different mind-set—you must be able to take a step back and consider what the ultimate aim is, and whether it's best expressed in the traditional C# manner, or whether a functional approach makes things clearer.

All the changes to delegate handling are useful, but they add complexity to the language, particularly when it comes to captured variables. Closures are always tricky in terms of determining exactly how the available environment is shared, and C# is no different in this respect. The reason the concept has lasted so long, though, is that it can make code simpler to understand and more immediate. The balancing act between complexity and simplicity is always a difficult one, and it's worth being cautious to start with. But over time you should expect to get better at working with captured variables and understanding how they behave. LINQ encourages their use even further, and a great deal of modern, idiomatic C# code uses closures frequently.

Anonymous methods aren't the only change in C# 2 that involves the compiler creating extra types behind the scenes and doing devious things with variables that appear to be local. You'll see a lot more of this in the next chapter, where the compiler effectively builds a whole state machine for you, in order to make it easier for you to implement iterators.

Implementing iterators
the easy way

6

This chapter covers

- Implementing iterators in C# 1
- Iterator blocks in C# 2
- Sample iterator usage
- Iterators as coroutines

The iterator pattern is an example of a *behavioral pattern*—a design pattern that simplifies communication between objects. It's one of the simplest patterns to understand, and it's incredibly easy to use. In essence, it allows you to access all the elements in a sequence of items without caring about what kind of sequence it is—an array, a list, a linked list, or none of the above. This can be effective for building a *data pipeline*, where an item of data enters the pipeline and goes through a number of different transformations or filters before coming out the other end. Indeed, this is one of the core patterns of LINQ, as you'll see in part 3 of the book.

In .NET, the iterator pattern is encapsulated by the IEnumerator and IEnumerable interfaces and their generic equivalents. (The naming is unfortunate—the pattern is normally called *iteration* to avoid confusing it with other meanings of the word *enumeration*. I've used *iterator* and *iterable* throughout this chapter.) If a type implements

IEnumerable, that means it can be iterated over; calling the GetEnumerator method will return the IEnumerator implementation, which is the iterator itself. You can think of the iterator as being like a database cursor: a position within the sequence. The iterator can only move forward within the sequence, and there can be many iterators operating on the same sequence at the same time.

As a language, C# 1 has built-in support for consuming iterators using the foreach statement. This makes it easy to iterate over collections—easier than using a straight for loop—and it's nicely expressive. The foreach statement compiles down to calls to the GetEnumerator and MoveNext methods and the Current property, with support for disposing of the iterator afterward if IDisposable has been implemented. It's a small but useful piece of syntactic sugar.

In C# 1, though, *implementing* an iterator is a relatively difficult task. C# 2 makes this much simpler, which can sometimes lead to the iterator pattern being worth implementing in cases where previously it would've caused more work than it saved.

In this chapter, we'll look at what's required to implement an iterator and at the support given by C# 2. After we've looked at the syntax in detail, we'll examine a few examples from the real world, including an exciting (if slightly off-the-wall) use of the iteration syntax in a concurrency library from Microsoft. I've held off providing the examples until the end of the description, because there isn't *very* much to learn, and the examples will be a lot clearer when you can understand what the code is doing. If you really want to read the examples first, they're in sections 6.3 and 6.4.

As in other chapters, let's start off by looking at what life was like before C# 2. We'll implement an iterator the hard way.

6.1   *C# 1: The pain of handwritten iterators*

You've already seen one example of an iterator implementation in section 3.4.3, when we looked at what happens when you iterate over a generic collection. In some ways, that was harder than a real C# 1 iterator implementation would've been, because you implemented the generic interfaces as well—but it was also easier in other ways because it wasn't actually iterating over anything useful.

To put the C# 2 features into context, we'll first implement an iterator that's about as simple as it can be while still providing real functionality. Suppose you wanted a new type of collection based on a circular buffer. In this example, you'll implement IEnumerable so that users of your new class can easily iterate over all the values in the collection. We'll ignore the guts of the collection here and just concentrate on the iteration side. Your collection will store its values in an array (object[]—no generics here), and the collection will have the interesting feature that you can set its logical starting point—so if the array had five elements, you could set the start point to 2 and expect elements 2, 3, 4, 0, and then 1 to be returned. I won't show the full circular buffer code here, but it's in the downloadable code.

To make the class easy to demonstrate, you'll provide both the values and the starting point in the constructor, so you should be able to write code such as the following to iterate over the collection.

Listing 6.1   Code using the (as yet unimplemented) new collection type

```
object[] values = {"a", "b", "c", "d", "e"};
IterationSample collection = new IterationSample(values, 3);
foreach (object x in collection)
{
    Console.WriteLine (x);
}
```

Running listing 6.1 should (eventually) produce output of d, e, a, b, and finally c because you specified a starting point of 3. Now that you know what you need to achieve, let's look at the skeleton of the class, as shown in the following listing.

Listing 6.2   Skeleton of the new collection type, with no iterator implementation

```
using System;
using System.Collections;

public class IterationSample : IEnumerable
{
    object[] values;
    int startingPoint;

    public IterationSample(object[] values, int startingPoint)
    {
        this.values = values;
        this.startingPoint = startingPoint;
    }

    public IEnumerator GetEnumerator()
    {
        throw new NotImplementedException();
    }
}
```

You haven't implemented GetEnumerator yet, but the rest of the code is ready to go. And how do you go about writing the GetEnumerator code? The first thing to understand is that you need to store some *state* somewhere. One important aspect of the iterator pattern is that you don't return all of the data in one go—the client asks for one element at a time. That means you need to keep track of how far you've already gone through your array. The stateful nature of iterators will be important when we look at what the C# 2 compiler does, so keep a close eye on the state required in this example.

Where should this state live? Suppose you tried to put it in the IterationSample class, making that implement IEnumerator as well as IEnumerable. At first glance, this looks like a good plan—after all, the *data* is in the right place, including the starting point. Your GetEnumerator method could just return this. But there's a big problem with this approach: if GetEnumerator is called several times, several independent iterators should be returned. For instance, you should be able to use two foreach statements, one inside another, to get all possible pairs of values. The two iterators need to be independent, which suggests you need to create a new object each time

GetEnumerator is called. You *could* still implement the functionality directly within IterationSample, but then you'd have a class that didn't have a single clear responsibility—it would be pretty confusing.

Instead, let's create another class to implement the iterator itself. You can use the fact that in C# a nested type has access to its enclosing type's private members, which means you can store a reference to the parent IterationSample, along with the state of how many iterations you've performed so far. This is shown in the following listing.

Listing 6.3   Nested class implementing the collection's iterator

```
class IterationSampleIterator : IEnumerator
{
    IterationSample parent;              ① Collection you're
    int position;                            iterating over

    internal IterationSampleIterator(IterationSample parent)     How far
    {                                                            you've
        this.parent = parent;                                 ② iterated
        position = -1;              ③ Starts before first element
    }

    public bool MoveNext()
    {
        if (position != parent.values.Length)     ④ Increments position if still going
        {
            position++;
        }
        return position < parent.values.Length;
    }

    public object Current
    {
        get
        {                                                   ⑤ Prevents access
            if (position == -1 ||                              before first or
                position == parent.values.Length)              after last element
            {
                throw new InvalidOperationException();
            }
            int index = position + parent.startingPoint;     ⑥ Implements
            index = index % parent.values.Length;               wraparound
            return parent.values[index];
        }
    }

    public void Reset()
    {                                       ⑦ Moves back to before
        position = -1;                         first element
    }
}
```

What a lot of code to perform such a simple task! You remember the original collection of values you're iterating over ① and keep track of where you'd be in a simple zero-based array ②. To return an element, you offset that index by the starting point ❻. In keeping with the interface, you consider your iterator to start logically before the first element ❸, so the client will have to call MoveNext before using the Current property for the first time. The conditional increment at ❹ makes the test at ❺ simple and correct even if MoveNext is called again after it's first reported that no more data is available. To reset the iterator, you set the logical position back to before the first element ❼.

Most of the logic involved is fairly straightforward, although there's plenty of room for off-by-one errors; my first implementation failed its unit tests for precisely that reason. The good news is that it works, and that you only need to implement IEnumerable in IterationSample to complete the example:

```
public IEnumerator GetEnumerator()
{
    return new IterationSampleIterator(this);
}
```

I won't reproduce the combined code here, but it's available on the book's website, including listing 6.1, which now produces the expected output.

It's worth bearing in mind that this is a relatively simple example—there's not a lot of state to keep track of, and there's no attempt to check whether the collection has changed between iterations. With such a large burden involved to implement a simple iterator, you shouldn't be surprised at how rarely this pattern was implemented in C# 1. Developers were generally happy to use foreach on the collections provided by the framework, but more direct (and collection-specific) access when it came to their own collections.

It took about 40 lines of code to implement the iterator in C# 1. Let's see if C# 2 can do any better.

6.2 C# 2: Simple iterators with yield statements

I've always been the kind of person who likes to stay up until midnight on Christmas Eve so I can open a present as soon as Christmas Day arrives. In the same way, I'd find it almost impossible to wait any significant amount of time before showing you how neat the solution is in C# 2.

6.2.1 Introducing iterator blocks and yield return

This chapter wouldn't exist if C# 2 didn't have a powerful feature that cuts down the amount of code you have to write to implement iterators. In some other topics the amount of code has only been reduced slightly, or the changes have just made something more elegant. In this case, though, the amount of code required is reduced *massively*. The following listing shows the complete implementation of the GetEnumerator method in C# 2.

Listing 6.4   Iterating through the sample collection with C# 2 and `yield return`

```
public IEnumerator GetEnumerator()
{
    for (int index = 0; index < values.Length; index++)
    {
        yield return values[(index + startingPoint) % values.Length];
    }
}
```

Four lines of implementation, two of which are just braces. To be clear, that replaces the whole of the `IterationSampleIterator` class. Completely. At least in the source code…Later on you'll see what the compiler has done behind the scenes and some of the quirks of the implementation it's provided, but for the moment let's look at the source code.

The method looks perfectly normal until you see the use of `yield return`. That's what tells the C# compiler that this isn't a normal method, but one implemented with an *iterator block*. The method is declared to return an `IEnumerator`, and you can only use iterator blocks to implement methods[1] that have a return type of `IEnumerable`, `IEnumerator`, or one of the generic equivalents. The *yield type* of the iterator block is `object` if the declared return type of the method is a nongeneric interface, or it's the type argument of the generic interface otherwise. For instance, a method declared to return `IEnumerable<string>` would have a yield type of `string`.

No normal `return` statements are allowed within iterator blocks—only `yield return`. All `yield return` statements in the block must try to return a value compatible with the yield type of the block. In the previous example, you couldn't write `yield return 1;` in a method declared to return `IEnumerable<string>`.

RESTRICTIONS ON YIELD RETURN   There are a few further restrictions on yield statements. You can't use `yield return` inside a `try` block if it has any `catch` blocks, and you can't use `yield return` or `yield break` (which we'll come to shortly) in a `finally` block. That doesn't mean you can't use `try/catch` or `try/finally` blocks inside iterators—it just restricts what you can do in them. If you want to know more about why these restrictions exist, Eric Lippert has a whole series of blog posts about these and other design decisions involving iterators: see http://mng.bz/EJ97.

The big idea that you need to get your head around when it comes to iterator blocks is that although you've written a method that looks like it executes sequentially, what you've actually asked the compiler to do is create a *state machine* for you. This is necessary for exactly the same reason you had to put so much effort into implementing the iterator in C# 1—the caller only wants to see one element at a time, so you need to keep track of what you were doing when you last returned a value.

---

[1]   Or properties, as you'll see later on. You can't use an iterator block in an anonymous method, though.

When the compiler encounters an iterator block, it creates a nested type for the state machine. This type remembers exactly where you are within the block and the values of local variables (including parameters). The generated class is *somewhat* similar to the longhand implementation you wrote earlier, in that it keeps all the necessary state as instance variables. Let's think about what this state machine has to do in order to implement the iterator:

- It has to have some initial state.
- Whenever `MoveNext` is called, it has to execute code from the `GetEnumerator` method until you're ready to provide the next value (in other words, until you hit a `yield return` statement).
- When the `Current` property is used, it has to return the last value you yielded.
- It has to know when you've finished yielding values so that `MoveNext` can return `false`.

The second point in this list is the tricky one, because the state machine always needs to restart the code from the point it had previously reached. Keeping track of the local variables (as they appear in the method) isn't too hard—they're represented by instance variables in the state machine. The restarting aspect is trickier, but the good news is that unless you're writing a C# compiler yourself, you needn't care about how it's achieved: the result from a black-box point of view is that it just works. You can write perfectly normal code within the iterator block, and the compiler is responsible for making sure that the flow of execution is exactly as it would be in any other method. The difference is that a `yield return` statement appears to only temporarily exit the method—you could think of it as being paused, effectively.

Next we'll examine the flow of execution in more detail and in a more visual way.

6.2.2 *Visualizing an iterator's workflow*

It may help to think about how iterators execute in terms of a sequence diagram. Rather than drawing the diagram by hand, the following listing prints it out. The iterator provides a sequence of numbers (0, 1, 2, -1) and then finishes. The interesting part isn't the numbers provided so much as the *flow* of the code.

Listing 6.5 Showing the sequence of calls between an iterator and its caller

```
static readonly string Padding = new string(' ', 30);

static IEnumerable<int> CreateEnumerable()
{
    Console.WriteLine("{0}Start of CreateEnumerable()", Padding);

    for (int i=0; i < 3; i++)
    {
        Console.WriteLine("{0}About to yield {1}", Padding, i);
        yield return i;
        Console.WriteLine("{0}After yield", Padding);
    }
    Console.WriteLine("{0}Yielding final value", Padding);
```

```
        yield return -1;

        Console.WriteLine("{0}End of CreateEnumerable()", Padding);
}
...
IEnumerable<int> iterable = CreateEnumerable();
IEnumerator<int> iterator = iterable.GetEnumerator();
Console.WriteLine("Starting to iterate");
while (true)
{
    Console.WriteLine("Calling MoveNext()...");
    bool result = iterator.MoveNext();
    Console.WriteLine("... MoveNext result={0}", result);
    if (!result)
    {
        break;
    }
    Console.WriteLine("Fetching Current...");
    Console.WriteLine("... Current result={0}", iterator.Current);
}
```

Listing 6.5 isn't pretty, particularly around the iteration side of things. In the normal course of events, you could just use a foreach loop, but to show exactly *what's* happening *when*, I had to break the use of the iterator out into pieces. This code broadly does what foreach does, although foreach also calls Dispose at the end. This is important for iterator blocks, as we'll discuss shortly. As you can see, there's no difference in the syntax within the iterator method, even though this time you're returning IEnumerable<int> instead of IEnumerator<int>. Usually you'll only want to return IEnumerator<T> in order to implement IEnumerable<T>; if you want to just yield a sequence from a method, return IEnumerable<T> instead.

Here's the output from listing 6.5:

```
Starting to iterate
Calling MoveNext()...
                                Start of CreateEnumerable()
                                About to yield 0
... MoveNext result=True
Fetching Current...
... Current result=0
Calling MoveNext()...
                                After yield
                                About to yield 1
... MoveNext result=True
Fetching Current...
... Current result=1
Calling MoveNext()...
                                After yield
                                About to yield 2
... MoveNext result=True
Fetching Current...
... Current result=2
Calling MoveNext()...
                                After yield
```

```
                              Yielding final value
... MoveNext result=True
Fetching Current...
... Current result=-1
Calling MoveNext()...
                              End of CreateEnumerable()
... MoveNext result=False
```

There are several important things to note in this output:

- None of the code in CreateEnumerable is called until the first call to MoveNext.
- It's only when you call MoveNext that any real work gets done. Fetching Current doesn't run any of your code.
- The code stops executing at yield return and picks up again just afterward at the next call to MoveNext.
- You can have multiple yield return statements in different places in the method.
- The code doesn't end at the last yield return. Instead, the call to MoveNext that causes you to reach the end of the method is the one that returns false.

The first point is particularly important, because it means you can't use an iterator block for any code that has to be executed immediately when the method is called, such as code for argument validation. If you put normal checking into a method implemented with an iterator block, it won't behave nicely. You'll almost certainly fall foul of this at some point—it's an extremely common error, and hard to understand until you think about what the iterator block is doing. You'll see the solution to the problem in section 6.3.3.

There are two things you haven't seen yet—an alternative way of halting the iteration, and how finally blocks work in this somewhat odd form of execution. Let's take a look at them now.

6.2.3   *Advanced iterator execution flow*

In normal methods, the return statement has two effects. First, it supplies the value the caller sees as the return value. Second, it terminates the execution of the method, executing any appropriate finally blocks on the way out. You've seen that the yield return statement temporarily exits the method, but only until MoveNext is called again, and we haven't examined the behavior of finally blocks at all. How can you *really* stop the method, and what happens to all of those finally blocks? We'll start with a fairly simple construct—the yield break statement.

ENDING AN ITERATOR WITH YIELD BREAK

You can always find a way to give a method a single exit point, and many people work hard to achieve this.[2] The same techniques can be applied in iterator blocks. But

---

[2]   I find that the hoops you have to jump through to achieve this often make the code much harder to read than having multiple return points, especially as try/finally is available for cleanup and you need to account for the possibility of exceptions occurring anyway. The point is that it can be done.

should you wish to have an early out, the `yield break` statement is your friend. This effectively terminates the iterator, making the current call to `MoveNext` return `false`.

The following listing demonstrates this by counting up to 100 but stopping early if it runs out of time. This code also demonstrates the use of a method parameter in an iterator block and proves that the name of the method is irrelevant.[3]

Listing 6.6   Demonstration of `yield break`

```csharp
static IEnumerable<int> CountWithTimeLimit(DateTime limit)
{
    for (int i = 1; i <= 100; i++)
    {
        if (DateTime.Now >= limit)
        {
            yield break;                 ⟵── Stops if the time is up
        }
        yield return i;
    }
}
...
DateTime stop = DateTime.Now.AddSeconds(2);
foreach (int i in CountWithTimeLimit(stop))
{
    Console.WriteLine("Received {0}", i);
    Thread.Sleep(300);
}
```

Typically when you run listing 6.6, you'll see about seven lines of output. The `foreach` loop terminates perfectly normally—as far as it's concerned, the iterator has just run out of elements to iterate over. The `yield break` statement behaves much like a return statement in a normal method.

So far, so simple. There's one last aspect of execution flow to explore: how and when `finally` blocks are executed.

EXECUTION OF FINALLY BLOCKS

You're used to `finally` blocks executing whenever you leave the relevant scope. Iterator blocks don't behave quite like normal methods, though. As you've seen, a `yield return` statement effectively pauses the method rather than exiting it. Following that logic, you wouldn't expect any `finally` blocks to be executed at that point, and they aren't. But appropriate `finally` blocks *are* executed when a `yield break` statement is hit, just as you'd expect them to be when returning from a normal method.[4]

The most common use of `finally` in an iterator block is to dispose of resources, typically with a convenient `using` statement. You'll see a real-world example of this in section 6.3.2, but for now we're just trying to see how and when `finally` blocks are

---

[3] Note that methods taking `ref` or `out` parameters can't be implemented with iterator blocks.

[4] `finally` blocks also work as expected when execution leaves the relevant scope without reaching either a `yield return` or a `yield break` statement. I'm only focusing on the behavior of the two `yield` statements here because that's where the flow of execution is new and different.

executed. The following listing shows this in action—it's the same code as in listing 6.6, but with a `finally` block. The changes are shown in bold.

Listing 6.7 Demonstration of `yield break` working with `try/finally`

```
static IEnumerable<int> CountWithTimeLimit(DateTime limit)
{
    try
    {
    for (int i = 1; i <= 100; i++)
    {
       if (DateTime.Now >= limit)
       {
          yield break;
       }
       yield return i;
    }
    }
    finally
    {
       Console.WriteLine("Stopping!");        ⟵── Executes however the loop ends
    }
}
...
DateTime stop = DateTime.Now.AddSeconds(2);
foreach (int i in CountWithTimeLimit(stop))
{
    Console.WriteLine("Received {0}", i);
    Thread.Sleep(300);
}
```

The `finally` block in listing 6.7 is executed whether the iterator block finishes by counting to 100 or due to the time limit being reached. (It would also execute if the code threw an exception.) But there are other ways you might try to avoid the `finally` block from being called...Let's try to be sneaky.

You've seen that code in the iterator block is only executed when `MoveNext` is called. So what happens if you never call `MoveNext`? Or if you call it a few times and then stop? Let's consider changing the calling part of listing 6.7 to this:

```
DateTime stop = DateTime.Now.AddSeconds(2);
foreach (int i in CountWithTimeLimit(stop))
{
    Console.WriteLine ("Received {0}", i);
    if (i > 3)
    {
       Console.WriteLine("Returning");
       return;
    }
    Thread.Sleep(300);
}
```

Here you're not stopping early in the iterator code—you're stopping early in the code *using* the iterator. The output is perhaps surprising:

```
Received 1
Received 2
Received 3
Received 4
Returning
Stopping!
```

You can see that code is being executed after the return statement in the foreach loop. That doesn't normally happen unless a finally block is involved—and in this case there are two! You already know about the finally block in the iterator method, but the question is what's causing it to be executed.

I gave a hint about this earlier—foreach calls Dispose on the iterator returned by GetEnumerator in its own finally block (just like the using statement). When you call Dispose on an iterator created with an iterator block before it's finished iterating, the state machine executes any finally blocks that are in the scope where the code is currently "paused." That's a complicated and somewhat detailed explanation, but the result is simpler to express: as long as callers use a foreach loop, finally works within iterator blocks in the way you want it to.

You can easily prove that it's the call to Dispose that triggers this by using the iterator manually:

```
DateTime stop = DateTime.Now.AddSeconds(2);
IEnumerable<int> iterable = CountWithTimeLimit(stop);
IEnumerator<int> iterator = iterable.GetEnumerator();

iterator.MoveNext();
Console.WriteLine("Received {0}", iterator.Current);

iterator.MoveNext();
Console.WriteLine("Received {0}", iterator.Current);
```

This time the stopping line is never printed. If you explicitly add a call to Dispose, you'll see the extra line in the output again. It's relatively rare that you'll want to terminate an iterator before it's finished, and it's relatively rare that you'll be iterating manually instead of using foreach, but if you *do*, remember to wrap the iterator in a using statement.

We've now covered most of the behavior of iterator blocks, but before we end this section, it's worth considering a few oddities to do with the current Microsoft implementation.

6.2.4 *Quirks in the implementation*

If you compile iterator blocks with the Microsoft C# 2 compiler and look at the resulting IL in either ildasm or Reflector, you'll see the nested type that the compiler has generated for you behind the scenes. In my case, when compiling listing 6.4, it was called IterationSample.<GetEnumerator>d__0 (where the angle brackets make it an unspeakable name—nothing to do with generics). I won't go through exactly what's generated in detail here, but it's worth looking at it in Reflector to get a feel for what's going on, preferably with the language specification next to you, open at section 10.14

("Iterators"); the specification defines different states the type can be in, and this description makes the generated code easier to follow. The bulk of the work is performed in MoveNext, which is generally a big switch statement.

Fortunately, as developers we don't need to care much about the hoops the compiler has to jump through. But there are a few quirks about the implementation that are worth knowing about:

- Before MoveNext is called the first time, the Current property will always return the default value for the yield type of the iterator.
- After MoveNext has returned false, the Current property will always return the final value yielded.
- Reset always throws an exception instead of resetting like your manual implementation did. This is required behavior, laid down in the specification.
- The nested class always implements both the generic and nongeneric forms of IEnumerator (and the generic and nongeneric IEnumerable, where appropriate).

Failing to implement Reset is reasonable—the compiler can't work out what you'd need to do in order to reset the iterator, or even whether it's feasible. Arguably Reset shouldn't have been in the IEnumerator interface to start with, and I can't remember the last time I called it. Many collections don't support it, so callers can't generally rely on it anyway.

Implementing extra interfaces does no harm either. It's interesting that if your method returns IEnumerable, you end up with one class implementing five interfaces (including IDisposable). The language specification explains it in detail, but the upshot is that as a developer you don't need to worry. The fact that it implements both IEnumerable and IEnumerator is slightly unusual—the compiler goes to some pains to make sure that the behavior is correct whatever you do with it, but it also manages to create a single instance of the nested type in the common case where you just iterate through the collection in the same thread that created it.

The behavior of Current is odd—in particular, keeping hold of the last item after supposedly moving off it could keep it from being garbage collected. It's possible that this may be fixed in a later release of the C# compiler, but it's unlikely, as it could break existing code (the Microsoft C# compilers shipping with .NET 3.5, 4, and 4.5 behave in the same way). Strictly speaking, it's correct from the point of view of the C# 2 language specification—the behavior of the Current property is undefined in this situation. It'd be nicer, though, if it implemented the property in the way that the framework documentation suggests, throwing exceptions at appropriate times.

Those are a few tiny drawbacks of using the autogenerated code, but *sensible* callers won't have any problems—and let's face it, you've saved a *lot* of code in order to come up with the implementation. This means it makes sense to use iterators more widely than you might've done in C# 1. The next section provides some sample code so you can check your understanding of iterator blocks and see how they're useful in real life rather than in theoretical scenarios.

6.3   *Real-life iterator examples*

Have you ever written some code that's really simple in itself but that makes your project *much* neater? It happens to me every so often, and it usually makes me happier than it probably ought to—enough to get strange looks from colleagues, anyway. That sort of childlike delight is particularly strong when it comes to using a new language feature in a way that's *clearly* nicer and you're not just doing it for the sake of playing with new toys.

Even now, after using iterators for a few years, I still come across situations where a solution using iterator blocks presents itself, and the resulting code is brief, clean, and easy to understand. In this section I'll share three such scenarios with you.

6.3.1   *Iterating over the dates in a timetable*

While working on a project involving timetables, I came across a few loops, all of which started like this:

```
for (DateTime day = timetable.StartDate;
     day <= timetable.EndDate;
     day = day.AddDays(1))
```

I was working on this area of code a lot, and I always hated that loop, but it was only when I was reading the code out loud to another developer as pseudocode that I realized I was missing a trick. I said something like, "For each day within the timetable..." In retrospect, it's obvious that what I really wanted was a foreach loop. (This may have been obvious to you from the start—apologies if this is the case. Fortunately I can't see you looking smug.) The loop is much nicer when rewritten as follows:

```
foreach (DateTime day in timetable.DateRange)
```

In C# 1, I might've looked at that as a fond dream but not bothered implementing it; you've seen how messy it is to implement an iterator by hand, and the end result only made a few for loops neater in this case. In C# 2, though, it was easy. Within the class representing the timetable, I simply added a property:

```
public IEnumerable<DateTime> DateRange
{
    get
    {
        for (DateTime day = StartDate;
             day <= EndDate;
             day = day.AddDays(1))
        {
            yield return day;
        }
    }
}
```

This moved the original loop into the timetable class, but that's okay—it's much nicer for it to be encapsulated there, in a property that just loops through the days, yielding them one at a time, than to be in business code that was dealing with those days. If I ever wanted to make it more complex (skipping weekends and public holidays, for instance), I could do it in one place and reap the rewards everywhere.

This one small change made a massive improvement to the readability of the code base. As it happens, I stopped refactoring at that point in the commercial code. I *thought* about introducing a Range<T> type to represent a general-purpose range, but as I only needed it in this one situation, it didn't make sense to expend any more effort on the problem. It turns out that was a wise move. In the first edition of this book, I created just such a type—but it had some shortcomings that were hard to address in a book-friendly manner. I redesigned it significantly for my utility library, but I still have a few misgivings. Types like this often sound simpler than they really are, and soon you end up with a corner case to be handled at every turn. The details of the difficulties I encountered don't really belong in this book—they're more points about general design than C#—but they're interesting in their own right, so I've written them up as an article on the book's website (see http://mng.bz/GAmS).

The next example is one of my favorites—it demonstrates everything I love about iterator blocks.

6.3.2 *Iterating over lines in a file*

How often have you read a text file line by line? It's an incredibly common task. As of .NET 4, the framework finally provides a method to make this easier in File.Read-Lines, but if you're using an earlier version of the framework, you can write your own version really easily, as I'll show in the next couple of pages.

I dread to think how often I've written code like this:

```
using (TextReader reader = File.OpenText(filename))
{
    string line;
    while ((line = reader.ReadLine()) != null)
    {
        // Do something with line
    }
}
```

We have four separate concepts here:

- How to obtain a TextReader
- Managing the lifetime of the TextReader
- Iterating over the lines returned by TextReader.ReadLine
- Doing something with each of those lines

Only the first and last of these are generally specific to the situation—the lifetime management and the mechanism for iterating are just boilerplate code. (At least, the lifetime management is simple in C#. Thank goodness for using statements!) There are two ways you could improve things. You could use a delegate—write a utility method that would take a reader and a delegate as parameters, call the delegate for each line in the file, and close the reader at the end. That's often used as an example of closures and delegates, but there's an alternative that I find more elegant and that fits in much better with LINQ. Instead of passing your logic into a method as a delegate, you can use an iterator to return a single line at a time from the file, so you can use the normal `foreach` loop.

You can achieve this using a whole type implementing `IEnumerable<string>` (I have a `LineReader` class in my MiscUtil library for this purpose), but a standalone method in another class will work fine, too. It's really simple, as the next listing proves.

Listing 6.8 Looping over the lines in a file using an iterator block

```
static IEnumerable<string> ReadLines(string filename)
{
    using (TextReader reader = File.OpenText(filename))
    {
        string line;
        while ((line = reader.ReadLine()) != null)
        {
            yield return line;
        }
    }
}
...
foreach (string line in ReadLines("test.txt"))
{
    Console.WriteLine(line);
}
```

The body of the method is pretty much exactly what you had before, except that what you're doing with the line is yielding it to the caller when it iterates over the collection. As before, you open the file, read a line at a time, and then close the reader when you've finished…although the concept of "when you've finished" is more interesting in this case than with a `using` statement in a normal method, where the flow control is more obvious.

This is why it's important that the `foreach` loop dispose of the iterator—because that's what makes sure the reader gets cleaned up. The `using` statement in the iterator method is acting as a `try`/`finally` block; that `finally` block will execute if *either* you get to the end of the file *or* you call `Dispose` on the `IEnumerator<string>` when you're part of the way through. It'd be possible for calling code to abuse the `IEnumerator <string>` returned by `ReadLines(...).GetEnumerator()` and end up with a resource leak, but that's usually the case with `IDisposable`—if you don't call `Dispose`, you may leak resources. It's rarely a problem though, as `foreach` does the right thing. It's important to be aware of this potential abuse—if you relied on some sort of `try/ finally` block in an iterator to grant some permission and then remove it again later, that really *would* be a security hole.

This method encapsulates the first three of the four concepts I listed earlier, but it's a bit restrictive. It's reasonable to lump together the lifetime management and iteration aspects, but what if you want to read text from a network stream instead? Or if you want to use an encoding other than UTF-8? You need to put the first part back in the control of the caller, and the most obvious approach would be to change the method signature to accept a `TextReader`, like this:

```
static IEnumerable<string> ReadLines(TextReader reader)
```

This is a bad idea, though. You want to take ownership of the reader so that you can clean it up conveniently for the caller, but the fact that you take responsibility for the cleanup means you *have* to clean it up, as long as the caller uses the result sensibly. The problem is, if something happens before the first call to `MoveNext()`, you're never going to have any chance to clean up: none of your code will run. The `IEnumerable<string>` itself isn't disposable, and yet it would've stored this piece of state, which required disposal. Another problem would occur if `GetEnumerator()` were called twice: that ought to generate two independent iterators, but they'd both be using the same reader. You could mitigate this somewhat by changing the return type to `IEnumerator<string>`, but that would mean the result couldn't be used in a `foreach` loop, and you still wouldn't get to run any cleanup code if you never got as far as the first `MoveNext()` call. Fortunately, there's a way around this.

Just as the code doesn't get to run immediately, you don't need the reader immediately. What you need is a way of getting the reader when you need it. You could use an interface to represent the idea of "I can provide a `TextReader` when you want one," but the idea of a single method interface should usually make you reach for a delegate. Instead, I'm going to cheat slightly by introducing a delegate that's part of .NET 3.5. It's overloaded by different numbers of type parameters, but you only need one:

```
public delegate TResult Func<TResult>()
```

As you can see, this delegate has no parameters, but it returns a result of the same type as the type parameter. It's a classic provider or factory signature. In this case, you want to get a `TextReader`, so you can use `Func<TextReader>`. The changes to the method are simple:

```
static IEnumerable<string> ReadLines(Func<TextReader> provider)
{
   using (TextReader reader = provider())
   {
      string line;
      while ((line = reader.ReadLine()) != null)
      {
         yield return line;
      }
   }
}
```

Now the resource is acquired just before you need it, and by that point you're in the context of `IDisposable`, so you can release the resource at the appropriate time. Furthermore, if `GetEnumerator()` is called multiple times on the returned value, each call will result in an independent `TextReader` being created.

You can easily use anonymous methods to add overloads to open files, optionally specifying an encoding:

```
static IEnumerable<string> ReadLines(string filename)
{
    return ReadLines(filename, Encoding.UTF8);
}

static IEnumerable<string> ReadLines(string filename, Encoding encoding)
{
    return ReadLines(delegate {
        return File.OpenText(filename, encoding);
    });
}
```

This example uses generics, an anonymous method (which captures parameters), and an iterator block. All that's missing is nullable value types and you'd have the full house of C# 2's major features. I've used this code on a number of occasions, and it's always much cleaner than the cumbersome code we started off with. As I mentioned earlier, if you're using a recent version of .NET, you've got all this available in `File.ReadLines` anyway, but it's still a neat example of just how useful iterator blocks can be.

As a final example, let's get a first taste of LINQ—even though we'll only use C# 2.

6.3.3 *Filtering items lazily using an iterator block and a predicate*

Even though we haven't started to look at LINQ properly yet, I'm sure you have some idea of what it's about: it allows you to query data in a simple and powerful way across multiple data sources, such as in-memory collections and databases. C# 2 doesn't have any of the language integration for query expressions, nor the lambda expressions and extension methods that can make it so concise, but you can still achieve some of the same effects.

One of the core features of LINQ is filtering with the `Where` method. You provide a collection and a predicate, and the result is a lazily evaluated query that'll yield only the items in the collection that match the predicate. This is a little like `List<T>.FindAll`, but it's lazy and works with any `IEnumerable<T>`. One of the beautiful things about LINQ[5] is that the cleverness is in the design. It's quite simple to implement LINQ to Objects as we'll prove now, at least for the `Where` method. Ironically, even though most of the language features that make LINQ shine are part of C# 3, these are almost all about how you can *access* methods such as `Where`, rather than how they're implemented.

The following listing shows a full example, including simple argument validation, and uses the filter to display all the `using` directives in the source file that contains the sample code itself.

---

[5] Or to be more precise, LINQ to Objects. LINQ providers for databases and the like are far more complex.

> ### Listing 6.9 Implementing LINQ's `Where` method using iterator blocks

```
public static IEnumerable<T> Where<T>(IEnumerable<T> source,
                                      Predicate<T> predicate)
{
    if (source == null || predicate == null)       ←─❶ Eagerly checks arguments
    {
        throw new ArgumentNullException();
    }
    return WhereImpl(source, predicate);            ←─❷ Lazily processes data
}

private static IEnumerable<T> WhereImpl<T>(IEnumerable<T> source,
                                           Predicate<T> predicate)
{
    foreach (T item in source)
    {
        if (predicate(item))       ←─❸ Tests current item against predicate
        {
            yield return item;
        }
    }
}
...
IEnumerable<string> lines = LineReader.ReadLines("../../FakeLinq.cs");
Predicate<string> predicate = delegate(string line)
    { return line.StartsWith("using"); };
foreach (string line in Where(lines, predicate))
{
    Console.WriteLine(line);
}
```

This example splits the implementation into two parts: argument validation and the real business logic of filtering. It's slightly ugly but entirely necessary for sensible error handling. Suppose you put everything in the same method—what would happen when you called `Where<string>(null, null)`? The answer is *nothing*...or, at least, the desired exception wouldn't be thrown. This is due to the lazy semantics of iterator blocks: none of the code in the body of the method runs until the first call to Move-Next(), as you saw in section 6.2.2. Typically you want to check the preconditions to the method *eagerly*—there's no point in delaying the exception, and it just makes debugging harder.

The standard workaround for this is to split the method in half, as in listing 6.9. First you check the arguments ❶ in a normal method, and then you call the method implemented using an iterator block to lazily process the data as and when it's requested ❷.

The iterator block itself is mind-numbingly straightforward: for each item in the original collection, you test the predicate ❸ and yield the value if it matches. If it doesn't match, you try the next item, and so on until you find something that *does* match, or you run out of items. It's straightforward, but a C# 1 implementation would've been much harder to follow (and couldn't have been generic, of course).

The final piece of code to demonstrate the method in action uses the previous example to provide the data—in this case, the source code of the implementation. The predicate simply tests a line to see whether it begins with "using"—it could contain far more complicated logic, of course. I've created separate variables for the data and the predicate just to make the formatting clearer, but it could all have been written inline. It's important to note the principal difference between this example and the equivalent that could've been achieved using `File.ReadAllLines` and `Array.FindAll<string>`. This implementation is entirely lazy and streaming. Only a single line from the source file is ever required in memory at a time. Of course, that wouldn't matter in this particular case where the file is small—but if you imagine a multigigabyte log file, you can see the benefits of this approach.

I hope these examples have given you an inkling of why iterator blocks are so important—as well as perhaps a desire to hurry on and find out more about LINQ. Before that, I'd like to mess with your mind a bit and introduce you to a thoroughly bizarre (but really neat) use of iterators.

6.4   *Pseudo-synchronous code with the Concurrency and Coordination Runtime*

The *Concurrency and Coordination Runtime* (CCR) is a library developed by Microsoft to offer an alternative way of writing asynchronous code that's amenable to complex coordination. At the time of this writing, it's only available as part of the Microsoft Robotics Studio (see http://www.microsoft.com/robotics). Microsoft has been putting a lot of resources into concurrency in various projects, most notably the Task Parallel Library introduced in .NET 4, and the asynchronous language features in C# 5 (supported by a lot of asynchronous APIs). But I wanted to use the CCR to show you how iterator blocks can change the whole execution model. Indeed, it's no coincidence that this early foray into an alternative approach to concurrency uses iterator blocks to change the execution model; the similarities between the state machines generated for iterator blocks and those used for asynchronous functions in C# 5 are striking.

The sample code does work (against dummy services) but the ideas are more important than the details.

Suppose you're writing a server that needs to handle lots of requests. As part of dealing with those requests, you need to first call a web service to fetch an authentication token, and then use that token to get data from two independent data sources (say, a database and another web service). You then process that data and return the result. Each of the fetch stages could take a while—perhaps a few seconds. Normally you might consider the simple synchronous route or the stock asynchronous approach. The synchronous version might look something like this:

```
HoldingsValue ComputeTotalStockValue(string user, string password)
{
    Token token = AuthService.Check(user, password);
    Holdings stocks = DbService.GetStockHoldings(token);
```

```
    StockRates rates = StockService.GetRates(token);
    return ProcessStocks(stocks, rates);
}
```

That's easy to understand, but if each request takes 2 seconds, the whole operation will take 6 seconds and tie up a thread for the whole time it's running. If you want to scale up to hundreds of thousands of requests running in parallel, you're in trouble.

Now let's consider a fairly simple asynchronous version, which avoids tying up a thread when nothing's happening[6] and uses parallel calls where possible:

```
void StartComputingTotalStockValue(string user, string password)
{
    AuthService.BeginCheck(user, password, AfterAuthCheck, null);
}

void AfterAuthCheck(IAsyncResult result)
{
    Token token = AuthService.EndCheck(result);
    IAsyncResult holdingsAsync = DbService.BeginGetStockHoldings
        (token, null, null);
    StockService.BeginGetRates(token, AfterGetRates, holdingsAsync);
}

void AfterGetRates(IAsyncResult result)
{
    IAsyncResult holdingsAsync = (IAsyncResult)result.AsyncState;
    StockRates rates = StockService.EndGetRates(result);
    Holdings stocks = DbService.EndGetStockHoldings(holdingsAsync);
    OnRequestComplete(ProcessStocks(stocks, rates));
}
```

This is much harder to read and understand—and that's only a simple version. The coordination of the two parallel calls is only achievable in a simple way because you don't need to pass any other state around, and even so it's not ideal. If the stock service call completes quickly, you'll still block a thread-pool thread waiting for the database call to complete. More importantly, it's far from obvious what's going on, because the code jumps between different methods.

By now you may be asking yourself where iterators come into the picture. Well, the iterator blocks provided by C# 2 effectively allow you to pause current execution at certain points of the flow through the block and then come back to the same place, with the same state. The clever folks designing the CCR realized that that's exactly what's needed for a *continuation-passing style* of coding. You need to tell the system that there are certain operations you need to perform—including starting other operations asynchronously—but that you're then happy to wait until the asynchronous operations have finished before you continue. You do this by providing the CCR with an implementation of IEnumerator<ITask> (where ITask is an interface defined by the CCR). Here's some code to achieve the same results using this style:

---

[6] Well, mostly. It might still be inefficient, as you'll see in a moment.

```
static IEnumerator<ITask> ComputeTotalStockVal.(str.user,str.pass)
{
    string token = null;
    yield return Arbiter.Receive(false, AuthService.CcrCheck(user, pass),
        delegate(string t) { token = t; });

    IEnumerable<Holding> stocks = null;
    IDictionary<string,decimal> rates = null;
    yield return Arbiter.JoinedReceive(false,
        DbService.CcrGetStockHoldings(token),
        StockService.CcrGetRates(token),
        delegate(IEnumerable<Holding> s, IDictionary<string,decimal> r)
          { stocks = s; rates = r; });

    OnRequestComplete(ComputeTotal(stocks, rates));
}
```

Confused? I certainly was when I first saw it, but now I'm in awe of how neat it is. The CCR calls into your code (with a call to MoveNext on the iterator), and you execute until and including the first yield return statement. The CcrCheck method within AuthService kicks off an asynchronous request, and the CCR waits (without using a dedicated thread) until it has completed, calling the supplied delegate to handle the result. It then calls MoveNext again, and your method continues. This time you kick off two requests in parallel and ask the CCR to call another delegate with the results of both operations when they've *both* finished. After that, MoveNext is called for a final time, and you get to complete the request processing.

Although it's obviously more complicated than the synchronous version, it's still all in one method, it gets executed in the order written, and the method itself can hold the state (in the local variables, which become state in the extra type generated by the compiler). It's fully asynchronous, using as few threads as it can get away with. I haven't shown any error handling, but that's also available in a sensible fashion that forces you to think about the issue at appropriate places.

I've deliberately not gone into the details of the Arbiter class, the ITask interface, and so forth here. I'm not trying to promote the CCR in this section, although it's fascinating to read about and experiment with; I suspect that asynchronous functions in C# 5 will have much more impact on mainstream developers. My point here has been to show that iterators can be used in radically different contexts that have little to do with traditional collections. At the heart of this use of them is the idea of a state machine: two of the tricky aspects of asynchronous development are handling state and effectively pausing until something interesting happens. Iterator blocks are a natural fit for both of these problems, although you'll see in chapter 15 how more targeted language support makes things much cleaner.

6.5   *Summary*

C# supports many patterns indirectly, in terms of it being feasible to implement them in C#. But relatively few patterns are *directly* supported in terms of language features being specifically targeted at a particular pattern. In C# 1, the iterator pattern was directly supported from the point of view of the calling code, but not from the perspective of the collection being iterated over. Writing a correct implementation of IEnumerable was time consuming and error-prone, without being interesting. In C# 2, the compiler does all the mundane work for you, building a state machine to cope with the callback nature of iterators.

It should be noted that iterator blocks have one aspect in common with the anonymous methods you saw in chapter 5, even though the actual features are very different. In both cases, extra types may be generated, and a potentially complicated code transformation is applied to the original source. Compare this with C# 1, where most of the transformations for syntactic sugar (lock, using, and foreach being the most obvious examples) were straightforward. You'll see this trend toward smarter compilation continuing with almost every aspect of C# 3.

I've shown you one piece of LINQ-related functionality in this chapter: filtering a collection. IEnumerable<T> is one of the most important types in LINQ, and if you ever want to write your own LINQ operators on top of LINQ to Objects,[7] you'll be eternally grateful to the C# team for including iterator blocks in the language.

In addition to seeing some real-life examples of the use of iterators, we've looked at how one particular library has used them in a fairly radical way that has little to do with what likely comes to mind when you think about iteration over a collection. It's worth bearing in mind that many languages have also looked at this sort of problem before—in computer science, the term *coroutine* is applied to concepts of this nature, and that's how they're referred to in the Unity 3D game development toolset, where again they're used for asynchrony. Different languages have historically supported them to a greater or lesser extent, with tricks being applicable to simulate them sometimes. For example, Simon Tatham has an excellent article on how even C can express coroutines if you're willing to bend coding standards somewhat (see his "Coroutines in C" article at http://mng.bz/H8YX). You've seen that C# 2 makes coroutines easy to write and use.

Now that you've seen some major and sometimes mind-warping language changes focused around a few key features, the next chapter will be a change of pace. It describes a number of small changes that make C# 2 more pleasant to work with than its predecessor. The designers learned from the little niggles of the past and produced a language that has fewer rough edges, more scope for dealing with awkward backward-compatibility cases, and a better story around working with generated code. Each feature is relatively straightforward, but there are quite a few of them.

---

[7] This is less daunting and more fun than it sounds. We'll look at a few guidelines around this topic in chapter 12.

Concluding C# 2:
the final features

7

So far we've looked at the four biggest new features in C# 2: generics, nullable types, delegate enhancements, and iterator blocks. Each addresses a fairly complex requirement, which is why we've gone into them in some depth. The remaining new features of C# 2 knock a few rough edges off C# 1. They're little niggles that the language designers decided to correct—either areas where the language needed a bit of improvement for its own sake, or where the experience of working with code generation and native code could be made more pleasant.

Over time, Microsoft has received a lot of feedback from the C# community (and its own developers, no doubt) about areas where C# hasn't gleamed quite as brightly as it might. Several smaller changes made it into C# 2 along with the larger ones, alleviating some of these small pain points.

None of the features in this chapter is particularly difficult, and we'll go through them fairly quickly. Don't underestimate how important they are, though. Just because a topic can be explored in a few pages doesn't mean it's useless. You're likely to use some of these features on a frequent basis. Here's a quick rundown of the features covered in this chapter and their uses, so you know what to expect:

- *Partial types*—The ability to write the code for a type in multiple source files. This is particularly handy for types where part of the code is autogenerated and the rest is written manually.
- *Static classes*—For tidying up utility classes so that the compiler can spot when you're trying to use them inappropriately, and making your intentions clearer.
- *Separate getter/setter property access*—Finally, the ability to have a public getter and a private setter for properties! (That's not the only combination available, but it's the most common.)
- *Namespace aliases*—Ways out of sticky situations where type names aren't unique.
- *Pragma directives*—Compiler-specific instructions for actions such as suppressing specific warnings for a particular section of code.
- *Fixed-size buffers*—More control over how structs handle arrays in unsafe code.
- *InternalsVisibleToAttribute (friend assemblies)*—A feature spanning language, framework, and runtime, this allows selected assemblies more access when required.

You may be itching to get on to the sexy stuff from C# 3 by this point, and I don't blame you. Nothing in this chapter is going to set the world on fire—but each of these features can make your life more pleasant, or dig you out of a hole in some cases. Having dampened your expectations somewhat, the first feature is actually pretty nifty.

7.1   Partial types

The first change we'll look at is in response to the power struggle that was usually involved when using code generators with C# 1. For Windows Forms, the designer in Visual Studio required its own regions of code that couldn't be touched by developers, within the same file that developers *had* to edit for user interface functionality. This was clearly a brittle situation.

In other cases, code generators create source that's compiled alongside manually written code. In C# 1, adding extra functionality involved deriving new classes from the autogenerated ones, which is ugly. There are plenty of other scenarios where having an unnecessary link in the inheritance chain can cause problems or reduce encapsulation. For instance, if two different parts of your code want to call each other, you need virtual methods for the parent type to call the child, and protected methods for the reverse situation, where normally you'd use two private nonvirtual methods.

C# 2 allows more than one file to contribute to a type, and IDEs can extend this notion so that some of the code used for a type may not even be visible as C# source code at all. Types built from multiple source files are called *partial types*.

In this section we'll also discuss *partial methods*, which are only relevant in partial types and allow a rich but efficient way of adding manually written hooks into auto-generated code. This is actually a C# 3 feature (this time based on feedback about C# 2), but it's more logical to discuss it when we examine partial types than to wait until the next part of the book.

7.1.1   *Creating a type with multiple files*

Creating a partial type is a cinch—you just need to include the `partial` contextual keyword in the declaration for the type in each file it occurs in. A partial type can be declared within as many files as you like, although all the examples in this section use two.

The compiler effectively combines all the source files together before compiling. This means that code in one file can call code in another and vice versa, as shown in figure 7.1—there's no need for forward references or other tricks.

You can't write half of a member in one file and half of it in another—each individual member has to be completely contained within its own file. You can't start a method in one file and finish it in another, for example.[1] There are a few obvious restrictions about the declarations of the type—the declarations have to be compatible. Any file can specify interfaces to be implemented (and they don't have to be implemented in that file), any file can specify the base type, and any file can specify constraints on a type parameter. But if multiple files specify a base type, those base types have to be the same, and if multiple files specify type constraints, the constraints have to be identical. The

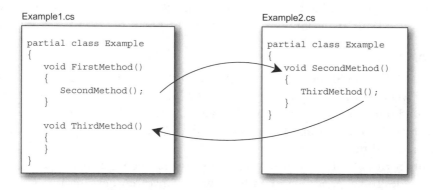

Figure 7.1   Code in partial types is able to see all of the members of the type, regardless of which file each member is in.

---

[1] There's an exception here: partial types can contain nested partial types spread across the same set of files.

following listing shows an example of the flexibility afforded (while not doing anything even remotely useful).

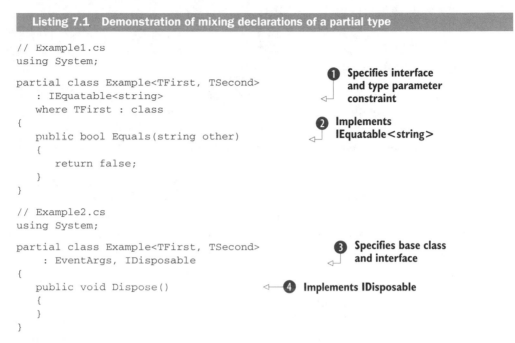

Listing 7.1 Demonstration of mixing declarations of a partial type

```
// Example1.cs
using System;

partial class Example<TFirst, TSecond>        ❶ Specifies interface
    : IEquatable<string>                          and type parameter
    where TFirst : class                          constraint
{
    public bool Equals(string other)          ❷ Implements
    {                                             IEquatable<string>
        return false;
    }
}

// Example2.cs
using System;

partial class Example<TFirst, TSecond>        ❸ Specifies base class
    : EventArgs, IDisposable                      and interface
{
    public void Dispose()                     ⟵ ❹ Implements IDisposable
    {
    }
}
```

I stress that this listing is *solely* for the purpose of talking about what's legal in a declaration—the types involved were only picked for convenience and familiarity. You can see that both declarations (❶ and ❸) contribute to the list of interfaces that must be implemented. In this example, each file implements the interfaces it declares, and that's a common scenario, but it would be legal to move the implementation of IDisposable ❹ to Example1.cs and the implementation of IEquatable<string> ❷ to Example2.cs. I've used the ability to specify interfaces separately from the implementation myself, encapsulating methods with the same signature generated for multiple different types into an interface. The code generator doesn't know about the interface, so it doesn't know to declare that the type implements it.

Only the first declaration ❶ specifies any type constraints, and only the second ❸ specifies a base class. If the first declaration ❶ had specified a base class, it would have to be EventArgs, and if the second declaration had specified any type constraints, they'd have to be exactly as in the first. In particular, you can't specify a type constraint for TSecond in the second declaration, even though it's not mentioned in the first. Both types have to have the same access modifier, if any—you can't make one declaration internal and the other public, for example. Essentially, the rules around combining files allow flexibility in most cases while encouraging consistency.

In single file types, the initialization of member and static variables is guaranteed to occur in the order they appear in the file, but there's no guaranteed order when multiple files are involved. Relying on the order of declaration within the file is brittle to start with—it leaves your code open to subtle bugs if a developer decides to "harmlessly" move things around—so it's worth avoiding this situation where you can. You should *particularly* avoid it with partial types.

Now that you know what you can and can't do, let's take a closer look at why you'd *want* to do it.

7.1.2   Uses of partial types

As I mentioned earlier, partial types are primarily useful in conjunction with designers and other code generators. If a code generator has to modify a file that's owned by a developer, there's always a risk of things going wrong. With the partial types model, a code generator can own the file where it'll work and completely overwrite the whole file every time it wants to.

Some code generators may choose not to generate a C# file at all until the build is well under way. For instance, Snippy has Extensible Application Markup Language (XAML) files that describe the user interface. When the project is built, each XAML file is converted into a C# file in the obj directory (the filenames end with *.g.cs* to show they've been generated) and compiled along with the partial class providing extra code for that type (typically event handlers and extra construction code). This completely prevents developers from tweaking the generated code, at least without going to the extreme lengths of hacking the build file.

I've been careful to use the phrase *code generator* instead of *designer* because there are plenty of code generators around other than designers. For instance, in Visual Studio, web service proxies are generated as partial classes, and you may have your own tools that generate code based on other data sources. One reasonably common example of this is object-relational mapping (ORM)—some ORM tools use database entity descriptions from a configuration file (or straight from the database) and generate partial classes representing those entities. Likewise my .NET port of the Google Protocol Buffers serialization framework generates partial classes—a feature that has proven useful even within the implementation itself.

This makes it straightforward to add behavior to the type—overriding virtual methods of the base class, adding new members with business logic, and so forth. It's a great way of letting the developer and the tool work together, rather than constantly squabbling about who's in charge.

One scenario that's occasionally useful is for one file to be generated containing multiple partial types, and then some of those types are enhanced in other files, with one manually generated file per type. To return to the ORM example, the tool could generate a single file containing all the entity definitions, and some of those entities could have extra code provided by the developer, using one file per entity. This keeps the number of automatically generated files low, but still provides good visibility of the manual code involved.

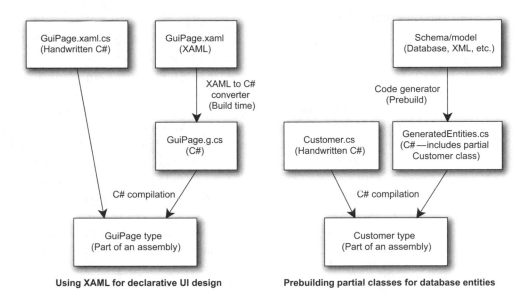

Figure 7.2 Comparison between XAML precompilation and autogenerated entity classes

Figure 7.2 shows how the uses of partial types for XAML and entities are similar, but with slightly different timing involved when it comes to creating the autogenerated C# code.

A somewhat different use of partial types is as an aid to refactoring. Sometimes a type gets too big and assumes too many responsibilities. One first step to dividing the bloated type into smaller, more coherent types can be to split it into a partial type over two or more files. This can be done with no risk and in an experimental manner, moving methods between files until each file addresses a single concern. Although the next step of splitting the type up is still far from automatic, it should be a lot easier to see the end goal.

One final use to mention: unit testing. Often the set of unit tests for a class can end up being much larger than the implementation itself. One way to split the tests into more understandable chunks is to use partial types. You can still easily run all the tests for a type in one go (since you still have a single test class), but you can easily see the tests for different areas of functionality in different files. By hand-editing the project file, you can even have the same parent/child expansion in Solution Explorer as you see when partial types are used for Visual Studio's generated code. This won't be to everyone's taste, but I've found it to be a useful way of managing tests.

When partial types first appeared in C# 2, no one knew exactly how they'd be used. One feature that was almost immediately requested was a way to provide optional extra code for generated methods to call. This need has been addressed by C# 3 with partial methods.

7.1.3   *Partial methods—C# 3 only!*

To reiterate my previous explanation, the rest of this part of the book just deals with C# 2 features, but partial methods don't fit with any of the other C# 3 features and they *do* fit in well when describing partial types. Apologies for any confusion this may cause.

Back to the feature: sometimes you want to be able to specify behavior in a manually created file and use that behavior from an automatically generated file. For instance, in a class that has lots of automatically generated properties, you might want to be able to specify code to be executed to validate a new value for some of those properties. Another common scenario is for a code generator to include constructors—manually written code may want to hook into object construction to set default values, perform some logging, and so forth.

In C# 2, these requirements can only be met either by using events that the manually generated code can subscribe to, or by making the automatically generated code *assume* that the handwritten code will include methods of a particular name—making all the code fail to compile unless the relevant methods are provided. Alternatively, the generated code can provide a base class with virtual methods that do nothing by default. The manually generated code can then derive from the class and override some or all of the methods.

All of these solutions are somewhat messy. C# 3's partial methods effectively provide *optional* hooks that have no cost whatsoever if they're not implemented—any calls to the unimplemented partial methods are removed by the compiler. This allows tools to be very generous in terms of the hooks they provide. In the compiled code, you only pay for what you use.

It's easiest to understand this with an example. The following listing shows a partial type specified in two files, with the constructor in the automatically generated code calling two partial methods, one of which is implemented in the manually generated code.

Listing 7.2   A partial method called from a constructor

```
// Generated.cs
using System;
partial class PartialMethodDemo
{
    public PartialMethodDemo()
    {
        OnConstructorStart();
        Console.WriteLine("Generated constructor");
        OnConstructorEnd();
    }

    partial void OnConstructorStart();
    partial void OnConstructorEnd();
}

// Handwritten.cs
```

```
using System;
partial class PartialMethodDemo
{
    partial void OnConstructorEnd()
    {
        Console.WriteLine("Manual code");
    }
}
```

As shown in listing 7.2, partial methods are declared just like abstract methods: by providing the signature without any implementation but using the `partial` modifier. Similarly, the actual implementations just have the `partial` modifier but are otherwise like normal methods.

Calling the parameterless constructor of `PartialMethodDemo` would result in `Generated constructor` and then `Manual code` being printed out. If you examined the IL for the constructor, you wouldn't see a call to `OnConstructorStart` because it no longer exists—there's no trace of it anywhere in the compiled type.

Because the method may not exist, partial methods must have a return type of `void`, and they can't take `out` parameters. They have to be private, but they can be static and/or generic. If the method isn't implemented in one of the files, the whole statement calling it is removed, *including any argument evaluations.*

If evaluating any of the arguments has a side effect that you want to occur whether or not the partial method is implemented, you should perform the evaluation separately. For instance, suppose you have the following code:

```
LogEntity(LoadAndCache(id));
```

Here `LogEntity` is a partial method, and `LoadAndCache` loads an entity from the database and inserts it into the cache. You might want to use this instead:

```
MyEntity entity = LoadAndCache(id);
LogEntity(entity);
```

That way, the entity is loaded and cached regardless of whether an implementation has been provided for `LogEntity`. Of course, if the entity can be loaded equally cheaply later on, and may not even be required, you should leave the statement in the first form and avoid an unnecessary load in some cases.

To be honest, unless you're writing your own code generators, you're more likely to be implementing partial methods than declaring and calling them. If you're only implementing them, you don't need to worry about the argument evaluation side of things.

In summary, partial methods in C# 3 allow generated code to interact with handwritten code in a rich manner without any performance penalties for situations where the interaction is unnecessary. This is a natural continuation of the C# 2 partial types feature, which enables a much more productive relationship between code generators and developers.

The next feature is entirely different. It's a way of telling the compiler more about the intended nature of a type so that it can perform more checking on both the type itself and any code using it.

7.2 Static classes

The second new feature is in some ways completely unnecessary—it just makes things tidier and more elegant when you write *utility classes.*

Everyone has utility classes. I haven't seen a significant project in either Java or C# that didn't have at least one class consisting solely of static methods. The classic example in developer code is a type with string helper methods, doing anything from escaping, reversing, smart replacing—you name it. An example from the framework is the System.Math class.

The key features of a utility class are as follows:

- All members are static (except a private constructor).
- The class derives directly from object.
- Typically there's no state at all, unless some caching or a singleton is involved.
- There are no visible constructors.
- The class is sealed if the developer remembers to do so.

The last two points are optional, and if there are no visible constructors (including protected ones), the class is *effectively* sealed anyway. Both of them help make the purpose of the class more obvious, though.

The following listing gives an example of a C# 1 utility class. Then we'll look at how C# 2 improves matters.

Listing 7.3   A typical C# 1 utility class

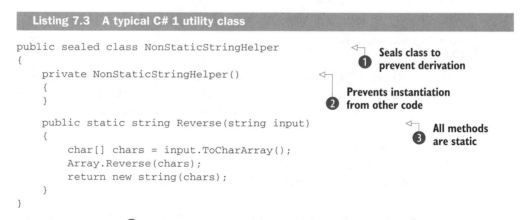

```
public sealed class NonStaticStringHelper          ◁      Seals class to
{                                                   ❶     prevent derivation
    private NonStaticStringHelper()        ◁
    {                                      ❷  Prevents instantiation
    }                                         from other code
    public static string Reverse(string input)      ◁   All methods
    {                                            ❸      are static
        char[] chars = input.ToCharArray();
        Array.Reverse(chars);
        return new string(chars);
    }
}
```

The class is sealed ❶ so that no one tries to derive from it. Inheritance is supposed to be about specialization, and there's nothing to specialize here, as all the members are static ❸ except the private constructor ❷. That constructor may seem odd at first sight—why have it at all if it's private and never going to be used? The reason is that if you don't supply any constructors for a class, the C# 1 compiler will always provide a *default constructor* that's public and parameterless. In this case, you don't want any visible constructors, so you have to provide a private one.

This pattern works reasonably well, but C# 2 makes it explicit and actively prevents the type from being misused. First, we'll look at what changes are needed to turn listing 7.3 into a proper static class, as defined in C# 2. As you can see in the following listing, little action is required.

Listing 7.4   The same utility class as in listing 7.3, but converted into a C# 2 static class

```
using System;

public static class StringHelper
{
    public static string Reverse(string input)
    {
        char[] chars = input.ToCharArray();
        Array.Reverse(chars);
        return new string(chars);
    }
}
```

You use the `static` modifier in the class declaration this time instead of `sealed`, and you don't include a constructor at all—those are the only code differences. The C# 2 compiler knows that a static class shouldn't have any constructors, so it doesn't provide a default one.

In fact, the compiler enforces a number of constraints on the class definition:

- It can't be declared as `abstract` or `sealed`, although it's implicitly both.
- It can't specify any implemented interfaces.
- It can't specify a base type.
- It can't include any nonstatic members, including constructors.
- It can't include any operators.
- It can't include any `protected` or `protected internal` members.

It's worth noting that although all the members must be static, you have to *explicitly* make them static. Although nested types are implicitly static members of the enclosing class, the nested type itself can be a nonstatic type if that's required.

The compiler doesn't just put constraints on the definition of static classes—it also guards against their misuse. Because it knows that there can never be any instances of the class, it prevents any use that would require one. For instance, all of the following are invalid when `StringHelper` is a static class:

```
StringHelper variable = null;
StringHelper[] array = null;
public void Method1(StringHelper x) {}
public StringHelper Method1() { return null; }
List<StringHelper> x = new List<StringHelper>();
```

None of these is prevented if the class follows the C# 1 pattern, but all of them are essentially useless. In short, static classes in C# 2 don't allow you to do anything you couldn't do before, but they prevent you from doing things that you *shouldn't* have been doing anyway. They also explicitly state your intentions. By making a class static, you're saying that you definitely *don't want* any instances to be created. It's not just a quirk of the implementation; it's a design choice.

The next feature on the list has a more positive feel. It's aimed at a specific—although widely encountered—situation, and allows a solution that's neither ugly nor breaks encapsulation, which was the choice available in C# 1.

7.3   *Separate getter/setter property access*

I'll admit to being bemused when I first saw that C# 1 didn't allow you to have a public getter and a private setter for properties. This isn't the only combination of access modifiers that's prohibited by C# 1, but it's the most commonly desired one. In fact, in C# 1 both the getter and the setter need to have the same accessibility—it's declared as part of the property declaration rather than as part of the getter or setter.

There are perfectly good reasons to want different accessibility for the getter and the setter. Often you may want some validation, logging, locking, or other code to be executed when changing a variable that backs the property, but you don't want to make the property writable to code outside the class. In C# 1 the alternatives were either to break encapsulation by making the property publicly writable against your better judgment or to write a SetXXX() method in the class to do the setting, which frankly looks ugly when you're used to real properties.

C# 2 fixes the problem by allowing either the getter or the setter to explicitly have more restrictive access than that declared for the property itself. This is most easily seen with an example:

```
string name;

public string Name
{
    get { return name; }
    private set
    {
        // Validation, logging etc here
        name = value;
    }
}
```

In this case, the Name property is effectively read-only to all other types,[2] but you can use the familiar property syntax for setting the property within the type itself. The same syntax is also available for indexers as well as properties. You *could* make the setter more public than the getter (a protected getter and a public setter, for example), but that's a pretty rare situation, in the same way that write-only properties are few and far between compared with read-only properties.

---

[2] Except nested types, which always have access to private members of their enclosing types.

TRIVIA: THE ONLY PLACE WHERE "PRIVATE" IS REQUIRED Everywhere else in C#, the default access modifier in any given situation is the most private one possible. For example, if something can be declared to be private, it will default to private if you don't specify any access modifiers. This is a nice element of language design, because it's hard to get it wrong accidentally; if you want something to be more public than it is, you'll notice when you try to use it. But if you accidentally make something too public, the compiler can't help you spot the problem. Specifying the access of a property getter or setter is the one exception to this rule—if you don't specify anything, the default is to give the getter or setter the same access as the overall property itself.

Note that you can't declare the property itself to be private and make the getter public—you can only make a particular getter or setter *more* private than the property. Also, you can't specify an access modifier for both the getter and the setter—that would be silly, as you could declare the property itself to be whichever is the more public of the two modifiers.

This aid to encapsulation is extremely welcome. There's still nothing in C# 2 to stop other code in the same class from bypassing the property and going directly to whatever fields are backing it, unfortunately. As you'll see in the next chapter, C# 3 fixes this in one particular case, but not in general.

We'll now move from a feature you may want to use regularly to one that you'll want to avoid most of the time—it allows your code to be absolutely explicit in terms of which types it's referring to, but at a significant cost to readability.

7.4   *Namespace aliases*

Namespaces are primarily intended as a means of organizing types into a useful hierarchy. They *also* allow you to keep fully qualified names of types distinct even when the unqualified names may be the same. This shouldn't be seen as an invitation to reuse unqualified type names without good cause, but there are times when it's the natural thing to do.

An example of this is the unqualified name `Button`. There are two classes with that name in the .NET 2.0 Framework: `System.Windows.Forms.Button` and `System.Web.UI.WebControls.Button`. Although they're both called `Button`, it's easy to tell them apart by their namespaces. This mirrors real life closely—you may know several people called Jon, but you're unlikely to know anyone else called Jon Skeet. If you're talking with friends in a particular context, you may be able to use just the name Jon without specifying which one you're talking about, but in other contexts you may need to provide more exact information.

The `using` directive of C# 1 (not to be confused with the `using` statement that calls `Dispose` automatically) was available in two flavors: one created an *alias* for a namespace or type (for example, `using Out = System.Console;`) and the other introduced a namespace into the list of contexts the compiler would search when looking for a type (for example, `using System.IO;`). By and large, this was adequate, but there were a few situations that the language couldn't cope with. In some other cases, automatically generated code would have to go out of its way to make absolutely sure that the right namespaces and types were being used whatever happened.

C# 2 fixes these problems, bringing additional expressiveness to the language. You can now write code that's guaranteed to mean what you want it to regardless of which other types, assemblies, and namespaces are introduced. These extreme measures are rarely needed outside automatically generated code, but it's nice to know that they're there when you need them.

In C# 2 there are three types of aliases: the namespace aliases of C# 1, the *global* namespace alias, and *extern* aliases. We'll start off with the one type of alias that was already present in C# 1, but we'll introduce a new way of using aliases to ensure that the compiler knows to treat it as an alias rather than checking to see whether it's the name of another namespace or type.

7.4.1   *Qualifying namespace aliases*

Even in C# 1, it was a good idea to avoid namespace aliases wherever possible. Every so often you might find that one type name clashed with another—as with the previous `Button` example—so you either had to specify the full name including the namespace every time you used it, or you needed an alias that distinguished the two, in some ways acting like a shortened form of the namespace. The following listing shows an example where the two types of `Button` are used, qualified by an alias.

Listing 7.5   Using aliases to distinguish between different `Button` types

```
using System;
using WinForms = System.Windows.Forms;
using WebForms = System.Web.UI.WebControls;

class Test
{
    static void Main()
    {
        Console.WriteLine(typeof(WinForms.Button));
        Console.WriteLine(typeof(WebForms.Button));
    }
}
```

Listing 7.5 compiles without any errors or warnings, although it's still not as pleasant as it would be if you only needed to deal with one kind of `Button` to start with. There's a problem, though—what if someone were to introduce a type or namespace called `WinForms` or `WebForms`? The compiler wouldn't know what `WinForms.Button` meant and would use the type or namespace in preference to the alias. You want to be able to tell the compiler that you need it to treat `WinForms` as an alias, even though it's available elsewhere.

C# 2 introduces the `::` *namespace alias qualifier* syntax to do this, as shown in the following listing.

Listing 7.6 Using : : to tell the compiler to use aliases

```
using System;
using WinForms = System.Windows.Forms;
using WebForms = System.Web.UI.WebControls;

class WinForms {}

class Test
{
    static void Main()
    {
        Console.WriteLine(typeof(WinForms::Button));
        Console.WriteLine(typeof(WebForms::Button));
    }
}
```

Instead of `WinForms.Button`, listing 7.6 uses `WinForms::Button`, and the compiler is happy. If you change the `::` back to `.` you'll get a compilation error.

So if you use `::` everywhere you use an alias, you'll be fine, right? Well, not quite…

7.4.2 *The global namespace alias*

There's one part of the namespace hierarchy that you can't define your own alias for: the root of it, or the *global* namespace. Suppose you have two classes, both named `Configuration`—one within a namespace of `MyCompany` and the other with no namespace specified at all. How can you refer to the root `Configuration` class from within the `MyCompany` namespace? You can't use a normal alias, and if you just specify `Configuration`, the compiler will use `MyCompany.Configuration`.

In C# 1, there was no way of getting around this. Again, C# 2 comes to the rescue, allowing you to use `global::Configuration` to tell the compiler exactly what you want. The following listing demonstrates both the problem and the solution.

```
using System;

class Configuration {}

namespace Chapter7
{
    class Configuration {}

    class Test
    {
        static void Main()
        {
            Console.WriteLine(typeof(Configuration));
            Console.WriteLine(typeof(global::Configuration));
            Console.WriteLine(typeof(global::Chapter7.Test));
        }
    }
}
```

Most of listing 7.7 just sets up the situation—the three lines within `Main` are the interesting ones. The first line prints `Chapter7.Configuration` as the compiler resolves `Configuration` to that type before moving out to the namespace root. The second line indicates that the type has to be in the global namespace, so it simply prints `Configuration`. I included the third line to demonstrate that by using the global alias, you can still refer to types within namespaces, but you have to specify the fully qualified name.

At this point, you can get to any uniquely named type, using the global namespace alias if necessary. If you ever write a code generator where the code doesn't need to be readable, you might want to use this feature liberally to make sure that you always refer to the correct type regardless of any other types that are present by the time the code is compiled. But what do you do if the type's name isn't unique even when you include its namespace? The plot thickens...

7.4.3   *Extern aliases*

At the start of this section, I referred to human names as examples of namespaces and contexts. I specifically said that you're unlikely to know more than one person called Jon Skeet. But I know that there *is* more than one person with my name, and it's not beyond the realm of possibility that you might know two or more of us. In this case, in order to specify which one you mean, you'd have to provide some more information beyond just the full name—the reason you know the particular person, or the country they live in, or something similarly distinctive.

C# 2 lets you specify that extra information in the form of an *extern alias*—a name that exists not only in your source code, but also in the parameters you pass to the compiler. For the Microsoft C# compiler, this means specifying the assembly that contains the types in question. Suppose that two assemblies—`First.dll` and `Second.dll`—both contain a type called `Demo.Example`. You can't just use the fully qualified name to distinguish them, as they both have the same fully qualified name. Instead, you can use extern aliases to specify which you mean. The following listing shows an example of the C# code involved, along with the command line needed to compile it.

Listing 7.8   Working with different types of the same type in different assemblies

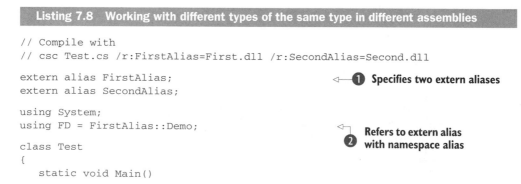

```
// Compile with
// csc Test.cs /r:FirstAlias=First.dll /r:SecondAlias=Second.dll

extern alias FirstAlias;                          ①  Specifies two extern aliases
extern alias SecondAlias;

using System;
using FD = FirstAlias::Demo;                       ②  Refers to extern alias
                                                       with namespace alias
class Test
{
    static void Main()
```

```
{
    Console.WriteLine(typeof(FD.Example));
    Console.WriteLine(typeof(SecondAlias::Demo.Example));
}
}
```

❸ Uses namespace alias

❹ Uses extern alias directly

The code in listing 7.8 is straightforward. The first thing you have to do is introduce the two extern aliases ❶. After that, you can use them either via namespace aliases (❷ and ❸) or directly ❹. In fact, a normal `using` directive without an alias (such as `using FirstAlias::Demo;`) would've allowed you to use the name `Example` without any further qualification at all. One extern alias can cover multiple assemblies, and several extern aliases can all refer to the same assembly, although I'd think carefully before using either of these features, and particularly before combining them.

To specify an extern alias in Visual Studio, just select the assembly reference within Solution Explorer and modify the Aliases value in the Properties window, as shown in figure 7.3.

Hopefully I don't need to persuade you to avoid this kind of situation whenever you can. It can be necessary to work with assemblies from different third parties who happen to have used the same fully qualified type names, at which point you'd otherwise be stuck. Where you have more control over the naming, though, make sure that your names never lead you into this territory.

The next feature is almost a metafeature. The exact functionality it provides depends on which compiler you're using, because its purpose is to enable control over compiler-specific features. We'll concentrate on the Microsoft compiler.

Figure 7.3 Part of the Properties window of Visual Studio 2010, showing an extern alias of FirstAlias for the First.dll reference

7.5 Pragma directives

Describing *pragma directives* in general is extremely easy: a pragma directive is a preprocessing directive represented by a line beginning with `#pragma`. The rest of the line can contain any text at all. The result of a pragma directive can't change the behavior of the program to contravene anything within the C# language specification, but it can do anything outside the scope of the specification. If the compiler doesn't understand a particular pragma directive, it can issue a warning, but not an error.

That's basically everything the specification has to say on the subject. The Microsoft C# compiler understands two pragma directives: warnings and checksums.

7.5.1 Warning pragmas

Occasionally, the C# compiler issues warnings that are justifiable but annoying. The correct response to a compiler warning is *almost always* to fix your code—it's rarely made any worse by fixing the cause of the warning, and usually it's improved.

But sometimes there's a good reason to ignore a warning, and that's what warning pragmas are available for. As an example, you'll create a private field that's never read from or written to. It's almost always going to be useless...unless you happen to know that it'll be used by reflection. The following listing is a complete class demonstrating this.

Listing 7.9   Class containing an unused field

```
public class FieldUsedOnlyByReflection
{
    int x;
}
```

If you try to compile listing 7.9, you'll get a warning message like this:

```
FieldUsedOnlyByReflection.cs(3,9): warning CS0169:
The private field 'FieldUsedOnlyByReflection.x' is never used
```

That's the output from the command-line compiler. In the Error List window of Visual Studio, you can see the same information (plus the project it's in) *except* that you don't get the warning number (CS0169). To find the number, you need to either select the warning and bring up the help related to it, or look in the Output window, where the full text is shown. You need the number in order to make the code compile without warnings, as shown in the following listing.

Listing 7.10   Disabling (and restoring) warning CS0169

```
public class FieldUsedOnlyByReflection
{
#pragma warning disable 0169
    int x;
#pragma warning restore 0169
}
```

Listing 7.10 is self-explanatory—the first pragma disables the specified warning, and the second one restores it. It's good practice to disable warnings for as short a time as you can, so that you don't miss any warnings you genuinely ought to fix. If you want to disable or restore multiple warnings in a single line, just use a comma-separated list of warning numbers. If you don't specify any warning numbers at all, the result is to disable or restore *all* warnings in one fell swoop, but that's a bad idea in almost every imaginable scenario.

7.5.2   *Checksum pragmas*

You're unlikely to need the second form of pragma recognized by the Microsoft compiler. It supports the debugger by allowing it to check that it's found the right source file. Normally when a C# file is compiled, the compiler generates a checksum from the file and includes it in the debugging information. When the debugger needs to locate a source file and finds multiple potential matches, it can generate the checksum itself for each of the candidate files and see which is correct.

When an ASP.NET page is converted into C#, the generated file is what the C# compiler sees. The generator calculates the checksum of the .aspx page and uses a checksum pragma to tell the C# compiler to use *that* checksum instead of calculating one from the generated page.

The syntax of the checksum pragma is

```
#pragma checksum "filename" "{guid}" "checksum bytes"
```

The GUID indicates which hashing algorithm has been used to calculate the checksum. The documentation for the `CodeChecksumPragma` class gives GUIDs for SHA-1 and MD5, should you ever wish to implement your own dynamic compilation framework with debugger support.

It's possible that future versions of the C# compiler will include more pragma directives, and other compilers (such as the Mono compiler, mcs) could have their own support for different features. Consult your compiler documentation for the most up-to-date information.

The next feature is another one that you may never use, but if you ever do, it's likely to make your life somewhat simpler.

7.6   *Fixed-size buffers in unsafe code*

When calling into native code with P/Invoke, it's not unusual to find yourself dealing with a structure that's defined to have a buffer of a particular length within it. Prior to C# 2, such structures were difficult to handle directly, even with unsafe code. Now you can declare a buffer of the right size to be embedded directly with the rest of the data for the structure.

This capability isn't just available for calling native code, although that's its primary use. You could use it to easily populate a data structure directly corresponding to a file format, for instance. The syntax is simple, and once again we'll demonstrate it with an example. To create a field that embeds an array of 20 bytes within its enclosing structure, you'd use

```
fixed byte data[20];
```

This would allow `data` to be used as if it were a `byte*` (a pointer to byte data), although the implementation used by the C# compiler is to create a new nested type within the declaring type and apply the new `FixedBuffer` attribute to the variable itself. The CLR then takes care of allocating the memory appropriately.

One downside of this feature is that it's only available within unsafe code: the enclosing structure has to be declared in an unsafe context, and you can only use the fixed-size buffer member within an unsafe context. This limits the situations in which it's useful, but it can still be a nice trick to have up your sleeve. Also, fixed-size buffers are only applicable to primitive types and can't be members of classes (only structures).

There are remarkably few Windows APIs where this feature is directly useful. Numerous situations call for a fixed array of characters—the `TIME_ZONE_INFORMATION` structure, for example—but unfortunately fixed-size buffers of characters appear to be handled poorly by P/Invoke, with the marshaler getting in the way.

The following listing shows one example, though—a console application that displays the colors available in the current console window. It uses an API function, `Get-ConsoleScreenBufferEx`, that was introduced in Windows Vista and Windows Server 2008 and that retrieves extended console information. The following listing displays all 16 colors in hexadecimal format (`bbggrr`).

Listing 7.11 Demonstration of fixed-size buffers to obtain console color information

```
using System;
using System.Runtime.InteropServices;

struct COORD
{
    public short X, Y;
}

struct SMALL_RECT
{
    public short Left, Top, Right, Bottom;
}

unsafe struct CONSOLE_SCREEN_BUFFER_INFOEX
{
    public int StructureSize;
    public COORD ConsoleSize, CursorPosition;
    public short Attributes;
    public SMALL_RECT DisplayWindow;
    public COORD MaximumWindowSize;
    public short PopupAttributes;
    public int FullScreenSupported;
    public fixed int ColorTable[16];
}

static class FixedSizeBufferDemo
{
    const int StdOutputHandle = -11;

    [DllImport("kernel32.dll")]
    static extern IntPtr GetStdHandle(int nStdHandle);

    [DllImport("kernel32.dll")]
    static extern bool GetConsoleScreenBufferInfoEx
        (IntPtr handle, ref CONSOLE_SCREEN_BUFFER_INFOEX info);

    unsafe static void Main()
    {
        IntPtr handle = GetStdHandle(StdOutputHandle);
        CONSOLE_SCREEN_BUFFER_INFOEX info;
        info = new CONSOLE_SCREEN_BUFFER_INFOEX();
        info.StructureSize = sizeof(CONSOLE_SCREEN_BUFFER_INFOEX);
        GetConsoleScreenBufferInfoEx(handle, ref info);

        for (int i=0; i < 16; i++)
        {
```

```
            Console.WriteLine ("{0:x6}", info.ColorTable[i]);
        }
    }
}
```

Listing 7.11 uses fixed-size buffers for the table of colors. Before fixed-size buffers, you could have used the API either with a field for each color table entry or by marshaling a normal array as `UnmanagedType.ByValArray`. But this would've created a separate array on the heap instead of keeping the information all within the structure. That's not a problem here, but in some high-performance situations it's nice to be able to keep lumps of data together. On a different performance note, if the buffer is part of a data structure on the managed heap, you have to pin it before accessing it. If you do this a lot, it can significantly affect the garbage collector. Stack-based structures don't have this problem, of course.

I don't claim that fixed-size buffers are a hugely important feature in C# 2—at least, not to most people. I've included them here for completeness, and doubtless someone, somewhere, will find them invaluable.

The final feature we'll look at can barely be called a C# 2 *language* feature at all, but it *just* about counts.

7.7   *Exposing internal members to selected assemblies*

Some features are obviously in the language—iterator blocks, for example. Some features obviously belong to the runtime, such as JIT compiler optimizations. Some clearly sit in both camps, such as generics. This last feature has a toe in both but is sufficiently odd that it doesn't merit a mention in *either* specification. In addition, it uses a term that has different meanings in C++ and VB.NET, adding a third meaning to the mix. To be fair, all the terms are used in the context of access permissions, but they have different effects.

7.7.1   *Friend assemblies in the simple case*

In .NET 1.1 it was entirely accurate to say that something defined to be *internal* (whether a type, a method, a property, a variable, or an event) could only be accessed within the same assembly in which it was declared.[3] In .NET 2.0 that's still *mostly* true, but there's a new attribute that lets you bend the rules slightly: `InternalsVisible-ToAttribute`, usually referred to as just `InternalsVisibleTo`. (When applying an attribute whose name ends with `Attribute`, the C# compiler will apply the suffix automatically.)

`InternalsVisibleTo` can only be applied to an assembly (not a specific member), and you can apply it multiple times to the same assembly. I'll call the assembly containing the attribute the *source assembly*, although this is unofficial terminology. When you apply the attribute, you have to specify another assembly, known as the *friend assembly*. The result is that the friend assembly can see all the internal members of the

---

[3] Using reflection when running with suitable permissions doesn't count.

source assembly as if they were public. This may sound alarming, but it can be useful, as you'll see in a minute.

The following listing shows this with three classes in three different assemblies.

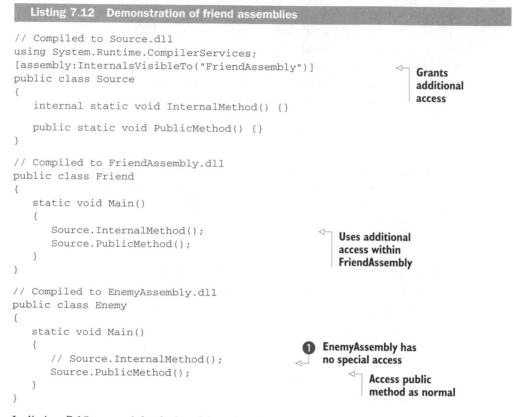

Listing 7.12   Demonstration of friend assemblies

```
// Compiled to Source.dll
using System.Runtime.CompilerServices;
[assembly:InternalsVisibleTo("FriendAssembly")]          Grants
public class Source                                      additional
{                                                        access
    internal static void InternalMethod() {}

    public static void PublicMethod() {}
}

// Compiled to FriendAssembly.dll
public class Friend
{
    static void Main()
    {
        Source.InternalMethod();        Uses additional
        Source.PublicMethod();          access within
    }                                   FriendAssembly
}

// Compiled to EnemyAssembly.dll
public class Enemy
{
    static void Main()
    {                                        EnemyAssembly has
        // Source.InternalMethod();          no special access
        Source.PublicMethod();
    }                                    Access public
}                                        method as normal
```

In listing 7.12, a special relationship exists between FriendAssembly.dll and Source.dll, although it only operates one way: Source.dll has no access to internal members of FriendAssembly.dll. If you were to uncomment the line at ❶, the Enemy class would fail to compile.

Why on earth would you want to open up your well-designed assembly to certain assemblies to start with?

7.7.2   *Why use InternalsVisibleTo?*

I rarely use InternalsVisibleTo between two production assemblies. I can see how it could be useful, and I've certainly used it for extra access when writing tools, but my primary use of it has always been unit testing.

Some say you should only test the public interface to code. Personally I'm happy to test whatever I can in the simplest manner possible. Friend assemblies make that a lot easier: suddenly it's trivial to test code that only has internal access without taking the dubious step of making members public just for the sake of testing or including the test code within the production assembly. (It does occasionally mean making members internal for the sake of testing where they might otherwise be private, but that's less worrying.)

The only downside to this is that the name of your test assembly lives on in your production assembly. In theory, this could represent a security attack vector if your assemblies aren't signed and if your code normally operates under a restricted set of permissions. (Anyone with full trust could use reflection to access the members in the first place. You could do that yourself for unit tests, but it's much nastier.) If this ever ends up as a genuine issue for anyone, I'll be very surprised. But it does bring the option of signing assemblies into the picture. Just when you thought this was a nice, simple little feature...

7.7.3 *InternalsVisibleTo and signed assemblies*

If a friend assembly is signed, the source assembly needs to specify the public key of the friend assembly, to make sure it's trusting the right code. You need the full public key, not just the public key token.

For instance, consider the following command line and output (rewrapped and modified slightly for formatting) used to discover the public key of a signed Friend-Assembly.dll:

```
c:\Users\Jon\Test>sn -Tp FriendAssembly.dll
Microsoft (R) .NET Framework Strong Name Utility Version 3.5.21022.8
Copyright (c) Microsoft Corporation. All rights reserved.
Public key is
0024000004800000940000000602000000240000525341310004000001
000100a51372c81ccfb8fba9c5fb84180c4129e50f0facdce932cf31fe
563d0fe3cb6b1d5129e28326060a3a539f287aaf59affc5aabc4d8f981
e1a82479ab795f410eab22e3266033c633400463ee7513378bb4ef41fc
0cae5fb03986d133677c82a865b278c48d99dc251201b9c43edd7bedef
d4b5306efd0dec7787ec6b664471c2

Public key token is 647b99330b7f792c
```

The source code for the Source class would now need to have this as the attribute:

```
[assembly:InternalsVisibleTo("FriendAssembly,PublicKey=" +
"0024000004800000940000000602000000240000525341310004000001" +
"000100a51372c81ccfb8fba9c5fb84180c4129e50f0facdce932cf31fe" +
"563d0fe3cb6b1d5129e28326060a3a539f287aaf59affc5aabc4d8f981" +
"e1a82479ab795f410eab22e3266033c633400463ee7513378bb4ef41fc" +
"0cae5fb03986d133677c82a865b278c48d99dc251201b9c43edd7bedef" +
"d4b5306efd0dec7787ec6b664471c2")]
```

Unfortunately, you need to either have the public key on one line or use string concatenation—whitespace in the public key will cause a compilation failure. It'd be a lot more pleasant to look at if you could specify the token instead of the whole key, but fortunately this ugliness is usually confined to AssemblyInfo.cs, so you won't need to see it often.

In theory, it's possible to have an unsigned source assembly and a signed friend assembly. In practice, that's not terribly useful, as the friend assembly typically wants to have a reference to the source assembly, and you can't refer to an unsigned assembly from one that's signed. Likewise, a signed assembly can't specify an unsigned friend assembly, so typically you end up with both assemblies being signed if either one of them is.

7.8   *Summary*

This completes our tour of the new features in C# 2. The topics we've looked at in this chapter have broadly fallen into two categories: "nice to have" improvements that streamline development, and "hope you don't need it" features that can get you out of tricky situations when you need them. To make an analogy between C# 2 and improvements to a house, the major features from our earlier chapters are comparable to full-scale additions. Some of the features we've seen in this chapter (such as partial types and static classes) are more like redecorating a bedroom, and features such as namespace aliases are akin to fitting smoke alarms—you may never see a benefit, but it's nice to know they're there if you ever need them.

The range of features in C# 2 is broad—the designers tackled many of the areas where developers were feeling pain, without any one overarching goal. That's not to say the features don't work well together—nullable value types wouldn't be feasible without generics, for instance—but there's no one aim that every feature contributes to, unless you count general productivity.

Now that we've finished examining C# 2, it's time to move on to C# 3, where the picture is very different. Nearly every feature in C# 3 forms part of the grand picture of LINQ, a conglomeration of technologies that massively simplifies many tasks.

Part 3

C# 3: Revolutionizing
data access

There's no doubt that C# 2 is a significant improvement over C# 1. The benefits of generics, in particular, are fundamental to other changes, not just in C# 2 but also in C# 3. But C# 2 is in some sense a piecemeal collection of features. Don't get me wrong: they fit together nicely enough, but they address a set of individual issues. That was appropriate at that stage of C#'s development, but C# 3 is different.

Almost every feature in C# 3 enables one specific technology: LINQ. Many of the features are useful outside this context, and you certainly shouldn't confine yourself to only using them when you happen to be writing a query expression, but it'd be equally silly not to recognize the complete picture created by the set of jigsaw puzzle pieces presented in the following five chapters.

When I originally wrote about C# 3 and LINQ in 2007, I was highly impressed on a somewhat academic level. The more deeply you study the language, the more clearly you see the harmony between the various elements that have been introduced. The elegance of query expressions—and in particular the ability to use the same syntax for both in-process queries and providers like LINQ to SQL—was very appealing. LINQ had a great deal of promise.

Now, years later, I can look back on the promises and see how they've played out. In my experience with the community—particularly on Stack Overflow—it's obvious that LINQ has been widely adopted and really has changed how we approach many data-oriented tasks. Database providers aren't restricted to those from Microsoft—LINQ to NHibernate and SubSonic are just two of the other options available. Microsoft hasn't stopped innovating around LINQ either; in chapter 12 you'll see Parallel LINQ and Reactive Extensions, two very different ways of handling data that still use the familiar LINQ operators. And then there's LINQ to Objects—the simplest, most predictable, almost mundane LINQ provider, and the one that's most pervasive in industry. The days of writing yet another filtering loop, yet another piece of code to find some maximum value, yet another check to see whether any items in a collection satisfy some condition have gone—and good riddance.

Despite the broad adoption of LINQ, I still see a number of questions that make it clear that some developers regard LINQ as a sort of magic black box. What's going to happen when I use a query expression, compared with using extension methods directly? When does the data actually get read? How can I make it work more efficiently? Though you can learn a lot of LINQ just by playing with it and looking at examples in blog posts, you'll get a great deal more out of it by seeing how it all works at a language level and then learning about what the various libraries do for you.

This is not a book about LINQ—I'm still concentrating on the language features that enable LINQ, rather than going into details of concurrency considerations for the Entity Framework and so on. But once you've seen the language elements individually and how they fit together, you'll be in a much better position to learn the details of specific providers.

Cutting fluff
with a smart compiler

8

This chapter covers

- Automatically implemented properties
- Implicitly typed local variables
- Object and collection initializers
- Implicitly typed arrays
- Anonymous types

We'll start looking at C# 3 in the same way that we finished looking at C# 2—with a collection of relatively simple features. These are just the first small steps on the path to LINQ. Each of them can be used outside that context, but almost all are important for simplifying code to the extent that LINQ requires in order to be effective.

One important point to note is that although two of the biggest features of C# 2—generics and nullable types—required CLR changes, there were no significant changes to the CLR that shipped with .NET 3.5. There were some tweaks, but nothing fundamental. The framework grew to support LINQ, and a few more features were introduced to the base class library, but that's a different matter. It's worth being clear in your mind which changes are only in the C# *language*, which are *library* changes, and which are *CLR* changes.

Almost all of the new features exposed in C# 3 are due to the compiler being willing to do more work for you. You saw some evidence of this in part of the book—particularly with anonymous methods and iterator blocks—and C# 3 continues in the same vein. In this chapter, you'll meet the following features that are new to C# 3:

- *Automatically implemented properties*—Remove the drudgery of writing simple properties backed directly by fields
- *Implicitly typed local variables*—Reduce redundancy from local variable declarations by inferring the variable type from the initial value
- *Object and collection initializers*—Simplify the creation and initialization of objects in single expressions
- *Implicitly typed arrays*—Reduce redundancy from array-creation expressions by inferring the array type from the contents
- *Anonymous types*—Enable the creation of ad hoc types to contain simple properties

In addition to describing what the new features do, I'll make recommendations about their use. Many of the features of C# 3 require a certain amount of discretion and restraint on the part of the developer. That's not to say they're not powerful and incredibly useful—quite the opposite—but the temptation to use the latest and greatest funky syntax shouldn't be allowed to overrule the drive toward clear and readable code.

The considerations I'll discuss in this chapter (and the rest of the book) will rarely be black and white. Perhaps more than ever before, readability is in the eye of the beholder, and as you become more comfortable with the new features, they're likely to become more readable to you. I should stress, though, that unless you have good reason to suppose you'll be the only one to ever read your code, you should consider the needs and views of your colleagues carefully.

That's enough navel gazing for the moment. We'll start off with a feature that shouldn't cause any controversy. Simple but effective, automatically implemented properties just make life better.

8.1   *Automatically implemented properties*

The first feature we'll discuss is probably the simplest in the whole of C# 3. It's even simpler than any of the new features in C# 2. Despite that—or possibly *because* of that—it's also immediately applicable in many, many situations. When you read about iterator blocks in chapter 6, you may not immediately have thought of any areas of your current code base that could be improved by using them, but I'd be surprised to find any nontrivial C# 2 program that couldn't be modified to use automatically implemented properties. This fabulously simple feature allows you to express trivial properties with less code than before.

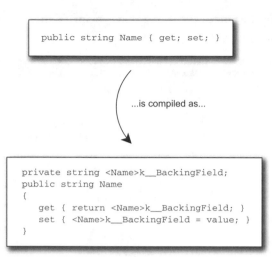

Figure 8.1 Transformation of an automatically implemented property

What do I mean by a *trivial property*? I mean one that's read/write and that stores its value in a straightforward private variable without any validation or other custom code. Trivial properties only take a few lines of code, but that's still a lot when you consider that you're expressing a very simple concept. C# 3 reduces the verbosity by applying a simple compile-time transformation, as shown in figure 8.1.

The code at the bottom of figure 8.1 isn't *quite* valid C#, of course. The field has an unspeakable name to prevent naming collisions, in the same way as you've seen before for anonymous methods and iterator blocks. But that's effectively the code that's generated by the automatically implemented property at the top.

Where previously you *might* have been tempted to use a public variable for the sake of simplicity, there's now even less excuse for not using a property instead. This is particularly true for throwaway code, which we all know tends to live far longer than anticipated.

> **TERMINOLOGY: AUTOMATIC PROPERTY OR AUTOMATICALLY IMPLEMENTED PROPERTY?** When automatically implemented properties were first discussed, long before the full C# 3 specification was published, they were called *automatic properties*. Personally, I find this less of a mouthful than the full name, and it's more widely used in the community. There's no risk of ambiguity, so for the rest of this book, I'll use *automatic property* and *automatically implemented property* synonymously.

The feature of C# 2 that allows you to specify different access for the getter and the setter is still available here, and you can also create static automatic properties. But static automatic properties are almost always pointless. Although most types don't claim to have thread-safe instance members, publicly visible static members usually *should* be thread-safe, and the compiler doesn't do anything to help you in this respect. The following listing gives an example of a safe, but useless, static automatic property that counts how many instances of a class have been created, along with instance properties for the name and age of a person.

```
public class Person
{
    public string Name { get; private set; }         Declares properties
    public int Age { get; private set; }              with public getters

    private static int InstanceCounter { get; set; }    Declares private
    private static readonly object counterLock = new object();   static property
                                                                 and lock
    public InstanceCountingPerson(string name, int age)
    {
        Name = name;
        Age = age;

        lock (counterLock)              Uses lock for safe
        {                               property access
            InstanceCounter++;
        }
    }
}
```

In this listing, you use a lock to make sure you don't have threading problems, and you'd also need to use the same lock whenever you accessed the property. There are better alternatives here involving the `Interlocked` class, but they require access to fields. In short, the only scenario in which I can see static automatic properties being useful is where the getter is public, the setter is private, and the setter is *only* called within the type initializer.

The other properties in listing 8.1, representing the name and age of the person, tell a much happier tale—using automatic properties is a no-brainer here. Where you have properties that you'd have implemented trivially in previous versions of C#, there's no benefit in *not* using automatic properties.[1]

One slight wrinkle occurs if you use automatic properties when writing your own structs: all of your constructors need to explicitly call the parameterless constructor—`this()`—so that the compiler knows that all the fields have been definitely assigned. You can't set the fields directly because they're anonymous, and you can't use the properties until all the fields have been set. The only way of proceeding is to call the parameterless constructor, which will set the fields to their default values. For example, if you wanted to create a struct with a single integer property, this wouldn't be valid:

```
public struct Foo
{
    public int Value { get; private set; }
```

---

[1] Certainly for read/write properties, anyway. If you're creating a read-only property, you may choose to use a read-only backing field and a property with just a getter to return it. This prevents you from accidentally writing to the property within the class, which would be possible with a "public read, private write" automatic property.

```
    public Foo(int value)
    {
        this.Value = value;
    }
}
```

But it's fine if you explicitly chain to the parameterless constructor:

```
public struct Foo
{
    public int Value { get; private set; }

    public Foo(int value) : this()
    {
        this.Value = value;
    }
}
```

That's all there is to automatically implemented properties. There are no bells and whistles to them. For instance, there's no way of declaring them with initial default values, and no way of making them genuinely read-only (a private setter is as close as you can get).

If all the C# 3 features were that simple, we could cover *everything* in a single chapter. Of course, that's not the case, but there are some features that don't take *too* much explanation. The next topic removes duplicate code in another common but specific situation—declaring local variables.

8.2 *Implicit typing of local variables*

In chapter 2 we discussed the nature of the C# 1 type system. In particular, I stated that it was static, explicit, and safe. That's still true in C# 2, and in C# 3 it's still *almost* completely true. The static and safe parts are still true (ignoring explicitly unsafe code, just as we did in chapter 2), and *most* of the time it's still explicitly typed—but you can ask the compiler to infer the types of local variables for you.[2]

8.2.1 *Using var to declare a local variable*

In order to use implicit typing, all you need to do is replace the type part of a normal local variable declaration with var. Certain restrictions exist (we'll come to those in a moment), but essentially it's as easy as changing this:

MyType variableName = someInitialValue;

to this:

var variableName = someInitialValue;

The results of the two lines (in terms of compiled code) are *exactly the same*, assuming that the type of someInitialValue is MyType. The compiler simply takes the compile-time type of the initialization expression and makes the variable have that type too.

---

[2] C# 4 changes the game yet again, allowing you to use dynamic typing where you want to, as you'll see in chapter 14. One step at a time—C# was still fully statically typed up to and including version 3.

```
int totalAge = 0;
foreach (var person in family)
{
    totalAge += person.Age;
}
```

(local variable) 'a person

Anonymous Types:
    'a is new { string Name, int Age }

Figure 8.2   Hovering over `var` in Visual Studio displays the type of the declared variable.

The type can be any normal .NET type, including generics, delegates, and interfaces. The variable is still statically typed; you just haven't written the name of the type in your code.

This is important to understand, as it goes to the heart of what a lot of developers initially fear when they see this feature—that `var` makes C# dynamic or weakly typed. That's not true at all. The best way of explaining this is to show you some invalid code:

INVALID
```
var stringVariable = "Hello, world.";
stringVariable = 0;
```

That doesn't compile because the type of `stringVariable` is `System.String`, and you can't assign the value `0` to a string variable. In many dynamic languages, the code *would* have compiled, leaving the variable with no particularly useful type as far as the compiler, IDE, or runtime environment is concerned. Using `var` is *not* like using a `VARIANT` type from COM or VB6. The variable is statically typed; the type has just been inferred by the compiler. I apologize if I seem to be laboring this point somewhat, but it's incredibly important, and it's been the cause of a lot of confusion.

In Visual Studio, you can tell which type the compiler has used for the variable by hovering over the `var` part of the declaration, as shown in figure 8.2. Note how the type parameters for the generic `Dictionary` type are also explained. If this looks familiar, that's because it's *exactly* the same behavior you get when you declare local variables explicitly.

Tooltips aren't just available at the point of declaration, either. As you'd probably expect, the tooltip displayed when you hover over the variable name later on in the code indicates the type of the variable too. This is shown in figure 8.3, where the same declaration is used and then I've hovered over a *use* of the variable. Again, that's exactly the same behavior as you'd see with a normal local variable declaration.

```
var namePeopleMap = new Dictionary<string, List<Person>>();

// Other code

Console.WriteLine(namePeopleMap.Count);
```

(local variable) Dictionary<string,List<Person>> namePeopleMap

Figure 8.3   Hovering over the use of an implicitly typed local variable displays its type.

There are two reasons for bringing up Visual Studio in this context. The first is that it's more evidence of the static typing involved—the compiler clearly knows the type of the variable. The second is to point out that you can easily discover the type involved, even from deep within a method. This'll be important when we talk about the pros and cons of using implicit typing in a minute. First, though, I ought to mention some limitations.

8.2.2 Restrictions on implicit typing

You can't use implicit typing for every variable in every case. You can only use it when all of the following points are true:

- The variable being declared is a local variable, rather than a static or instance field.
- The variable is initialized as part of the declaration.
- The initialization expression isn't a method group or anonymous function[3] (without casting).
- The initialization expression isn't null.
- Only one variable is declared in the statement.
- The type you want the variable to have is the compile-time type of the initialization expression.
- The initialization expression doesn't involve the variable being declared.[4]

The third and fourth points are interesting. You can't write this:

INVALID

```
var starter = delegate() { Console.WriteLine(); };
```

That's because the compiler doesn't know what type to use. You *can* write this:

```
var starter = (ThreadStart) delegate() { Console.WriteLine(); };
```

But if you're going to do that, you'd be better off explicitly declaring the variable in the first place. The same is true in the null case—you could cast the null appropriately, but there'd be no point.

Note that you *can* use the result of method calls or properties as the initialization expression—you're not limited to constants and constructor calls. For instance, you could use this:

```
var args = Environment.GetCommandLineArgs();
```

In that case, args would be of type string[]. In fact, initializing a variable with the result of a method call is likely to be the most common situation where implicit typing is used, as part of LINQ. You'll see all that later on—just bear it in mind as the examples progress.

---

[3] The term *anonymous function* covers both anonymous methods and lambda expressions, which we'll delve into in chapter 9.
[4] It'd be highly unusual to do so anyway, but with normal declarations it's possible if you try hard enough.

It's also worth noting that you *are* allowed to use implicit typing for the local variables declared in the first part of a using, for, or foreach statement. For example, the following are all valid (with appropriate bodies, of course):

```
for (var i = 0; i < 10; i++)
using (var x = File.OpenText("test.dat"))
foreach (var s in Environment.GetCommandLineArgs())
```

These variables would end up with types of int, StreamReader, and string, respectively.

Of course, just because you *can* do this doesn't mean you *should*. Let's look at the reasons for and against using implicit typing.

8.2.3   *Pros and cons of implicit typing*

The question of when it's a good idea to use implicit typing is the cause of a lot of community discussion. Views range from "everywhere" to "nowhere" with plenty of more balanced approaches between the two. You'll see in section 8.5 that in order to use another of C# 3's features—anonymous types—you often *need* to use implicit typing. You could avoid anonymous types as well, of course, but that's throwing the baby out with the bathwater.

The main reason *for* using implicit typing (leaving anonymous types aside for the moment) is not that it reduces the number of keystrokes required to enter the code, but that it makes the code less cluttered (and therefore more readable) on the screen. In particular, when generics are involved, the type names can get very long. Figures 8.2 and 8.3 used a type of Dictionary<string, List<Person>>, which is 33 characters. By the time you have that twice on a line (once for the declaration and once for the initialization), you end up with a massive line just for declaring and initializing a single variable. An alternative is to use an alias, but that puts the real type involved a long way (conceptually at least) from the code that uses it.

When reading the code, there's no point in seeing the same long type name twice on the same line when it's obvious that they *should* be the same. If the declaration isn't visible on the screen, you're in the same boat whether implicit typing was used or not (all the ways you'd use to find out the variable type are still valid), and if it *is* visible, the expression used to initialize the variable tells you the type anyway.

Additionally, using var changes the emphasis of the code. Sometimes you want the reader to pay close attention to the precise types involved because they're significant. For example, even though the generic SortedList and SortedDictionary types have similar APIs, they have different performance characteristics, and that may be important for your particular piece of code. Other times, all you really care about is the operations that are being performed; you wouldn't really mind if the expression used to initialize the variable changed, as long as you could achieve the same goals.[5] Using

---

[5] I realize this sounds a little like duck typing: "As long as it can quack, I'm happy." The difference is that you're still checking quackability at compile time, not execution time.

var allows the reader to focus on the *use* of a variable rather than the declaration—the *what* rather than the *how* of the code.

All of this sounds good, so what are the arguments *against* implicit typing? Paradoxically enough, readability is the most important one, despite also being an argument in favor of implicit typing! By not being explicit about what type of variable you're declaring, you may be making it harder to work it out when reading the code. It breaks the "state what you're declaring, then what value it'll start off with" mindset that keeps the declaration and the initialization separate. To what extent that's an issue depends on both the reader and the initialization expression involved.

If you're explicitly calling a constructor, it'll always be pretty obvious what type you're creating. If you're calling a method or using a property, it depends on how obvious the return type is when looking at the call. Integer literals are an example where it's harder to guess the type of an expression than you might suppose. How quickly can you work out the type of each of the variables declared here?

```
var a = 2147483647;
var b = 2147483648;
var c = 4294967295;
var d = 4294967296;
var e = 9223372036854775807;
var f = 9223372036854775808;
```

The answers are int, uint, uint, long, long, and ulong, respectively—the type used depends on the value of the expression. There's nothing new here in terms of the handling of literals—C# has always behaved like this—but implicit typing makes it easier to write obscure code in this case.

The argument that's rarely explicitly stated but that I believe is behind a lot of the concern over implicit typing is, "It just doesn't feel right." If you've been writing in a C-like language for years and years, there's something unnerving about the whole business, however much you tell yourself that it's still static typing under the covers. This may not be a rational concern, but that doesn't make it any less real. If you're uncomfortable, you're likely to be less productive. If the advantages don't outweigh your negative feelings, that's fine. Depending on your personality, you may try to push yourself to *become* more comfortable with implicit typing, but you certainly don't have to.

8.2.4 Recommendations

Here are some recommendations based on my experience with implicit typing. That's all they are—recommendations—and you should feel free to take them with a pinch of salt:

- If it's important that someone reading the code knows the type of the variable at a glance, use explicit typing.
- If the variable is directly initialized with a constructor and the type name is long (which often occurs with generics), consider using implicit typing.

- If the precise type of the variable isn't important, but its general nature is clear from the context, use implicit typing to de-emphasize *how* the code achieves its aim and concentrate on the higher level of *what* it's achieving.
- Consult your teammates on the matter when embarking on a new project.
- When in doubt, try a line both ways and go with your gut feelings.

I used to use explicit typing for production code, except in situations where there was a clear and significant benefit to using implicit typing. Most of my uses of implicit typing were in test code (and throwaway code). Nowadays I'm more ambivalent and frankly inconsistent. I'll happily use implicit typing in production code just for a bit of added simplicity, even when the type names involved aren't too onerous. Although consistency in some aspects of coding style is quite important, I haven't found this mix-and-match approach to cause any problems.

Effectively, my recommendation boils down to *not* using implicit typing just because it saves a few keystrokes. Where it keeps the code tidier, allowing you to concentrate on the most important elements of the code, go for it. I'll use implicit typing extensively in the rest of the book, for the simple reason that code is harder to format in print than on a screen—not as much width is available.

We'll come back to implicit typing when we look at anonymous types, as they create situations where you're forced to ask the compiler to infer the types of some variables. Before that, let's look at how C# 3 makes it easier to construct and populate a new object in one expression.

8.3   *Simplified initialization*

One would've thought that object-oriented languages would've streamlined object creation long ago. After all, before you start using an object, *something* has to create it, whether it's through your code directly or a factory method of some sort. Despite this, few language features in C# 2 are geared toward making life easier when it comes to initialization. If you can't do what you want using constructor arguments, you're basically out of luck—you need to create the object, and then manually initialize it with property calls and the like.

This is particularly annoying when you want to create a whole bunch of objects in one go, such as in an array or other collection. Without a single-expression way of initializing an object, you're forced to either use local variables for temporary manipulation or create a helper method that performs the appropriate initialization based on parameters.

C# 3 comes to the rescue in a number of ways, as you'll see in this section.

8.3.1   *Defining some sample types*

The expressions we'll use in this section are called *object initializers*. These are just ways of specifying initialization that should occur after an object has been created. You can set properties, set properties of properties (don't worry, it's simpler than it sounds), and add to collections that are accessible via properties.

To demonstrate all this, we'll use a `Person` class again. It has the name and age we've used before, exposed as writable properties. We'll provide both a parameterless constructor and one that accepts the name as a parameter. We'll also add a list of friends and the person's home location, both of which are accessible as read-only properties but can still be modified by manipulating the retrieved objects. A simple `Location` class provides `Country` and `Town` properties to represent the person's home. The following listing shows the complete code for the classes.

Listing 8.2 A fairly simple `Person` class used for further demonstrations

```
public class Person
{
    public int Age { get; set; }
    public string Name { get; set; }

    List<Person> friends = new List<Person>();
    public List<Person> Friends { get { return friends; } }

    Location home = new Location();
    public Location Home { get { return home; } }

    public Person() { }

    public Person(string name)
    {
        Name = name;
    }
}
public class Location
{
    public string Country { get; set; }
    public string Town { get; set; }
}
```

Listing 8.2 is straightforward, but it's worth noting that both the list of friends and the home location are created in a blank way when the person is created, rather than being left as null references. The friends and home location properties are read-only, too. That'll be important later on—but for the moment let's look at the properties representing the name and age of a person.

8.3.2 *Setting simple properties*

Now that you have a `Person` type, it's time to create some instances of it using the new features of C# 3. In this section, we'll look at setting the `Name` and `Age` properties—we'll come to the others later.

Object initializers are most commonly used to set properties, but everything shown here also applies to fields. In a well-encapsulated system, though, you're unlikely to have access to fields unless you're creating an instance of a type within that type's own code. It's worth knowing that you *can* use fields, of course—so for the rest of the section, just read *property and field* whenever the text says *property*.

With that out of the way, let's get down to business. Suppose you want to create a person called *Tom*, who is 9 years old. Prior to C# 3, there were two ways this could be achieved:

```
Person tom1 = new Person();
tom1.Name = "Tom";
tom1.Age = 9;

Person tom2 = new Person("Tom");
tom2.Age = 9;
```

The first version uses the parameterless constructor and then sets both properties. The second version uses the constructor overload, which sets the name, and then sets the age afterward. Both of these options are still available in C# 3, but there are other alternatives:

```
Person tom3 = new Person() { Name = "Tom", Age = 9 };
Person tom4 = new Person { Name = "Tom", Age = 9 };
Person tom5 = new Person("Tom") { Age = 9 };
```

The part in braces at the end of each line is the object initializer. Again, it's just compiler trickery. The IL used to initialize tom3 and tom4 is identical, and is nearly the same as that used for tom1.[6] Predictably, the code for tom5 is nearly the same as for tom2. Note how the initialization of tom4 omits the parentheses for the constructor. You can use this shorthand for types with a parameterless constructor, which is what gets called in the compiled code.

After the constructor has been called, the specified properties are set in the obvious way. They're set in the order specified in the object initializer, and you can only specify a particular property once—you can't set the Name property twice, for example. (You could call the constructor taking the name as a parameter, and then set the Name property. It would be pointless, but the compiler wouldn't stop you from doing it.) The expression used as the value for a property can be any expression that isn't itself an assignment—you can call methods, create new objects (potentially using another object initializer), pretty much anything.

You may be wondering just how useful this is—you've saved one or two lines of code, but surely that's not a good enough reason to make the language more complicated, is it? There's a subtle point here, though: you haven't just created an object in one *line*—you've created it in one *expression*. That difference can be very important.

Suppose you want to create an array of type Person[] with some predefined data in it. Even without using the implicit array typing you'll see later, the code is neat and readable:

---

[6] In fact, tom1's new value isn't assigned until all the properties have been set. A temporary local variable is used until then. This is rarely important but worth knowing to avoid confusion if you happen to break into the debugger halfway through the initializer.

```
Person[] family = new Person[]
{
    new Person { Name = "Holly", Age = 36 },
    new Person { Name = "Jon", Age = 36 },
    new Person { Name = "Tom", Age = 9 },
    new Person { Name = "William", Age = 6 },
    new Person { Name = "Robin", Age = 6 }
};
```

In a simple example like this, you could've written a constructor taking both the name and age as parameters and initialized the array in a similar way in C# 1 or 2. But appropriate constructors aren't always available, and if there are several constructor parameters, it's often not clear which one means what, just from the position. By the time a constructor needs to take five or six parameters, I often find myself relying on IntelliSense more than I want to. Using the property names is a great boon to readability in such cases.[7]

This form of object initializer is the one you'll probably use most often. But there are two other forms—one for setting subproperties, and one for adding to collections. Let's look at subproperties—properties of properties—first.

8.3.3 *Setting properties on embedded objects*

So far it's been easy to set the Name and Age properties, but you can't set the Home property in the same way—it's read-only. You *can* set the town and the country of a person, though, by first fetching the Home property and then setting properties on the result. The language specification refers to this as setting the properties of an *embedded object*.

Just to make it clear, what we're talking about is the following C# 1 code:

```
Person tom = new Person("Tom");
tom.Age = 9;
tom.Home.Country = "UK";
tom.Home.Town = "Reading";
```

When you're populating the home location, each statement is doing a get to retrieve the Location instance, and then a set on the relevant property on that instance. There's nothing new in that, but it's worth slowing your mind down to look at it carefully; otherwise it's easy to miss what's going on behind the scenes.

C# 3 allows all of this to be done in one expression, as shown here:

```
Person tom = new Person("Tom")
{
    Age = 9,
    Home = { Country = "UK", Town = "Reading" }
};
```

---

[7] C# 4 provides an alternative approach here using named arguments, which you'll meet in chapter 13.

The compiled code for these snippets is effectively the same. The compiler spots that to the right side of the = sign is another object initializer, and it applies the properties to the embedded object appropriately.

The absence of the `new` keyword in the part initializing `Home` is significant. If you need to work out where the compiler is going to create new objects and where it's going to set properties on existing ones, look for occurrences of `new` in the initializer. Every time a new object is created, the `new` keyword appears *somewhere*.

> **FORMATTING OBJECT INITIALIZER CODE**   As with almost all C# features, object initializers are whitespace-independent. You can collapse the whitespace in the object initializer, putting it all on one line if you like. It's up to you to work out where the sweet spot is in balancing long lines against lots of lines.

We've dealt with the `Home` property, but what about Tom's friends? There are properties you can set on a `List<Person>`, but none of them will add entries to the list. It's time for the next feature—collection initializers.

8.3.4   *Collection initializers*

Creating a collection with some initial values is an extremely common task. Until C# 3 arrived, the only language feature that gave any assistance was array creation, and even that was clumsy in many situations. C# 3 has *collection initializers*, which allow you to use the same type of syntax as array initializers but with arbitrary collections and with more flexibility.

CREATING NEW COLLECTIONS WITH COLLECTION INITIALIZERS

As a first example, let's use the now-familiar `List<T>` type. In C# 2, you could populate a list either by passing in an existing collection or by calling `Add` repeatedly after creating an empty list. Collection initializers in C# 3 take the latter approach.

Suppose we want to populate a list of strings with some names—here's the C# 2 code (on the left) and the close equivalent in C# 3 (on the right):

```
List<string> names = new List<string>();   |   var names = new List<string>
names.Add("Holly");                         |   {
names.Add("Jon");                           |       "Holly", "Jon", "Tom",
names.Add("Tom");                           |       "Robin", "William"
names.Add("Robin");                         |   };
names.Add("William");                       |
```

Just as with object initializers, you can specify constructor arguments if you want, or use a parameterless constructor either explicitly or implicitly. The use of implicit typing here was partly for space reasons—the `names` variable could equally well have been declared explicitly. Reducing the number of lines of code (without reducing readability) is nice, but there are two bigger benefits of collection initializers:

- The create-and-initialize part counts as a single expression.
- There's a lot less clutter in the code.

The first point becomes important when you want to use a collection as either an argument to a method or as one element in a larger collection. That happens *relatively* rarely (although often enough to still be useful). The second point is the real reason this is a killer feature in my view. If you look at the code on the right, you can easily see the information you need, with each piece of information written only once. The variable name occurs once, the type being used occurs once, and each of the elements of the initialized collection appears once. It's all extremely simple, and much clearer than the C# 2 code, which contains a lot of fluff around the *useful* bits.

Collection initializers aren't limited to just lists. You can use them with any type that implements IEnumerable, as long as it has an appropriate Add method for each element in the initializer. You can use an Add method with more than one parameter by putting the values within another set of braces. The most common use for this is creating dictionaries. For example, if you wanted a dictionary mapping names to ages, you could use the following code:

```
Dictionary<string,int> nameAgeMap = new Dictionary<string,int>
{
    { "Holly", 36 },
    { "Jon", 36 },
    { "Tom", 9 }
};
```

In this case, the Add(string, int) method would be called three times. If multiple Add methods are available, different elements of the initializer can call different overloads. If no compatible overload is available for a specified element, the code will fail to compile. There are two interesting points about the design decision here:

- The fact that the type has to implement IEnumerable is never used by the compiler.
- The Add method is only found by name—there's no interface requirement specifying it.

These are both pragmatic decisions. Requiring IEnumerable to be implemented is a reasonable attempt to check that the type really is a collection of some sort, and using any accessible overload of the Add method (rather than requiring an exact signature) allows for simple initializations, such as the earlier dictionary example.

An early draft of the C# 3 specification required ICollection<T> to be implemented instead, and the implementation of the single-parameter Add method (as specified by the interface) was called rather than allowing different overloads. This sounds more pure, but there are far more types that implement IEnumerable than ICollection<T>, and using the single-parameter Add method would be inconvenient. For example, in this case it would've forced you to explicitly create an instance of a KeyValuePair<string,int> for each element of the initializer. Sacrificing a bit of academic purity has made the language far more useful in real life.

POPULATING COLLECTIONS WITHIN OTHER OBJECT INITIALIZERS

So far we've only looked at collection initializers used in a standalone fashion to create whole new collections. They can also be combined with object initializers to populate embedded collections. To demonstrate this, we'll go back to the `Person` example. The `Friends` property is read-only, so you can't create a new collection and specify that as the collection of friends, but you *can* add to whatever collection is returned by the property's getter. The way you do this is similar to the syntax you've already seen for setting properties of embedded objects, but you just specify a collection initializer instead of a sequence of properties.

Let's see this in action by creating another `Person` instance for Tom, this time with some of his friends.

Listing 8.3   Building up a rich object using object and collection initializers

```
Person tom = new Person                              ⟵┐ Implicitly calls
{                                                     │ parameterless
    Name = "Tom",          ⟵ Sets properties directly │ constructor
    Age = 9,
    Home = { Town = "Reading", Country = "UK" },     ⟵── Initializes embedded object
    Friends =
    {
        new Person { Name = "Alberto" },             ⟵┐ Initializes collection
        new Person("Max"),                            │ with further object
        new Person { Name = "Zak", Age = 7 },         │ initializers
        new Person("Ben"),
        new Person("Alice"),
        {
            Age = 9,
            Home = { Town = "Twyford", Country = "UK" }
        }
    }
};
```

Listing 8.3 uses all the features of object and collection initializers we've come across. The main part of interest is the collection initializer, which itself uses lots of different forms of object initializers internally. Note that you're not creating a new collection here, just adding to an existing one. (If the property had a setter, you *could* create a new collection and still use collection initializer syntax.)

You could've gone further, specifying friends of friends, friends of friends of friends, and so forth. But you couldn't specify that Tom is Alberto's friend. While you're still initializing an object, you don't have access to it, so you can't express cyclic relationships. This can be awkward in a few cases, but it usually isn't a problem.

Collection initialization within object initializers works as a sort of cross between standalone collection initializers and setting embedded object properties. For each element in the collection initializer, the collection property getter (`Friends`, in this case) is called, and then the appropriate `Add` method is called on the returned value. The collection isn't cleared in any way before elements are added. For example, if you were to decide that a person should always be his own friend, and added `this` to the list of friends within the `Person` constructor, using a collection initializer would only add extra friends.

As you can see, the combination of collection and object initializers can be used to populate whole trees of objects. But when and where is this likely to actually happen?

8.3.5 Uses of initialization features

Trying to pin down exactly where these features are useful is reminiscent of being in a Monty Python sketch about the Spanish Inquisition—every time you think you have a reasonably complete list, another common example pops up. I'll just mention three examples, which I hope will encourage you to consider where else *you* might use them.

CONSTANT COLLECTIONS

It's not uncommon for me to want some kind of collection (often a map) that's effectively constant. Of course, it can't be a constant as far as the C# language is concerned, but it *can* be declared static and read-only, with big warnings to say that it shouldn't be changed. (It's usually private, so that's good enough. Alternatively, you can use `Read-OnlyCollection<T>`.) Typically, this used to involve writing a static constructor or a helper method, just to populate the map. With C# 3's collection initializers, it's easy to set the whole thing up inline.

SETTING UP UNIT TESTS

When writing unit tests, I frequently want to populate an object just for one test, often passing it in as an argument to the method I'm trying to test at the time. Writing all of the initialization longhand can be long-winded and also hides the essential structure of the object from the reader of the code, just as XML creation code can often obscure what the document would look like if you viewed it (appropriately formatted) in a text editor. With appropriate indentation of object initializers, the nested structure of the object hierarchy can become obvious in the very shape of the code, as well as make the values stand out more than they would otherwise.

THE BUILDER PATTERN

For various reasons, sometimes you want to specify a lot of values for a single method or constructor call. The most common situation in my experience is creating an immutable object. Instead of having a huge set of parameters (which can become a readability problem as the meaning of each argument becomes unclear[8]), you can use the *builder pattern*—create a mutable type with appropriate properties, and then pass an instance of the builder into the constructor or method. The framework `Process-StartInfo` type is a good example of this—the designers *could* have overloaded `Process.Start` with many different sets of parameters, but using `ProcessStartInfo` makes everything clearer.

Object and collection initializers allow you to create the builder object in a clearer manner—you can even specify it inline when you call the original member if you want. Admittedly, you still have to write the builder type in the first place, but automatic properties help on that front.

---

[8] Named arguments in C# 4 help in this area, admittedly.

<INSERT YOUR FAVORITE USE HERE>

Of course, there are uses beyond these three in ordinary code, and I don't want to put you off using the new features elsewhere. There's little reason *not* to use them, other than possibly confusing developers who aren't familiar with C# 3 yet. You may decide that using an object initializer just to set one property (as opposed to explicitly setting it in a separate statement) is over the top—that's a matter of aesthetics, and I can't give you much objective guidance there. As with implicit typing, it's a good idea to try the code both ways, and learn to predict your own (and your team's) reading preferences.

So far we've looked at a fairly diverse range of features: implementing properties easily, simplifying local variable declarations, and populating objects in single expressions. In the remainder of this chapter, we'll gradually bring these topics together, using more implicit typing and more object population, and creating whole *types* without giving any implementation details.

The next topic appears to be quite similar to collection initializers when you look at code using it. I mentioned earlier that array initialization was a bit clumsy in C# 1 and 2. I'm sure it won't surprise you to learn that it's been streamlined for C# 3. Let's take a look.

8.4   *Implicitly typed arrays*

In C# 1 and 2, initializing an array as part of a variable declaration and initialization statement was quite neat, but if you wanted to do it anywhere else, you had to specify the exact array type involved. For example, this compiles without any problem:

```
string[] names = {"Holly", "Jon", "Tom", "Robin", "William"};
```

This doesn't work for parameters, though—suppose you wanted to make a call to MyMethod, declared as void MyMethod(string[] names). This code won't work:

 MyMethod({"Holly", "Jon", "Tom", "Robin", "William"});

Instead, you have to tell the compiler what type of array you want to initialize:

```
MyMethod(new string[] {"Holly", "Jon", "Tom", "Robin", "William"});
```

C# 3 allows something in between:

```
MyMethod(new[] {"Holly", "Jon", "Tom", "Robin", "William"});
```

Clearly the compiler needs to work out what type of array to use. It starts by forming a set containing all the compile-time types of the expressions inside the braces. If there's exactly one type in that set that all the others can be implicitly converted to, that's the type of the array. Otherwise (or if all the values are typeless expressions, such as constant null values or anonymous methods, with no casts) the code won't compile.

Note that only the types of the expressions are considered as candidates for the overall array type. This means that occasionally you might have to explicitly cast a value to a *less*-specific type. For instance, this won't compile:

INVALID new[] { new MemoryStream(), new StringWriter() }

There's no conversion from MemoryStream to StringWriter or vice versa. Both are implicitly convertible to object and IDisposable, but the compiler only considers types that are in the original set produced by the expressions themselves. If you change one of the expressions in this situation so that its type is either object or IDisposable, the code compiles:

```
new[] { (IDisposable) new MemoryStream(), new StringWriter() }
```

The type of this last expression is implicitly IDisposable[]. Of course, at that point you might as well explicitly state the type of the array just as you would in C# 1 and 2, to make it clearer what you're trying to achieve.

Compared with the earlier features, implicitly typed arrays are a bit of an anticlimax. I find it hard to get excited about them, even though they *do* make life simpler in cases where an array is passed as an argument. The designers haven't gone mad, though—there's one important situation in which this implicit typing is absolutely crucial. That's when you don't know (and *can't* know) the name of the type of the elements of the array. How can you possibly get into this peculiar state? Read on…

8.5 Anonymous types

Implicit typing, object and collection initializers, and implicit array typing are all useful in their own right, to a greater or lesser extent. But they also serve a higher purpose—they make it possible to work with this chapter's final feature, *anonymous types*. In turn, anonymous types serve the higher purpose of LINQ.

8.5.1 First encounters of the anonymous kind

It's much easier to explain anonymous types when you already have some idea of what they are through an example. I'm sorry to say that without the use of extension methods and lambda expressions, the examples in this section are likely to be a little contrived, but there's a chicken-and-egg situation here: anonymous types are most useful within the context of the more advanced features, but we need to cover the building blocks before we can look at much of the bigger picture. Stick with it—it *will* make sense in the long run, I promise.

Let's pretend we didn't have the Person class, and the only properties we cared about were the name and age. The following listing shows how you could still build objects with those properties, without ever declaring a type.

Listing 8.4 Creating objects of an anonymous type with Name and Age properties

```
var tom= new { Name = "Tom", Age = 9 };
var holly = new { Name = "Holly", Age = 36 };
var jon = new { Name = "Jon", Age = 36 } ;

Console.WriteLine("{0} is {1} years old", jon.Name, jon.Age);
```

As you can tell from listing 8.4, the syntax for initializing an anonymous type is similar to the object initializers you saw in section 8.3.2—it's just that the name of the type is missing between `new` and the opening brace. Here you're using implicitly typed local variables because that's all you *can* use (other than `object` of course)—you don't have a type name to declare the variable with. As you can see from the last line, the type has properties for `Name` and `Age`, both of which can be read and which will have the values specified in the *anonymous object initializer* used to create the instance, so in this case the output is `Jon is 36 years old`. The properties have the same types as the expressions in the initializers—`string` for `Name` and `int` for `Age`. Just as in normal object initializers, the expressions used in anonymous object initializers can call methods or constructors, fetch properties, perform calculations—whatever you need to do.

You might now be starting to see why implicitly typed arrays are important. Suppose you want to create an array containing the whole family, and then iterate through it to work out the total age.[9] The following listing does just that, and it demonstrates a few other interesting features of anonymous types at the same time.

Listing 8.5   Populating an array using anonymous types and then finding the total age

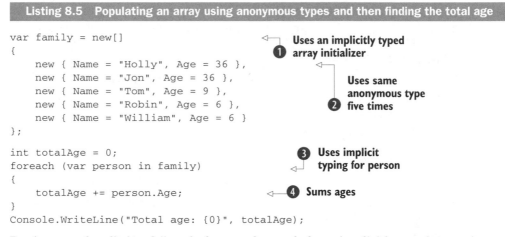

```
var family = new[]                                    ①  Uses an implicitly typed
{                                                         array initializer
    new { Name = "Holly", Age = 36 },
    new { Name = "Jon", Age = 36 },                      Uses same
    new { Name = "Tom", Age = 9 },                       anonymous type
    new { Name = "Robin", Age = 6 },                  ②  five times
    new { Name = "William", Age = 6 }
};

int totalAge = 0;                                     ③  Uses implicit
foreach (var person in family)                            typing for person
{
    totalAge += person.Age;                           ④  Sums ages
}
Console.WriteLine("Total age: {0}", totalAge);
```

Putting together listing 8.5 and what you learned about implicitly typed arrays in section 8.4, you can deduce something important: *all the people in the family are of the same type.* If each use of an anonymous object initializer ② referred to a different type, the compiler couldn't infer an appropriate type for the array ①. Within any given assembly, the compiler treats two anonymous object initializers as the same type if there are the same number of properties, with the same names and types in the same order. In other words, if you swapped the `Name` and `Age` properties in one of the initializers, there'd be two different types involved; likewise, if you introduced an extra property in one line, or used a `long` instead of an `int` for the age of one person, another anonymous type would've been introduced. At that point, the type inference for the array would fail.

---

[9] If you already know LINQ, you may feel that this is a quaint way of summing the ages. I agree, calling `family.Sum(p => p.Age)` would be a lot neater—but let's take things one step at a time.

```
int totalAge = 0;
foreach (var person in family)
{
    totalAge += person.Age;
}
```

```
(local variable) 'a person

Anonymous Types:
    'a is new { string Name, int Age }
```

Figure 8.4 Hovering over a variable that's declared (implicitly) to be of an anonymous type shows the details of that anonymous type.

IMPLEMENTATION DETAIL: HOW MANY TYPES? If you ever decide to look at the IL (or decompiled C#) for an anonymous type generated by Microsoft's compiler, be aware that although two anonymous object initializers with the same property names in the same order but using different property types will produce two different types, they'll actually be generated from a single generic type. The generic type is parameterized, but the closed, constructed types will be different because they'll be given different type arguments for the different initializers.

Notice that you can use a `foreach` statement to iterate over the array, just as you would any other collection. The type involved is inferred ❸, and the type of the `person` variable is the same anonymous type you used in the array. Again, you can use the same variable for different instances because they're all of the same type.

Listing 8.5 also proves that the `Age` property really is strongly typed as an `int`—otherwise trying to sum the ages ❹ wouldn't compile. The compiler knows about the anonymous type, and Visual Studio is even willing to share the information via tooltips, in case you're uncertain. Figure 8.4 shows the result of hovering over the `person` part of the `person.Age` expression from listing 8.5.

Now that you've seen anonymous types in action, let's go back and look at what the compiler is actually doing.

8.5.2 Members of anonymous types

Anonymous types are created by the compiler and included in the compiled assembly in the same way as the extra types for anonymous methods and iterator blocks. The CLR treats them as perfectly ordinary types, and so they are—if you later move from an anonymous type to a normal, manually coded type with the behavior described in this section, you shouldn't see anything change.

Anonymous types contain the following members:

- A constructor taking all the initialization values. The parameters are in the same order as they were specified in the anonymous object initializer, and they have the same names and types.
- Public read-only properties.
- Private read-only fields backing the properties.
- Overrides for `Equals`, `GetHashCode`, and `ToString`.

That's it. There are no implemented interfaces, no cloning or serialization capabilities—just a constructor, some properties, and the normal methods from `object`.

The constructor and the properties do the obvious things. Equality between two instances of the same anonymous type is determined in the natural manner, comparing each property value in turn using the property type's `Equals` method. The hash code generation is similar, calling `GetHashCode` on each property value in turn and combining the results. The exact method for combining the various hash codes together to form one composite hash is unspecified, and you shouldn't write code that depends on it anyway—you just need to be confident that two equal instances will return the same hash, and two unequal instances will *usually* return different hashes. All of this only works if the `Equals` and `GetHashCode` implementations of all the different types involved as properties conform to the normal rules, of course.

Because the properties are read-only, all anonymous types are immutable as long as the types used for their properties are immutable. This provides you with all the normal benefits of immutability—being able to pass values to methods without fear of them changing, simple sharing of data across threads, and so forth.

> **VB ANONYMOUS TYPE PROPERTIES ARE MUTABLE BY DEFAULT** Anonymous types are also available in Visual Basic 9 onward. But, by default, their properties are mutable; you need to declare any properties you want to be immutable with the `Key` modifier. Only properties declared as keys are used in hashing and equality comparisons. This is easy to overlook when converting code from one language to another.

We're almost done with anonymous types now. But there's one slight wrinkle still to talk about—a shortcut for a situation that's fairly common in LINQ.

8.5.3 *Projection initializers*

The anonymous object initializers you've seen so far have all been lists of name/value pairs—`Name="Jon"`, `Age=36` and the like. As it happens, I've always used constants because they make for smaller examples, but in real code you often want to copy properties from an existing object. Sometimes you'll want to manipulate the values in some way, but often a straight copy is enough.

Again, without LINQ it's hard to give convincing examples of this, but let's go back to our `Person` class and *suppose* we had a good reason to want to convert a collection of `Person` instances into a similar collection where each element has just a name and a flag to say whether that person is an adult. Given an appropriate `person` variable, you could use something like this:

```
new { Name = person.Name, IsAdult = (person.Age >= 18) }
```

That works, and for just a single property the syntax for setting the name (the part in bold) isn't too clumsy, but if you were copying several properties it would get tiresome.

C# 3 provides a shortcut: if you don't specify the property name, but just the expression to evaluate for the value, it'll use the last part of the expression as the name, provided it's a simple field or property. This is called a *projection initializer.* It means you can rewrite the previous code as follows:

```
new { person.Name, IsAdult = (person.Age >= 18) }
```

It's common for all the bits of an anonymous object initializer to be projection initializers—it typically happens when you're taking some properties from one object and some properties from another, often as part of a join operation. Anyway, I'm getting ahead of myself.

The following listing shows the previous code in action, using the List<T>.ConvertAll method and an anonymous method.

Listing 8.6 Transformation from `Person` to a name and adulthood flag

```
List<Person> family = new List<Person>
{
    new Person { Name = "Holly", Age = 36 },
    new Person { Name = "Jon", Age = 36 },
    new Person { Name = "Tom", Age = 9 },
    new Person { Name = "Robin", Age = 6 },
    new Person { Name = "William", Age = 6 }
};
var converted = family.ConvertAll(delegate(Person person)
    { return new { person.Name, IsAdult = (person.Age >= 18) }; }
);
foreach (var person in converted)
{
    Console.WriteLine("{0} is an adult? {1}",
                    person.Name, person.IsAdult);
}
```

In addition to the use of a projection initializer for the Name property, listing 8.6 shows the value of delegate type inference and anonymous methods. Without them, you couldn't have retained the strong typing of converted, because you wouldn't have been able to specify what the TOutput type parameter of Converter should be. As it is, you can iterate through the new list and access the Name and IsAdult properties as if you were using any other type.

Don't spend too long thinking about projection initializers at this point—the important thing is to be aware that they exist so you won't get confused when you see them later. In fact, that advice applies to this entire section on anonymous types, so without going into details, let's look at why they're present at all.

8.5.4 What's the point?

I hope you're not feeling cheated at this point, but I sympathize if you are. Anonymous types are a fairly complex solution to a problem we haven't really encountered yet. But I bet you *have* seen part of the problem before, really.

If you've ever done any real-life work involving databases, you'll know that you don't always want all of the data that's available on all the rows that match your query criteria. Often it's not a problem to fetch more than you need, but if you only need 2 columns out of the 50 in the table, you wouldn't bother to select all 50, would you?

The same problem occurs in nondatabase code. Suppose you have a class that reads a log file and produces a sequence of log lines with many fields. Keeping all of the information might be far too memory-intensive if you only care about a couple of fields from the log. LINQ lets you filter that information easily.

But what's the result of that filtering? How can you keep some data and discard the rest? How can you easily keep some *derived* data that isn't directly represented in the original form? How can you combine pieces of data that may not initially have been consciously associated, or that may only have a relationship in a particular situation? Effectively, you want a new data type, but manually creating such a type in every situation is tedious, particularly when you have tools such as LINQ available that make the rest of the process so simple. Figure 8.5 shows the three elements that make anonymous types a powerful feature.

If you find yourself creating a type that's only used in a single method, and that only contains fields and trivial properties, consider whether an anonymous type would be appropriate. I suspect that usually, when you find yourself leaning toward anonymous types, you could also use LINQ to help you.

If you find yourself using the same sequence of properties for the same purpose in several places, though, you might want to consider creating a normal type for the purpose, even if it still just contains trivial properties. Anonymous types naturally infect whatever code they're used in with implicit typing, which is often fine, but can be a nuisance at other times. In particular, it means you can't easily create a method to return an instance of that type in a strongly typed way. As with the previous features, use anonymous types when they genuinely make the code simpler to work with, not just because they're new and cool.

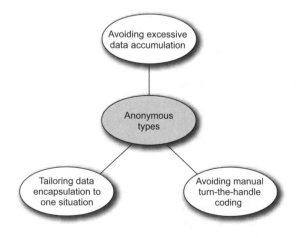

Figure 8.5 **Anonymous types allow you to keep just the data you need for a particular situation, in a form that's tailored to that situation, without the tedium of writing a fresh type each time.**

8.6 *Summary*

What a seemingly mixed bag of features! You've seen four features that are quite similar, at least in syntax: object initializers, collection initializers, implicitly typed arrays, and anonymous types. The other two features—automatic properties and implicitly typed local variables—are somewhat different. Likewise, most of the features would've been useful individually in C# 2, whereas implicitly typed arrays and anonymous types only pay back the cost of learning about them when the rest of the C# 3 features are brought into play.

So what do these features really have in common? *They all relieve the developer of tedious coding.* I'm sure you don't enjoy writing trivial properties any more than I do, or setting several properties, one at a time, using a local variable—particularly when you're trying to build up a collection of similar objects. Not only do the new features of C# 3 make it easier to *write* the code, they also make it easier to *read* it, at least when they're applied sensibly.

In the next chapter, we'll look at a major new language feature, along with a framework feature it provides direct support for. If you thought anonymous methods made creating delegates easy, just wait until you see lambda expressions.

Lambda expressions and expression trees

In chapter 5 you saw how C# 2 made delegates much easier to use due to implicit conversions of method groups, anonymous methods, and return type and parameter variance. This is enough to make event subscription significantly simpler and more readable, but delegates in C# 2 are still too bulky to be used all the time; a page of code full of anonymous methods is painful to read, and you wouldn't want to start putting multiple anonymous methods in a single statement on a regular basis.

One of the fundamental building blocks of LINQ is the ability to create pipelines of operations, along with any state required by those operations. These operations can express all kinds of logic about data: how to filter it, how to order it, how to join different data sources together, and much more. When LINQ queries are executed in-process, those operations are usually represented by delegates.

Statements containing several delegates are common when manipulating data with LINQ to Objects,[1] and *lambda expressions* in C# 3 make all of this possible without sacrificing readability. (While I'm mentioning readability, this chapter uses *lambda expression* and *lambda* interchangeably.)

> **IT'S ALL GREEK TO ME**   The term *lambda expression* comes from *lambda calculus,* also written as λ-calculus, where λ is the Greek letter lambda. This is an area of math and computer science dealing with defining and applying functions. It's been around for a long time and is the basis of functional languages such as ML. The good news is that you don't need to know lambda calculus to use lambda expressions in C# 3.

Executing delegates is only part of the LINQ story. To use databases and other query engines efficiently, you need a different representation of the operations in the pipeline—a way to treat code as data that can be examined programmatically. The logic within the operations can then be transformed into a different form, such as a web service call, a SQL or LDAP query—whatever's appropriate.

Although it's possible to build up representations of queries in a particular API, it's usually tricky to read and it sacrifices a lot of compiler support. This is where lambdas save the day again: not only can they be used to create delegate instances, but the C# compiler can also transform them into *expression trees*—data structures representing the logic of the lambda expressions—so that other code can examine it. In short, lambda expressions are the idiomatic way of representing the operations in LINQ data pipelines—but we'll take things one step at a time, examining them in a fairly isolated way before we embrace the whole of LINQ.

In this chapter we'll look at both ways of using lambda expressions, although for the moment our coverage of expression trees will be relatively basic—we won't create any SQL just yet. With that theory under your belt, you should be relatively comfortable with lambda expressions and expression trees by the time we hit the really impressive stuff in chapter 12.

In the final part of this chapter we'll examine how type inference has changed for C# 3, mostly due to lambdas with implicit parameter types. This is a bit like learning how to tie shoelaces: far from exciting, but without this ability you'll trip over yourself when you start running.

Let's begin by seeing what lambda expressions look like. We'll start with an anonymous method and gradually transform it into shorter and shorter forms.

---

[1]   LINQ to Objects handles sequences of data within the same process. By contrast, providers such as LINQ to SQL offload the work to other out-of-process systems—databases, for example.

9.1   Lambda expressions as delegates

In many ways, lambda expressions can be seen as an evolution of anonymous methods from C# 2. Lambda expressions can do almost everything that anonymous methods can, and they're almost always more readable and compact.[2] In particular, the behavior of captured variables is exactly the same in lambda expressions as in anonymous methods. In the most explicit form, not much difference exists between the two, but lambda expressions have a lot of shortcuts available that make them compact in common situations. Like anonymous methods, lambda expressions have special conversion rules—the type of the expression isn't a delegate type in itself, but it can be converted into a delegate instance in various ways, both implicitly and explicitly. The term *anonymous function* covers anonymous methods and lambda expressions, and in many cases the same conversion rules apply to both of them.

We'll start with a simple example, initially expressed as an anonymous method. You'll create a delegate instance that takes a `string` parameter and returns an `int` (which is the length of the string). First you need to choose a delegate type to use; fortunately, .NET 3.5 comes with a whole family of generic delegate types to help you out.

9.1.1   Preliminaries: Introducing the Func<...> delegate types

There are five generic `Func` delegate types in .NET 3.5's `System` namespace. There's nothing special about `Func`—it's just handy to have some predefined generic types that are capable of handling many situations. Each delegate signature takes between zero and four parameters, the types of which are specified as type parameters.[3] The last type parameter is used for the return type in each case.

Here are the signatures of all the `Func` delegate types in .NET 3.5:

```
TResult Func<TResult>()
TResult Func<T,TResult>(T arg)
TResult Func<T1,T2,TResult>(T1 arg1, T2 arg2)
TResult Func<T1,T2,T3,TResult>(T1 arg1, T2 arg2, T3 arg3)
TResult Func<T1,T2,T3,T4,TResult>(T1 arg1, T2 arg2, T3 arg3, T4 arg4)
```

For example, `Func<string,double,int>` is equivalent to a delegate type of the form

```
public delegate int SomeDelegate(string arg1, double arg2)
```

The `Action<...>` set of delegates provides the equivalent functionality when you want a void return type. The single parameter form of `Action` existed in .NET 2.0, but the rest are new to .NET 3.5. If four arguments aren't enough for you, then .NET 4 has the answer: it expands both the `Action<...>` and `Func<...>` families to take up to 16 arguments, so `Func<T1,...,T16,TResult>` has an eye-watering 17 type parameters. This is primarily to help support the Dynamic Language Runtime (DLR) that you'll meet in chapter 14, and you're unlikely to need to deal with it directly.

---

[2]   The one feature available to anonymous methods but not lambda expressions is the ability to concisely ignore parameters. Look back at section 5.4.3 for more details if you're interested, but in practice it's not something you'll really miss with lambda expressions.

[3]   You may remember that you met the version without any parameters (but one type parameter) in chapter 6.

For this example, you need a type that takes a string parameter and returns an int, so you can use Func<string,int>.

9.1.2 *First transformation to a lambda expression*

Now that you know the delegate type, you can use an anonymous method to create your delegate instance. The following listing shows this and executes the delegate instance afterward, so you can see it working.

Listing 9.1 Using an anonymous method to create a delegate instance

```
Func<string,int> returnLength;
returnLength = delegate (string text) { return text.Length; };

Console.WriteLine(returnLength("Hello"));
```

Listing 9.1 prints 5, just as you'd expect it to. I've separated the declaration of return-Length from the assignment to it, to keep it on one line—it's easier to keep track of that way. The anonymous method expression is the part in bold; that's the part you'll convert into a lambda expression.

The most long-winded form of a lambda expression is this:

```
(explicitly-typed-parameter-list) => { statements }
```

The => part is new to C# 3 and tells the compiler that you're using a lambda expression. Most of the time, lambda expressions are used with a delegate type that has a nonvoid return type, and the syntax is slightly less intuitive when there isn't a result. This is another indication of the changes in idiom between C# 1 and C# 3. In C# 1, delegates were usually used for events and rarely returned anything. In LINQ they're usually used as part of a data pipeline, taking input and returning a result to say what the projected value is, or whether the item matches the current filter, and so forth.

With the explicit parameters and statements in braces, this version looks very similar to an anonymous method. The following listing is equivalent to listing 9.1, but it uses a lambda expression.

Listing 9.2 A long-winded first lambda expression, similar to an anonymous method

```
Func<string,int> returnLength;
returnLength = (string text) => { return text.Length; };

Console.WriteLine(returnLength("Hello"));
```

Again, I've used bold to indicate the expression used to create the delegate instance. When reading lambda expressions, it helps to think of the => part as "goes to," so the example in listing 9.2 could be read "text goes to text.Length." Since this is the only part of the listing that's interesting for a while, I'll show it alone from now on. You can replace the bold text from listing 9.2 with any of the lambda expressions listed in this section and the result will be the same.

The same rules that govern return statements in anonymous methods apply to lambdas: you can't try to return a value from a lambda expression with a void return type, whereas if there's a nonvoid return type, every code path has to return a compatible value.[4] It's all pretty intuitive and rarely gets in the way.

So far, we haven't saved much space or made things particularly easy to read. Let's start applying the shortcuts.

9.1.3 Using a single expression as the body

The form we've looked at so far uses a full block of code to return the value. This is flexible—you can have multiple statements, perform loops, return from different places in the block, and so on, just as with anonymous methods. But most of the time, you can easily express the whole of the body in a single expression, the value of which is the result of the lambda.[5] In these cases, you can specify just that expression, without any braces, return statements, or semicolons. The format then is

```
(explicitly-typed-parameter-list) => expression
```

In our example, this means that the lambda expression becomes

```
(string text) => text.Length
```

That's starting to look simpler already. Now, what about that parameter type? The compiler already knows that instances of Func<string,int> take a single string parameter, so you should be able to just name that parameter.

9.1.4 Implicitly typed parameter lists

Most of the time, the compiler can guess the parameter types without you explicitly stating them. In these cases, you can write the lambda expression as

```
(implicitly-typed-parameter-list) => expression
```

An implicitly typed parameter list is just a comma-separated list of names, without the types. You can't mix and match for different parameters—either the whole list is explicitly typed, or it's all implicitly typed. Also, if any of the parameters are out or ref parameters, you're forced to use explicit typing. In our example, it's fine, so your lambda expression is just

```
(text) => text.Length
```

That's getting pretty short now. There's not a lot more you could get rid of. The parentheses seem redundant, though.

---

[4] Code paths throwing exceptions don't need to return a value, of course, and neither do detectable infinite loops.

[5] You can still use this syntax for a delegate with a void return type if you only need one statement. You omit the semicolon and the braces, basically.

9.1.5 *Shortcut for a single parameter*

When the lambda expression only needs a single parameter, and that parameter can be implicitly typed, C# 3 allows you to omit the parentheses, so it now has this form:

```
parameter-name => expression
```

The final form of your lambda expression is therefore

```
text => text.Length
```

You may be wondering why there are so many special cases with lambda expressions—none of the rest of the language cares whether a method has one parameter or more, for instance. Well, what sounds like a very specific case actually turns out to be *extremely* common, and the improvement in readability from removing the parentheses from the parameter list can be significant when there are many lambdas in a short piece of code.

It's worth noting that you can put parentheses around the whole lambda expression if you want to, just like other expressions. Occasionally this helps readability, such as when you're assigning the lambda to a variable or property—otherwise, the equals symbols can get confusing, at least to start with. Most of the time it's perfectly readable without any extra syntax at all. The following listing shows this in the context of our original code.

Listing 9.3 A concise lambda expression

```
Func<string,int> returnLength;
returnLength = text => text.Length;

Console.WriteLine(returnLength("Hello"));
```

At first you may find listing 9.3 confusing to read, in the same way that anonymous methods appear strange to many developers until they get used to them. In normal use, you'd declare the variable and assign the value to it in the same expression, making it even clearer. When you *are* used to lambda expressions, though, you can appreciate how concise they are. It'd be hard to imagine a shorter, clearer way of creating a delegate instance.[6] You could change the variable name text to something like x, and in full LINQ that's often useful, but longer names give valuable information to the reader.

I've shown this transformation over the course of a few pages, but figure 9.1 makes it clear just how much extraneous syntax you've saved.

The decision of whether to use the short form for the body of the lambda expression, specifying just an expression instead of a whole block, is completely independent from the decision about whether to use explicit or implicit parameters. This example has taken us down one route of shortening the lambda, but we could've started off by

---

[6] That's not to say it's impossible. Some languages allow closures to be represented as simple blocks of code with a magic variable name to represent the common case of a single parameter.

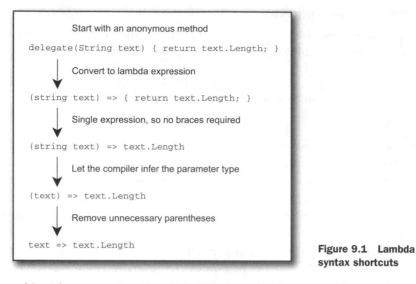

Figure 9.1 **Lambda syntax shortcuts**

making the parameters implicit. When you're comfortable with lambda expressions, you won't think about this at all—you'll just write the shortest available form naturally.

> **HIGHER-ORDER FUNCTIONS**   The body of a lambda expression can itself contain a lambda expression, and this tends to be as confusing as it sounds. Alternatively, the parameter to a lambda expression can be another delegate, which is just as bad. Both of these are examples of *higher-order functions*. If you enjoy feeling dazed and confused, have a look at some of the downloadable source code. Although I'm being flippant, this approach is common in functional programming and can be useful. It just takes a certain degree of perseverance to get into the right mindset.

So far we've only dealt with a single lambda expression, putting it into different forms. Let's look at a few examples to make things more concrete before we examine the details.

9.2   *Simple examples using List<T> and events*

When we look at extension methods in chapter 10, we'll use lambda expressions all the time. Until then, List<T> and event handlers give us the best examples. We'll start off with lists, using automatically implemented properties, implicitly typed local variables, and collection initializers for the sake of brevity. We'll then call methods that take delegate parameters, using lambda expressions to create the delegates, of course.

9.2.1   *Filtering, sorting, and actions on lists*

Remember the FindAll method on List<T>—it takes a Predicate<T> and returns a new list with all the elements from the original list that match the predicate. The Sort method takes a Comparison<T> and sorts the list accordingly. Finally, the ForEach method takes an Action<T> to perform on each element.

Listing 9.4 uses lambda expressions to provide the delegate instance to each of these methods. The sample data in question is the name and year of release for various films. You print out the original list, then create and print out a filtered list of only old films, and then sort and print out the original list ordered by name. (It's interesting to consider how much more code would've been required to do the same thing in C# 1.)

Listing 9.4   Manipulating a list of films using lambda expressions

```
class Film
{
    public string Name { get; set; }
    public int Year { get; set; }
}
...
var films = new List<Film>
{
    new Film { Name = "Jaws", Year = 1975 },
    new Film { Name = "Singing in the Rain", Year = 1952 },
    new Film { Name = "Some like it Hot", Year = 1959 },
    new Film { Name = "The Wizard of Oz", Year = 1939 },
    new Film { Name = "It's a Wonderful Life", Year = 1946 },
    new Film { Name = "American Beauty", Year = 1999 },
    new Film { Name = "High Fidelity", Year = 2000 },
    new Film { Name = "The Usual Suspects", Year = 1995 }
};

Action<Film> print =                                    ❶ Creates reusable
    film => Console.WriteLine("Name={0}, Year={1}",        list-printing delegate
                             film.Name, film.Year);

films.ForEach(print);                                   ❷ Prints original list

films.FindAll(film => film.Year < 1960)                 ❸ Creates filtered list
    .ForEach(print);

films.Sort((f1, f2) => f1.Name.CompareTo(f2.Name));     ❹ Sorts original list
films.ForEach(print);
```

The first half of listing 9.4 involves setting up the data. This code uses a named type just to make life easier—an anonymous type would've meant a few more hoops to jump through in this particular case.

Before you use the newly created list, you create a delegate instance ❶, which you'll use to print out the items of the list. You use this delegate instance three times, which is why I created a variable to hold it rather than using a separate lambda expression each time. It just prints a single element, but by passing it into List<T>.ForEach you can dump the whole list to the console. A subtle but important point is that the semicolon at the end of this statement is part of the assignment statement, not part of the lambda expression. If you were using the same lambda expression as an argument in a method call, there wouldn't be a semicolon directly after Console.WriteLine(...).

The first list you print out is just the original one without any modifications ❷. You then find all the films in your list that were made before 1960 and print those out ❸. This is done with another lambda expression, which is executed for each film in the list—it only has to determine whether a single film should be included in the filtered list. The source code uses the lambda expression as a method argument, but really the compiler has created a method like this:

```
private static bool SomeAutoGeneratedName(Film film)
{
    return film.Year < 1960;
}
```

The method call to `FindAll` is then effectively this:

```
films.FindAll(new Predicate<Film>(SomeAutoGeneratedName))
```

The lambda expression support here is just like the anonymous method support in C# 2; it's all cleverness on the part of the compiler. (In fact, the Microsoft compiler is even smarter in this case—it realizes it can get away with reusing the delegate instance if the code is ever called again, so it caches it.)

Sorting the list is also achieved using a lambda expression ❹, which compares any two films using their names. I have to confess that explicitly calling `CompareTo` yourself is a bit ugly. In the next chapter you'll see how the `OrderBy` extension method allows you to express ordering in a neater way.

Let's look at another example, this time using lambda expressions with event handling.

9.2.2 *Logging in an event handler*

If you think back to chapter 5, in section 5.9 you saw an easy way of using anonymous methods to log which events were occurring, but you could only use a compact syntax because you didn't mind losing the parameter information. What if you wanted to log both the nature of the event *and* information about its sender and arguments? Lambda expressions enable this in a neat way, as shown in the following listing.

Listing 9.5 Logging events using lambda expressions

```
static void Log(string title, object sender, EventArgs e)
{
    Console.WriteLine("Event: {0}", title);
    Console.WriteLine(" Sender: {0}", sender);
    Console.WriteLine(" Arguments: {0}", e.GetType());
    foreach (PropertyDescriptor prop in
            TypeDescriptor.GetProperties(e))
    {
        string name = prop.DisplayName;
        object value = prop.GetValue(e);
        Console.WriteLine("    {0}={1}", name, value);
    }
}
```

```
...
Button button = new Button { Text = "Click me" };
button.Click      += (src, e) => Log("Click", src, e);
button.KeyPress   += (src, e) => Log("KeyPress", src, e);
button.MouseClick += (src, e) => Log("MouseClick", src, e);

Form form = new Form { AutoSize = true, Controls = { button } };
Application.Run(form);
```

Listing 9.5 uses lambda expressions to pass the event name *and parameters* to the Log method, which logs details of the event. You don't log the details of the event source, beyond whatever its ToString override returns, because an overwhelming amount of information is associated with controls. But you use reflection over property descriptors to show the details of the EventArgs instance passed to you.

Here's some sample output from when you click the button:

```
Event: Click
  Sender: System.Windows.Forms.Button, Text: Click me
  Arguments: System.Windows.Forms.MouseEventArgs
    Button=Left
    Clicks=1
    X=53
    Y=17
    Delta=0
    Location={X=53,Y=17}
Event: MouseClick
  Sender: System.Windows.Forms.Button, Text: Click me
  Arguments: System.Windows.Forms.MouseEventArgs
    Button=Left
    Clicks=1
    X=53
    Y=17
    Delta=0
    Location={X=53,Y=17}
```

All of this is *possible* without lambda expressions, of course, but it's a lot neater than it would've been otherwise.

Now that you've seen lambdas being converted into delegate instances, it's time to look at expression trees, which represent lambda expressions as data instead of code.

9.3 *Expression trees*

The idea of *code as data* is an old one, but it hasn't been used much in popular programming languages. You could argue that all .NET programs use the concept, because the IL code is treated as data by the JIT, which then converts it into native code to run on your CPU. That's deeply hidden though, and although libraries that manipulate IL programmatically exist, they're not widely used.

Expression trees in .NET 3.5 provide an abstract way of representing some code as a tree of objects. It's like CodeDOM but operating at a slightly higher level. The primary use of expression trees is in LINQ, and later in this section you'll see how crucial expression trees are to the whole LINQ story.

C# 3 provides built-in support for converting lambda expressions to expression trees, but before we cover that, let's explore how they fit into the .NET Framework without using any compiler tricks.

9.3.1 *Building expression trees programmatically*

Expression trees aren't as mystical as they sound, although some of the uses they're put to look like magic. As the name suggests, they're trees of objects, where each node in the tree is an expression in itself. Different types of expressions represent the different operations that can be performed in code: binary operations, such as addition; unary operations, such as taking the length of an array; method calls; constructor calls; and so forth.

The `System.Linq.Expressions` namespace contains the various classes that represent expressions. All of them derive from the `Expression` class, which is abstract and mostly consists of static factory methods to create instances of other expression classes. It exposes two properties, though:

- The `Type` property represents the .NET type of the evaluated expression—you can think of it like a return type. The type of an expression that fetches the `Length` property of a string would be `int`, for example.
- The `NodeType` property returns the kind of expression represented as a member of the `ExpressionType` enumeration, with values such as `LessThan`, `Multiply`, and `Invoke`. To use the same example, in `myString.Length` the property access part would have a node type of `MemberAccess`.

There are many classes derived from `Expression`, and some of them can have many different node types. `BinaryExpression`, for instance, represents any operation with two operands: arithmetic, logic, comparisons, array indexing, and the like. This is where the `NodeType` property is important, as it distinguishes between different kinds of expressions that are represented by the same class.

I don't intend to cover every expression class or node type—there are far too many, and MSDN does a perfectly good job of explaining them (see http://mng.bz/3vW3). Instead, we'll try to get a general feel for what you can do with expression trees.

Let's start off by creating one of the simplest possible expression trees, adding two constant integers together. The following listing creates an expression tree to represent 2+3.

Listing 9.6 A simple expression tree, adding 2 and 3

```
Expression firstArg = Expression.Constant(2);
Expression secondArg = Expression.Constant(3);
Expression add = Expression.Add(firstArg, secondArg);

Console.WriteLine(add);
```

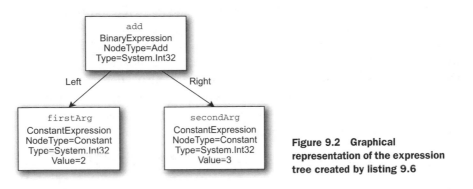

Figure 9.2 **Graphical representation of the expression tree created by listing 9.6**

Running listing 9.6 will produce the output (2 + 3), which demonstrates that the various expression classes override ToString to produce human-readable output. Figure 9.2 depicts the tree generated by the code.

It's worth noting that the leaf expressions are created first in the code: you build expressions from the bottom up. This is enforced by the fact that expressions are immutable—once you've created an expression, it'll never change, so you can cache and reuse expressions at will.

Now that you've built up an expression tree, it's time to execute it.

9.3.2 *Compiling expression trees into delegates*

One of the types derived from Expression is LambdaExpression. The generic class Expression<TDelegate> then derives from LambdaExpression. It's all slightly confusing—figure 9.3 shows the type hierarchy to make things clearer.

The difference between Expression and Expression<TDelegate> is that the generic class is statically typed to indicate what kind of expression it is, in terms of return type and parameters. Obviously, this is expressed by the TDelegate type parameter, which must be a delegate type. For instance, the simple addition expression takes no parameters and returns an integer—this is matched by the signature of Func<int>, so you could use an Expression<Func<int>> to represent the expression in a statically typed manner. You do this using the Expression.Lambda method, which has a number of overloads. The examples we've looked at use the generic method, which uses a

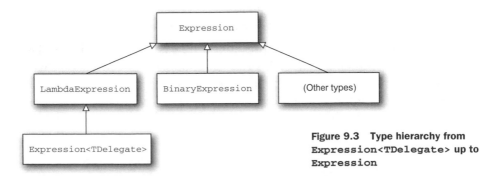

Figure 9.3 **Type hierarchy from Expression<TDelegate> up to Expression**

type parameter to indicate the type of delegate we wanted to represent. See MSDN for alternatives.

So, what's the point of doing this? Well, `LambdaExpression` has a `Compile` method that creates a delegate of the appropriate type; `Expression<TDelegate>` has another method by the same name, but statically typed to return a delegate of type `TDelegate`. This delegate can now be executed in the normal manner, as if it had been created using a normal method or any other means. The following listing shows this in action, with the same expression as before.

Listing 9.7   Compiling and executing an expression tree

```
Expression firstArg = Expression.Constant(2);
Expression secondArg = Expression.Constant(3);
Expression add = Expression.Add(firstArg, secondArg);

Func<int> compiled = Expression.Lambda<Func<int>>(add).Compile();
Console.WriteLine(compiled());
```

Arguably, listing 9.7 is one of the most convoluted ways of printing out 5 that you could ask for. At the same time, it's also rather impressive. You're programmatically creating some logical blocks and representing them as normal objects, and then asking the framework to compile the whole thing into real code that can be executed. You may never need to use expression trees this way, or even build them up programmatically at all, but it's useful background information that will help you understand how LINQ works.

As I said at the beginning of this section, expression trees aren't too far removed from CodeDOM—Snippy compiles and executes C# code that's been entered as plain text, for instance. But two significant differences exist between CodeDOM and expression trees.

First, in .NET 3.5, expression trees were only able to represent single expressions. They weren't designed for whole classes, methods, or even just statements. This has changed somewhat in .NET 4, where they're used to support dynamic typing—you can now create blocks, assign values to variables, and so on. But there are still significant restrictions compared with CodeDOM.

Second, C# supports expression trees directly in the language, through lambda expressions. Let's take a look at that now.

9.3.3   *Converting C# lambda expressions to expression trees*

As you've already seen, lambda expressions can be converted to appropriate delegate instances, either implicitly or explicitly. That's not the only conversion that's available. You can also ask the compiler to build an expression tree from your lambda expression, creating an instance of `Expression<TDelegate>` at execution time. For example, the following listing shows a much shorter way of creating the "return 5" expression, compiling it, and then invoking the resulting delegate.

Listing 9.8　Using lambda expressions to create expression trees

```
Expression<Func<int>> return5 = () => 5;
Func<int> compiled = return5.Compile();
Console.WriteLine(compiled());
```

In the first line of listing 9.8, the () => 5 part is the lambda expression. You don't need any casts because the compiler can verify everything as it goes. You could've written 2+3 instead of 5, but the compiler would've optimized the addition away for you. The important point to take away is that the lambda expression has been converted into an expression tree.

> **THERE ARE LIMITATIONS** Not *all* lambda expressions can be converted to expression trees. You can't convert a lambda with a block of statements (even just one return statement) into an expression tree—it has to be in the form that evaluates a single expression, and that expression can't contain assignments. This restriction applies even in .NET 4 with its extended abilities for expression trees. Although these are the most common restrictions, they're not the only ones—the full list isn't worth describing here, as this issue comes up so rarely. If there's a problem with an attempted conversion, you'll find out at compile time.

Let's look at a more complicated example to see how things work, particularly with respect to parameters. This time you'll write a predicate that takes two strings and checks to see if the first one begins with the second. The code is simple when written as a lambda expression.

Listing 9.9　Demonstration of a more complicated expression tree

```
Expression<Func<string, string, bool>> expression =
    (x, y) => x.StartsWith(y);

var compiled = expression.Compile();

Console.WriteLine(compiled("First", "Second"));
Console.WriteLine(compiled("First", "Fir"));
```

The expression tree itself is more complicated, especially by the time you've converted it into an instance of LambdaExpression. The next listing shows how it could be built in code.

Listing 9.10　Building a method call expression tree in code

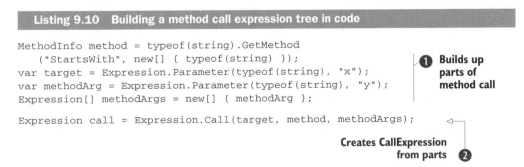

```
MethodInfo method = typeof(string).GetMethod
    ("StartsWith", new[] { typeof(string) });
var target = Expression.Parameter(typeof(string), "x");
var methodArg = Expression.Parameter(typeof(string), "y");
Expression[] methodArgs = new[] { methodArg };

Expression call = Expression.Call(target, method, methodArgs);
```

❶ Builds up parts of method call

Creates CallExpression from parts ❷

```
var lambdaParameters = new[] { target, methodArg };
var lambda = Expression.Lambda<Func<string, string, bool>>
    (call, lambdaParameters);

var compiled = lambda.Compile();

Console.WriteLine(compiled("First", "Second"));
Console.WriteLine(compiled("First", "Fir"));
```

Converts call into LambdaExpression ❸

As you can see, listing 9.10 is considerably more involved than the version with the C# lambda expression. But it does make it more obvious exactly what's involved in the tree and how parameters are bound.

You start off by working out everything you need to know about the method call that forms the body of the final expression ❶: the target of the method (the string you're calling `StartsWith` on); the method itself (as a `MethodInfo`); and the list of arguments (in this case, just the one). It so happens that your method target and argument will both be parameters passed into the expression, but they could be other types of expressions—constants, the results of other method calls, property evaluations, and so forth.

After building the method call as an expression ❷, you then need to convert it into a lambda expression ❸, binding the parameters as you go. You reuse the same `ParameterExpression` values you created as information for the method call: the order in which they're specified when creating the lambda expression is the order in which they'll be picked up when you eventually call the delegate.

Figure 9.4 shows the same final expression tree graphically. To be picky, even though it's still called an expression tree, the fact that you reuse the parameter expressions (and you have to—creating a new one with the same name and attempting to bind parameters that way causes an exception at execution time) means that it's not really a tree in the purest sense.

Glancing at the complexity of figure 9.4 and listing 9.10 without trying to look at the details, you'd be forgiven for thinking that you were doing something really complicated, when in fact it's just a single method call. Imagine what the expression tree for a genuinely complex expression would look like—and then be grateful that C# 3 can create expression trees from lambda expressions!

For one final way of looking at the same idea, Visual Studio 2010 and 2012 provide a built-in visualizer for expression trees.[7] This can be useful if you're trying to work out how to build up an expression tree in code, and you want to get an idea of what it should look like; write a lambda expression that does what you want with some dummy data, look at the visualization in the debugger, and then work out how to build similar trees with the information you have in your real code. The visualizer relies on changes within .NET 4, so it won't work with projects targeting .NET 3.5. Figure 9.5 shows the visualization for the `StartsWith` example.

---

[7] If you're using Visual Studio 2008, you can download some sample code from MSDN to build a similar visualizer (see http://mng.bz/g6xd), but obviously it's easier to use the one shipped with Visual Studio if you have a recent enough version.

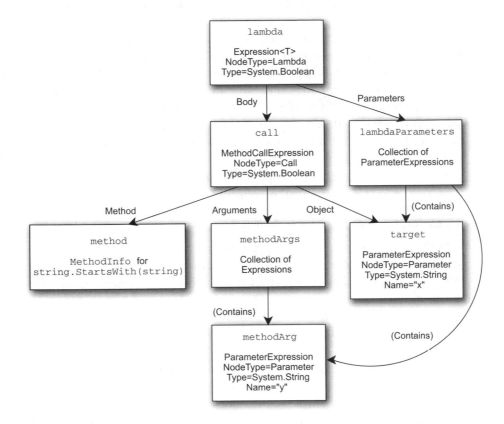

Figure 9.4 Graphical representation of an expression tree that calls a method and uses parameters from a lambda expression

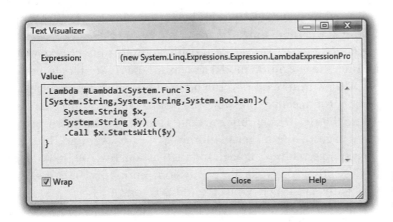

Figure 9.5 Debugger visualization of an expression tree

The `.Lambda` and `.Call` parts of the visualization correspond to your calls to `Expression.Lambda` and `Expression.Call`; $x and $y correspond to the parameter expressions. The visualization is the same whether the expression tree has been built up explicitly through code or using a lambda expression conversion.

One small point to note is that although the C# compiler builds expression trees in the compiled code using code similar to listing 9.10, it has one shortcut up its sleeve: it doesn't need to use normal reflection to get the `MethodInfo` for `string.StartsWith`. Instead, it uses the method equivalent of the `typeof` operator. This is only available in IL, not in C# itself, and the same operator is used to create delegate instances from method groups.

Now that you've seen how expression trees and lambda expressions are linked, let's take a brief look at why they're so useful.

9.3.4   *Expression trees at the heart of LINQ*

Without lambda expressions, expression trees would have relatively little value. They'd be an alternative to CodeDOM in cases where you only wanted to model a single expression instead of whole statements, methods, types, and so forth, but the benefit would still be limited.

The reverse is also true to a limited extent: without expression trees, lambda expressions would certainly be *less* useful. Having a more compact way of creating delegate instances would still be welcome, and the shift toward a more functional mode of development would still be viable. Lambda expressions are particularly effective when combined with extension methods, as you'll see in the next chapter, but with expression trees in the picture as well, things get a lot more interesting.

What do you get when you combine lambda expressions, expression trees, and extension methods? The answer is, "the language side of LINQ," pretty much. The extra syntax you'll see in chapter 11 is icing on the cake, but the story would still have been compelling with just those three ingredients. For a long time you could have *either* nice compile-time checking *or* the ability to tell another platform to run some code, usually expressed as text (SQL queries being the most obvious example). But you couldn't do both at the same time.

By combining lambda expressions that provide compile-time checks with expression trees that abstract the execution model away from the desired logic, you can have the best of both worlds, within reason. At the heart of out-of-process LINQ providers is the idea that you can produce an expression tree from a familiar source language (C#, in this case) and use the result as an intermediate format that can then be converted into the native language of the target platform—SQL, for example. In some cases, there may not be a simple native language so much as a native API, making different web service calls depending on what the expression represents, perhaps. Figure 9.6 shows the different paths of LINQ to Objects and LINQ to SQL.

In some cases, the conversion may try to perform *all* the logic on the target platform, whereas other cases may use the compilation facilities of expression trees to

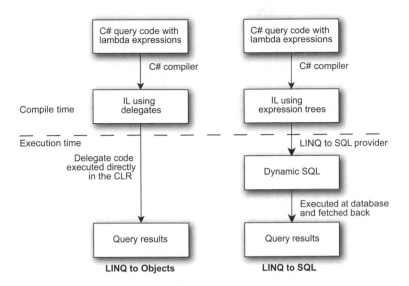

Figure 9.6 Both LINQ to Objects and LINQ to SQL start with C# code and end with query results. The ability to execute the code remotely comes through expression trees.

execute some of the expression locally and some elsewhere. We'll look at some of the details of this conversion step in chapter 12, but you should bear this end goal in mind as we explore extension methods and LINQ syntax in chapters 10 and 11.

> **NOT ALL CHECKING CAN BE DONE BY THE COMPILER** When expression trees are examined by some sort of converter, some cases generally have to be rejected. For instance, although it's possible to convert a call to `string.StartsWith` into a similar SQL expression, a call to `string.IsInterned` doesn't make sense in a database environment. Expression trees allow a large amount of compile-time safety, but the compiler can only check that the lambda expression can be converted into a valid expression tree; it can't make sure that the expression tree will be suitable for its eventual use.

Although the most common uses of expression trees are related to LINQ, that's not always the case...

9.3.5 *Expression trees beyond LINQ*

Bjarne Stroustrup once said, "I wouldn't like to build a tool that could only do what I had been able to imagine for it." Though expression trees were introduced into .NET primarily for LINQ, both the community and Microsoft have found other uses for them since then. This section is far from comprehensive, but it might give you a few ideas of where expression trees might help you.

OPTIMIZING THE DYNAMIC LANGUAGE RUNTIME

We'll see a lot more of the Dynamic Language Runtime (DLR) in chapter 14, when we talk about dynamic typing in C#, but expression trees are a core part of the architecture. They have three properties that make them attractive to the DLR:

- They're immutable, so you can cache them safely.
- They're composable, so you can build complex behavior out of simple building blocks.
- They can be compiled into delegates that are JIT-compiled into native code as normal.

The DLR has to make decisions about how to handle various expressions where the meaning can change subtly based on different rules. Expression trees allow these rules (and the results) to be transformed into code that's close to what you'd write by hand if you knew all the rules and results you'd seen so far. It's a powerful concept, and one that allows dynamic code to execute surprisingly quickly.

REFACTOR-PROOF REFERENCES TO MEMBERS

In section 9.3.3 I mentioned that the compiler can emit references to `MethodInfo` values much like the `typeof` operator can. Unfortunately, C# doesn't have the same ability, which means the only way of telling one piece of general-purpose, reflection-based code to "use the property called `BirthDate` defined in my type" has previously been to use a string literal and make sure that if you change the name of the property, you also change the literal. Using C# 3, you can build an expression tree representing a property reference using a lambda expression. The method can then dissect the expression tree, work out the property you mean, and do whatever it likes with the information. It can also compile the expression tree into a delegate and use it directly, of course.

As an example of how this might be used, you could write this:

```
serializationContext.AddProperty(x => x.BirthDate);
```

The serialization context would then know that you wanted to serialize the `BirthDate` property, and it could record appropriate metadata and retrieve the value. (Serialization is just one area where you may want a property or method reference; it's fairly common within reflection-driven code.) If you refactor the `BirthDate` property to call it `DateOfBirth`, the lambda expression will change too. Of course, it's not foolproof—there's no compile-time check that the expression really evaluates a simple property; that has to be an execution-time check in the `AddProperty` code.

It's possible that one day C# will gain the ability to do this within the language itself. Such an operator has already been named: `infoof`, pronounced either "info-of" or "in-foof," depending on your level of light-heartedness. This has been on the C# team's possible-feature list for a while, and unsurprisingly Eric Lippert has blogged about it (see http://mng.bz/24y7), but it hasn't made the cut yet. Maybe in C# 6.

SIMPLER REFLECTION

The final use I want to mention before we delve into the murky depths of type inference is also about reflection. As I mentioned in chapter 3, arithmetic operators don't play nicely with generics, which makes it hard to write generic code to (say) add up a series of values. Marc Gravell used expression trees to great effect to provide a generic `Operator` class and a nongeneric helper class, allowing you to write code such as this:

```
T runningTotal = initialValue;
foreach (T item in values)
{
    runningTotal = Operator.Add(runningTotal, item);
}
```

This will even work in cases where the values are a different type than the running total—adding a whole sequence of `TimeSpan` values to a `DateTime`, for example. It's *possible* to do this in C# 2, but it's significantly more fiddly due to the ways that operators are exposed via reflection, particularly for the primitive types. Expression trees allow the implementation of this magic to be quite clean, and the fact that they're compiled to normal IL, which is then JIT-compiled, gives great performance.

These are just some examples, and no doubt there are many developers busy working on completely different uses. But they mark an end to our direct coverage of lambda expressions and expression trees. You'll see a good deal more of them when we look at LINQ, but before we go any further, there are a few changes to C# that need some explanation. These are changes to type inference and how the compiler selects between overloaded methods.

9.4   *Changes to type inference and overload resolution*

The steps involved in type inference and overload resolution were altered in C# 3 to accommodate lambda expressions and to make anonymous methods more useful. This may not count as a new feature of C# as such, but it can be important to understand what the compiler is going to do. If you find details like this tedious and irrelevant, feel free to skip to the chapter summary, but remember that this section exists, so you can read it if you run across a compilation error related to this topic and can't understand why your code doesn't work. (Alternatively, you might want to come back to this section if you find your code *does* compile, but you don't think it should!)

Even within this section, I won't go into every nook and cranny—that's what the language specification is for; the details are in the C# 5 specification, section 7.5.2 ("Type inference"). Instead, I'll give an overview of the new behavior, providing examples of common cases. The primary reason for changing the specification is to allow lambda expressions to work in a concise fashion, which is why I've included the topic in this particular chapter.

Let's first look a little deeper at what problems you'd have run into if the C# team had stuck with the old rules.

9.4.1   *Reasons for change: streamlining generic method calls*

Type inference occurs in a few situations. You've already seen it apply to implicitly typed arrays, and it's also required when you try to implicitly convert a method group to a delegate type. This can be particularly confusing when the conversion occurs when you're using a method group as an argument to another method. With overloading of the method being called, *and* overloading of methods within the method group, *and* the possibility of generic methods getting involved, the set of potential conversions may be enormous.

By far the most common situation for type inference is when you're calling a generic method without specifying any type arguments. This happens all the time in LINQ—the way that query expressions work depends heavily on this ability. It's all handled so smoothly that it's easy to ignore how much the compiler has to work out on your behalf, all for the sake of making your code clearer and more concise.

The rules were *reasonably* straightforward in C# 2, although method groups and anonymous methods weren't always handled as well as you might've liked. The type inference process didn't deduce any information from them, leading to situations where the desired behavior was obvious to developers but not to the compiler. Life is more complicated in C# 3 due to lambda expressions. If you call a generic method using a lambda expression with an implicitly typed parameter list, the compiler needs to work out what types you're talking about before it can check the lambda expression's body.

This is much easier to see in code than in words. The following listing gives an example of the kind of issue I'm referring to: calling a generic method using a lambda expression.

Listing 9.11   Example of code requiring the new type inference rules

```
static void PrintConvertedValue<TInput,TOutput>
    (TInput input, Converter<TInput,TOutput> converter)
{
    Console.WriteLine(converter(input));
}
...
PrintConvertedValue("I'm a string", x => x.Length);
```

The `PrintConvertedValue` method in listing 9.11 simply takes an input value and a delegate that can convert that value into a different type. It's completely generic—it makes no assumptions about the type parameters `TInput` and `TOutput`. Now, look at the types of the arguments you're calling it with in the bottom line of the listing. The first argument is clearly a string, but what about the second? It's a lambda expression, so you need to convert it into a `Converter<TInput,TOutput>`, and that means you need to know the types of `TInput` and `TOutput`.

Remember from section 3.3.2 that the type inference rules of C# 2 were applied to each argument individually, with no way of using the types inferred from one argument to another. In this case, these rules would've stopped you from finding the types of TInput and TOutput for the second argument, so the code in listing 9.11 would've failed to compile.

Our eventual goal is to understand what makes listing 9.11 compile in C# 3 (and it does, I promise you), but we'll start with something more modest.

9.4.2 *Inferred return types of anonymous functions*

The following listing shows another example of some code that looks like it should compile but doesn't under the type inference rules of C# 2.

Listing 9.12 Attempting to infer the return type of an anonymous method

```
delegate T MyFunc<T>();          ◁── Declares delegate type: Func<T> isn't in .NET 2.0

static void WriteResult<T>(MyFunc<T> function)     ◁┐
{                                                   │ Declares generic
    Console.WriteLine(function());                  │ method with
}                                                   │ delegate parameter
...
WriteResult(delegate { return 5; });     ◁── Requires type inference for T
```

Compiling listing 9.12 under C# 2 gives an error like this:

```
error CS0411: The type arguments for method
'Snippet.WriteResult<T>(Snippet.MyFunc<T>)' cannot be inferred from the
usage. Try specifying the type arguments explicitly.
```

You can fix the error in two ways—either specify the type argument explicitly (as suggested by the compiler) or cast the anonymous method to a concrete delegate type:

```
WriteResult<int>(delegate { return 5; });
WriteResult((MyFunc<int>)delegate { return 5; });
```

Both of these work, but they're ugly. You might *like* the compiler to perform the same kind of type inference as for nondelegate types, using the type of the returned expression to infer the type of T. That's exactly what C# 3 does for both anonymous methods and lambda expressions, but there's one catch. Although in many cases only one return statement is involved, there can sometimes be more.

The following listing is a slightly modified version of listing 9.12, where the anonymous method sometimes returns an integer and sometimes returns an object.

Listing 9.13 Code returning an integer or an object depending on the time of day

```
delegate T MyFunc<T>();

static void WriteResult<T>(MyFunc<T> function)
{
    Console.WriteLine(function());
}
...
WriteResult(delegate
{
    if (DateTime.Now.Hour < 12)
```

```
    {
        return 10;              ◁───  Return type is int
    }
    else
    {
        return new object();    ◁──Return type is object
    }
});
```

The compiler uses the same logic to determine the return type in this situation as it does for implicitly typed arrays, as described in section 8.4. It forms a set of all the types from the return statements in the body of the anonymous function[8] (in this case, `int` and `object`) and checks to see if exactly one of the types can be implicitly converted to from all the others. There's an implicit conversion from `int` to `object` (via boxing) but not from `object` to `int`, so the inference succeeds with `object` as the inferred return type. If there are no types matching that criterion (or more than one), no return type can be inferred and you'll get a compilation error.

Now you know how to work out the *return* type of an anonymous function, but what about lambda expressions where the parameter types can be implicitly defined?

9.4.3   *Two-phase type inference*

The details of type inference in C# 3 are *much* more complicated than they are for C# 2. It's rare that you'll need to reference the specification for the exact behavior, but if you do, I recommend you write down all the type parameters, arguments, and so forth on a piece of paper, and then follow the specification step by step, carefully noting down every action it requires. You'll end up with a sheet full of *fixed* and *unfixed* type variables, with a different set of *bounds* for each of them. A *fixed* type variable is one that the compiler has decided the value of; otherwise it's *unfixed*. A *bound* is a piece of information about a type variable. In addition to a bunch of notes, I suspect you'll get a headache; this stuff isn't pretty.

I'll present a more fuzzy way of thinking about type inference—one that's likely to serve just as well as knowing the specification and that will be a lot easier to understand. The fact is, if the compiler doesn't perform type inference in exactly the way you want it to, it'll almost certainly result in a compilation error rather than code that builds but doesn't behave properly. If your code doesn't build, try giving the compiler more information—it's as simple as that. But here's *roughly* what's changed for C# 3.

The first big difference is that the method arguments work as a team in C# 3. In C# 2, every argument was used to try to pin down some type parameters *exactly*, and the compiler would complain if any two arguments came up with different results for a particular type parameter, even if they were compatible. In C# 3, arguments can

---

[8] Returned expressions that don't have a type, such as `null` or another lambda expression, aren't included in this set. Their validity is checked later, once a return type has been determined, but they don't contribute to that decision.

contribute *pieces* of information—types that must be implicitly convertible to the final fixed value of a particular type variable. The logic used to come up with that fixed value is the same as for inferred return types and implicitly typed arrays.

The following listing shows an example of this without using any lambda expressions or even anonymous methods.

Listing 9.14 Flexible type inference combining information from multiple arguments

```
static void PrintType<T>(T first, T second)
{
    Console.WriteLine(typeof(T));
}
...
PrintType(1, new object());
```

Although the code in listing 9.14 is *syntactically* valid in C# 2, it wouldn't build; type inference would fail, because the first parameter would decide that T must be int and the second parameter would decide that T must be object. In C# 3, the compiler determines that T should be object in exactly the same way that it did for the inferred return type in listing 9.13. In fact, the inferred return type rules are effectively one example of the more general process in C# 3.

The second change is that type inference is now performed in two phases. The first phase deals with normal arguments where the types involved are known to begin with. This includes anonymous functions where the parameter list is explicitly typed.

The second phase then kicks in, where implicitly typed lambda expressions and method groups have their types inferred. The idea is to see whether any of the information the compiler has pieced together so far is enough to work out the parameter types of the lambda expression (or method group). If it is, the compiler can then examine the body of the lambda expression and work out the inferred return type which is often another of the type parameters it's looking for. If the second phase gives some more information, the compiler goes through it again, repeating until either it runs out of clues or it's worked out all the type parameters involved.

Figure 9.7 shows this in flowchart form, but please bear in mind that this is a heavily simplified version of the algorithm.

Let's look at two examples to show how it works. First we'll take the code we started the section with—listing 9.11:

```
static void PrintConvertedValue<TInput,TOutput>
    (TInput input, Converter<TInput,TOutput> converter)
{
    Console.WriteLine(converter(input));
}
...
PrintConvertedValue("I'm a string", x => x.Length);
```

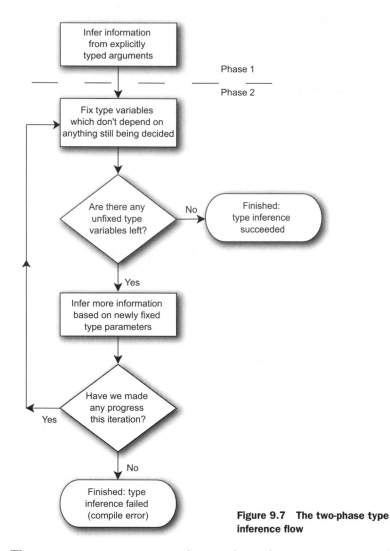

Figure 9.7   The two-phase type inference flow

The type parameters you need to work out here are TInput and TOutput. The steps performed are as follows:

1 Phase 1 begins.
2 The first parameter is of type TInput, and the first argument is of type string. You infer that there must be an implicit conversion from string to TInput.
3 The second parameter is of type Converter<TInput,TOutput>, and the second argument is an implicitly typed lambda expression. No inference is performed—you don't have enough information.
4 Phase 2 begins.
5 TInput doesn't depend on any unfixed type parameters, so it's fixed to string.

6 The second argument now has a fixed *input* type but an unfixed *output* type. You can consider it to be (string x) => x.Length and infer the return type as int. Therefore an implicit conversion must take place from int to TOutput.

7 Phase 2 repeats.

8 TOutput doesn't depend on anything unfixed, so it's fixed to int.

9 There are now no unfixed type parameters, so inference succeeds.

Complicated, eh? Still, it does the job—the result is what you'd want (TInput=string, TOutput=int), and everything compiles without any problems.

The importance of phase 2 repeating is best shown with another example. Listing 9.15 shows *two* conversions being performed, with the output of the first one becoming the input of the second. Until you've worked out the output type of the first conversion, you don't know the input type of the second, so you can't infer its output type either.

Listing 9.15 Multistage type inference

```
static void ConvertTwice<TInput,TMiddle,TOutput>
    (TInput input,
     Converter<TInput,TMiddle> firstConversion,
     Converter<TMiddle,TOutput> secondConversion)
{
    TMiddle middle = firstConversion(input);
    TOutput output = secondConversion(middle);
    Console.WriteLine(output);
}
...
ConvertTwice("Another string",
            text => text.Length,
            length => Math.Sqrt(length));
```

The first thing to notice is that the method signature appears to be pretty horrific. It's not too bad when you stop being scared and just look at it carefully, and certainly the example usage makes it more obvious. You take a string and perform a conversion on it—the same conversion as before, just a length calculation. You then take that length (an int) and find its square root (a double).

Phase 1 of type inference tells the compiler that there must be a conversion from string to TInput. The first time through phase 2, TInput is fixed to string and you infer that there must be a conversion from int to TMiddle. The second time through phase 2, TMiddle is fixed to int and you infer that there must be a conversion from double to TOutput. The third time through phase 2, TOutput is fixed to double and type inference succeeds. When type inference has finished, the compiler can look at the code within the lambda expression properly.

CHECKING THE BODY OF A LAMBDA EXPRESSION The body of a lambda expression *cannot be checked* until the input parameter types are known. The lambda expression x => x.Length is valid if x is an array or a string, but invalid in many other cases. This isn't a problem when the parameter types are explicitly declared, but with an implicit parameter list, the compiler needs to wait until it's performed the relevant type inference before it can try to work out what the lambda expression means.

These examples have shown only one change working at a time, but in practice there can be several pieces of information about different type variables, potentially discovered in different iterations of the process. In an effort to save your sanity (and mine), I won't present any more complicated examples—hopefully you understand the general mechanism, even if the exact details are hazy.

Although it may seem as if this kind of situation will occur so rarely that it's not worth having such complex rules to cover it, in fact it's common in C# 3, particularly with LINQ. You could easily use type inference extensively without thinking about it—it's likely to become second nature to you. If it fails and you wonder why, you can always revisit this section and the language specification.

We need to cover one more change, but you'll be glad to hear it's easier than type inference. Let's look at method overloading.

9.4.4 *Picking the right overloaded method*

Overloading occurs when there are multiple methods available with the same name but different signatures. Sometimes it's obvious which method is appropriate, because it's the only one with the right number of parameters, or it's the only one where all the arguments can be converted into the corresponding parameter types.

The tricky bit comes when there are multiple methods that *could* be the right one. The rules in section 7.5.3 of the specification ("Overload Resolution") are quite complicated (yes, *again*), but the key part is the way that each argument type is converted into the parameter type.[9] For instance, consider these method signatures as if they were both declared in the same type:

```
void Write(int x)
void Write(double y)
```

The meaning of a call to Write(1.5) is obvious, because there's no implicit conversion from double to int, but a call to Write(1) is trickier. There *is* an implicit conversion from int to double, so both methods are possible. At that point, the compiler considers the conversion from int to int and from int to double. A conversion from any type to itself is defined to be *better than* any conversion to a different type, so the Write(int x) method is better than Write(double y) for this particular call.

When there are multiple parameters, the compiler has to make sure there's a best method to use. One method is better than another if all the argument conversions involved are *at least as good as* the corresponding conversions in the other method, and at least one conversion is strictly better. As a simple example, suppose you had this:

---

[9] I'm assuming that all the methods are declared in the same class. When inheritance is involved as well, it becomes even *more* complicated. That aspect hasn't changed in C# 3, though.

```
void Write(int x, double y)
void Write(double x, int y)
```

A call to `Write(1, 1)` would be ambiguous, and the compiler would force you to add a cast to at least one of the parameters to make it clear which method you meant to call. Each overload has one better argument conversion, so neither of them is the best method.

That logic still applies to C# 3, but with one extra rule about anonymous functions, which never specify a return type. In this case, the inferred return type (as described in section 9.4.2) is used in the better-conversion rules.

Let's look at an example of the kind of situation that needs the new rule. The following listing contains two methods with the name `Execute` and a call using a lambda expression.

Listing 9.16 Sample of overloading choice influenced by delegate return type

```
static void Execute(Func<int> action)
{
    Console.WriteLine("action returns an int: " + action());
}
static void Execute(Func<double> action)
{
    Console.WriteLine("action returns a double: " + action());
}
...

Execute(() => 1);
```

The call to `Execute` in listing 9.16 could've been written with an anonymous method or a method group instead—the same rules are applied whatever kind of conversion is involved. Which `Execute` method should be called? The overloading rules say that when two methods are both applicable after performing conversions on the arguments, those argument conversions are examined to see which one is better. The conversions here aren't from a normal .NET type to the parameter type—they're from a lambda expression to two different delegate types. Which conversion is better?

Surprisingly enough, the same situation in C# 2 would result in a compilation error—there was no language rule covering this case. In C# 3, the method with the `Func<int>` parameter would be chosen. The extra rule that has been added can be paraphrased this way:

> *If an anonymous function can be converted to two delegate types that have the same parameter list but different return types, the delegate conversions are judged by the conversions from the inferred return type to the delegates' return types.*

That's pretty much gibberish without referring to an example. Let's look back at listing 9.16 where you're converting from a lambda expression with no parameters and an inferred return type of `int` to either `Func<int>` or `Func<double>`. The parameter lists are the same (empty) for both delegate types, so the rule applies. You then just need to find the better conversion: `int` to `int`, or `int` to `double`. This puts you in more familiar territory; as you saw earlier, the `int` to `int` conversion is better. Listing 9.16 therefore prints out `action returns an int: 1`.

9.4.5   *Wrapping up type inference and overload resolution*

This section has been pretty heavy. I would've loved to have made it simpler, but it's a fundamentally complicated topic. The terminology involved doesn't make it any easier, especially as *parameter type* and *type parameter* mean completely different things! Congratulations if you made it through and actually understood it all. Don't worry if you didn't; hopefully next time you read through the section, it'll shed more light on the topic—particularly after you've run into situations where it's relevant to your own code. For the moment, here are the most important points:

- Anonymous functions (anonymous methods and lambda expressions) have inferred return types based on the types of all the return statements.
- Lambda expressions can only be understood by the compiler when the types of all the parameters are known.
- Type inference no longer requires that each argument independently come to exactly the same conclusion about type parameters, as long as the results stay compatible.
- Type inference is now multistage: the inferred return type of one anonymous function can be used as a parameter type for another.
- Finding the best overloaded method when anonymous functions are involved takes the inferred return type into account.

Even that short list is pretty daunting in terms of the sheer density of technical terms. Again, don't fret if it doesn't all make sense. In my experience things just work the way you want them to most of the time.

9.5   *Summary*

In C# 3, lambda expressions almost entirely replace anonymous methods. Anonymous methods are supported for the sake of backward compatibility, but idiomatic, freshly written C# 3 code will contain few of them.

You've seen how lambda expressions are more than just a compact syntax for delegate creation. They can be converted into expression trees, subject to some limitations. The expression trees can then be processed by other code, possibly performing equivalent actions in different execution environments. Without this ability, LINQ would be restricted to in-process queries.

Our discussion of type inference and overloading was a necessary evil to some extent; very few people actually *enjoy* discussing the sort of rules that are required, but it's important to have at least a passing understanding of what's going on. Before we all feel too sorry for ourselves, spare a thought for the poor language designers who have to live and breathe this kind of thing, making sure the rules are consistent and don't fall apart in nasty situations. Then pity the testers who have to try to break the implementation.

That's it in terms of *describing* lambda expressions, but you'll see a lot more of them in the rest of the book. For instance, the next chapter is all about *extension methods*. Superficially, they're completely separate from lambda expressions, but in reality the two features are often used together.

Extension methods

I'm not a fan of inheritance. Or rather, I'm not a fan of a number of places where inheritance has been used in code that I've maintained, or class libraries I've worked with. As with so many things, it's powerful when used properly, but its design overhead is often overlooked and can become painful over time. It's sometimes used as a way of adding extra behavior and functionality to a class, even when no real information about the object is being added—where nothing is being specialized.

Sometimes that's appropriate—if objects of the new type should carry around the details of the extra behavior—but often it's not. Often it's just not possible to use inheritance in this way in the first place, such as when you're working with a value type, a sealed class, or an interface. The alternative is usually to write a bunch of static methods, most of which take an instance of the type in question as at least one of their parameters. This works fine, without the design penalty of inheritance, but it tends to make code look ugly.

C# 3 introduced the idea of *extension methods*, which have the benefits of the static methods solution and also improve the readability of code that calls them. They let you call static methods as if they were instance methods of a completely different class. Don't panic—it's not as crazy or as arbitrary as it sounds.

In this chapter we'll first look at how to use extension methods and how to write them. We'll then examine a few of the extension methods provided by .NET 3.5 and see how they can be chained together easily. This chaining ability is an important part of the reason for introducing extension methods to the language in the first place, and it's an important part of LINQ.[1] Finally, we'll consider some of the pros and cons of using extension methods instead of plain static methods.

First, though, let's take a closer look at why extension methods are sometimes desirable compared with what's available in C# 1 and 2, particularly when you create utility classes.

10.1   *Life before extension methods*

You may be getting a sense of déjà vu at this point, because utility classes came up in chapter 7 when we looked at static classes. If you wrote a lot of C# 2 code before using C# 3, you should look at your static classes—many of the methods in them may be good candidates for converting into extension methods. That's not to say that all existing static classes are a good fit, but you may well recognize the following traits:

- You want to add some members to a type.
- You don't need to add any more data to the instances of the type.
- You can't change the type itself, because it's in someone else's code.

One slight variation on this is where you want to work with an interface instead of a class, adding useful behavior while only calling methods on the interface. A good example of this is IList<T>. Wouldn't it be nice to be able to sort any (mutable) implementation of IList<T>? It'd be horrendous to force each implementation of the interface to implement sorting, but it'd be nice from the point of view of the *user* of the list.

The thing is, IList<T> provides all the building blocks for a completely generic sort routine (several, in fact), but you can't put that implementation in the interface. IList<T> could've been specified as an abstract class instead, and the sorting functionality included that way, but as C# and .NET have single inheritance of implementation, that would've placed a significant restriction on the types deriving from it. An extension method on IList<T> would allow you to sort any IList<T> implementation, making it *appear* as if the list itself provided the functionality.

---

[1]   If you're getting fed up with hearing about how many features are "an important part of LINQ," I don't blame you, but that's part of its greatness. There are lots of small parts, but the sum of them is very shiny. The fact that each feature can be used independently is an added bonus.

You'll see later that a lot of the functionality of LINQ is built on extension methods over interfaces. For the moment, though, we'll use a different type for our examples: System.IO.Stream, the bedrock of binary communication in .NET. Stream itself is an abstract class with several concrete derived classes, such as NetworkStream, FileStream, and MemoryStream. Unfortunately, there are a few pieces of functionality that would've been handy to include in Stream that just aren't there.

The missing features I'm most often aware of are the ability to read the whole of a stream into memory as a byte array, and the ability to copy the contents of one stream into another.[2] Both of these features are frequently implemented badly, making assumptions about streams that just aren't valid—the most common misconception being that Stream.Read will completely fill the buffer if the data doesn't run out first.

NOT SO "MISSING" AFTER ALL   One of these features has been added to .NET 4: Stream now has a CopyTo method. This is useful in terms of demonstrating one slightly brittle aspect of extension methods, and we'll come back to it in section 10.2.3. ReadFully is still missing, but it should be used carefully anyway: you should only try to read the entirety of a stream if you're confident it actually has an end and that all the data fits into memory. Streams are under no obligation to have a finite amount of data.

It'd be nice to have the functionality in a single place, rather than duplicating it in several projects. That's why I wrote the StreamUtil class in my miscellaneous utility library. The real code contains a fair amount of error checking and other functionality, but the following listing shows a cut-down version that's more than adequate for our needs.

Listing 10.1   A simple utility class to provide extra functionality for streams

```
using System.IO;

public static class StreamUtil
{
    const int BufferSize = 8192;

    public static void Copy(Stream input, Stream output)
    {
        byte[] buffer = new byte[BufferSize];
        int read;
        while ((read = input.Read(buffer, 0, buffer.Length)) > 0)
        {
            output.Write(buffer, 0, read);
        }
    }
    public static byte[] ReadFully(Stream input)
    {
        using (MemoryStream tempStream = new MemoryStream())
```

---

[2] Due to the nature of streams, this copying doesn't necessarily *duplicate* the data—it just reads it from one stream and writes it to another. Although *copy* isn't a strictly accurate term in this sense, the difference is usually irrelevant.

```
        {
            Copy(input, tempStream);
            return tempStream.ToArray();
        }
    }
}
```

The implementation details don't matter much, although it's worth noting that the ReadFully method calls the Copy method—that'll be useful to demonstrate a point about extension methods later.

The class is easy to use—the following listing shows how you can write a web response to disk, for example.

Listing 10.2 Using `StreamUtil` to copy a web response stream to a file

```
WebRequest request = WebRequest.Create("http://manning.com");
using (WebResponse response = request.GetResponse())
using (Stream responseStream = response.GetResponseStream())
using (FileStream output = File.Create("response.dat"))
{
    StreamUtil.Copy(responseStream, output);
}
```

Listing 10.2 is quite compact, and the StreamUtil class has taken care of looping and asking the response stream for more data until it's all been received. It's done its job as a utility class perfectly reasonably. Even so, it doesn't feel very object-oriented. It'd be better to ask the response stream to copy itself to the output stream, just like the MemoryStream class has a WriteTo method. It's not a *big* problem, but it's a little ugly as it is.

Inheritance wouldn't help you in this situation (you want this behavior to be available for all streams, not just ones you're responsible for), and you can't go changing the Stream class itself, so what can you do? With C# 2, you were out of options—you had to stick with the static methods and live with the clumsiness. C# 3 allows you to change your static class to expose its members as extension methods, so you can pretend that the methods have been part of Stream all along. Let's see what changes are required.

10.2 Extension method syntax

Extension methods are almost embarrassingly easy to create, and they're simple to use, too. The considerations around when and how to use them are significantly deeper than the difficulties involved in learning how to write them in the first place. Let's start by converting the StreamUtil class so it has a couple of extension methods.

10.2.1 Declaring extension methods

You can't use just any method as an extension method—it must have the following characteristics:

- It must be in a non-nested, nongeneric static class (and therefore must be a static method).
- It must have at least one parameter.
- The first parameter must be prefixed with the `this` keyword.
- The first parameter can't have any other modifiers (such as `out` or `ref`).
- The type of the first parameter must not be a pointer type.

That's it—the method can be generic, return a value, have `ref`/`out` parameters other than the first one, be implemented with an iterator block, be part of a partial class, use nullable types—anything, as long as the preceding constraints are met.

We'll call the type of the first parameter the *extended type* of the method and say that the method *extends* that type—in this case, we're extending `Stream`. This isn't official terminology from the specification, but it's a useful piece of shorthand.

Not only does the previous list provide all the restrictions, but it also gives the details of what you need to do to turn a normal static method in a static class into an extension method—just add the `this` keyword. The following listing shows the same class as in listing 10.1, but this time with both methods as extension methods.

Listing 10.3 The `StreamUtil` class again, but this time with extension methods

```
public static class StreamUtil
{
    const int BufferSize = 8192;

    public static void CopyTo(this Stream input, Stream output)
    {
        byte[] buffer = new byte[BufferSize];
        int read;
        while ((read = input.Read(buffer, 0, buffer.Length)) > 0)
        {
            output.Write(buffer, 0, read);
        }
    }

    public static byte[] ReadFully(this Stream input)
    {
        using (MemoryStream tempStream = new MemoryStream())
        {
            CopyTo(input, tempStream);
            return tempStream.ToArray();
        }
    }
}
```

Yes, the only big change in listing 10.3 is the addition of the two modifiers shown in bold. I've also changed the name of the method from `Copy` to `CopyTo`. As you'll see in a minute, that'll allow calling code to read more naturally, although it does look slightly strange in the `ReadFully` method at the moment.

Now, it's not much use *having* extension methods if you can't *use* them…

10.2.2 Calling extension methods

I've mentioned it in passing, but you haven't yet seen what an extension method actually *does*. Simply put, it pretends to be an instance method of another type—the type of the first parameter of the method.

The transformation of code that uses `StreamUtil` is as simple as the transformation of the utility class itself. This time, instead of adding something in, we'll take it away. The following listing is a repeat performance of listing 10.2, but using the new syntax to call `CopyTo`. I say "new," but it's really not new at all—it's the same syntax you've always used for calling instance methods.

Listing 10.4 Copying a stream using an extension method

```
WebRequest request = WebRequest.Create("http://manning.com");
using (WebResponse response = request.GetResponse())
using (Stream responseStream = response.GetResponseStream())
using (FileStream output = File.Create("response.dat"))
{
    responseStream.CopyTo(output);
}
```

In listing 10.4 it at least *looks* like you're asking the response stream to do the copying. It's still `StreamUtil` doing the work behind the scenes, but the code reads in a more natural way. In fact, the compiler has converted the `CopyTo` call into a normal static method call to `StreamUtil.CopyTo`, passing the value of `responseStream` as the first argument (followed by `output` as normal).

Now that you can see the code in question, I hope you understand why I changed the method name from `Copy` to `CopyTo`. Some names work just as well for static methods as instance methods, but you'll find that others need tweaking to get the maximum readability benefit.

If you want to make the `StreamUtil` code slightly more pleasant, you can change the line of `ReadFully` that calls `CopyTo` like this:

```
input.CopyTo(tempStream);
```

At this point, the name change is fully appropriate for all the uses—although there's nothing to stop you from using the extension method as a normal static method, which is useful when you're migrating a lot of code.

You may have noticed that nothing in these method calls indicates that you're using an extension method instead of a regular instance method of `Stream`. This can be seen in two ways: it's a good thing if your aim is to make extension methods blend in as much as possible and cause little alarm, but it's a bad thing if you want to be able to immediately see what's *really* going on.

If you're using Visual Studio, you can hover over a method call and get an indication in the tooltip when it's an extension method, as shown in figure 10.1. IntelliSense also indicates when it's offering an extension method, in both the icon for the method and the tooltip when it's selected. Of course, you don't want to have to hover

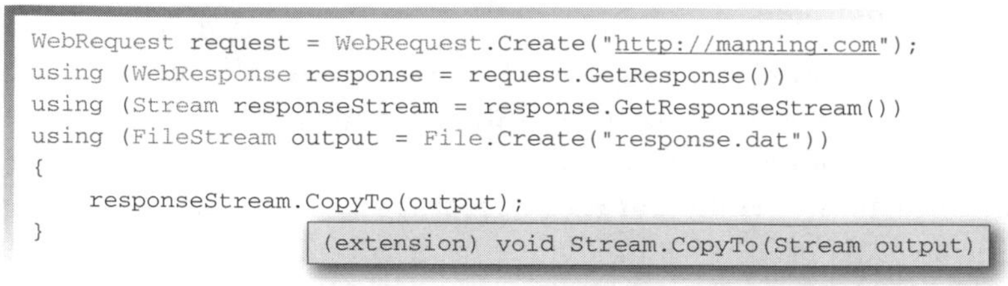

```
WebRequest request = WebRequest.Create("http://manning.com");
using (WebResponse response = request.GetResponse())
using (Stream responseStream = response.GetResponseStream())
using (FileStream output = File.Create("response.dat"))
{
    responseStream.CopyTo(output);
}                         (extension) void Stream.CopyTo(Stream output)
```

Figure 10.1   Hovering over a method call in Visual Studio reveals whether the method is an extension method.

over every method call you make or be super careful with IntelliSense, but most of the time it doesn't matter whether you're calling an instance or extension method.

There's still one rather strange thing about this calling code—it doesn't mention StreamUtil anywhere! How does the compiler know to use the extension method in the first place?

10.2.3 *Extension method discovery*

It's important to know how to call extension methods, but it's also important to know how to *not* call them—how to avoid being presented with unwanted options. To achieve that, you need to know how the compiler decides which extension methods to use in the first place.

Extension methods are made available to the code in the same way that classes are made available without qualification—with using directives. When the compiler sees an expression that looks like it's trying to use an instance method, but none of the instance methods are compatible with the method call (if there's no method with that name, for instance, or no overload matches the arguments given), it then looks for an appropriate extension method. It considers all the extension methods in all the imported namespaces and the current namespaces, and matches ones where there's an implicit conversion from the expression type to the extended type.

> **Implementation detail: how does the compiler spot an extension method?**
> To work out whether it should use an extension method, the compiler has to be able to tell the difference between an extension method and other methods within a static class that happen to have an appropriate signature. It does this by checking whether System.Runtime.CompilerServices.ExtensionAttribute has been applied to the method and the class. This attribute was introduced in .NET 3.5, but the compiler doesn't check which assembly the attribute comes from. This means that you can still use extension methods even if your project targets .NET 2.0—you just need to define your own attribute with the right name in the right namespace. You can then declare your extension methods as normal, and the attribute will be applied automatically. The compiler also applies the attribute to the assembly *containing* the extension method, but it doesn't currently require this when searching for extension methods.

Introducing your own copies of system types can become problematic when you later need to use a version of the framework that already defines those types. If you do use this technique, it's worth using preprocessor symbols to only declare the attribute conditionally. You can then build one version of your code targeting .NET 2.0 and another targeting .NET 3.5 and higher.

If multiple applicable extension methods are available for different extended types (using implicit conversions), the most appropriate one is chosen with the better conversion rules used in overloading. For instance, if `IDerived` inherits from `IBase`, and there's an extension method with the same name for both, then the `IDerived` extension method is used in preference to the one on `IBase`. Again, this feature is used in LINQ, as you'll see in section 12.2, where you'll meet the `IQueryable<T>` interface.

It's important to note that if an applicable instance method is available, that will always be used before searching for extension methods, but the compiler doesn't issue a warning if an extension method also matches an existing instance method. For example, .NET 4 has a new `Stream` method that's also called `CopyTo`. It has two overloads, one of which conflicts with the extension method you just created. The result is that the new method is picked in preference to the extension method, so if you compile listing 10.4 against .NET 4, you'll end up using `Stream.CopyTo` instead of `Stream-Util.CopyTo`. You can still call the `StreamUtil` method statically using the normal syntax of `StreamUtil.CopyTo(input, output)`, but it'll never be picked as an extension method. In this case, there's no harm to existing code: the new instance method has the same meaning as your extension method, so it doesn't matter which one is used. In other cases, there could be subtle differences in semantics that might be hard to spot until the code breaks.

Another potential problem with the way that extension methods are made available to code is that it's very wide-ranging. If there are two classes in the same namespace containing methods with the same extended type, there's no way of only using the extension methods from one of the classes. Likewise, there's no way of importing a namespace for the sake of making types available using only their simple names, but without making the extension methods within that namespace available at the same time. You may want to use a namespace that solely contains static classes with extension methods to mitigate this problem, unless the rest of the functionality of the namespace is heavily dependent on the extension methods already (as is the case for `System.Linq`, for example).

One aspect of extension methods can be quite surprising when you first encounter it, but it's also useful in some situations. It's all about null references—let's take a look.

10.2.4 *Calling a method on a null reference*

Anyone who does a significant amount of .NET programming is bound to encounter a `NullReferenceException` caused by calling a method via a variable whose value turns out to be a null reference. You can't call instance methods on null references in C# (although IL itself supports it for nonvirtual calls), but you *can* call extension methods with a null reference. This is demonstrated by the following listing. Note that this isn't a snippet, since nested classes can't contain extension methods.

Listing 10.5   Extension method being called on a null reference
---

```
using System;
public static class NullUtil
{
    public static bool IsNull(this object x)
    {
        return x == null;
    }
}
public class Test
{
    static void Main()
    {
        object y = null;
        Console.WriteLine(y.IsNull());
        y = new object();
        Console.WriteLine(y.IsNull());
    }
}
```

The output of listing 10.5 is `True`, and then `False`. If `IsNull` had been a normal instance method, an exception would've been thrown in the second line of `Main`; instead, `IsNull` was called with `null` as the argument. Prior to the advent of extension methods, C# had no way of letting you write the more readable `y.IsNull()` form safely, requiring `NullUtil.IsNull(y)` instead.

There's one particularly obvious example in the framework where this aspect of the behavior of extension methods could be useful: `string.IsNullOrEmpty`. C# 3 allows you to write an extension method that has the same signature (other than the extra parameter for the extended type) as an existing static method on the extended type. To save you reading through that sentence several times, here's an example—even though the `string` class has a static, parameterless method `IsNullOrEmpty`, you can still create and use the following extension method:

```
public static bool IsNullOrEmpty(this string text)
{
    return string.IsNullOrEmpty(text);
}
```

At first it seems odd to be able to call `IsNullOrEmpty` on a variable that's null without an exception being thrown, particularly if you're familiar with it as a static method from .NET 2.0. But in my view, code using the extension method is more easily understandable. For instance, if you read the expression `if (name.IsNullOrEmpty())` out loud, it says exactly what it's doing.

As always, experiment to see what works for you, but be aware of the possibility of other people using this technique if you're debugging code. Don't assume that an exception will be thrown on a method call unless you're sure it's not an extension method. Also, think carefully before reusing an existing name for an extension method—the previous extension method could confuse readers who are only familiar with the static method from the framework.

> **CHECKING FOR NULLITY** I'm sure that, as a conscientious developer, your production methods always check their arguments' validity before proceeding. One question that naturally arises from this quirky feature of extension methods is what exception you should throw when the first argument is null (assuming it's not meant to be). Should it be `ArgumentNullException`, as if it were a normal argument, or should it be `NullReferenceException`, which is what would've happened if the extension method had been an instance method to start with? I recommend the former: it's still an argument, even if the extension method syntax doesn't make that obvious. This is the route that Microsoft has taken for the extension methods in the framework, so it has the benefit of consistency too. Finally, bear in mind that extension methods can still be called as normal static methods, and in that situation, `Argument-NullException` is clearly the preferred result.

Now that you know the syntax and behavior of extension methods, we can look at some examples of the ones provided in .NET 3.5 as part of the framework.

10.3 Extension methods in .NET 3.5

The biggest use of extension methods in the framework is for LINQ. Some LINQ providers have a few extension methods to help them along, but there are two classes that stand out, both of them appearing in the `System.Linq` namespace: `Enumerable` and `Queryable`. These contain many, many extension methods; most of the ones in `Enumerable` operate on `IEnumerable<T>` and most of those in `Queryable` operate on `IQueryable<T>`. We'll look at the purpose of `IQueryable<T>` in chapter 12, but for the moment let's concentrate on `Enumerable`.

10.3.1 First steps with Enumerable

`Enumerable` has a *lot* of methods in it, and the purpose of this section isn't to cover all of them, but to give you enough of a feel for them that you're comfortable going off and experimenting. It's a joy to play with everything available in `Enumerable`, and it's definitely worth firing up Visual Studio or LINQPad for your experiments (rather than using Snippy), as IntelliSense is handy for this kind of activity. Appendix A gives a quick rundown of the behavior of all `Enumerable`'s methods too.

All the complete examples in this section deal with a simple situation: we'll start with a collection of integers and transform it in various ways. Real-life situations are likely to be somewhat more complicated, usually dealing with business-related types, so at the end of this section I'll present a couple examples of the transformation side of things applied to possible business situations, with full source code available on the book's website. But those examples are harder to play with than a straightforward collection of numbers.

It's worth considering some recent projects you've been working on as you read this chapter; see if you can think of situations where you could make your code simpler or more readable by using the kind of operations described here.

There are a few methods in `Enumerable` that aren't extension methods, and we'll use one of them in the examples for the rest of the chapter. The `Range` method takes two `int` parameters: the number to start with and how many results to yield. The result is an `IEnumerable<int>` that returns one number at a time in the obvious way.

To demonstrate the `Range` method and create a framework to play with, let's print out the numbers 0 to 9, as shown in the following listing.

Listing 10.6   Using `Enumerable.Range` to print out the numbers 0 to 9

```
var collection = Enumerable.Range(0, 10);

foreach (var element in collection)
{
    Console.WriteLine(element);
}
```

No extension methods are called in listing 10.6, just a plain static method. And yes, it really does just print the numbers 0 to 9—I never claimed this code would set the world on fire.

> **DEFERRED EXECUTION**   The `Range` method doesn't build a list with the appropriate numbers—it just yields them at the appropriate time. In other words, constructing the enumerable instance doesn't do the bulk of the work; it gets things ready, so that the data can be provided in a just-in-time fashion at the appropriate point. This is called *deferred execution*—you saw this sort of behavior when we looked at iterator blocks in chapter 6, but you'll see much more of it in the next chapter.

Pretty much the simplest thing you can do with a sequence of numbers that's already in order is to reverse it. The following listing uses the `Reverse` extension method to do this—it returns an `IEnumerable<T>` that yields the same elements as the original sequence, but in the reverse order.

Listing 10.7   Reversing a collection with the `Reverse` method

```
var collection = Enumerable.Range(0, 10)
                           .Reverse();

foreach (var element in collection)
{
    Console.WriteLine(element);
}
```

Efficiency: buffering versus streaming

The extension methods provided by the framework stream or pipe data wherever possible. When an iterator is asked for its next element, it'll often take an element from the iterator it's chained to, process that element, and then return something appropriate, preferably without using any more storage itself. Simple transformations and filters can do this easily, and it's a powerful way of efficiently processing data where it's possible, but some operations, such as reversing the order or sorting, require all the data to be available, so it's all loaded into memory for bulk processing. The difference between this buffered approach and piping is similar to the difference between reading data by loading a whole `DataSet` versus using a `DataReader` to process one record at a time. It's important to consider what's required when using LINQ—a single method call can have significant performance implications.

Streaming is also known as *lazy evaluation*, and buffering is also known as *eager evaluation*. For example, the `Reverse` method uses deferred execution (it does nothing until the first call to `MoveNext`), but it then eagerly evaluates its data source. Personally, I dislike the terms *lazy* and *eager*, as they mean different things to different people (a topic I discuss more in my "Just how lazy are you?" blog entry: http://mng.bz/3LLM).

Predictably enough, this prints out 9, then 8, then 7, and so on right down to 0. You called `Reverse` (seemingly) on an `IEnumerable<int>`, and the same type has been returned. This pattern of returning one enumerable based on another is pervasive in the `Enumerable` class.

Let's do something more adventurous now—we'll use a lambda expression to remove the even numbers.

10.3.2 *Filtering with Where and chaining method calls together*

The `Where` extension method is a simple but powerful way of filtering collections. It accepts a predicate, which it applies to each of the elements of the original collection. It returns an `IEnumerable<T>`, and any element that matches the predicate is included in the resulting collection.

Listing 10.8 demonstrates this, applying the odd/even filter to the collection of integers before reversing it. You don't *have* to use a lambda expression here; for instance, you could use a delegate you'd created earlier, or an anonymous method. In this case (and in many other real-life situations), it's simple to put the filtering logic inline, and lambda expressions keep the code concise.

> **Listing 10.8 Using the `Where` method with a lambda expression to find odd numbers**

```
var collection = Enumerable.Range(0, 10)
                           .Where(x => x % 2 != 0)
                           .Reverse();
foreach (var element in collection)
{
   Console.WriteLine(element);
}
```

Listing 10.8 prints out the numbers 9, 7, 5, 3, and 1. Hopefully, you'll have noticed a pattern forming—you're chaining the method calls together. The chaining idea itself isn't new. For example, `StringBuilder.Replace` always returns the instance you call it on, allowing code like this:

```
builder = builder.Replace("<", "&lt;")
                 .Replace(">", "&gt;")
                 ...
```

In contrast, `String.Replace` returns a string, but a new one each time—this allows chaining, but in a slightly different way. Both patterns are handy to know about; the "return the same reference" pattern works well for mutable types, whereas "return a new instance that's a copy of the original with some changes" is required for immutable types.

Chaining with instance methods like `String.Replace` and `StringBuilder` `.Replace` has always been simple, but extension methods allow *static* method calls to be chained together. *This is one of the primary reasons why extension methods exist.* They're *useful* for other utility classes, but their true power is revealed in this ability to chain static methods in a natural way. That's why extension methods primarily show up in `Enumerable` and `Queryable` in .NET: LINQ is geared toward this approach to data processing, with information effectively traveling through pipelines constructed of individual operations chained together.

> **EFFICIENCY CONSIDERATION: REORDERING METHOD CALLS TO AVOID WASTE**   I'm not a fan of micro-optimization without good cause, but it's worth looking at the ordering of the method calls in listing 10.8. You could've added the `Where` call after the `Reverse` call and achieved the same results, but that would've wasted some effort—the `Reverse` call would've had to work out where the even numbers should come in the sequence even though they'll be discarded from the final result. In this case, it won't make much difference, but it can have a significant effect on performance in real situations; if you can reduce the amount of wasted work without compromising readability, that's a good thing. That doesn't mean you should always put filters at the start of the pipeline, though; you need to think carefully about any reordering to make sure you get the correct results.

There are two obvious ways of writing the first part of listing 10.8 without using the fact that `Reverse` and `Where` are extension methods. One is to use a temporary variable, which keeps the structure intact:

```
var collection = Enumerable.Range(0, 10);
collection      = Enumerable.Where(collection, x => x % 2 != 0)
collection      = Enumerable.Reverse(collection);
```

I hope you'll agree that the meaning of the code is far less clear here than in listing 10.8.

It gets even worse with the other option, which is to keep the single-statement style:

```
var collection = Enumerable.Reverse
                    (Enumerable.Where
                        (Enumerable.Range(0, 10),
                            x => x % 2 != 0));
```

The method call order appears to be reversed, because the innermost method call (Range) will be performed first, then the others, with execution working its way outward. Even with just three method calls it's ugly—it becomes far worse for queries involving more operators.

Before we move on, let's think a bit about what the Where method does.

10.3.3 *Interlude: haven't we seen the Where method before?*

If the Where method feels familiar, it's because you implemented it in chapter 6. All you need to do is convert listing 6.9 into an extension method and change the delegate type from Predicate<T> to Func<T,bool> and you have a perfectly good alternative implementation to Enumerable.Where:

```
public static IEnumerable<T> Where<T>(this  IEnumerable<T> source,
                                      Func<T, bool> predicate)
{
    if (source == null || predicate == null)
    {
        throw new ArgumentNullException();
    }
    return WhereImpl(source, predicate);
}
private static IEnumerable<T> WhereImpl<T>(IEnumerable<T> source,
                                           Func<T, bool>  predicate)
{
    foreach (T item in source)
    {
        if (predicate(item))
        {
            yield return item;
        }
    }
}
```

You can change the last part of listing 6.9 to make it look more LINQ-like, too:

```
foreach (string line in LineReader.ReadLines("../../FakeLinq.cs")
                            .Where(line => line.StartsWith("using")))
{
    Console.WriteLine(line);
}
```

This is effectively a LINQ query without using the System.Linq namespace. It would work perfectly well in .NET 2.0 if you declared the appropriate Func delegate and [ExtensionAttribute]. You could even use that implementation for the where clause in a query expression (while still targeting .NET 2.0), as you'll see in the next chapter—but let's not get ahead of ourselves.

Filtering is one of the simplest operations in a query, and another is transforming or *projecting* the results.

10.3.4 *Projections using the Select method and anonymous types*

The most commonly used projection method in `Enumerable` is `Select`. It operates on an `IEnumerable<TSource>` and projects it into an `IEnumerable<TResult>` by way of a `Func<TSource,TResult>`, which is the transformation to use on each element, specified as a delegate. It's much like the `ConvertAll` method in `List<T>`, but it operates on any enumerable collection and uses deferred execution to perform the projection when each element is requested.

When I introduced anonymous types, I said they were useful with lambda expressions and LINQ—here's an example of the kind of thing you can do with them. You currently have the odd numbers from 0 to 9 (in reverse order)—let's create a type that encapsulates the square root of the number as well as the original number. The following listing shows both the projection and a slightly modified way of writing out the results. I've adjusted the whitespace solely for the sake of space on the printed page.

> **Listing 10.9   Projection using a lambda expression and an anonymous type**

```
var collection = Enumerable.Range(0, 10)
    .Where(x => x % 2 != 0)
    .Reverse()
    .Select(x => new { Original = x, SquareRoot = Math.Sqrt(x) } );

foreach (var element in collection)
{
    Console.WriteLine("sqrt({0})={1}",
                    element.Original,
                    element.SquareRoot);
}
```

This time the type of `collection` isn't `IEnumerable<int>`—it's `IEnumerable<Something>`, where `Something` is the anonymous type created by the compiler. You can't give the collection variable an explicit type other than the nongeneric `IEnumerable` type or `object`. Implicit typing (with `var`) is what allows you to use the `Original` and `SquareRoot` properties when writing out the results.

The output of listing 10.9 is as follows:

```
sqrt(9)=3
sqrt(7)=2.64575131106459
sqrt(5)=2.23606797749979
sqrt(3)=1.73205080756888
sqrt(1)=1
```

Of course, a `Select` method doesn't *have* to use an anonymous type at all—you could've selected just the square root of the number, discarding the original. In that case, the result would've been `IEnumerable<double>`. Alternatively, you could've manually written a type to encapsulate an integer and its square root—it was just easiest to use an anonymous type in this case.

Let's look at one last method to round off our coverage of `Enumerable` for the moment: `OrderBy`.

10.3.5 *Sorting using the OrderBy method*

Sorting is a common requirement when processing data, and in LINQ this is usually performed by using the `OrderBy` or `OrderByDescending` methods. The first call is sometimes followed by `ThenBy` or `ThenByDescending` if you need to sort by more than one property of the data. This ability to sort on multiple properties has always been available the hard way using a complicated comparison, but it's much clearer to be able to present a series of simple comparisons.

To demonstrate this, let's make a small change to the operations involved. You'll start off with the integers –5 to 5 (inclusive, so there are 11 elements in total), and then project to an anonymous type containing the original number and its square (rather than square root). Finally, you'll sort by the square and then the original number. The following listing shows all of this.

Listing 10.10 Ordering a sequence by two properties

```
var collection = Enumerable.Range(-5, 11)
    .Select(x => new { Original = x, Square = x * x })
    .OrderBy(x => x.Square)
    .ThenBy(x => x.Original);

foreach (var element in collection)
{
    Console.WriteLine(element);
}
```

Note how aside from the call to `Enumerable.Range`, the code reads almost exactly like the textual description. The anonymous type's `ToString` implementation does the formatting this time, and here are the results:

```
{ Original = 0, Square = 0 }
{ Original = -1, Square = 1 }
{ Original = 1, Square = 1 }
{ Original = -2, Square = 4 }
{ Original = 2, Square = 4 }
{ Original = -3, Square = 9 }
{ Original = 3, Square = 9 }
{ Original = -4, Square = 16 }
{ Original = 4, Square = 16 }
{ Original = -5, Square = 25 }
{ Original = 5, Square = 25 }
```

As intended, the main sorting property is `Square`, but when two values have the same square, the negative original number is always sorted before the positive one. Writing a single comparison to do the same kind of thing (in a general case—there are mathematical tricks to cope with this particular example) would've been significantly more complicated, to the extent that you wouldn't want to include the code inline in the lambda expression.

One thing to note is that the ordering doesn't change an existing collection—it returns a new sequence that yields the same data as the input sequence, except sorted. Contrast this with List<T>.Sort or Array.Sort, which both change the element order within the list or array. LINQ operators are intended to be *side-effect free*: they don't affect their input, and they don't make any other changes to the environment, unless you're iterating through a naturally stateful sequence (such as reading from a network stream) or a delegate argument has side effects. This is an approach from functional programming, and it leads to code that's more readable, testable, composable, predictable, thread-safe, and robust.

We've looked at just a few of the many extension methods available in Enumerable, but hopefully you can appreciate how neatly they can be chained together. In the next chapter you'll see how this can be expressed in a different way using extra syntax provided by C# 3 (query expressions), and we'll look at some other operations we haven't covered here. It's worth remembering that you don't *have* to use query expressions—often it can be simpler to make a couple of calls to methods in Enumerable, using extension methods to chain operations together.

Now that you've seen how all these apply to the collection-of-numbers example, it's time for me to make good on the promise of showing you some business-related examples.

10.3.6 *Business examples involving chaining*

Much of what we do as developers involves moving data around. In fact, for many applications that's the *only* meaningful thing we do—the user interface, web services, database, and other components often exist solely to get data from one place to another, or from one form into another. It should come as no surprise that the extension methods we've looked at in this section are well suited to many business problems.

I'll just give a couple of examples here. I'm sure you'll be able to imagine how C# 3 and the Enumerable class can help you solve problems involving your business requirements more expressively than before. For each example, I'll only include a sample query—it should be enough to help you understand the purpose of the code, but without all the baggage. Full working code is on the book's website.

AGGREGATION: SUMMING SALARIES

The first example involves a company composed of several departments. Each department has a number of employees, each of whom has a salary. Suppose you want to report on total salary cost by department, with the most expensive department listed first. The query is simply as follows:

```
company.Departments
      .Select(dept => new
      {
         dept.Name,
         Cost = dept.Employees.Sum(person => person.Salary)
      })
      .OrderByDescending(deptWithCost => deptWithCost.Cost);
```

This query uses an anonymous type to keep the department name (using a projection initializer) and the sum of the salaries of all the employees within that department. The salary summation uses a self-explanatory `Sum` extension method, again part of `Enumerable`.

In the result, the department name and total salary can be retrieved as properties. If you wanted the original department reference, you'd just need to change the anonymous type used in the `Select` method.

GROUPING: COUNTING BUGS ASSIGNED TO DEVELOPERS

If you're a professional developer, I'm sure you've seen many project management tools giving you different metrics. If you have access to the raw data, LINQ can help you transform it in practically any way you choose.

As a simple example, let's look at a list of developers and how many bugs they have assigned to them at the moment:

```
bugs.GroupBy(bug => bug.AssignedTo)
    .Select(list => new { Developer = list.Key, Count = list.Count() })
    .OrderByDescending(x => x.Count);
```

This query uses the `GroupBy` extension method, which groups the original collection by a projection (the developer assigned to fix the bug, in this case), resulting in an `IGrouping<TKey,TElement>`. There are many overloads of `GroupBy`, but this example uses the simplest one and then selects just the key (the name of the developer) and the number of bugs assigned to him. After that you order the result to show the developers with the most bugs first.

One of the problems when looking at the `Enumerable` class can be working out exactly what's going on; for example, one of the overloads of `GroupBy` has four type parameters and five normal parameters (three of which are delegates). Don't panic—just follow the steps shown in chapter 3, assigning different types to different type parameters until you have a concrete example of what the method would look like. That usually makes it a lot easier to understand what's going on.

These examples aren't particularly involved, but I hope you can see the power of chaining method calls together, where each method takes an original collection and returns another one in some form or other, whether by filtering out some values, ordering values, transforming each element, aggregating some values, or using other options. In many cases, the resulting code can be read aloud and understood immediately, and in other situations it's still usually a lot simpler than the equivalent code would've been in previous versions of C#.

We'll use the example of defect tracking as our sample data when we look at query expressions in the next chapter. Now that you've seen some of the extension methods that are provided, let's consider just how and when it makes sense to write them yourself.

10.4   Usage ideas and guidelines

Like implicit typing of local variables, extension methods are controversial. It'd be difficult to claim that they make the overall aim of the code harder to understand in many cases, but at the same time they *do* obscure the details of which method is getting called. In the words of one of the lecturers at my university, "I'm hiding the truth in order to show you a *bigger* truth." If you believe that the most important aspect of the code is its result, extension methods are great. If the implementation is more important to you, then explicitly calling a static method is more clear. Effectively, it's the difference between the *what* and the *how.*

We've already looked at using extension methods for utility classes and method chaining, but before we discuss the pros and cons further, it's worth calling out a couple of aspects that may not be obvious.

10.4.1   "Extending the world" and making interfaces richer

Wes Dyer, a former developer on the C# compiler team, has a fantastic blog covering all kinds of subject matter (see http://blogs.msdn.com/b/wesdyer/). One of his posts about extension methods particularly caught my attention (see http://mng.bz/I4F2). It's called "Extending the World," and it talks about how extension methods can make code easier to read by effectively adapting your environment to your needs:

> *Typically for a given problem, a programmer is accustomed to building up a solution until it finally meets the requirements. Now, it is possible to extend the world to meet the solution instead of solely just building up until we get to it. That library doesn't provide what you need, just extend the library to meet your needs.*

This has implications beyond situations where you'd use a utility class. Typically developers only start creating utility classes when they've seen the same kind of code reproduced in dozens of places, but extending a library is about clarity of expression as much as avoiding duplication. Extension methods can make the calling code feel like the library is richer than it really is.

You've already seen this with `IEnumerable<T>`, where even the simplest implementation *appears* to have a wide set of operations available, such as sorting, grouping, projection, and filtering. The benefits aren't limited to interfaces—you can also "extend the world" with enums, abstract classes, and so forth.

The .NET Framework also provides a good example of another use for extension methods: fluent interfaces.

10.4.2   Fluent interfaces

There used to be a television program in the United Kingdom called *Catchphrase.* The idea was that contestants would watch a screen where an animation would show some cryptic version of a phrase or saying, which they'd have to guess. The host would often try to help by instructing them: "Say what you see." That's pretty much the idea behind *fluent interfaces*—that if you read the code verbatim, its purpose will leap off the screen as if it were written in a natural human language. The term "fluent interfaces" was originally coined by Martin Fowler (see his blog entry at http://mng.bz/ 3T9T) and Eric Evans.

If you're familiar with *domain-specific languages* (DSLs), you may be wondering what the differences are between a fluent interface and a DSL. A lot has been written on the subject, but the consensus seems to be that a DSL has more freedom to create its own syntax and grammar, whereas a fluent interface is constrained by the host language (C#, in our case).

Some good examples of fluent interfaces in the framework are the `OrderBy` and `ThenBy` methods: with a bit of interpretation of lambda expressions, the code explains exactly what it does. In the case of listing 10.10 earlier, you could read "order by the square, then by the original number" without much work. Statements end up reading as whole sentences rather than individual noun-verb phrases.

Writing fluent interfaces can require a change of mindset. Method names defy the normal descriptive-verb form, with *And, Then,* and *If* sometimes being suitable methods in a fluent interface. The methods themselves often do little more than set up context for future calls, often returning a type whose sole purpose is to act as a bridge between calls. Figure 10.2 illustrates how this bridging works. It only uses two extension methods (on `int` and `TimeSpan`), but they make all the difference in the readability.

The grammar of the example in figure 10.2 could have many different forms; you may be able to add additional attendees to an `UntimedMeeting` or create an `UnattendedMeeting` at a particular time before specifying the attendees, for instance. For a lot more guidance on DSLs, see *DSLs in Boo: Domain-Specific Languages in .NET* by Ayende Rahien (Manning, 2010).

C# 3 only supports extension *methods* rather than extension *properties*, which restricts fluent interfaces slightly. It means you can't have expressions such as `1.week.from.now` or `2.days + 10.hours` (which are both valid in Groovy with an appropriate package— see Groovy's Google Data Support: http://groovy.codehaus.org/Google+Data+ Support), but with a few superfluous parentheses you can achieve similar results. At first it looks odd to call a method on a number (such as `2.Dollars()` or `3.Meters()`), but it's hard to deny that the meaning is clear. Without extension methods, this sort of clarity isn't possible when you need to act on types such as numbers that aren't under your control.

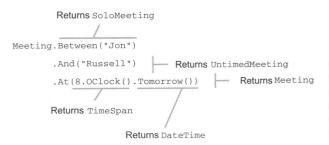

Figure 10.2 Pulling apart a fluent interface expression to create a meeting. The time of the meeting is specified using extension methods to create a `TimeSpan` from an `int`, and a `DateTime` from a `TimeSpan`.

At the time of this writing, the development community is still on the fence about fluent interfaces: they're relatively rare in most fields, although many mocking and unit testing libraries have at least some fluent aspects. They're certainly not universally applicable, but in the right situations they can radically transform the readability of the calling code. As an example, with appropriate extension methods from my Misc-Util library, I can iterate over every day I've been alive in a readable way:

```
foreach (DateTime day in 19.June(1976).To(DateTime.Today)
                                       .Step(1.Days()))
```

Although the range-related implementation details are complicated, the extension methods allowing `19.June(1976)` and `1.Days()` are extremely simple. This is culture-specific code, which you may not want to expose in your production code, but it can make unit tests a great deal more pleasant.

These aren't the only uses available for extension methods, of course. I've used them for argument validation, implementing alternative approaches to LINQ, adding my own operators to LINQ to Objects, making composite comparisons easier to build, adding more flag-related functionality to enums, and much more. I'm constantly amazed at how such a simple feature can have such a profound impact on readability when used appropriately. The key word there is "appropriately," which is easier to say than describe.

10.4.3　*Using extension methods sensibly*

I'm in no position to dictate how you write your code. It may be possible to write tests to objectively measure readability for an average developer, but it only matters for those who're going to use and maintain your code. You need to consult with the relevant people as far as you can, presenting different options and getting appropriate feedback. Extension methods make this particularly easy in many cases, as you can demonstrate both options in working code simultaneously—turning a method into an extension method doesn't stop you from calling it explicitly in the same way as before.

The main question to ask is the one I referred to at the start of this section: is the "what does it do" aspect of the code more important than the "how does it do it" aspect? That varies by person and situation, but here are some guidelines to bear in mind:

- Everyone on the development team should be aware of extension methods and where they might be used. Where possible, avoid surprising code maintainers.
- By putting extensions in their own namespace, you make it hard to use them accidentally. Even if it's not obvious when *reading* the code, the developers *writing* it should be aware of what they're doing. Use a project-wide or company-wide convention for naming the namespace. You may choose to take this one step further and use a single namespace for each extended type. For instance, you could create a `TypeExtensions` namespace for classes that extend `System.Type`.

- Think carefully before you extend widely used types, such as numbers or `object`, or before you write a method where the extended type is a type parameter. Some guidelines go as far as to recommend that you shouldn't do this at all; I think such extensions have their place, but they should have to really earn their place in your library. In this situation, it's even more important that the extension method be either internal or in its own namespace; I wouldn't want IntelliSense to be suggesting the `June` extension method everywhere I used an integer, for example—only in classes that used at least *some* extension methods related to date and time.

- The decision to write an extension method should always be a conscious one. It shouldn't become habitual. Not every static method deserves to be an extension method.

- Document whether the first parameter (the value your method appears to be called on) is allowed to be null—if it's not, check the value in the method and throw an `ArgumentNullException` if necessary.

- Be careful not to use a method name that already has a meaning in the extended type. If the extended type is a framework type or comes from a third-party library, check all your extended method names whenever you change versions of the library. If you're lucky (as I was with `Stream.CopyTo`), the new meaning is the same as the old, but even so, you may wish to deprecate your extension method.

- Question your instincts, but acknowledge that they affect your productivity. Just like with implicit typing, there's little point in forcing yourself to use a feature you instinctively dislike.

- Try to group extension methods into static classes dealing with the same extended type. Sometimes related classes (such as `DateTime` and `TimeSpan`) can be sensibly grouped together, but avoid grouping extension methods targeting disparate types such as `Stream` and `string` within the same class.

- Think *really* carefully before adding extension methods with the same extended type and same name in two different namespaces, particularly if there are situations where the different methods may both be applicable (they have the same number of parameters). It's reasonable for adding or removing a `using` directive to make a program fail to build, but it's nasty if it still builds but changes the behavior.

Few of these guidelines are particularly clear-cut; to some extent you'll have to feel your own way to the best use or avoidance of extension methods. It's perfectly reasonable to never write your own extension methods at all, and to use the LINQ-related ones for the readability gains available there. But it's worth at least *thinking* about what's possible.

10.5 *Summary*

The mechanical aspect of extension methods is straightforward—the feature is simple to describe and demonstrate. The benefits (and costs) of them are harder to talk about in a definitive manner—it's a touchy-feely topic, and different people are bound to have different views on the value provided.

In this chapter I've tried to show a bit of everything. Early on, we looked at what the feature achieves in the language, and then we looked at some of the capabilities available through the framework. In some ways, this was a relatively gentle introduction to LINQ; we'll revisit some of the extension methods you've seen so far, and look at some new ones, when we delve into query expressions in the next chapter.

A wide variety of methods is available within the `Enumerable` class, and we've only scratched the surface in this chapter. It's fun to come up with a scenario of your own devising (whether hypothetical or in a real project) and browse through MSDN to see what's available to help you. I urge you to use a sandbox project of some sort to play with the extension methods provided—it does feel like play rather than work, and you're unlikely to want to limit yourself to just the methods you need to achieve your most immediate goal. Appendix A has a list of the standard query operators from LINQ, which covers many of the methods within `Enumerable`.

New patterns and practices keep emerging in software engineering, and ideas from some systems often cross-pollinate to others. That's one of the things that keeps development exciting. Extension methods allow code to be written in a way that was previously unavailable in C#, creating fluent interfaces and changing the environment to suit your code rather than the other way around. Those are just the techniques we've looked at in this chapter—there are bound to be interesting future developments using the new C# features, whether individually or combined.

The revolution obviously doesn't end here. For a few calls, extension methods are fine. In the next chapter, we'll look at the real power tools: query expressions and full-blown LINQ.

Query expressions and LINQ to Objects

You may be tired of all the hyperbole around LINQ by now. You've already seen some examples in the book, and you've almost certainly read a lot about it on the web. This is where we separate myth from reality:

- LINQ doesn't turn the most complicated query into a one-liner.
- LINQ doesn't mean you never need to look at raw SQL again.
- LINQ doesn't magically imbue you with architectural genius.

Given all that, LINQ is still the best way of expressing queries that I've seen within an object-oriented environment. It's not a silver bullet, but it's a *very* powerful tool to have in your development armory. We'll explore two distinct aspects of LINQ: the framework support and the compiler translation of *query expressions*. The latter can look odd to start with, but I'm sure you'll learn to love them.

Query expressions are effectively preprocessed by the compiler into "normal" C# 3, which is then compiled in an ordinary way. This is a neat way of integrating queries into the language without changing the specification in more than one small section. Most of this chapter is a list of the preprocessing translations performed by the compiler, as well as the effects achieved when the result uses the `Enumerable` extension methods.

You won't see any SQL or XML here—that awaits you in chapter 12. But with this chapter as a foundation, you should be able to understand what the more exciting LINQ providers do when you meet them. Call me a spoilsport, but I want to take away some of their magic. Even without the air of mystery, LINQ is still very cool.

First let's consider the basis of LINQ, and how we'll go about exploring it.

11.1   Introducing LINQ

With a topic as large as LINQ, you need a certain amount of background before you're ready to see it in action. In this section we'll look at a few of the core principles behind LINQ and at the data model we'll use for the examples in this chapter and the next. I know you're likely to be itching to get into the code, so I'll keep this fairly brief.

11.1.1   Fundamental concepts in LINQ

One of the problems with reducing the impedance mismatch between two data models is that it usually involves creating yet another model to act as the bridge. This section describes the LINQ model, beginning with its most important aspect: sequences.

SEQUENCES

You're already familiar with the concept of a sequence: it's encapsulated by the `IEnumerable` and `IEnumerable<T>` interfaces, and we looked at those fairly closely in chapter 6 when we studied iterators. A sequence is like a conveyor belt of items—you fetch them one at a time until either you're no longer interested or the sequence runs out of data.

The key difference between a sequence and other collection data structures, such as lists and arrays, is that when you're reading from a sequence, you don't generally know how many more items are waiting, and you don't have access to arbitrary items—just the current one. Indeed, some sequences could be never-ending; you could easily have an infinite sequence of random numbers, for example. Lists and arrays can *act* as sequences, just as `List<T>` implements `IEnumerable<T>`, but the reverse isn't always true. You can't have an infinite array or list, for example.

Sequences are LINQ's bread and butter. When you read a query expression, you should think about the sequences involved; there's always at least one sequence to start with, and it's usually transformed into other sequences along the way, possibly being joined with yet more sequences. LINQ query examples on the web frequently have little explanation, but when you take them apart by looking at each sequence in turn, things make a lot more sense. As well as being an aid to *reading* code, this approach can also help a lot when *writing* it. Thinking in sequences can be tricky—it's a bit of a mental leap sometimes—but if you can get there, it'll help you immeasurably when you're working with LINQ.

As a simple example, let's take a query expression running against a list of people. We'll apply a filter first, and then a projection, so that we end up with a sequence of the names of adults:

```
var adultNames = from person in people
                 where person.Age >= 18
                 select person.Name;
```

Figure 11.1 shows this query expression graphically, breaking it down into its individual steps.

Each arrow represents a sequence—the description is on the left side and some sample data is on the right. Each box is a step in the query expression. Initially, you have the whole family (as `Person` objects); then, after filtering, the sequence only contains adults (again, as `Person` objects); and the final result has the names of those adults as strings. Each time, you take one sequence and apply an operation to produce a new sequence. The result isn't the strings `Holly` and `Jon`—instead, it's an `IEnumerable<string>`, which, when asked for its elements one by one, will first yield `Holly` and then `Jon`.

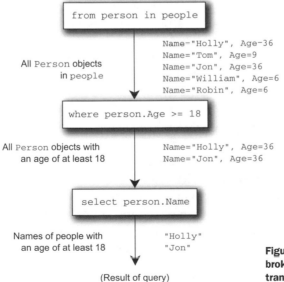

Figure 11.1 A simple query expression broken down into the sequences and transformations involved

This example was straightforward to start with, but we'll apply the same technique later to more complicated query expressions in order to understand them more easily. Some advanced operations involve more than one sequence as input, but it's still a lot less to worry about than trying to understand the whole query in one go.

And why are sequences so important? They're the basis for a streaming model for data handling—one that allows you to fetch and process data only when you need it.

DEFERRED EXECUTION AND STREAMING

When the query expression shown in figure 11.1 is created, no data is processed. The original list of people isn't accessed *at all*.[1] Instead, a representation of the query is built up in memory. Delegate instances are used to represent the predicate testing for adulthood and the conversion from a person to that person's name. The wheels only start turning when the resulting IEnumerable<string> is asked for its first element.

This aspect of LINQ is called *deferred execution*. When the first element of the result is requested, the Select transformation asks the Where transformation for its first element. The Where transformation asks the list for its first element, checks whether the predicate matches (which it does, in this case), and returns that element back to Select. That in turn extracts the name and returns it as the result.

> **HAVEN'T WE SEEN THIS BEFORE?**   You may be getting a sense of déjà vu here, because I did mention all of this in chapter 10. But it's such an important topic that it's worth covering a second time, in more detail.

That's a mouthful, but a sequence diagram makes it all much clearer. I'll collapse the calls to MoveNext and Current to a single fetch operation; it makes the diagram a lot simpler. Just remember that each time the fetch occurs, it's effectively checking for the end of the sequence as well. Figure 11.2 shows the first few stages of the sample query expression in operation, when you print out each element of the result using a foreach loop.

As you can see in figure 11.2, only one element of data is processed at a time. If you decided to stop printing output after Holly, you'd never execute any of the operations on the other elements of the original sequence. Although several stages are involved here, processing data in a *streaming* manner like this is efficient and flexible. Regardless of how much source data there is, you don't need to know about more than one element at any point in time.

This is a best-case scenario. There are times where in order to fetch the first result of a query, you have to evaluate *all* of the data from the source. We've already looked at one example of this in the previous chapter: the Enumerable.Reverse method needs to fetch all the data available in order to return the last original element as the first element of the resulting sequence. This makes Reverse a *buffering* operation, which can have a huge effect on the efficiency (or even feasibility) of your overall

---

[1]   The various parameters involved are checked for nullity, though. This is important to bear in mind if you implement your own LINQ operators, as you'll see in chapter 12.

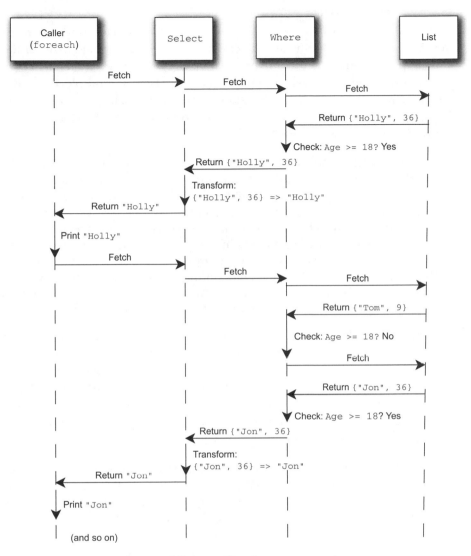

Figure 11.2 Sequence diagram of the execution of a query expression

operation. If you can't afford to have all the data in memory at one time, you can't use buffering operations.

Just as streaming depends on which operation you perform, some transformations take place as soon as you call them, rather than using deferred execution. This is called *immediate execution*. Generally speaking, operations that return another sequence (usually an IEnumerable<T> or IQueryable<T>) use deferred execution, whereas operations that return a single value use immediate execution.

The operations that are widely available in LINQ are known as the standard query operators—let's take a brief look at them now.

STANDARD QUERY OPERATORS

LINQ's *standard query operators* are a collection of transformations whose meanings are well understood. LINQ providers are encouraged to implement as many of these operators as possible, making the implementation obey the expected behavior. This is crucial in providing a consistent query framework across multiple data sources. Of course, some LINQ providers may expose more functionality, and some of the operators may not map appropriately to the target domain of the provider, but at least the opportunity for consistency is there.

> **IMPLEMENTATION-SPECIFIC DETAILS OF STANDARD OPERATORS**   Just because the standard query operators have common general meanings doesn't mean they'll work exactly the same way for every implementation. For example, some LINQ providers may load the data for a whole query as soon as they need the first item—if you're accessing a web service, that may make perfect sense. Likewise, a query that works in LINQ to Objects may have subtly different semantics in LINQ to SQL. This doesn't mean that LINQ has failed, just that you need to consider which data source you're accessing when you write a query. There's still a huge advantage in having a single set of query operators and a consistent query syntax, even though it's not a panacea.

C# 3 has support for some of the standard query operators built into the language via query expressions, but you can always choose to call them manually if you find that makes the code clearer. You may be interested to know that VB9 has more of the operators present in the language; as ever, there's a trade-off between the added complexity of including a feature in the language and the benefits that feature brings. Personally, I think the C# team has done an admirable job; I've always been a fan of a relatively small language with a large library behind it.

> **OPERATOR OVERLOADING**   The term *operator* is used to describe both query operators (methods such as `Select` and `Where`) and the familiar operators such as addition, equality, and so on. Usually it should be obvious which one I mean from the context—if I'm talking about LINQ, *operator* will almost always refer to a method used as part of a query.

You'll see some of these operators in the examples as we go through this chapter and the next, but I don't aim to give a comprehensive guide to them here; this book is primarily about C#, not the whole of LINQ. You don't need to know all of the operators in order to be productive in LINQ, but your experience is likely to grow over time. Appendix A gives a brief description of each of the standard query operators, and MSDN gives more details of each specific overload. When you run into a problem, check the list: if it feels like there *ought* to be a built-in method to help you, there probably is! That's not always the case, though—I founded the MoreLINQ open source project to add some extra operators to LINQ to Objects (see http://code.google.com/p/morelinq/). Likewise the Reactive Extensions package (see http://mng.bz/R7ip) has additions for the pull model of LINQ to Objects as well as the push model we'll look at later. If the standard operators fail you, check both projects before building your own solution. It's not a disaster if you *do* have to write your own operator, though; it can be a lot of fun. In chapter 12 I'll give a few tips on this subject.

Having mentioned examples, it's time I introduced the data model that most of the rest of the sample code in this chapter will use.

11.1.2 *Defining the sample data model*

In section 10.3.4 I gave a brief example of defect tracking as a real use for extension methods and lambda expressions. We'll use the same idea for almost all of the sample code in this chapter—it's a fairly simple model, but one that can be manipulated in many different ways to give useful information. Defect tracking is also a domain that most professional developers are all too familiar with, unfortunately.

Our fictional setting is SkeetySoft, a small software company with big ambitions. The founders have decided to create an office suite, a media player, and an instant messaging application. After all, there are no big players in those markets, are there?

The development department of SkeetySoft consists of five people: two developers (Deborah and Darren), two testers (Tara and Tim), and a manager (Mary). There's currently a single customer: Colin. The aforementioned products are SkeetyOffice, SkeetyMediaPlayer, and SkeetyTalk, respectively.[2] We'll look at defects logged during May 2013, using the data model shown in figure 11.3.

As you can see, there's not a lot of data being recorded here. In particular, there's no real history to the defects, but there's enough here to let you work with the query expression features of C# 3.

For the purposes of this chapter, all the data is stored in memory. You have a class named `SampleData` with properties `AllDefects`, `AllUsers`, `AllProjects`, and `AllSubscriptions`, which each return an appropriate type of `IEnumerable<T>`. The `Start` and `End` properties return `DateTime` instances for the start and end of May, respectively, and there are nested classes `Users` and `Projects` within `SampleData` to provide easy access to a particular user or project. The one type that may not be immediately obvious is `NotificationSubscription`; the idea behind this is to send an email to the specified address every time a defect is created or changed in the relevant project.

There are 41 defects in the sample data, created using C# 3 object initializers. All of the code is available on the book's website, along with the sample data.

Now that the preliminaries are dealt with, let's get cracking with some queries!

---

[2] The marketing department of SkeetySoft isn't particularly creative.

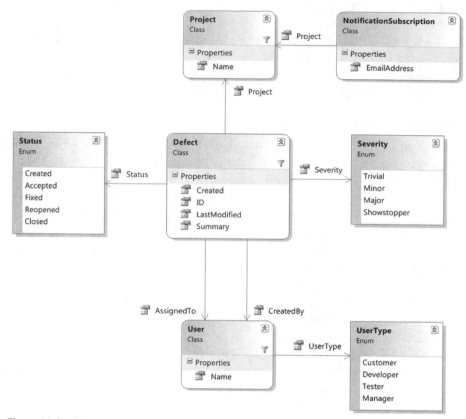

Figure 11.3   Class diagram of the SkeetySoft defect data model

11.2   *Simple beginnings: selecting elements*

We've already discussed some general LINQ concepts—I'll introduce the concepts that are specific to C# 3 as they arise in the course of the chapter. We'll start with a simple query (even simpler than the one you saw earlier) and work up to some complicated ones, not only building up your understanding of what the C# 3 compiler is doing, but also teaching you how to read LINQ code.

All of the examples will follow the pattern of defining a query and then printing the results to the console. We won't look at binding queries to data grids or anything like that—it's all important, but not directly relevant to learning C# 3.

You can use a simple expression that prints out all the users as the starting point for examining what the compiler is doing behind the scenes and learning about *range variables*.

11.2.1 Starting with a source and ending with a selection

Every query expression in C# 3 starts off in the same way—stating the source of a sequence of data:

```
from element in source
```

The `element` part is just an identifier, with an optional type name before it. Most of the time you won't need the type name, and we won't have one for the first example. The `source` part is a normal expression. Lots of different things can happen after that first clause, but sooner or later you always end with a `select` clause or a `group` clause.

We'll start off with a `select` clause to keep things nice and simple. The syntax for a `select` clause is also easy:

```
select expression
```

The `select` clause is known as a *projection*.

Combining the two together and using a trivial expression gives a simple (and practically useless) query, as shown in the following listing.

Listing 11.1   Trivial query to print the list of users

```
var query = from user in SampleData.AllUsers
            select user;
foreach (var user in query)
{
    Console.WriteLine(user);
}
```

The query expression is the part in bold. I've overridden `ToString` for each of the entities in the model, so the results of listing 11.1 are as follows:

```
User: Tim Trotter (Tester)
User: Tara Tutu (Tester)
User: Deborah Denton (Developer)
User: Darren Dahlia (Developer)
User: Mary Malcop (Manager)
User: Colin Carton (Customer)
```

You may be wondering how useful this is as an example; after all, you could just use `SampleData.AllUsers` directly in the `foreach` statement. But we'll use this query expression—trivial though it is—to introduce two new concepts. First we'll look at the general nature of the *translation* process the compiler uses when it encounters a query expression, and then we'll discuss range variables.

11.2.2 Compiler translations as the basis of query expressions

The C# 3 query expression support is based on the compiler translating query expressions into normal C# code. It does this in a mechanical manner that doesn't try to understand the code, apply type inference, check the validity of method calls, or perform any of the normal business of a compiler. That's all done later, after the translation. In many ways, this first phase can be regarded as a preprocessor step.

The compiler translates listing 11.1 into the following code before doing the *real* compilation.

Listing 11.2   The query expression of listing 11.1 translated into a method call

```
var query = SampleData.AllUsers.Select(user => user);

foreach (var user in query)
{
    Console.WriteLine(user);
}
```

The C# 3 compiler translates the query expression into *exactly* this code before properly compiling it further. In particular, it doesn't assume that it should use `Enumerable` `.Select`, or that `List<T>` will contain a method called `Select`. It merely translates the code and then lets the next phase of compilation deal with finding an appropriate method—whether as a straightforward member or as an extension method.[3] The parameter can be a suitable delegate type or an `Expression<T>` for an appropriate type `T`.

This is where it's important that lambda expressions can be converted into both delegate instances and expression trees. All the examples in this chapter will use delegates, but you'll see how expression trees are used when we look at the other LINQ providers in chapter 12. When I present the signatures for some of the methods called by the compiler later on, remember that these are just the ones called in LINQ to Objects—whenever the parameter is a delegate type (which most of them are), the compiler will use a lambda expression as the argument and then try to find a method with a suitable signature.

It's also important to remember that wherever a normal variable (such as a local variable within the method) appears within a lambda expression after translation has been performed, it'll become a captured variable in the same way that you saw back in chapter 5. This is normal lambda expression behavior, but unless you understand which variables will be captured, you could easily be confused by the results of your queries.

The language specification gives details of the *query expression pattern*, which must be implemented for all query expressions to work, but this isn't defined as an interface as you might expect. That makes a lot of sense: it allows LINQ to be applied to interfaces such as `IEnumerable<T>` using extension methods. This chapter tackles each element of the query expression pattern, one at a time. If you want to see exactly how the language specification defines each translation, see section 7.16 ("Query Expressions").

---

[3]   It's even more general than that—the compiler doesn't require `Select` to be a method or `SampleData` `.AllUsers` to be a property access. So long as the translated code compiles, it's happy. In almost every sensible case, you'll access either standard or extension methods, but I have a blog post with some particularly odd queries that the compiler's perfectly happy with (see http://mng.bz/7E3i). I haven't found queries like this to be useful in practice, but I do like this example as a way of hammering home how mechanical the translation process is and how it doesn't care about the *meaning* of the translated code.

Listing 11.3 illustrates how the compiler translation works: it provides a dummy implementation of both `Select` and `Where`, with `Select` as a normal instance method and `Where` as an extension method. Our original simple query expression only contained a `select` clause, but this one includes a `where` clause to show both kinds of methods in use. This is a full listing rather than a snippet as extension methods can only be declared in top-level static classes.

Listing 11.3 Compiler translation calling methods on a dummy LINQ implementation

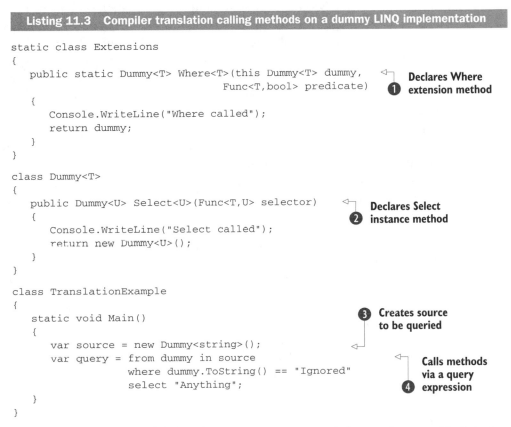

```
static class Extensions
{
    public static Dummy<T> Where<T>(this Dummy<T> dummy,        Declares Where
                            Func<T,bool> predicate)         ❶ extension method
    {
        Console.WriteLine("Where called");
        return dummy;
    }
}

class Dummy<T>
{
    public Dummy<U> Select<U>(Func<T,U> selector)          Declares Select
    {                                                   ❷ instance method
        Console.WriteLine("Select called");
        return new Dummy<U>();
    }
}

class TranslationExample
{
    static void Main()                            ❸ Creates source
    {                                                to be queried
        var source = new Dummy<string>();
        var query = from dummy in source                Calls methods
                    where dummy.ToString() == "Ignored" via a query
                    select "Anything";              ❹ expression
    }
}
```

When you run listing 11.3, it prints `Where called` and then `Select called`, just as you'd expect, because the query expression has been translated into this code:

```
var query = source.Where(dummy => dummy.ToString() == "Ignored")
                  .Select(dummy => "Anything");
```

Of course, you're not doing any querying or transformation here, but it shows how the compiler is translating the query expression. If you're puzzled as to why the lambda expression in the `Select` call returns `"Anything"` instead of just `dummy`, it's because a projection of `dummy` (which is a do-nothing projection) would be removed by the compiler in this particular case. We'll look at that in section 11.3.2, but for the moment the important idea is the overall type of translation involved. You only need to learn what translations the C# compiler will use, and then you can take any query expression, convert it into the form that doesn't use query expressions, and then look at what it's doing from that point of view.

Note that you don't implement `IEnumerable<T>` at all in `Dummy<T>`. The translation from query expressions to normal code doesn't depend on it, but in practice most LINQ providers will expose data either as `IEnumerable<T>` or `IQueryable<T>` (which we'll look at in chapter 12). The fact that the translation doesn't depend on any particular types but merely on the method names and parameters is a sort of compile-time form of duck typing. This is similar to the way that the collection initializers presented in chapter 8 find a public method called `Add` using normal overload resolution rather than using an interface containing an `Add` method with a particular signature. Query expressions take this idea one step further—the translation occurs early in the compilation process in order to allow the compiler to pick either instance methods or extension methods. You could even consider the translation to be the work of a separate preprocessing engine.

You may think I'm banging on about this a lot, but it's all part of removing the mist that sometimes shrouds LINQ. If you rewrite a query expression as a series of method calls, effectively doing what the compiler would've done, you won't change the performance and your query won't behave any differently. They're just two different ways of representing the same code.

> **WHY FROM...WHERE...SELECT INSTEAD OF SELECT...FROM...WHERE?**   Many developers find the order of the clauses in query expressions confusing to start with. It looks just like SQL—except back to front. If you look back to the translation into methods, you'll see the main reason behind it. The query expression is processed in the same order that it's written: you start with a source in the `from` clause, then filter it in the `where` clause, and then project it in the `select` clause. Another way of looking at it is to consider the diagrams throughout this chapter. The data flows from top to bottom, and the boxes appear in the diagram in the same order as their corresponding clauses appear in the query expression. Once you get over any initial discomfort due to unfamiliarity, you may find this approach appealing—I know I do. You may even find yourself asking the equivalent question about SQL.

You now know that a source level translation is involved, but there's another crucial concept to understand before we move on any further.

11.2.3 *Range variables and nontrivial projections*

Let's look back at this chapter's original query expression in more depth. We haven't examined the identifier in the `from` clause or the expression in the `select` clause. Figure 11.4 shows the query expression again, with each part labeled to explain its purpose.

The contextual keywords are easy to explain—they specify to the compiler what you want to do with the data. Likewise, the source expression is a normal C# expression—a property in this case, but it could just as easily have been a method call or a variable.

The tricky bits are the range variable declaration and the projection expression. Range variables aren't like any other type of variable. In some ways they're not variables at all! They're only available in query expressions, and they're effectively present to propagate context from one expression to another. They represent one element of a particular sequence at a time, and they're used in the compiler translation to allow other expressions to be turned into lambda expressions easily.

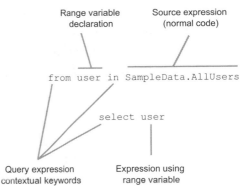

Figure 11.4 A simple query expression broken down into its constituent parts

You've already seen that the original query expression was turned into

```
SampleData.AllUsers.Select(user => user)
```

The left side of the lambda expression—the part that provides the parameter name—comes from the range variable declaration. The right side comes from the `select` clause. The translation is as simple as that (in this case). It all works out okay because the same name is used on both sides.

Suppose you'd written the query expression like this:

```
from user in SampleData.AllUsers
select person
```

In that case, the translated version would've been

```
SampleData.AllUsers.Select(user => person)
```

At that point, the compiler would've complained because it wouldn't have known what `person` referred to.

Now that you know how simple the process is, it becomes easier to understand a query expression that has a slightly more complicated projection. The following listing prints out just the names of our users.

Listing 11.4 Query selecting just the names of the users

```
IEnumerable<string> query = from user in SampleData.AllUsers
                            select user.Name;

foreach (string name in query)
{
    Console.WriteLine(name);
}
```

This time you're using `user.Name` as the projection, and the result is a sequence of strings, not of `User` objects. (I've used an explicitly typed variable to emphasize this point.) The translation of the query expression follows the same rules as before, and becomes

```
SampleData.AllUsers.Select(user => user.Name)
```

The compiler allows this, because the chosen `Select` extension method from Enumerable has this signature:[4]

```
static IEnumerable<TResult> Select<TSource,TResult>
    (this IEnumerable<TSource> source,
     Func<TSource,TResult> selector)
```

The type inference described in chapter 9 kicks in, converting the lambda expression into a `Func<TSource,TResult>`. First it infers that `TSource` is `User` due to the type of `SampleData.AllUsers`. At that point, it knows about the parameter type for the lambda expression, so it can resolve `user.Name` as a property access expression returning type `string`, thus inferring that `TResult` is `string`. This is why lambda expressions allow implicitly typed parameters, and why there are such complicated type inference rules; these are the gears and pistons of the LINQ engine.

> **WHY DO YOU NEED TO KNOW ALL THIS?** You can almost ignore what's going on with range variables a lot of the time. You may have seen many, many queries and understood what they achieve without ever knowing about what's going on behind the scenes. That's fine when things are working (as they tend to with examples in tutorials), but when things go wrong, it pays to know about the details. If you have a query expression that won't compile because the compiler is complaining that it doesn't know about a particular identifier, you should look at the range variables involved.

So far we've only looked at implicitly typed range variables. What happens when you include a type in the declaration? The answer lies in the `Cast` and `OfType` standard query operators.

11.2.4   *Cast, OfType, and explicitly typed range variables*

Most of the time, range variables can be implicitly typed; you're likely to be working with generic collections where the specified type is all you need. What if that weren't the case, though? What if you had an `ArrayList`, or perhaps an `object[]` that you wanted to perform a query on? It would be a pity if LINQ couldn't be applied in those situations. Fortunately, there are two standard query operators that come to the rescue: `Cast` and `OfType`. Only `Cast` is supported directly by the query expression syntax, but we'll look at both in this section.

The two operators are similar: both take an arbitrary untyped sequence (they're extension methods on the nongeneric `IEnumerable` type) and return a strongly typed sequence. `Cast` does this by casting each element to the target type (and failing on any element that isn't of the right type), and `OfType` does a test first, skipping any elements of the wrong type.

---

[4] In order to allow all the methods' signatures in this chapter to fit on the printed page, I've omitted the `public` modifier. In reality they *are* all public though.

The following listing demonstrates both of these operators, used as simple extension methods from `Enumerable`. For a change, we won't use the SkeetySoft defect system for sample data—after all, that's all strongly typed! Instead, we'll use two `ArrayList` objects.

Listing 11.5 Using `Cast` and `OfType` to work with weakly typed collections

```
ArrayList list = new ArrayList { "First", "Second", "Third" };
IEnumerable<string> strings = list.Cast<string>();
foreach (string item in strings)
{
    Console.WriteLine(item);
}

list = new ArrayList { 1, "not an int", 2, 3 };
IEnumerable<int> ints = list.OfType<int>();
foreach (int item in ints)
{
    Console.WriteLine(item);
}
```

The first list contains only strings, so it's safe to use `Cast<string>` to obtain a sequence of strings. The second list has mixed content, so in order to fetch just the integers from it you use `OfType<int>`. If you'd used `Cast<int>` on the second list, an exception would've been thrown when you tried to cast "not an int" to int. Note that this would only have happened *after* you'd returned 1—both operators stream their data, converting elements as they fetch them.

> **IDENTITY, REFERENCE, AND UNBOXING CONVERSIONS ONLY** The behavior of `Cast` changed subtly in .NET 3.5 SP1. In the original .NET 3.5, it would perform more conversions, so using `Cast<int>` on a `List<short>` would convert each `short` into a int as it was fetched. In .NET 3.5 service pack 1 and all later releases, this will throw an exception. If you want any conversion other than a reference conversion or an unboxing conversion (or the no-op identity conversion), use a `Select` projection instead. `OfType` only performs these conversions too, but it doesn't throw an exception if they fail.

When you introduce a range variable with an explicit type, the compiler uses a call to `Cast` to make sure the sequence used by the rest of the query expression is of the appropriate type. The following listing shows this, with a projection using the `Substring` method to prove that the sequence generated by the `from` clause is a sequence of strings.

Listing 11.6 Using an explicitly typed range variable to automatically call `Cast`

```
ArrayList list = new ArrayList { "First", "Second", "Third"};
var strings = from string entry in list
              select entry.Substring(0, 3);
foreach (string start in strings)
```

```
{
    Console.WriteLine(start);
}
```

The output of listing 11.6 is `Fir`, `Sec`, `Thi`, but what's more interesting is the translated query expression:

```
list.Cast<string>().Select(entry => entry.Substring(0,3));
```

Without the cast, you wouldn't be able to call `Select` at all, because the extension method is only defined for `IEnumerable<T>` rather than `IEnumerable`. Even when you're using a strongly typed collection, you might still want to use an explicitly typed range variable. For instance, you could have a collection that's defined to be a `List<ISomeInterface>` but you know that all the elements are instances of `MyImplementation`. Using a range variable with an explicit type of `MyImplementation` allows you to access all the members of `MyImplementation` without manually inserting casts all over the code.

We've covered a lot of important conceptual ground so far, even though we haven't achieved any impressive results. To recap the most important points briefly:

- LINQ is based on sequences of data, which are streamed wherever possible.
- Creating a query doesn't usually execute it; most operations use deferred execution.
- Query expressions in C# 3 involve a preprocessing phase that converts the expression into normal C#, which is then compiled properly with all the normal rules of type inference, overloading, lambda expressions, and so forth.
- The variables declared in query expressions don't act like anything else; they're range variables that allow you to refer to data consistently within the query expression.

I know that there's been a lot of somewhat abstract information to take in. Don't worry if you're beginning to wonder if LINQ is worth all this trouble. I promise you that it is. With a lot of the groundwork out of the way, we can start doing genuinely useful things—such as filtering data and then ordering it.

11.3 *Filtering and ordering a sequence*

You may be surprised to learn that filtering and ordering are two of the simplest operations to explain in terms of compiler translations. This is because they always return a sequence with the same element type as their input, which means you don't need to worry about any new range variables being introduced. It also helps that you've seen the corresponding extension methods in chapter 10.

11.3.1 *Filtering using a where clause*

It's remarkably easy to understand the `where` clause. The syntax is just

```
where filter-expression
```

The compiler translates this into a call to the Where method with a lambda expression, which uses the appropriate range variable as the parameter and the filter expression as the body. The filter expression is applied as a predicate to each element of the incoming stream of data, and only those that return true are present in the resulting sequence.

Using multiple where clauses results in multiple chained Where calls—only elements that match *all* of the predicates are part of the resulting sequence. The following listing demonstrates a query expression that finds all open defects assigned to Tim.

Listing 11.7 Query expression using multiple `where` clauses

```
User tim = SampleData.Users.TesterTim;

var query = from defect in SampleData.AllDefects
            where defect.Status != Status.Closed
            where defect.AssignedTo == tim
            select defect.Summary;
foreach (var summary in query)
{
    Console.WriteLine(summary);
}
```

The query expression in listing 11.7 is translated into this:

```
SampleData.AllDefects.Where (defect => defect.Status != Status.Closed)
                     .Where(defect => defect.AssignedTo == tim)
                     .Select(defect => defect.Summary)
```

The output of listing 11.7 is as follows:

```
Installation is slow
Subtitles only work in Welsh
Play button points the wrong way
Webcam makes me look bald
Network is saturated when playing WAV file
```

Of course, you could write a single where clause that combined the two conditions as an alternative to using multiple where clauses. In some cases this might improve performance, but it's worth bearing the readability of the query expression in mind too, and this is likely to be fairly subjective. My personal inclination is to combine conditions that are logically related but keep others separate. In this case both parts of the expression deal directly with a defect (as that's all our sequence contains), so it'd be reasonable to combine them. As before, it's worth trying both forms to see which is clearer.

In a moment you'll start applying some ordering rules to the query, but first we should look at a small detail to do with the select clause.

11.3.2 Degenerate query expressions

While we have a fairly simple translation to work with, let's revisit a point I glossed over earlier in section 11.2.2 when I first introduced the compiler translations. So far, all our translated query expressions have included a call to Select. What happens if the `select` clause does nothing, effectively returning the same sequence it's given? The answer is that the compiler removes that call to `Select`, but only if there are other operations being performed within the query expression.

For example, the following query expression just selects all the defects in the system:

```
from defect in SampleData.AllDefects
select defect
```

This is known as a *degenerate query expression*. The compiler deliberately generates a call to `Select` even though it seems to do nothing:

```
SampleData.AllDefects.Select(defect => defect)
```

There's a big difference between this and using `SampleData.AllDefects` as a simple expression, though. The items returned by the two sequences are the same, but the result of the `Select` method is *just* the sequence of items, not the source itself. The result of a query expression is never the same object as the source data, unless the LINQ provider has been poorly coded. This can be important from a data integrity point of view—a provider can return a mutable result object, knowing that changes to the returned data sequence won't affect the master, even in the face of a degenerate query.

When other operations are involved, there's no need for the compiler to keep no-op `select` clauses. For example, suppose you change the query expression in listing 11.7 to select the whole defect rather than just the name:

```
from defect in SampleData.AllDefects
where defect.Status != Status.Closed
where defect.AssignedTo == SampleData.Users.TesterTim
select defect
```

You now don't need the final call to `Select`, so the translated code is just this:

```
SampleData.AllDefects.Where(defect => defect.Status != Status.Closed)
                .Where(defect => defect.AssignedTo == tim)
```

These rules rarely get in the way when you're writing query expressions, but they can cause confusion if you decompile the code with a tool such as Reflector—it can be surprising to see the `Select` call go missing for no apparent reason.

With that knowledge in hand, it's time to improve the query so that you know what Tim should work on next.

11.3.3 *Ordering using an orderby clause*

It's not uncommon for developers and testers to be asked to work on the most critical defects before they tackle more trivial ones. You can use a simple query to tell Tim the order in which he should tackle the open defects assigned to him. The following listing does exactly this using an `orderby` clause, printing out all the details of the defects in descending order of priority.

Listing 11.8 Sorting by the severity of a defect, from high to low priority

```
User tim = SampleData.Users.TesterTim;

var query = from defect in SampleData.AllDefects
            where defect.Status != Status.Closed
            where defect.AssignedTo == tim
            orderby defect.Severity descending
            select defect;

foreach (var defect in query)
{
    Console.WriteLine("{0}: {1}", defect.Severity, defect.Summary);
}
```

The output of listing 11.8 shows that you've sorted the results appropriately:

```
Showstopper: Webcam makes me look bald
Major: Subtitles only work in Welsh
Major: Play button points the wrong way
Minor: Network is saturated when playing WAV file
Trivial: Installation is slow
```

You have two major defects. Which order should those be tackled in? Currently no clear ordering is involved.

Let's change the query so that after sorting by severity in descending order, you sort by last modified time in *ascending* order. This means that Tim will test the defects that were fixed a long time ago before those addressed more recently. This just requires an extra expression in the orderby clause, as shown in the following listing.

Listing 11.9 Ordering by severity and then last modified time

```
User tim = SampleData.Users.TesterTim;

var query = from defect in SampleData.AllDefects
            where defect.Status != Status.Closed
            where defect.AssignedTo == tim
            orderby defect.Severity descending, defect.LastModified
            select defect;
foreach (var defect in query)
{
    Console.WriteLine("{0}: {1} ({2:d})",
                defect.Severity, defect.Summary, defect.LastModified);
}
```

The results of listing 11.9 are shown here. Note how the order of the two major defects has been reversed:

```
Showstopper: Webcam makes me look bald (05/27/2013)
Major: Play button points the wrong way (05/17/2013)
Major: Subtitles only work in Welsh (05/23/2013)
Minor: Network is saturated when playing WAV file (05/31/2013)
Trivial: Installation is slow (05/15/2013)
```

That's what the query expression looks like, but what does the compiler do? It simply calls the `OrderBy` and `ThenBy` methods (or `OrderByDescending`/`ThenByDescending` for descending orders). Your query expression is translated into this:

```
SampleData.AllDefects.Where(defect => defect.Status != Status.Closed)
                     .Where(defect => defect.AssignedTo == tim)
                     .OrderByDescending(defect => defect.Severity)
                     .ThenBy(defect => defect.LastModified)
```

Now that you've seen an example, we can look at the general syntax of `orderby` clauses. They're basically the contextual keyword `orderby` followed by one or more orderings. An *ordering* is just an expression (which can use range variables) optionally followed by `ascending` or `descending`, which have the obvious meanings. (The default order is ascending.) The translation for the primary ordering is a call to `OrderBy` or `OrderByDescending`, followed by as many calls to `ThenBy` or `ThenBy-Descending` as you have subsequent orderings.

The difference between `OrderBy` and `ThenBy` is simple: `OrderBy` assumes it has primary control over the ordering, whereas `ThenBy` understands that it's subservient to one or more previous orderings. For LINQ to Objects, `ThenBy` is only defined as an extension method for `IOrderedEnumerable<T>`, which is the type returned by `OrderBy` (and by `ThenBy` itself, to allow further chaining).

It's important to note that although you can use multiple `orderby` clauses, each one will start with its own `OrderBy` or `OrderByDescending` clause, which means the last one will effectively win. I've yet to see a situation in which this is useful unless you do something else to the query between `orderby` clauses; you should almost always use a single clause containing multiple orderings instead.

As noted in chapter 10, applying an ordering requires all the data to be loaded (at least for LINQ to Objects)—you can't order an infinite sequence, for example. Hopefully the reason for this is obvious: you don't know which element should come at the start of the resulting sequence until you've seen all the elements.

We're about halfway through learning about query expressions, and you may be surprised that we haven't looked at any *joins* yet. Obviously they're important in LINQ, just as they're important in SQL, but they're also complicated. I promise we'll get to them in due course, but in order to introduce just one new concept at a time, we'll detour through `let` clauses first. That way we can discuss transparent identifiers before we hit joins.

11.4   *Let clauses and transparent identifiers*

Most of the rest of the operators we still need to look at involve *transparent identifiers*. Just like range variables, you can get along perfectly well without understanding transparent identifiers if you only want to have a fairly shallow grasp of query expressions. If you've bought this book, though, you probably want to know C# at a deeper level, which will (among other things) enable you to look compilation errors in the face and know what they're talking about.

You don't need to know *everything* about transparent identifiers, but I'll teach you enough so that if you see one in the language specification, you won't feel like running and hiding. You'll also understand why they're needed at all—and that's where an example will come in handy. The `let` clause is the simplest transformation available that uses transparent identifiers.

11.4.1 Introducing an intermediate computation with let

A `let` clause introduces a new range variable with a value that can be based on other range variables. The syntax is as easy as pie:

```
let identifier = expression
```

To explain this operator in terms that don't use any other complicated operators, I'll resort to a very artificial example. Suspend your disbelief, and imagine that finding the length of a string is a costly operation. Now imagine that you have a completely bizarre system requirement to order your users by the lengths of their names and then display the name and its length. Yes, I know it's unlikely. The following listing shows one way of doing this without a `let` clause.

Listing 11.10 Sorting by the lengths of user names without a `let` clause

```
var query = from user in SampleData.AllUsers
            orderby user.Name.Length
            select user.Name;

foreach (var name in query)
{
    Console.WriteLine("{0}: {1}", name.Length, name);
}
```

That works fine, but it uses the dreaded `Length` property twice—once to sort the users, and once in the display side. Surely not even the fastest supercomputer could cope with finding the lengths of six strings *twice*! No, you need to avoid that redundant computation.

You can do so with the `let` clause, which evaluates an expression and introduces it as a new range variable. The following code achieves the same result as listing 11.10, but only uses the `Length` property once per user.

Listing 11.11 Using a `let` clause to remove redundant calculations

```
var query = from user in SampleData.AllUsers
            let length = user.Name.Length
            orderby length
            select new { Name = user.Name, Length = length };

foreach (var entry in query)
{
    Console.WriteLine("{0}: {1}", entry.Length, entry.Name);
}
```

Listing 11.11 introduces a new range variable called `length`, which contains the length of the user's name (for the current user in the original sequence). You then use that new range variable both for sorting and the projection at the end. Have you spotted the problem yet? You need to use two range variables, but the lambda expression passed to `Select` only takes one parameter! This is where transparent identifiers come on the scene.

11.4.2 *Transparent identifiers*

In listing 11.11 you have *two* range variables involved in the final projection, but the `Select` method only acts on a single sequence. How can you combine the range variables?

The answer is to create an anonymous type that contains both variables, and then to apply a clever translation to make it *look* as if you actually have two parameters for the `select` and `orderby` clauses. Figure 11.5 shows the sequences involved.

The `let` clause achieves its objectives by using another call to `Select`, creating an anonymous type for the resulting sequence, and effectively creating a new range

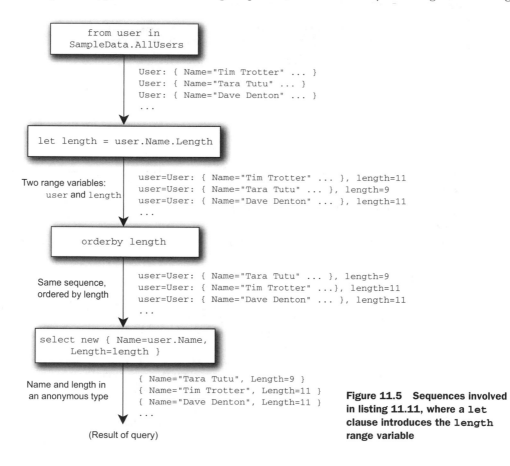

Figure 11.5 Sequences involved in listing 11.11, where a `let` clause introduces the `length` range variable

variable whose name can never be seen or used in source code. The query expression from listing 11.11 is translated into something like this:

```
SampleData.AllUsers
        .Select(user => new { user, length = user.Name.Length })
        .OrderBy(z => z.length)
        .Select(z => new { Name = z.user.Name, Length = z.length })
```

Each part of the query has been adjusted appropriately: where the original query expression referenced `user` or `length` directly, if the reference occurs after the `let` clause, it's replaced by `z.user` or `z.length`. The choice of `z` as the name here is arbitrary—it's all hidden by the compiler.

> **ANONYMOUS TYPES ARE AN IMPLEMENTATION DETAIL** Strictly speaking, it's up to the C# compiler implementation to decide how to group together different range variables to make transparent identifiers work. The Microsoft implementation uses anonymous types, and the specification shows the translations in those terms as well, so I've followed the trend. Even if another compiler chose a different approach, it shouldn't affect the results.

If you consult the language specification about `let` clauses (section 7.16.2.4), you'll see that the translation it describes is from one query expression to another. It uses an asterisk (*) to represent the transparent identifier introduced. The transparent identifier is then *erased* as a final step in translation. I won't use that notation in this chapter, as it's hard to come to grips with and unnecessary at the level of detail we're going into. Hopefully with this background the specification won't be quite as impenetrable as it might be otherwise, should you need to refer to it.

The good news is that we can now look at the rest of the translations making up C# 3's query expression support. I won't go into the details of every transparent identifier introduced, but I'll mention the situations in which they occur. Let's look at the support for joins first.

11.5 Joins

If you've ever read *anything* about SQL, you probably have an idea what a database join is. It takes two tables (or views, or table-valued functions, and so forth) and creates a result by matching one set of rows against another set of rows. A LINQ join is similar, except it works on sequences. Three types of join are available, although not all of them use the `join` keyword in the query expression. We'll start with the join that's closest to a SQL inner join.

11.5.1 Inner joins using join clauses

Inner joins involve two sequences. One *key selector* expression is applied to each element of the first sequence, and another key selector (which may be totally different) is applied to each element of the second sequence. The result of the join is a sequence of all the pairs of elements where the key from the first element is the same as the key from the second element.

TERMINOLOGY CLASH! INNER AND OUTER SEQUENCES   The MSDN documentation for the `Join` method used to evaluate inner joins calls the sequences involved `inner` and `outer`, and the real method parameters are based on these names too. This has nothing to do with inner joins and outer joins—it's just a way of differentiating between the sequences. You can think of them as first and second, left and right, Bert and Ernie—anything you like that helps you. I'll use left and right for this chapter, so that it's clear which is which in the diagrams. Usually, *outer* corresponds with *left* and *inner* corresponds with *right*.

The two sequences can be anything you like; the right sequence can even be the same as the left sequence, if that's useful. (Imagine finding pairs of people who were born on the same day, for example.) The only thing that matters is that the two key selector expressions must result in the same type of key.[5]

You can't join a sequence of people to a sequence of cities by saying that the birth date of the person is the same as the population of the city—it doesn't make any sense. But one important possibility is to use an anonymous type for the key; this works because anonymous types implement equality and hashing appropriately. If you need to effectively create a multicolumn key, anonymous types are the way to go. This is also applicable for the grouping operations we'll look at later.

The syntax for an inner join looks more complicated than it is:

```
[query selecting the left sequence]
join right-range-variable in right-sequence
    on left-key-selector equals right-key-selector
```

Seeing `equals` as a contextual keyword rather than using symbols can be disconcerting, but it makes it easier to distinguish the left key selector from the right key selector. Often (but not always) at least one of the key selectors is a trivial one that just selects the exact element from that sequence. The contextual keyword is used by the compiler to separate the key selectors into different lambda expressions. The query processor's ability to obtain the keys for each value (on each side of the join) is important both for performance in LINQ to Objects and for the feasibility of translating the query into other forms, such as SQL.

Let's look at an example from our defect system. Suppose you've just added the notification feature and want to send the first batch of emails for all the existing defects. You need to join the list of notifications against the list of defects where their projects match. The following listing performs just such a join.

Listing 11.12   Joining the defects and notification subscriptions based on project

```
var query = from defect in SampleData.AllDefects
            join subscription in SampleData.AllSubscriptions
                on defect.Project equals subscription.Project
```

---

[5]   It's also valid for there to be two key types involved, with an implicit conversion from one to the other. One of the types must be a better choice than the other, in the same way that the compiler infers the type of an implicitly typed array. In my experience, you rarely need to consciously consider this detail.

```
        select new { defect.Summary, subscription.EmailAddress };
foreach (var entry in query)
{
    Console.WriteLine("{0}: {1}", entry.EmailAddress, entry.Summary);
}
```

Listing 11.12 will show each of the media player defects twice—once for mediabugs @skeetysoft.com and once for theboss@skeetysoft.com (because the boss really cares about the media player project).

In this particular case, you could easily have made the join the other way around, reversing the left and right sequences. The result would've been the same entries but in a different order. The implementation in LINQ to Objects returns entries such that all the pairs using the first element of the left sequence are returned (in the order of the right sequence), then all the pairs using the second element of the left sequence, and so on. The right sequence is buffered, but the left sequence is streamed, so if you want to join a massive sequence to a tiny one, it's worth using the tiny one as the right sequence if you can. The operation is still deferred: it waits until you ask for the first pair before reading any data from either sequence. At that point, it reads the entirety of the right sequence in order to build a lookup from keys to the values producing those keys. After that, it doesn't need to read from the right sequence again, and can begin to iterate over the left sequence, yielding pairs appropriately.

One error that might trip you up is putting the key selectors the wrong way around. In the left key selector, only the left sequence range variable is in scope; in the right key selector, only the right range variable is in scope. If you reverse the left and right sequences, you have to reverse the left and right key selectors too. Fortunately, the compiler knows that this is a common mistake and suggests the appropriate course of action.

Just to make it more obvious what's going on, figure 11.6 shows the sequences as they're processed.

Often you'll want to filter the sequence, and filtering before the join occurs is more efficient than filtering it afterward. At this stage, the query expression is simpler if the left sequence is the one requiring filtering. For instance, if you wanted to show only defects that are closed, you could use this query expression:

```
from defect in SampleData.AllDefects
where defect.Status == Status.Closed
join subscription in SampleData.AllSubscriptions
    on defect.Project equals subscription.Project
select new { defect.Summary, subscription.EmailAddress }
```

You *can* perform the same query with the sequences reversed, but it's messier:

```
from subscription in SampleData.AllSubscriptions
join defect in (from defect in SampleData.AllDefects
                where defect.Status == Status.Closed
                select defect)
    on subscription.Project equals defect.Project
select new { defect.Summary, subscription.EmailAddress }
```

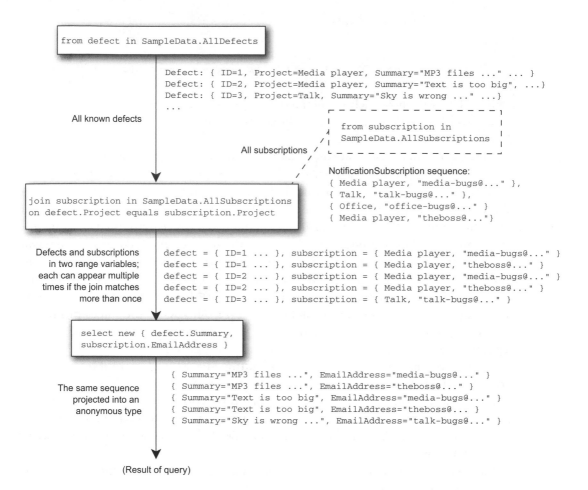

Figure 11.6   The join from listing 11.12 in graphical form, showing two different sequences (defects and subscriptions) used as data sources

Note how you can use one query expression inside another—the language specification describes many of the compiler translations in these terms. Nested query expressions are useful but hurt readability as well; it's often worth looking for an alternative, or using a variable for the sequence on the right in order to make the code clearer.

ARE INNER JOINS USEFUL IN LINQ TO OBJECTS?   Inner joins are used all the time in SQL. They're effectively the way that you navigate from one entity to a related one, usually joining a foreign key in one table to the primary key in another. In the object-oriented model, you tend to navigate from one object to another via references. For instance, retrieving the summary of a defect and the name of the user assigned to work on it would require a join in SQL— in C# you often just use a chain of properties. If you'd had a reverse association from Project to the list of NotificationSubscription objects associated with it in the model, you wouldn't have needed the join to achieve the goal of this example, either. That's not to say that inner joins aren't sometimes useful within object-oriented models, but they don't naturally occur as often as in relational models.

Inner joins are translated by the compiler into calls to the `Join` method, like this:

```
leftSequence.Join(rightSequence,
                  leftKeySelector,
                  rightKeySelector,
                  resultSelector)
```

The signature of the overload used for LINQ to Objects is as follows (this is the real signature, with the real parameter names—hence the *inner* and *outer* references):

```
static IEnumerable<TResult> Join<TOuter,TInner,TKey,TResult> (
    this IEnumerable<TOuter> outer,
    IEnumerable<TInner> inner,
    Func<TOuter,TKey> outerKeySelector,
    Func<TInner,TKey> innerKeySelector,
    Func<TOuter,TInner,TResult> resultSelector
)
```

The first three parameters are self-explanatory when you've remembered to treat *inner* and *outer* as *right* and *left*, respectively, but the last one is more interesting. It's a projection from two elements (one from the left sequence and one from the right sequence) into a single element of the resulting sequence.

When the join is followed by anything other than a `select` clause, the C# 3 compiler introduces a transparent identifier in order to make the range variables used in both sequences available for later clauses, and creates an anonymous type and a simple mapping to use for the `resultSelector` parameter.

But if the next part of the query expression is a `select` clause, the projection from the `select` clause is used directly as the `resultSelector` parameter—there's no point in creating a pair and then calling `Select` when you can do the transformation in one step. You can still *think* about it as a "join" step followed by a "select" step, despite the two being squished into a single method call. This leads to a more consistent mental model in my view, and one that's easier to reason about. Unless you're looking at the generated code, just ignore the optimization the compiler is performing for you.

The good news is that, having learned about inner joins, you'll find the next type of join much easier to approach.

11.5.2 *Group joins with join...into clauses*

You've seen that the result sequence from a normal `join` clause consists of pairs of elements, one from each of the input sequences. A *group join* looks similar in terms of the query expression but has a significantly different outcome. Each element of a group join result consists of an element from the left sequence (using its original range variable) and a *sequence* of all the matching elements of the right sequence, exposed as a new range variable specified by the identifier coming after `into` in the `join` clause.

Let's change the previous example to use a group join. The following listing again shows all the defects and the notifications required for each of them, but it breaks them out in a per-defect manner. Pay particular attention to how the results are displayed with a nested `foreach` loop.

Listing 11.13   Joining defects and subscriptions with a group join

```
var query = from defect in SampleData.AllDefects
            join subscription in SampleData.AllSubscriptions
                on defect.Project equals subscription.Project
                into groupedSubscriptions
            select new { Defect = defect,
                         Subscriptions = groupedSubscriptions };

foreach (var entry in query)
{
   Console.WriteLine(entry.Defect.Summary);
   foreach (var subscription in entry.Subscriptions)
   {
      Console.WriteLine (" {0}", subscription.EmailAddress);
   }
}
```

The `Subscriptions` property of each entry is the embedded sequence of subscriptions matching that entry's defect. Figure 11.7 shows how the two initial sequences are combined.

One important difference between an inner join and a group join—and between a group join and a normal grouping—is that a group join has a one-to-one correspondence between the left sequence and the result sequence, even if some of the elements in the left sequence don't match any elements of the right sequence. This can be important and is sometimes used to simulate a *left outer join* from SQL. The embedded sequence is empty when the left element doesn't match any right elements. As with an inner join, a group join buffers the right sequence but streams the left one.

Listing 11.14 shows an example of this, counting the number of defects created on each day in May. It uses a `DateTimeRange` type to generate a sequence of dates in May as the left sequence, and a projection that calls `Count()` on the embedded sequence in the result of the group join.[6]

Listing 11.14   Counting the number of defects raised on each day in May

```
var dates = new DateTimeRange(SampleData.Start, SampleData.End);

var query = from date in dates
            join defect in SampleData.AllDefects
                on date equals defect.Created.Date
                into joined
            select new { Date = date, Count = joined.Count() };
```

---

[6] This is a simple implementation for the sake of the example—not a full-blown, general-purpose range.

```
foreach (var grouped in query)
{
    Console.WriteLine("{0:d}: {1}", grouped.Date, grouped.Count);
}
```

The Count() method uses immediate execution, iterating through all the elements of the sequence it's called on—but you're only calling it in the projection part of the query expression, so it becomes part of a lambda expression. This means you still have deferred execution; nothing is evaluated until you start the foreach loop.

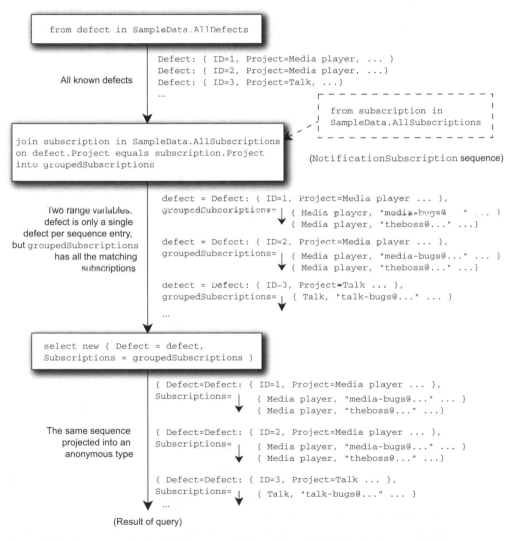

Figure 11.7 Sequences involved in the group join from listing 11.13. The short arrows indicate embedded sequences within the result entries. In the output, some entries contain multiple email addresses for the same defect.

Here's the first part of the results of listing 11.14, showing the number of defects created each day in the first week of May:

```
05/01/2013: 1
05/02/2013: 0
05/03/2013: 2
05/04/2013: 1
05/05/2013: 0
05/06/2013: 1
05/07/2013: 1
```

The compiler translation involved for a group join is simply a call to the `GroupJoin` method in the same way that an inner join translates to a call to `Join`. Here's the signature for `Enumerable.GroupJoin`:

```
static IEnumerable<TResult> GroupJoin<TOuter,TInner,TKey,TResult>(
    this IEnumerable<TOuter> outer,
    IEnumerable<TInner> inner,
    Func<TOuter,TKey> outerKeySelector,
    Func<TInner,TKey> innerKeySelector,
    Func<TOuter,IEnumerable<TInner>,TResult> resultSelector
)
```

This is exactly the same as for inner joins, except that the `resultSelector` parameter has to work with a sequence of right-hand elements, not just a single one. As with inner joins, if a group join is followed by a `select` clause, the projection is used as the result selector of the `GroupJoin` call; otherwise, a transparent identifier is introduced. In this case you have a `select` clause immediately after the group join, so the translated query looks like this:

```
dates.GroupJoin(SampleData.AllDefects,
            date => date,
            defect => defect.Created.Date,
            (date, joined) => new  { Date = date,
                                    Count = joined.Count() })
```

The final type of join is known as a *cross join*, but it's not as straightforward as it might initially seem.

11.5.3 *Cross joins and flattening sequences using multiple from clauses*

So far all our joins have been *equijoins*—a match has been performed between elements of the left and right sequences. Cross joins don't perform any matching between the sequences; the result contains every possible pair of elements. This is achieved by simply using two (or more) `from` clauses. For the sake of sanity, we'll only consider two `from` clauses for the moment—when there are more, just mentally perform a cross join on the first two `from` clauses, then cross join the resulting sequence with the next `from` clause, and so on. Each extra `from` clause adds its own range variable via a transparent identifier.

The following listing shows a simple (but useless) cross join in action, producing a sequence where each entry consists of a user and a project. I've deliberately picked two completely unrelated initial sequences to show that no matching is performed.

Listing 11.15 Cross joining users against projects

```
var query = from user in SampleData.AllUsers
            from project in SampleData.AllProjects
            select new { User = user, Project = project };
foreach (var pair in query)
{
    Console.WriteLine("{0}/{1}",
                      pair.User.Name,
                      pair.Project.Name);
}
```

The output of listing 11.15 begins like this:

```
Tim Trotter/Skeety Media Player
Tim Trotter/Skeety Talk
Tim Trotter/Skeety Office
Tara Tutu/Skeety Media Player
Tara Tutu/Skeety Talk
Tara Tutu/Skeety Office
```

Figure 11.8 shows the sequences involved to get this result.

If you're familiar with SQL, you're probably comfortable so far—it looks just like a Cartesian product obtained from a query specifying multiple tables. But more power is available when you want it: the right sequence can depend on the current value of the left sequence. In other words, each element of the left sequence is used to generate a right sequence, and then that left element is paired with each element of the new sequence. When this is the case, it's not a cross join in the normal sense of the term. Instead, it's effectively flattening a sequence of sequences into one single sequence. The query expression translation is the same whether or not you're using a true cross join, so you need to understand the more complicated scenario in order to understand the translation process.

Before we dive into the details, let's see the effect it produces. The following listing shows a simple example, using sequences of integers.

Listing 11.16 Cross join where the right sequence depends on the left element

```
var query = from left in Enumerable.Range(1, 4)
            from right in Enumerable.Range(11, left)
            select new { Left = left, Right = right };

foreach (var pair in query)
{
    Console.WriteLine("Left={0}; Right={1}",
                      pair.Left, pair.Right);
}
```

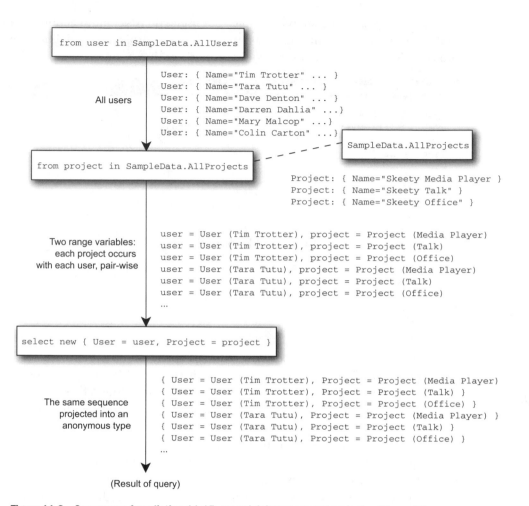

Figure 11.8   Sequences from listing 11.15, cross joining users and projects. All possible combinations are returned in the results.

Listing 11.16 starts with a simple range of integers, 1 to 4. For each of those integers, you create another range, beginning at 11 and having as many elements as the original integer. By using multiple `from` clauses, the left sequence is joined with each of the generated right sequences, resulting in this output:

```
Left=1; Right=11
Left=2; Right=11
Left=2; Right=12
Left=3; Right=11
Left=3; Right=12
Left=3; Right=13
Left=4; Right=11
Left=4; Right=12
Left=4; Right=13
Left=4; Right=14
```

The method the compiler calls to generate this sequence is SelectMany. It takes a single input sequence (the *left* sequence in our terminology), a delegate to *generate* another sequence from any element of the left sequence, and a delegate to generate a result element given an element of each of the sequences. Here's the signature of Enumerable.SelectMany:

```
static IEnumerable<TResult> SelectMany<TSource,TCollection,TResult>(
    this IEnumerable<TSource> source,
    Func<TSource,IEnumerable<TCollection>> collectionSelector,
    Func<TSource,TCollection,TResult> resultSelector
)
```

As with the other joins, if the part of the query expression following the join is a select clause, that projection is used as the final argument; otherwise, a transparent identifier is introduced to make the range variables of both the left and right sequences available later in the query.

Just to make this all a bit more concrete, here's the query expression of listing 11.16 as the translated source code:

```
Enumerable.Range(1, 4)
        .SelectMany(left => Enumerable.Range(11, left),
                   (left, right) => new {Left = left, Right = right})
```

One interesting feature of SelectMany is that the execution is completely streamed—it only needs to process one element of each sequence at a time, because it uses a freshly generated right sequence for each different element of the left sequence. Compare this with inner joins and group joins: they both load the right sequence completely before starting to return any results.

The flattening behavior of SelectMany can be very useful. Consider a situation where you want to process a lot of log files, a line at a time. You can process a seamless sequence of lines with barely any work. The following pseudocode is filled in more thoroughly in the downloadable source code, but the overall meaning and usefulness should be clear:

```
var query = from file in Directory.GetFiles(logDirectory, "*.log")
            from line in ReadLines(file)
            let entry = new LogEntry(line)
            where entry.Type == EntryType.Error
            select entry;
```

In just five lines of code, you can retrieve, parse, and filter a whole collection of log files, returning a sequence of entries representing errors. Crucially, you don't have to load even a single full log file into memory in one go, let alone all of the files—all the data is streamed.

Having tackled joins, the last items we need to look at are slightly easier to understand. We'll look at grouping elements by a key and continuing a query expression after a group ... by or select clause.

11.6 Groupings and continuations

One common requirement is to group a sequence of elements by one of its properties. LINQ makes this easy with the group ... by clause. In addition to describing this final type of clause in this section, we'll also revisit select to see a feature called *query continuations* that can be applied to both groupings and projections. Let's start with a simple grouping.

11.6.1 Grouping with the group...by clause

Grouping is largely intuitive, and LINQ makes it simple. To group a sequence in a query expression, all you need to do is use the group ... by clause, with this syntax:

```
group projection by grouping
```

This clause comes at the end of a query expression in the same way a select clause does. The similarities between these clauses don't end there: the *projection* expression is the same kind of projection that select clauses use. The outcome is somewhat different, though.

The *grouping* expression determines what the sequence is grouped by—it's the *key selector* of the grouping operation. The overall result is a sequence where each element is a group. Each group is a sequence of projected elements that also has a Key property, which is the key for that group; this combination is encapsulated in the IGrouping<TKey,TElement> interface, which extends IEnumerable<TElement>. Again, if you want to group by multiple values, you can use an anonymous type for the key.

Let's look at a simple example from the SkeetySoft defect system: grouping defects by their current assignee. The following listing does this with the simplest form of projection, so that the resulting sequence has the assignee as the key and a sequence of defects embedded in each entry.

Listing 11.17 Grouping defects by assignee—trivial projection

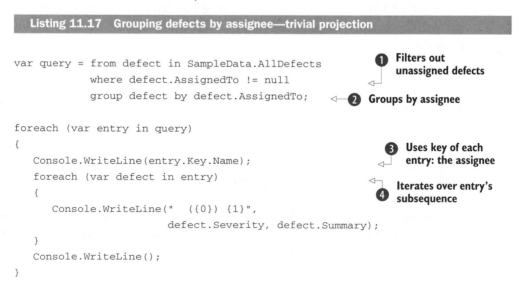

```
var query = from defect in SampleData.AllDefects          ❶ Filters out
            where defect.AssignedTo != null                 unassigned defects
            group defect by defect.AssignedTo;    ←  ❷ Groups by assignee

foreach (var entry in query)
{
                                                   ❸ Uses key of each
    Console.WriteLine(entry.Key.Name);                entry: the assignee
    foreach (var defect in entry)                  ❹ Iterates over entry's
    {                                                 subsequence
        Console.WriteLine("  ({0}) {1}",
                        defect.Severity, defect.Summary);
    }
    Console.WriteLine();
}
```

Listing 11.17 might be useful in a daily build report, to quickly see what defects each person needs to look at. It filters out all the defects that don't need any more attention ❶ and then groups using the `AssignedTo` property. Although this time you're just using a property, the grouping expression can be anything you like—it's applied to each entry in the incoming sequence, and the sequence is grouped based on the result of the expression. Note that grouping can't stream the results; it applies the key selection and projection to each element in the input and buffers the grouped sequences of projected elements. But even though it's not streamed, execution is still deferred until you start retrieving the results.

The projection applied in the grouping ❷ is trivial—it just selects the original element. As you go through the resulting sequence, each entry has a `Key` property, which is of type `User` ❸, and each entry also implements `IEnumerable<Defect>`, which is the sequence of defects assigned to that user ❹.

The results of listing 11.17 start like this:

```
Darren Dahlia
  (Showstopper) MP3 files crash system
  (Major) Can't play files more than 200 bytes long
  (Major) DivX is choppy on Pentium 100
  (Trivial) User interface should be more caramelly
```

After all of Darren's defects have been returned, you'll see Tara's, then Tim's, and so on. The implementation effectively keeps a list of the assignees it's seen so far, and adds a new one every time it needs to. Figure 11.9 shows the sequences generated throughout the query expression, which may make this ordering more clear.

Within each entry's subsequence, the order of the defects is the same as in the original defect sequence. If you actively care about the ordering, consider explicitly stating it in the query expression, to make it more readable.

If you run listing 11.17, you'll see that Mary Malcop doesn't appear in the output at all, because she doesn't have any defects assigned to her. If you wanted to produce a full list of users and defects assigned to each of them, you'd need to use a group join like the one in listing 11.14.

The compiler always uses a method called `GroupBy` for grouping clauses. When the projection in a grouping clause is trivial—when each entry in the original sequence maps directly to the exact same object in a subsequence—the compiler uses a simple method call that only requires the grouping expression, so it knows how to map each element to a key. For instance, the query expression in listing 11.17 is translated into this:

```
SampleData.AllDefects.Where(defect => defect.AssignedTo != null)
                .GroupBy(defect => defect.AssignedTo)
```

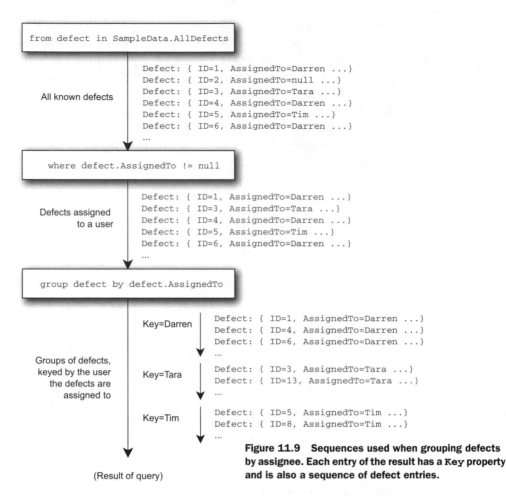

Figure 11.9 Sequences used when grouping defects by assignee. Each entry of the result has a Key property and is also a sequence of defect entries.

When the projection is nontrivial, a slightly more complicated version is used. The following listing gives an example of a projection where you only capture the summary of each defect rather than the Defect object itself.

Listing 11.18 Grouping defects by assignee—projection retains just the summary

```
var query = from defect in SampleData.AllDefects
            where defect.AssignedTo != null
            group defect.Summary by defect.AssignedTo;

foreach (var entry in query)
{
   Console.WriteLine(entry.Key.Name);
   foreach (var summary in entry)
   {
      Console.WriteLine(" {0}", summary);
   }
   Console.WriteLine();
}
```

I've highlighted the differences between listings 11.18 and 11.17 in bold. Because each defect is projected to just its summary, the embedded sequence in each entry is just an `IEnumerable<string>`. In this case the compiler uses an overload of `GroupBy` with another parameter to represent the projection. The query expression in listing 11.18 is translated into the following expression:

```
SampleData.AllDefects.Where(defect => defect.AssignedTo != null)
              .GroupBy(defect => defect.AssignedTo,
                       defect => defect.Summary)
```

Grouping clauses are relatively simple but useful. Even in the defect-tracking system, you could easily imagine wanting to group defects by project, creator, severity, or status, as well as by the assignee used in these examples.

So far, you've ended each query expression with a `select` or `group ... by` clause, and that's been the end of the expression. But there are times when you'll want to do more with the results, and that's when *query continuations* are used.

11.6.2 *Query continuations*

Query continuations provide a way of using the result of one query expression as the initial sequence of another. They apply to both `group ... by` and `select` clauses, and the syntax is the same for both—you simply use the contextual keyword `into` and then provide the name of a new range variable. That range variable can then be used in the next part of the query expression.

The specification explains this in terms of a translation from one query expression to another, changing

```
first-query into identifier
second query-body
```

into

```
from identifier in (first-query)
second-query-body
```

An example will make this clearer. Let's go back to the grouping of defects by assignee, but this time imagine you only want the count of the defects assigned to each person. You can't do that with the projection in the grouping clause, because that only applies to each individual defect. You want to project each group, which contains an assignee and the sequence of their defects, into a single element consisting of the assignee and the count of defects in the group. This can be achieved with the following code.

Listing 11.19 Continuing a grouping with another projection

```
var query = from defect in SampleData.AllDefects
            where defect.AssignedTo != null
            group defect by defect.AssignedTo into grouped
            select new { Assignee = grouped.Key,
                         Count = grouped.Count() };

foreach (var entry in query)
```

```
{
    Console.WriteLine("{0}: {1}",
                      entry.Assignee.Name, entry.Count);
}
```

The changes to the query expression are highlighted in bold. You can use the grouped range variable in the second part of the query, but the defect range variable is no longer available—you can think of it as being out of scope. This projection simply creates an anonymous type with Assignee and Count properties, using the key of each group as the assignee, and counting the sequence of defects associated with each group.

The results of listing 11.19 are as follows:

```
Darren Dahlia: 14
Tara Tutu: 5
Tim Trotter: 5
Deborah Denton: 9
Colin Carton: 2
```

Following the specification, the query expression from listing 11.19 is translated into this one:

```
from grouped in (from defect in SampleData.AllDefects
                 where defect.AssignedTo != null
                 group defect by defect.AssignedTo)
select new { Assignee = grouped.Key, Count = grouped.Count() }
```

The rest of the translations are then performed, resulting in the following code:

```
SampleData.AllDefects
          .Where(defect => defect.AssignedTo != null)
          .GroupBy(defect => defect.AssignedTo)
          .Select(grouped => new { Assignee = grouped.Key,
                                   Count = grouped.Count() })
```

An alternative way of understanding continuations is to think of two separate statements. This isn't as accurate in terms of the actual compiler translation, but I find it makes it easier to see what's going on. In this case, the query expression (and assignment to the query variable) can be thought of as the following two statements:

```
var tmp = from defect in SampleData.AllDefects
          where defect.AssignedTo != null
          group defect by defect.AssignedTo;

var query = from grouped in tmp
            select new { Assignee = grouped.Key,
                         Count = grouped.Count() };
```

Of course, if you find this easier to read, there's nothing to stop you from breaking up the original expression into this form in your source code. Nothing will be evaluated until you start trying to step through the query results anyway, due to deferred execution.

> **JOIN...INTO ISN'T A CONTINUATION**   It's easy to fall into the trap of thinking that wherever you see the contextual keyword into, you have a continuation. This isn't true for joins—the join ... into clause (which is used for group joins)

doesn't form a continuation. The important difference is that with a group join, all the earlier range variables (apart from the one used to name the right side of the join) can still be used. Compare that with the queries we're looking at in this section, where the continuation wipes the slate clean; the *only* range variable available afterward is the one declared by the continuation.

Let's extend this example to see how multiple continuations can be used. The results are currently unordered—let's change that so you can see who has the most defects assigned to them first. You could use a let clause after the first continuation, but the following listing shows an alternative with a second continuation after the current expression.

Listing 11.20 Query expression continuations from `group` and `select`

```
var query = from defect in SampleData.AllDefects
            where defect.AssignedTo != null
            group defect by defect.AssignedTo into grouped
            select new { Assignee = grouped.Key,
                         Count = grouped.Count() } into result
            orderby result.Count descending
            select result;

foreach (var entry in query)
{
   Console.WriteLine("{0}: {1}",
                     entry.Assignee.Name,
                     entry.Count);
}
```

The changes between listings 11.19 and 11.20 are highlighted in bold. You didn't need to change any of the output code, because you had the same type of sequence— you just needed to apply an ordering to it.

This time the translated query expression is as follows:

```
SampleData.AllDefects
        .Where(defect => defect.AssignedTo != null)
        .GroupBy(defect => defect.AssignedTo)
        .Select(grouped => new { Assignee = grouped.Key,
                                 Count = grouped.Count() })
        .OrderByDescending(result => result.Count);
```

By pure coincidence, this is remarkably similar to the first defect-tracking query we looked at, in section 10.3.6. The final select clause effectively does nothing, so the C# compiler ignores it. It's required in the query expression, though, as all query expressions must end with either a select or a group ... by clause. There's nothing to stop you from using a different projection or performing other operations with the continued query—joins, further groupings, and so forth. Just keep an eye on the readability of the query expression as it grows.

Speaking of readability, there are options to consider when you're writing LINQ queries.

11.7   *Choosing between query expressions and dot notation*

As you've seen throughout this chapter, query expressions are translated into normal C# before being compiled any further. There isn't an official name for a call to the LINQ query operators written using normal C# rather than as a query expression, but many developers now refer to this as *dot notation*.[7] Every query expression can be written in dot notation, but the reverse isn't true: many LINQ operators don't have a query expression equivalent in C#. The big question is this: When should you use which syntax?

11.7.1   *Operations that require dot notation*

The most obvious situation where you're forced to use dot notation is when you're calling a method such as `Reverse` or `ToDictionary` that isn't represented in query expression syntax at all. But even when you use a query operator that's supported by query expressions, it's quite possible for the overload you want to be unavailable.

For example, `Enumerable.Where` has an overload where the index into the parent sequence is supplied as another argument to the delegate. In such a situation, you could use code like the following to take every other item from a sequence:

```
sequence.Where((item, index) => index % 2 == 0)
```

There's a similar overload for `Select`, so if you wanted to be able to get at the original index in a sequence after ordering, you could do something like this:

```
sequence.Select((Item, Index) => new { Item, Index })
       .OrderBy(x => x.Item.Name)
```

This example shows another option you might want to consider: if you're going to use a lambda expression parameter directly in an anonymous type, you could buck the normal convention of starting the parameter name with a lowercase letter, and then use a projection initializer to avoid writing `new { Item = item, Index = index }`, which can be distracting. Of course, you can ignore the convention about property names instead, and make your anonymous type have properties beginning with a lowercase letter (`item` and `index`, for example). All of this is entirely up to you, and it's worth experimenting. Although consistency is usually important, it doesn't matter too much here, as the impact of inconsistency is confined to the method in question; you're not exposing these names in your public API or throughout the rest of your class.

Many of the query operators also support custom comparisons—ordering and joining being the most obvious examples. These are unlikely to be required often, in my experience, but they're occasionally invaluable. For example, if you want to perform a join on a person's name in a case-insensitive manner, you can specify `String-Comparer.OrdinalIgnoreCase` (or a culture-specific comparer) as the final argument to a `Join` call. Again, if you feel that an operator *nearly* does what you want but doesn't quite cut it, check the documentation for other overloads.

---

[7] That's the term I'll use from now on, but if you hear others talking about *fluent notation*, they probably mean the same thing.

When you're forced to use dot notation, the decision to use it is easy, but what about cases where a query expression *could* be used?

11.7.2 *Query expressions where dot notation may be simpler*

Some developers use query expressions everywhere they can get away with it; personally, I look at what the query is doing and decide which approach will be more readable.

For example, take this query expression, which is similar to one near the start of this chapter:

```
var adults = from person in people
             where person.Age >= 18
             select person;
```

This is three lines of code with a lot of baggage, even though all it's doing is filtering. In this case I'd use dot notation:

```
var adults = people.Where(person => person.Age >= 18);
```

I find that clearer—every part of it mentions something you're actually interested in.

Another area where using dot notation throughout a query expression can give more clarity is when you're forced to use it for part of the query anyway. For example, suppose you're going to use the ToList() extension method to end up with a list of the names of adults. (I'm performing a projection as well, in this case, so that it's a more balanced comparison.) Here's the query expression:

```
var adultNames = (from person in people
                  where person.Age >= 18
                  select person.Name).ToList();
```

Here's the dot notation equivalent:

```
var adultNames = people.Where(person => person.Age >= 18)
                       .Select(person => person.Name)
                       .ToList();
```

Something about the need for parentheses around the query expression in the first case makes it seem uglier *to me*. This is very much a case of personal choice—this section is really just raising your awareness that there *is* a choice, and that you can pick and choose. If you're going to use LINQ to any significant extent, you really should be comfortable with both notations, and there's no harm in switching style based on the query in question. As you've seen, the generated code is absolutely equivalent. None of this is to say that I dislike query expressions, of course.

11.7.3 *Where query expressions shine*

Having explained where you might find dot notation beneficial, I should point out that when it comes to any operations where the query expression would use transparent identifiers—particularly joins—dot notation starts to suffer in terms of readability. The beauty of transparent identifiers is that they're transparent—so transparent that you can't see them at all when you only have to look at the query expression. Even a simple `let` clause can be enough to swing the decision in favor of query expressions; introducing a new anonymous type just to propagate context through the query gets annoying quickly.

The other area where query expressions win is in situations where multiple lambda expressions would be required, or even multiple method calls. Again, this includes joins, where you have to specify the key selector for each side of the join as well as the result selector. For example, here's a cut-down version of an earlier query where I introduced inner joins:

```
from defect in SampleData.AllDefects
join subscription in SampleData.AllSubscriptions
    on defect.Project equals subscription.Project
select new { defect.Summary, subscription.EmailAddress }
```

In an IDE, it'd be reasonable to put the whole `join` clause on one line, leading to fairly easy-to-read code. The dot notation equivalent is fairly horrible, though:

```
SampleData.AllDefects.Join(SampleData.AllSubscriptions,
    defect => defect.Project,
    subscription => subscription.Project,
    (defect, subscription) => new { defect.Summary,
                                    subscription.EmailAddress })
```

The last argument could all fit on one line in an IDE, but it's still pretty ugly because the lambda expressions don't have much context; you can't immediately tell which argument means what. Named arguments in C# 4 can help there, but that adds even more bulk to the query.

Complex orderings can be similarly unpleasant in dot notation. Consider which you'd rather read—this `orderby` clause

```
orderby item.Rating descending, item.Price, item.Name
```

or three method calls:

```
.OrderByDescending(item => item.Rating)
.ThenBy(item => item.Price)
.ThenBy(item => item.Name)
```

Changing the priority of these orderings is simple in the query expression—just switch them around. In dot notation, you may also have to switch from `OrderBy` to `ThenBy` or vice versa.

To reiterate, I'm not trying to press my own personal preferences onto your code. I simply want you to know what's available, and to think about the choices you make. Of course, this is only one aspect of writing readable code, but it's a whole new area to consider in C#.

11.8   *Summary*

In this chapter, we've looked at how LINQ to Objects and C# 3 interact, focusing on the way query expressions are first translated into code that *doesn't* involve query expressions and then are compiled in the usual way. You've seen how all query expressions form a series of sequences, applying a transformation of some description at each step. In many cases these sequences are evaluated using deferred execution, fetching data only when it's first required.

Compared with all the other features of C# 3, query expressions look somewhat alien—more like SQL than the C# you're used to. One of the reasons they look so odd is that they're *declarative* instead of *imperative*—a query talks about the features of the end result rather than the exact steps required to achieve it. This goes hand in hand with a more functional way of thinking. It can take a while to click, and it's not suitable for every situation, but where declarative syntax is appropriate, it can vastly improve readability as well as make code easier to test and parallelize.

Don't be fooled into thinking that LINQ should only be used with databases. Plain in-memory manipulation of collections is common, and you've seen how well it's supported by query expressions and the extension methods in `Enumerable`.

In a real sense, you've now seen all the features introduced in C# 3! We haven't looked at any other LINQ providers yet, but you have a clearer understanding of what the compiler will do for you when you ask it to handle XML and SQL. The compiler itself doesn't know the difference between LINQ to Objects, LINQ to SQL, or any of the other providers; it just follows the same rules blindly.

In the next chapter you'll see how these rules form the final piece of the LINQ jigsaw puzzle when they convert lambda expressions into expression trees so that the various clauses of query expressions can be executed on different platforms. You'll also see some other examples of what LINQ can do.

LINQ beyond collections

This chapter covers

- LINQ to SQL
- IQueryable and expression tree queries
- LINQ to XML
- Parallel LINQ
- Reactive Extensions for .NET
- Writing your own operators

Suppose an alien visited you and asked you to describe *culture*. How could you capture the diversity of human culture in a short space of time? You might decide to spend that time *showing* him culture rather than describing it in the abstract: a visit to a New Orleans jazz club, opera in La Scala, the Louvre gallery in Paris, a Shakespeare play in Stratford-upon-Avon, and so on.

Would this alien know everything about culture afterward? Could he compose a tune, write a book, dance a ballet, craft a sculpture? Absolutely not. But he'd hopefully leave with a *sense* of culture—its richness and variety, its ability to light up people's lives.

So it is with this chapter. You've now seen all of the features of C# 3, but without seeing more of LINQ, you don't have enough context to really appreciate them.

When the first edition of this book was published, not many LINQ technologies were available, but now there's a glut of them, both from Microsoft and from third parties. That in itself hasn't surprised me, but I've been fascinated to see the different *natures* of these technologies.

We'll look at various ways in which LINQ manifests itself, with an example of each. I've chosen to demonstrate Microsoft technologies in the main, because they're the most typical ones. This isn't meant to imply that third parties aren't welcome in the LINQ ecosystem: there are a number of projects, both commercial and open source, providing access to varied data sources and building extra features on top of existing providers.

In contrast to the rest of this book, we'll only skim the surface of each of the topics here—the point isn't to learn the details, but to immerse yourself in the *spirit* of LINQ. To investigate any of these technologies further, I recommend that you get a book dedicated to the subject or read the relevant documentation carefully. I've resisted the temptation to say, "There's more to LINQ to [xxx] than this" at the end of each section, but please take it as read. Each technology has many capabilities beyond querying, but I've focused here on the areas that are directly related to LINQ.

Let's start off with the provider that generally got the most attention when LINQ was first introduced: LINQ to SQL.

12.1 Querying a database with LINQ to SQL

I'm sure by now you've absorbed the message that LINQ to SQL converts query expressions into SQL, which is then executed on the database. It's more than that—it's a full ORM solution—but I'll concentrate on the query side of LINQ to SQL rather than go into concurrency handling and the other details that an ORM has to deal with. I'll show you just enough so that you can experiment with it yourself—the database and code are available on the book's website (http://csharpindepth.com). The database is in SQL Server 2005 format to make it easy to play with, even if you don't have the latest version of SQL Server installed, although obviously Microsoft has made sure that LINQ to SQL works against newer versions too.

> **WHY LINQ TO SQL RATHER THAN THE ENTITY FRAMEWORK?** Speaking of "newer versions," you may be wondering why I've chosen to demonstrate LINQ to SQL instead of the Entity Framework, which is now Microsoft's preferred solution (and which also supports LINQ). The answer is merely simplicity; the Entity Framework is undoubtedly more powerful than LINQ to SQL in various ways, but it requires extra concepts that would take too much space to explain here. I'm trying to give you a sense of the consistency (and occasional inconsistency) that LINQ provides, and that's as applicable to LINQ to SQL as to the Entity Framework.

Before you start writing any queries, you need a database and a model to represent it in code.

12.1.1 *Getting started: the database and model*

LINQ to SQL needs metadata about the database to know which classes correspond to which database tables, and so on. There are various ways of representing that metadata, and this section will use the LINQ to SQL designer built into Visual Studio. You can design the entities first and ask LINQ to create the database, or design your database and let Visual Studio work out what the entities should look like. Personally, I favor the second approach, but there are pros and cons for both ways.

CREATING THE DATABASE SCHEMA

The mapping from the classes in chapter 11 to database tables is straightforward. Each table has an auto-incrementing integer ID column with an appropriate name: ProjectID, DefectID, and so on. The references between tables simply use the same name, so the Defect table has a ProjectID column, for instance, with a foreign key constraint.

There are a few exceptions to this simple set of rules:

- User is a reserved word in T-SQL, so the User class is mapped to the DefectUser table.
- The enumerations (status, severity, and user type) don't have tables. Their values are mapped to tinyint columns in the Defect and DefectUser tables.
- The Defect table has two links to the DefectUser table: one for the user who created the defect and one for the current assignee. These are represented with the CreatedByUserId and AssignedToUserId columns, respectively.

CREATING THE ENTITY CLASSES

Once your tables are created, generating the entity classes from Visual Studio is easy. Simply open Server Explorer (View > Server Explorer) and add a data source to the SkeetySoftDefects database (right-click on Data Connections and select Add Connection). You should be able to see four tables: Defect, DefectUser, Project, and NotificationSubscription.

You can then add a new item of type "LINQ to SQL classes" to the project. This name will be the basis for a generated class representing the overall database model; I've used the name DefectModel, which leads to a class called DefectModelDataContext. The designer will open when you've created the new item.

You can then drag the four tables from Server Explorer into the designer, and it'll figure out all the associations. After that, you can rearrange the diagram and adjust various properties of the entities. Here's a list of what I changed:

- I renamed the DefectID property to ID to match the previous model.
- I renamed DefectUser to User (so although the table is still called DefectUser, it'll generate a class called User, just like before).
- I changed the type of the Severity, Status, and UserType properties to their enum equivalents (having copied those enumerations into the project).

- I renamed the parent and child properties used for the associations between `Defect` and `DefectUser`—the designer guessed suitable names for the other associations but had trouble here because there were two associations between the same pair of tables. I named the relationships `AssignedTo/Assigned-Defects` and `CreatedBy/CreatedDefects`.

Figure 12.1 shows the designer diagram after all of these changes. As you can see, it looks much like the class diagram in figure 11.3, but without the enumerations.

If you look in the C# code generated by the designer (DefectModel.designer.cs), you'll find five partial classes: one for each of the entities, and the `DefectModelData-Context` class I mentioned earlier. The fact that they're partial is useful; in this case I added extra constructors to match the ones from the original in-memory classes, so the code from chapter 11 to create the sample data can be reused without much extra work. For the sake of brevity, I didn't include the insertion code here, but if you look at PopulateDatabase.cs in the source code, you should be able to follow it easily enough. Of course, you don't have to run this yourself—the downloadable database is already populated.

Now that you have a schema in SQL, an entity model in C#, and some sample data, it's time to get querying.

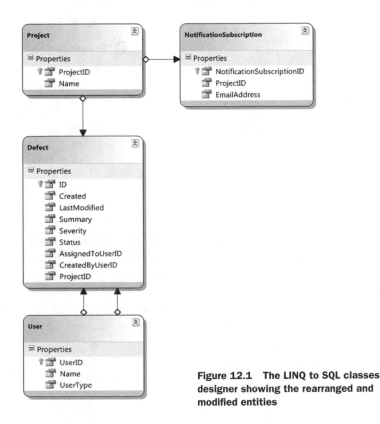

Figure 12.1   The LINQ to SQL classes designer showing the rearranged and modified entities

12.1.2 *Initial queries*

I'm sure you've guessed what's coming, but hopefully that won't make it any less impressive. We'll execute query expressions against the data source, watching LINQ to SQL convert the query into SQL on the fly. For the sake of familiarity, we'll use some of the same queries we executed against the in-memory collections in chapter 11.

FIRST QUERY: FINDING DEFECTS ASSIGNED TO TIM

I'll skip over the trivial examples from early in chapter 11 and start instead with the query from listing 11.7 that checks for open defects assigned to Tim. Here's the query part of listing 11.7, for the sake of comparison:

```
User tim = SampleData.Users.TesterTim;

var query = from defect in SampleData.AllDefects
            where defect.Status != Status.Closed
            where defect.AssignedTo == tim
            select defect.Summary;
```

The full LINQ to SQL equivalent of listing 11.7 is as follows.

Listing 12.1   Querying the database to find all Tim's open defects

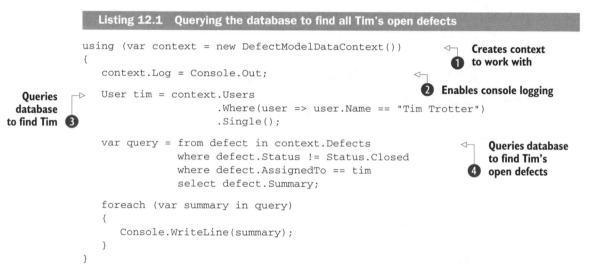

```
using (var context = new DefectModelDataContext())        ⟵  Creates context
{                                                          ①  to work with
    context.Log = Console.Out;                         ⟵
                                                       ②  Enables console logging
    User tim = context.Users
                      .Where(user => user.Name == "Tim Trotter")
                      .Single();

    var query = from defect in context.Defects            ⟵  Queries database
                where defect.Status != Status.Closed          to find Tim's
                where defect.AssignedTo == tim            ④  open defects
                select defect.Summary;

    foreach (var summary in query)
    {
        Console.WriteLine(summary);
    }
}
```

Queries database to find Tim ③

Listing 12.1 requires a certain amount of explanation, because it's all new. First you create a new *data context* to work with ①. Data contexts are pretty multifunctional, taking responsibility for connection and transaction management, query translation, tracking changes in entities, and dealing with identity. For the purposes of this chapter, you can regard a data context as your point of contact with the database. I don't show the more advanced features here, but you do take advantage of one useful capability here: you tell the data context to write out all the SQL commands it executes to the console ②. The model-related properties used in the code for this section (`Defects`, `Users`, and so on) are all of type `Table<T>` for the relevant entity type. They act as the data sources for your queries.

You can't use `SampleData.Users.TesterTim` to identify Tim in the main query because that object doesn't know the ID of the relevant row in the `DefectUser` table. Instead, you use a separate query to load Tim's user entity ❸. I used dot notation for this, but a query expression would've worked just as well. The `Single` method just returns a single result from a query, throwing an exception if there isn't exactly one element. In a real-life situation, you may have the entity as a product of other operations, such as logging in, and if you don't have the full entity, you may have its ID, which can be used equally well within the main query. As an alternative in this case, you could've change the open defects query to filter based on the assignee's name. That wouldn't have quite been in the spirit of the original query, though.

Within the query expression ❹, the only difference between the in-memory query and the LINQ to SQL query is the data source—instead of using `SampleData.All-Defects`, you use `context.Defects`. The final results are the same (although the ordering isn't guaranteed), but the work has been done on the database.

Because you asked the data context to log the generated SQL, you can see exactly what's going on when you run the code. The console output shows both of the queries executed on the database, along with the query parameter values:[1]

```
SELECT [t0].[UserID], [t0].[Name], [t0].[UserType]
FROM [dbo].[DefectUser] AS [t0]
WHERE [t0].[Name] = @p0
-- @p0: Input String (Size = 11; Prec = 0; Scale = 0) [Tim Trotter]

SELECT [t0].[Summary]
FROM [dbo].[Defect] AS [t0]
WHERE ([t0].[AssignedToUserID] = @p0) AND ([t0].[Status] <> @p1)
-- @p0: Input Int32 (Size = 0; Prec = 0; Scale = 0) [2]
-- @p1: Input Int32 (Size = 0; Prec = 0; Scale = 0) [4]
```

Note how the first query fetches all of the properties of the user because you're populating a whole entity, but the second query only fetches the summary, as that's all you need. LINQ to SQL has also converted the two separate `where` clauses in the second query into a single filter on the database.

LINQ to SQL is capable of translating a wide range of expressions. Let's try a slightly more complicated query from chapter 11, just to see what SQL is generated.

SQL GENERATION FOR A MORE COMPLEX QUERY: A LET CLAUSE

The next query shows what happens when you introduce a sort of temporary variable with a `let` clause. In chapter 11 we considered a bizarre situation, if you remember—pretending that calculating the length of a string took a long time. Again, the query expression here is exactly the same as in listing 11.11, with the exception of the data source. The following listing shows the LINQ to SQL code.

---

[1] Additional log output is generated showing some details of the data context, which I've omitted here to avoid distracting from the SQL. The console output also contains the summaries printed by the `foreach` loop, of course.

Listing 12.2   Using a `let` clause in LINQ to SQL

```
using (var context = new DefectModelDataContext())
{
    context.Log = Console.Out;

    var query = from user in context.Users
                let length = user.Name.Length
                orderby length
                select new { Name = user.Name, Length = length };

    foreach (var entry in query)
    {
        Console.WriteLine("{0}: {1}", entry.Length, entry.Name);
    }
}
```

The generated SQL is close to the spirit of the sequences we saw in figure 11.5. The innermost sequence (the first one in that diagram) is the list of users; that's transformed into a sequence of name/length pairs (as the nested `select`), and then the no-op projection is applied, with an ordering by length:

```
SELECT [t1].[Name], [t1].[value]
FROM (
    SELECT LEN([t0].[Name]) AS [value], [t0].[Name]
    FROM [dbo].[DefectUser] AS [t0]
    ) AS [t1]
ORDER BY [t1].[value]
```

This is a good example of where the generated SQL is wordier than it needs to be. Although you couldn't reference the elements of the final output sequence when performing an ordering on the query expression, you can in SQL. This simpler query would've worked fine:

```
SELECT LEN([t0].[Name]) AS [value], [t0].[Name]
FROM [dbo].[DefectUser] AS [t0]
ORDER BY [value]
```

Of course, what's important is what the query optimizer does on the database—the execution plan displayed in SQL Server Management Studio Express is the same for both queries, so it doesn't look like you're losing out.

The final set of LINQ to SQL queries we'll look at are all joins.

12.1.3 *Queries involving joins*

We'll try both inner joins and group joins, using the examples of joining notification subscriptions against projects. I suspect you're used to the drill now—the pattern of the code is the same for each query, so from here on I'll just show the query expression and the generated SQL, unless something else is going on.

EXPLICIT JOINS: MATCHING DEFECTS WITH NOTIFICATION SUBSCRIPTIONS

The first query is the simplest kind of join—an inner equijoin using a LINQ join clause:

```
// Query expression (modified from listing 11.12)
from defect in context.Defects
join subscription in context.NotificationSubscriptions
    on defect.Project equals subscription.Project
select new { defect.Summary, subscription.EmailAddress }

-- Generated SQL
SELECT [t0].[Summary], [t1].[EmailAddress]
FROM [dbo].[Defect] AS [t0]
INNER JOIN [dbo].[NotificationSubscription] AS [t1]
ON [t0].[ProjectID] = [t1].[ProjectID]
```

Unsurprisingly, it uses an inner join in SQL. It'd be easy to guess at the generated SQL in this case. How about a group join, though? This is where things get slightly more hectic:

```
// Query expression (modified from listing 11.13)
from defect in context.Defects
join subscription in context.NotificationSubscriptions
    on defect.Project equals subscription.Project
    into groupedSubscriptions
select new { Defect = defect, Subscriptions = groupedSubscriptions }

-- Generated SQL
SELECT [t0].[DefectID] AS [ID], [t0].[Created],
[t0].[LastModified], [t0].[Summary], [t0].[Severity],
[t0].[Status], [t0].[AssignedToUserID],
[t0].[CreatedByUserID], [t0].[ProjectID],
[t1].[NotificationSubscriptionID],
[t1].[ProjectID] AS [ProjectID2], [t1].[EmailAddress],
    (SELECT COUNT(*)
     FROM [dbo].[NotificationSubscription] AS [t2]
     WHERE [t0].[ProjectID] = [t2].[ProjectID]) AS [count]
FROM [dbo].[Defect] AS [t0]
LEFT OUTER JOIN [dbo].[NotificationSubscription] AS [t1]
ON [t0].[ProjectID] = [t1].[ProjectID]
ORDER BY [t0].[DefectID], [t1].[NotificationSubscriptionID]
```

That's a major change in the amount of SQL generated! There are two important things to notice. First, it uses a *left outer join* instead of an inner join, so you'd still see a defect even if it didn't have anyone subscribing to its project. If you want a left outer join but without the grouping, the conventional way of expressing this is to use a group join and then an extra `from` clause, using the `DefaultIfEmpty` extension method on the embedded sequence. It looks odd, but it works well.

The second odd thing about the previous query is that it calculates the count for each group within the database. This is effectively a trick performed by LINQ to SQL to make sure that all the processing can be done on the server. A naive implementation would have to perform the grouping in memory after fetching all the results. In some cases, the provider could do tricks to avoid needing the count, simply spotting when the grouping ID changes, but there are issues with this approach for some queries. It's possible that a later implementation of LINQ to SQL will be able to switch courses of action depending on the exact query.

You don't need to explicitly write a join in the query expression to see one in the SQL. Our final queries will show joins implicitly created through property access expressions.

IMPLICIT JOINS: SHOWING DEFECT SUMMARIES AND PROJECT NAMES

Let's take a simple example. Suppose you want to list each defect, showing its summary and the name of the project it's part of. The query expression is just a matter of a projection:

```
// Query expression
from defect in context.Defects
select new { defect.Summary, ProjectName = defect.Project.Name }

-- Generated SQL
SELECT [t0].[Summary], [t1].[Name]
FROM [dbo].[Defect] AS [t0]
INNER JOIN [dbo].[Project] AS [t1]
ON [t1].[ProjectID] = [t0].[ProjectID]
```

Note how you navigate from the defect to the project via a property—LINQ to SQL has converted that navigation into an inner join. It can use an inner join here because the schema has a non-nullable constraint on the `ProjectID` column of the `Defect` table—every defect has a project. Not every defect has an assignee, though, because the `AssignedToUserID` field is nullable, so if you use the assignee in a projection instead, a left outer join is generated:

```
// Query expression
from defect in context.Defects
select new { defect.Summary, Assignee = defect.AssignedTo.Name }

-- Generated SQL
SELECT [t0].[Summary], [t1].[Name]
FROM [dbo].[Defect] AS [t0]
LEFT OUTER JOIN [dbo].[DefectUser] AS [t1]
ON [t1].[UserID] = [t0].[AssignedToUserID]
```

Of course, if you navigate via more properties, the joins get more and more complicated. I'm not going into the details here—the important thing is that LINQ to SQL has to do a lot of analysis of the query expression to work out what SQL is required. In order to perform that analysis, it clearly needs to be able to look at the query you've specified.

Let's move away from LINQ to SQL specifically, and think in general terms about what LINQ providers of this kind need to do. This will apply to any provider that needs to introspect the query, rather than just being handed a delegate. At long last, it's time to see why expression trees were added as a feature of C# 3.

12.2　*Translations using IQueryable and IQueryProvider*

In this section I'll show you the basics of how LINQ to SQL manages to convert your query expressions into SQL. This is the starting point for implementing your own

LINQ provider, should you wish to. (Please don't underestimate the technical difficulties involved in doing so—but if you like a challenge, implementing a LINQ provider is certainly interesting.) This is the most theoretical section in the chapter, but it's useful to have some insight as to how LINQ decides whether to use in-memory processing, a database, or some other query engine.

In all the query expressions we've looked at in LINQ to SQL, the source has been a `Table<T>`. But if you look at `Table<T>`, you'll see it doesn't have a `Where` method, or `Select`, or `Join`, or any of the other standard query operators. Instead, it uses the same trick that LINQ to Objects does; just as the source in LINQ to Objects always implements `IEnumerable<T>` (possibly after a call to `Cast` or `OfType`) and then uses the extension methods in `Enumerable`, so `Table<T>` implements `IQueryable<T>` and then uses the extension methods in `Queryable`. You'll see how LINQ builds up an expression tree and then allows a provider to execute it at the appropriate time.

Let's start by looking at what `IQueryable<T>` consists of.

12.2.1 Introducing IQueryable<T> and related interfaces

If you look up `IQueryable<T>` in the documentation and see what members it contains directly (rather than inheriting), you may be disappointed. There aren't any. Instead, it inherits from `IEnumerable<T>` and the nongeneric `IQueryable`, which in turn inherits from the nongeneric `IEnumerable`. So `IQueryable` is where the new and exciting members are, right? Well, nearly. In fact, `IQueryable` just has three properties: `QueryProvider`, `ElementType`, and `Expression`. The `QueryProvider` property is of type `IQueryProvider`—yet another new interface to consider.

Lost? Perhaps figure 12.2 will help out—it's a class diagram of all the interfaces directly involved.

The easiest way of thinking about `IQueryable` is that it represents a query that'll yield a sequence of results when you execute it. The details of the query in LINQ terms are held in an expression tree, as returned by the `Expression` property of the `IQueryable`. The query is executed by iterating through the `IQueryable` (in other words, calling the `GetEnumerator` method and then `MoveNext` on the result) or by calling the `Execute` method on an `IQueryProvider`, passing in an expression tree.

Now that you have at least some grasp of what `IQueryable` is for, what's `IQueryProvider`? You can do more with a query than just execute it; you can also use it to build a bigger query, which is the purpose of the standard query operators in LINQ.[2] To build up a query, you need to use the `CreateQuery` method on the relevant `IQueryProvider`.[3]

Think of a data source as a simple query (`SELECT * FROM SomeTable` in SQL, for instance)—calling `Where`, `Select`, `OrderBy`, and similar methods results in a different

---

[2] Well, the ones that keep deferring execution, such as `Where` and `Join`. You'll see what happens with the aggregations such as `Count` in a while.

[3] Both `Execute` and `CreateQuery` have generic and nongeneric overloads. The nongeneric versions make it easier to create queries dynamically in code. Compile-time query expressions use the generic version.

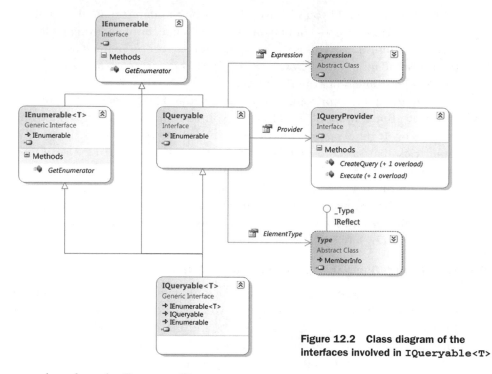

Figure 12.2   Class diagram of the interfaces involved in `IQueryable<T>`

query based on the first one. Given any `IQueryable` query, you can create a new query by performing the following steps:

1 Ask the existing query for its query expression tree (using the `Expression` property).
2 Build a new expression tree that contains the original expression and the extra functionality you want (a filter, projection, or ordering, for instance).
3 Ask the existing query for its query provider (using the `Provider` property).
4 Call `CreateQuery` on the provider, passing in the new expression tree.

Of those steps, the only tricky one is creating the new expression tree. Fortunately, there are a bunch of extension methods on the static `Queryable` class that can do all that for you. Enough theory—let's start implementing the interfaces so we can see all this in action.

12.2.2 *Faking it: interface implementations to log calls*

Before you get too excited, you're not going to build a full-fledged query provider in this chapter. But if you understand everything in this section, you'll be in a much better position to build one if you ever need to—and possibly more important, you'll understand what's going on when you issue LINQ to SQL queries. Most of the hard work of query providers goes on at the point of execution, where they need to parse an expression tree and convert it into the appropriate form for the target platform.

We'll concentrate on the work that happens before that—how LINQ *prepares* to execute a query.

We'll look at implementations of IQueryable and IQueryProvider and then try to run a few queries against them. The interesting part isn't the results—the queries won't do anything useful—but the series of calls made up to the point of execution. We'll focus on two types: FakeQueryProvider and FakeQuery. The implementation of each interface method writes out the current expression involved, using a simple logging method (not shown here).

Let's look first at FakeQuery, as shown in the following listing.

Listing 12.3 A simple implementation of `IQueryable` that logs method calls

```
class FakeQuery<T> : IQueryable<T>
{
    public Expression Expression { get; private set; }          Declares simple
    public IQueryProvider Provider { get; private set; }        automatic
    public Type ElementType { get; private set; }            ❶ properties

    internal FakeQuery(IQueryProvider provider,
                    Expression expression)
    {
        Expression = expression;
        Provider = provider;
        ElementType = typeof(T);
    }

    internal FakeQuery() : this(new FakeQueryProvider(), null)
    {
        Expression = Expression.Constant(this);           Uses this query
    }                                                     as initial
                                                       ❷ expression
    public IEnumerator<T> GetEnumerator()
    {
        Logger.Log(this, Expression);
        return Enumerable.Empty<T>().GetEnumerator();
    }
                                                       ❸ Returns empty
    IEnumerator IEnumerable.GetEnumerator()                result sequence
    {
        Logger.Log(this, Expression);
        return Enumerable.Empty<T>().GetEnumerator();
    }

    public override string ToString()                   ❹ Overrides ToString
    {                                                      for the sake of
        return "FakeQuery";                                logging
    }
}
```

The property members of IQueryable are implemented in FakeQuery with automatic properties ❶, which are set by the constructors. There are two constructors: a parameterless one that's used by the main program to create a plain source for the query, and one that's called by FakeQueryProvider with the current query expression.

The use of `Expression.Constant(this)` as the initial source expression ❷ is just a way of showing that the query initially represents the original object. (Imagine an implementation representing a table, for example—until you apply any query operators, the query would just return the whole table.) When the constant expression is logged, it uses the overridden `ToString` method, which is why you give a short, constant description ❹. This makes the final expression much cleaner than it would've been without the override. When you're asked to iterate over the results of the query, you always return an empty sequence ❸ to make life easy. Production implementations would parse the expression here, or (more likely) call `Execute` on their query provider and return the result.

As you can see, not a lot is going on in `FakeQuery`, and the following listing shows that `FakeQueryProvider` is simple too.

Listing 12.4   An implementation of `IQueryProvider` that uses `FakeQuery`

```
class FakeQueryProvider : IQueryProvider
{
    public IQueryable<T> CreateQuery<T>(Expression expression)
    {
        Logger.Log(this, expression);
        return new FakeQuery<T>(this, expression);
    }

    public IQueryable CreateQuery(Expression expression)
    {
        Type queryType = typeof(FakeQuery<>).MakeGenericType(expression.Type);
        object[] constructorArgs = new object[] { this, expression };
        return (IQueryable)Activator.CreateInstance(queryType, constructorArgs);
    }

    public T Execute<T>(Expression expression)
    {
        Logger.Log(this, expression);
        return default(T);
    }

    public object Execute(Expression expression)
    {
        Logger.Log(this, expression);
        return null;
    }
}
```

There's even less to say about the implementation of `FakeQueryProvider` than there was for `FakeQuery<T>`. The `CreateQuery` methods do no real processing but act as factory methods for the query. The only tricky bit is that the nongeneric overload still needs to provide the right type argument for `FakeQuery<T>` based on the `Type` property of the given expression. The `Execute` method overloads return empty results after logging the call. This is where a lot of analysis would *normally* be done, along with the actual call to the web service, database, or other target platform.

Even though you've done no real work, interesting things start to happen when you start to use FakeQuery as the source in a query expression. I've already let slip that you're able to write query expressions without explicitly writing methods to handle the standard query operators: it's all about extension methods—this time the ones in the Queryable class.

12.2.3 *Gluing expressions together: the Queryable extension methods*

Just as the Enumerable type contains extension methods on IEnumerable<T> to implement the LINQ standard query operators, the Queryable type contains extension methods on IQueryable<T>. There are two big differences between the implementations in Enumerable and those in Queryable.

First, the Enumerable methods all use delegates as their parameters—the Select method takes a Func<TSource,TResult>, for example. That's fine for in-memory manipulation, but for LINQ providers that execute the query elsewhere, you need a format you can examine more closely—expression trees. For example, the corresponding overload of Select in Queryable takes a parameter of type Expression<Func <TSource,TResult>>. The compiler doesn't mind at all—after query translation, it has a lambda expression that it needs to pass as an argument to the method, and lambda expressions can be converted to either delegate instances or expression trees.

This is how LINQ to SQL can work so seamlessly. The four key elements involved are all new features of C# 3: lambda expressions, the translation of query expressions into normal expressions that *use* lambda expressions, extension methods, and expression trees. Without all four, there'd be problems. If query expressions were always translated into delegates, for instance, they couldn't be used with a provider such as LINQ to SQL, which requires expression trees. Figure 12.3 shows two possible paths taken by query expressions; they differ only in what interfaces their data source implements.

Note how in figure 12.3 the early parts of the compilation process are independent of the data source. The same query expression is used, and it's translated in exactly the same way. It's only when the compiler looks at the translated query to find the appropriate Select and Where methods to use that the data source is truly important. At that point, the lambda expressions can be converted to either delegate instances or expression trees, potentially giving radically different implementations: typically in-memory for the left path, and SQL executing against a database in the right path.

Just to hammer home a familiar point, the decision in figure 12.3 of whether to use Enumerable or Queryable has no explicit support in the C# compiler. These aren't the only two possible paths, as you'll see later with Parallel LINQ and Reactive LINQ. You can create your own interface and implement extension methods following the query pattern, or even create a type with appropriate instance methods.

The second big difference between Enumerable and Queryable is that the Enumerable extension methods do the actual work associated with the corresponding query operator (or at least they build iterators that do the work). There's code in

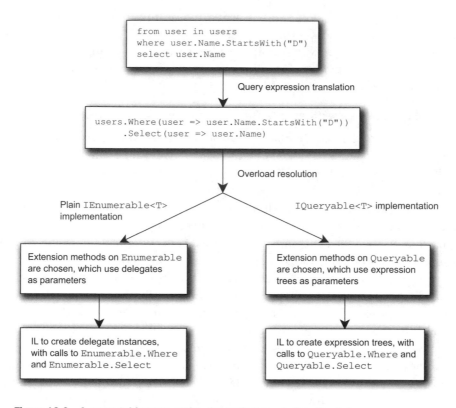

Figure 12.3   A query taking two paths, depending on whether the data source implements IQueryable or only IEnumerable

`Enumerable.Where` to execute the specified filter and only yield appropriate elements as the result sequence, for example. By contrast, the query operator implementations in `Queryable` do little: they just create a new query based on the parameters or they call `Execute` on the query provider, as described at the end of section 12.2.1. In other words, they're only used to build up queries and request that they be executed—they don't contain the logic behind the operators. This means they're suitable for any LINQ provider that uses expression trees, but they're useless on their own. They're the glue between your code and the details of the provider.

With the `Queryable` extension methods available and ready to use the `IQueryable` and `IQueryProvider` implementations, it's finally time to see what happens when you use a query expression with your custom provider.

12.2.4   *The fake query provider in action*

Listing 12.5 shows a simple query expression, which (supposedly) finds all the strings in the fake source, beginning with abc, and projects the results into a sequence listing the lengths of the matching strings. You iterate through the results but don't do anything with them, as you know already that they'll be empty. That's because you have no source data, and you haven't written any code to do any real filtering—you're just logging which calls are made by LINQ in the course of creating the query expression, and iterating through the results.

Listing 12.5   A simple query expression using the fake query classes

```
var query = from x in new FakeQuery<string>()
            where x.StartsWith("abc")
            select x.Length;
foreach (int i in query) { }
```

What would you expect the results of running listing 12.5 to be? In particular, what would you like to be logged *last*, at the point where you'd normally expect to do some real work with the expression tree? Here are the results, reformatted slightly for clarity:

```
FakeQueryProvider.CreateQuery
Expression=FakeQuery.Where(x => x.StartsWith("abc"))

FakeQueryProvider.CreateQuery
Expression=FakeQuery.Where(x => x.StartsWith("abc"))
                    .Select(x => x.Length)

FakeQuery<Int32>.GetEnumerator
Expression=FakeQuery.Where(x => x.StartsWith("abc"))
                    .Select(x => x.Length)
```

The two important things to note are that GetEnumerator is only called at the end, not on any intermediate queries; by the time GetEnumerator is called, you have all the information present in the original query expression. You haven't manually had to keep track of earlier parts of the expression in each step—a single expression tree captures all the information so far.

Don't be fooled by the concise output, by the way—the actual expression tree is deep and complicated, particularly due to the where clause including an extra method call. This expression tree is what LINQ to SQL will examine to work out what query to execute. LINQ providers *could* build up their own queries (in whatever form they may need) when calls to CreateQuery are made, but usually looking at the final tree when GetEnumerator is called is simpler, because all the necessary information is available in one place.

The final call logged by listing 12.5 was to FakeQuery.GetEnumerator, and you may be wondering why you *also* need an Execute method on IQueryProvider. Well, not all query expressions generate sequences. If you use an aggregation operator such as Sum, Count, or Average, you're no longer really creating a source—you're evaluating a result immediately. That's when Execute is called, as shown by the following listing and its output.

Listing 12.6   `IQueryProvider.Execute`

```
var query = from x in new FakeQuery<string>()
            where x.StartsWith("abc")
            select x.Length;
```

```
double mean = query.Average();

// Output
FakeQueryProvider.CreateQuery
Expression=FakeQuery.Where(x => x.StartsWith("abc"))

FakeQueryProvider.CreateQuery
Expression=FakeQuery.Where(x => x.StartsWith("abc"))
                    .Select(x => x.Length)

FakeQueryProvider.Execute
Expression=FakeQuery.Where(x => x.StartsWith("abc"))
                    .Select(x => x.Length)
                    .Average()
```

The `FakeQueryProvider` can be quite useful when it comes to understanding what the C# compiler is doing behind the scenes with query expressions. It'll show the transparent identifiers introduced within a query expression, along with the translated calls to `SelectMany`, `GroupJoin`, and the like.

12.2.5 *Wrapping up IQueryable*

You haven't written any of the significant code that a real query provider would need in order to get useful work done, but hopefully this fake provider has given you insight into how LINQ providers get their information from query expressions. It's all built up by the `Queryable` extension methods, given an appropriate implementation of `IQueryable` and `IQueryProvider`.

We've gone into a bit more detail in this section than we will for the rest of the chapter, as it involved the foundations that underpin the LINQ to SQL code we saw earlier. Even though you're unlikely to need to implement query interfaces yourself, the steps involved in taking a C# query expression and (at execution time) running some SQL on a database are quite profound and lie at the heart of the big features of C# 3. Understanding why C# has gained these features will help keep you more in tune with the language.

This is the end of our coverage of LINQ using expression trees. The rest of the chapter involves in-process queries using delegates, but as you'll see, there can still be a great deal of variety and innovation in how LINQ can be used. Our first port of call is LINQ to XML, which is "merely" an XML API designed to integrate well with LINQ to Objects.

12.3 *LINQ-friendly APIs and LINQ to XML*

LINQ to XML is by far the most pleasant XML API I've ever used. Whether you're consuming existing XML, generating a new document, or a bit of both, it's easy to use and understand. Part of that is completely independent of LINQ, but a lot of it's due to how well it interacts with the rest of LINQ. As in section 12.1, I'll give you just enough introductory information to understand the examples, and then you'll see how LINQ to XML blends its own query operators with those in LINQ to Objects. By the end of the section, you may have some ideas about how you can make your own APIs work in harmony with the framework.

12.3.1 Core types in LINQ to XML

LINQ to XML lives in the `System.Xml.Linq` assembly, and most of the types are in the `System.Xml.Linq` namespace too.[4] Almost all of the types in that namespace have a prefix of X, so whereas the normal DOM API has an `XmlElement` type, the LINQ to XML equivalent is `XElement`. This makes it easy to spot when code is using LINQ to XML, even if you're not immediately familiar with the exact type involved. Figure 12.4 shows the types you'll use most often.

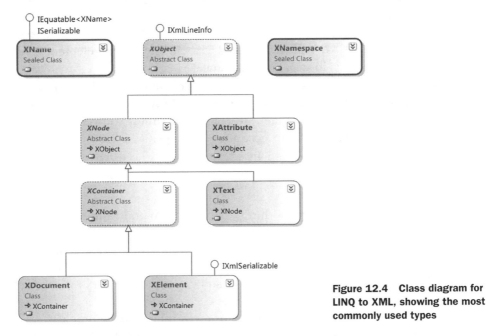

Figure 12.4 Class diagram for LINQ to XML, showing the most commonly used types

Here's a brief rundown of the types shown:

- `XName` is used for names of elements and attributes. Instances are usually created using an implicit conversion from a string (in which case no namespace is used) or via the `+(XNamespace, string)` overloaded operator.
- `XNamespace` represents an XML namespace—a URI, basically. Instances are usually created by the implicit conversion from string.
- `XObject` is the common ancestor of both `XNode` and `XAttribute`; unlike in the DOM API, an attribute isn't a node in LINQ to XML. Methods returning child nodes don't include attributes, for example.
- `XNode` represents a node in the XML tree. It defines various members to manipulate and query the tree. There are several other classes derived from `XNode` that aren't shown in figure 12.4, such as `XComment` and `XDeclaration`. These are

---

[4] I used to forget whether it was `System.Xml.Linq` or `System.Linq.Xml`. If you remember that it's an XML API first and foremost, you should be okay.

used relatively infrequently—the most common node types are documents, elements, and text.

- XAttribute is an attribute with a name and a value. The value is intrinsically text, but there are explicit conversions to many other data types, such as int and DateTime.

- XContainer is a node in the XML tree that can have child content—it's an element or a document, basically.

- XText is a text node, and a further derived type XCData is used to represent CDATA text nodes. (A CDATA node is roughly equivalent to a verbatim string literal—less escaping is required.) XText is rarely instantiated directly in user code; instead, when a string is used as the content of an element or document, that's converted into an XText instance.

- XElement is an element. This is the most commonly used class in LINQ to XML, along with XAttribute. Unlike in the DOM API, you can create an XElement without creating a document to contain it. Unless you really *need* a document object (for a custom XML declaration, perhaps), you can often just use elements.

- XDocument is a document. Its root element is accessed using the Root property—this is the equivalent to XmlDocument.DocumentElement. As noted earlier, this often isn't required.

More types are available even within the document model, and there are a few other types for things such as loading and saving options—but this list covers the most important ones. Of the preceding types, the only ones you regularly need to reference explicitly are XElement and XAttribute. If you use namespaces, you'll use XNamespace as well, but most of the rest of the types can be ignored the rest of the time. It's amazing how much you can do with so few types.

Speaking of amazing, I can't resist showing you how the namespace support works in LINQ to XML. We won't use namespaces anywhere else, but it's a good example of how a well-designed set of conversions and operators can make life easier. It'll also ease us into our next topic: constructing elements.

If you only need to specify the name of an element or attribute without a namespace, you can use a string. You won't find any constructors for either type with parameters of type string though—they all accept an XName. An implicit conversion exists from string to XName, and also from string to XNamespace. Adding together a namespace and a string also gives you an XName. There's a fine line between operator abuse and genius, but in this case LINQ to XML really makes it work.

Here's some code to create two elements—one within a namespace and one not:

```
XElement noNamespace = new XElement("no-namespace");
XNamespace ns = "http://csharpindepth.com/sample/namespace";
XElement withNamespace = new XElement(ns + "in-namespace");
```

This makes for readable code even when namespaces are involved, which comes as a welcome relief from some other APIs. But this just creates two empty elements. How do you give them some content?

12.3.2 *Declarative construction*

Normally in the DOM API, you create an element and then add content to it. You can do that in LINQ to XML via the Add method inherited from XContainer, but that's not the idiomatic LINQ to XML way of doing things.[5] It's still worth looking at the signature of XContainer.Add though, because it introduces the content model. You might've expected a signature of Add(XNode) or perhaps Add(XObject), but it's just Add(object). The same pattern is used for the XElement (and XDocument) constructor signatures. The XElement constructors all have one parameter for the name of the element, but after that you can specify nothing (to create an empty element), a single object (to create an element with a single child node), or an array of objects to create multiple child nodes. In the multiple children case, a parameter array is used (the params keyword in C#), which means the compiler will create the array for you—you can just keep listing arguments.

The use of plain object for the content type may sound crazy, but it's incredibly useful. When you add content—whether it's through a constructor or the Add method—the following points are considered:

- Null references are ignored.
- XNode and XAttribute instances are added in a relatively straightforward manner; they're cloned if they already have parents, but otherwise no conversion is required. (Some other sanity checks are performed, such as making sure you don't have duplicate attributes in a single element.)
- Strings, numbers, dates, times, and so on are added by converting them into XText nodes using standard XML formatting.
- If the argument implements IEnumerable (and isn't covered by anything else), Add will iterate over its contents and add each value in turn, recursing where necessary.
- Anything that doesn't have special-case handling is converted into text by just calling ToString().

This means that you often don't need to prepare your content in a special way before adding it to an element—LINQ to XML does the right thing for you. The details are explicitly documented, so you don't need to worry about it being too magical—but it really works.

Constructing nested elements leads to code that naturally resembles the hierarchical structure of the tree. This is best shown with an example. Here's a snippet of LINQ to XML code:

```
new XElement("root",
    new XElement("child",
        new XElement("grandchild", "text")),
    new XElement("other-child"));
```

---

[5] In some ways, it's a shame that XElement doesn't implement IEnumerable, as otherwise collection initializers would be another approach to construction. But using the constructor works neatly anyway.

And here's the XML of the created element—note the visual similarity between the code and the output:

```
<root>
  <child>
    <grandchild>text</grandchild>
  </child>
  <other-child />
</root>
```

So far, so good, but the important part is the fourth bullet in the earlier list, where sequences are processed recursively, because that lets you build an XML structure out of a LINQ query in a natural way. For example, the book's website has some code to generate an RSS feed from its database. The statement to construct the XML document is 28 lines long—which I'd normally expect to be an abomination—but it's remarkably pleasant to read.[6] That statement contains two LINQ queries—one to populate an attribute value, and the other to provide a sequence of elements, each representing a news item. As you read the code, it's obvious what the resulting XML will look like.

To make this more concrete, let's take two simple examples from the defect-tracking system. I'll demonstrate using the LINQ to Objects sample data, but you could use almost identical queries to work with another LINQ provider instead. First, you need to build an element containing all the users in the system. In this case, you just need a projection, so the following listing uses dot notation.

Listing 12.7   Creating elements from the sample users

```
var users = new XElement("users",
    SampleData.AllUsers.Select(user => new XElement("user",
        new XAttribute("name", user.Name),
        new XAttribute("type", user.UserType)))
);
Console.WriteLine(users);

// Output
<users>
  <user name="Tim Trotter" type="Tester" />
  <user name="Tara Tutu" type="Tester" />
  <user name="Deborah Denton" type="Developer" />
  <user name="Darren Dahlia" type="Developer" />
  <user name="Mary Malcop" type="Manager" />
  <user name="Colin Carton" type="Customer" />
</users>
```

If you want to make a slightly more complex query, it's probably worth using a query expression. The following listing creates another list of users, but this time only the

---

[6] One contributing factor to the readability is an extension method I created to convert anonymous types into elements, using the properties for child elements. If you're interested, the code is freely available as part of my MiscUtil project (see http://mng.bz/xDMt). It only helps when the XML structure you need fits a certain pattern, but in that case it can reduce the clutter of XElement constructor calls significantly.

developers within SkeetySoft. For a bit of variety, this time each developer's name is a text node within an element instead of an attribute value.

Listing 12.8   Creating elements with text nodes

```
var developers = new XElement("developers",
    from user in SampleData.AllUsers
    where user.UserType == UserType.Developer
    select new XElement("developer", user.Name)
);
Console.WriteLine(developers);

// Output
<developers>
  <developer>Deborah Denton</developer>
  <developer>Darren Dahlia</developer>
</developers>
```

This sort of thing can be applied to all the sample data, producing a document structure like this:

```
<defect-system>
  <projects>
    <project name="..." id="...">
      <subscription email="..." />
    </project>
  </projects>
  <users>
    <user name="..." id="..." type="..." />
  </users>
  <defects>
    <defect id="..." summary="..." created="..." project="..."
            assigned-to="..." created-by="..." status="..."
            severity="..." last-modified="..." />
  </defects>
</defect-system>
```

You can see the code to generate all of this in XmlSampleData.cs in the downloadable solution. It demonstrates an alternative to the one-huge-statement approach: each of the elements under the top level is created separately, and then glued together like this:

```
XElement root = new XElement("defect-system", projects, users, defects);
```

We'll use this XML to demonstrate the next LINQ integration point: queries. Let's start with the query methods available on a single node.

12.3.3   Queries on single nodes

You may be expecting me to reveal that XElement implements IEnumerable and that LINQ queries come for free. It's not *quite* that simple, because there are so many different things that an XElement could iterate through. XElement contains a number of *axis methods* that are used as query sources. If you're familiar with XPath, the idea of an axis will no doubt be familiar to you.

Here are the axis methods used directly for querying a single node, each of which returns an appropriate IEnumerable<T>:

- Ancestors
- Annotations
- Descendants
- AncestorsAndSelf
- Attributes
- DescendantsAndSelf

- DescendantNodes
- Elements
- ElementsBeforeSelf
- DescendantNodesAndSelf
- ElementsAfterSelf
- Nodes

All of these are fairly self-explanatory (and the MSDN documentation provides more details). There are useful overloads to retrieve only nodes with an appropriate name; calling Descendants("user") on an XElement will return all user elements underneath the element you call it on, for instance.

In addition to these calls returning sequences, some methods return a single result—Attribute and Element are the most important, returning the named attribute and the first child element with the specified name, respectively. Additionally, there are explicit conversions from an XAttribute or XElement to any number of other types, such as int, string, and DateTime. These are important for both filtering and projecting results. Each conversion to a non-nullable value type also has a conversion to its nullable equivalent—these (and the conversion to string) return a null value if you invoke them on a null reference. This null propagation means you don't have to check for the presence or absence of attributes or elements within the query— you can use the query results instead.

What does this have to do with LINQ? Well, the fact that multiple search results are returned in terms of IEnumerable<T> means you can use the normal LINQ to Objects methods after finding some elements. The following listing shows an example of finding the names and types of the users, this time starting off with the sample data in XML.

Listing 12.9   Displaying the users within an XML structure

```
XElement root = XmlSampleData.GetElement();

var query = root.Element("users").Elements().Select(user => new
            {
                Name = (string) user.Attribute("name"),
                UserType = (string) user.Attribute("type")
            });
foreach (var user in query)
{
    Console.WriteLine ("{0}: {1}", user.Name, user.UserType);
}
```

After creating the data at the start, you navigate down to the users element and ask it for its direct child elements. This two-step fetch could be shortened to just root.Descendants("user"), but it's good to know about the more rigid navigation so you can use it where necessary. It's also more robust in the face of changes to the document structure, such as another (unrelated) user element being added else-where in the document.

The rest of the query expression is merely a projection of an XElement into an anonymous type. I'll admit that this is slightly cheating with the user type: it's kept as a string instead of calling Enum.Parse to convert it into a proper UserType value. The latter approach works perfectly well, but it's quite long-winded when you only need the string form, and the code becomes hard to format sensibly within the strict limits of the printed page.

There's nothing particularly special here—returning query results as sequences is fairly common, after all. It's worth noting how seamlessly you can go from domain-specific query operators to general-purpose ones. That's not the end of the story, though. LINQ to XML has some extra extension methods to add as well.

12.3.4 *Flattened query operators*

You've seen how the result of one part of a query is often a sequence, and in LINQ to XML it's often a sequence of elements. What if you wanted to then perform an XML-specific query on each of those elements? To present a somewhat contrived example, you can find all the projects in the sample data with root.Element("projects").Elements(), but how can you find the subscription elements within them? You need to apply another query to each element and then flatten the results. (Again, you could use root.Descendants("subscription"), but imagine a more complex document model where that wouldn't work.)

This may sound familiar, and it is—LINQ to Objects already provides the Select-Many operator (represented by multiple from clauses in a query expression) to do this. You could write the query as follows:

```
from project in root.Element("projects").Elements()
from subscription in project.Elements("subscription")
select subscription
```

As there are no elements within a project other than subscription, you could use the overload of Elements that doesn't specify a name. I find it clearer to specify the element name in this case, but it's often just a matter of taste. (The same argument could be made for calling Element("projects").Elements("project") to start with, admittedly.)

Here's the same query written using dot notation and an overload of SelectMany that only returns the flattened sequence, without performing any further projections:

```
root.Element("projects").Elements()
    .SelectMany(project => project.Elements("subscription"))
```

Neither of these queries are completely unreadable by any means, but they're not ideal. LINQ to XML provides a number of extension methods (in the System .Xml.Linq.Extensions class), which either act on a specific sequence type or are generic with a constrained type argument, to cope with the lack of generic interface covariance prior to C# 4. There's InDocumentOrder, which does exactly what it sounds like, and most of the axis methods mentioned in section 12.4.3 are also available as extension methods. This means that you can convert the previous query into this simpler form:

```
root.Element("projects").Elements().Elements("subscription")
```

This sort of construction makes it easy to write XPath-like queries in LINQ to XML without everything being a string. If you want to use XPath, that's available too via more extension methods, but the query methods have served me well more often than not. You can also mix the axis methods with the operators of LINQ to Objects. For example, to find all the subscriptions for projects with a name including *Media*, you could use this query:

```
root.Element("projects").Elements()
    .Where(project => ((string) project.Attribute("name"))
                                        .Contains("Media"))
    .Elements("subscription")
```

Before we move on to Parallel LINQ, let's think about how the design of LINQ to XML merits the "LINQ" part of its title, and how you could potentially apply the same techniques to your own API.

12.3.5   *Working in harmony with LINQ*

Some of the design decisions in LINQ to XML seem odd if you take them in isolation as part of an XML API, but in the context of LINQ they make perfect sense. The designers clearly imagined how their types could be used within LINQ queries, and how they could interact with other data sources. If you're writing your own data access API, in whatever context that might be, it's worth taking the same things into account. If someone uses your methods in the middle of a query expression, are they left with something useful? Will they be able to use some of your query methods, then some from LINQ to Objects, and then some more of yours in one fluent expression?

We've seen three ways in which LINQ to XML has accommodated the rest of LINQ:

- It's good at *consuming* sequences with its approach to construction. LINQ is deliberately declarative, and LINQ to XML supports this with a declarative way of creating XML structures.
- It *returns* sequences from its query methods. This is probably the most obvious step that data access APIs would already take: returning query results as `IEnumerable<T>` or a class implementing it is pretty much a no-brainer.
- It *extends* the set of queries you can perform on sequences of XML types; this makes it feel like a unified querying API, even though some of it is XML-specific.

You may be able to think of other ways in which your own libraries can play nicely with LINQ; these aren't the only options you should consider, but they're a good starting point. Above all, I'd urge you to put yourself in the shoes of a developer wanting to use your API within code that's already using LINQ. What might such a developer want to achieve? Can LINQ and your API be mixed easily, or are they really aiming for different goals?

We're roughly halfway through our whirlwind tour of different approaches to LINQ. Our next stop is in some ways reassuring and in some ways terrifying: we're back to querying simple sequences, but this time in parallel…

12.4 *Replacing LINQ to Objects with Parallel LINQ*

I've been following Parallel LINQ for a long time. I first came across it when Joe Duffy introduced it in his blog on September 2006 (see http://mng.bz/vYCO). The first Community Technology Preview (CTP) was released in November 2007, and the overall feature set has evolved over time too. It's now part of a wider effort called Parallel Extensions, which is part of .NET 4, aiming to provide higher-level building blocks for concurrent programming than the relatively small set of primitives we've had to work with until now. There's a lot more to Parallel Extensions than Parallel LINQ—or *PLINQ*, as it's often known—but we'll only look at the LINQ aspect here.

The idea behind Parallel LINQ is that you should be able to take a LINQ to Objects query that's taking a long time and make it run faster by using multiple threads to take advantage of multiple cores—with as few changes to the query as possible. As with anything to do with concurrency, it's not quite as simple as that, but you may be surprised at what can be achieved. Of course, we're still trying to think bigger than individual LINQ technologies—we're thinking about the different models of interaction involved, rather than the precise details. But if you're interested in concurrency, I heartily recommend that you dive into Parallel Extensions—it's one of the most promising approaches to parallelism that I've come across recently.

I'll use a single example for this section: rendering a Mandelbrot set image (see Wikipedia for an explanation of Mandelbrot sets: http://en.wikipedia.org/wiki/Mandelbrot_set). Let's start off by trying to get it right with a single thread before moving into trickier territory.

12.4.1 *Plotting the Mandelbrot set with a single thread*

Before any mathematicians attack me, I should point out that I'm using the term *Mandelbrot set* loosely here. The details aren't really important, but these aspects are:

- You'll create a rectangular image, given various options such as width, height, origin, and search depth.
- For each pixel in the image, you'll calculate a byte value that will end up as the index into a 256-entry palette.
- The calculation of one pixel value doesn't rely on any other results.

The last point is absolutely crucial—it means this task is *embarrassingly parallel*. In other words, there's nothing in the task itself that makes it hard to parallelize. You still need a mechanism for distributing the workload across threads and then gathering the results together, but the rest should be easy. PLINQ will be responsible for the distribution and collation (with a little help and care); you just need to express the range of pixels, and how each pixel's color should be computed.

For the purposes of demonstrating multiple approaches, I've put together an abstract base class that's responsible for setting things up, running the query, and displaying the results; it also has a method to compute the color of an individual pixel. An abstract method is responsible for creating a byte array of values, which are then converted into the image. The first row of pixels comes first, left to right, then the second row, and so on. Each example here is just an implementation of this method.

I should note that using LINQ really isn't an ideal solution here—there are various inefficiencies in this approach. Don't focus on that side of things: concentrate on the idea that we have an embarrassingly parallel query, and we want to execute it across multiple cores.

The following listing shows the single-threaded version of the method in all its simple glory.

Listing 12.10   Single-threaded Mandelbrot generation query

```
var query = from row in Enumerable.Range(0, Height)
            from column in Enumerable.Range(0, Width)
            select ComputeIndex(row, column);

return query.ToArray();
```

You iterate over every row and every column within each row, computing the index of the relevant pixel. Calling `ToArray()` evaluates the resulting sequence, converting it into an array. Figure 12.5 shows the beautiful results.

This took about 5.5 seconds to generate on my old dual-core laptop. The `ComputeIndex` method performs more iterations than you really need, but it makes the timing differences more obvious.[7] Now that you have a benchmark in terms of both timing and what the results should look like, it's time to parallelize the query.

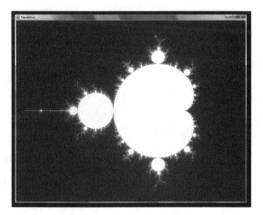

Figure 12.5   Mandelbrot image generated on a single thread

12.4.2   *Introducing ParallelEnumerable, ParallelQuery, and AsParallel*

Parallel LINQ brings with it several new types, but in many cases you'll never see their names mentioned. They live in the `System.Linq` namespace, so you don't

---

[7]   Proper benchmarking is hard, particularly when threading is involved. I haven't attempted to do rigorous measurements here. The timings given are just meant to indicate *faster* and *slower*; please take the numbers with a pinch of salt.

even need to change using directives. ParallelEnumerable is a static class, similar to Enumerable—it mostly contains extension methods, the majority of which extend a new ParallelQuery type.

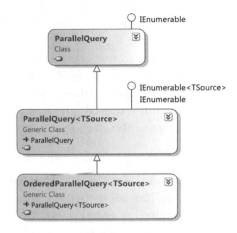

This latter type has both nongeneric and generic forms (ParallelQuery and ParallelQuery<TSource>), but most of the time you'll use the generic form, just as IEnumerable<T> is more widely used than IEnumerable. Additionally, there's Ordered-ParallelQuery<TSource>, which is the parallel equivalent of IOrderedEnumerable<T>. The relationships between all of these types are shown in figure 12.6.

Figure 12.6 Class diagram for Parallel LINQ, including relationship to normal LINQ interfaces

As you can see, ParallelQuery<TSource> implements IEnumerable<TSource>, so once you've constructed a query appropriately, you can iterate through the results in the normal way. When you have a parallel query, the extension methods in Parallel-Enumerable take precedence over the ones in Enumerable (because ParallelQuery<T> is more specific than IEnumerable<T>; see section 10.2.3 if you need a reminder of the rules); this is how the parallelism is maintained throughout a query. There's a parallel equivalent to all the LINQ standard query operators, but you should be careful if you've created any of your own extension methods. You'll still be able to call them, but they'll force the query to be single-threaded from that point onward.

How do you get a parallel query to start with? By calling AsParallel, an extension method in ParallelEnumerable that extends IEnumerable<T>. This means you can parallelize the Mandelbrot query incredibly simply, as shown in the following listing.

Listing 12.11 First attempt at a multithreaded Mandelbrot generation query

```
var query = from row in Enumerable.Range(0, Height)
                        .AsParallel()
            from column in Enumerable.Range(0, Width)
            select ComputeIndex(row, column);

return query.ToArray();
```

Job done? Well, not quite. This query *does* run in parallel, but the results aren't quite what you need: it doesn't maintain the order in which you process the rows. Instead of the beautiful Mandelbrot image, we get something like figure 12.7, but the exact details change every time, of course.

Oops. On the bright side, this rendered in about 3.2 seconds, so my machine was clearly making use of its second core. But getting the right answer is pretty important.

You may be surprised to hear that this is a deliberate *feature* of Parallel LINQ. Ordering a parallel query requires more coordination between the threads, and the whole purpose of parallelization is to improve performance, so PLINQ defaults to an unordered query. It's a bit of a nuisance in this case, though.

12.4.3 *Tweaking parallel queries*

Fortunately, there's a way out of this—you just need to force the query to be treated as ordered, which can be done with the `AsOrdered` extension method. The following listing shows the fixed code, which produces the original image.

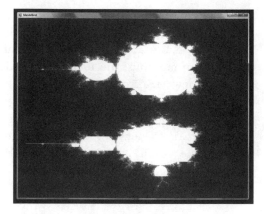

Figure 12.7   Mandelbrot image generated using an unordered query, resulting in some sections being incorrectly placed

It's slightly slower than the unordered query, but still significantly faster than the single-threaded version.

Listing 12.12   Multithreaded Mandelbrot query maintaining ordering

```
var query = from row in Enumerable.Range(0, Height)
                              .AsParallel().AsOrdered()
            from column in Enumerable.Range(0, Width)
            select ComputeIndex(row, column);

return query.ToArray();
```

The nuances of ordering are beyond the scope of this book, but I recommend that you read the "PLINQ Ordering" MSDN blog post (http://mng.bz/9x9U), which goes into the gory details.

A number of other methods can be used to alter how the query behaves:

- `AsUnordered`—Makes an ordered query unordered; if you only need results to be ordered for the first part of a query, this allows later stages to be executed more efficiently.

- `WithCancellation`—Specifies a *cancellation token* to be used with this query. Cancellation tokens are used throughout Parallel Extensions to allow tasks to be canceled in a safe, controlled manner.

- `WithDegreeOfParallelism`—Allows you to specify the maximum number of concurrent tasks used to execute the query. You could use this to limit the number of threads used if you wanted to avoid swamping the machine, or to increase the number of threads used for a query that wasn't CPU-bound.

- `WithExecutionMode`—Can be used to force the query to execute in parallel, even if Parallel LINQ thinks it'd execute faster as a single-threaded query.

- `WithMergeOptions`—Allows you to tweak how the results are buffered. Disabling buffering gives the shortest time before the first result is returned, but also lower throughput; full buffering gives the highest throughput, but no results are returned until the query has executed completely. The default is a compromise between the two.

The important point is that aside from ordering, these methods shouldn't affect the *results* of the query. You can design your query and test it in LINQ to Objects, then parallelize it, work out your ordering requirements, and tweak it if necessary to perform just how you want it to. If you showed the final query to someone who knew LINQ but not PLINQ, you'd only have to explain the PLINQ-specific method calls—the rest of the query would be familiar. Have you ever seen such an easy way to achieve concurrency? (The rest of Parallel Extensions is aimed at achieving simplicity where possible too.)

PLAY WITH THE CODE YOURSELF A couple of further points are demonstrated in the downloadable source code. If you parallelize across the whole query of pixels rather than just the rows, then an unordered query looks even weirder, and there's a `ParallelEnumerable.Range` method that gives PLINQ a bit more information than calling `Enumerable.Range(...).AsParallel()`. I used `AsParallel()` in this section, because that's the more general way of parallelizing a query; most queries don't start with a range.

Changing the in-process query model from single-threaded to parallel is quite a small conceptual leap, really. In the next section we'll turn the model on its head.

12.5 *Inverting the query model with LINQ to Rx*

All of the LINQ libraries you've seen so far have one thing in common: you pull data from them using `IEnumerable<T>`. At first sight, that seems so obvious that it's not worth saying—what would be the alternative? Well, how about if you *push* the data instead of pulling it? Instead of the data consumer being in control, the provider can be in the driving seat, letting the data consumer *react* when new data is available. Don't worry too much if this sounds dauntingly different; you actually know about the fundamental concept already, in the form of events. If you're comfortable with the idea of subscribing to an event, reacting to it, and unsubscribing later, that's a good starting point.

Reactive Extensions for .NET is a Microsoft project (http://mng.bz/R7ip); there are multiple versions available, including one targeting JavaScript. These days, the simplest way of obtaining the latest version is via NuGet. You may hear Reactive Extensions going by various names, but *Rx* and *LINQ to Rx* are the most common abbreviations, and they're the ones I'll use here. Even more so than for the other technologies covered in this chapter, we'll barely scratch the surface here. Not only is there a lot to learn about the library itself, but it's a whole different way of thinking. There are loads of videos on Channel 9 (see http://channel9.msdn.com/tags/Rx/)—some are based on the mathematical aspects, whereas others are more practical. In this section I'll emphasize the way that the LINQ concepts can be applied to this push model for data flow.

Enough of the introduction...let's meet the two interfaces that form the basis of LINQ to Rx.

12.5.1 *IObservable<T> and IObserver<T>*

The data model of LINQ to Rx is the *mathematical dual* of the normal IEnumerable<T> model.[8] When you iterate over a pull collection, you effectively start off by saying, "Please give me an iterator" (the call to GetEnumerator) and then repeatedly ask, "Is there another item? If so, I'd like it now" (via calls to MoveNext and Current). LINQ to Rx reverses this. Instead of requesting an iterator, you provide an observer. Then, instead of requesting the next item, your code is told when one is ready—or when an error occurs or the end of the data is reached.

Here are the declarations of the two interfaces involved:

```
public interface IObservable<T>
{
    IDisposable Subscribe(IObserver<T> observer);
}

public interface IObserver<T>
{
    void OnNext(T value);
    void OnCompleted();
    void OnException(Exception error);
}
```

These interfaces are actually part of .NET 4 (in the System namespace), even though the rest of LINQ to Rx is in a separate download. In fact, they're IObservable<out T> and IObserver<in T> in .NET 4, expressing the covariance of IObservable and the contravariance of IObserver. You'll learn more about generic variance in the next chapter, but I'm presenting the interfaces here as if they were invariant for the sake of simplicity. One concept at a time!

Figure 12.8 shows the duality in terms of how data flows in each model.

I suspect I'm not alone in finding the push model harder to think about, as it has the natural ability to work asynchronously. But look at how much simpler it is than the pull model, in terms of the flow diagram. This is partly due to the multiple method approach of the pull model; if IEnumerator<T> just had a method with a signature of bool TryGetNext(out T item), it'd be somewhat simpler.

Earlier I mentioned that LINQ to Rx is similar to the events you're already familiar with. Calling Subscribe on an observable is like using += with an event to register a handler. The disposable value returned by Subscribe remembers the observer you passed in; disposing of it is like using -= with the same handler. In many cases, you don't need to unsubscribe from the observable; this is just available in case you need to unsubscribe halfway through a sequence—the equivalent of breaking out of a foreach loop early. Failing to dispose of an IDisposable value may feel like anathema

---

[8] For a more detailed examination of this duality—and the essence of LINQ itself—I recommend Bart de Smet's "The Essence of LINQ—MINLINQ" blog post at http://mng.bz/96Wh.

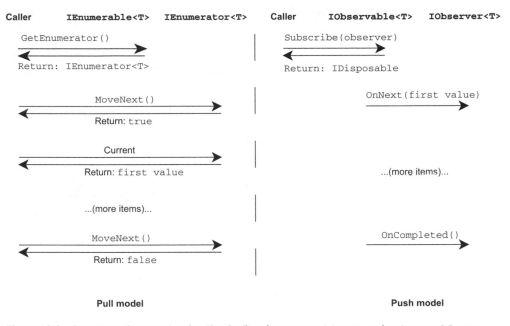

Figure 12.8 Sequence diagram showing the duality of `IEnumerable<T>` and `IObservable<T>`

to you, but it's often safe in LINQ to Rx. None of the examples in this chapter use the return value of `Subscribe`.

That's all there is to `IObservable<T>`, but what about the observer itself? Why does it have three methods? Consider the normal pull model where for any `MoveNext`/`Current` pair of calls, three things can happen:

- You may be at the end of the sequence, in which case `MoveNext` returns `false`.
- You may not have reached the end of the sequence, in which case `MoveNext` returns `true` and `Current` returns the new value.
- An error may occur—reading the next line from a network connection could fail, for example. In this case, an exception would be thrown.

The `IObserver<T>` interface represents each of these options as a separate method. Typically an observer will have its `OnNext` method called repeatedly, and then finally `OnCompleted`, unless there's an error of some kind, in which case `OnError` will be called instead. After the sequence has completed or encountered an error, no further method calls will be made. You rarely need to implement `IObserver<T>` directly, though. There are many extension methods on `IObservable<T>`, including overloads for `Subscribe`, and these allow you to subscribe to an observable by just providing appropriate delegates. Usually you provide a delegate to be executed for each item, and then optionally one to be executed on completion, on error, or both.

With that bit of theory out of the way, let's look at some actual code using LINQ to Rx.

12.5.2 Starting simply (again)

We'll demonstrate LINQ to Rx in the same way we started off with LINQ to Objects—using a range. Instead of `Enumerable.Range`, we'll use `Observable.Range`, which creates an observable range. Each time an observer subscribes to the range, the numbers are emitted to that observer using `OnNext`, followed by `OnCompleted`. We'll start off as simply as we can, just printing out each value as it's received, and printing a confirmation message at the end or if an error occurs.

The following listing shows that this involves less code than you'd need for the pull model.

Listing 12.13   First contact with `IObservable<T>`

```
var observable = Observable.Range(0, 10);
observable.Subscribe(x => Console.WriteLine("Received {0}", x),
                     e => Console.WriteLine("Error: {0}", e),
                     () => Console.WriteLine("Finished"));
```

In this case, it's hard to see how you could get an error, but I've included the error notification delegate for completeness. The results are as you'd expect:

```
Received 0
Received 1
...
Received 9
Finished
```

The observable returned by the `Range` method is known as a *cold observable*: it lies dormant until an observer subscribes to it, at which point it'll emit the values to that individual observer. If you subscribe with another observer, that will see another copy of the range. This isn't quite the same as a normal event such as a button click, where several observers could be subscribed to the same actual sequence of values, and the values may be effectively yielded whether there are any observers or not. (You can click a button even if there aren't any event handlers attached, after all.) Sequences like this are known as *hot observables*. It's important to know which type you're dealing with, even though the same set of operations applies to both kinds.

Now that you've done the simplest thing possible, let's try some familiar LINQ operators.

12.5.3 Querying observables

By now I'm sure you're familiar with the pattern—there are various extension methods in a static class (called `Observable`, somewhat predictably) that perform appropriate transformations. We'll look at just a few of the available operators and think a little about what's *not* available, and why it's not.

FILTERING AND PROJECTING

Let's jump straight into a query expression that takes a sequence of numbers, filters out the odd ones, and squares anything that's left. Then we'll subscribe `Console`

.WriteLine to the final result of the query, so that any items produced will be displayed. The following listing shows the code—look at how the query expression could easily be a LINQ to Objects query.

Listing 12.14 Filtering and projecting in LINQ to Rx

```
var numbers = Observable.Range(0, 10);
var query = from number in numbers
            where number % 2 == 0
            select number * number;
query.Subscribe(Console.WriteLine);
```

For simplicity's sake, I haven't added handlers for completion or error, and using the conversion from the Console.WriteLine method group to an Action<int> keeps the code nice and short. This produces the same results it would in LINQ to Objects: 0, 4, 16 and so on. Let's move on to grouping.

GROUPING

A group by query expression in LINQ to Rx produces a new IGroupedObservable<T> for each group, although what you then *do* with the grouping isn't always obvious. For example, it's not uncommon to have a nested subscription so that each time a new group is produced, you subscribe an observer to that group. The results *within* each group are produced as they're received by the grouping construct—effectively it acts as a sort of redirection choice, like an usher at a play examining each person's ticket as they arrive, and directing them to the relevant section of the theater. By contrast, LINQ to Objects collects a whole group together before returning it, which means it has to read to the end of the sequence, buffering all the results.

The following listing shows an example of this nested subscription, and also demonstrates how group results are emitted.

Listing 12.15 Grouping numbers mod 3

```
var numbers = Observable.Range(0, 10);
var query = from number in numbers
            group number by number % 3;
query.Subscribe(group => group.Subscribe
    (x => Console.WriteLine("Value: {0}; Group: {1}", x, group.Key)));
```

The best way to understand this is probably to remember that dealing with groups in LINQ to Objects often involves having a nested foreach loop—so you have nested subscriptions in LINQ to Rx.

When in doubt, try to find the duality between the two data models. In LINQ to Objects, you'd normally process each whole group in turn, whereas the order in LINQ to Rx means the output of listing 12.15 looks like this:

```
Value: 0; Group: 0
Value: 1; Group: 1
Value: 2; Group: 2
Value: 3; Group: 0
```

```
Value: 4; Group: 1
Value: 5; Group: 2
Value: 6; Group: 0
Value: 7; Group: 1
Value: 8; Group: 2
Value: 9; Group: 0
```

This makes perfect sense when you think of the push model, and in some cases it means that operations that would've required a lot of data buffering in LINQ to Objects can be implemented in LINQ to Rx much more efficiently.

As a final example, let's look at another operator that uses multiple sequences.

FLATTENING

LINQ to Rx supplies a few overloads of `SelectMany`, and the idea is still the same as in LINQ to Objects: each item in the original sequence produces a new sequence, and the result is the combination of all these new sequences, flattened. The following listing shows this in action—it's a little like listing 11.16, when we first discussed `Select-Many` in LINQ to Objects.

Listing 12.16   `SelectMany` producing multiple ranges

```
var query = from x in Observable.Range(1, 3)
            from y in Observable.Range(1, x)
            select new { x, y };
query.Subscribe(Console.WriteLine);
```

Here are the results, which should be reasonably predictable:

```
{ x = 1, y = 1 }
{ x = 2, y = 1 }
{ x = 2, y = 2 }
{ x = 3, y = 1 }
{ x = 3, y = 2 }
{ x = 3, y = 3 }
```

In this case, the results are deterministic, but that's only because, by default, `Observable.Range` emits items on the current thread. It's entirely possible to have multiple sequences being produced on multiple threads.

For fun, you might want to change the second call to `Observable.Range` to specify `Scheduler.ThreadPool` as a third argument. In that case, each of the inner sequences comes out in order with respect to itself, but those separate sequences can be mixed up among each other. Imagine a sports stadium with one official firing a starting pistol for several different races in quick succession—even if you know the winner of each race, you don't know which race will finish first.

Apologies if this makes you want to go and lie down. If it's any consolation, it gives me the same feeling. I do find it fascinating at the same time though.

WHAT'S IN AND WHAT'S OUT?

You already know that a `let` clause works by just calling `Select`, so that naturally works in LINQ to Rx, but not all LINQ to Objects operators are implemented in LINQ to Rx.

The missing operators are generally the ones that would have to buffer all their output and return a new observable. For example, there's no `Reverse` method, and no `OrderBy`. C# is quite happy with that—it just won't let you use an `orderby` clause in a query expression based on observables. There's a `Join` method, but that doesn't deal with observables directly—it handles *join plans*. This is part of the Rx implementation of the join-calculus, and it's well beyond the scope of this book. Likewise there's no `GroupJoin` method, so `join...into` isn't supported.

For the various LINQ standard query operators that aren't covered by the query expression syntax—and to see the range of extra methods it makes available—see the `System.Reactive` documentation. Although you may start off being disappointed about the familiar functionality from LINQ to Objects that's missing in LINQ to Rx (usually because it just doesn't make sense), you may be surprised by how rich the set of available methods really is. Many of the new methods are then ported to LINQ to Objects in the `System.Interactive` assembly.

12.5.4 What's the point?

I'm well aware that I haven't provided any compelling reasons to use LINQ to Rx yet. This is deliberate, as I don't intend to show a full, useful example—it's incidental to the point of this chapter, and would take too much space. But Rx provides an elegant way of thinking about all kinds of asynchronous processes, such as normal .NET events (which can be viewed as an observable using `Observable.FromEvent`), asynchronous I/O, and calls to web services. It provides a way of managing the complexity and concurrency in an efficient manner. There's no doubt that it *is* harder to get your head around than LINQ to Objects, but if you're in the kind of situation where it'd be useful, you're already facing a mountain of complexity.

The reason I wanted to cover Rx in this book, despite not being able to do it any sort of justice, is because it shows why LINQ was designed the way it was. Although there are conversion methods available between `IEnumerable<T>` and `IObservable<T>`, there's no inheritance relationship. If the language had made any requirement that the types involved in LINQ had to be pull sequences, there would've been no query expression support for Rx at all. It would've been even more disastrous if extension methods had been limited to `IEnumerable<T>` in some way. Likewise, you've seen that not all the normal LINQ operators are applicable to Rx, which is why it's important that the language specifies query translations in terms of a pattern that should be supported as far as it makes sense for the given provider. I hope you have a sense that even though the push and pull models are very different to work with, LINQ acts as a sort of unifying force where possible.

You may be relieved to hear that our last topic is a lot simpler—it's back on the home ground of LINQ to Objects, but this time we're writing our own extension methods.

12.6 *Extending LINQ to Objects*

One of the nice things about LINQ is that it's extensible. Not only can you come up with your own query providers and data models, you can also add to existing ones. In my experience, the most common situation where this is useful is with LINQ to Objects. If you need a particular type of query that isn't directly supported (or is awkward or inefficient with the standard query operators), you can write your own. Of course, writing a general-purpose generic method can be more challenging than just solving your immediate problem, but if you find yourself writing similar code a few times, it's worth considering whether you could refactor it into a new operator.

Personally, I enjoy writing query operators. There are interesting technical challenges, but it rarely requires a huge amount of code, and the results can be elegant. In this section, we'll look at some of the ways you can make your custom operators behave efficiently and predictably, followed by a full sample for selecting a random element from a sequence.

12.6.1 *Design and implementation guidelines*

Most of these guidelines may seem fairly obvious, but this section can form a useful checklist when you write an operator.

UNIT TESTS

It's generally pretty easy to write a good set of unit tests for operators, although you may be surprised at how many you end up with for what originally appeared to be simple code. Don't forget to test corner cases, such as empty sequences, as well as invalid arguments. MoreLINQ (http://code.google.com/p/morelinq/) has some helper methods in its unit test project that you might want to use for your own tests.

ARGUMENT CHECKING

Good methods check their arguments, but there's a problem when it comes to LINQ operators. Many operators return another sequence, as you've already seen, and iterator blocks are the easiest way to implement this functionality. But you should really perform the argument checking as soon as your method is called, rather than waiting until the caller decides to iterate over the results. If you're going to use an iterator block, split your method into two: perform argument checking in a public method and then call a private method to do the iteration.

OPTIMIZATION

IEnumerable<T> itself is fairly weak in terms of the operations it supports, but the execution-time type of a sequence you're working on may have considerably more functionality. For example, the Count() operator will always work, but it'll generally be an O(n) operation. If you call it on an implementation of ICollection<T>, though, it can use the Count property directly, which will generally be O(1). In .NET 4, this optimization is extended to cover ICollection as well. Likewise, retrieving a specific element by index is slow in the general case, but can be efficient if the sequence implements IList<T>.

If your operator can benefit from these optimizations, you can have different execution paths depending on the execution-time type. To test the slow path in unit tests, you can always call `Select(x => x)` on a `List<T>` to retrieve a nonlist sequence. `LinkedList<T>` can test the case where you want an `ICollection<T>` that doesn't implement `IList<T>`.

DOCUMENTATION

It's important to document what your code will do with its inputs, and also the expected performance of the operator. This is particularly important if your method needs to work with multiple sequences: which one will be evaluated first, and how far? Does your code stream its data, buffer it, or is it a mixture? Does it use deferred or immediate execution? Can any parameters be null, and if so, does that have a special meaning?

ITERATE ONCE WHERE POSSIBLE

At an interface level, `IEnumerable<T>` will let you iterate over the same sequence multiple times—you can have multiple iterators active at the same time over the same sequence, potentially. But this is rarely a good idea within an operator. Wherever possible, it's wise to iterate over your input sequences just once. This means your code will work even for nonrepeatable sequences, such as lines read from a network stream. If you do need to read the sequence multiple times (and you don't want to buffer the whole sequence, like `Reverse` does), you should draw particular attention to this in the documentation.

REMEMBER TO DISPOSE OF ITERATORS

In most cases, you can use a `foreach` statement to iterate over your data source. But it's sometimes useful to treat the first item differently, in which case using an iterator directly can lead to the simplest code. In that situation, remember to include a `using` block for the iterator. You probably aren't used to disposing of iterators yourself because normally `foreach` does it for you, which can make it hard to spot the bug.

SUPPORT CUSTOM COMPARISONS

Many LINQ operators have overloads that allow you to specify an appropriate `IEqualityComparer<T>` or `IComparer<T>`. If you're building a general-purpose library for others (potentially developers who you aren't in contact with), it may be worth providing similar overloads yourself. On the other hand, if you're the sole user, or it's just going to be members of your team using it, you can do this on a need-to-implement basis. It's easy, though: typically the simpler overloads just call a more complex one, passing `EqualityComparer<T>.Default` or `Comparer<T>.Default` as the comparison.

Now that I've talked the talk, let's check whether I can actually walk the walk.

12.6.2 *Sample extension: selecting a random element*

The aim of the extension method we'll look at here is simple: given a sequence and an instance of `Random`, return a random element from the sequence. You could add an overload that doesn't require the instance of `Random`, but I prefer to make the dependency on a random number generator explicit. Randomness is a tricky topic for various reasons, and rather than discuss it here, I've included an article on the book's website (see http://mng.bz/h483). Also for reasons of space, I haven't included the XML documentation or unit tests in the following listing, but of course they're in the downloadable code.

Listing 12.17   Extension method to choose a random element from a sequence

```
public static T RandomElement<T>(this IEnumerable<T> source,
                                 Random random)
{
   if (source == null)                                    ◁── ❶ Validates arguments
   {
      throw new ArgumentNullException("source");
   }
   if (random == null)
   {
      throw new ArgumentNullException("random");
   }
   ICollection collection = source as ICollection;        ◁┐ Optimizes for
   if (collection != null)                                ❷ collections
   {
      int count = collection.Count;
      if (count == 0)
      {
         throw new InvalidOperationException("Sequence was empty.");
      }
      int index = random.Next(count);                     │ ElementAt
      return source.ElementAt(index);                     ◁┘ optimizes further
   }
   using (IEnumerator<T> iterator = source.GetEnumerator())  ◁┐ Handles
   {                                                       ❸ slow case
      if (!iterator.MoveNext())
      {
         throw new InvalidOperationException("Sequence was empty.");
      }
      int countSoFar = 1;
      T current = iterator.Current;
      while (iterator.MoveNext())
      {                                           ❹ Replaces current guess
         countSoFar++;                               with appropriate
         if (random.Next(countSoFar) == 0)        ◁┘ probability
         {
            current = iterator.Current;
         }
      }
      return current;
   }
}
```

Listing 12.17 doesn't show the technique of splitting an extension method into argument validation and then implementation, because it doesn't use an iterator block. Look back at the implementation of the Where operator in section 10.3.3 for an example of this. No custom comparisons are required either, but apart from that, every item on the checklist is appropriate.

First you validate your arguments in the obvious way ❶. Things get more interesting where the source sequence implements `ICollection` ❷.[9] This allows you to take the count cheaply and then generate a single random number to work out which element to pick. You don't *explicitly* handle the case where the source sequence implements `IList<T>`; instead, you rely on `ElementAt` to do that for you (as it's documented to do).

If you're dealing with a noncollection sequence (such as the result of another query operator), you want to avoid taking the count and then picking an element; that would require you to either buffer the contents of the sequence or iterate over it twice. Instead you step through it once, explicitly fetching the iterator ❸ so that you can test for an empty sequence easily. The clever bit[10] is at ❹—you replace your current idea of a random element with the element from the iterator with a probability of $1/n$, where n is the number of elements you've seen so far. There's a one-half chance of replacing the first element with the second, a one-third chance of replacing the result after two elements with the third element, and so on. The final result is that each element in the sequence has an equal chance of being picked, and you've managed to iterate just once.

Of course, the important point isn't what this particular method does—it's the potential issues that had to be considered as you implemented it. Once you know what to look for, it really doesn't take much effort to implement a robust method like this, and your personal toolbox will grow over time.

12.7 Summary

Phew! This chapter has been the exact opposite of most of the rest of the book. Instead of focusing on a single topic in great detail, we've covered a range of LINQ technologies, but at a shallow level.

I wouldn't expect you to feel particularly familiar with any one of the specific technologies we've looked at here, but I hope you have a deeper understanding of why LINQ is important. It's not about XML, or in-memory queries, SQL queries, observables, or enumerators—it's about consistency of expression, and giving the C# compiler the opportunity to validate your queries to at least some extent, regardless of their final execution platform.

You should now appreciate why expression trees are so important that they're among the few *framework* elements that the C# compiler has direct intimate knowledge of (along with strings, `IDisposable`, `IEnumerable<T>`, and `Nullable<T>`, for example). They act as passports, allowing behavior to cross the border of the local machine, expressing logic in whatever foreign tongue is catered for by a LINQ provider.

---

[9] The downloadable code contains the same test for implementations of `ICollection<T>`, just like `Count()` does in .NET 4. It's exactly the same block of code, just with a different type and a different variable name.

[10] I'm comfortable claiming this is clever because, even though it's my implementation, it's not my idea.

It's not just expression trees—we've also relied on the query expression translation employed by the compiler, and the way that lambda expressions can be converted to both delegates and expression trees. But extension methods are also important, as without them each provider would have to give implementations of all the relevant methods. If you look back at all the new features of C#, you'll find few that don't contribute significantly to LINQ in some way or another. That's part of the reason for this chapter's existence: to show the connections between all the features.

I shouldn't wax lyrical for too long, though. As well as the upsides of LINQ, we've seen a few gotchas. LINQ won't always allow you to express everything you need in a query, nor does it hide *all* the details of the underlying data source. When it comes to database LINQ providers, the impedance mismatches that have caused developers so much trouble in the past are still with us: you can reduce their impact with ORM systems and the like, but without a proper understanding of the query being executed on your behalf, you're likely to run into significant issues. In particular, don't think of LINQ as a way of removing your need to understand SQL—think of it as a way of hiding the SQL when you're not interested in the details. Likewise, in order to plan an effective parallel query, you've got to know where ordering matters and where it doesn't, and perhaps help the framework along a bit by giving it more tuning information.

Since .NET 3.5 came out, I've been delighted to see how wholeheartedly the community has embraced LINQ. Likewise, there have been plenty of interesting uses of the features of C# 4, which you'll see in the next part of the book.

Part 4

C# 4: Playing nicely with others

C# 4 is a funny beast. It doesn't have the "several, almost unrelated, major new features" feeling of C# 2, nor the "all in the cause of LINQ" feeling of C# 3. Instead, the new features of C# 4 fall somewhere between the two. Interoperability is a major theme, but many of the features are equally useful even if you never need to work with other environments.

My personal favorite features from C# 4 are optional parameters and named arguments. They're relatively simple but can be put to good use in many places, improving the readability of code and generally making life more pleasant. Do you waste time working out which argument means what? Put some names on them. Are you tired of writing endless overloads to avoid callers having to specify everything? Make some parameters optional.

If you work with COM, C# 4 will be a breath of fresh air for you. To start with, the features I just described make some APIs much simpler to work with, where the component designers have pretty much assumed that you'll be working with a language supporting optional parameters and named arguments. Beyond that, there's a better deployment story, support for named indexers, and a helpful shortcut to avoid having to pass arguments by reference everywhere. The biggest feature of C# 4—dynamic typing—also makes COM integration easier.

We'll look at all of these areas in chapter 13, along with the brain-busting topic of generic variance applied to interfaces and delegates. Don't worry; we'll take that reasonably slowly, and the best part is that most of the time you don't need to know the details—it just makes code work where you might've expected it to in C# 3 anyway!

Chapter 14 covers dynamic typing and the Dynamic Language Runtime (DLR). This is an enormous topic. I've concentrated on how the C# language implements dynamic typing, but we'll also look at a few examples of interoperating with dynamic languages such as IronPython, and see examples of how a type can dynamically respond to method calls, property accesses, and so on. It's worth applying a little perspective here: the fact that this is a major feature doesn't mean that you should expect to see dynamic expressions cropping up all over your code base. This won't be as pervasive as LINQ, for example, but when you do want dynamic typing, you'll find it well implemented in C# 4.

13

Minor changes
to simplify code

This chapter covers

- Optional parameters
- Named arguments
- Streamlining ref parameters in COM
- Embedding COM Primary Interop Assemblies
- Calling named indexers declared in COM
- Generic variance for interfaces and delegates
- Changes in locking and field-like events

Just as with previous versions, C# 4 has a few minor features that don't merit individual chapters to themselves. In fact, there's only one really *big* feature in C# 4—dynamic typing—which we'll cover in the next chapter. The changes we'll cover here just make C# that little bit more pleasant to work with, particularly if you work with COM on a regular basis. These features generally make code clearer, remove drudgery from COM calls, or simplify deployment.

Will any of these features make your heart race with excitement? It's unlikely. But they're nice features all the same, and some of them may be widely applicable. Let's start by looking at how we call methods.

13.1 *Optional parameters and named arguments*

These are perhaps the Batman and Robin[1] features of C# 4. They're distinct, but usually seen together. I'll keep them apart for the moment so we can examine each in turn, but then we'll use them together for some more interesting examples.

Parameters and arguments

This section obviously talks about parameters and arguments a lot. In casual conversation, the two terms are often used interchangeably, but I'll use them in line with their formal definitions. Just to remind you, a *parameter* (also known as a *formal parameter*) is the variable that's part of the method or indexer declaration. An *argument* is an expression used when calling the method or indexer. For example, consider this snippet:

```
void Foo(int x, int y)
{
    // Do something with x and y
}
...
int a = 10;
Foo(a, 20);
```

Here the parameters are x and y, and the arguments are a and 20.

We'll start by looking at optional parameters.

13.1.1 *Optional parameters*

Visual Basic has had optional parameters for ages, and they've been in the CLR from .NET 1.0. The concept is as obvious as it sounds: some parameters are optional, so their values don't have to be explicitly specified by the caller. Any parameter that hasn't been specified as an argument by the caller is given a default value.

MOTIVATION

Optional parameters are usually used when several values are required for an operation, and the same values are used a lot of the time. For example, suppose you wanted to read a text file; you might want to provide a method that allows the caller to specify the name of the file and the encoding to use. The encoding is almost always UTF-8, though, so it's nice to be able to use that automatically if it's all you need.

Historically the idiomatic way of allowing this in C# has been to use method overloading: declare one method with all the possible parameters, and others that call that

---

[1] Or Cavalleria rusticana and Pagliacci if you're feeling more highly cultured.

method, passing in default values where appropriate. For instance, you might create methods like this:

```
public IList<Customer> LoadCustomers(string filename,
                                     Encoding encoding)
{
    ...                                              <─── Do real work here
}

public IList<Customer> LoadCustomers(string filename)
{
    return LoadCustomers(filename, Encoding.UTF8);   <─── Default to UTF-8
}
```

This works fine for a single parameter, but it becomes complicated when there are multiple options, as each extra option doubles the number of possible overloads. If two of them are of the same type, this approach would naturally lead to multiple methods with the same signature, which is invalid. Often the same set of overloads is also required for multiple parameter types. For example, the XmlReader.Create() method can create an XmlReader from a Stream, a TextReader, or a string, but it also provides the option of specifying an XmlReaderSettings and other arguments. Due to this duplication, there are 12 overloads for the method.

This could be significantly reduced with optional parameters. Let's see how it's done.

DECLARING OPTIONAL PARAMETERS AND OMITTING THEM WHEN SUPPLYING ARGUMENTS

Making a parameter optional is as simple as supplying a default value for it, using what looks like a variable initializer. Figure 13.1 shows a method with three parameters: two are optional, one is required.

All this method does is print out the arguments, but that's enough to see what's going on. The following listing gives the full code and calls the method three times, specifying a different number of arguments for each call.

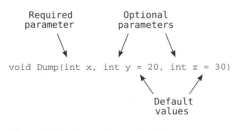

Figure 13.1 Declaring optional parameters

Listing 13.1 Declaring and calling a method with optional parameters

```
static void Dump(int x, int y = 20, int z = 30)      ❶ Declares method
{                                                       with optional
    Console.WriteLine("x={0} y={1} z={2}", x, y, z);    parameters
}
...
Dump(1, 2, 3);                                       ❷ Calls method with
Dump(1, 2);              <──❸ Omits one argument        all arguments
Dump(1);
        ❹ Omits two arguments
```

The *optional parameters* are the ones with default values specified ❶. If the caller doesn't specify y, its initial value will be 20, and likewise z has a default value of 30. The first call ❷ explicitly specifies all the arguments; the remaining calls (❸ and ❹) omit one or two arguments, respectively, so the default values are used. When there's one argument missing, the compiler assumes that the final parameter has been omitted, then the penultimate one, and so on. The output is as follows:

```
x=1 y=2 z=3
x=1 y=2 z=30
x=1 y=20 z=30
```

Note that although the compiler *could* use some clever analysis of the types of the optional parameters and the arguments in order to work out what's been left out, it doesn't: it assumes that you're supplying arguments in the same order as the parameters.[2] This means that the following code is invalid:

INVALID ▷
```
static void TwoOptionalParameters(int x = 10,
                                  string y = "default")
{
    Console.WriteLine("x={0} y={1}", x, y);
}
...
TwoOptionalParameters("second parameter");    ⟵— Error!
```

This tries to call the TwoOptionalParameters method specifying a string for the *first* argument. There's no overload with a first parameter that's convertible from a string, so the compiler issues an error. This is a good thing—overload resolution is tricky enough (particularly when generic type inference gets involved) without the compiler trying all kinds of different permutations to find something you *might* be trying to call. If you want to omit the value for one optional parameter but specify a later one, you need to use named arguments.

RESTRICTIONS ON OPTIONAL PARAMETERS

There are a few rules for optional parameters. All optional parameters must come after required parameters. The exception to this is a *parameter array* (as declared with the params modifier), which still has to come at the end of a parameter list, but can come after optional parameters. A parameter array can't be declared as an optional parameter—if the caller doesn't specify any values for it, an empty array will be used instead. Optional parameters can't have ref or out modifiers either.

An optional parameter can be of any type, but there are restrictions on the default value specified. You can always use constants: numeric and string literals, null, const members, enum members, and the default(T) operator. Additionally, for value types, you can call the parameterless constructor, although this is equivalent to using the default (...) operator anyway. There has to be an implicit conversion from the specified value to the parameter type, but this must *not* be a user-defined conversion. Table 13.1 shows some examples of valid parameter lists.

---

[2]   Unless you're using named arguments, of course—you'll learn about those soon.

Table 13.1   Valid method parameter lists using optional parameters

Declaration	Notes
`Foo(int x, int y = 10)`	Numeric literal used for default value
`Foo(decimal x = 10)`	Implicit built-in conversion from `int` to `decimal`
`Foo(string name = "default")`	String literal used for default value
`Foo(DateTime dt = new DateTime())`	Zero value of `DateTime`
`Foo(DateTime dt = default(DateTime))`	Alternative syntax for the zero value
`Foo<T>(T value = default(T))`	Default value operator works with type parameters
`Foo(int? x = null)`	Nullable conversion
`Foo(int x, int y = 10, params int[] z)`	Parameter array after optional parameters

In contrast, table 13.2 shows some invalid parameter lists and explains why they're not allowed.

Table 13.2   Invalid method parameter lists using optional parameters

Declaration (invalid)	Notes
`Foo(int x = 0, int y)`	Required non-`params` parameter after optional parameter
`Foo(DateTime dt = DateTime.Now)`	Default values must be constants
`Foo(XName name = "default")`	Conversion from `string` to `XName` is user-defined
`Foo(params string[] names = null)`	Parameter arrays can't be optional
`Foo(ref string name = "default")`	`ref`/`out` parameters can't be optional

The fact that the default value has to be constant is a pain in two different ways. One of them is familiar from a slightly different context, as we'll look at now.

VERSIONING AND OPTIONAL PARAMETERS

The restrictions on default values for optional parameters may remind you of the restrictions on `const` fields or attribute values, and they behave very similarly. In both cases, when the compiler references the value, it copies it directly into the output. The generated IL acts exactly as if your original source code had contained the default value. This means if you ever *change* the default value without recompiling everything that references it, the old callers will still be using the old default value.

To make this concrete, imagine this set of steps:

1 Create a class library (Library.dll) with a class like this:

```
public class LibraryDemo
{
    public static void PrintValue(int value = 10)
    {
        System.Console.WriteLine(value);
    }
}
```

2 Create a console application (Application.exe) that references the class library:

```
public class Program
{
    static void Main()
    {
        LibraryDemo.PrintValue();
    }
}
```

3 Run the application—it'll print 10, predictably.

4 Change the declaration of PrintValue as follows, and then recompile *just* the class library:

```
public static void PrintValue(int value = 20)
```

5 Rerun the application—it'll still print 10. The value has been compiled directly into the executable.

6 Recompile the application and rerun it—this time it'll print 20.

This versioning issue can cause bugs that are hard to track down, because all the code *looks* correct. Essentially, you're restricted to using genuine constants that should never change as default values for optional parameters.[3] There's one benefit of this setup: it gives the caller a guarantee that the value it knew about at compile time is the one that'll be used. Developers may feel more comfortable with that than with a dynamically computed value, or one that depends on the version of the library used at execution time.

Of course, this also means you can't use any values that can't be expressed as constants anyway. You can't create a method with a default value of "the current time," for example.

MAKING DEFAULTS MORE FLEXIBLE WITH NULLITY

Fortunately, there's a way around the restriction that default values must be constants. Essentially, you introduce a magic value to represent the default, and then replace that magic value with the *real* default within the method itself. If the phrase *magic value* bothers you, I'm not surprised, but we'll use null for the magic value, which already represents the absence of a normal value. If the parameter type would normally be a value type, we'll simply make it the corresponding nullable value type, at which point we can still specify that the default value is null.

---

[3] Or you could just accept that you'll need to recompile everything if you change the value. In many contexts that's a reasonable trade-off.

As an example of this, let's look at a situation similar to the one I used to introduce the whole topic: allowing the caller to supply an appropriate text encoding to a method, but defaulting to UTF-8. You can't specify the default encoding as `Encoding.UTF8` as that's not a constant value, but you can treat a null parameter value as "use the default." To demonstrate how you can handle value types, let's make the method append a timestamp to a text file with a message. We'll default the encoding to UTF-8 and the timestamp to the current time. The following listing shows the complete code and a few examples of using it.

Listing 13.2 Using null default values to handle nonconstant situations

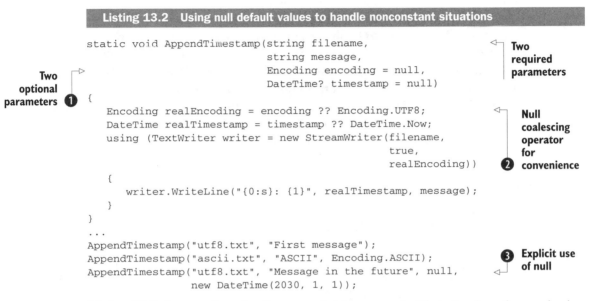

```
static void AppendTimestamp(string filename,              ◁─┐  Two
                           string message,                   │  required
                           Encoding encoding = null,         │  parameters
                           DateTime? timestamp = null)
{
    Encoding realEncoding = encoding ?? Encoding.UTF8;    ◁─┐  Null
    DateTime realTimestamp = timestamp ?? DateTime.Now;      │  coalescing
    using (TextWriter writer = new StreamWriter(filename,    │  operator
                                      true,                  │  for
                                      realEncoding))       ❷ │  convenience
    {
        writer.WriteLine("{0:s}: {1}", realTimestamp, message);
    }
}
...
AppendTimestamp("utf8.txt", "First message");
AppendTimestamp("ascii.txt", "ASCII", Encoding.ASCII);     ❸  Explicit use
AppendTimestamp("utf8.txt", "Message in the future", null,    of null
            new DateTime(2030, 1, 1));                    ◁─┘
```

Two optional parameters ❶ points to the opening `{`.

Listing 13.2 shows a few nice features of this approach. First, it solves the versioning problem. The default values for the optional parameters are null ❶, but the *effective* values are "the UTF-8 encoding" and "the current date and time." Neither of these could be expressed as constants, and should you ever want to change the effective default—for example, to use the current UTC time instead of the local time—you could do so without having to recompile everything that called `AppendTimestamp`. Of course, changing the effective default changes the behavior of the method; you need to take the same sort of care with this as you would with any other code change. At this point, you (as the library author) are in charge of the versioning story—you're taking responsibility for not breaking clients, effectively. At least it's more familiar territory; you know that all callers will experience the same behavior, regardless of recompilation.

This listing also introduces an extra level of flexibility. Not only do optional parameters mean you can make the calls shorter, but having a specific "use the default" value means that should you ever wish to, you can *explicitly* make a call allowing the method to choose the appropriate value. At the moment, this is the only way you know to specify the timestamp explicitly without also providing an encoding ❸, but that'll change when we look at named arguments.

The optional parameter values are simple to deal with, thanks to the null coalescing operator ❷. This example uses separate variables for the sake of printed formatting, but in real code you'd probably use the same expressions directly in the calls to the StreamWriter constructor and the WriteLine method.

There are two downsides to this approach: first, it means that if a caller *accidentally* passes in null due to a bug, it'll get the default value instead of an exception. In cases where you're using a nullable value type and callers will either explicitly use null or have a non-nullable argument, that's not much of a problem, but for reference types it could be an issue.

On a related note, it requires that you don't want to use null as a "real" value.[4] There are occasions where you want *null* to mean *null*, and if you don't want that to be the default value, you'll have to find a different constant or just leave the parameter as a required one. But in other cases, where there isn't an obvious constant value that'll clearly *always* be the right default, I recommend this approach to optional parameters as one that's easy to follow consistently and removes some of the normal difficulties.

We'll need to look at how optional parameters affect overload resolution, but it makes sense to wait until you've seen how named arguments work. Speaking of which…

13.1.2 *Named arguments*

The basic idea of named arguments is that when you specify an argument value, you can also specify the name of the parameter it's supplying the value for. The compiler then makes sure that there *is* a parameter of the right name and uses the value for that parameter. Even on its own, this can increase readability in some cases. In practice, named arguments are most useful in cases where optional parameters are also likely to appear, but we'll look at the simple situation first.

> **INDEXERS, OPTIONAL PARAMETERS, AND NAMED ARGUMENTS** You *can* use optional parameters and named arguments with indexers as well as methods. But this is only useful for indexers with more than one parameter: you can't access an indexer without specifying at least one argument anyway. Given this limitation, I don't expect to see the feature used much with indexers, and I haven't demonstrated it in the book. It works exactly as you'd expect it to, though.

I'm sure you've seen code that looks something like this:

```
MessageBox.Show("Please do not press this button again", // text
                "Ouch!"); // title
```

I've chosen a pretty tame example; it can get a lot worse when there are loads of arguments, especially if a lot of them are the same type. But this is still realistic; even with

---

[4] We almost need a second null-like special value, meaning "please use the default value for this parameter," and then we could allow that special value to be supplied either automatically for missing arguments or explicitly in the argument list. I'm sure this would cause dozens of problems, but it's an interesting thought experiment.

just two parameters, I'd find myself guessing which argument meant what based on the text when reading this code, unless it had comments like the ones I have here. There's a problem though: comments can lie about the code they describe. Nothing is checking them at all. In contrast, named arguments ask the compiler to help.

SYNTAX

All you need to do to the previous example to make the code clearer is prefix each argument with the name of the corresponding parameter and a colon:

```
MessageBox.Show(text: "Please do not press this button again",
                caption: "Ouch!");
```

Admittedly, you now don't get to choose the name you find most meaningful (I prefer `title` to `caption`), but at least you'll know if you get something wrong.

Of course, the most common way in which you could get something wrong here is to get the arguments the wrong way around. Without named arguments, this would be a problem: you'd end up with the pieces of text switched in the message box. With named arguments, the ordering becomes largely irrelevant. You can rewrite the previous code like this:

```
MessageBox.Show(caption: "Ouch!",
                text: "Please do not press this button again");
```

You'd still have the right text in the right place, because the compiler would work out what you meant based on the names.

For another example, look at the `StreamWriter` constructor call in listing 13.2. The second argument is just `true`—what does this mean? Is it going to force a stream flush after every write? Include a byte order mark? Append to an existing file instead of creating a new one? Here's the equivalent call using named arguments:

```
new StreamWriter(path: filename,
                 append: true,
                 encoding: realEncoding)
```

In both of these examples, you've seen how named arguments effectively attach semantic *meaning* to values. In the never-ending quest to make code communicate better with humans as well as computers, this is a definite step forward.

I'm not suggesting that named arguments should be used when the meaning is already obvious, of course. Like all features, it should be used with discretion and thought.

Named arguments with out and ref

If you want to specify the name of an argument for a `ref` or `out` parameter, you put the `ref` or `out` modifier after the name and before the argument. Using `int.TryParse` as an example, you might have code like this:

```
int number;
bool success = int.TryParse("10", result: out number);
```

To explore some other aspects of the syntax, the following listing shows a method with three integer parameters, just like the one we used to start looking at optional parameters.

Listing 13.3   Simple examples of using named arguments

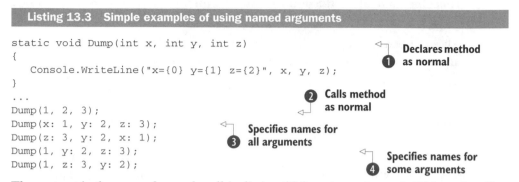

```
static void Dump(int x, int y, int z)                    ◁⌐  Declares method
{                                                         ❶   as normal
    Console.WriteLine("x={0} y={1} z={2}", x, y, z);
}
...
Dump(1, 2, 3);                          ❷  Calls method
Dump(x: 1, y: 2, z: 3);      ◁⌐              as normal
Dump(z: 3, y: 2, x: 1);      ❸  Specifies names for
Dump(1, y: 2, z: 3);            all arguments
Dump(1, z: 3, y: 2);                     ◁⌐  Specifies names for
                                         ❹   some arguments
```

The output is the same for each call in listing 13.3: x=1, y=2, z=3. This code effectively makes the same method call in five different ways. It's worth noting that there are no tricks in the method declaration ❶; you can use named arguments with any method that has parameters. First, you call the method in the normal way, without using any new features ❷. This is a sort of control point to make sure that the other calls really are equivalent. You then make two calls to the method using just named arguments ❸. The second of these calls reverses the order of the arguments, but the result is still the same, because the arguments are matched up with the parameters by name, not position. Finally, there are two calls using a mixture of named arguments and *positional arguments* ❹. A positional argument is one that isn't named, so every argument in valid C# 3 code is a positional argument from the point of view of C# 4.

Figure 13.2 shows how the final line of code works.

All named arguments have to come after positional arguments—you can't switch between the styles. Positional arguments *always* refer to the corresponding parameter in the method declaration—you can't make positional arguments skip a parameter by specifying it later with a named argument. This means that these method calls would both be invalid:

- Dump(z: 3, 1, y: 2)—Positional arguments must come before named ones.
- Dump(2, x: 1, z: 3)—x has already been specified by the first positional argument, so you can't specify it again with a named argument.

Now, although in *this particular case* the method calls are equivalent, that's not *always* the case. Let's look at why reordering arguments might change behavior.

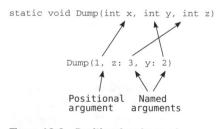

Figure 13.2   Positional and named arguments in the same call

ARGUMENT EVALUATION ORDER

You're used to C# evaluating its arguments in the order they're specified, which, until C# 4, has always been the order in which the parameters have been declared too. In C# 4, only the first part is still true: the arguments are still evaluated in the order they're written, even if that's not the same as the order in which they're declared as parameters. This matters if evaluating the arguments has side effects.

It's *usually* worth trying to avoid having side effects in arguments, but there are cases where it can make the code clearer. A more realistic rule is to try to avoid side effects that might interfere with each other. For the sake of demonstrating execution order, we'll break both of these rules. Please don't treat this as a recommendation that you do the same thing.

First we'll create a relatively harmless example, introducing a method that logs its input and returns it—a sort of logging echo. We'll use the return values of three calls to this to call the Dump method (which isn't shown, as it hasn't changed). The following listing shows two calls to Dump that result in slightly different output.

Listing 13.4 Logging argument evaluation

```
static int Log(int value)
{
    Console.WriteLine("Log: {0}", value);
    return value;
}
...
Dump(x: Log(1), y: Log(2), z: Log(3));
Dump(z: Log(3), x: Log(1), y: Log(2));
```

The results of running listing 13.4 show what happens:

```
Log: 1
Log: 2
Log: 3
x=1 y=2 z=3
Log: 3
Log: 1
Log: 2
x=1 y=2 z=3
```

In both cases, the parameters x, y, and z in the Dump method still have the values 1, 2, and 3, respectively. But you can see that although they were evaluated in that order in the first call (which was equivalent to using positional arguments), the second call evaluated the value used for the z parameter first.

You can make the effect even more significant by using side effects that change the results of the argument evaluation, as shown in the following listing, again using the same Dump method.

Listing 13.5   Abusing argument evaluation order

```
int i = 0;
Dump(x: ++i, y: ++i, z: ++i);
i = 0;
Dump(z: ++i, x: ++i, y: ++i);
```

The results of listing 13.5 may be best expressed in terms of the blood spatter pattern at a murder scene, after someone maintaining code like this has gone after the original author with an axe. Yes, *technically speaking* the last line results are x=2 y=3 z=1, but I'm sure you see what I'm getting at. Just say *No* to code like this.

By all means, reorder your arguments for the sake of readability. You may think that laying out a call to `MessageBox.Show` with the title coming above the text in the code itself reflects the onscreen layout more closely, for example. If you want to rely on a particular evaluation order for the arguments, though, introduce some local variables to execute the relevant code in separate statements. The compiler won't care either way—it'll follow the rules of the spec—but this reduces the risk of a "harmless refactoring" that inadvertently introduces a subtle bug.

To return to cheerier matters, let's combine the two features (optional parameters and named arguments) and see how much tidier the code can be.

13.1.3 *Putting the two together*

Optional parameters and named arguments work in tandem with no extra effort required on your part. It's not uncommon to have a bunch of parameters where there are obvious defaults, but where it's hard to predict which ones a caller will want to specify explicitly. Figure 13.3 shows just about every combination: a required parameter, two optional parameters, a positional argument, a named argument, and a missing argument for an optional parameter.

Going back to an earlier example, in listing 13.2 you wanted to append a timestamp to a file using the default encoding of UTF-8, but with a particular timestamp. That code used `null` for the encoding argument, but now you can write the same code more simply, as shown in the following listing.

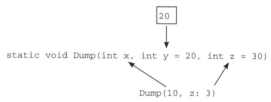

Figure 13.3   Mixing named arguments and optional parameters

Listing 13.6   Combining named arguments and optional parameters

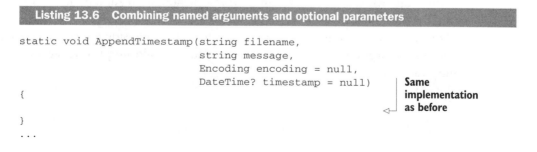

```
static void AppendTimestamp(string filename,
                           string message,
                           Encoding encoding = null,
                           DateTime? timestamp = null)
{

}
...
```

Same
implementation
as before

```
AppendTimestamp("utf8.txt", "Message in the future",    ◁─── Encoding is omitted
            timestamp: new DateTime(2030, 1, 1));    ◁─┐
                                                       │ Named timestamp
                                                       │ argument
```

In this fairly simple situation, the benefit isn't particularly huge, but in cases where you want to omit three or four arguments but specify the final one, it's a real blessing.

You've seen how optional parameters reduce the need for huge long lists of overloads, but one specific pattern where this is worth mentioning is with respect to immutability.

IMMUTABILITY AND OBJECT INITIALIZATION

One aspect of C# 4 that disappoints me somewhat is that it hasn't done much *explicitly* to make immutability easier. Immutable types are a core part of functional programming, and C# has been gradually supporting the functional style more and more... except for immutability. Object and collection initializers make it easy to work with *mutable* types, but immutable types have been left out in the cold. (Automatically implemented properties fall into this category too.) Fortunately, though they're not particularly designed to aid immutability, named arguments and optional parameters allow you to write object initializer–like code that calls a constructor or other factory method.

For instance, suppose you were creating a `Message` class, which required a *from* address, a *to* address, and a *body*, with the subject and attachment being optional. (We'll stick with single recipients in order to keep the example as simple as possible.) You *could* create a mutable type with appropriate writable properties, and construct instances like this:

```
Message message = new Message {
    From = "skeet@pobox.com",
    To = "csharp-in-depth-readers@everywhere.com",
    Body = "Hope you like the third edition",
    Subject = "A quick message"
};
```

That has two problems: first, it doesn't enforce the required data to be provided. You could force those to be supplied to the constructor, but then (before C# 4) it wouldn't be obvious which argument meant what:

```
Message message = new Message(
    "skeet@pobox.com",
    "csharp-in-depth-readers@everywhere.com",
    "Hope you like the third edition")
{
    Subject = "A quick message"
};
```

The second problem is that this initialization pattern simply doesn't work for immutable types. The compiler has to call a property setter *after* it has initialized the object.

But you can use optional parameters and named arguments to come up with something that has the nice features of the first form (only specifying what you're interested in and supplying names) without losing the validation of which aspects of the message are required or the benefits of immutability. The following listing shows a possible constructor signature and the construction step for the same message as before.

Listing 13.7   Using optional parameters and named arguments for immutability

```
public Message(string from, string to,
               string body, string subject = null,
               byte[] attachment = null)                    Normal
{                                                           initialization
                                                         ⊲┘ code goes here
}
...
Message message = new Message(
    from: "skeet@pobox.com",
    to: "csharp-in-depth-readers@everywhere.com",
    body: "I hope you like the third edition",
    subject: "A quick message"
);
```

I really like this in terms of readability and general cleanliness. You don't need hundreds of constructor overloads—just one with some of the parameters being optional. The same syntax will also work with static creation methods, unlike object initializers. The only downside is that it really relies on your code being consumed by a language that supports optional parameters and named arguments; otherwise callers will be forced to write ugly code to specify values for all the optional parameters. Obviously there's more to immutability than getting values to the initialization code, but this is a welcome step in the right direction nonetheless.

There are a couple of final points to make about these features before we move on to COM—points concerning the details of how the compiler handles your code and the difficulty of good API design.

OVERLOAD RESOLUTION

Clearly both named arguments and optional parameters affect how the compiler resolves overloads—if there are multiple method signatures available with the same name, which one should it pick? Optional parameters can *increase* the number of applicable methods (if some methods have more parameters than the number of specified arguments) and named arguments can *decrease* the number of applicable methods (by ruling out methods that don't have the appropriate parameter names).

For the most part, the changes are intuitive: to check whether any particular method is applicable, the compiler tries to build a list of the arguments it *would* pass in, using the positional arguments in order, and then matching the named arguments up with the remaining parameters. If a required parameter hasn't been specified or if a named argument doesn't match any remaining parameters, the method isn't applicable. The specification gives more detail about this in section 7.5.3, but there are two situations I'd like to draw particular attention to.

First, if two methods are both applicable and one of them has been given *all* of its arguments explicitly, whereas the other uses an optional parameter filled in with a default value, the method that doesn't use any default values will win. But this doesn't extend to just comparing the number of default values used—it's a strict "does it use default values or not" divide. For example, consider the following:

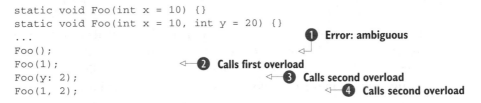

```
static void Foo(int x = 10) {}
static void Foo(int x = 10, int y = 20) {}
...                                              ❶ Error: ambiguous
Foo();
Foo(1);                          ←—❷ Calls first overload
Foo(y: 2);                              ←—❸ Calls second overload
Foo(1, 2);                                   ←—❹ Calls second overload
```

In the first call ❶, both methods are applicable because of their optional parameters. But the compiler can't work out which one you meant to call; it'll raise an error. In the second call ❷, both methods are still applicable, but the first overload is used because it can be applied without using any default values, whereas the second overload uses the default value for y. For both the third and fourth calls, only the second overload is applicable. The third call ❸ names the y argument, and the fourth call ❹ has two arguments; both of these mean the first overload isn't applicable.

> **OVERLOADS AND INHERITANCE DON'T ALWAYS MIX NICELY** All of this assumes that the compiler has gone as far as finding multiple overloads to choose between. If some methods are declared in a base type, but there are applicable methods in a more derived type, the latter will win. This has always been the case, and it can cause some surprising results (see the book's website for more details and examples: http://mng.bz/aEmE), but now optional parameters mean there may be more applicable methods than you'd expect. I advise you to avoid overloading a base class method within a derived class unless you get a huge benefit.

The second point is that sometimes named arguments can be an alternative to casting in order to help the compiler resolve overloads. Sometimes a call can be ambiguous because the arguments can be converted to the parameter types in two different methods, but neither method is better than the other in all respects. For instance, consider the following method signatures and call:

```
void Method(int x, object y) { ... }
void Method(object a, int b) { ... }
...
Method(10, 10);                  ←— Ambiguous call
```

Both methods are applicable, and neither is better than the other. There are two ways to resolve this, assuming you can't change the method names to make them unambiguous that way. (That's my preferred approach. Make each method name more informative and specific, which will improve the general readability of the code.) You can either cast one of the arguments explicitly, or use named arguments to resolve the ambiguity:

```
void Method(int x, object y) { ... }
void Method(object a, int b) { ... }
...
Method(10, (object) 10);
Method(x: 10, y: 10);
```

Casting to resolve ambiguity

Naming to resolve ambiguity

Of course, this only works if the parameters have different names in the different methods, but it's a handy trick to know. Sometimes the cast will give more readable code; sometimes the name will. It's just an extra weapon in the fight for clear code.

Unfortunately, it does have a downside, along with named arguments in general: it's another thing to be careful about when you change parameter names.

THE SILENT HORROR OF CHANGING NAMES

In the past, parameter names haven't mattered much if you've only been using C#. Other languages may have cared, but in C# the only times that parameter names were important were when you were looking at IntelliSense and when you were looking at the method code itself. Now the parameter names of a method are effectively part of the API even if you're only using C#. If you change them at a later date, code can break—anything that was using a named argument to refer to one of your parameters will fail to compile if you decide to change it. This may not be much of an issue if your code is only consumed by itself, but if you're writing a public API, be aware that changing a parameter name is a big deal. It always has been, really, but if everything calling the code was written in C#, you've been able to ignore that until now.

Renaming parameters is bad; switching the names around is worse. The calling code may still compile, but with a different meaning. A particularly evil form of this is to override a method and switch the parameter names in the overridden version. The compiler will always look at the deepest override it knows about, based on the static type of the expression used as the target of the method call. You don't want to get into a situation where calling the same method implementation with the same argument list results in different behavior based on the static type of a variable.

IN CONCLUSION...

Named arguments and optional parameters are possibly two of the simplest-sounding features of C# 4, and yet they have a fair amount of complexity, as you've seen. The basic ideas are easily expressed and understood, and the good news is that most of the time that's all you need to care about. You can take advantage of optional parameters to reduce the number of overloads you write, and named arguments can make code much more readable when several easily confusable arguments are used.

The trickiest bit is probably deciding which default values to use, bearing in mind potential versioning issues. Likewise, it's now more obvious than before that parameter names matter, and you need to be careful when overriding existing methods, to avoid being evil to your callers.

Speaking of evil, let's move on to the new features relating to COM. I'm only kidding...mostly, anyway.

13.2 Improvements for COM interoperability

I readily admit to being far from a COM expert. When I tried to use it before .NET came along, I always ran into issues that were no doubt partially caused by my lack of knowledge and partially caused by the components I was working with being poorly designed or implemented. My overall impression of COM as a sort of black magic has lingered, though. I've been reliably informed that there's a lot to like about it, but unfortunately I haven't found myself going back to learn it in detail—and there seems to be a *lot* of detail to study.

THIS SECTION IS MICROSOFT-SPECIFIC The changes for COM interoperability won't make sense for all C# compilers, and a compiler can still be deemed compliant with the specification without implementing these features.

.NET has made COM somewhat friendlier in general, but until now there have been distinct advantages to using it from Visual Basic instead of C#. The playing field has been leveled significantly by C# 4, as you'll see in this section. For the sake of familiarity, I'll use Word for the example in this chapter and Excel in the next chapter. There's nothing Office-specific about the new features, though; you should find the experience of working with COM to be nicer in C# 4 whatever you're doing.

13.2.1 The horrors of automating Word before C# 4

Our example is simple—it's just going to start Word, create a document with a single paragraph of text, save it, and then exit. Sounds easy, right? If only that were so. The following listing shows the code required before C# 4.

Listing 13.8 Creating and saving a document in C# 3

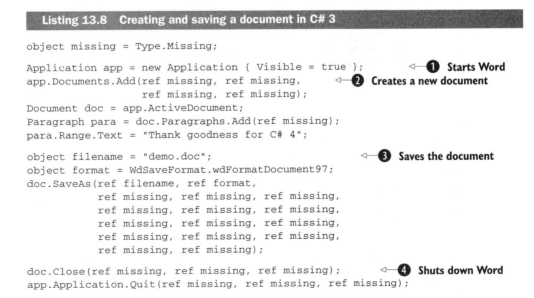

```
object missing = Type.Missing;

Application app = new Application { Visible = true };          ←①  Starts Word
app.Documents.Add(ref missing, ref missing,           ←②  Creates a new document
                  ref missing, ref missing);
Document doc = app.ActiveDocument;
Paragraph para = doc.Paragraphs.Add(ref missing);
para.Range.Text = "Thank goodness for C# 4";

object filename = "demo.doc";                         ←③  Saves the document
object format = WdSaveFormat.wdFormatDocument97;
doc.SaveAs(ref filename, ref format,
           ref missing, ref missing, ref missing,
           ref missing, ref missing, ref missing,
           ref missing, ref missing, ref missing,
           ref missing, ref missing, ref missing,
           ref missing, ref missing);

doc.Close(ref missing, ref missing, ref missing);     ←④  Shuts down Word
app.Application.Quit(ref missing, ref missing, ref missing);
```

Each step in this code sounds simple: first you create an instance of the COM type ❶ and make it visible using an object initializer expression; then you create and fill in a new document ❷. The mechanism for inserting some text into a document isn't quite as straightforward as you might expect, but it's worth remembering that a Word document can have a fairly complex structure; this isn't as bad as it might be. A couple of the method calls here have optional by-reference parameters; you don't need them, so you pass a local variable by reference with a value of `Type.Missing`. If you've ever done any COM work before, you're probably very familiar with this pattern.

Next comes the really nasty bit: saving the document ❸. Yes, the `SaveAs` method really does have 16 parameters, of which you're only using 2. Even those 2 need to be passed by reference, which means creating local variables for them. In terms of readability, this is a complete nightmare. Don't worry—we'll soon sort it out.

Finally, you close the document and the application ❹. Aside from the fact that both calls have three optional parameters that you don't care about, there's nothing interesting here.

Let's start off by using the features we've already seen in this chapter—they're sufficient in themselves to cut the example down significantly.

13.2.2 *The revenge of optional parameters and named arguments*

First things first: let's get rid of all those arguments corresponding to optional parameters you're not interested in. That also means you don't need the `missing` variable.

That still leaves you with 2 parameters out of a possible 16 for the `SaveAs` method. At the moment it's obvious which is which based on the local variable names, but what if you have them the wrong way around? All the parameters are weakly typed, so you're really going on guesswork. You can easily give the arguments names to clarify the call. If you wanted to use one of the later parameters, you'd have to specify the name anyway, just to skip the ones you're not interested in.

The following listing shows the code—it looks a lot cleaner already.

Listing 13.9   Automating Word using normal C# 4 features

```csharp
Application app = new Application { Visible = true };
app.Documents.Add();
Document doc = app.ActiveDocument;
Paragraph para = doc.Paragraphs.Add();
para.Range.Text = "Thank goodness for C# 4";

object filename = "demo.doc";
object format = WdSaveFormat.wdFormatDocument97;
doc.SaveAs(FileName: ref filename, FileFormat: ref format);

doc.Close();
app.Application.Quit();
```

That's much better, although it's still ugly to have to create local variables for the `SaveAs` arguments you *are* specifying. Also, if you've been reading carefully, you may be concerned about the optional parameters that have been removed. They were `ref` parameters—but optional—which isn't a combination C# normally supports. What's going on?

13.2.3 *When is a ref parameter not a ref parameter?*

C# normally takes a pretty strict line on `ref` parameters. You have to mark the argument with `ref` as well as the parameter, to show that you understand what's going on—that your variable may have its value changed by the method you're calling. That's all fine in normal code, but COM APIs often use `ref` parameters for almost *everything*, for perceived performance reasons—they usually don't modify the variable you pass in. Passing arguments by reference is slightly painful in C#. Not only do you have to specify the `ref` modifier, you also must have a variable. You can't just pass *values* by reference.

In C# 4, the compiler makes this a lot easier by letting you pass an argument by value into a COM method, even if it's for a `ref` parameter. Consider a call like this, where `argument` might happen to be a variable of type `string`, but the parameter is declared as `ref object`:

```
comObject.SomeMethod(argument);
```

The compiler emits code that's equivalent to this:

```
object tmp = argument;
comObject.SomeMethod(ref tmp);
```

Note that any changes made by `SomeMethod` are discarded, so the call really does behave as if you were passing `argument` by value. This same process is used for optional `ref` parameters; each involves a local variable initialized to `Type.Missing` and passed by reference into the COM method. If you decompile the slimlined C# code, you'll see that the IL emitted is pretty bulky with all of those extra variables.

You can now apply the finishing touches to the Word example, as shown in the following listing.

Listing 13.10 Passing arguments by value in COM methods

```
Application app = new Application { Visible = true };
app.Documents.Add();
Document doc = app.ActiveDocument;
Paragraph para = doc.Paragraphs.Add();
para.Range.Text = "Thank goodness for C# 4";
doc.SaveAs(FileName: "test.doc",                    ◁── Arguments passed by value
           FileFormat: WdSaveFormat.wdFormatDocument97);
doc.Close();
app.Application.Quit();
```

As you can see, the final result is much cleaner code than you started with. With an API like Word, you still need to work through a somewhat bewildering set of methods, properties, and events in the core types, such as `Application` and `Document`, but at least your code will be a lot easier to read.

In terms of changes to source code, there's one final aspect of the COM support to look at before we move on to the deployment improvements available in C# 4.

13.2.4 *Calling named indexers*

Several aspects of C# 4 provide support for features that Visual Basic has enjoyed for a long time, and this is another one. The CLR, COM, and Visual Basic all permit nondefault properties with parameters—*named indexers* in C# terms. Until version 4, C# has not only forbidden you to directly declare your own named indexers,[5] but it hasn't provided a way of *accessing* them using property syntax either. The only indexer you can use from C# is the one declared as the *default property* for the type. This hasn't been a great issue for .NET components written in Visual Basic, as named indexers are generally discouraged. But COM components, such as those for Office, use them more heavily. C# 4 allows you to call named indexers in a more natural fashion, but you still can't declare them for your own C# types.

> **TERMINOLOGY CLASHES AGAIN**   I've used the term *indexer* throughout this section to describe what in VB terms would be known as a *parameterized property*. The CLI specification calls it an *indexed property*. Whatever the terminology, it's declared as a property in the IL, and it has parameters. The normal indexer (as far as C# is concerned) is defined by the *default member* (or *default property*) for the type—for example, the default member of StringBuilder is the Chars property (which has an Int32 parameter). When I talk about *named indexers* here, I'm talking about ones that *aren't* the default for the type, so you have to refer to them by name.

We'll use Word for the example again, this time showing the different meanings for words. The _Application type in Word defines an indexer called SynonymInfo with a declaration like this:

```
SynonymInfo SynonymInfo[string Word,
                    ref object LanguageId = Type.Missing]
```

That's not valid C# syntax, because you can't declare a named indexer, but hopefully it's obvious what it means. The name of the indexer is SynonymInfo. It *returns* a reference to a SynonymInfo object and has two parameters, one of which is optional. (The fact that the name of the indexer and the name of the return type are the same in this case is entirely coincidental.)

The SynonymInfo can be used to find meanings for the word and synonyms for each meaning. The following listing shows three different ways of using the indexer to display the number of meanings for three different words.

---

[5] Directly, anyway. You can apply System.Runtime.CompilerServices.IndexerNameAttribute manually, but it's not something that C# is aware of as a language.

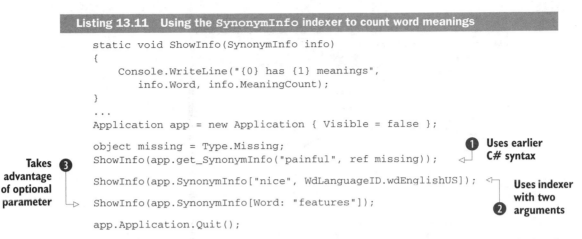

Listing 13.11 Using the `SynonymInfo` indexer to count word meanings

```
static void ShowInfo(SynonymInfo info)
{
    Console.WriteLine("{0} has {1} meanings",
        info.Word, info.MeaningCount);
}
...
Application app = new Application { Visible = false };

object missing = Type.Missing;                                 ❶ Uses earlier
ShowInfo(app.get_SynonymInfo("painful", ref missing));    ⟵      C# syntax

ShowInfo(app.SynonymInfo["nice", WdLanguageID.wdEnglishUS]);  ⟵  Uses indexer
                                                                  with two
ShowInfo(app.SynonymInfo[Word: "features"]);                  ❷ arguments

app.Application.Quit();
```

Takes ❸ advantage of optional parameter

Even without named indexers, the previous features you've seen would've helped alleviate the pain of the earlier C# syntax ❶; you could've called `app.get_SynonymInfo("better")` and taken advantage of optional parameters, for example. But you can see from the second and third `ShowInfo` calls (❷ and ❸) that the indexer syntax looks less awkward than the `get_` call. You could argue that this should be a method call anyway, or that there should be a parameterless `SynonymInfo` property that returns a collection with an appropriate default indexer. That's one case of the general argument given by the C# designers for not implementing *full* support for named indexers, including declaring them within C#. But the point is that it already is an indexer in Word, so it's nice to be able to use it that way.[6] The second `ShowInfo` call ❷ uses the implicit `ref` parameter feature from section 13.2.3, and the third ❸ omits the optional parameter and names the remaining argument just for kicks.

There's one slight twist to optional parameters and indexers: if *all* of the parameters are optional, and you don't want to specify any arguments, you have to omit the square brackets. Instead of writing `foo.Indexer[]`, you'd use `foo.Indexer`. All of this applies both for getting from the indexer and setting to it.

So far, so good—but writing the code is only part of the battle. You usually need to be able to deploy it onto other machines as well. Again, C# 4 makes this task easier.

13.2.5 Linking primary interop assemblies

When you build against a COM type, you use an assembly generated for the component library. Usually you use a *Primary Interop Assembly* (PIA), which is the canonical interop assembly for a COM library, signed by the publisher. You can generate these using the Type Library Importer tool (`tlbimp`) for your own COM libraries. PIAs make life easier in terms of having one true way of accessing the COM types, but they're a pain in other ways. They can be quite large, and the whole PIA needs to be present

---

[6] It might've been more interesting to display the actual meanings, but that leads to interop problems that aren't relevant to this chapter.

Properties   ▼ ⊕ ×

Microsoft.Office.Interop.Word Reference Properties   ▾

(Name)	Microsoft.Office.Interop.Word
Aliases	**global**
Copy Local	False
Culture	
Description	
Embed Interop Types	**True**
File Type	Assembly
Identity	Microsoft.Office.Interop.Word
Path	C:\Program Files\Microsoft Visual Studio
Resolved	True
Runtime Version	v1.1.4322
Specific Version	**True**
Strong Name	True
Version	12.0.0.0

Figure 13.4   Linking PIAs in Visual Studio 2010

even if you're only using a small subset of the functionality. Also, you need to have the same version of the PIA on the deployment machine as the one you compiled against. This can be awkward in situations where licensing issues prevent you from redistributing the PIA itself, relying on the right version being installed already. If there are a number of versions available, but they all expose the functionality you need, you might have to ship different versions of *your* code to make the references work.

C# 4 allows a very different approach. Instead of *referencing* a PIA like any other assembly, you can *link* it. In Visual Studio 2010 and higher, this is an option in the properties of the assembly reference, as shown in figure 13.4.

Command-line fans can use the /l (or /link) option instead of /r (or /reference) to link instead of reference:

```
csc /l:Path\To\PIA.dll MyCode.cs
```

When you link a PIA, the compiler embeds just the bits it needs from the PIA directly into your own assembly. It only takes the types it needs, and only the members within those types. For example, the compiler creates these types for the code we've looked at in this chapter:

```
namespace Microsoft.Office.Interop.Word
{
    [ComImport, TypeIdentifier, CompilerGenerated, Guid("...")]
    public interface _Application

    [ComImport, TypeIdentifier, CompilerGenerated, Guid("...")]
    public interface _Document

    [ComImport, CompilerGenerated, TypeIdentifier, Guid("...")]
    public interface Application : _Application

    [ComImport, Guid("..."), TypeIdentifier, CompilerGenerated]
    public interface Document : _Document
```

```
[ComImport, TypeIdentifier, CompilerGenerated, Guid("...")]
public interface Documents : IEnumerable

[TypeIdentifier("...", "WdSaveFormat"), CompilerGenerated]
public enum WdSaveFormat
}
```

If you look in the _Application interface, it looks like this:

```
[ComImport, TypeIdentifier, CompilerGenerated, Guid("...")]
public interface _Application
{
    void_VtblGap 1_4();
    Documents Documents { [...] get; }
    void_VtblGap2_1();
    Document ActiveDocument { [...] get; }
}
```

I've omitted the GUIDs and the property attributes here just for the sake of space, but you can always use Reflector to look at the embedded types. These are just interfaces and enums—there's no implementation. Whereas a normal PIA has a CoClass representing the actual implementation (but proxying everything to the real COM type, of course), when the compiler needs to create an instance of a COM type via a linked PIA, it creates the instance using the GUID associated with the type. For example, the line in the Word example that creates an instance of Application is translated into this code when linking is enabled:[7]

```
Application application = (Application) Activator.CreateInstance(
    Type.GetTypeFromCLSID (new Guid("...")));
```

Figure 13.5 shows how this works at execution time.

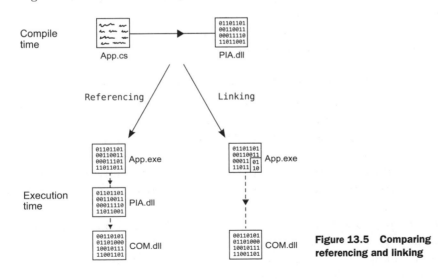

Figure 13.5 Comparing referencing and linking

---

[7] Well, nearly. The object initializer makes it slightly more complicated, because the compiler uses an extra temporary variable.

There are various benefits to embedding type libraries:

- Deployment is easier: the original PIA isn't needed, so you don't have to rely on the right version being present already, or have to ship the PIA yourself.
- Versioning is simpler: as long as you only use members from the version of the COM library that's *actually* installed, it doesn't matter if you compile against an earlier or later PIA.
- Variants are treated as dynamic types, reducing the amount of casting required.

Don't worry about the last point for now—I need to explain dynamic typing before it'll make much sense. All will be revealed in the next chapter.

As you can see, Microsoft has really taken COM interoperability seriously for C# 4, making the whole development process less painful. Of course, the degree of pain has always been variable depending on the COM library you're developing against—some will benefit more than others from the new features.

The next feature is entirely separate from COM, named arguments, and optional parameters, but again it eases development a bit.

13.3   *Generic variance for interfaces and delegates*

You may remember that in chapter 3 I mentioned that the CLR had some support for variance in generic types, but that C# hadn't exposed that support yet. That's changed with C# 4. C# has gained the syntax required to declare generic variance, and the compiler now knows about the possible conversions for interfaces and delegates.

This isn't a life-changing feature—it's more a case of flattening some speed bumps you may have hit occasionally. It doesn't even remove all the bumps; there are various limitations, mostly in the name of keeping generics absolutely type-safe. But it's still a nice feature to have up your sleeve.

Just in case you need a reminder of what variance is all about, let's start with a recap of the two basic forms it comes in.

13.3.1   *Types of variance: covariance and contravariance*

In essence, variance is about being able to use an object of one type as if it were another, in a type-safe way. You're used to variance in terms of normal inheritance: if a method has a declared return type of `Stream`, you can return a `MemoryStream` from the implementation, for example. Generic variance is the same concept, but applied to generics, where it becomes a bit more complicated. The variance is applied to the type parameters within the interfaces and delegate types. That's the bit you need to concentrate on.

Ultimately, it doesn't matter whether you remember the terminology I'll use in this section. It'll be useful while you're reading the chapter, but you're unlikely to find yourself needing it in conversation. The concepts are far more important.

There are two types of variance: *covariance* and *contravariance*. They're essentially the same idea but are used in the context of values moving in different directions. We'll start with covariance, which is generally easier to understand.

COVARIANCE: VALUES COMING OUT OF AN API

Covariance is all about values being returned from an operation back to the caller. Let's imagine a very simple generic interface representing the factory pattern. It has a single method, `CreateInstance`, which will return an instance of the appropriate type. Here's the code:

```
interface IFactory<T>
{
    T CreateInstance();
}
```

Now, `T` only occurs once in the interface (aside from the name). It's only used as the *return value*—it's the *output* of the method. That means it makes sense to be able to treat a factory of a specific type as a factory of a more general type. To put it in real-world terms, you can think of a pizza factory as a food factory.

CONTRAVARIANCE: VALUES GOING INTO AN API

Contravariance is the opposite way around. It's about values being passed *into* the API by the caller: the API is consuming the values instead of producing them. Let's imagine another simple interface—one that can pretty-print a particular document type to the console. Again, there's just one method, this time called `Print`:

```
interface IPrettyPrinter<T>
{
    void Print(T document);
}
```

This time `T` only occurs in the *input* positions in the interface, as a parameter. To put this into concrete terms again, if you had an implementation of `IPrettyPrinter <SourceCode>`, you should be able to use it as an `IPrettyPrinter<CSharpCode>`.

INVARIANCE: VALUES GOING BOTH WAYS

If covariance applies when values only come *out* of an API, and contravariance applies when values only go *into* the API, what happens when a value goes both ways? In short: nothing. That type would be *invariant.*

Here's an interface representing a type that can serialize and deserialize a data type:

```
interface IStorage<T>
{
    byte[] Serialize(T value);
    T Deserialize(byte[] data);
}
```

This time, if you have an instance of `IStorage<T>` for a particular type `T`, you can't treat it as an implementation of the interface for either a more or less specific type. If you try to use it in a covariant way (for example, using an `IStorage<Customer>` as an `IStorage<Person>`), you might make a call to `Serialize` with an object that it can't handle. Similarly, if you try to use it in a contravariant way, you might get an unexpected type out when you deserialized some data.

If it helps, you can think of invariance as being like `ref` parameters; to pass a variable by reference, it has to be *exactly* the same type as the parameter itself, because the value goes into the method and effectively comes out again too.

13.3.2 *Using variance in interfaces*

C# 4 allows you to specify in the declaration of a generic interface or delegate that a type parameter can be used covariantly by using the `out` modifier, or contravariantly using the `in` modifier. Once the type has been declared, the relevant types of conversion are available implicitly. This works exactly the same way in both interfaces and delegates, but I'll show them separately for clarity. Let's start with interfaces, as they may be a bit more familiar and we've used them already to describe variance.

> **VARIANT CONVERSIONS ARE REFERENCE CONVERSIONS**   Any conversion using variance or covariance is a *reference conversion*, which means that the same reference is returned after the conversion. It doesn't create a new object; it just treats the existing reference as if it matched the target type. This is the same as casting between reference types in a hierarchy: if you cast a `Stream` to `MemoryStream` (or use the implicit conversion the other way), there's still just one object. The nature of these conversions introduces some limitations, as you'll see later, but it means they're efficient, and it makes the behavior easier to understand in terms of object identity.

This time we'll use familiar interfaces to demonstrate the ideas, with some simple user-defined types for the type arguments.

EXPRESSING VARIANCE WITH IN AND OUT

There are two interfaces that demonstrate variance particularly effectively: `IEnumerable<T>` is covariant in `T`, and `IComparer<T>` is contravariant in `T`. Here are their new type declarations in .NET 4:

```
public interface IEnumerable<out T>
public interface IComparer<in T>
```

It's easy enough to remember: if a type parameter is only used for output, you can use `out`; if it's only used for input, you can use `in`. The compiler doesn't know whether you can remember which form is called covariance and which is called contravariance!

Unfortunately, the framework doesn't contain many inheritance hierarchies that would help me demonstrate variance particularly clearly, so I'll fall back to the standard object-oriented example of shapes. The downloadable source code includes the definitions for `IShape`, `Circle`, and `Square`, which are fairly obvious. The interface exposes properties for the bounding box of the shape and its area. I'll use two lists a lot in the following examples, so I'll show their construction code just for reference:

```
List<Circle> circles = new List<Circle>
{
    new Circle(new Point(0, 0), 15),
    new Circle(new Point(10, 5), 20),
};

List<Square> squares = new List<Square>
{
    new Square(new Point(5, 10), 5),
    new Square(new Point(-10, 0), 2)
};
```

The only important point concerns the types of the variables—they're declared as List<Circle> and List<Square> rather than List<IShape>. This can often be useful—if you were to access the list of circles elsewhere, you might want to get at circle-specific members without having to cast, for example. The actual values involved in the construction code are entirely irrelevant; I'll use the names circles and squares elsewhere to refer to the same lists, but without duplicating the code.[8]

USING INTERFACE COVARIANCE

To demonstrate covariance, we'll try to build a list of shapes from a list of circles and a list of squares. The following listing shows two different approaches, neither of which would've worked in C# 3.

Listing 13.12 Using variance to build a list of general shapes from specific lists

```
List<IShape> shapesByAdding = new List<IShape>();        ⟵❶ Adds lists directly
shapesByAdding.AddRange(circles);
shapesByAdding.AddRange(squares);                        Uses LINQ for concatenation ❷

List<IShape> shapesByConcat = circles.Concat<IShape>(squares).ToList();   ⟵┘
```

Effectively, listing 13.12 shows covariance in four places, each converting a sequence of circles or squares into a sequence of general shapes, as far as the type system is concerned. First you create a new List<IShape> and call AddRange to add the circle and square lists to it ❶. (You could've passed one of them into the constructor instead, and then called AddRange once.) The parameter for List<T>.AddRange is of type IEnumerable<T>, so in this case you're treating each list as an IEnumerable <IShape>—something that wouldn't have been possible before. AddRange *could* have been written as a generic method with its own type parameter, but it wasn't—doing this would've made some optimizations hard or impossible.

Another way of creating a list that contains the data in two existing sequences is to use LINQ ❷. You can't directly call circles.Concat(squares), as it would confuse the type inference mechanism, but by specifying the type argument explicitly, all is well. Both circles and squares are implicitly converted to IEnumerable<IShape> via covariance. This conversion isn't actually changing the value—just how the compiler

---

[8] In the full source code solution, these are exposed as properties on the static Shapes class, but in the snippets version I've included the construction code where it's needed, so you can tweak it easily if you want to.

treats the value. It isn't building a separate copy, which is the important point. Covariance is particularly important in LINQ to Objects, because so much of the API is expressed in terms of IEnumerable<T>—contravariance isn't as important, because fewer of the types involved are contravariant.

In C# 3 there would certainly have been other ways to approach the same problem. You could've built List<IShape> instances instead of List<Circle> and List<Square> for the original shapes; you could've used the LINQ Cast operator to convert the specific lists to more general ones; you could've written your own list class with a generic AddRange method. But none of these would've been as convenient or as efficient as the alternatives offered here.

USING INTERFACE CONTRAVARIANCE

We'll use the same shape types to demonstrate contravariance. This time we'll only use the list of circles, but a comparer that's able to compare *any* two shapes by just comparing the areas. We couldn't do this before C# 4 because an IComparer<IShape> couldn't be used as an IComparer<Circle>, but the following listing shows contravariance coming to the rescue.

Listing 13.13 Sorting circles using a general-purpose comparer and contravariance

```
class AreaComparer : IComparer<IShape>          ◁─❶ Compares shapes by area
{
    public int Compare(IShape x, IShape y)
    {
        return x.Area.CompareTo(y.Area);
    }
}
...
IComparer<IShape> areaComparer = new AreaComparer();          ❷ Sorts using
circles.Sort(areaComparer);                                      contravariance
```

There's nothing complicated here. The AreaComparer class ❶ is about as simple as an implementation of IComparer<T> can be; it doesn't need any state, for example. There'd normally be some null handling in the Compare method, but that's not necessary to demonstrate variance.

Once you have an IComparer<IShape>, you use it to sort a list of circles ❷. The argument to circles.Sort needs to be an IComparer<Circle>, but contravariance allows you to convert your comparer implicitly. It's as simple as that.

> **SURPRISE, SURPRISE** If someone had presented you with this code as if it were C# 3, you might've looked at it and expected it to work. It seems obvious that it *should* be able to work, and this is a common feeling; the invariance in C# 2 and 3 often is an unwelcome surprise. The new abilities of C# 4 in this area aren't introducing new concepts you'd never have thought of before; they just allow you more flexibility.

These have both been simple examples using single-method interfaces, but the same principles apply for more complex APIs. Of course, the more complex the interface is, the more likely that a type parameter will be used for both input and output, which would make it invariant. We'll come back to some tricky examples later, but first we'll look at delegates.

13.3.3 *Using variance in delegates*

Now that you've seen how to use variance with interfaces, applying the same knowledge to delegates is easy. We'll use some familiar types again:

```
delegate T Func<out T>()
delegate void Action<in T>(T obj)
```

These are really equivalent to the `IFactory<T>` and `IPrettyPrinter<T>` interfaces we started off with. Using lambda expressions, we can demonstrate both of these easily, and even chain the two together. The following listing shows an example using the shape types.

Listing 13.14 Using variance with simple `Func<T>` and `Action<T>` delegates

```
Func<Square> squareFactory = () => new Square(new Point(5, 5), 10);
Func<IShape> shapeFactory = squareFactory;              Converts Func<T>
                                                      ❶ using covariance

Action<IShape> shapePrinter = shape => Console.WriteLine(shape.Area);
Action<Square> squarePrinter = shapePrinter;            Converts Action<T>
                                                      ❷ using contravariance

squarePrinter(squareFactory());      ◁── Sanity checking...
shapePrinter(shapeFactory());
```

Hopefully by now the code will need little explanation. The square factory always produces a square at the same position, with sides of length 10. Covariance allows you to treat a square factory as a general shape factory with no fuss ❶. You then create a general-purpose action that prints out the area of whatever shape is given to it. This time you use a contravariant conversion to treat the action as one that can be applied to any square ❷. Finally, you feed the square action with the result of calling the square factory, and the shape action with the result of calling the shape factory. Both print `100`, as you'd expect.

Of course, you've only used delegates with a single type parameter here. What happens if you use delegates or interfaces with multiple type parameters? What about type arguments that are themselves generic delegate types? Well, it can all get quite complicated.

13.3.4 *Complex situations*

Before I try to make your head spin, I should provide a little comfort. Although we'll do some weird and wonderful things in this section, the compiler will stop you from making mistakes. You may still get confused by the error messages if you've used several type parameters in funky ways, but once you have it compiling, you should be safe. Complexity is possible in both the delegate and interface forms of variance, although the delegate version is usually more concise to work with. Let's start off with a relatively simple example.

SIMULTANEOUS COVARIANCE AND CONTRAVARIANCE WITH CONVERTER<TINPUT, TOUTPUT> The `Converter<TInput, TOutput>` delegate type has been around since .NET 2.0. It's effectively `Func<T, TResult>`, but with a clearer expected purpose. In .NET 4 this becomes `Converter<in TInput, out TOutput>`, which shows which type parameter has which kind of variance.

The following listing shows a few combinations of variance using a simple converter.

Listing 13.15   Demonstrating covariance and contravariance with a single type

```
Converter<object, string> converter = x => x.ToString();   ◁   Converts
Converter<string, string> contravariance = converter;              objects to
Converter<object, object> covariance = converter;          ❶   strings
Converter<string, object> both = converter;
```

❷ Converts strings to objects

Listing 13.15 shows the variance conversions available on a delegate of type `Converter<object, string>`—a delegate that takes any object and produces a string. First you implement the delegate using a simple lambda expression that calls `ToString` ❶. As it happens, you never actually *call* the delegate, so you could've used a null reference, but I find it easier to think about variance if you can pin down a concrete action that *would* happen if you called it.

The next two lines are relatively straightforward, as long as you only concentrate on one type parameter at a time. The `TInput` type parameter is only used in an input position, so it makes sense that you can use it contravariantly, using a `Converter<object, string>` as a `Converter<Button, string>`. In other words, if you can pass *any* object reference into the converter, you can certainly hand it a `Button` reference. Likewise, the `TOutput` type parameter is only used in an output position (the return type), so it makes sense to use that covariantly; if the converter always returns a string reference, you can safely use it where you only need to guarantee that it'll return an object reference.

The final line is just a logical extension of this idea ❷. It uses both contravariance and covariance in the same conversion to end up with a converter that only accepts buttons and only declares that it'll return an object reference. Note that you *can't* convert this back to the original conversion type without a cast—you've essentially relaxed the guarantees at every point, and you can't tighten them up again implicitly.

Let's up the ante a little and see just how complex things can get if you try hard enough.

HIGHER-ORDER FUNCTION INSANITY

The really weird stuff starts happening when you combine variant types together. I won't go into a lot of detail here—I just want you to appreciate the potential for complexity.

Let's look at four delegate declarations:

```
delegate Func<T> FuncFunc<out T>();
delegate void ActionAction<out T>(Action<T> action);
delegate void ActionFunc<in T>(Func<T> function);
delegate Action<T> FuncAction<in T>();
```

Each of these declarations is equivalent to nesting one of the standard delegates inside another. For example, `FuncAction<T>` is equivalent to `Func<Action<T>>`. Both represent a function that will return an `Action` that can be passed a `T`. But should this be covariant or contravariant? Well, the function is going to *return* something to do with `T`, so it sounds covariant, but that something then *takes* a `T`, so it sounds contravariant. The answer is that the delegate *is* contravariant in `T`, which is why it's declared with the `in` modifier.

As a quick rule of thumb, you can think of nested contravariance as reversing the previous variance, whereas covariance doesn't, so whereas `Action<Action<T>>` is covariant in `T`, `Action<Action<Action<T>>>` is contravariant. Compare that with `Func<T>` variance, where you can write `Func<Func<Func<...Func<T>...>>>` with as many levels of nesting as you like and still get covariance.

Just to give a similar example using interfaces, imagine you have something that can compare sequences. If it can compare two sequences of arbitrary objects, it can certainly compare two sequences of strings, but not vice versa. Converting this to code (without implementing the interface!), you can see this as follows:

```
IComparer<IEnumerable<object>> objectsComparer = ...;
IComparer<IEnumerable<string>> stringsComparer = objectsComparer;
```

This conversion is legal: `IEnumerable<string>` is a "smaller" type than `IEnumerable<object>` due to the covariance of `IEnumerable<T>`. The contravariance of `IComparer<T>` then allows the conversion from a comparer of a "bigger" type to a comparer of a smaller type.

Of course, we've only looked at delegates and interfaces with a single type parameter in this section—it can all apply to multiple type parameters too. Don't worry, though: you're unlikely to need this sort of brain-busting variance very often, and when you do, you have the compiler to help you. I really just wanted to make you aware of the possibilities.

On the flip side, there are some things you may expect to be able to do, but that aren't supported.

13.3.5 *Restrictions and notes*

The variance support provided by C# 4 is mostly limited by what's provided by the CLR. It'd be hard for the language to support conversions that were prohibited by the underlying platform. This can lead to a few surprises.

NO VARIANCE FOR TYPE PARAMETERS IN CLASSES

Only interfaces and delegates can have variant type parameters. Even if you have a class that only uses the type parameter for input (or only uses it for output), you can't specify the `in` or `out` modifiers. For example, `Comparer<T>`, the common implementation of `IComparer<T>`, is invariant—there's no conversion from `Comparer<IShape>` to `Comparer<Circle>`.

Aside from any implementation difficulties that this might've incurred, I'd say it makes a certain amount of sense conceptually. Interfaces represent a way of looking at an object from a particular perspective, whereas classes are more rooted in the object's *actual* type. This argument is weakened somewhat by inheritance letting you treat an object as an instance of any of the classes in its inheritance hierarchy, admittedly. Either way, the CLR doesn't allow it.

VARIANCE ONLY SUPPORTS REFERENCE CONVERSIONS

You can't use variance between two arbitrary type arguments just because there's a conversion between them. It has to be a *reference conversion*. Basically, that limits it to conversions that operate on reference types and that don't affect the binary representation of the reference. This is so that the CLR can know that operations will be type-safe without having to inject any actual conversion code anywhere. As I mentioned in section 13.3.2, variant conversions are themselves reference conversions, so there wouldn't be anywhere for the extra code to go anyway.

In particular, this restriction prohibits any conversions of value types and user-defined conversions. For example, the following conversions are all invalid:

- `IEnumerable<int>` to `IEnumerable<object>`—Boxing conversion
- `IEnumerable<short>` to `IEnumerable<int>`—Value type conversion
- `IEnumerable<string>` to `IEnumerable<XName>`—User-defined conversion

User-defined conversions aren't likely to be a problem as they're relatively rare, but you may find the restriction around value types a pain.

OUT PARAMETERS AREN'T OUTPUT POSITIONS

This one came as a surprise to me, although it makes sense in retrospect. Consider a delegate with the following definition:

```
delegate bool TryParser<T>(string input, out T value)
```

You might expect that you could make `T` covariant—after all, it's only used in an output position...or is it?

The CLR doesn't really know about `out` parameters. As far as it's concerned, they're just `ref` parameters with an `[Out]` attribute applied to them. C# attaches special meaning to the attribute in terms of definite assignment, but the CLR doesn't. `ref` parameters mean data going both ways, so if you have a `ref` parameter of type `T`, that means `T` is invariant.

In fact, even if the CLR did support out parameters natively, it still wouldn't be safe, because it can be used in an input position within the method itself; after you've written to the variable, you can read from it as well. It'd be okay if out parameters were treated as "copy value at return time," but it essentially aliases the argument and parameter, which would cause problems if they weren't exactly the same type. It's slightly fiddly to demonstrate, but there's an example on the book's website.

Delegates and interfaces using out parameters are rare, so this may never affect you anyway, but it's worth knowing about just in case.

VARIANCE HAS TO BE EXPLICIT

When I introduced the syntax for expressing variance—applying the in or out modifiers to type parameters—you may have wondered why you needed to bother at all. The compiler is able to *check* that whatever variance you try to apply is valid, so why doesn't it just apply it automatically?

It *could* do that—at least, in many cases—but I'm glad it doesn't. Normally you can add methods to an interface and only affect implementations rather than callers. But if you've declared that a type parameter is variant and you then want to add a method that breaks that variance, all the *callers* are affected too. I can see this causing a lot of confusion. Variance requires some thought about what you might want to do in the future, and forcing developers to explicitly include the modifier encourages them to plan carefully before committing to variance.

There's less of an argument for this explicit nature when it comes to delegates; any change to the signature that would affect the variance would probably break existing uses anyway. But there's a lot to be said for consistency—it would feel odd if you had to specify the variance in interfaces but not in delegate declarations.

BEWARE OF BREAKING CHANGES

Whenever new conversions become available, there's the risk of your current code breaking. For instance, if you rely on the results of the is or as operators *not* allowing for variance, your code will behave differently when running under .NET 4. Likewise, there are cases where overload resolution will choose a different method due to there being more applicable options now. This is another reason for variance to be explicitly specified: it reduces the risk of breaking your code.

These situations should be quite rare, and the benefit from variance is more significant than the potential drawbacks. You *do* have unit tests to catch subtle changes, right? In all seriousness, the C# team takes code breakage very seriously, but sometimes there's no way of introducing a new feature without breaking code.

MULTICAST DELEGATES AND VARIANCE DON'T MIX

Normally, generics make sure that unless you have casts involved, you won't run into type-safety issues at execution time. Unfortunately, there's a nasty situation with variant delegate types when it comes to combining them together. This is best demonstrated in code:

```
Func<string> stringFunc = () => "";
Func<object> objectFunc = () => new object();
Func<object> combined = objectFunc + stringFunc;
```

This compiles with no problem because there's a covariant reference conversion from an expression of type Func<string> to Func<object>. But the object itself is still a Func<string>, and the Delegate.Combine method that does the work requires its arguments to be the same type—otherwise it doesn't know what type of delegate it's meant to create. The preceding code will throw an ArgumentException at execution time.

This problem was found relatively late in the .NET 4 release cycle, but Microsoft is aware of it, and there's hope that it may be fixed for the majority of cases in a future release (it wasn't fixed in .NET 4.5). Until then, there's a workaround: you can create a new delegate object of the correct type based on the variant one, and combine that with another delegate of the same type. For example, you can modify the preceding code slightly to make it work:

```
Func<string> stringFunc = () => "";
Func<object> defensiveCopy = new Func<object>(stringFunc);
Func<object> objectFunc = () => new object();
Func<object> combined = objectFunc + defensiveCopy;
```

Fortunately, this is rarely an issue, in my experience.

NO CALLER-SPECIFIED OR PARTIAL VARIANCE

This is really a matter of interest and comparison rather than anything else, but it's worth noting that C#'s variance is *very* different from Java's system. Java's generic variance manages to be extremely flexible by approaching it from the other side: instead of the type itself declaring the variance, code *using* the type can express the variance it needs.

> **WANT TO KNOW MORE?**   This book isn't about Java generics, but if this little teaser has piqued your interest, you may want to check out Angelika Langer's "Java Generics FAQs" (http://mng.bz/3qgO). Be warned: it's a huge and complex topic!

For example, the List<T> interface in Java is roughly equivalent to IList<T> in C#. It contains methods to both add items and fetch them, so clearly in C# it's invariant, but in Java you can decorate the type at the calling code to explain what variance you want. The compiler then stops you from using the members that go against that variance. For example, the following code would be perfectly valid:

```
List<Shape> shapes1 = new ArrayList<Shape>();
List<? super Square> squares = shapes1;          Declaration using
squares.add(new Square(10, 10, 20, 20));         contravariance

List<Circle> circles = new ArrayList<Circle>();
circles.add(new Circle(10, 10, 20));
List<? extends Shape> shapes2 = circles;         Declaration using
Shape shape = shapes2.get(0);                    covariance
```

For the most part, I prefer generics in C# to Java, and type erasure in particular can be a pain in many cases. But I find this treatment of variance really interesting. I don't expect to see anything similar in future versions of C#, so think carefully about how you can split your interfaces to allow for flexibility, but without introducing more complexity than is really warranted.

Just before I close the chapter, there are two almost trivial changes to cover—how the C# compiler handles `lock` statements and field-like events.

13.4 Teeny tiny changes to locking and field-like events

I don't want to make too much of these changes; chances are they'll never affect you. But if you're ever looking at compiled code and wondering why it looks the way it does, it's helpful to know what's going on.

13.4.1 Robust locking

Let's consider a simple piece of C# code that uses a lock. The details of what happens inside the block aren't important, but I've included a single statement just for the sake of clarity:

```
lock (listLock)
{
    list.Add("item");
}
```

Prior to C# 4—and including C# 4 if you're targeting anything earlier than .NET 4—that would effectively be compiled into this code:

```
object tmp = listLock;
Monitor.Enter(tmp);
try
{
    list.Add("item");
}
finally
{
    Monitor.Exit(tmp);
}
```

❶ Copies reference for locking

◁ Acquires lock before try

Releases lock whatever Add does ◁

This is *nearly* okay—in particular, it avoids a couple of problems. You want to make sure that you release the same monitor you acquire, so first you copy the reference into a temporary local variable ❶. This also means that the locking expression is only evaluated once. Next you acquire the lock *before* the `try` block. This is so that you don't try to release the lock in the `finally` block if the thread is aborted without successfully acquiring it in the first place. That leads to a different problem: now if the thread is aborted *after* the lock is acquired but *before* you enter the `try` block, you won't have released the lock. That could feasibly lead to a deadlock—another thread could be waiting eternally for this one to release the lock. Though the CLR has historically tried hard to stop this from happening, it's not quite impossible.

What you want is some way of atomically acquiring the lock and knowing that it was acquired. Fortunately that's exposed in .NET 4 via a new overload to `Monitor.Enter`, which the C# 4 compiler uses in this way:

```
bool acquired = false;
object tmp = listLock;
try
{
    Monitor.Enter(tmp, ref acquired);      <--- Acquires lock inside try block
    list.Add("item");
}
finally
{
    if (acquired)
    {                                      | Conditionally
        Monitor.Release(tmp);              | releases lock
    }
}
```

Now the lock will be released if and only if you successfully acquired it in the first place, consistently.

It should be noted that in some cases a deadlock isn't the worst result; occasionally it's more dangerous for an application to continue at all than for it to simply halt.[9] But it'd be ridiculous to *rely* on the deadlock condition; better to avoid aborting threads if at all possible. (Aborting the currently executing thread is somewhat better, as you're more in control—this is what `Response.Redirect` does in ASP.NET, for example, but I'd still generally suggest finding better forms of flow control.)

There's one last tweak to cover before we move on to the really big feature of C# 4.

13.4.2 Changes to field-like events

There are two changes to the way *field-like events* are implemented in C# 4 that are worth mentioning briefly. They're unlikely to affect you, although they're *potentially* breaking changes.

Just to recap, field-like events are events that are declared as if they're fields, with no explicit add/remove blocks, like this:

```
public event EventHandler Click;
```

First, the way that thread safety is achieved has been changed. Before C# 4, field-like events resulted in code that would lock on either `this` (for instance events) or the declaring type (for static events). As of C# 4, the compiler achieves thread-safe, atomic subscription and unsubscription using `Interlocked.CompareExchange<T>`. Unlike the previous change to the `lock` statement, this applies even when targeting earlier versions of the .NET Framework.

---

[9] Eric Lippert has an excellent blog post on this topic, entitled "Locks and exceptions do not mix": http://mng.bz/Qy7p.

Second, the meaning of the event's name *within the declaring class* has changed. Previously, if you subscribed to (or unsubscribed from) the event within the class that contained the declaration—such as with `Click += DefaultClickHandler;`—that would go straight to the backing field, skipping the add/remove implementation completely. Now it doesn't; when you're using `+=` or `-=`, the name of the event refers to the event itself, not the backing field. When the name is used for any other purpose (typically assignment or invocation), it still refers directly to the backing field.

These are both sensible changes that make everything neater, although you probably wouldn't have noticed them in daily use. Chris Burrows goes into the topic in detail in his blog, if you want to know more (see http://mng.bz/Kyr4).

13.5 Summary

This has been a bit of a pick-and-mix chapter, with various distinct areas. Having said that, COM greatly benefits from named arguments and optional parameters, so there's some overlap between them.

I suspect it'll take a while for C# developers to get the hang of how best to use the new features for parameters and arguments. Overloading still provides extra portability for languages that don't support optional parameters, and named arguments may look strange in some situations until you get used to them. The benefits can be significant, though, as I demonstrated with the example of building instances of immutable types. You'll need to take some care when assigning default values to optional parameters, but I hope that you'll find the suggestion of using `null` as a "default default value" to be a useful and flexible one that effectively sidesteps some of the limitations and pitfalls you might otherwise encounter.

Working with COM has come a *long* way in C# 4. I still prefer to use purely managed solutions where they're available, but at least the code calling into COM is a lot more readable now, as well as having a better deployment story. We haven't looked at all of the improvements to COM interop yet, as the dynamic typing features we'll discuss in the next chapter have an impact on COM too, but even without taking that into account, we've seen a short sample become a lot more pleasant just by applying a few simple steps.

The last major topic in this chapter was the generic variance now available for interfaces and delegates. Sometimes you may end up using variance without even knowing it, and I think most developers are more likely to use the variance declared in the framework interfaces and delegates rather than creating their own. I apologize if it occasionally became tricky, but it's good to know just what's out there. If it's any consolation to you, former C# team member Eric Lippert has publicly acknowledged in a blog post (see http://mng.bz/79d8) that higher-order functions make even *his* head hurt, so you're in good company. Eric's post is one in a long series about variance (see http://mng.bz/94H3), which is, as much as anything, a dialogue about the design decisions involved. If you haven't had enough of variance by now, it's an excellent read.

For the sake of completeness, we also took a quick peek at the changes to how the C# compiler handles locking and field-like events.

This chapter dealt with *relatively* small changes to C#. Chapter 14 deals with something far more fundamental: the ability to use C# in a dynamic manner.

14

Dynamic binding in a static language

This chapter covers

- What it means to be dynamic
- How to use dynamic typing in C# 4
- Examples with COM, Python, and reflection
- How dynamic typing is implemented
- Reacting dynamically

C# has always been a statically typed language, with no exceptions. There have been a few areas where the compiler has looked for particular names rather than interfaces, such as finding appropriate `Add` methods for collection initializers, but there's been nothing truly dynamic in the language beyond normal polymorphism. That changes with C# 4—at least partially. The simplest way of explaining it is that there's a new static type called `dynamic`, which you can try to do almost anything with at compile time and let the framework sort it out at execution time. Of course, there's more to it than that, but that's the executive summary.

Given that C# is still a statically typed language everywhere that you're *not* using `dynamic`, I don't expect fans of dynamic programming to suddenly become C#

409

advocates. That's not why the feature was introduced: it's aimed primarily at interoperability. When dynamic languages such as IronRuby and IronPython joined the .NET ecosystem, it would have been crazy not to be able to call into C# code from IronPython and vice versa. Likewise, developing against COM APIs used to be awkward in C#, with an abundance of casts cluttering the code. Dynamic typing addresses all of these concerns. On the other hand, there are plenty of projects that use dynamic typing within C# to make data access boundaries simpler.

One word of warning that I'll repeat throughout the chapter—it's worth being careful with dynamic typing. It's fun to explore, and it's been well implemented, but I still recommend that you think carefully before using it heavily. Just like any other new feature, weigh the pros and cons rather than rushing into it just because it's neat (which it undoubtedly is). The framework does a fine job of optimizing dynamic code, but it'll be slower than static code in most cases. More important, you lose a lot of compile-time safety. Whereas unit testing will help you find a lot of the mistakes that can crop up when the compiler isn't able to help you much, I still prefer the immediate feedback of the compiler telling me if I'm trying to use a method that doesn't exist or can't be called with a given set of arguments.

On the other hand, there are situations where the level of safety given to you by the compiler isn't very strong to start with. For example, there are far more things that can go wrong with code that uses reflection than just the errors a compiler can spot. If you're trying to invoke a method with its name, does that method exist? Is it accessible to your code? Are you providing appropriate arguments? The compiler can't help you with any of that. The equivalent dynamic code still can't spot those errors at compile time, but at least the code may be considerably easier to read and understand. It's all a matter of using the most appropriate approach for the particular problem you're working on.

Dynamic behavior can be useful in situations where you're naturally dealing with dynamic environments or data, but if you're really looking to write large chunks of your code dynamically, I suggest you use a language where that's the *normal* style instead of the exception. C# is still a language that was *designed* for static typing; languages that have been dynamic from the start often have various features to help you work more productively with dynamic behavior. Now that you can easily call into such languages from C#, you can separate the parts of your code that benefit from a largely dynamic style from those where static typing works better.

I don't want to put too much of a damper on things. Where dynamic typing *is* useful, it can be a lot simpler than the alternatives. In this chapter we'll look at the basic rules of dynamic typing in C# 4, and then dive into some examples: using COM dynamically, calling into some IronPython code, and making reflection a lot simpler. You can do all of this without knowing the details, but once you have the flavor of dynamic typing, we'll look at what's going on under the hood. In particular, we'll discuss the Dynamic Language Runtime and what the C# compiler does when it encounters dynamic code. Finally, you'll see how you can make your own types respond dynamically to method calls, property accesses, and the like. But first, let's take a step back.

14.1 What? When? Why? How?

Before we get to any code showing off this new feature of C# 4, it's worth getting a better handle on why it was introduced in the first place. I don't know any other languages that have gone from being purely static to partially dynamic; this is a significant step in C#'s evolution, whether you use it often or only occasionally.

We'll start by taking a fresh look at what *dynamic* and *static* mean, considering some of the major use cases for dynamic typing in C#, and then we'll delve into how it's implemented in C# 4.

14.1.1 What is dynamic typing?

In chapter 2 I explained the characteristics of a type system and described how C# has previously been a statically typed language. The compiler knows the type of expressions in the code and knows the members available on any type. It applies a fairly complex set of rules to determine which exact member should be used when. This includes overload resolution; the only choice left until later is to pick the implementation of virtual methods depending on the execution-time type of the object. The process of working out which member to use is called *binding*, and in a statically typed language it occurs at compile time.

In a dynamically typed language, all of this binding occurs at execution time. A compiler or parser can check that the code is *syntactically* correct, but it can't check that the methods you call and the properties you access are actually present. It's a bit like a word processor with no dictionary: it may be able to check your punctuation, but not your spelling, so if you're to have any sort of confidence in your code, you really need a good set of unit tests. Some dynamic languages are always interpreted, with no compiler involved at all. Others provide both an interpreter and a compiler, to allow rapid development with a *REPL*—a read, evaluate, print loop.

> **REPL AND C#** Strictly speaking, REPL isn't solely associated with dynamic languages. Some statically typed languages have *interpreters* that compile on the fly. Notably, F# comes with a tool called *F# Interactive*, which does exactly this. But interpreters are much more common for dynamic languages than static ones.
>
> C# does have similar tools: the expression evaluator underlying the Watch and Immediate windows in Visual Studio can be considered a form of REPL, and Mono has a C# Shell (see www.mono-project.com/CsharpRepl).

It's worth noting that the new dynamic features of C# 4 *don't* include interpreting C# source code at execution time; there's no direct equivalent to the JavaScript `eval` function, for example. To execute code based on data in strings, you need to use either the CodeDOM API (and `CSharpCodeProvider` in particular) or simple reflection to invoke individual members. The Roslyn project is another option here, although it's still in Community Technology Preview as I write this.

Of course, the same kind of work has to be done at *some* point in time, no matter what approach you're taking. By asking the compiler to do more work before execution, static systems usually perform better than dynamic ones. Given the downsides I've mentioned so far, you might be wondering why anyone would want to bother with dynamic typing in the first place.

14.1.2 *When is dynamic typing useful, and why?*

Dynamic typing has two important points in its favor. First, if you know the name of a member you want to call, the arguments you want to call it with, and the object you want to call it on, that's all you need. That may sound like all the information you could have anyway, but the C# compiler would normally want to know more. Crucially, in order to identify the member exactly (modulo overriding), it'd need to know the type of the object you're calling it on and the types of the arguments. Sometimes you don't know those types at compile time, even though you *do* know enough to be sure that the member will be present and correct when the code runs.

For example, if you know that the object you're using has a `Length` property you want to use, it doesn't matter whether it's a `String`, a `StringBuilder`, an `Array`, a `Stream`, or any of the other types with that property. You don't need that property to be defined by some common base class or interface, which can be useful if there isn't such a type. This is called *duck typing,* from the notion that "if it walks like a duck and quacks like a duck, I'd call it a duck."[1] Even when there *is* a type that offers everything you need, it can sometimes be irritating to tell the compiler exactly which type you're talking about. This is particularly relevant when using Microsoft Office APIs via COM. Many methods and properties are declared to just return VARIANT, which means that C# code using these calls is often peppered with casts. Duck typing allows you to omit all of these casts, as long as you're confident about what you're doing.

The second important feature of dynamic typing is the ability of an object to respond to a call by analyzing the name and arguments provided to it. It can behave as if the member had been declared by the type in the normal way, even if the member names couldn't possibly be known until execution time. For example, consider the following call:

```
books.FindByAuthor("Joshua Bloch")
```

Normally this would require the `FindByAuthor` member to be declared by the designer of the type involved. In a dynamic data layer, there can be a single smart piece of code to analyze calls like this. It can detect that there's an `Author` property in the associated data (whether that's from a database, XML document, hardcoded data, or anything else) and act accordingly.

---

[1] The Wikipedia article on duck typing has more information about the history of the term: http://en.wikipedia.org/wiki/Duck_typing.

In this case, it would decide that you want to perform a query using the specified argument as the author. In some ways, that's just a more complex way of writing something like this:

```
books.Find("Author", "Joshua Bloch")
```

But the first snippet feels more appropriate; the calling code knows the Author part statically, even if the receiving code doesn't. This approach can be used to mimic domain-specific languages (DSLs) in some situations. It can also be used to create a natural API for exploring data structures such as XML trees.

Another feature of programming with dynamic languages *tends* to be an experimental style of programming using an appropriate interpreter, as I mentioned earlier. This isn't *directly* relevant to C# 4, but the fact that C# 4 can interoperate richly with dynamic languages running on the Dynamic Language Runtime (DLR) means that if you're dealing with a problem that would benefit from this style, you'll be able to use the results directly from C# instead of having to port them to C# afterward.

We'll look at these scenarios in more depth, and at some concrete examples, when we've discussed the basics of C# 4's dynamic abilities. It's worth briefly pointing out that if these benefits *don't* apply to you, dynamic typing is more likely to be a hindrance than a help. Many developers won't need to use dynamic typing much in their day-to-day coding, and even when it *is* required, it may only be for a small part of the code. Just like any feature, it can be overused. In my view, it's usually worth thinking carefully about whether any alternative designs would allow static typing to solve the same problem elegantly. But I'm biased due to having a background in statically typed languages—it's worth reading books on dynamically typed languages such as Python and Ruby to see a wider variety of benefits than the ones I present in this chapter.

You're probably getting anxious to see some real code by now, so we'll just get a brief overview of what's going on, and then dive into some examples.

14.1.3 *How does C# 4 provide dynamic typing?*

C# 4 introduces a new type called `dynamic`. The compiler treats this type differently than any normal CLR type.[2] Any expression that uses a dynamic value causes the compiler to change its behavior radically. Instead of trying to work out *exactly* what the code means, binding each member access appropriately, performing overload resolution, and so on, the compiler just parses the source code to work out what *kind* of operation you're trying to perform, its name, what arguments are involved, and any other relevant information. Instead of emitting IL to execute the code directly, the compiler generates code that calls into the DLR with all the required information. The rest of the work is performed at execution time.

---

[2] In fact, `dynamic` doesn't represent a specific CLR type. It's really just `System.Object` in conjunction with `System.Dynamic.DynamicAttribute`. We'll look at this in more detail in section 14.4, but for the moment you can pretend it's a real type.

In many ways, this is similar to the different kinds of code generated by lambda expression conversions. These can either result in code to perform the required actions (when converting to a delegate type) or result in code that builds a *description* of the required actions (when converting to an expression tree). You'll see later that expression trees are extremely important in the DLR, and often the C# compiler will use expression trees to describe the code. (In the simplest cases, where there's nothing but a member invocation, there's no need for an expression tree.)

When the DLR comes to bind the relevant call at execution time, it goes through a complicated process to determine what should happen. This not only has to take into account the normal C# rules for method overloads and so on, but also the possibility that the object itself will want to be part of the decision, as you saw in the FindBy-Author example earlier.

Most of this happens under the hood—the source code you write to use dynamic typing can be really simple.

14.2   *The five-minute guide to dynamic*

Do you remember how many new bits of syntax were involved when you learned about LINQ? Well, dynamic typing is just the opposite: there's a single contextual keyword, dynamic, which you can use in most places where you'd use a type name. That's all the new syntax that's required, and the main rules about dynamic are easily expressed, if you don't mind a bit of hand-waving to start with:

- An implicit conversion exists from almost any CLR type to dynamic.
- An implicit conversion exists from any expression of type dynamic to almost any CLR type.
- Expressions that use a value of type dynamic are usually evaluated dynamically.
- The static type of a dynamically evaluated expression is usually deemed to be dynamic.

The detailed rules are more complicated, as you'll see in section 14.4, but for the moment let's stick with the simplified version.

The following listing provides a complete example demonstrating each point.

Listing 14.1   Using dynamic to iterate through a list, concatenating strings

```
dynamic items = new List<string> { "First", "Second", "Third" };
dynamic valueToAdd = "!";
foreach (dynamic item in items)
{
    string result = item + valueToAdd;
    Console.WriteLine(result);
}
```

The result of listing 14.1 shouldn't come as much of a surprise: it prints First!, Second!, and Third!. You could easily have specified the types of the items and valueToAdd variables explicitly in this case, and it would all have worked in the normal way, but imagine that the variables are getting their values from other data sources instead of having them hardcoded. What would happen if you wanted to add an integer instead of a string?

The next listing is just a slight variation. The *declaration* of valueToAdd hasn't been changed; just the assignment expression.

Listing 14.2 Adding integers to strings dynamically

```
dynamic items = new List<string> { "First", "Second", "Third" };
dynamic valueToAdd = 2;
foreach (dynamic item in items)
{                                                        string + int
    string result = item + valueToAdd;         ⟵┘   concatenation
    Console.WriteLine(result);
}
```

This time the first result is First2, which is hopefully what you'd expect. Using static typing, you'd have to explicitly change the declaration of valueToAdd from string to int. The addition operator is still building a string, though.

What if you changed the items to be integers as well? Let's try that one simple change, as shown in the following listing.

Listing 14.3 Adding integers to integers

```
dynamic items = new List<int> { 1, 2, 3 };
dynamic valueToAdd = 2;
foreach (dynamic item in items)
{
    string result = item + valueToAdd;        ⟵— int + int addition
    Console.WriteLine(result);
}
```

Disaster! You're still trying to convert the result of the addition to a string. The only conversions that are allowed are the same ones that are present in C# normally, so there's no conversion from int to string. The result is an exception (at execution time, of course):

```
Unhandled Exception:
   Microsoft.CSharp.RuntimeBinder.RuntimeBinderException:
Cannot implicitly convert type 'int' to 'string'
   at CallSite.Target(Closure , CallSite , Object )
   at System.Dynamic.UpdateDelegates.UpdateAndExecute1[T0,TRet]
        (CallSite site, T0 arg0)
   . . .
```

Unless you're perfect, you're likely to encounter RuntimeBinderException a lot when you start using dynamic typing. It's the new NullReferenceException in some ways; you're bound to come across it, but with any luck it'll be in the context of unit tests rather than customer bug reports. Anyway, you can fix it by changing the type of result to dynamic, so that the conversion isn't required.

Come to think of it, why bother with the result variable in the first place? You could just call `Console.WriteLine` immediately. The following listing shows the changes.

Listing 14.4   Adding integers to integer—but without the exception

```
dynamic items = new List<int> { 1, 2, 3 };
dynamic valueToAdd = 2;
foreach (dynamic item in items)
{
    Console.WriteLine(item + valueToAdd);        Calls overload
}                                                 with int argument
```

This prints 3, 4, and 5, as you'd expect. Changing the input data would now not only change the operator that was chosen at execution time—it would also change which overload of `Console.WriteLine` was called. With the original data, it would call `Console.WriteLine(string)`; with the updated variables, it would call `Console.WriteLine(int)`. The data could even contain a mixture of values, making the exact call change on every iteration!

You can also use `dynamic` as the declared type for fields, parameters, and return types. This is in stark contrast to the use of `var`, which is restricted to local variables.

> **DIFFERENCES BETWEEN VAR AND DYNAMIC**   In many of the examples so far, when you've really known the types at compile time, you could've used `var` to declare the variables. At first glance, the two features look very similar. In both cases, it looks like you're declaring a variable without specifying its type, but by using `dynamic` you're explicitly setting the type to be dynamic. You can only use `var` when the compiler is able to infer the type you mean *statically*, and the type system really does remain entirely static. Of course, if you use `var` for a variable that's initialized with an expression of type `dynamic`, the variable ends up being (statically) typed to be `dynamic` too. Given the confusion this could cause, I strongly caution against it.

The compiler is smart about the information it records, and the code that then *uses* that information at execution time is clever too: it's a mini C# compiler in its own right. It uses whatever static type information was known at compile time to make the code behave as intuitively as possible.

Other than a few details of what you *can't* do with dynamic typing, that's all you really need to know in order to start using it in your own code. Later on we'll come back to those restrictions, as well as details of what the compiler is actually doing, but first let's see dynamic typing doing something genuinely *useful*.

14.3   *Examples of dynamic typing*

Dynamic typing is a bit like unsafe code, or interoperability with native code using P/Invoke. Many developers will have no need for it, or will use it once in a blue moon. For other developers—particularly those dealing with Microsoft Office—it'll give a huge productivity boost, either by making their existing code simpler or by allowing radically different approaches to their problems.

This section isn't meant to be exhaustive by any means. Since the second edition of this book was published, several open source projects have used dynamic typing to great effect, including Massive (https://github.com/robconery/massive), Dapper (http://code.google.com/p/dapper-dot-net/), and Json.NET (http://json.code-plex.com). These examples are all at data boundaries—whether that's when talking to a database, or serializing and deserializing JSON. That's not to say that dynamic typing is only useful at data boundaries, of course, and I'm loathe to predict what novel uses the community may come up with in the future.

We'll look at three examples here: working with Excel, calling into Python, and using normal managed .NET types in a more flexible way.

14.3.1 COM in general, and Microsoft Office in particular

You've already seen most of the new features C# 4 brings to COM interop, but there was one that we couldn't cover in chapter 13 because you hadn't seen dynamic typing yet. If you choose to embed the interop types you're using into the assembly (by using the `/l` compiler switch, or setting the Embed Interop Types property to `true`), then anything in the API that would otherwise be declared as `object` is changed to `dynamic`. This makes it much easier to work with somewhat weakly typed APIs such as those exposed by Office. (Although the object model in Office is reasonably strong in itself, many properties are exposed as *variants* because they can deal with numbers, strings, dates, and so on.)

Again, I'll just show you a short example here—one that does even less than the Word example in chapter 13. The dynamic aspect is easy to understand from this one scenario. We'll set the first 20 cells of the top row of a new Excel worksheet to the numbers 1 to 20. The following listing shows an initial, statically typed piece of code to achieve this.

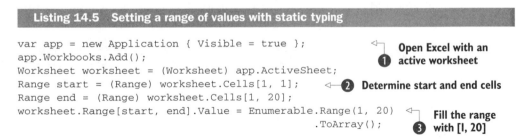

Listing 14.5 Setting a range of values with static typing

```
var app = new Application { Visible = true };      Open Excel with an
app.Workbooks.Add();                          ❶ active worksheet
Worksheet worksheet = (Worksheet) app.ActiveSheet;
Range start = (Range) worksheet.Cells[1, 1];   ❷ Determine start and end cells
Range end = (Range) worksheet.Cells[1, 20];
worksheet.Range[start, end].Value = Enumerable.Range(1, 20)   Fill the range
                                    .ToArray();   ❸ with [I, 20]
```

This code relies on a `using` directive for the `Microsoft.Office.Interop.Excel` namespace (not shown here), so this time the `Application` type refers to Excel, not Word. You're still using the new features of C# 4 by not specifying an argument for the optional parameter in the `Workbooks.Add()` call while you're setting things up ❶ and also by using a named indexer ❷.

When Excel is up and running, you work out the start and end cells of the overall range. In this case they're both on the same row, but you could've created a rectangular range instead by selecting two opposite corners. You *could* have created the range in a single call to `Range["A1:T1"]`, but I personally find it easier to work with just numbers. Cell names like B3 are great for humans, but harder to use in a program.

Once you have the range, you set all the values in it by setting the `Value` property with an array of integers ❸. You can use a one-dimensional array, as you're only setting a single row; to set a range spanning multiple rows you'd need to use a rectangular array.

This all works, but you've had to use three casts in six lines of code. The indexer you call via `Cells` and the `ActiveSheet` property are both declared to return `object` normally. (Various parameters are *also* declared as type `object`, but that doesn't matter as much because there's an implicit conversion from any nonpointer type to `object`—only coming the other way requires the cast.) This code doesn't close Excel at the end of the listing, just so you can see the open worksheet at the end.

With the primary interop assembly set to embed the required types into your own binary, all of these examples become `dynamic`. With the implicit conversion from `dynamic` to other types, you can remove all the casts, as shown in the following listing.

Listing 14.6   Using implicit conversions from `dynamic` in Excel

```
var app = new Application { Visible = true };
app.Workbooks.Add();
Worksheet worksheet = app.ActiveSheet;
Range start = worksheet.Cells[1, 1];
Range end = worksheet.Cells[1, 20];
worksheet.Range[start, end].Value = Enumerable.Range(1, 20)
                                              .ToArray();
```

This is exactly the same code as listing 14.5, but without the casts.

It's worth noting that the conversions are still checked at execution time. If you changed the declaration of `start` to be `Worksheet`, the conversion would fail and an exception would be thrown. Of course, you don't *have* to perform the conversion. You *could* just leave everything as `dynamic`, as shown in the following listing.

Listing 14.7   Using `dynamic` everywhere

```
var app = new Application { Visible = true };
app.Workbooks.Add();
dynamic worksheet = app.ActiveSheet;
dynamic start = worksheet.Cells[1, 1];
dynamic end = worksheet.Cells[1, 20];
worksheet.Range[start, end].Value = Enumerable.Range(1, 20)
                                              .ToArray();
```

Which is clearer? I'm an old-fashioned static typing fan, so I prefer the version in listing 14.6. It states the types I expect on each line, so if there are any problems, I get to find out immediately rather than waiting until I try to use a value in a way that may not be supported.

In terms of productivity when initially developing, there are pros and cons to both approaches. Using `dynamic`, you don't need to work out which particular type you expect; you can just use the value, and as long as all the necessary operations are supported, you're okay. On the other hand, by using static typing, you can see what's available at every stage via IntelliSense. You're still using dynamic typing to provide the implicit conversion to `Worksheet` and `Range`—you're just using it for one step at a time rather than wholesale. The change from static typing to dynamic may not look like much to start with, because the example is relatively simple, but as the complexity of the code increases, so does the readability benefit of removing all those casts.

In some ways this has all been a blast from the past—COM is a relatively old technology. Now we'll jump to interoperating with something much more recent: IronPython.

14.3.2 Dynamic languages such as IronPython

In this section I'll only use IronPython as an example, but that's certainly not the only dynamic language available for the DLR. It's arguably the most mature, but there are already alternatives such as IronRuby and IronScheme. One of the stated aims of the DLR is to make it easier for budding language designers to create a working language that has access to the huge .NET Framework libraries as well as good interoperability with other DLR languages and the traditional .NET languages such as C#.

WHY WOULD I WANT TO USE IRONPYTHON FROM C#?

There are many reasons you might want to interoperate with a dynamic language, just as it's been beneficial to interoperate with other managed languages from .NET's infancy. It's clearly useful for a VB developer to be able to use a class library written in C# and vice versa, so why would the same not be true of dynamic languages? I asked Michael Foord, one of the authors of *Iron Python in Action* (Manning, 2009), to come up with a few ideas for using IronPython within a C# application. Here's his list:

- User scripting
- Writing a layer of your application in IronPython
- Using Python as a configuration language
- Using Python as a rules engine with rules stored as text (even in a database)
- Using a library that's available in Python, but has no .NET equivalent
- Putting a live interpreter into your application for debugging

If you're still skeptical, you might want to consider that embedding a scripting language in a mainstream application is far from uncommon—Sid Meier's *Civilization IV* computer game[3] is scriptable with Python. This isn't just an afterthought for modifications, either—a lot of the core gameplay is written in Python. Once they'd built the engine, the developers found it to be a more powerful development environment than they'd originally imagined.

For this chapter I'll work with the single example of using Python as a configuration language. Just as with the COM example, I'll keep it simple, but hopefully it'll provide enough of a starting point for you to experiment more with it if you're interested.

---

[3] Or way of life, depending on how you view the world and your level of addiction to playing the game.

GETTING STARTED: EMBEDDING "HELLO, WORLD"

There are various types available if you want to *host* or *embed* another language within a C# application, depending on the level of flexibility and control you want to achieve. We'll only use `ScriptEngine` and `ScriptScope` here, because our requirements are primitive. In this example, you know you're always going to use Python, so you can ask the IronPython framework to create a `ScriptEngine` directly; in more general situations, you can use a `ScriptRuntime` to pick language implementations dynamically by name. More demanding scenarios may require you to work with `ScriptHost` and `ScriptSource`, as well as use more of the features of the other types, too.

Not content with merely printing `hello, world` once, this initial example will do so *twice*, first by using text passed directly into the engine as a string, and then by loading a file called HelloWorld.py. The following listing shows everything you need.

> **Listing 14.8 Printing `hello, world` twice using Python embedded in C#**

```
ScriptEngine engine = Python.CreateEngine();
engine.Execute("print 'hello, world'");
engine.ExecuteFile("HelloWorld.py");
```

You may find this listing either quite dull or very exciting, both for the same reason. It's simple to understand, requiring little explanation. It does little, in terms of actual output…and yet the fact that it *is* so easy to embed Python code into C# is a cause for celebration. True, the level of interaction is somewhat minimal so far, but it really couldn't be much easier than this.

> **PYTHON'S MANY STRING LITERAL FORMS**   The Python file contains a single line: `print "hello, world"`. Note the double quotes in the file, compared with the single quotes in the string literal that were passed into `engine.Execute()`. Either would've been fine in either source. Python has various string literal representations, including triple single quotes or triple double quotes for multiline literals. I only mention this because it's useful not to have to escape double quotes any time you want to put Python code into a C# string literal.

The next type we'll look at is `ScriptScope`, which will be crucial to the configuration script.

STORING AND RETRIEVING INFORMATION FROM A SCRIPTSCOPE

The execution methods we've used both have overloads with a second parameter—a scope. In its simplest terms, this can be regarded as a dictionary of names and values. Scripting languages often allow variables to be assigned without any explicit declaration, and when this is done in the top level of a program (instead of in a function or class), this usually affects a *global scope.*

When a `ScriptScope` instance is passed into an execution method, that's used as the global scope for the script you've asked the engine to execute. The script can retrieve existing values from the scope and create new values, as shown in the following listing.

Listing 14.9 Passing information between a host and a script using `ScriptScope`

```
string python = @"
text = 'hello'
output = input + 1
";
ScriptEngine engine = Python.CreateEngine();
ScriptScope scope = engine.CreateScope();
scope.SetVariable("input", 10);
engine.Execute(python, scope);
Console.WriteLine(scope.GetVariable("text"));
Console.WriteLine(scope.GetVariable("input"));
Console.WriteLine(scope.GetVariable("output"));
```

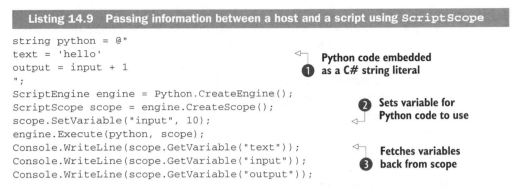

❶ Python code embedded as a C# string literal

❷ Sets variable for Python code to use

❸ Fetches variables back from scope

In this code the Python source code is embedded into the C# code as a verbatim string literal ❶ rather than putting it in a file, so that it's easier to see all the code in one place. I don't recommend that you do this in production code, partly because Python is sensitive to whitespace—reformatting the code in a seemingly harmless way can make it fail completely at execution time.

The `SetVariable` and `GetVariable` methods simply put values into the scope ❷ and fetch them out again ❸ in the obvious way. They're declared in terms of `object` rather than `dynamic`, as you might've expected. But `GetVariable` also allows you to specify a type argument, which acts as a conversion request.

This isn't quite the same as casting the result of the nongeneric method, as the latter just unboxes the value, which means you need to cast it to exactly the right type. For example, you can put an integer into the scope, but retrieve it as a `double`:

```
scope.SetVariable("num", 20)
double x = scope.GetVariable<double>("num")
double y = (double) scope.GetVariable("num");
```

❶ Converts successfully to double

❷ Unboxing throws exception

The first call succeeds: you're explicitly telling `GetVariable` what type you want ❶, so it knows to coerce the value appropriately. The second call ❷ will throw an `Invalid-CastException`, just as it would in any other situation where you try to unbox a value using the wrong type.

The scope can also hold functions, which you can retrieve and then call dynamically, passing arguments and returning values. The easiest way of doing this is to use the `dynamic` type, as shown in the following listing.

Listing 14.10 Calling a function declared in a `ScriptScope`

```
string python = @"
def sayHello(user):
    print 'Hello %(name)s' % {'name' : user}
";
ScriptEngine engine = Python.CreateEngine();
ScriptScope scope = engine.CreateScope();
engine.Execute(python, scope);
dynamic function = scope.GetVariable("sayHello");
function("Jon");
```

Configuration files might not often need this ability, but it can be useful in other situations. For example, you could easily use Python to script a graph-drawing program by providing a function to be called on each input point. A simple example of this can be found on the book's website at http://mng.bz/6yGi.

There are a number of situations in which it's useful to have some sort of expression evaluator running user code entered at execution time, such as evaluating business rules for discounts, shipping costs, and so on. It can also be useful to be able to change these rules in text form without having to recompile or redeploy binaries. Listing 14.10 is quite tame—another example in the downloadable source code weaves in and out of the two languages rather more tortuously, showing that the calls can go both ways: from C# to IronPython, as you've seen, and from IronPython to C#.

PUTTING IT ALL TOGETHER

Now that you can get values into your scope, you're essentially done. You could potentially wrap the scope in another object, providing access via an indexer, or even access the values dynamically using the techniques shown in section 14.5. The application code might look something like this:

```
static Configuration LoadConfiguration()
{
    ScriptEngine engine = Python.CreateEngine();
    ScriptScope scope = engine.CreateScope();
    engine.ExecuteFile("configuration.py", scope);
    return Configuration.FromScriptScope(scope);
}
```

The exact form of the `Configuration` type will depend on your application, but it's unlikely to be terribly exciting code. I've provided a sample dynamic implementation in the full source that allows you to retrieve values as properties and call functions directly too. Of course, you're not limited to using primitive types in your configuration: the Python code could be arbitrarily complex, building collections, wiring up components and services, and so forth. It could perform a lot of the roles of a normal dependency injection or inversion of control container.

The important thing is that you now have a configuration file that's *active* instead of the traditional passive XML and .ini files. Of course, you could've embedded your own programming language into previous configuration files, but the result would probably have been less powerful and would've taken a lot more effort to implement. As an example of where this could be useful in a simpler situation than full dependency injection, you might want to configure the number of threads to use for some background processing component in your application. You might normally use as many threads as you have processors in the system, but occasionally reduce it in order to help another application run smoothly on the same system. The configuration file would simply change from something like this

```
agentThreads = System.Environment.ProcessorCount
agentThreadName = 'Processing agent'
```

to this

```
agentThreads = 1
agentThreadName = 'Processing agent (single thread only)'
```

This change wouldn't require the application to be rebuilt or redeployed—you'd just need to edit the file and restart the application. Particularly smart applications could even choose to reconfigure themselves on the fly. (I've found that usually this ability is more painful to implement than the extra value it brings, but in certain places it can make a big difference. The ability to change logging levels either for a particular bit of code or even just a specific user who's having difficulties can make debugging much easier.)

Other than executing functions, we haven't really looked at using Python in a particularly dynamic way. The full power of Python is available, and by using the `dynamic` type in your C# code, you can take advantage of metaprogramming and all the other dynamic features. The C# compiler is responsible for representing your code in an appropriate fashion, and the script engine is responsible for taking that code and working out what it means for Python. Just don't feel you *have* to be doing anything particularly clever for it to be worth embedding the script engine in your application. It's a simple step toward a more powerful application.

> **HOW MUCH POWER DO YOU WANT TO GIVE TO YOUR SCRIPT AUTHORS?** If you're executing arbitrary code, particularly code entered by external users of the system, you should think seriously about security, and possibly run the script in some sort of sandboxed environment. Discussion of this topic is outside the scope of this book, but it needs to be considered carefully.

So far our examples have been interoperating with other systems. Dynamic typing can make sense even within a purely managed system, though. Let's visit a few examples.

14.3.3 Dynamic typing in purely managed code

You've almost certainly used something *like* dynamic typing in the past, even if it wasn't your own code that had to do the work. Data binding is the simplest example of this—any time you specify something like `ListControl.DisplayMember`, you're asking the framework to find a property at execution time based on its name. If you've ever used reflection directly in your own code, you're again using information that's only available at execution time.

In my experience, reflection is error-prone, and even when it works, you may need to put in extra effort to optimize it. In some cases, dynamic typing can completely replace that reflection-based code; it may be faster too, depending on exactly what you're doing.

It's particularly tricky to use generic types and methods from reflection. For instance, if you have an object that you know implements `IList<T>` for some type argument `T`, it can be difficult to work out exactly what `T` is. If the only reason for discovering `T` is to then call another generic method, you really want to just ask the compiler to call whatever it *would* have called if you knew the actual type. Of course, that's exactly what dynamic typing does. I'll use this scenario as our first example.

EXECUTION-TIME TYPE INFERENCE

If you want to do more than just call a single method, it's often best to wrap all the additional work in a generic method. You can then call the generic method dynamically, but write all the rest of the code using static typing. Listing 14.11 shows a simple example of this.

Pretend you've been given a list of some type and a new element by some other part of the system. You've been promised that they're compatible, but you don't know their types statically. There are various reasons this could happen—this could be the result of deserialization elsewhere, for example. Anyway, your code is meant to add the new element to the end of the list, but only if there are fewer than 10 elements in the list at the moment. The method returns whether or not the element was actually added. Obviously, in real life the business logic would be more complicated, but the point is that you'd really like to be able to use the strong types for these operations. The following listing shows the statically typed method and the dynamic call into it.

Listing 14.11   Using dynamic type inference

```
private static bool AddConditionallyImpl<T>(IList<T> list, T item)
{
    if (list.Count < 10)                    ◁┐    Normal statically
    {                                        ❶    typed code
        list.Add(item);
        return true;
    }
    return false;
}

public static bool AddConditionally(dynamic list, dynamic item)
{
    return AddConditionallyImpl(list, item);    ◁┐    Calls helper method
}                                               ❷    dynamically
...
object list = new List<string> { "x", "y" };
object item = "z";                              ┤    Eventually calls
AddConditionally(list, item);                   ◁┘    AddConditionallyImpl<string>
```

The public method has dynamic parameters; in previous versions of C# it would perhaps have taken `IEnumerable` and `Object`, relying on complicated checks with reflection to work out the type of the list and then invoke the generic method with reflection. With dynamic typing, you can just call a strongly typed implementation ❶ using the dynamic arguments ❷, isolating the dynamic access to the single call in the wrapper method. Of course, the call could still fail, but you've been saved the effort of trying to determine the appropriate type argument.

You could also expose the strongly typed method publicly to avoid the dynamic typing for callers who knew their list types statically. It'd be worth keeping the names different in that case, to avoid accidentally calling the dynamic version due to a slight mistake with the static types of the arguments. (It's also a lot easier to make the right call within the dynamic version when the names are different!)

As another example of dynamic typing in purely managed code, I've already bemoaned the lack of generic operator support in C#. There's no concept of specifying a constraint saying "T must have an operator that allows me to add two values of type T together." You saw this in our initial demonstration of dynamic typing (see listing 14.4), so mentioning it here should come as no surprise. Let's take the `Sum` query operator from LINQ and make it dynamic.

COMPENSATING FOR THE LACK OF GENERIC OPERATORS

Have you ever looked at the list of overloads for `Enumerable.Sum`? It's pretty long. Admittedly, half of the overloads are due to a projection, but even so there are 10 overloads, each of which just takes a sequence of elements and adds them together, and that doesn't even cover summing unsigned values, or bytes, or shorts. Why not use dynamic typing to try to do it all in one method?

Even though we'll use dynamic typing internally, the method shown in listing 14.12 is statically typed. You could declare it as a nongeneric method summing an `IEnumerable <dynamic>`, but that wouldn't work well due to the limitations of covariance. I named the method `DynamicSum` rather than `Sum` to avoid clashing with the methods in `Enumerable`. The compiler will pick a nongeneric overload over a generic one where both signatures have the same parameter types, and it's simpler to avoid the collision in the first place.

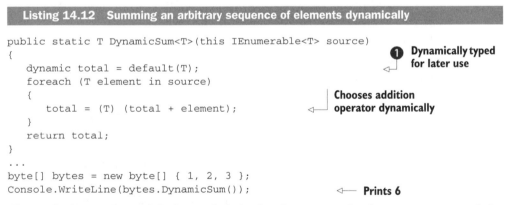

Listing 14.12   Summing an arbitrary sequence of elements dynamically

```
public static T DynamicSum<T>(this IEnumerable<T> source)
{                                                            ❶ Dynamically typed
    dynamic total = default(T);                                 for later use
    foreach (T element in source)
    {                                                         Chooses addition
        total = (T) (total + element);                        operator dynamically
    }
    return total;
}
...
byte[] bytes = new byte[] { 1, 2, 3 };
Console.WriteLine(bytes.DynamicSum());                       ⟵— Prints 6
```

The code is mostly straightforward; it looks almost exactly the same as any of the implementations of the normal `Sum` overloads would. It omits checking whether `source` is null just for brevity, but most of the rest is simple enough. There are a couple of interesting points.

First, you use `default(T)` to initialize `total`, which is declared as `dynamic` so that you get the desired dynamic behavior ❶. You have to start off with an initial value somehow; you could try to use the first value in the sequence, but then you'd be stuck if the sequence were empty. For non-nullable value types, `default(T)` is almost always an appropriate value anyway: it's a natural zero. For reference types, you'll end up adding the first element of the sequence to `null`, which may or may not be appropriate. For nullable value types, you'll end up trying to add the first element to the null value for that type, which certainly *won't* be appropriate.

Second, you cast the result of the addition back to `T`, even though it's then assigned to a dynamic variable. This may seem odd, but you need to think about the results of summing two bytes together. The C# compiler would normally promote each operand to `int` before performing the addition. Without the cast, the `total` variable would end up storing an `int` value, which would then cause an exception when the return statement attempted to convert it back to `byte`.

Both of these points lead to deeper questions, but that's not the point of this section. I've written up a more detailed investigation of dynamic summation on the book's website (see http://mng.bz/0N37).

Just to prove that our code is capable of more than arithmetic on normal numbers, listing 14.13 shows an example of summing `TimeSpan` values.

Listing 14.13   **Summing a list of `TimeSpan` elements dynamically**

```
var times = new List<TimeSpan>
{
    2.Hours(), 25.Minutes(), 30.Seconds(),
    45.Seconds(), 40.Minutes()
};
Console.WriteLine(times.DynamicSum());
```

The `TimeSpan` values are created using extension methods for convenience, but the summation is entirely dynamic, resulting in a total span of 3 hours, 6 minutes, and 15 seconds.

DUCK TYPING

Sometimes you know that a member with a particular name will be available at execution time, but you can't tell the compiler exactly which member you're talking about because it'll depend on the type. In some ways this is a more general example of the same problem that we've just solved, except using normal methods and properties instead of operators.

There is a difference: usually you'd try to capture the commonality in an interface or abstract base class. You can't do this with operators, but it's the normal approach for methods and properties. Unfortunately it doesn't always work—particularly if multiple libraries are involved. The .NET Framework is mostly consistent here, but you've already seen one example where it doesn't quite work. In chapter 12 we looked at the optimizations available for counting a sequence and saw that both `ICollection` and `ICollection<T>` have a `Count` property—but they have no common ancestor interface with that property, so you have to handle them separately.

Duck typing lets you just access `Count` without performing the type checking yourself, as shown in the following listing.

Listing 14.14 Accessing a Count property with duck typing

```
static void PrintCount(IEnumerable collection)
{
    dynamic d = collection;
    int count = d.Count;
    Console.WriteLine(count);
}
...
PrintCount(new BitArray(10));
PrintCount(new HashSet<int> { 3, 5 });
PrintCount(new List<int> { 1, 2, 3 });
```

The `PrintCount` method is restricted to implementations of `IEnumerable` for the same reason that collection initializers are: it's a pretty good indication that the `Count` property you end up using is an appropriate one. The test collections are a `BitArray` (which only implements `ICollection`), a `HashSet<int>` (which only implements `ICollection<int>`), and a `List<int>` (which implements both). In all cases, the correct property is found at execution time.

Explicit interface implementation and dynamic don't mix well

When I first tried to test this code, I used an `int[]`, which is implicitly convertible to both of the interfaces involved. I was therefore surprised when the `PrintCount` method failed at execution time...until I thought about it more closely. The execution-time binding is performed using the actual type of the object, which in this case is an `int[]`. Array types don't publicly expose a `Count` property—they use explicit interface implementation for that. You can only use `Count` when you view an array object in a particular way.

This is just one example where dynamic typing can behave in a way that's logical but can be unexpected unless you're careful. I'm collecting an ongoing list of such oddities on the book's website (see http://mng.bz/5y7M); please let me know if you find any new ones.

We'll stick with the example of retrieving the count of items, but this time we'll look at how execution-time overload resolution can offer an alternative to explicit type testing.

MULTIPLE DISPATCH

With static typing, C# uses *single dispatch*: at execution, the exact method called only depends on the actual type of the target of the method call, through overriding. Overloading is decided at compile time. Occasionally *multiple dispatch* is useful to find the most specialized implementation of a method based on the execution-time types of the arguments—again, this is what dynamic typing provides.

The following listing demonstrates how multiple dispatch would allow for a more varied and robust implementation of optimized counting.

Listing 14.15 Counting different types efficiently using multiple dispatch

```
private static int CountImpl<T>(ICollection<T> collection)
{
    return collection.Count;
}

private static int CountImpl(ICollection collection)
{
    return collection.Count;
}

private static int CountImpl(string text)
{
    return text.Length;
}

private static int CountImpl(IEnumerable collection)
{
    int count = 0;
    foreach (object item in collection)
    {
        count++;
    }
    return count;
}

public static void PrintCount(IEnumerable collection)
{
    dynamic d = collection;
    int count = CountImpl(d);
    Console.WriteLine(count);
}
...
PrintCount(new BitArray(5));
PrintCount(new HashSet<int> { 1, 2 });
PrintCount("ABC");
PrintCount("ABCDEF".Where(c => c > 'B'));
```

You know that at least one overload of CountImpl will be appropriate at execution time because the parameter for PrintCount is of type IEnumerable. You rely on dynamic typing to perform the same job as the explicit "if it's an ICollection<T>, use this implementation; if it's an ICollection, use this implementation" steps we used when picking a random element in listing 12.17. As an example of how this is more than just using the Count property if it's available, listing 14.15 includes an optimization for strings, where you can use the Length property to obtain the right result quickly.

Even using multiple dispatch here, you could still run into problems at execution time: what if the actual type implemented both ICollection<string> and ICollection<int> via explicit interface implementation? There would be two possible results depending on which Count implementation was picked. In this case the binding would be ambiguous, leading to an exception. Fortunately such pathological cases are likely to be rare.

These are just a few examples of areas where you *might* want to use dynamic typing even if you're not trying to interoperate with anything else. Next, we'll delve into how all these effects are achieved, before we finish off the chapter by implementing our own dynamic behavior.

I should warn you that things are about to get tricky. In fact, it's all extremely elegant, but it's complicated because programming languages provide a rich set of operations, and representing all the necessary information about those operations as data and then acting on it appropriately are complex jobs. The good news is that you don't need to understand it all intimately. As ever, you'll get more out of dynamic typing the more familiar you are with the machinery behind it, but even if you just use the techniques you've seen so far, there may be situations where it makes you a lot more productive.

14.4 Looking behind the scenes

Despite the warning of the previous paragraph, I won't go into *huge* amounts of detail about the inner workings of dynamic typing. That would be a lot of ground to cover, with reference to both the framework and language changes. It's not often that I shy away from the nitty-gritty of specifications, but in this case I truly believe there's not much to be gained from learning it all. I'll cover the most important (and interesting) points, and I can thoroughly recommend Sam Ng's blog (http://blogs.msdn.com/b/samng/), the C# language specification, and the DLR project page (http://mng.bz/0M6A) for more information if you need to dig into a particular scenario.

My eventual goal is to help you understand what the C# compiler is doing and the code it emits to achieve dynamic binding at execution time. Unfortunately, none of the generated code will make any sense until you see the mechanism that underpins it all—the DLR. You might like to think of a statically typed program as a conventional stage play with a fixed script, and a dynamically typed program as more like an improvisation show. The DLR takes the place of the actors' brains frantically coming up with something to say in response to audience suggestions. Let's meet our quick-thinking star performer.

14.4.1 Introducing the Dynamic Language Runtime

I've been bandying the acronym *DLR* around for a while now, occasionally expanding it to Dynamic Language Runtime, but never explaining what it is. This has been deliberate: I've been trying to get across the nature of dynamic typing and how it affects developers, rather than the details of the implementation. But that excuse was never going to last until the end of the chapter, so here we are. In its barest terms, the Dynamic Language Runtime is a library that all dynamic languages and the C# compiler use to execute code dynamically.

Amazingly enough, it really is just a library. Despite its name, it isn't at the same level as the CLR (Common Language Runtime)—it doesn't deal in JIT compilation, native API marshaling, garbage collection, and so forth. But it builds on a lot of the

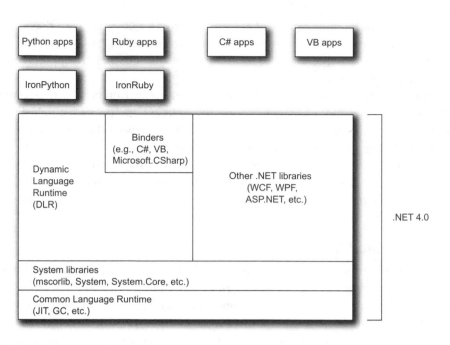

Figure 14.1 How the components of .NET 4 fit together, allowing static and dynamic languages to execute on the same underlying platform

work in .NET 2.0 and 3.5, particularly the `DynamicMethod` and `Expression` types. The expression tree API has been expanded in .NET 4 to allow the DLR to express more concepts, too. Figure 14.1 shows how it all fits together.

In addition to the DLR, figure 14.1 shows another library that may be new to you. One of the assemblies in the binders part of the diagram is `Microsoft.CSharp`. It contains a number of types that are referenced by the C# compiler when you use `dynamic` in your code. Confusingly, this doesn't include the existing `Microsoft.CSharp .Compiler` and `Microsoft.CSharp.CodeDomProvider`. (They're not even in the same assembly as each other!) You'll see exactly what the new types are used for in section 14.4.2, where we'll decompile some code written using `dynamic`.

One other important aspect differentiates the DLR from the rest of the .NET Framework: it's provided as open source. The complete code lives in a CodePlex project (http://dlr.codeplex.com), so you can download it and see the inner workings. One of the benefits of this approach is that the DLR hasn't had to be reimplemented for Mono (http://mono-project.com): the same code runs on both .NET and its cross-platform cousin.

Although the DLR doesn't handle native code directly, you can think of it as doing a job *similar* to the CLR in one sense: just as the CLR converts IL (Intermediate Language) into native code, the DLR converts code represented using binders, call sites, meta-objects, and various other concepts into expression trees that can then be compiled down into IL and eventually native code by the CLR. Figure 14.2 shows a simplified view of the lifecycle of a single evaluation of a dynamic expression.

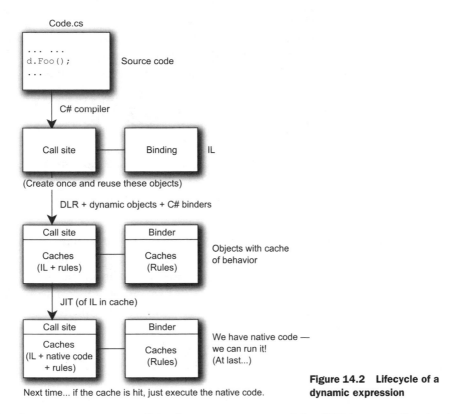

Figure 14.2 Lifecycle of a dynamic expression

As you can see, one of the important aspects of the DLR is a multilevel cache. This is crucial for performance reasons, but to understand that and the other concepts I've already mentioned, we'll need to dive one layer deeper.

14.4.2 *DLR core concepts*

We can summarize the purpose of the DLR in *very* general terms as taking a high-level representation of code and executing that code, based on various pieces of information that may only be known at execution time. In this section I'll introduce a lot of terminology to describe how the DLR works, but it's all contributing to that common aim.

CALL SITES

The first concept we need is a *call site*. This is sort of the atom of the DLR—the smallest piece of code that can be considered as a single executable unit. One expression may contain a lot of call sites, but the behavior is built up in the natural way, evaluating one call site at a time.

For the rest of the discussion, we'll only consider a single call site. It'll be useful to have a small example of a call site to refer to, so here's a simple one, where d is a variable of type dynamic:

```
d.Foo(10);
```

The call site is represented in code as a `System.Runtime.CompilerServices.Call-`
`Site<T>`. You'll see a full example of how call sites are created and used in the next section, when we look at what the C# compiler does at compile time, but here's an example
of the code that might be called to create the site for the previous snippet:

```
CallSite<Action<CallSite, object, int>>.Create(Binder.InvokeMember(
  CSharpBinderFlags.ResultDiscarded, "Foo", null, typeof(Test),
  new CSharpArgumentInfo[] {
  CSharpArgumentInfo.Create(CSharpArgumentInfoFlags.None, null),
  CSharpArgumentInfo.Create(CSharpArgumentInfoFlags.Constant |
                            CSharpArgumentInfoFlags.UseCompileTimeType,
                            null) }));
```

Now that we have a call site, can we execute the code? Not quite.

RECEIVERS AND BINDERS

As well as a call site, we need something to decide what it means and how to execute it.
In the DLR, two entities can decide this: the *receiver* of a call and the *binder*. The
receiver of a call is simply the object that a member is called on. In our sample call
site, the receiver is the object that d refers to at execution time. The binder will
depend on the calling language and is part of the call site—in this case, you can see
that the C# compiler emits code to create a binder using `Binder.InvokeMember`. The
`Binder` class, in this case, is `Microsoft.CSharp.RuntimeBinder.Binder`, so it really is
C#-specific. The C# binder is also COM-aware and will perform appropriate COM binding if the receiver is an `IDispatch` object.

The DLR always gives precedence to the receiver: if it's a dynamic object that knows
how to handle the call, then it'll use whatever execution path the object provides. An
object can advertise itself as being dynamic by implementing the new `IDynamicMeta-`
`ObjectProvider` interface. The name is a mouthful, but it only contains a single member: `GetMetaObject`. You'll need to be an expression-tree ninja and know the DLR
quite well to implement `GetMetaObject` correctly. But in the right hands, this can be a
powerful tool, giving you lower-level interaction with the DLR and its execution cache.
If you need to implement dynamic behavior in a high-performance fashion, it's worth
the investment to learn the details.

There are two public implementations of `IDynamicMetaObjectProvider` included
in the framework to make it easy to implement dynamic behavior in situations where
performance isn't quite as critical. We'll look at all of this in more detail in section
14.5, but for now you just need to be aware of the interface itself, and that it represents the ability of an object to react dynamically.

If the receiver isn't dynamic, the binder gets to decide how the code should be executed. In C# code, it would apply C#-specific rules to the code and work out what to
do. If you were creating your own dynamic language, you could implement your own
binder to decide how it should behave in general (when the object doesn't override
the behavior). That lies well beyond the scope of this book, but it's an interesting
topic in and of itself; one of the aims of the DLR is to make it easier to implement your
own languages.

RULES AND CACHES

The decision about how to execute a call is represented as a *rule*. Fundamentally, this consists of two elements of logic: the circumstances under which the call site should behave this way, and the behavior itself.

The first part is really for optimization. Suppose you have a call site that represents addition of two dynamic values, and the first time it's evaluated, both values are of type `byte`. The binder has gone to a fair amount of effort to work out that this means both operands should be promoted to `int`, and the result should be the sum of those integers. It can reuse that operation any time the operands turn out to both be `byte`. Checking a set of previous results for validity can save a lot of time. The rule I've used as an example (the operand types must be exactly the same as the ones I've just seen) is a common one, but the DLR supports other rules too.

The second part of a rule is the code to use when the rule matches, and it's represented as an expression tree. It *could* have been stored as a compiled delegate to call, but keeping the expression tree representation means the cache can optimize heavily. There are three levels of cache in the DLR: L0, L1, and L2. The caches store information in different ways, and with a different scope. Each call site has its own L0 and L1 caches, but an L2 cache may be shared between several similar call sites, as shown in figure 14.3.

The set of call sites that share an L2 cache is determined by their binders—each binder has an L2 cache associated with it. The compiler (or whatever is creating the call sites) decides how many binders it wants to use. It can only use a binder for multiple call sites that represent very similar code, where, if the context is the same at execution time, the call sites should execute in the same way. In fact, the C# compiler doesn't use this facility—it creates a new binder for every call site,[4] so there's not much difference between the L1 and L2 caches for C# developers. Genuinely dynamic languages, such as IronRuby and IronPython, make more use of it, though.

The caches themselves are executable, which takes a while to understand. The C# compiler generates code to simply execute the call site's L0 cache (which is a delegate accessed through the `Target` property). That's it! The L0 cache has a single rule,

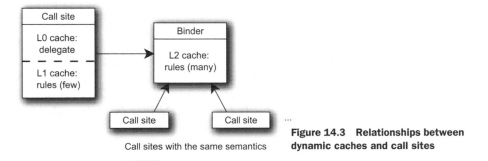

Call sites with the same semantics

Figure 14.3 Relationships between dynamic caches and call sites

---

[4] A lot of information is specific to a particular call site, as the binding rules will be different depending on things like which class it's being called from.

which it checks when it's called. If the rule matches, it executes the associated behavior. If the rule doesn't match (or if this is the first call, so it doesn't have even one rule), it calls into the L1 cache, which in turn calls into the L2 cache. If the L2 cache can't find any matching rules, it asks the receiver or the binder to resolve the call. The results are then put into the cache for next time.

In the case of our earlier snippet, the execution part would look something like this:

```
callSite.Target(callSite, d, 10);
```

The L1 and L2 caches look through their rules in a fairly standard way—each has a collection of rules, and each rule is asked whether or not it matches. The L0 cache is somewhat different. The two parts of its behavior (checking its rule and delegating to the L1 cache) are combined into a single method that is then JIT compiled. Updating the L0 cache consists of rebuilding the method from the new rule.

The result of all of this is that typical call sites that see similar context repeatedly are very fast; the dispatch mechanism is about as lean as you could make it if you hand-coded the tests yourself. Of course, this has to be weighed against the cost of all the dynamic code generation involved, but the multilevel cache is complicated precisely because it tries to achieve a balance across various scenarios.

Now that you know a bit about the machinery in the DLR, you'll be able to understand what the C# compiler does to set it all in motion.

14.4.3   *How the C# compiler handles dynamic*

The main jobs of the C# compiler when it comes to dynamic code are to work out when dynamic behavior is required, and to capture all the necessary context so that the binder and receiver have enough information to resolve the call at execution time.

IF IT USES DYNAMIC, IT'S DYNAMIC!

One situation is obviously dynamic: when the target of a member call is dynamic. The compiler has no way of knowing how that'll be resolved. It may be a truly dynamic object that'll perform the resolution itself, or it may end up with the C# binder resolving it with reflection later. Either way, there's no opportunity for the call to be resolved statically.

But when the dynamic value is being used as an *argument* for the call, there are some situations where you *might* expect the call to be resolved statically—particularly if there's a suitable overload that has a parameter type of dynamic. The rule is that if any part of a call is dynamic, the call becomes dynamic and will resolve the overload with the execution-time type of the dynamic value. The following listing demonstrates this using a method with two overloads, and invoking it in a number of different ways.

Listing 14.16   Experimenting with method overloading and dynamic values

```
static void Execute(string x)
{
    Console.WriteLine("String overload");
}

static void Execute(dynamic x)
{
    Console.WriteLine("Dynamic overload");
}
...
dynamic text = "text";
Execute(text);                    ⟵── Prints "String overload"
dynamic number = 10;
Execute(number);                  ⟵── Prints "Dynamic overload"
```

Both calls to Execute are bound dynamically. At execution time, they're resolved using the types of the actual values, namely, string and int. The parameter of type dynamic is treated as if it were declared with type object everywhere except within the method itself—if you look at the compiled code, you'll see it *is* a parameter of type object, just with an extra attribute applied. This also means you can't have two methods whose signatures differ just by dynamic/object parameter types.

That's an example of resolving method calls, but there are plenty of other expressions to consider. Sometimes the situation isn't quite as straightforward as I've led you to believe...

IT'S DYNAMIC...EXCEPT WHEN IT ISN'T

When I introduced dynamic in 14.2 I had to be careful not to generalize too far, because there are exceptions to almost every rule. Although you should know about these, you don't need to worry about them—they're unlikely to cause you any problems.

Let's get them out of the way quickly.

Conversions between CLR types and dynamic

The conversions between CLR types and dynamic are restricted in the same way that you can't convert from *every* CLR type to object; the exceptions are types such as pointers and System.TypedReference. Given that dynamic is just object at the CLR level, it's not surprising that these types are excluded.

You may have also noticed that I wrote about a conversion "from an expression of type dynamic" to a CLR type, not a conversion from the dynamic type itself. This subtlety helps during type inference and other situations that need to consider implicit conversions between types; in general, life gets unpleasant when there are two types with implicit conversions both ways. It basically limits the situations in which the conversion is considered. For example, consider this implicitly typed array:

```
dynamic d = 0;
string x = "text";
var array = new[] { d, x };
```

What should the inferred type of array be? If there were an implicit conversion from `dynamic` to `string`, then it could be either `string[]` or `dynamic[]`, so you'd end up with ambiguity and a compile-time error. But as the conversion only exists from a dynamic *expression*, the compiler sees a conversion from `string` to `dynamic` but not the other way, and `array` is of type `dynamic[]`. It's probably best not to worry about this subtlety unless you're trying to work through a particular scenario with the specification beside you.

Expressions using dynamic aren't always evaluated dynamically

There are some cases where the CLR is quite capable of evaluating an expression using the normal static execution paths, even if one of the subexpressions is dynamic. For example, consider the `as` operator:

```
dynamic d = GetValueDynamically();
string x = d as string;
```

There's nothing that can happen dynamically here—either the value of `d` is a reference to a string or it isn't. User-defined conversions aren't applied when the `as` operator is used, so the C# compiler can use exactly the same IL that it would if the variable were of type `object`.

Dynamically evaluated expressions aren't always of type dynamic

In some cases, the compiler doesn't know exactly how it's going to evaluate an expression, but it knows the exact type of the result (assuming an exception isn't thrown). For example, consider making a constructor call using a dynamic value as an argument:

```
dynamic d = GetValueDynamically();
SomeType x = new SomeType(d);
```

The constructor call itself has to be evaluated dynamically. There may be several overloads to be resolved at execution time, but the result is always going to be a `SomeType` reference. The assignment to x can therefore happen without a dynamic conversion.

There are a few other cases like this; using a dynamic array index into a statically typed array can only result in a value of the array element type, for example. But you shouldn't assume it'll always happen where you might expect it to. You could have several overloads of a method, all of which have the same static return type, but the type of that method invocation expression will still be `dynamic`.

That's enough about when dynamic evaluation *doesn't* happen, or doesn't result in a dynamic value—let's get back to the situations where it does and see what the C# compiler does to make it all work.

CREATING CALL SITES AND BINDERS

You don't need to know the exact details of what the compiler does with dynamic expressions in order to use them, but it can be instructive to see what the compiled code looks like. In particular, if you need to decompile your code for any other reason, you won't be surprised by what the dynamic parts look like. My tool of choice for this kind of work is Reflector (see http://mng.bz/pMXJ), but you could use ildasm if you wanted to read the IL directly.

We're only going to look at a single example—I'm sure I could fill a whole chapter by looking at implementation details, but the idea is only to give you the gist of what the compiler is up to. If you find this example interesting, you may want to experiment more on your own. Just remember that the exact details are implementation-specific; they may change in future compiler versions, so long as the behavior is equivalent.

Here's the sample snippet, which exists in a Main method in the normal manner for Snippy:

```
string text = "text to cut";
dynamic startIndex = 2;
string substring = text.Substring(startIndex);
```

Pretty simple, right? But it actually contains two dynamic operations—one to call Substring, and one (implicit) to dynamically convert the result (which is just dynamic at compile time) to a string. Listing 14.17 shows the decompiled code for the Snippet class.[5] I've omitted the class declaration itself and the implicit parameterless constructor to save space, and I've reformatted the code with less whitespace for the same reason.

Listing 14.17 The results of compiling dynamic code

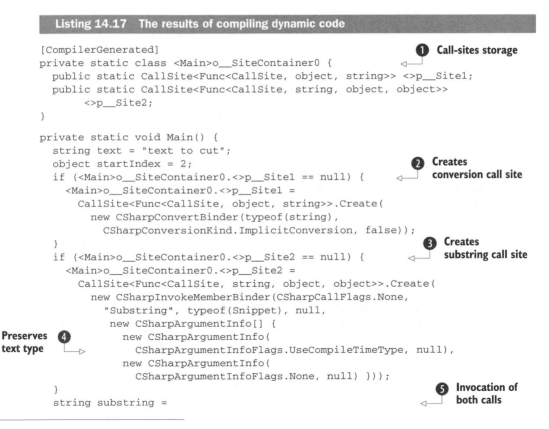

```
[CompilerGenerated]                                              ❶ Call-sites storage
private static class <Main>o__SiteContainer0 {
  public static CallSite<Func<CallSite, object, string>> <>p__Site1;
  public static CallSite<Func<CallSite, string, object, object>>
      <>p__Site2;
}

private static void Main() {
  string text = "text to cut";
  object startIndex = 2;                                         ❷ Creates
  if (<Main>o__SiteContainer0.<>p__Site1 == null) {                 conversion call site
    <Main>o__SiteContainer0.<>p__Site1 =
      CallSite<Func<CallSite, object, string>>.Create(
        new CSharpConvertBinder(typeof(string),
          CSharpConversionKind.ImplicitConversion, false));
  }                                                              ❸ Creates
  if (<Main>o__SiteContainer0.<>p__Site2 == null) {                 substring call site
    <Main>o__SiteContainer0.<>p__Site2 =
      CallSite<Func<CallSite, string, object, object>>.Create(
        new CSharpInvokeMemberBinder(CSharpCallFlags.None,
          "Substring", typeof(Snippet), null,
            new CSharpArgumentInfo[] {
```
Preserves text type ❹
```
              new CSharpArgumentInfo(
                CSharpArgumentInfoFlags.UseCompileTimeType, null),
              new CSharpArgumentInfo(
                CSharpArgumentInfoFlags.None, null) }));
  }                                                              ❺ Invocation of
  string substring =                                               both calls
```

---

[5] Just as a reminder, Snippet is the class generated by Snippy automatically.

```
        <Main>o__SiteContainer0.<>p__Site1.Target.Invoke(
          <Main>o__SiteContainer0.<>p__Site1,
          <Main>o__SiteContainer0.<>p__Site2.Target.Invoke(
            <Main>o__SiteContainer0.<>p__Site2, text, startIndex));
}
```

I don't know about you, but I'm glad that I never have to write or encounter code like that, other than for the purpose of learning about what's going on. There's nothing new about that, though—the generated code for iterator blocks, expression trees, and anonymous functions can be pretty gruesome too.

A nested static class is used to store all the call sites ❶ for the method, as they only need to be created once. (If they were created each time, the cache would be useless!) It's possible that the call sites *could* be created more than once due to multithreading, but if that happens it's just slightly inefficient, and it means the lazy creation is achieved with no locking at all. It doesn't really matter if one call site instance is replaced with another. Each method using dynamic binding has a separate site container; this *has* to be the case for generic methods, as the call site needs to vary based on the type arguments. Another compiler implementation could choose to use one site container for all the nongeneric methods, one for all generic methods with a single type parameter, and so on.

After the call sites are created (❷ and ❸), they're invoked. The Substring call is invoked first (read the code from the innermost part of the statement outward) and then the conversion is invoked on the result ❺. At this point, you have a statically typed value again, so you can assign it to the substring variable.

I'd like to highlight one more aspect of the code: the way that some static type information is preserved in the call site. The type information itself is present in the delegate signature used for the type argument of the call site (Func<CallSite, string, object, object>), and a flag in the corresponding CSharpArgumentInfo indicates that this type information should be used in the binder ❹. (Even though this is the target of the method, it's represented as an argument; instance methods are treated as static methods with an implicit first parameter of this.) This is a crucial part of making the binder behave as if it were just recompiling your code at execution time. Let's look at why this is so important.

14.4.4 *The C# compiler gets even smarter*

C# 4 lets you straddle the static/dynamic boundary not only by having some of your code bound statically and some bound dynamically, but also by combining the two ideas within a single binding. It remembers everything it needs to know within the call site, and then cleverly merges this information with the types of the dynamic values at execution time.

PRESERVING COMPILER BEHAVIOR AT EXECUTION TIME

The ideal model for working out how the binder should behave is to imagine that instead of having a dynamic value in your source code, you have a value of exactly the right type: the type of the actual value at execution time.[6] This *only* applies to dynamic values within the expression; any types that are known at compile time are still used for lookups, such as member resolution. I'll give two examples of where this makes a difference.

The following listing shows a simple overloaded method in a single type.

Listing 14.18 Dynamic overload resolution within a single type

```
static void Execute(dynamic x, string y)
{
    Console.WriteLine("dynamic, string");
}

static void Execute(dynamic x, object y)
{
    Console.WriteLine("dynamic, object");
}
...
object text = "text";
dynamic d = 10;                          Prints
Execute(d, text);              ←——      "dynamic, object"
```

The important variable here is text. Its *compile-time* type is object, but at *execution time* its value is a string reference. The call to Execute is dynamic because you're using the dynamic variable d as one of the arguments, but the overload resolution uses the static type of text, so the result is dynamic, object. If the text variable had been declared as dynamic as well, it would've used the other overload.

The next listing is similar, but this time it's the receiver of the call that matters.

Listing 14.19 Dynamic overload resolution within a class hierarchy

```
class Base
{
    public void Execute(object x)
    {
        Console.WriteLine("object");
    }
}

class Derived : Base
{
    public void Execute(string x)
    {
        Console.WriteLine("string");
    }
}
...
Base receiver = new Derived();
dynamic d = "text";
receiver.Execute(d);                        ←—— Prints "object"
```

---

[6] It's slightly more complicated than that—what if the actual type is internal to another assembly? You wouldn't want that to be used as the type argument of a generic method via type inference, for example. The binder has the notion of a "best accessible type" based on the calling context and the actual type.

In listing 14.19 the type of `receiver` is `Derived` at execution time, so you might've expected the overload introduced in `Derived` to be called. But the compile-time type of `receiver` is `Base`, so the binder restricts the set of methods it considers to just the ones that *would* have been available if you'd been binding the method statically.

Despite all of these decisions that have to be taken later, some compile-time checks are available, even for code that'll be fully bound at execution time.

COMPILE-TIME ERRORS FOR DYNAMIC CODE

As I said near the start of this chapter, one of the disadvantages of dynamic typing is that some errors that would normally be detected by the compiler are delayed until execution time, at which point an exception is thrown. There are many situations where the compiler has to just hope you know what you're doing, but where it *can* help you, it will.

The simplest example of this is when you try to call a method with a statically typed receiver (or a static method) and none of the overloads can possibly be valid, whatever type the dynamic value has at execution time. The following listing shows three examples of invalid calls, two of which are caught by the compiler.

Listing 14.20   Catching errors in dynamic calls at compile time

```
string text = "cut me up";
dynamic guid = Guid.NewGuid();
text.Substring(guid);
text.Substring("x", guid);
text.Substring(guid, guid, guid);
```

Here you have three calls to `string.Substring`. The compiler knows the exact set of possible overloads, because it knows the type of `text` statically. It doesn't complain at the first call, because it can't tell what type `guid` will be—if it turns out to be an integer, all will be well. But the final two lines throw up errors—there are no overloads that take a string as the first argument, and there are no overloads with three parameters. The compiler can *guarantee* that these would fail at execution time, so it's reasonable for it to fail at compile time instead.

A slightly trickier example is with type inference. If a dynamic value is used to infer a type argument in a call to a generic method, the actual type argument won't be known until execution time and no validation can occur beforehand. But any type argument that would be inferred without using *any* dynamic values can cause type inference to fail at compile time. The following listing shows an example of this.

Listing 14.21   Generic type inference with mixed static and dynamic values

```
void Execute<T>(T first, T second, string other) where T : struct
{
}
...
dynamic guid = Guid.NewGuid();
Execute(10, 0, guid);
```

```
Execute(10, false, guid);
Execute("hello", "hello", guid);
```

Again, the first call compiles but would fail at execution time. The second call won't compile because T can't be both int and bool, and there are no conversions between the two of them. The third call won't compile because T is inferred to be string, which violates the constraint that it must be a value type.

The compiler is conservative: it'll only fail with an error if it can tell that some code can't possibly succeed, and it only performs relatively simple tests on this front. There are some situations where it may be obvious (and provable) to a human that the code won't work, but where the compiler allows the code through. Of course, if a particular line of code will never work, then a single unit test that executes it will fail, so the simplistic nature of the compiler's checking doesn't matter if you have good code coverage. Think of it as a bonus in the cases where it *does* spot a problem.

That covers the most important points in terms of what the compiler *can* do for you. But you can't use dynamic absolutely everywhere. There are limitations, some of which are painful, but most of which are quite obscure.

14.4.5 *Restrictions on dynamic code*

You can *mostly* use dynamic wherever you'd normally use a type name, and then write normal C#. But there are a few exceptions. This isn't an exhaustive list, but it covers the cases you're most likely to run into.

EXTENSION METHODS AREN'T RESOLVED DYNAMICALLY

The compiler emits *some* of the context of the call into the call site, as you've already seen. In particular, the site knows the static types that the compiler was aware of. But in current versions of C#, it *doesn't* know which using directives occurred in the source file containing the call. That means it doesn't know which extension methods are available at execution time.

Not only does that mean that you can't call extension methods *on* dynamic values—it means you can't pass them in to extension methods as arguments either. There are two workarounds, both of which are helpfully suggested by the compiler. If you know which overload you want, you can cast the dynamic value to the right type within the method call. Otherwise, assuming you know which static class contains the extension method, you can call it as a normal static method. The following listing shows an example of a failing call and both workarounds.

Listing 14.22 Calling extension methods with dynamic arguments

```
dynamic size = 5;
var numbers = Enumerable.Range(10, 10);
var error = numbers.Take(size);                  ⟵── Compile-time error
var workaround1 = numbers.Take((int) size);
var workaround2 = Enumerable.Take(numbers, size);
```

Both approaches will work if you want to call the extension method with the dynamic value as the implicit `this` value, too, although the cast becomes pretty ugly in that case.

DELEGATE CONVERSION RESTRICTIONS WITH DYNAMIC

The compiler has to know the exact delegate (or expression) type involved when converting a lambda expression, an anonymous method, or a method group. You can't assign any of these to a plain `Delegate` or `object` variable without casting, and the same is true for `dynamic`. But a cast is enough to keep the compiler happy. This could be useful in some situations if you want to execute the delegate dynamically later. You can also use a delegate with a dynamic type as one of its parameters, if that's useful.

Listing 14.23 shows some examples that'll compile, and some that won't.

Listing 14.23   Dynamic types and lambda expressions

```
dynamic badMethodGroup = Console.WriteLine;
dynamic goodMethodGroup = (Action<string>) Console.WriteLine;

dynamic badLambda = y => y + 1;
dynamic goodLambda = (Func<int, int>) (y => y + 1);

dynamic veryDynamic = (Func<dynamic, dynamic>) (d => d.SomeMethod());
```

Note that because of the way overload resolution works, this means you can't use lambda expressions in dynamically bound calls at all without casting—even if the only method that could possibly be invoked has a known delegate type at compile time. For example, this code won't compile:

```
void Method(Action<string> action, string value)
{
    action(value);
}
...
dynamic text = "error";
Method(x => Console.WriteLine(x), text);        ⟵ Compile-time error
```

It's worth pointing out that all is not lost in terms of LINQ and `dynamic` interacting. You can have a strongly typed collection with an element type of `dynamic`, at which point you can still use extension methods, lambda expressions, and even query expressions. The collection can contain objects of different types, and they'll behave appropriately at execution time, as shown in the following listing.

Listing 14.24   Querying a collection of dynamic elements

```
var list = new List<dynamic> { 50, 5m, 5d };
var query = from number in list
            where number > 4
            select (number / 20) * 10;

foreach (var item in query)
{
    Console.WriteLine(item);
}
```

This prints 20, 2.50, and 2.5. I deliberately divided by 20 and then multiplied by 10 to show the difference between decimal and double: the decimal type keeps track of precision without normalizing, which is why 2.50 is displayed instead of 2.5. The first value is an integer, so integer division is used; hence the value of 20 instead of 25.

CONSTRUCTORS AND STATIC METHODS

You can call constructors and static methods dynamically in the sense that you can specify dynamic arguments, but you can't resolve a constructor or static method against a dynamic type. There's just no way of specifying which type you mean.

If you run into a situation where you *want* to be able to do this dynamically in some way, try to think of ways to use instance methods instead, such as by creating a factory type. You may find that you can get the dynamic behavior you want using simple polymorphism or interfaces, but within static typing.

TYPE DECLARATIONS AND GENERIC TYPE PARAMETERS

You can't declare that a type has a base class of dynamic. You also can't use dynamic in a type parameter constraint, or as part of the set of interfaces that your type implements. You *can* use it as a type argument for a base class, or when you're specifying an interface for a variable declaration. For example, these declarations are invalid:

- class BaseTypeOfDynamic : dynamic
- class DynamicTypeConstraint<T> where T : dynamic
- class DynamicTypeConstraint<T> where T : List<dynamic>
- class DynamicInterface : IEnumerable<dynamic>

But these are valid:

- class GenericDynamicBaseClass : List<dynamic>
- IEnumerable<dynamic> variable;

Most of these restrictions around generics are the result of the dynamic type not really existing as a .NET type. The CLR doesn't know about it—any uses in your code are translated into objects with the DynamicAttribute applied appropriately. (For types such as List<dynamic> or Dictionary<string, dynamic>, the attribute indicates exactly which parts of the type are dynamic.) DynamicAttribute is only applied when the dynamic nature needs to be represented in metadata; local variables don't require the attribute, as nothing needs to inspect them after compilation to spot their dynamic nature.

All the dynamic behavior is achieved through compiler cleverness in deciding how the source code should be translated, and *library* cleverness at execution time. This equivalence between dynamic and object is evident in various places, but it's perhaps most obvious if you look at typeof(dynamic) and typeof(object), which return the same reference. In general, if you find you can't do what you want with the dynamic type, remember what it looks like to the CLR and see if that explains the problem. It may not suggest a solution, but at least you'll get better at predicting what'll work ahead of time.

That's all the detail I'll give about how C# 4 treats `dynamic`, but there's another aspect of the dynamic typing picture that we really need to look at to get a well-rounded view of the topic: reacting dynamically. It's one thing to be able to *call* code dynamically, but it's another to be able to *respond* dynamically to those calls.

Of course, if you're just calling into third-party code dynamically—or even using techniques such as multiple dispatch, shown earlier—you don't need to worry about this. I understand if you feel you've already had your fill of dynamic typing, at least for the moment; we've already covered an awful lot of ground. You can safely skip the next section and come back to it another time—nothing in the rest of the book relies on it. On the other hand, it's kind of fun.

14.5 Implementing dynamic behavior

The C# language doesn't offer any specific help in implementing dynamic behavior, but the framework does. A type has to implement `IDynamicMetaObjectProvider` in order to react dynamically, but there are two built-in implementations that can take a lot of the work away in many cases. We'll look at both of these, as well as a *very* simple implementation of `IDynamicMetaObjectProvider`, just to show you what's involved. These three approaches are really different, and we'll start with the simplest of them: `ExpandoObject`.

14.5.1 Using ExpandoObject

`System.Dynamic.ExpandoObject` looks like a funny beast at first glance. Its single public constructor has no parameters. It has no public methods, unless you count the explicit implementation of various interfaces—crucially, `IDynamicMetaObjectProvider` and `IDictionary<string, object>`. (The other interfaces it implements are all due to `IDictionary<,>` extending other interfaces.) Oh, and it's sealed, so it's not a matter of deriving from it to implement useful behavior. No, `ExpandoObject` is *only* useful if you refer to it via `dynamic` or one of the interfaces it implements.

SETTING AND RETRIEVING INDIVIDUAL PROPERTIES

The dictionary interface gives a hint as to its purpose—it's basically a way of storing objects via names. But those names can also be used as properties via dynamic typing. The following listing shows this working both ways.

Listing 14.25 Storing and retrieving values with `ExpandoObject`

```
dynamic expando = new ExpandoObject();
IDictionary<string, object> dictionary = expando;
expando.First = "value set dynamically";
Console.WriteLine(dictionary["First"]);

dictionary["Second"] = "value set with dictionary";
Console.WriteLine(expando.Second);
```

Listing 14.25 just uses strings as the values for convenience—you can use any object, as you'd expect with an `IDictionary<string, object>`. If you specify a delegate as the value, you can then call the delegate as if it were a method on the expando, as follows.

Listing 14.26 Faking methods on an `ExpandoObject` with delegates

```
dynamic expando = new ExpandoObject();
expando.AddOne = (Func<int, int>) (x => x + 1);
Console.Write(expando.AddOne(10));
```

Although this looks like a method access, you can also think of it as a property access that returns a delegate, and then an invocation of the delegate. If you created a statically typed class with an `AddOne` property of type `Func<int, int>`, you could use exactly the same syntax. The C# generated to call `AddOne` does in fact use an "invoke member" operation rather than trying to access it as a property and then invoke it, but `ExpandoObject` knows what to do. You can also access the property to retrieve the delegate if you want to.

Let's move on to a slightly larger example, although we're still not going to do anything particularly tricky.

CREATING A DOM TREE

We'll create a tree of expandos that mirrors an XML DOM tree. This is a pretty crude implementation, designed for simplicity of demonstration rather than real-world use. In particular, it assumes we don't have any XML namespaces to worry about.

Each node in the tree has two name/value pairs that'll always be present: `XElement`, which stores the original LINQ to XML element used to create the node, and `ToXml`, which stores a delegate that just returns the node as an XML string. You could just call `node.XElement.ToString()`, but this way gives another example of how delegates work with `ExpandoObject`. One point to mention is that we'll use `ToXml` instead of `ToString`, because setting the `ToString` property on an expando *doesn't* override the normal `ToString` method. This could lead to confusing bugs, so we'll use the different name instead.

The interesting part isn't the fixed names; it's the ones that depend on the real XML. We'll ignore attributes completely, but any *elements* in the original XML that are children of the original element are accessible via properties of the same name. For instance, consider the following XML:

```
<root>
  <branch>
    <leaf />
  </branch>
</root>
```

Assuming a dynamic variable called `root` representing the `root` element, you could access the leaf node with two simple property accesses, which can occur in a single statement:

```
dynamic leaf = root.branch.leaf;
```

If an element occurs more than once within a parent, the property refers to the first element with that name. To make the other elements accessible, each element will also be exposed via a property using the element name with a suffix of *List*, which returns a `List<dynamic>` containing each of the elements with that name in document order. In other words, the access could also be represented as `root.branchList[0].leaf`, or perhaps `root.branchList[0].leafList[0]`. Note that the indexer here is being applied to the list—you can't define your own indexer behavior for expandos.

The implementation of all of this is remarkably simple, with a single recursive method doing all the work, as shown in the following listing.

Listing 14.27 Implementing a simplistic XML DOM conversion with `ExpandoObject`

```
public static dynamic CreateDynamicXml(XElement element)
{
    dynamic expando = new ExpandoObject();
    expando.XElement = element;                                    ❶ Assigns a simple property
    expando.ToXml = (Func<string>)element.ToString;
                                                                   ❷ Converts a method
                                                                       group to delegate
    IDictionary<string, object> dictionary = expando;                 to use as property
    foreach (XElement subElement in element.Elements())
    {
        dynamic subNode = CreateDynamicXml(subElement);           ❸ Recursively
        string name = subElement.Name.LocalName;                      processes
        string listName = name + "List";                              subelement
        if (dictionary.ContainsKey(name))
        {
            ((List<dynamic>) dictionary[listName]).Add(subNode);  ❹ Adds repeated
        }                                                             element to list
        else
        {
            dictionary[name] = subNode;                           ❺ Creates new list
            dictionary[listName] = new List<dynamic> { subNode };     and sets properties
        }
    }
    return expando;
}
```

Without the list handling, listing 14.27 would've been even simpler. You set the `XElement` and `ToXml` properties dynamically (❶ and ❷), but you can't do that for the elements or their lists, because you don't know the names at compile time.[7] You use the dictionary representation instead (❹ and ❺), which also allows you to check for repeated elements easily. You can't tell whether an expando contains a value for a particular key just by accessing it as a property; any attempt to access a property that hasn't already been defined results in an exception. The recursive handling of subelements is as straightforward in dynamic code as it'd be in statically typed code; you just

---

[7] There's a certain irony here—the names you know statically can be set dynamically, but the names you know dynamically have to use static typing.

call the method recursively ❸ with each subelement, using its result to populate the appropriate properties.

You'll need some XML to use as an example, but it's helpful to picture it graphically as well as in its raw format. We'll use a simple structure representing books. Each book has a single name represented as an attribute, and may have multiple authors, each with their own element. Figure 14.4 shows the whole file as a tree; the following text is the raw XML:

```
<books>
  <book name="Mortal Engines">
    <author name="Philip Reeve" />
  </book>
  <book name="The Talisman">
    <author name="Stephen King" />
    <author name="Peter Straub" />
  </book>
  <book name="Rose">
    <author name="Holly Webb" />
    <excerpt>
      Rose was remembering the illustrations from
      Morally Instructive Tales for the Nursery.
    </excerpt>
  </book>
</books>
```

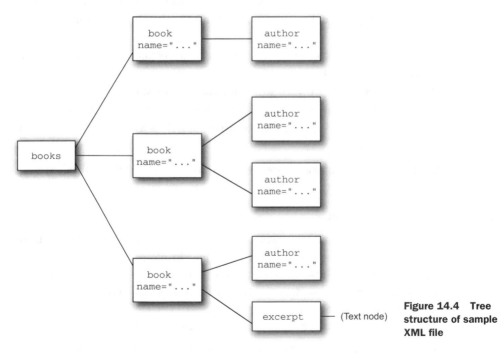

Figure 14.4 Tree structure of sample XML file

The following listing shows a brief example of how the expando code can be used with this XML document, including the `ToXml` and `XElement` properties. The books.xml file contains the XML document shown in the figure.

Listing 14.28   Using a dynamic DOM created from expandos

```
XDocument doc = XDocument.Load("books.xml");
dynamic root = CreateDynamicXml(doc.Root);
Console.WriteLine(root.book.author.ToXml());
Console.WriteLine(root.bookList[2].excerpt.XElement.Value);
```

Listing 14.28 should hold no surprises, unless you're unfamiliar with the `XElement.Value` property, which simply returns the text within an element. The output of the listing is as you'd expect:

```
<author name="Philip Reeve" />
Rose was remembering the illustrations from
Morally Instructive Tales for the Nursery.
```

This is all good, but there are a few issues with the DOM we've used:

- It doesn't handle attributes at all.
- Two properties are required for each element name, due to the need to represent lists.
- It'd be nice to override `ToString()` instead of adding an extra property.
- The result is mutable—there's nothing to stop code from adding its own properties afterward.
- Although the expando is mutable, it won't reflect any changes to the underlying `XElement` (which is also mutable).
- There are many opportunities for naming clashes, such as a node containing elements `Foo` and `FooList`, or elements called `XElement` or `ToXml`.
- The entire tree is populated up front, which is a lot of work if you only need a few nodes.

Fixing these issues requires more control than just being able to set properties. Enter `DynamicObject`.

14.5.2 *Using DynamicObject*

`DynamicObject` is a more powerful way of interacting with the DLR than using `ExpandoObject`, but it's a lot simpler than implementing `IDynamicMetaObject-Provider`. Although it's not *actually* an abstract class, you really need to derive from it to do anything useful—and the only constructor is protected, so it might as well be abstract for all practical purposes.

There are four kinds of methods that you might want to override:

- `TryXXX()` invocation methods, representing dynamic calls to the object
- `GetDynamicMemberNames()`, which can return a list of the available members

- The normal `Equals()`, `GetHashCode()`, and `ToString()` methods, which can be overridden as usual
- `GetMetaObject()`, which returns the meta-object used by the DLR

We'll look at all but the last of these to improve the XML DOM representation, and we'll discuss meta-objects in the next section when we implement `IDynamicMeta-ObjectProvider` from scratch. In addition, it can be useful to create new members in a derived type, even if callers are likely to use instances as dynamic values. Before we take any of these steps, we'll need a class to hold all these members.

GETTING STARTED

As we're deriving from `DynamicObject` instead of just calling methods on it, we need to start with a class declaration. The following listing shows the basic skeleton that we'll flesh out.

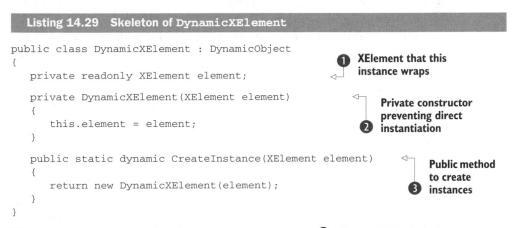

Listing 14.29 Skeleton of `DynamicXElement`

```
public class DynamicXElement : DynamicObject
{
    private readonly XElement element;          // 1 XElement that this instance wraps

    private DynamicXElement(XElement element)   // 2 Private constructor preventing direct instantiation
    {
        this.element = element;
    }

    public static dynamic CreateInstance(XElement element)  // 3 Public method to create instances
    {
        return new DynamicXElement(element);
    }
}
```

The `DynamicXElement` class just wraps an `XElement` **1**. This will be all the state you have, which is a significant design decision in itself. In the `ExpandoObject` earlier, you recursed into its structure and populated a whole mirrored tree. You really had to do that, because you couldn't intercept property accesses with custom code later on. Obviously this is more expensive than the `DynamicXElement` approach, where you'll only ever wrap the elements of the tree when you actually have to. Additionally, it means that any changes to the `XElement` after you've created the expando are effectively lost; if you add more subelements, for example, they won't appear as properties because they weren't present when you took the snapshot. The lightweight wrapping approach is always "live"—any changes you make in the tree will be visible through the wrapper.

The *disadvantage* of this is that you no longer provide the same idea of identity that you had before. With the expando, the expression `root.book.author` would evaluate to the same reference if you used it twice. Using `DynamicXElement`, each time the expression is evaluated it'll create new instances to wrap the subelements. You *could* implement some sort of smart caching to get around this, but it could end up getting very complicated, very quickly.

In listing 14.29 the constructor of DynamicXElement is private ❷, and there's a public static method to create instances ❸. The method has a return type of dynamic, because that's how you expect developers to use the class. A slight alternative would've been to create a separate public static class with an extension method to XElement, and to keep DynamicXElement itself internal. The class itself is an implementation detail; there's not much point in using it unless you're working dynamically.

With this skeleton in place, you can start adding features. We'll start with really simple stuff: adding methods and indexers as if this were a normal class.

DYNAMICOBJECT SUPPORT FOR SIMPLE MEMBERS

When we discussed expandos, there were two members we *always* added: the ToXml method and the XElement property. This time you don't need a new method to convert the object to a string representation; you can override the normal ToString() method. You can also provide the XElement property as if you were writing any other class.

One of the nice things about DynamicObject is that when some behavior doesn't need to be truly dynamic, you don't have to implement it dynamically. Before the associated meta-object uses any of the TryXXX methods, it checks whether the member already exists as a straightforward CLR member. If it does, that member will be called. This makes life significantly simpler.

We'll have two indexers in DynamicXElement as well, to provide access to attributes and replace the element lists. The following listing shows the new code to be added to the class.

Listing 14.30 Adding nondynamic members to DynamicXElement

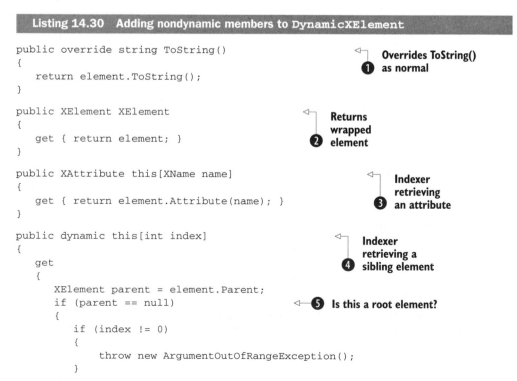

```
public override string ToString()                    ◁┐  Overrides ToString()
{                                                    ❶  as normal
    return element.ToString();
}

public XElement XElement                             ◁┐  Returns
{                                                        wrapped
    get { return element; }                          ❷  element
}

public XAttribute this[XName name]                   ◁┐  Indexer
{                                                        retrieving
    get { return element.Attribute(name); }          ❸  an attribute
}

public dynamic this[int index]                       ◁┐  Indexer
{                                                        retrieving a
    get                                              ❹  sibling element
    {
        XElement parent = element.Parent;
        if (parent == null)                          ◁─❺  Is this a root element?
        {
            if (index != 0)
            {
                throw new ArgumentOutOfRangeException();
            }
        }
```

```
        return this;                                        ⑥ Find
    }                                                          appropriate
    XElement sibling = parent.Elements(element.Name)    ◁┘    sibling
                            .ElementAt(index);
    return element == sibling ? this
                             : new DynamicXElement(sibling);
    }
}
```

There's a fair amount of code in listing 14.30, but most of it is straightforward. You override ToString() ❶ by proxying the call to the XElement, and if you wanted to implement value equality, you could do something similar for Equals() and GetHash-Code(). The property returning the underlying element ❷ and the indexer for attributes ❸ are also simple, although it's worth noting that you only need to use an XName for the parameter to the attribute indexer; if you provide a string at execution time, DynamicObject will take care of calling the implicit conversion to XName for you.

The trickiest part of the code is understanding what the indexer with the int parameter ❹ is meant to be doing. It's probably easiest to explain this in terms of expected usage. The idea is to avoid having the extra list property by making an element act as both a single element and a list of child elements of the same name. Figure 14.5 shows the previous sample XML with a few expressions to reach different nodes within it.

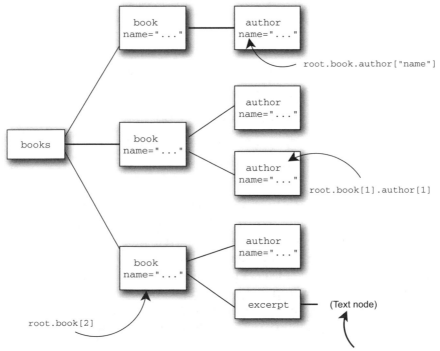

Figure 14.5 Selecting data using `DynamicXElement`

Once you understand what the indexer is meant to do, the implementation is fairly simple, complicated only by the possibility that you could already be at the top of the tree ❺. Otherwise you just have to ask the element for all its siblings, and then pick the one you've been asked for ❻.

So far we haven't looked at anything dynamic except in terms of the return type of CreateInstance()—none of these examples will work because you haven't written the code to fetch subelements. Let's fix that now.

OVERRIDING TRYXXX METHODS

In DynamicObject you respond to calls dynamically by overriding one of the TryXXX methods. There are 12 of them, representing different types of operations, as shown in table 14.1.

Table 14.1   Virtual TryXXX methods in DynamicObject

Name	Type of call represented (where x is the dynamic object)
TryBinaryOperation	Binary operation, such as x + y
TryConvert	Conversions, such as (Target) x
TryCreateInstance	Object creation expressions; no equivalent in C#
TryDeleteIndex	Indexer removal operation; no equivalent in C#
TryDeleteMember	Property removal operation; no equivalent in C#
TryGetIndex	Indexer getter, such as x[10]
TryGetMember	Property getter, such as x.Property
TryInvoke	Direct invocation treating x like a delegate, such as x(10)
TryInvokeMember	Invocation of a member, such as x.Method()
TrySetIndex	Indexer setter, such as x[10] = 20
TrySetMember	Property setter, such as x.Property = 10
TryUnaryOperation	Unary operation, such as !x or -x

Each of these methods has a Boolean return type to indicate whether the binding was successful. Each takes an appropriate binder as the first parameter, and if the operation logically has arguments (for instance, the arguments to a method, or the indexes for an indexer), these are represented as an object[]. Finally, if the operation might have a return value (which includes everything except the set and delete operations), there's an out parameter of type object to capture that value.

The exact type of the binder depends on the operation; there's a different binder type for each of the operations. For example, the full signature of TryInvokeMember is

```
public virtual bool TryInvokeMember(InvokeMemberBinder binder,
    object[] args, out object result)
```

You only need to override the methods representing operations you support dynamically. In this case, you have dynamic read-only properties (for the elements) so you need to override `TryGetMember()`, as shown in the following listing.

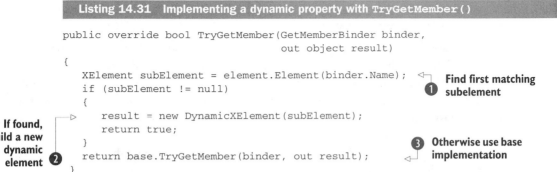

Listing 14.31 Implementing a dynamic property with `TryGetMember()`

```
public override bool TryGetMember(GetMemberBinder binder,
                                  out object result)
{
    XElement subElement = element.Element(binder.Name);        ◁┐  Find first matching
    if (subElement != null)                                      ❶  subelement
    {
        result = new DynamicXElement(subElement);
        return true;
    }
    return base.TryGetMember(binder, out result);              ◁┘  Otherwise use base
}                                                                ❸  implementation
```

If found, build a new dynamic element ❷

The implementation in listing 14.31 is simple. The binder contains the name of the requested property, so you look for the appropriate subelement in the tree ❶. If there is one, you create a new `DynamicXElement` with it, assign that to the output parameter result, and return `true` to indicate that the call was bound successfully ❷. If there was no subelement with the right name, you just call the base implementation of `Try-GetMember()` ❸. The base implementation of each of the `TryXXX` methods just returns `false` and sets the output parameter to `null`, if there is one. You could easily have done this explicitly, but you'd have had two separate statements: one to set the output parameter and one to return `false`. If you prefer the slightly longer code, there's no reason not to write it—the base implementations are just slightly convenient in terms of doing everything required to indicate that the binding failed.

I've sidestepped one bit of complexity: the binder has another property (`Ignore-Case`) that indicates whether the property should be bound in a case-insensitive way. For example, Visual Basic is case-insensitive, so its binder implementation would return `true` for this property, whereas C#'s would return `false`. In this situation, it's slightly awkward. Not only would it be more work for `TryGetMember` to find the element in a case-insensitive manner ("more work" is always unpleasant, but it's not a good reason not to implement it), but there's the more philosophical problem of what happens when you then use the indexer (by number) to select siblings. Should the object remember whether it's case-sensitive, and select siblings in the same way later on? You could easily get into situations where the behavior is both hard to predict and hard to explain in documentation. This sort of impedance mismatch is likely to happen in other similar situations too. If you aim for perfection, you're likely to tie yourself up in knots. Instead, find a pragmatic solution that you're confident you can implement and maintain, and then document the restrictions.

With all this in place, you can test `DynamicXElement`, as shown in the following listing.

Listing 14.32   Testing `DynamicXElement`

```
XDocument doc = XDocument.Load("books.xml");
dynamic root = DynamicXElement.CreateInstance(doc.Root);
Console.WriteLine(root.book[2]["name"]);
Console.WriteLine(root.book[1].author[1]);
Console.WriteLine(root.book);
```

You could add more complexity to the class, of course. You could add a `Parent` property to go back up the tree, or you might want to change the code to use methods to access subelements and make property access represent attributes. The principle would be exactly the same: where you know the name in advance, implement it as a normal class member. If you need it to be dynamic, override the appropriate `DynamicObject` method.

There's one more piece of polish to apply to `DynamicXElement` before we leave it. It's time to advertise what you've got to offer.

OVERRIDING GetDynamicMemberNames

Some languages, such as Python, allow you to ask an object what names it knows about. For example, you can use the `dir` function in Python to output a list. This information is useful in a REPL environment, and it can also be handy when you're debugging in an IDE. The DLR makes this information available through the `GetDynamicMemberNames()` method of both `DynamicObject` and `DynamicMetaObject` (you'll meet the latter in a minute). All you have to do is override this method to provide a sequence of the dynamic member names, and your object's properties are more discoverable. The following listing shows the implementation for `DynamicXElement`.

Listing 14.33   Implementing `GetDynamicMemberNames` in `DynamicXElement`

```
public override IEnumerable<string> GetDynamicMemberNames()
{
    return element.Elements()
                  .Select(x => x.Name.LocalName)
                  .Distinct()
                  .OrderBy(x => x);
}
```

As you can see, all you need is a simple LINQ query. That won't *always* be the case, but I suspect many dynamic implementations will be able to use LINQ in this way.

You need to make sure that you don't return the same value more than once if there's more than one element with any particular name, and the results are sorted for consistency. In the Visual Studio 2010 debugger, you can expand the Dynamic View of a dynamic object and see the property names and values, as shown in figure 14.6.

You can drill down through the dynamic object, showing the Dynamic View at each level. For figure 14.6 I've drilled down from the document, to the first book, to the author. The Dynamic View of the author shows that there's no further information in the hierarchy.

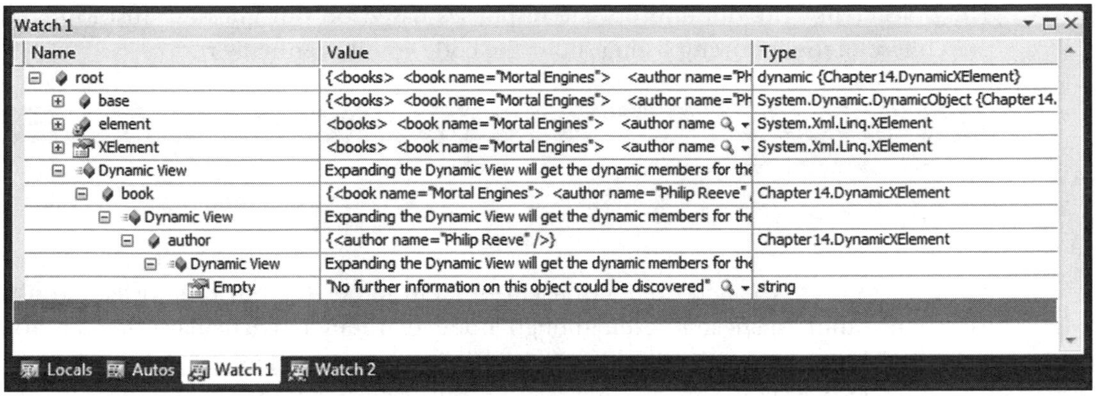

Figure 14.6   Visual Studio 2010 displaying dynamic properties of a `DynamicXElement`

We've now finished the `DynamicXElement` class, at least as far as we're going to take it in this book. I believe that `DynamicObject` hits a sweet spot between control and simplicity: it's fairly easy to get it right, and it has far fewer restrictions than `Expando-Object`. But if you really need total control over binding, you'll need to implement `IDynamicMetaObjectProvider` directly.

14.5.3 Implementing IDynamicMetaObjectProvider

I won't go into a lot of detail here, but I really want to show at least one example of low-level dynamic behavior. The tough bit of implementing `IDynamicMetaObject-Provider` isn't the interface itself—it's creating the `DynamicMetaObject` to return from the interface's sole method. `DynamicMetaObject` is a bit like `DynamicObject` in that it contains a lot of methods, and you override individual ones to affect the behavior; where you've previously overridden `DynamicObject.TryGetMember`, you'd override `DynamicMetaObject.BindGetMember`. But within the overridden methods, instead of taking the required action directly, the idea is to build up an expression tree *describing* the required action and the circumstances in which that action should be taken. That extra level of indirection is why it's a *meta-object*.

I'll leap straight into an example, and then leap out with only a brief explanation. I really want to get across the difference in level of interaction here—it's a bit like tinkering with the guts of the JIT compiler. Most C# developers won't need to know the details, and if you do need to do this, it probably means you're trying to write a library that responds dynamically but has to perform well too. Alternatively, it may mean that you're trying to build your own dynamic language. If that's the case, then good luck—and please find a more comprehensive resource than this meager example.

The example isn't meant to be clever; it's a Rumpelstiltskin type. We'll create an instance of Rumpelstiltskin with a given name (stored in a perfectly ordinary string variable) and call methods on the object until we call a method with the right name.

The object will write out appropriate responses based on our guesses.[8] Just to make this concrete, the following listing shows the code you'll eventually run.

Listing 14.34   The final aim: calling methods dynamically until you hit the right name

```
dynamic x = new Rumpelstiltskin("Hermione");
x.Harry();
x.Ron();
x.Hermione();
```

The object won't be called Rumpelstiltskin—that would be too obvious. Instead, you'll use some other magicians, even though none of them is particularly famous for alchemy. The aim is for the first two method calls to result in denials, and the third to admit defeat. You'll also make your method calls return a Boolean value to indicate whether the guess was successful, but for brevity we won't use the result here.

Let's look at the Rumpelstiltskin type first. Don't forget that this *isn't* the meta-object—that'll come later. The next listing shows the complete code.

Listing 14.35   The `Rumpelstiltskin` type, without its meta-object code

```
public sealed class Rumpelstiltskin : IDynamicMetaObjectProvider
{
    private readonly string name;
    public Rumpelstiltskin(string name)        ←—❶ Constructs a new instance
    {
        this.name = name;
    }

    public DynamicMetaObject GetMetaObject(Expression expression) ←┑ Exposes
    {                                                              ❷ dynamic
        return new MetaRumpelstiltskin(expression, this);            behavior
    }

    private object RespondToWrongGuess(string guess)   ←┑ Responds
    {                                                   ❸ to guesses
        Console.WriteLine("No, I'm not {0}! (I'm {1}.)",
            guess, name);
        return false;
    }

    private object RespondToRightGuess()
    {
        Console.WriteLine("Curses! Foiled again!");
        return true;
    }
}
```

There are three aspects to this class. There's construction ❶, which is perfectly ordinary. There's the implementation of IDynamicMetaObjectProvider's sole method ❷, and then there are two methods you'll use to perform the real work ❸.

---

[8] If you're not familiar with the fairy tale of Rumpelstiltskin, look at its Wikipedia article (http://en.wikipedia.org/wiki/Rumpelstiltskin). The example will make more sense afterward!

The meta-object constructed at ❷ needs to know which instance it's responding to and which expression tree refers to the instance within the calling code. You're given the expression tree as a parameter, and you know your own instance via the `this` reference, so you just pass those on in the constructor.

> **WHY DO THE METHODS RETURN OBJECT?** You may be wondering why the methods are declared to return `object` rather than `bool`. My original implementation actually had `void` methods, but unfortunately dynamic method invocations are expected to return something, and the binder always expects `object`, in my experience. (There's a `ReturnType` property you can check.) That makes a call to a `void` method throw an exception at execution time, and the same is true for a `bool` method; you need to perform the boxing yourself to make the types match up properly. You could build the boxing into the expression tree, but that's more painful than changing the return type of the method. These are the kinds of subtleties you'll need to deal with if you ever implement `IDynamicMetaObjectProvider` in real life.

Strictly speaking, you don't *need* the two response methods. When you build up the behavior to react to the incoming method calls, you *could* express that logic directly in an expression tree. But it'd be relatively painful to do so, compared with just returning an expression tree that calls the right method. More to the point, though, it wouldn't be too hard in this case; in other situations it could be much worse. You'll effectively create a bridge between the static and dynamic worlds, responding to dynamic method calls by redirecting them to static ones with appropriate arguments. This leads to simpler code in the meta-object.

Speaking of which, let's finally look at the code for `MetaRumpelstiltskin`—it's in the following listing, and it's a private nested class inside `Rumpelstiltskin`.

Listing 14.36 The real dynamic guts of `Rumpelstiltskin`—its meta-object

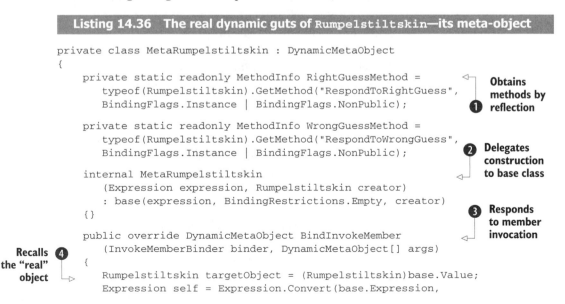

```
private class MetaRumpelstiltskin : DynamicMetaObject
{
    private static readonly MethodInfo RightGuessMethod =          Obtains
        typeof(Rumpelstiltskin).GetMethod("RespondToRightGuess",    methods by
        BindingFlags.Instance | BindingFlags.NonPublic);          ❶ reflection

    private static readonly MethodInfo WrongGuessMethod =
        typeof(Rumpelstiltskin).GetMethod("RespondToWrongGuess",    Delegates
        BindingFlags.Instance | BindingFlags.NonPublic);          ❷ construction
                                                                     to base class
    internal MetaRumpelstiltskin
        (Expression expression, Rumpelstiltskin creator)
        : base(expression, BindingRestrictions.Empty, creator)      Responds
    {}                                                            ❸ to member
                                                                     invocation
    public override DynamicMetaObject BindInvokeMember
        (InvokeMemberBinder binder, DynamicMetaObject[] args)
    {
        Rumpelstiltskin targetObject = (Rumpelstiltskin)base.Value;
        Expression self = Expression.Convert(base.Expression,
```

Recalls the "real" object ❹

```
        typeof(Rumpelstiltskin));
```

⑤ **Determines appropriate behavior**

```
Expression targetBehavior;
if (binder.Name == targetObject.name)
{
    targetBehavior = Expression.Call(self, RightGuessMethod);
}
else
{
    targetBehavior = Expression.Call(self, WrongGuessMethod,
        Expression.Constant(binder.Name));
}
```

Responds with behavior and restrictions ⑥

```
var restrictions = BindingRestrictions.GetInstanceRestriction
    (self, targetObject);
return new DynamicMetaObject(targetBehavior, restrictions);
    }
}
```

As I type this, I can almost see your eyes glazing over. Listing 14.36 is dense code, and it looks like an awful lot of work to get a simple job done. Just remember: you're unlikely to ever need to do this, so just relax and let the general flavor of the code sink in while the details wash over you.

The first half of the code is genuinely easy. You stash the `MethodInfo` for the two response methods in static variables ❶ (they don't change for different instances) and declare a constructor that does nothing but pass its parameters up to the base class ❷. All of the real work is done in `BindInvokeMember` ❸, which has to work out two things—how the object should react to the method call, and the circumstances in which that decision is valid.

You want to react by calling either `RespondToRightGuess` or `RespondToWrongGuess` based on whether the name of the method call is the same as the name of the object. The meta-object knows what the real instance is, because you passed it in to the constructor. You access it again using the `Value` property and remember it using the `targetObject` variable ❹. You also need the expression tree that was originally used to create the meta-object, so that you can bind the appropriate method call entirely within expression trees. The `Expression.Convert` method is the expression-tree equivalent of the cast in the previous line.

Once you know the real object, you can check its name against the method call that you're binding, which is available via the `InvokeMemberBinder.Name` property. You build a call to the appropriate method using `Expression.Call`, passing in the name of the method as an argument if the guess was wrong ❺. Again, I'd like to stress that at this point you're not actually calling the method—you're describing the method call.

The restrictions in this case are simple: this call will always be bound in the same way if it's calling the same argument, but it'd be bound differently if it were called on a different object, because it could have a different name. `GetInstanceRestriction` returns an appropriate restriction; if you wanted to always behave the same way regardless of which instance the method was called on, you might use GetType-Restriction instead, to indicate that the call would be handled the same way for any instance of Rumpelstiltskin. The full source code includes an alternative implementation that does exactly this, by always passing in the actual method name, putting the condition testing inside the normal method.

Finally, you create a new DynamicMetaObject representing the results of the binding ❻. It's fairly confusing for the result to be of the same type as the object that's working out the binding, but that's how the DLR works.

At this point, you're done—cross your fingers, run the code, and see if it works... Then debug it a few times to work out exactly what's wrong, if you're anything like me. As I've said, this isn't something that most developers will need to take on—it's a bit like LINQ, in that far more people will use LINQ than implement their own IQueryable-based LINQ provider. It's useful to get a peek at how it all works instead of treating it as magic, but most of the time you can just sit back and enjoy the hard work of the DLR team.

14.6 Summary

It feels like we've come a long way from mainstream, statically typed C#. We've looked at some situations where dynamic typing can be useful, at how C# 4 makes it possible (both in terms of the code you write and how it works under the surface), and at how to respond dynamically to calls. Along the way, you've seen a bit of COM, a bit of Python, some reflection, and you've learned a little about the Dynamic Language Runtime.

This has *not* been a complete guide to how the DLR works, or even how C# operates with it. The truth is, this is a deep topic with many dark corners. Many of the problems are obscure enough that you won't bump into them—and most developers won't even use the simple scenarios often. I'm sure whole books will be written about the DLR, but I hope I've given enough detail here to let 99 percent of C# developers get on with their jobs without needing any more information. If you want to know more, the documentation on the DLR website is a good starting point (see http:// mng.bz/0M6A).

If you never use the dynamic type, you can pretty much ignore dynamic typing entirely. I recommend that you do exactly that for the majority of your code—in particular, I wouldn't use it as a crutch to avoid creating appropriate interfaces, base classes, and so on. Where you *do* need dynamic typing, I'd use it as sparingly as possible. Don't take the attitude, "I'm using dynamic in this method, so I might as well make *everything* dynamic."

I don't want to sound too negative. If you find yourself in a situation where dynamic typing is helpful, I'm sure you'll be thankful that it's present in C# 4. Even if you never need it for production code, I'd encourage you to give it a try for the fun of it—I've found it fascinating to delve into. You may also find the DLR useful without really using dynamic typing; most of this chapter's Python example didn't use any features of dynamic typing, but it used the DLR to execute the Python script containing the configuration data.

Between this chapter and the previous one, that covers all the new features in C# 4. Next up, C# 5, which has an even narrower focus than C# 4 did with dynamic typing. It's really *all* about asynchrony…

Part 5

C# 5: Asynchrony made simple

It's simple to describe C# 5: it has exactly one big feature (asynchronous functions) and two tiny ones.

Chapter 15 is all about asynchrony. The aim of the asynchronous functions feature (often just called *async/await* for short) is to make asynchronous programming easy…or at least easier than it was before. It doesn't try to remove the *inherent* complexity of asynchrony; you still need to consider the consequences of operations completing in an unexpected order, or the user pressing another button before the first operation has completed, but it removes a lot of the incidental complexity. This allows you to see the wood for the trees, and build robust, readable solutions to those inherent complexities.

In the past, asynchronous code has often turned into spaghetti, with the logical execution path jumping from method to method as one asynchronous call completes and starts another one. With asynchronous functions, you can write code that *looks* synchronous, with familiar control structures such as loops and `try`/`catch`/`finally` blocks, but with an asynchronous execution flow triggered by a new contextual keyword (`await`). The difference in readability is simply staggering, in my experience. We'll go into a lot of depth on this topic, not just in terms of how the language behaves, but how it's implemented by the Microsoft C# compiler.

That just leaves the two features covered in chapter 16: a slight change to the irritating `foreach` behavior you saw in chapter 5, and some new attributes that work with the optional parameters feature from C# 4 to allow the line number, member name, and source file of a piece of code to be automatically provided by the compiler. I'll then wrap up this edition of the book in my customary way with a few closing thoughts.

You may be forgiven for thinking that this doesn't sound like a lot, particularly as I've been deliberately dismissive of the features covered in chapter 16. Don't be fooled; asynchronous functions are a really big deal, particularly if you're writing any Windows Store applications using WinRT. The API exposed by WinRT is built around asynchrony, in order to combat unresponsive user interfaces. Without asynchronous functions, it would be a huge pain to use. With the features of C# 5, you still need to think, but the code can be as clear as I can imagine asynchronous code ever becoming. So, rather than more description of how wonderful it is, let's get on and meet the feature...

Asynchrony with async/await

This chapter covers

- The fundamental aims of asynchrony
- Writing async methods and delegates
- Compiler transformations for async
- The task-based asynchronous pattern
- Asynchrony in WinRT

Asynchrony has been a thorn in the side of developers for years. It's been known to be *useful* as a way of avoiding tying up a thread while waiting for some arbitrary task to complete, but it's also been a pain in the neck to implement correctly.

Even within the .NET Framework (which is still relatively young in the grand scheme of things), we've had three different models to try to make things simpler:

- The `BeginFoo` / `EndFoo` approach from .NET 1.x, using `IAsyncResult` and `AsyncCallback` to propagate results
- The event-based asynchronous pattern from .NET 2.0, as implemented by `BackgroundWorker` and `WebClient`
- The Task Parallel Library (TPL) introduced in .NET 4 and expanded in .NET 4.5

Despite its generally excellent design, writing robust and readable asynchronous code with the TPL was hard. Although the support for parallelism was great, there are some aspects of general asynchrony that are much better fixed in a language instead of purely in libraries.

ASYNC/AWAIT WILL ROCK YOUR WORLD   The introductory list of topics may make this chapter sound rather dull. It's an accurate list, but it fails to convey the excitement I feel about this feature. I've been playing with async/await for about two years now, and it still makes me feel like a giddy schoolboy. I firmly believe it will do for asynchrony what LINQ did for data handling when C# 3 came out—except that dealing with asynchrony was a far harder problem. To achieve the proper effect, please read this chapter in an overexcited mental voice. Hopefully I'll infect you with my enthusiasm for the feature along the way.

The main feature of C# 5 builds on the TPL so that you can write synchronous-looking code that uses asynchrony where appropriate. Gone is the spaghetti of callbacks, event subscriptions, and fragmented error handling; instead, asynchronous code expresses its intentions clearly, and in a form that builds on the structures developers are already familiar with. A new language construct allows you to "await" an asynchronous operation. This "awaiting" looks very much like a normal blocking call, in that the rest of your code won't continue until the operation has completed, but it manages to do this without blocking the currently executing thread. Don't worry if that statement sounds completely contradictory—all will become clear over the course of the chapter.

The .NET Framework has embraced asynchrony wholeheartedly in version 4.5, exposing asynchronous versions of a great many operations, following a newly documented *task-based asynchronous pattern* to give a consistent experience across multiple APIs. Additionally, the new Windows Runtime platform[1] used to create Windows Store applications in Windows 8 enforces asynchrony for all long-running (or potentially long-running) operations. In short, the future is asynchronous, and you'd be foolish not to take advantage of the new language features when trying to manage the additional complexity. Even if you're not using .NET 4.5, Microsoft has created a NuGet package (`Microsoft.Bcl.Async`) that allows you to use the new features when targeting .NET 4, Silverlight 4 or 5, or Windows Phone 7.5 or 8.

Just to be clear, C# hasn't become omniscient, guessing where you might want to perform operations concurrently or asynchronously. The compiler is smart, but it doesn't attempt to remove the *inherent* complexity of asynchronous execution. You still need to think carefully, but the beauty of C# 5 is that all the tedious and confusing boilerplate code that used to be required has gone. Without the distraction of all the fluff required to make your code asynchronous to start with, you can concentrate on the hard bits.

---

[1] This is commonly known as WinRT; it's not to be confused with Windows RT, which is the version of Windows 8 that runs on ARM processors.

A word of warning: this topic is reasonably advanced. It has the unfortunate properties of being incredibly important (realistically, even entry-level developers will need to have a passing understanding of it in a few years) but also quite tricky to get your head around to start with. Just as in the rest of this book, I won't shy away from the complexity—we'll look at what's going on in a fair amount of detail.

It's just possible that I may break your brain a little, hopefully putting it back together again later on. If it all starts sounding a little crazy, don't worry—it's not just you; bafflement is an entirely natural reaction. The good news is that when you're *using* C# 5, it all makes sense on the surface. It's only when you try to think of exactly what's going on behind the scenes that things get tough. Of course, we'll do exactly that later on—as well as look at how to use the feature effectively.

Let's make a start.

15.1 Introducing asynchronous functions

So far I've claimed that C# 5 makes async easier, but I've only given a tiny description of the features involved. Let's fix that, and then look at an example.

C# 5 introduces the concept of an *asynchronous function*. This is always either a method or an anonymous function[2] that's declared with the `async` modifier, and it can include `await` expressions. These `await` expressions are the points where things get interesting from a language perspective: if the value that the expression is awaiting isn't available yet, the asynchronous function will return immediately, and it will then continue where it left off (in an appropriate thread) when the value becomes available. The natural flow of "don't execute the next statement until this one has completed" is still maintained, but without blocking.

I'll break that woolly description down into more concrete terms and behavior later on, but you really need to see an example of it before it's likely to make any sense.

15.1.1 First encounters of the asynchronous kind

Let's start with something very simple, but that demonstrates asynchrony in a practical way. We often curse network latency for causing delays in our real applications, but latency does make it easy to show why asynchrony is so important. Take a look at the following listing.

Listing 15.1 Displaying a page length asynchronously

```
class AsyncForm : Form
{
    Label label;
    Button button;

    public AsyncForm()
    {
        label = new Label { Location = new Point(10, 20),
                            Text = "Length" };
```

---

[2] Just as a reminder, an anonymous function is either a lambda expression or an anonymous method.

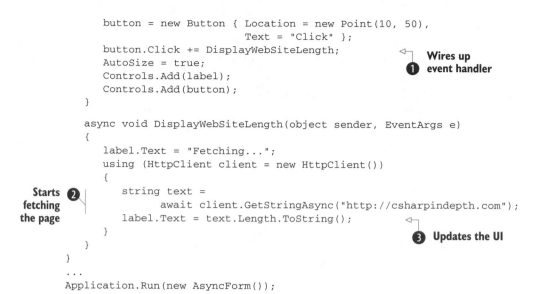

```
        button = new Button { Location = new Point(10, 50),
                              Text = "Click" };
        button.Click += DisplayWebSiteLength;
        AutoSize = true;
        Controls.Add(label);
        Controls.Add(button);
    }

    async void DisplayWebSiteLength(object sender, EventArgs e)
    {
        label.Text = "Fetching...";
        using (HttpClient client = new HttpClient())
        {
            string text =
                await client.GetStringAsync("http://csharpindepth.com");
            label.Text = text.Length.ToString();
        }
    }
}
...
Application.Run(new AsyncForm());
```

Wires up ① **event handler**

Starts ② **fetching the page**

③ **Updates the UI**

The first part of listing 15.1 simply creates the UI and hooks up an event handler for the button in a straightforward way ①. It's the `DisplayWebSiteLength` method that's of interest here. When you click on the button, the text of the book's home page is fetched ②, and the label is updated to display the HTML length in characters ③. The `HttpClient` is also disposed appropriately, whether the operation succeeds or fails—something that would be all too easy to forget if you were writing similar asynchronous code in C# 4.

> **DISPOSING OF TASKS** I'm careful to dispose of the `HttpClient` when I'm finished using it, but I'm not disposing of the task returned by `GetStringAsync`, even though `Task` implements `IDisposable`. Fortunately, you really don't need to dispose of tasks in general. The background of this is somewhat complicated, but Stephen Toub explains it in a blog post dedicated to the topic: http://mng.bz/E6L3.

I could have written a smaller example program as a console app, but hopefully listing 15.1 makes a more convincing demo. In particular, if you remove the `async` and `await` contextual keywords, change `HttpClient` to `WebClient`, and change `GetStringAsync` to `DownloadString`, the code will still compile and work...but the UI will freeze while it fetches the contents of the page.[3] If you run the async version (ideally over a slow network connection), you'll see that the UI is responsive—you can still move the window around while the web page is fetching.

---

[3] `HttpClient` is in some senses the "new and improved" `WebClient`—it's the preferred HTTP API for .NET 4.5 onwards, and it *only* contains asynchronous operations. If you're writing a Windows Store app, you don't even have the option of using `WebClient`.

Most developers are familiar with the two golden rules of threading in Windows Forms development:

- Don't perform any time-consuming action on the UI thread.
- Don't access any UI controls *other* than on the UI thread.

These are easier to state than to obey. As an exercise, you might want to try a few different ways of creating code similar to listing 15.1 *without* using the new features of C# 5. For this extremely simple example, it's not actually too bad to use the event-based `WebClient.DownloadStringAsync` method, but as soon as more complex flow control (error handling, waiting for multiple pages to complete, and so on) comes into the equation, the "legacy" code quickly becomes hard to maintain, whereas the C# 5 code can be modified in a natural way.

At this point, the `DisplayWebSiteLength` method feels somewhat magical: you know it does what you need it to, but you have no idea how. Let's take it apart just a little bit, saving the really gory details for later.

15.1.2 Breaking down the first example

We'll start by expanding the method very slightly—splitting the call to `Http-Client.GetStringAsync` from the `await` expression to highlight the types involved:

```
async void DisplayWebSiteLength(object sender, EventArgs e)
{
    label.Text = "Fetching...";
    using (HttpClient client = new HttpClient())
    {
        Task<string> task =
            client.GetStringAsync("http://csharpindepth.com");
        string text = await task;
        label.Text = text.Length.ToString();
    }
}
```

Notice how the type of `task` is `Task<string>`, but the type of the `await task` expression is just `string`. In this sense, an `await` expression performs an "unwrapping" operation—at least when the value being awaited is a `Task<TResult>`. (You can await other types too, as you'll see, but `Task<TResult>` is a good starting point.) That's one aspect of `await` that doesn't seem directly related to asynchrony but makes life easier.

The main purpose of `await` is to avoid blocking while you wait for time-consuming operations to complete. You may be wondering how this all works in the concrete terms of threading. You're setting `label.Text` at both the start and end of the method, so it's reasonable to assume that both of those statements are executed on the UI thread...and yet you're clearly *not* blocking the UI thread while you wait for the web page to download.

The trick is that the method actually returns as soon as you hit the `await` expression. Up until that point, it executes synchronously on the UI thread, just as any other event handler would. If you put a breakpoint on the first line and hit it in the debugger, you'll see that the stack trace shows that the button is busy raising its `Click` event, including the `Button.OnClick` method. When you reach the `await`, the code checks whether the result is already available, and if it's not (which will almost certainly be the case) it schedules a *continuation* to be executed when the web operation has completed. In this example, the continuation executes the rest of the method, effectively jumping to the end of the `await` expression, back in the UI thread, just as you want in order to manipulate the UI.

> **CONTINUATIONS**   A continuation is effectively a callback to be executed when an asynchronous operation (or indeed any `Task`) has completed. In an async method, the continuation maintains the control state of the method; just as a closure maintains its environment in terms of variables, a continuation remembers where it had got to, so it can continue from there when it's executed. The `Task` class has a method specifically for attaching continuations: `Task.ContinueWith`.

If you then put a breakpoint in the code *after* the `await` expression, you'll see that the stack trace no longer has the `Button.OnClick` method in it (assuming that the `await` expression needed to schedule the continuation). That method finished executing long ago. The call stack will now effectively be the bare Windows Forms event loop, with a few layers of async infrastructure on top. The call stack will be very similar to what you'd see if you called `Control.Invoke` from a background thread in order to update the UI appropriately, but it's all been done for you. At first it can be unnerving to notice the call stack change dramatically under your feet, but it's absolutely necessary for asynchrony to be effective.

In case you're wondering, all of this is handled by the compiler creating a complicated state machine. That's an implementation detail, and it's instructive to examine it to get a better grasp of what's going on, but first we need a more concrete description of what we're trying to achieve and what the language actually specifies.

15.2 *Thinking about asynchrony*

If you ask a developer to describe asynchronous execution, chances are they'll start talking about multithreading. Although that's an important part of *typical* uses of asynchrony, it's not really required for asynchronous execution. To fully appreciate how the async feature of C# 5 works, it's best to strip away any thoughts of threading and go back to basics.

15.2.1 *Fundamentals of asynchronous execution*

Asynchrony strikes at the very heart of the execution model that C# developers are familiar with. Consider simple code like this:

```
Console.WriteLine("First");
Console.WriteLine("Second");
```

You expect the first call to complete, and then the second call to start. Execution flows from one statement to the next, in order. But an asynchronous execution model doesn't work that way. Instead, it's all about *continuations*. When you start doing something, you tell that operation what you want to happen when that operation has completed. You may have heard (or used) the term *callback* for the same idea, but that has a broader meaning than the one we're after here. In the context of asynchrony, I'm using the term to refer to callbacks that preserve the control state of the program— not arbitrary callbacks for other purposes, such as GUI event handlers.

Continuations are naturally represented as delegates in .NET, and they're typically actions that receive the results of the asynchronous operation. That's why, to use the asynchronous methods in `WebClient` prior to C# 5, you would wire up various events to say what code should be executed in the case of success, failure, and so on. The trouble is, creating all those delegates for a complicated sequence of steps ends up being very complicated, even with the benefit of lambda expressions. It's even worse when you try to make sure that your error handling is correct. (On a good day, I can be reasonably confident that the success paths of handwritten asynchronous code are correct. I'm typically less certain that it reacts the right way on failure.)

Essentially, all that `await` in C# does is ask the compiler to build a continuation for you. For an idea that can be expressed so simply, however, the consequences for readability and developer sanity are remarkable.

My earlier description of asynchrony was an idealized one. The reality in the task-based asynchronous pattern is slightly different. Instead of the continuation being passed to the asynchronous operation, the asynchronous operation starts and returns a token you can use to provide the continuation later. It represents the ongoing operation, which may have completed before it's returned to the calling code, or may still be in progress. That token is then used whenever you want to express this idea: "I can't proceed any further until this operation has completed." Typically the token is in the form of a `Task` or `Task<TResult>`, but it doesn't have to be.

The execution flow in an asynchronous method in C# 5 typically follows these lines:

1. Do some work.
2. Start an asynchronous operation, and remember the token it returns.
3. Possibly do some more work. (Often you can't make any further progress until the asynchronous operation has completed, in which case this step is empty.)
4. Wait for the asynchronous operation to complete (via the token).
5. Do some more work.
6. Finish.

If you didn't care about exactly what the "wait" part meant, you could do all of this in C# 4. If you're happy to *block* until the asynchronous operation completes, the token will normally provide you some way of doing so. For a `Task`, you could just call `Wait()`. At that point though, you're taking up a valuable resource (a thread) and not doing any useful work. It's a little like phoning for a delivery pizza, and then standing at the front door until it arrives. What you really want to do is get on with something else, ignoring the pizza until it arrives. That's where `await` comes in.

When you "wait" for an asynchronous operation, you're really saying, "I've gone as far as I can go for now. Keep going when the operation has completed." But if you're not going to block the thread, what can you do? Very simply, you can return right then and there. You'll continue asynchronously yourself. And if you want your *caller* to know when your asynchronous method has completed, you'll pass a token back to them, which they can block on if they want, or (more likely) use with another continuation. Often you'll end up with a whole stack of asynchronous methods calling each other—it's almost as if you go into an "async mode" for a section of code. There's nothing in the language that states that it *has* to be done that way, but the fact that the same code that *consumes* asynchronous operations also *behaves as* an asynchronous operation certainly encourages it.

> ### Synchronization contexts
>
> Earlier I mentioned that one of the golden rules of UI code is that you mustn't update the user interface unless you're on the right thread. In the "check the web page length" example (listing 15.1) you need to ensure that the code after the `await` expression executes on the UI thread. Asynchronous functions get back to the right thread using `SynchronizationContext`—a class that's existed since .NET 2.0 and is used by other components such as `BackgroundWorker`. A `Synchronization-Context` generalizes the idea of executing a delegate "on an appropriate thread"; its `Post` (asynchronous) and `Send` (synchronous) messages are similar to `Control.BeginInvoke` and `Control.Invoke` in Windows Forms.
>
> Different execution environments use different contexts; for example, one context may let any thread from the thread pool execute the action it's given. There's more contextual information around than just the synchronization context, but if you start wondering how asynchronous methods manage to execute exactly where you want them to, bear this sidebar in mind.
>
> For more information on `SynchronizationContext`, read Stephen Cleary's MSDN magazine article on the topic (http://mng.bz/5cDw). In particular, pay careful attention if you're an ASP.NET developer: the ASP.NET context can easily trap unwary developers into creating deadlocks within code that *looks* fine.

With the theory out of the way, let's take a closer look at the concrete details of asynchronous methods. Asynchronous anonymous functions fit into the same mental model, but it's much easier to talk about asynchronous methods.

15.2.2 *Modeling asynchronous methods*

I find it very useful to think about asynchronous methods as shown in figure 15.1.

Here you have three blocks of code (the methods) and two boundaries (the method return types). As a very simple example, you might have code like this:

```
static async Task<int> GetPageLengthAsync(string url)
{
    using (HttpClient client = new HttpClient())
    {
        Task<string> fetchTextTask = client.GetStringAsync(url);
        int length = (await fetchTextTask).Length;
        return length;
    }
}

static void PrintPageLength()
{
    Task<int> lengthTask =
        GetPageLengthAsync("http://csharpindepth.com");
    Console.WriteLine(lengthTask.Result);
}
```

The five parts of figure 15.1 correspond to the preceding code like this:

- The *calling method* is `PrintPageLength`.
- The *async method* is `GetPageLengthAsync`.
- The *asynchronous operation* is `HttpClient.GetStringAsync`.
- The boundary between the calling method and the async method is `Task<int>`.
- The boundary between the async method and the asynchronous operation is `Task<string>`.

We're mainly interested in the async method itself, but I've included the other methods so you can see how they all interact. In particular, you definitely need to know about the valid types at the method boundaries.

I'll refer to these blocks and boundaries repeatedly in the rest of this chapter, so keep figure 15.1 in mind as you read on.

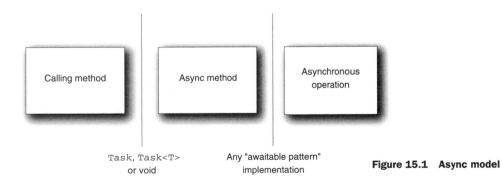

Figure 15.1   Async model

15.3 Syntax and semantics

We're finally ready to look at how to write async methods and how they'll behave. There's a lot to cover here, as "what you can do" and "what happens when you do it" blend together to a large extent.

There are only two new pieces of syntax: async is a modifier used when declaring an asynchronous method, and await expressions consume asynchronous operations. But following how information is transferred between different parts of your program gets complicated really quickly, especially when you have to consider what happens when things go wrong. I've tried to separate out the different aspects, but your code will be dealing with everything at once. If you find yourself asking, "But what about...?" while reading this section, keep reading—chances are your question will be dealt with soon.

Let's start with the method declaration itself—that's the easiest bit...

15.3.1 Declaring an async method

The syntax for an async method declaration is exactly the same as for any other method, except it has to include the async contextual keyword. This can appear anywhere before the return type. All of these are valid:

```
public static async Task<int> FooAsync() { ... }
public async static Task<int> FooAsync() { ... }
async public Task<int> FooAsync() { ... }
public async virtual Task<int> FooAsync() { ... }
```

My personal preference is to keep the async modifier just before the return type, but there's no reason you shouldn't come up with your own convention. As ever, discuss it with your team and try to be consistent within one code base.

Now, the async contextual keyword has a dirty secret: *the language designers didn't really need to include it at all.* Just as the compiler goes into a sort of "iterator block mode" when you try to use yield return or yield break in a method with a suitable return type, the compiler *could* have just spotted the use of await inside a method and used that to go into "async mode." But I'm personally pleased that async is required, as it makes it much easier to *read* code written using asynchronous methods. It sets your expectations immediately, so you're actively looking for await expressions—and you can actively look for any blocking calls that *should* be turned into an async call and an await expression.

The fact that the async modifier has no representation[4] in the generated code is important, though. As far as the calling method is concerned, it's just a normal method, possibly returning a task. You can change an existing method (with an appropriate signature) to use async, or you could go in the other direction—it's a compatible change in terms of both source and binary.

---

[4] Well, sort of. In practice there *is* an attribute applied, as you'll see later, but it's not part of the signature of the method, and it can be ignored as far as humans are concerned. It's really used to help tools identify where the "real" code has gone.

15.3.2 *Return types from async methods*

Communication between the caller and the async method is effectively in terms of the value returned. Asynchronous functions are limited to the following return types:

- `void`
- `Task`
- `Task<TResult>` (for some type `TResult`, which could itself be a type parameter)

The .NET 4 `Task` and `Task<TResult>` types both represent an operation that may not have completed yet; `Task<TResult>` derives from `Task`. The difference between the two is essentially that `Task<TResult>` represents an operation that returns a value of type `T`, whereas `Task` need not produce a result at all. It's still useful to return a `Task`, though, as it allows the caller to attach their own continuations to the returned task, detect when the task has failed or completed, and so on. In some senses, you can think of `Task` as being like a `Task<void>` type, if such a thing were valid.

The ability to return `void` from an async method is designed for compatibility with event handlers. For example, you might have a UI button click handler like this:

```
private async void LoadStockPrice(object sender, EventArgs e)
{
    string ticker = tickerInput.Text;
    decimal price = await stockPriceService.FetchPriceAsync(ticker);
    priceDisplay.Text = price.ToString("c");
}
```

This is an asynchronous method, but the calling code (the button `OnClick` method or whatever piece of framework code is raising the event) doesn't really care. It doesn't need to know when you've really *finished* handling the event—when you've loaded the stock price and updated the UI. It just calls the event handler it's been given. The fact that the code generated by the compiler will end up with a state machine attaching a continuation to whatever is returned by `FetchPriceAsync` is effectively an implementation detail.

You can subscribe to an event with the preceding method as if it were any other event handler:

```
loadStockPriceButton.Click += LoadStockPrice;
```

After all (and yes, I'm laboring this deliberately), it's *just a normal method* as far as calling code is concerned. It has a `void` return type and parameters of type `object` and `EventArgs`, which makes it suitable as the action for an `EventHandler` delegate instance.

Event subscription is pretty much the *only* time I'd recommend returning `void` from an asynchronous method. Any other time you don't need to return a specific value, it's best to declare the method to return `Task`. That way, the caller is able to await the operation completing, detect failures, and so on.

One additional restriction around the signature of an async method: none of the parameters can use the `out` or `ref` modifiers. This makes sense as those modifiers are for communicating information back to the calling code; because some of the async method may not have run by the time control returns to the caller, the value of the by-reference parameter might not have been set. Indeed, it could get stranger than that: imagine passing a local variable as an argument for a `ref` parameter—the async method could end up trying to set that variable after the calling method had already completed. It doesn't make a lot of sense to try to do this, so the compiler prohibits it.

Once you've declared the method, you can start writing the body and awaiting other asynchronous operations.

15.3.3   *The awaitable pattern*

An async method can basically contain almost anything a regular C# method can contain, plus `await` expressions. You can use all kinds of control flow—loops, exceptions, `using` statements, anything. The code will behave just as normal. The only interesting bits are what `await` expressions do and how return values are propagated.

Restrictions on await

Just like `yield return`, there are restrictions around where you can use `await` expressions. You can't use them in `catch` or `finally` blocks, non-async anonymous functions,[5] the body of a `lock` statement, or unsafe code.

These restrictions are for your safety—particularly the restriction around locks. If you ever find yourself *wanting* to hold a lock while an asynchronous operation completes, you should redesign your code. *Don't* work around the compiler restriction by calling `Monitor.TryEnter` and `Monitor.Exit` manually with a `try`/`finally` block—change your code so you don't need the lock during the operation. If this is really, really awkward in your situation, consider using `SemaphoreSlim` instead, with its `WaitAsync` method.

An `await` expression is very simple—it's just `await` before another expression. But there are limits on what you can await, of course. Just as a reminder, we're talking about the second boundary from figure 15.1—how the async method interacts with another asynchronous operation. Informally, you can only await something that describes an asynchronous operation. In other words, something that provides you with the means of

- Telling whether or not it's already finished
- Attaching a continuation if it hasn't finished
- Getting the result, which may be a return value but at least is an indication of success or failure

---

[5]   Lambda expressions and anonymous methods that aren't declared with `async`—so any anonymous function declaration that would have been valid C# 4. You'll see async anonymous functions in section 15.4.

You might *expect* this to be expressed via interfaces, but it's (mostly) not. There's only one interface involved, and it just covers the "attaching a continuation" part. Even that is very simple—and you'll almost never need to deal with it directly. It's in the `System.Runtime.CompilerServices` namespace and looks like this:

```
// Real interface in System.Runtime.CompilerServices
public interface INotifyCompletion
{
    void OnCompleted(Action continuation);
}
```

The bulk of the work is expressed via patterns, a bit like `foreach` and LINQ queries. To make the shape of the pattern clearer, I'll briefly present it *as if* there were interfaces involved, but there really aren't. I'll cover reality in a moment. Let's have a look at the imaginary interfaces:

```
// Warning: these don't really exist
// Imaginary interfaces for asynchronous operations returning values
public interface IAwaitable<T>
{
    IAwaiter<T> GetAwaiter();
}

public interface IAwaiter<T> : INotifyCompletion
{
    bool IsCompleted { get; }
    T GetResult();

    // Inherited from INotifyCompletion
    // void OnCompleted(Action continuation);
}

// Imaginary interfaces for "void" asynchronous operations
public interface IAwaitable
{
    IAwaiter GetAwaiter();
}

public interface IAwaiter : INotifyCompletion
{
    bool IsCompleted { get; }
    void GetResult();

    // Inherited from INotifyCompletion
    // void OnCompleted(Action continuation);
}
```

These probably remind you of `IEnumerable<T>` and `IEnumerator<T>`. In order to iterate over a collection in a `foreach` loop, the compiler generates code that calls `GetEnumerator()` first, and then uses `MoveNext()` and `Current`. Likewise, in async methods, whenever you write an `await` expression, the compiler will generate code that first calls `GetAwaiter()`, and then uses the members of the awaiter to await the result appropriately.

The C# compiler *does* require the awaiter to implement INotifyCompletion. This is primarily for efficiency reasons; some prerelease versions of the compiler didn't have the interface at all.

All the other members are checked by the compiler just by signature. Importantly, the GetAwaiter() method itself doesn't have to be a normal instance method. It can be an extension method on whatever you want to use an await expression with. The IsCompleted and GetResult members have to be real members of whatever type is returned from GetAwaiter(), but they don't have to be public—they just need to be accessible to the code containing the await expression.

The preceding text describes what's required for an expression to be used as the target of the await keyword, but the whole expression itself also has an interesting type: if the GetResult() returns void, then the overall type of the await expression is nothing—the await expression has to be a standalone statement. Otherwise, the overall type is the same as the return type of GetResult().

For example, Task<TResult>.GetAwaiter() returns a TaskAwaiter<TResult>, which has a GetResult() method returning TResult. (No surprise there, hopefully.) The rule about the type of the await expression is what allows us to write this:

```
using (var client = new HttpClient())
{
    Task<string> task = client.GetStringAsync(...);
    string result = await task;
}
```

Compare that with the static Task.Yield() method, which returns a YieldAwaitable. That, in turn, has a GetAwaiter() method returning a YieldAwaitable.Yield-Awaiter, which has a GetResult method returning void. That means you can *only* use it like this:

```
await Task.Yield();
```

Or if you really wanted to split things up—odd though it would be:

```
YieldAwaitable yielder = Task.Yield();
await yielder;
```

The await expression here doesn't return a value of any kind, so you can't assign it to a variable, or pass it as a method argument, or do anything else you might with expressions classified as values.

One important point to note is that because both Task and Task<TResult> implement the awaitable pattern, you can call one async method from another, and so on:

```
public async Task<int> FooAsync()
{
    string bar = await BarAsync();
    // Obviously this would usually be more complicated...
    return bar.Length;
}
```

```
public async Task<string> BarAsync()
{
    // Some async code that could call more async methods...
}
```

This ability to compose asynchronous operations is one of the aspects of the async feature that really makes it shine. Once you're in an async mode, it's very easy to stay there, writing code that flows very naturally.

But I'm getting ahead of myself. I've described what the compiler needs in order for you to await something, but not what it actually does.

15.3.4 *The flow of await expressions*

One of the most curious aspects of the async feature in C# 5 is how await can be simultaneously intuitive and extremely confusing. If you don't think too hard about it, it's really simple. If you just accept that it will do what you want, without really defining exactly what you want to start with, you'll probably be fine...at least until something goes wrong.

Once you start trying to work out exactly what must be going on to achieve the desired effect, things become a bit trickier. Given that you're reading a book with "In Depth" in the title, I'll assume you want to know about these details. In the long run, I promise it will allow you to use await with more confidence, and use it more effectively.

Even so, I urge you to try to develop the ability to read asynchronous code on two different levels, depending on your context: when you don't *need* to think about the individual steps listed here, let them breeze past you. Read the code almost as if it were synchronous, just taking note of where the code waits asynchronously for some operation or other to complete. Then, when you get stuck on some thorny problem where the code isn't behaving as you expect it to, you can switch into the more forensic mode, working out which threads will be involved where, and what the call stack will be at any point in time. (I'm not saying this will be simple, but understanding the machinery will at least make it more feasible.)

EXPANDING COMPLEX EXPRESSIONS

Let's start by simplifying things a bit. Sometimes await is used with the result of a method call or occasionally a property, like this:[6]

```
string pageText = await new HttpClient().GetStringAsync(url);
```

This makes it look as if await can modify the meaning of the whole expression. The truth is that await just operates on a single value. The preceding line is equivalent to this:

```
Task<string> task = new HttpClient().GetStringAsync(url);
string pageText = await task;
```

---

[6] This example is slightly contrived, as you would normally use a using statement for the HttpClient, but I hope you'll forgive me for not disposing resources just this once.

Similarly, the result of an `await` expression can be used as a method argument or within some other expression. Again, it helps if you can separate out the `await`-specific part from everything else.

Imagine you have two methods, `GetHourlyRateAsync()` and `GetHoursWorked-Async()`, returning a `Task<decimal>` and a `Task<int>`, respectively. You might have this complicated statement:

```
AddPayment(await employee.GetHourlyRateAsync() *
        await timeSheet.GetHoursWorkedAsync(employee.Id));
```

The normal rules of C# expression evaluation apply, and the left operand of the `*` operator has to be completely evaluated before the right operand is evaluated, so the preceding statement can be expanded as follows:

```
Task<decimal> hourlyRateTask = employee.GetHourlyRateAsync();
decimal hourlyRate = await hourlyRateTask;
Task<int> hoursWorkedTask = timeSheet.GetHoursWorkedAsync(employee.Id);
int hoursWorked = await hoursWorkedTask;
AddPayment(hourlyRate * hoursWorked);
```

This expansion reveals a potential inefficiency in the original statement—you could introduce parallelism into this code by starting *both* tasks (calling both `Get...Async` methods) before awaiting either of them.

For the moment, the more useful result is that you only need to examine the behavior of `await` in the context of a *value*. Even if that value originally came from a method call, you can ignore that method call for the purpose of talking about asynchrony.

VISIBLE BEHAVIOR

When execution reaches the `await` expression, there are two possibilities—either the asynchronous operation you're awaiting has already completed, or it hasn't.

If the operation has already completed, the execution flow is really simple—it keeps going. If the operation failed and it's captured an exception to represent that failure, the exception is thrown. Otherwise, any result from the operation is obtained—for example, extracting the `string` from a `Task<string>`—and you move on to the next part of the program. All of this is done without any thread context switching or attaching continuations to anything.

You might be wondering why an operation that completes immediately would be represented with asynchrony in the first place. It's a little bit like calling the `Count()` method on a sequence in LINQ: in the general case you may need to iterate over every item in the sequence, but in some situations (such as when the sequence turns out to be a `List<T>`) there's an easy optimization available. It's useful to have a single abstraction that covers both scenarios, but without paying an execution-time price. As a real-world example in the asynchronous API case, consider reading asynchronously from a stream associated with a file on disk. All the data you want to read may already have been fetched from disk into memory, perhaps as part of previous `ReadAsync` call request, so it makes sense to use it immediately, without going through all the other async machinery.

The more interesting scenario is where the asynchronous operation is still ongoing. In this case, the method waits asynchronously for the operation to complete, and then continues in an appropriate context. This "asynchronous waiting" really means the method isn't executing at all. A continuation is attached to the asynchronous operation, and the method returns. It's up to the asynchronous operation to make sure that the method resumes on the right thread—typically either a thread-pool thread (where it doesn't matter which thread is used) or the UI thread where that makes sense.

From the developer's point of view, this *feels* like the method is just paused while the asynchronous operation completes. The compiler makes sure that all the local variables used within the

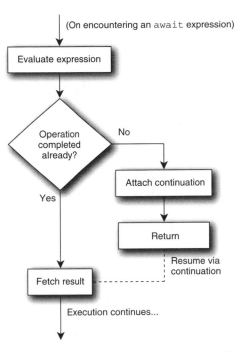

Figure 15.2 User-visible model of await handling

method have the same values as they did before the continuation—just as it does with iterator blocks.

I've attempted to capture this flow in figure 15.2, although classic flowcharts weren't really designed with asynchronous behavior in mind.

You could think of the dotted line as being another line coming into the top of the flowchart as an alternative. Note that I'm assuming the target of the await expression has a result. If you're just awaiting a plain Task or something similar, "fetch result" really means "check the operation completed successfully."

It's worth stopping to think briefly about what it means to "return" from an asynchronous method. Again, there are two possibilities:

- This is the first await expression you've actually had to wait for, so you still have the original caller somewhere in your stack. (Remember that until you really need to wait, the method executes synchronously.)
- You've already awaited something else, so you're in a continuation that has been called by *something*. Your call stack will almost certainly have changed very significantly from the one you'd have seen when you first entered the method.

In the first case, you'll usually end up returning a Task or Task<T> to the caller. Obviously you don't have the actual result of the method yet—even if there's no value to return as such, you don't know whether the method will complete without exceptions. Because of this, the task you'll be returning has to be an uncompleted one.

In the latter case, the "something" calling you back depends on your context. For example, in a Windows Forms UI, if you started your async method on the UI thread and didn't deliberately switch away from it, the whole method would execute on the UI thread. For the first part of the method, you'll be in some event handler or other—whatever kicked off the async method. Later on, however, you'd be called back by the message pump pretty directly, as if you were using `Control.Begin-Invoke(continuation)`. Here, the calling code—whether it's the Windows Forms message pump, part of the thread pool machinery, or something else—doesn't care about your task.

Note that until you hit the first truly asynchronous `await` expression, the method executes entirely synchronously. Calling an asynchronous method is *not* like firing up a new task in a separate thread, and it's up to you to make sure that you always write async methods so they return quickly. Admittedly, it depends on the context in which you're writing code, but you should generally avoid performing long-running work in an async method. Separate it out into another method that you can create a `Task` for.

THE USE OF AWAITABLE PATTERN MEMBERS
Now that you understand what you need to achieve, it's reasonably easy to see how the members of the await-able pattern are used. Figure 15.3 is really just the same as figure 15.2, but fleshed out to include the calls to the pattern.

When it's written like this, you might be wondering what all the fuss is about—why is it worth having language support at all? Attaching a continuation is more complex than you might imagine, though. In very simple cases, when the control flow is entirely linear (do some work, await something, do some more work, await something else), it's pretty easy to imagine what the continuation might look like as a lambda expression, even if it wouldn't be very pleasant. As soon as the code contains loops or conditions, however, and you want to

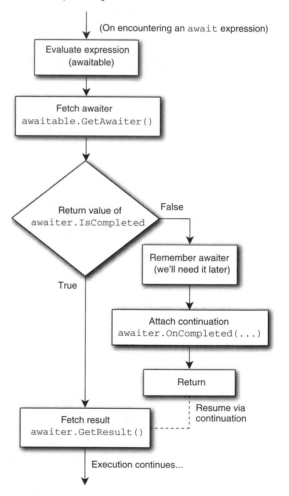

Figure 15.3   Await handling via the awaitable pattern

keep the code within one method, life becomes very much more complicated. It's here that the benefits of C# 5 really kick in. Although you could argue that the compiler is just applying syntactic sugar, there's an enormous difference in readability between manually creating the continuations and getting the compiler to do so for you.

Unlike simple transformations, such as automatically implemented properties, the code generated by the compiler is quite different from what you'd probably write by hand, even when the async method itself is almost trivial. We'll look at a little bit of this transformation in a later section, but you can already see some of the "man behind the curtain"—hopefully async methods are feeling a little less mysterious now.

I've already described the limitations on async method return types, and you've seen how an await expression unwraps asynchronous operation results via the Get-Result() method, but I haven't talked about the link between the two, or how you can return values from async methods.

15.3.5 *Returning from an async method*

You've already seen an example that returned data, but let's look at it again, this time focusing on the return aspect alone:

```
static async Task<int> GetPageLengthAsync(string url)
{
    using (HttpClient client = new HttpClient())
    {
        Task<string> fetchTextTask = client.GetStringAsync(url);
        int length = (await fetchTextTask).Length;
        return length;
    }
}
```

You can see that the type of length is int, but the return type of the method is Task<int>. The generated code takes care of the wrapping for you, so that the caller gets a Task<int>, which will eventually have the value returned from the method when it completes. A method returning just Task is like a normal void method—it doesn't need a return statement at all, and any return statements it *does* have must be simply return; rather than trying to specify a value. In either case, the task will also propagate any exception thrown within the async method.

Hopefully by now you should have a good intuition about why this wrapping is necessary: you're almost certainly returning to the caller before you hit the return statement, and you've got to propagate the information to that caller somehow. A Task<T> (often known as a *future* in computer science) is the promise of a value—or an exception—at a later time.

Just as with normal execution flow, if the return statement occurs within the scope of a try block that has an associated finally block (including when all of this happens due to a using statement), the expression used to compute the return value is *evaluated* immediately, but it doesn't become the result of the task until everything has been cleaned up. This means that if the `finally` block throws an exception, you don't get a task that both succeeds and fails—the whole thing will fail.

To reiterate a point I made earlier, it's the combination of automatic wrapping and unwrapping that makes the async feature work so well with composition. You can think of this as being a bit like LINQ: you write operations on each *element* of a sequence in LINQ, and the wrapping and unwrapping means you can apply those operations to sequences and get sequences back. In an async world, you rarely need to explicitly handle a task—instead you `await` the task to consume it, and produce a result task automatically as part of the mechanism of the async method.

15.3.6 *Exceptions*

Of course, things don't always work smoothly, and the idiomatic way of representing failures in .NET is via exceptions. Like returning a value to the caller, exception handling requires extra support from the language. When you want to throw an exception, the original caller of the async method may not be on the stack; and when you `await` an asynchronous operation that's failed, it may well not have executed on the same thread, so you need a way of marshaling the failure across. If you think of failure as just another kind of result, it makes sense that exceptions and return values are handled similarly.

In this section we'll look at how exceptions cross over both of the boundaries in figure 15.1. Let's start with the boundary between the async method and the asynchronous operation it's awaiting.

UNWRAPPING EXCEPTIONS WHEN AWAITING

Just as the `GetResult()` method of an awaiter is meant to fetch the return value if there is one, it's also responsible for propagating any exceptions from the asynchronous operation back to the method. This isn't *quite* as simple as it sounds, because in an asynchronous world a single `Task` can represent multiple operations, leading to multiple failures. Although other awaitable pattern implementations are available, it's worth considering `Task` specifically, as it's the type you're likely to be awaiting for the vast majority of the time.

`Task` indicates exceptions in a number of ways:

- The `Status` of a task becomes `Faulted` when the asynchronous operation has failed (and `IsFaulted` returns `true`).
- The `Exception` property returns an `AggregateException` containing all the (potentially multiple) exceptions that caused the task to fail, or `null` if the task isn't faulted.
- The `Wait()` method will throw an `AggregateException` if the task ends up in a faulted state.
- The `Result` property of `Task<T>` (which also waits for completion) will likewise throw an `AggregateException`.

Additionally, tasks support the idea of cancellation, via `CancellationTokenSource` and `CancellationToken`. If a task is canceled, the `Wait()` method and `Result` properties will throw an `AggregateException` containing an `OperationCanceledException` (in practice, a `TaskCanceledException`, which derives from `OperationCanceled-Exception`), but the status becomes `Canceled` instead of `Faulted`.

When you await a task, if it's either faulted or canceled, an exception will be thrown—but not the `AggregateException`. Instead, for convenience (in most cases), the first exception *within* the `AggregateException` is thrown. In most cases, this is really what you want. It's in the spirit of the async feature to allow you to write asynchronous code that looks very much like the synchronous code you'd otherwise write. For example, consider something like this:

```
async Task<string> FetchFirstSuccessfulAsync(IEnumerable<string> urls)
{
    // TODO: Validate that we've actually got some URLs...
    foreach (string url in urls)
    {
        try
        {
            using (var client = new HttpClient())
            {
                return await client.GetStringAsync(url);
            }
        }
        catch (WebException exception)
        {
            // TODO: Logging, update statistics etc.
        }
    }
    throw new WebException("No URLs succeeded");
}
```

For the moment, ignore the fact that you're losing all the original exceptions, and that you're fetching all the pages sequentially. The point I'm trying to make is that catching `WebException` is what you'd expect here—you're trying an asynchronous operation with an `HttpClient`, and if something fails it'll throw a `WebException`. You want to catch and handle that...right? That certainly *feels* like what you'd want to do— but, of course, `GetStringAsync()` can't throw a `WebException` for an error such as the server timing out because the method only *starts* the operation. All it can do is return a task that is faulted *containing* a `WebException`. If you simply called `Wait()` on the task, an `AggregateException` would be thrown, containing the `WebException` within it. The task awaiter's `GetResult` method just throws the `WebException` instead, and it's caught in the preceding code.

Of course, this *can* lose information. If there are multiple exceptions in a faulted task, `GetResult` can only throw one of them, and it arbitrarily uses the first. You might want to rewrite the preceding code so that on failure, the caller can catch an `AggregateException` and examine *all* the causes of the failure. Importantly, some framework methods such as `Task.WhenAll()` do exactly this—`WhenAll()` is a method that will asynchronously wait for multiple tasks (specified in the method call) to complete. If any of them fails, the result is a failure that will contain the exceptions from all the faulted tasks. But if you just await the task returned by `WhenAll()`, you'll only see the first exception.

Fortunately, it doesn't take very much work to fix this. You can use your knowledge of the awaitable pattern and write an extension method on `Task<T>` to create a special awaitable that will throw the original `AggregateException` from a task. The full code is a little unwieldy for the printed page, but the gist of it is shown in the following listing.

Listing 15.2   Rewrapping multiple exceptions from task failures

```
public static AggregatedExceptionAwaitable WithAggregatedExceptions(
                                                 this Task task)
{
    return new AggregatedExceptionAwaitable(task);
}

// In AggregatedExceptionAwaitable
public AggregatedExceptionAwaiter GetAwaiter()
{
    return new AggregatedExceptionAwaiter(task);
}

// In AggregatedExceptionAwaiter
public bool IsCompleted
{
    get { return task.GetAwaiter().IsCompleted; }     ◁┐
}                                                       │  ❶ Delegates to
public void OnCompleted(Action continuation)            │     task awaiter
{                                                       │
    task.GetAwaiter().OnCompleted(continuation);      ◁┘
}
public void GetResult()              ❷ Throws AggregateException
{                                  ◁┐   directly on failure
    task.Wait();
}
```

You'd probably want a similar approach for `Task<T>`, using `return task.Result;` in `GetResult()` instead of calling `Wait()`. The important point is that you delegate to the task's normal awaiter for the bits you don't want to handle yourself ❶, but side-step the usual behavior of `GetResult()`, which is where the exception unwrapping takes place. By the time `GetResult` is called, you *know* that the task is in a terminal state, so the `Wait()` call ❷ will complete immediately—this doesn't violate the asynchrony you're trying to achieve.

To use the code, you just need to call the extension method and await the result, as shown next.

Listing 15.3 Catching multiple exceptions as `AggregateException`

```
private async static Task CatchMultipleExceptions()
{
    Task task1 = Task.Run(() => { throw new Exception("Message 1");
    });
    Task task2 = Task.Run(() => { throw new Exception("Message 2");
    });
    try
    {
        await Task.WhenAll(task1, task2).WithAggregatedExceptions();
    }
    catch (AggregateException e)
    {
        Console.WriteLine("Caught {0} exceptions: {1}",
            e.InnerExceptions.Count,
            string.Join(", ",
                e.InnerExceptions.Select(x => x.Message)));
    }
}
```

`WithAggregatedExceptions()` returns your custom awaitable; `GetAwaiter()` from that, in turn, supplies the custom awaiter, which supports the operations the C# compiler requires to await the result. Note that you could have coalesced the awaitable and the awaiter—there's nothing to say they *have* to be different types—but it feels a little cleaner to separate them.

Here's the output of listing 15.3:

```
Caught 2 exceptions: Message 1, Message 2
```

It's relatively rare that you'll want to do this—sufficiently rare that Microsoft didn't include any support for it in the framework—but it's worth knowing about this option.

That's all you need to know about exception handling for the second boundary, at least for now. But what about the first boundary, between the async method and the caller?

WRAPPING EXCEPTIONS WHEN THROWING

You may well be able to predict what's coming here: async methods *never* throw exceptions directly when called. Instead, for async methods returning `Task` or `Task<T>`, any exceptions thrown within the method (including those propagated up from other operations, whether synchronous or asynchronous) are simply transferred to the task, as you've already seen. If the caller waits on the task directly, they'll get an `AggregateException` containing the exception, but if the caller uses `await` instead, the exception will be unwrapped from the task. Async methods that return `void` will report the exception to the original `SynchronizationContext`—how that handles it is up to the context.[7]

---

[7] We'll discuss contexts in more detail in section 15.6.4.

Unless you really care about the wrapping and unwrapping for a particular context, you can just catch the exception the nested async method has thrown. The following listing demonstrates how familiar this feels:

Listing 15.4   Handling asynchronous exceptions in a familiar style

```
static async Task MainAsync()
{
    Task<string> task = ReadFileAsync("garbage file");      ◁┐   Starts the
    try                                                      ❶   async read
    {
        string text = await task;                           ◁┐   Waits for
            Console.WriteLine("File contents: {0}", text);   ❷   the contents
    }
    catch (IOException e)                                   ◁─❸  Handles IO failures
    {
        Console.WriteLine("Caught IOException: {0}", e.Message);
    }
}

static async Task<string> ReadFileAsync(string filename)
{
    using (var reader = File.OpenText(filename))            ◁┐   Opens the file
    {                                                        ❹   synchronously
        return await reader.ReadToEndAsync();
    }
}
```

Here you'll get an `IOException` in the `File.OpenText` call ❹ (unless you create a file called "garbage file"), but you'd see the same execution path if the task returned by `ReadToEndAsync` failed. Within `MainAsync`, the call to `ReadFileAsync` ❶ happens *before* you enter the `try` block, but it's only when you await the task ❷ that the exception is seen by the caller and caught by the `catch` block ❸, just like with the `WebException` example earlier. Again, it behaves in a very familiar way—except perhaps for the timing of the exception.

Just like iterator blocks, this is a bit of a pain in terms of argument validation. Suppose you want to do some work in an async method after validating that the parameters don't have null values. If you validate the parameters as you would in a normal synchronous code, the caller won't have any indication of the problem until the task is awaited. The following listing gives an example of this.

Listing 15.5   Broken argument validation in an async method

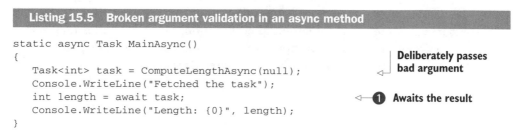

```
static async Task MainAsync()
{
    Task<int> task = ComputeLengthAsync(null);     |   Deliberately passes
    Console.WriteLine("Fetched the task");         ◁┘  bad argument
    int length = await task;                       ◁─❶  Awaits the result
    Console.WriteLine("Length: {0}", length);
}
```

```
static async Task<int> ComputeLengthAsync(string text)
{
    if (text == null)
    {
        throw new ArgumentNullException("text");        ❷  Throws exception
    }                                                       immediately
    await Task.Delay(500);                        Simulates real
    return text.Length;                           asynchronous work
}
```

Listing 15.5 outputs `Fetched the task` before it fails. The exception has actually been thrown synchronously before that output is written, as there are no `await` expressions before the validation ❷, but the calling code won't see it until it awaits the returned task ❶. Generally, for argument validation that can sensibly be done up front without taking a long time (or incurring other asynchronous operations), it would be better if the failure were reported immediately, before the system can get itself into further trouble. As an example of this, `HttpClient.GetStringAsync` will throw an exception immediately if you pass it a null reference.

There are two approaches to forcing the exception to be thrown "eagerly" in C# 5. The first is to split the argument validation from the implementation, in the same way you did for iterator blocks in listing 6.9. The following listing shows a fixed version of `ComputeLengthAsync`.

Listing 15.6 Splitting argument validation from async implementation

```
static Task<int> ComputeLengthAsync(string text)
{
    if (text == null)
    {
        throw new ArgumentNullException("text");
    }
    return ComputeLengthAsyncImpl(text);
}

static async Task<int> ComputeLengthAsyncImpl(string text)
{
    await Task.Delay(500); // Simulate real asynchronous work
    return text.Length;
}
```

In listing 15.6, `ComputeLengthAsync` itself isn't an asynchronous method as far as the language is concerned—it doesn't have the `async` modifier. It executes using the normal execution flow, so if the argument validation at the start of the method throws an exception, it really throws an exception. If that passes, however, the task returned is the one created by the `ComputeLengthAsyncImpl` method, which is where the real work occurs. In a more real-world scenario, `ComputeLengthAsync` would probably be a public or internal method, and `ComputeLengthAsyncImpl` should be private, because it *assumes* that the argument validation has already been performed.

The other approach to eager validation is to use *asynchronous anonymous functions*—we'll revisit this example when we look at those in section 15.4.

There's one other kind of exception that's handled differently within asynchronous methods: cancellation.

HANDLING CANCELLATION

The Task Parallel Library (TPL) introduced a uniform cancellation model into .NET 4 using two types: `CancellationTokenSource` and `CancellationToken`. The idea is that you can create a `CancellationTokenSource`, and then ask it for a `CancellationToken`, which is passed to an asynchronous operation. You can only perform the cancellation on the source, but that is reflected to the token. (This means you can pass out the same token to multiple operations and not worry about them interfering with each other.) There are various ways of using the cancellation token, but the most idiomatic approach is to call `ThrowIfCancellationRequested`, which will throw `Operation-CanceledException` if the token has been canceled and do nothing otherwise. The same exception is thrown by synchronous calls (such as `Task.Wait`) if they're canceled.

How this interacts with asynchronous methods is undocumented in the C# 5 specification. According to the specification, if an asynchronous method body throws *any* exception, the task returned by the method will be in a faulted state. The exact meaning of "faulted" is implementation-specific, but in reality if an asynchronous method throws an `OperationCanceledException` (or a derived exception type, such as `Task-CanceledException`), the returned task will end up with a status of `Canceled`. The following listing proves that it really is an exception that causes the task to be canceled.

Listing 15.7   Creating a canceled task by throwing `OperationCanceledException`

```
static async Task ThrowCancellationException()
{
    throw new OperationCanceledException();
}
...
Task task = ThrowCancellationException();
Console.WriteLine(task.Status);
```

This outputs `Canceled` rather than the `Faulted` you might expect from the specification. If you `Wait()` on the task, or ask for its result (in the case of a `Task<T>`), the exception is still thrown within an `AggregateException`, so it's not like you need to explicitly start checking for cancellation on every task you use.

OFF TO THE RACES? You might be wondering if there's a race condition in listing 15.7. After all, you're calling an asynchronous method and then immediately expecting the status to be fixed. If you were actually starting a new thread, that would be dangerous...but you're not. Remember that before the first `await` expression, an asynchronous method runs synchronously—it still performs result and exception wrapping, but the fact that it's in an asynchronous method does *not* necessarily mean there are any more threads involved. The `ThrowCancellationException` method doesn't contain any `await` expressions, so the whole method (all one line of it) runs synchronously; you know that you'll have a result by the time it returns. Visual Studio actually warns you about an asynchronous method without any `await` expressions in it, but in this case it's exactly what you want.

Importantly, if you await an operation that's canceled, the original `Operation-CanceledException` is thrown. This means that unless you take any direct action, the task returned from the asynchronous method will also be canceled—cancellation is propagated in a natural fashion.

The following listing gives a slightly more realistic example of task cancellation.

Listing 15.8 Cancellation of an async method via a canceled delay

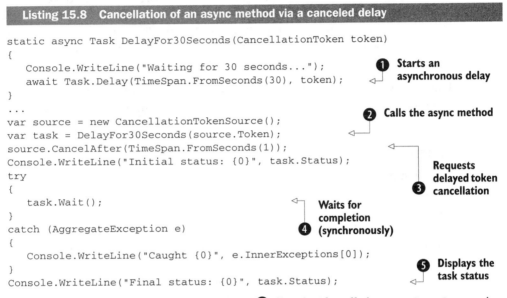

```
static async Task DelayFor30Seconds(CancellationToken token)
{
    Console.WriteLine("Waiting for 30 seconds...");        ❶ Starts an
    await Task.Delay(TimeSpan.FromSeconds(30), token);        asynchronous delay
}
...
var source = new CancellationTokenSource();             ❷ Calls the async method
var task = DelayFor30Seconds(source.Token);
source.CancelAfter(TimeSpan.FromSeconds(1));
Console.WriteLine("Initial status: {0}", task.Status);    Requests
try                                                       delayed token
{                                                       ❸ cancellation
    task.Wait();                            Waits for
}                                           completion
catch (AggregateException e)               ❹ (synchronously)
{
    Console.WriteLine("Caught {0}", e.InnerExceptions[0]);
}                                                        ❺ Displays the
Console.WriteLine("Final status: {0}", task.Status);        task status
```

Here you start an asynchronous operation ❷ that simply calls into `Task.Delay` to simulate real work ❶, but provides a cancellation token. This time, you really *do* have multiple threads involved: when it hits the `await` expression, control returns to the calling method, at which point you ask the cancellation token to be canceled in 1 second ❸. You then wait (synchronously) for the task to finish ❹, fully expecting it to end with an exception. Finally, you show the status of the task ❺.

The output of 15.8 looks like this:

```
Waiting for 30 seconds...
Initial status: WaitingForActivation
Caught System.Threading.Tasks.TaskCanceledException: A task was canceled.
Final status: Canceled
```

You can think of this in terms of cancellation being transitive by default: if operation A is waiting for operation B, and operation B is canceled, then you regard operation A as being canceled too.

Of course, you don't have to leave it that way. You could have caught the `Operation-CanceledException` in the `DelayFor30Seconds` method and either continued to do something else, or returned immediately, or even thrown a different exception. Again, the async feature isn't removing control; it's just giving you useful default behavior.

CAREFUL WHERE YOU RUN THIS!   Listing 15.8 works fine in a console application, or when called from a thread-pool thread, but if you execute it on a Windows Forms UI thread (or any other single-thread synchronization context), it will deadlock. Can you see why? Think about which thread the `DelayFor-30Seconds` method will try to return to when the delayed task completes, and then think about which thread the `task.Wait()` call is running on. This is a relatively simple example, but the same type of mistake has caused problems for several developers when they first started out with asynchronous code. Fundamentally, the problem is in using the `Wait()` method call, or the `Result` property, both of which will block until the relevant task completes. I'm not saying you shouldn't use them, but you should think very carefully any time you *do* use them. You should usually be using `await` to asynchronously wait for the results of tasks instead.

That pretty much covers the behavior of asynchronous methods. It's likely that most of your use of the async feature in C# 5 will be via asynchronous methods, but they do have a close sibling...

15.4   *Asynchronous anonymous functions*

I won't spend much time on asynchronous anonymous functions. As you'd probably expect, they're a combination of two features: anonymous functions (lambda expressions and anonymous methods) and asynchronous functions (code that can include `await` expressions). Basically, they allow you to create delegates[8] that represent asynchronous operations. Everything you've learned so far about asynchronous methods applies to asynchronous anonymous functions too.

You create an asynchronous anonymous function just like any other anonymous method or lambda expression, just with the `async` modifier at the start. Here's an example:

```
Func<Task> lambda = async () => await Task.Delay(1000);
Func<Task<int>> anonMethod = async delegate()
{
    Console.WriteLine("Started");
    await Task.Delay(1000);
    Console.WriteLine("Finished");
    return 10;
};
```

The delegate you create has to have a signature with a return type of `void`, `Task`, or `Task<T>`, just as with an asynchronous method. You can capture variables, as with other anonymous functions, and add parameters. Also, the asynchronous operation doesn't start until the delegate is invoked, and multiple invocations create multiple operations. Delegate invocation really *does* start the operation though; just as before, it's not awaiting that starts an operation, and you don't *have* to use `await` with the result of an asynchronous anonymous function at all.

---

[8] In case you were wondering, you can't use asynchronous anonymous functions to create expression trees.

The following listing shows a slightly fuller (although still pointless) example.

Listing 15.9 Creating and calling an asynchronous function using a lambda expression

```
Func<int, Task<int>> function = async x =>
{
    Console.WriteLine("Starting... x={0}", x);
    await Task.Delay(x * 1000);
    Console.WriteLine("Finished... x={0}", x);
    return x * 2;
};

Task<int> first = function(5);
Task<int> second = function(3);
Console.WriteLine("First result: {0}", first.Result);
Console.WriteLine("Second result: {0}", second.Result);
```

I've deliberately chosen the values here so that the second operation completes quicker than the first. But because you wait for the first to finish before printing the results (using the `Result` property, which blocks until the task has completed—again, be careful where you run this!), the output looks like this:

```
Starting... x=5
Starting... x=3
Finished... x=3
Finished... x=5
First result: 10
Second result: 6
```

Again, this is exactly the same as if you'd put the asynchronous code into an asynchronous method.

I find it hard to get terribly excited about asynchronous anonymous functions, but they have their uses. Although you can't include them in LINQ query expressions, there are still cases where you might want to perform data transformations asynchronously. You just need to think about the whole process in a slightly different way.

We'll come back to that idea when we discuss composition, but first I want to show you one area where they really are very useful indeed. I promised earlier that I'd show another way of performing eager argument validation at the start of an asynchronous method. You'll remember that we wanted to check a parameter value for nullity before launching into the main operation. The following listing is a single method that achieves the same result as the split implementation in listing 15.6.

Listing 15.10 Argument validation using an async anonymous function

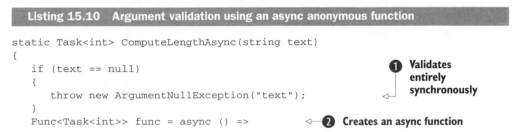

```
static Task<int> ComputeLengthAsync(string text)
{
    if (text == null)
    {
        throw new ArgumentNullException("text");
    }
    Func<Task<int>> func = async () =>
}
```

❶ Validates entirely synchronously

❷ Creates an async function

```
    {
        await Task.Delay(500);        ◁——— Simulates real asynchronous work
        return text.Length;
    };
    return func();                    ◁—❸ Calls the async function
}
```

You'll note that this *isn't* an asynchronous method. If it were, the exception would be wrapped up in a task instead of being thrown immediately. You still want to return a task though, so after the validation ❶, you just wrap the work up in an asynchronous anonymous function ❷, call the delegate ❸, and return the result.

While this is still a *little* bit ugly, it's cleaner than having to split the method in two. There's a performance penalty to be aware of though: this extra wrapping doesn't come for free. In most cases that's fine, but if you're writing a library that may be used in performance-critical work, you should check the cost in your actual scenario before deciding which approach to use.

> **VB SUPERIORITY?**   In version 11, Visual Basic finally gained the iterator block support that C# has had since version 2. The delay has allowed the team to reflect on C#'s shortcomings though—the Visual Basic implementation allows anonymous iterator functions, permitting the same kind of in-method split between eager and deferred execution. The feature hasn't (yet) been added to C#…

You've now seen pretty much all there is in terms of the async feature in C# 5. For the remainder of the chapter, we'll dig into some implementation details and then look at how to get the most out of the feature. All of this will assume that you're reasonably comfortable with everything that's gone before—if you haven't tried any of the sample code yet (or ideally your own experimental code), now would be a great time to do so. Even if you think you understand the theory, it's well worth playing with `async` and `await` to really get the *feeling* of what it's like to program asynchrony in a somewhat-synchronous style.

15.5 *Implementation details: compiler transformation*

I vividly remember the evening of October 28, 2010. Anders Hejlsberg was presenting async/await at PDC, and shortly before his talk started, an avalanche of downloadable material was made available—including a draft of the changes to the C# specification, a CTP (Community Technology Preview) of the C# 5 compiler, and the slides Anders was presenting. At one point I was watching the talk live and skimming through the slides while the CTP installed. By the time Anders had finished, I was writing async code and trying things out.

In the next few weeks, I started taking bits apart—looking at exactly what code the compiler was generating, trying to write my own simplistic implementation of the library that came with the CTP, and generally poking at it from every angle. As new versions came out, I worked out what had changed and became more and more comfortable with what was going on behind the scenes. The more I saw, the more I appreciated how much boilerplate code the compiler is happy to write on our behalf. It's like looking at a beautiful flower under a microscope: the beauty is still there to be admired, but there's so much more to it than can be seen at first glance.

Not everyone is like me, of course. If you just want to rely on the behavior I've already described, and simply trust that the compiler will do the right thing, that's *absolutely fine*. Alternatively, you won't miss out on anything if you skip this section for now and come back to it at a later date—none of the rest of the chapter relies on it. It's unlikely that you'll ever have to debug your code down to the level that we'll look at here…but I believe this section will give you more insight into how the whole feature hangs together. The awaitable pattern certainly makes a lot more sense once you've looked at the generated code, and you'll see some of the types that the framework provides to help the compiler. Some of the scariest details are only present due to optimization; the design and implementation are very carefully tuned to avoid unnecessary heap allocations and context switches, for example.

As a rough approximation, we'll pretend the C# compiler performs a transformation from "C# code using async/await" to "C# code without using async/await." In reality, the internals of the compiler aren't available to us, and it's more than likely that this transformation occurs at a lower level than C#. Certainly the generated IL can't always be expressed in non-async C#, as C# has tighter restrictions around flow control than IL does. But it's simpler for us to think of it as C#, in terms of how the jigsaw of code fits together.

The generated code is somewhat like an onion, with layers of complexity. We'll start from the very outside, working our way in toward the tricky bit—await expressions and the dance of awaiters and continuations.

15.5.1 *Overview of the generated code*

Still with me? Let's get started. I won't go into *all* the depth I could here—that could fill hundreds of pages—but I'll give you enough background to understand the overall structure, and then you can either read the various blog posts I've written over the past couple of years for more intricate detail, or simply write some asynchronous code and decompile it. Also, I'll only cover asynchronous methods—that will include all the interesting machinery, and you won't need to deal with the extra layer of indirection that asynchronous anonymous functions present.

> **WARNING, BRAVE TRAVELER—HERE BE IMPLEMENTATION DETAILS!** This section documents some aspects of the implementation found in the Microsoft C# 5 compiler, released with .NET 4.5. A few details changed pretty substantially between CTP versions and in the beta, and they may well change again in the future. But I think it unlikely that the fundamental *ideas* will change much though. If you understand enough of this section to be comfortable that there's no magic involved, just really clever compiler-generated code, you should be able to take any future changes to the details in your stride.

As I've mentioned a couple of times, the implementation (both in this approximation and in the code generated by the real compiler) is basically in the form of a *state machine*. The compiler will generate a private nested struct to represent the asynchronous method, and it must also include a method with the same signature as the one you've declared. I call this the *skeleton method*—there's not much to it, but everything else hangs off it.

The skeleton method needs to create the state machine, make it perform a single step (where a *step* is whatever code executes before the first genuinely waiting `await` expression), and then return a task to represent the state machine's progress. (Don't forget that until you hit the first `await` expression that actually needs to wait, execution is synchronous.) After that, the method's job is done—the state machine looks after everything else, and continuations attached to other asynchronous operations simply tell the state machine to perform another step. The state machine signals when it's reached the end by giving the appropriate result to the task that was returned earlier. Figure 15.4 shows a flow diagram of this, as best I can represent it.

Of course the "execute method body" step only starts from the beginning of the method the first time it's called, from the skeleton method. After that, each time you get to that block, it's via a continuation, at which point execution effectively continues from where it left off.

We now have two things to look at: the skeleton method and the state machine. For most of the remainder of this section, I'll use a single sample asynchronous method, shown in the following listing.

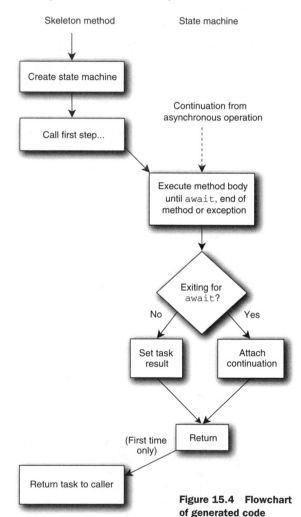

Figure 15.4 Flowchart of generated code

Listing 15.11   Simple async method to demonstrate compiler transformations

```
static async Task<int> SumCharactersAsync(IEnumerable<char> text)
{
    int total = 0;
    foreach (char ch in text)
    {
        int unicode = ch;
        await Task.Delay(unicode);
        total += unicode;
    }
    await Task.Yield();
    return total;
}
```

Listing 15.11 doesn't do anything *useful*, but we're really just interested in the control flow. It's worth noting a few points before we start:

- The method has a parameter (text).
- It contains a loop that you effectively need to jump back into when the continuation executes.
- It has two await expressions of different types: Task.Delay returns a Task, but Task.Yield() returns a YieldAwaitable.
- It has obvious local variables (total, ch, and unicode) that you'll need to keep track of across calls.
- It has an implicit local variable created by calling text.GetEnumerator().
- It returns a value at the end of the method.

The original version of this code had text as a string parameter, but the C# compiler knows about iterating over strings in an efficient way, using the Length property and the indexer, which made the decompiled code more complicated.

I won't present the *complete* decompiled code, although it's in the downloadable source. In the next few sections we'll look at a few of the most important parts. You won't see exactly this code if you decompile the code yourself; I've renamed variables and types so they're rather more legible, but it's effectively the same code.

Let's start off with the simplest bit—the skeleton method.

15.5.2 *Structure of the skeleton method*

Although the code in the skeleton method is simple, it offers some hints about the state machine's responsibilities. The skeleton method generated for listing 15.11 looks like this:

```
[DebuggerStepThrough]
[AsyncStateMachine(typeof(DemoStateMachine))]
static Task<int> SumCharactersAsync(IEnumerable<char> text)
{
    var machine = new DemoStateMachine();
    machine.text = text;
    machine.builder = AsyncTaskMethodBuilder<int>.Create();
```

```
        machine.state = -1;
        machine.builder.Start(ref machine);
        return machine.builder.Task;
}
```

The `AsyncStateMachineAttribute` type is just one of the new attributes introduced for async. It's really for the benefit of tools—you're unlikely to ever need to consume it yourself, and you shouldn't start decorating your own methods with it.

You can see three of the fields of the state machine already:

- One for the parameter (`text`). Obviously there are as many fields here as there are parameters.
- One for an `AsyncTaskMethodBuilder<int>`. This struct is effectively responsible for tying the state machine and the skeleton method together. There's a nongeneric equivalent for methods returning just `Task` and an `AsyncVoidMethodBuilder` structure for methods returning `void`.
- One for `state`, starting off with a value of `-1`. The initial value is always `-1`, and we'll take a look at what various possible values mean later.

Given that the state machine is a struct, and `AsyncTaskMethodBuilder<int>` is a struct, you haven't knowingly performed *any* heap allocation yet. It's entirely possible for the various calls you're making to have done so for you, of course, but it's worth noting that the code tries to avoid them as far as possible. The nature of asynchrony means that if any `await` expressions need to really wait, you'll need a lot of these values on the heap, but the code makes sure that they're only boxed when they need to be. All of this is an implementation detail, just like the heap and the stack are implementation details, but in order for async to be practical in as many situations as possible, the teams involved in Microsoft have worked closely to reduce allocations to the bare minimum.

The `machine.builder.Start(ref machine)` call is an interesting one. The use of pass-by-reference here allows you to avoid creating a copy of the state machine (and thus a copy of the builder)—this is for both performance and correctness. The compiler would really *like* to treat both the state machine and the builder as classes, so `ref` is used liberally throughout the code. In order to use interfaces, various methods take the builder (or awaiter) as a parameter using a generic type parameter that's constrained to implement an interface (such as `IAsyncStateMachine` for the state machine). That allows the members of the interface to be called without any boxing being required. The *action* of the method is simple to describe—it makes the state machine take the first step, synchronously, returning only when the method has either completed or reached a point where it needs to wait for an asynchronous operation.

Once that first step has completed, the skeleton method asks the builder for the task to return. The state machine uses the builder to set results or exceptions when it finishes.

15.5.3 *Structure of the state machine*

The overall structure of the state machine is pretty straightforward. It always implements the IAsyncStateMachine interface (introduced in .NET 4.5) using explicit interface implementation. The two methods declared by that interface (MoveNext and SetStateMachine) are the only two methods it contains. It also has a bunch of fields—some private, some public.

For example, this is the collapsed declaration of the state machine for listing 15.11:

```
[CompilerGenerated]
private struct DemoStateMachine : IAsyncStateMachine
{                                                        ❶ Fields for
    public IEnumerable<char> text;                          parameters

    public IEnumerator<char> iterator;
    public char ch;                                      ❷ Fields for local
    public int total;                                       variables
    public int unicode;

    private TaskAwaiter taskAwaiter;                        Fields for
    private YieldAwaitable.YieldAwaiter yieldAwaiter;    ❸ awaiters
    public int state;
    public AsyncTaskMethodBuilder<int> builder;          ❹ Common
    private object stack;                                   infrastructure

    void IAsyncStateMachine.MoveNext() { ... }

    [DebuggerHidden]
    void IAsyncStateMachine.SetStateMachine(IAsyncStateMachine machine)
    { ... }
}
```

In this example I've split the fields up into various sections. You've already seen that the text field ❶ representing the original parameter is set by the skeleton method, along with the builder and state fields, which are common infrastructure shared by all state machines.

Each local variable also has its own field ❷, as you need to preserve the values across invocations of the MoveNext() method. Sometimes there are local variables that are only ever used between two particular await expressions, and don't really *need* to be preserved in fields, but in my experience the current implementation always hoists them up to be fields anyway. Aside from anything else, this improves the debugging experience, as you wouldn't generally expect local variables to lose their values, even if there's nothing in the code that uses them any further.

There's a single field for each type of awaiter used in the asynchronous method if they're value types, and one field for all awaiters that are reference types (in terms of their compile-time type). In this case, you've got two await expressions that use two different types of awaiter structures, so you've got two fields ❸. If the second await expression had also used a TaskAwaiter, or if TaskAwaiter and YieldAwaiter were both classes, you'd just have a single field. Only one awaiter can ever be live at a time, so it doesn't matter that you can only store one value at a time. You have to propagate awaiters across `await` expressions so that once the operation has finished, you can get the result.

Out of the common infrastructure fields ❹, you've already seen `state` and `builder`. Just as a reminder, `state` is used to keep track of where you've got to, so the continuation can get to the right point in the code. `builder` is used for various things, including creating a `Task` or `Task<T>` for the skeleton method to return—a task that will then be populated with the right result when the asynchronous method finishes. The `stack` field is a little more arcane—it's used when an `await` expression occurs as part of a statement that needs to keep track of some extra state that isn't represented by normal local variables. You'll see an example of that in section 15.5.6—it's not used in the state machine generated for listing 15.11.

The `MoveNext()` method is where all the compiler smarts really come into play, but before I describe that, we'll take a *very* quick look at `SetStateMachine`. It has the same implementation in every state machine, and it looks like this:

```
void IAsyncStateMachine.SetStateMachine(IAsyncStateMachine machine)
{
    builder.SetStateMachine(machine);
}
```

In brief, this method is used to allow a boxed copy of the state machine to have a reference to itself, within the builder. I won't go into the details of how all the boxing is managed—all you need to understand is that the state machine *is* boxed where necessary, and the various aspects of the async machinery ensure that after boxing, the single boxed copy is used consistently. This is really important, as we're talking about a *mutable value type* (shudder!). If some changes were applied to one copy of the state machine, and some changes were applied to another copy, the whole thing would fall apart very quickly.

If you want to think of it another way—and this will be important if you ever start *really* thinking about how the instance variables of the state machine are propagated—the state machine is a `struct` to avoid unnecessary heap allocations early on, but most of the code tries to *act* like it's really a class. The reference juggling around `Set-StateMachine` makes it all work.

Right…now we've got everything in place except for the actual code that was in the asynchronous method. Let's dive into `MoveNext()`.

15.5.4 *One entry point to rule them all*

If you ever decompile an async method—and I really hope you will—you'll see that the `MoveNext()` method in the state machine gets very long, very fast, mostly as a function of how many `await` expressions you have. It contains all the logic in the original method, *and* the delicate ballet required to handle all the state transitions,[9] *and* some wrapper code to handle the overall result or exception.

---

[9] It really does feel like a dance, with intricate steps that have to be performed at exactly the right time and place.

When writing asynchronous code by hand, you'd typically put continuations into separate methods: start in one method, then continue in another, and maybe finish in a third. But that makes it hard to handle flow control, such as loops, and it's unnecessary for the C# compiler. It's not like the readability of the generated code matters. The state machine has a single entry point, MoveNext(), which is used from the start and for the continuations for all await expressions. Each time MoveNext() is called, the state machine works out where in the method to get to via the state field. This is either the logical starting point of the method or the end of an await expression, when you're ready to evaluate the result. Each state machine is executed only once. Effectively there's a switch statement based on state, with different cases corresponding to goto statements with different labels.

The MoveNext() method typically looks something like this:

```
void IStateMachine.MoveNext()
{
    // For an asynchronous method declared to return Task<int>
    int result;
    try
    {
        bool doFinallyBodies = true;
        switch (state)
        {
            // Code to jump to the right place...
        }

        // Main body of the method
    }
    catch (Exception e)
    {
        state = -2;
        builder.SetException(e);
        return;
    }
    state = -2;
    builder.SetResult(result);
}
```

The initial state is always -1, and that's *also* the state when the method is executing your code (as opposed to being paused while awaiting). Any non-negative states indicate the target of a continuation. The state machine ends up in state -2 when it's completed. In state machines created in debug configurations, you'll see reference to a state of -3—it's never expected that you'll actually *end up* in that state. It's there to avoid having a degenerate switch statement, which would result in a poorer debugging experience.

The result variable is set during the course of the method, at the point where the original async method had a return statement. This is then used in the builder .SetResult() call, when you reach the logical end of the method. Even the nongeneric AsyncTaskMethodBuilder and AsyncVoidMethodBuilder types have Set-Result() methods; the former communicates the fact that the method has completed to the task returned from the skeleton method, and the latter signals completion to the original `SynchronizationContext`. (Exceptions are propagated to the original `SynchronizationContext` in the same way. It's a rather dirtier way of keeping track of what's going on, but it provides a solution for situations where you really *must* have `void` methods.)

The `doFinallyBodies` variable is used to work out whether any `finally` blocks in the original code (including implicit ones from `using` or `foreach` statements) should be executed when execution leaves the scope of a `try` block. Conceptually, you only want to execute a `finally` block when you leave the `try` block in a normal way. If you're just returning from the method early having attached a continuation to an awaiter, the method is logically "paused" so you don't want to execute the `finally` block. Any `finally` blocks would appear within the `Main` body of the method section of code, along with the associated `try` block.

Most of the body of the method is recognizable in terms of the original async method. Admittedly, you need to get used to all the local variables now appearing as instance variables in the state machine, but that's not too hard. The tricky bits are all around `await` expressions—as you might expect.

15.5.5 *Control around await expressions*

Just as a reminder, any `await` expression represents a fork in terms of possible execution paths. First the awaiter is fetched for the asynchronous operation being awaited, and then its `IsCompleted` property is checked. If that returns `true`, you can get the results immediately and continue. Otherwise, you need to do the following:

- Remember the awaiter for later
- Update the state to indicate where to continue from
- Attach a continuation to the awaiter
- Return from `MoveNext()`, ensuring that any `finally` blocks are *not* executed

Then, when the continuation is called, you need to jump to the right point, retrieve the awaiter, and reset your state before continuing.

As an example, the first `await` expression in listing 15.11 looks like this:

```
await Task.Delay(unicode);
```

The generated code looks like this:

```
TaskAwaiter localTaskAwaiter = Task.Delay(unicode).GetAwaiter();
    if (localTaskAwaiter.IsCompleted)
    {
        goto DemoAwaitCompletion;
    }
    state = 0;
    taskAwaiter = localTaskAwaiter;
    builder.AwaitUnsafeOnCompleted(ref localTaskAwaiter, ref this);
    doFinallyBodies = false;
    return;
DemoAwaitContinuation:
    localTaskAwaiter = taskAwaiter;
```

```
      taskAwaiter = default(TaskAwaiter);
      state = -1;
DemoAwaitCompletion:
   localTaskAwaiter.GetResult();
   localTaskAwaiter = default(TaskAwaiter);
```

If you'd been awaiting an operation that returned a value—for example assigning the result of `await client.GetStringAsync(...)` using an `HttpClient`—the `Get-Result()` call near the end would be where you'd get the value.

The `AwaitUnsafeOnCompleted` method attaches the continuation to the awaiter, and the `switch` statement at the start of the `MoveNext()` method would ensure that when `MoveNext()` executes again, control passes to `DemoAwaitContinuation`.

> **AWAITONCOMPLETED VS. AWAITUNSAFEONCOMPLETED** Earlier, I showed you a notional set of interfaces, where `IAwaiter<T>` extended `INotifyCompletion` with its `OnCompleted` method. There's also an `ICriticalNotifyCompletion` interface, with an `UnsafeOnCompleted` method. The state machine calls `builder.AwaitUnsafeOnCompleted` for awaiters that implement `ICritical-NotifyCompletion`, or `builder.AwaitOnCompleted` for awaiters that only implement `INotifyCompletion`. We'll look at the differences between these two calls in section 15.6.4 when we discuss how the awaitable pattern interacts with contexts.

Note that the compiler wipes both the local and instance variables for the awaiter, so that it can be garbage-collected where appropriate.

Once you can identify a block like this as corresponding to a single `await` expression, the generated code really isn't *too* bad to read in decompiled form. There may be more `goto` statements (and corresponding labels) than you'd expect, due to CLR restrictions, but getting your head round the `await` pattern is the biggest hump in understanding, in my experience.

There's one thing I still need to explain—the mysterious `stack` variable in the state machine…

15.5.6 *Keeping track of a stack*

When you think of a stack frame, you probably think about the local variables you've declared in the method. Sure, you may be aware of some hidden local variables like the iterator for a `foreach` loop, but that's not all that goes on the stack…at least logically.[10] In various situations, there are intermediate expressions that can't be used until some other expressions are evaluated. The simplest examples of these are binary operations like addition, and method invocations.

As a trivial example, consider this line:

```
var x = y * z;
```

---

[10] As Eric Lippert is fond of saying, the stack is an implementation detail—some variables you might *expect* to go on the stack actually end up on the heap, and some variables may end up only existing in registers. For the purposes of this section, we're just talking about what logically happens on the stack.

In stack-based pseudocode, that's something like this:

```
push y
push z
multiply
store x
```

Now suppose you have an `await` expression in there:

```
var x = y * await z;
```

You need to evaluate y and store it somewhere before you await z, but you might well end up returning from the `MoveNext()` method immediately, so you need a logical stack to store y on. When the continuation executes, you can restore the value and perform the multiplication. In this case, the compiler can assign the value of y to the `stack` instance variable. This does involve boxing, but it means you get to use a single variable.

That's a simple example. Imagine you had something where multiple values needed to be stored, like this:

```
Console.WriteLine("{0}: {1}", x, await task);
```

You need both the format string and the value of x on your logical stack. This time, the compiler creates a `Tuple<string, int>` containing the two values, and stores that reference in `stack`. Like the awaiter, you only ever need a single logical stack at a time, so it's fine to always use the same variable.[11] In the continuation, the individual arguments can be fetched from the tuple and used in the method call. The downloadable source code contains a complete decompilation of this sample, with both of the preceding statements (`LogicalStack.cs` and `LogicalStackDecompiled.cs`).

The second statement ends up using code like this:

```
string localArg0 = "{0} {1}";
int localArg1 = x;
localAwaiter = task.GetAwaiter();
if (localAwaiter.IsCompleted)
{
    goto SecondAwaitCompletion;
}
var localTuple = new Tuple<string, int>(localArg0, localArg1);
stack = localTuple;
state = 1;
awaiter = localAwaiter;
builder.AwaitUnsafeOnCompleted(ref awaiter, ref this);
doFinallyBodies = false;
return;
SecondAwaitContinuation:
    localTuple = (Tuple<string, int>) stack;
    localArg0 = localTuple.Item1;
    localArg1 = localTuple.Item2;
    stack = null;
```

---

[11] Admittedly there are times when the compiler could be smarter about the type of the variable, or avoid including one at all if it's never needed, but all of that may be added in a later version, as a further optimization.

```
    localAwaiter = awaiter;
    awaiter = default(TaskAwaiter<int>);
    state = -1;
SecondAwaitCompletion:
    int localArg2 = localAwaiter.GetResult();
    Console.WriteLine(localArg0, localArg1, localArg2);  // Bold
```

The bold lines here are the ones involving elements of the logical stack.

At this point, we've probably gone as far as we need to—if you've made it this far successfully, you know more about the details of what's going on under the hood than 99 percent of developers are ever likely to. It's fine if you didn't quite follow everything first time through—if your experience is anything like mine has been when reading the code of these state machines, you'll want to wait a little while, and then come back to it.

15.5.7 *Finding out more*

Want even more details? Crack out a decompiler. I'd urge you to use very small programs to investigate what the compiler does—it's very easy to get lost in a maze of twisty little continuations, all alike, if you write anything nontrivial. You may need to reduce the level of optimization the decompiler performs in order to get it to show you a fairly close-to-the-metal view of the code, rather than an interpretation. After all, a perfect decompiler would just reproduce your async functions, which would defeat the whole purpose of the exercise!

The code that the compiler generates can't always be decompiled into valid C#. There's *always* the problem of it deliberately using unspeakable names for both variables and types, but more important, there are some cases where valid IL has no direct equivalent in C#. For example, in IL it's legitimate to branch to an instruction that's within a loop—after all, IL doesn't even *have* the concept of a loop, as such. In C#, you can't goto a label within a loop from outside the loop, so such an instruction can't be represented entirely correctly. Even the C# compiler can't have it all its own way: IL still has some restrictions on jump targets, so you'll often find the compiler has to go through a series of jumps to get to the right place.

Similarly, I've seen some decompilers get a little confused as to the exact ordering of assignment statements around the logical stack, occasionally moving the assignment of the temporary variables (localArg0 and localArg1, for example) to the wrong side of the IsCompleted check. I believe this is due to the code not being quite like the normal output of the C# compiler. It's not too bad when you know what to look for, but it does mean that occasionally you'll probably end up dropping down to IL.

15.6 *Using async/await effectively*

I've shown you how asynchronous functions behave, and what they look like behind the scenes. You're now an expert at asynchronous programming, right? Obviously not.[12] Like many aspects of programming, there's a lot to be said for experience... and very few people have had a great deal of experience with asynchronous functions so far. While I can't give you experience, I can provide some hints and tips that should make your life slightly easier.

As I write this, the teams who know the most about asynchronous programming using C# 5 are the ones within Microsoft, who have lived and breathed it during development and received feedback from beta testers and the like. To that end, I *thoroughly* recommend the Parallel Programming Team's blog (http://blogs.msdn.com/b/pfxteam/), which has a lot more advice than I have room to give here.

Of course, that doesn't mean I don't have some suggestions...

15.6.1 *The task-based asynchronous pattern*

One of the benefits of the asynchronous function feature in C# 5 is that it gives a consistent approach to asynchrony. But that could easily be undermined if everyone came up with their own ways of using it—how to name asynchronous methods, how exceptions should be raised, and the like. Microsoft has addressed this by publishing the *Task-based Asynchronous Pattern* (TAP)—a set of conventions for everyone to follow. It's available as a standalone document (http://mng.bz/B68W) or on MSDN as separate pages (http://mng.bz/4N39).

Of course, Microsoft has also been following this—.NET 4.5 contains a huge number of asynchronous APIs for all kinds of scenarios. Just like with normal .NET conventions for naming, type design, and the like, if you follow the same conventions as the rest of the framework, other developers will find your code much easier to work with.

The TAP is very readable, and it's only 38 pages long—I strongly advise you to read the full document. In the rest of this section, I'll cover what I consider to be the most important parts.

Asynchronous methods should end with the suffix *Async*—`GetAuthenticationTokenAsync`, `FetchUserPortfolioAsync`, and so on. In the .NET Framework this has already caused some collisions—`WebClient` already had methods such as `DownloadStringAsync` following the event-based asynchronous pattern, which is why the new TAP-based methods have the slightly ugly names of `DownloadStringTaskAsync`, `UploadDataTaskAsync`, and the like. `TaskAsync` is the recommended suffix if you have your own naming collisions, too. Where the asynchrony is obvious, the suffix can be dropped entirely—`Task.Delay` and `Task.WhenAll` are examples of this. As a general rule, if the entire business of the method is asynchrony, rather than achieving some business goal, it's *probably* safe to drop the suffix.

TAP methods generally return `Task` or `Task<T>`—again, there are exceptions such as `Task.Yield`, where the awaitable pattern comes in, but these should be few and far between. Importantly, the task returned from a TAP method should be *hot*. In other words, the operation it represents should already be in progress—the caller shouldn't

---

[12] Of course, you *might* be an expert at asynchronous programming, but just reading this chapter won't have done that for you.

need to start it manually. For most developers, this probably sounds obvious, but there are other platforms where the convention is to create a cold task that doesn't start until you explicitly ask it to—a little bit like an iterator block in C#. In particular, F# follows this convention, and it's also something you need to consider in Reactive Extensions (Rx).

There are generally four overloads to *consider* providing when you create an asynchronous method. All would take the same basic parameters, but they'd provide different options in terms of both progress reporting and cancellation. Suppose you were considering developing an asynchronous method that would be logically equivalent to a synchronous method like this:

```
Employee LoadEmployeeById(string id)
```

Following TAP conventions, you could provide any or all of these:

```
// NOTE TO PRODUCTION: Please consult with Jon on formatting.
Do not abbreviate!
Task<Employee> LoadEmployeeById(string id)
Task<Employee> LoadEmployeeById(string id, CancellationToken cancellationToken)
Task<Employee> LoadEmployeeById(string id, IProgress<int> progress)
Task<Employee> LoadEmployeeById(string id,
    CancellationToken cancellationToken, IProgress<int> progress)
```

Here the `IProgress<int>` could be an `IProgress<T>` for any type `T` that's appropriate to use for progress reporting. For example, if your asynchronous method found a collection of records and then processed them one by one, you could accept an `IProgress<Tuple<int, int>>`, which could report both the number of reports processed so far and the number of reports in total.

I'd avoid trying to shoehorn progress reporting into operations where it really doesn't make sense. Cancellation is generally easier to support, because so many framework methods support it. If your asynchronous method basically consists of performing several other asynchronous operations (possibly with dependencies), you may find it's easier to just accept a cancellation token and pass it downstream.

Asynchronous operations should check for usage errors—typically invalid arguments—synchronously. This is slightly awkward, but it can be implemented either using a split method, as shown in section 15.3.6, or with a single method using an anonymous asynchronous function, as shown in section 15.4. Although it's tempting to validate arguments lazily, you'll curse yourself when you're trying to address a failure that's harder to diagnose than it needs to be.

IO-based operations—where you're handing off a job to either a disk or another computer—are great candidates for asynchrony, with no obvious downside. CPU-bound tasks are less so. It's easy to offload some work onto the thread pool, and even easier in .NET 4.5 than it was before, thanks to the `Task.Run` method, but doing so within library code would be making assumptions on behalf of the caller. Different callers may well have different requirements; if you just expose a synchronous method, you give the caller the flexibility to work in the most appropriate fashion.

They can either start a new task if they need to, or call it synchronously if they're happy for the current thread to be busy executing the method for some time.

Tasks that are a mixture of waiting for results from other systems and then processing them in a potentially time-consuming manner are trickier. Although I think hard-and-fast guidelines are unlikely to be helpful, it's important to *document* the behavior. If you're going to end up taking a lot of CPU in the caller's context, you should make that very clear.

Another option is to avoid using the caller's context, using the `Task.Configure-Await` method. This method currently only has a single parameter, `continueOn-CapturedContext`, although for clarity it's worth using a named argument to specify it. The method returns an implementation of the awaitable pattern. When the argument is `true`, the awaitable behaves exactly as normal, so if the async method is called on a UI thread, for example, the continuation after the `await` expression will still execute on the UI thread. That's handy *if* you want to access UI elements. If you don't have any special requirements, however, you can specify `false` for the argument, in which case the continuation will usually execute in the same context that the original operation completed.[13]

For a mixed workload that fetches some data, processes it, and then saves it to a database, you might have code like this:

```
public static async Task<int> ProcessRecords()
{
    List<Record> records = await FetchRecordsAsync()
        .ConfigureAwait(continueOnCapturedContext: false);

    // ... record handling here ...
    await SaveResultsAsync(results)
        .ConfigureAwait(continueOnCapturedContext: false);

    // Let the caller know how many records were processed
    return records.Count;
}
```

Most of this method is likely to execute on a thread from the thread pool; this is exactly what you want, as you're not doing anything that requires execution in the original thread. (The jargon for this is that the operation doesn't have any *thread affinity*.) This doesn't affect the caller, however; if an async UI method awaits the result of calling `ProcessRecords`, that async method will still continue on the UI thread. It's only the code within `ProcessRecords` that's declaring that it doesn't care about its execution context.

Arguably, you don't really need to call `ConfigureAwait` on the second `await` expression here, as there's so little work remaining, but in general you should use it

---

[13] Usually, but not always. The details aren't explicitly documented, but there are times when you really don't want to execute in the same context. You should consider `ConfigureAwait(false)` to be saying, "I don't mind where the continuation executes," rather than explicitly attaching it to a specific context.

on *every* await expression, and it's a good idea to get into the habit of doing so consistently. If you want to give the caller flexibility about the context in which the method executes, you could potentially make this a parameter to the asynchronous method.

Note that ConfigureAwait only affects the *synchronization* part of the execution context. Other aspects such as impersonation are propagated regardless, as you'll see in section 15.6.4.

> **TPL DATAFLOW** Although TAP is just a set of conventions and some examples, Microsoft has also made a separate library called "TPL Dataflow," which is available to provide higher-level building blocks for specific scenarios, particularly those that can be modeled using producer/consumer patterns. The simplest way to get started is probably via the NuGet package (Microsoft .Tpl.Dataflow). It's free to use, and there's lots of guidance around it. Even if you don't use it directly, it's worth looking at, just to get more of a feeling for how parallel programs *can* be designed.

Even without any extra libraries, you can still build elegant asynchronous code following normal design principles, and one of the most important aspects of that is composition.

15.6.2 *Composing async operations*

One of the things I love most about the asynchrony in C# 5 is the way it composes so naturally. This manifests itself in two different ways. Most obviously, asynchronous methods return tasks and typically involve calling other methods that return tasks. Those could be direct asynchronous operations (the bottom of the chain, so to speak) or just more asynchronous methods. All the wrapping and unwrapping required to turn results into tasks and vice versa is handled by the compiler.

The other form of composition is the way that you can create operation-neutral building blocks to govern how tasks are handled. These building blocks don't need to know anything about what the tasks are doing—they stay purely at the abstraction level of Task<T>. They're a little bit like the LINQ operators, but they work on tasks instead of sequences. Some building blocks are built into the framework, but you can write your own.

COLLECTING RESULTS IN A SINGLE CALL

As an example, let's consider the task of fetching lots of URLs. In section 15.3.6 you did this one at a time, stopping as soon as you were successful. Suppose this time you want to launch the requests in parallel, and then log the result for each URL. Remembering that asynchronous methods return already-running tasks, you can start a task for each URL fairly easily:

```
var tasks = urls.Select(async url =>
{
    using (var client = new HttpClient())
    {
```

```
        return await client.GetStringAsync(url);
    }
}).ToList();
```

Note that the `ToList()` is required in order to materialize the LINQ query. This ensures that you start each task once and only once—otherwise each time you iterated over `tasks`, you'd start another set of fetches. (The code would be even simpler if you didn't care about disposing of the `HttpClient`, but even with that wrinkle, it's not too bad.)

The TPL provides a method `Task.WhenAll` that combines the results of lots of tasks, each providing a single result, into a single task with multiple results. The signature of the overload you'll use looks like this:

```
static Task<TResult[]> WhenAll<TResult>(IEnumerable<Task<TResult>> tasks)
```

That's a fearsome-looking declaration, but the purpose of the method is quite simple when you start to use it. You've got a `List<Task<string>>`, so you can write this:

```
string[] results = await Task.WhenAll(tasks);
```

That will wait until all the tasks have finished and gather the results together into an array. This is one of those occasions where if several tasks throw exceptions, only the first will be thrown immediately, but you can always iterate over the tasks to work out which ones have failed and why, or use the `WithAggregatedExceptions` extension method shown in listing 15.2.

If you only care about the first request to come back, there's another method called `Task.WhenAny` that doesn't wait for the first *successful* task completion; it just waits for the first task to reach a terminal state.

In this case, you may want something a little different. It might be more useful to report all the results as they come in.

COLLECTING RESULTS AS THEY ARRIVE

Although `Task.WhenAll` was an example of a transformational building block that's built into .NET, the next example shows how you can build your own methods in a similar way. The TAP documentation gives some very similar sample code, creating a method called `Interleaved`, and we'll look at a slightly alternative version.

The idea of listing 15.12 is to allow you to pass in a sequence of input tasks, and the method will return a sequence of output tasks. The results of the tasks in the two sequences will be the same, but with one crucial difference: the output tasks will complete in the order they're provided, so you can `await` them one at a time and know you'll get the results as soon as they're available. Now, this may sound like magic—it does to me—so let's look at the code and see how it works.

Listing 15.12 **Transforming a task sequence into a new collection in completion order**

```
public static IEnumerable<Task<T>> InCompletionOrder<T>
    (this IEnumerable<Task<T>> source)
{
    var inputs = source.ToList();
    var boxes = inputs.Select(x => new TaskCompletionSource<T>())
                      .ToList();

    int currentIndex = -1;
    foreach (var task in inputs)
    {
        task.ContinueWith(completed =>
        {
            var nextBox = boxes[Interlocked.Increment(ref currentIndex)];
            PropagateResult(completed, nextBox);
        }, TaskContinuationOptions.ExecuteSynchronously);
    }
    return boxes.Select(box => box.Task);
}
```

Listing 15.12 relies on a very important type in the TPL—TaskCompletionSource<T>. This type allows you to create a Task with no result yet, and then provide a result (or an exception) later on. This is built on the same underlying infrastructure that AsyncTaskMethodBuilder<T> uses to provide a Task for an asynchronous method to return, allowing the task to be populated with the result when the method body completes.

To explain the slightly curious variable names, I often think of tasks as being like cardboard boxes, with the promise that at some point they'll have a value inside (or a fault). A TaskCompletionSource<T> is like a box with a hole in the back—you can give it to someone and then sneakily poke the value through the hole later on.[14] That's exactly what the PropagateResult method does—it's not terribly interesting, so I've omitted it here, but basically it propagates the result of a completed Task<T> into a TaskCompletionSource<T>. If the original task completes normally, the return value is copied into the task completion source. If the original task faults, the exception is copied into the task completion source. If the original task was canceled, the task completion source is canceled.

The really clever part here (and I take no credit for this—the suggestion was emailed to me) is that when this method runs, it doesn't know which Task-CompletionSource<T> will correspond with which input task. Instead, it simply attaches the same continuation to each task, and that continuation says, "Find the next TaskCompletionSource<T> (by atomically incrementing a counter) and propagate the result." In other words, the boxes are filled in the output order as the original tasks complete.

---

[14] Any resemblance to quantum physics is purely coincidental, and I won't be held responsible for any experiments involving Task<Cat>.

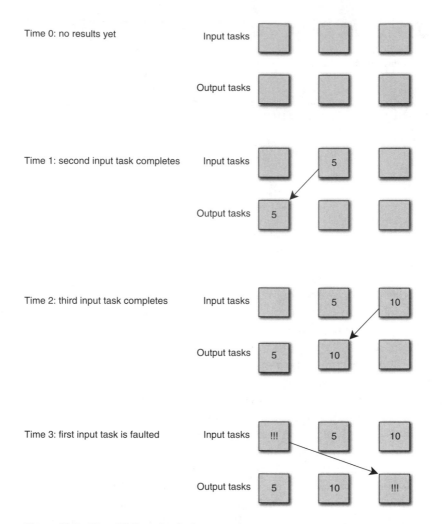

Figure 15.5   Visualization of ordering

Figure 15.5 shows three input tasks and the corresponding output tasks returned by the method. The output tasks complete in the returned order, even though the input tasks complete in a different order.

With this wonderful extension method in place, you can then write the following code, which takes a collection of URLs, launches requests for each of them in parallel, writes out each page length as it completes, and returns the total length.

Listing 15.13   Displaying page lengths as the data is returned

```
static async Task<int> ShowPageLengthsAsync(params string[] urls)
{
   var tasks = urls.Select(async url =>
   {
```

```
    using (var client = new HttpClient())
    {
        return await client.GetStringAsync(url);
    }
}).ToList();

int total = 0;
foreach (var task in tasks.InCompletionOrder())
{
    string page = await task;
    Console.WriteLine("Got page length {0}", page.Length);
    total += page.Length;
}
return total;
}
```

There are two slight issues with listing15.13:

- As soon as one task fails, the whole asynchronous operation fails with no indication of the remaining results. That *may* be okay, or you may want to make sure that you log every failure. (Unlike in .NET 4, letting task exceptions go unobserved won't bring down the process by default, but you should at least *think* about what you want to happen to other tasks.)
- You lose track of which page went with which URL.

Both of these are reasonably easily fixed with a little bit more code, and they might even suggest further reusable building blocks. The point of showing these examples wasn't to examine the individual requirements—it was to open your mind to the possibilities provided by composition.

`Interleaved` isn't the only example in the TAP white paper—it's got lots of ideas, with sample code to help you.

15.6.3 *Unit testing asynchronous code*

I'm slightly nervous about even starting to write this section. At the moment, I don't believe that the community has enough experience to come up with definitive answers about how to test asynchronous code. I'm sure there will be some missteps along the way, and no doubt several competing approaches will be explored. The important point is that, just like synchronous code, if you design for testability from the start, you can unit test asynchronous code effectively.

INJECTING ASYNCHRONY SAFELY

In this section I'll present an approach for situations where you're able to control the asynchronous operations that your own asynchronous code depends on. It doesn't try to address the difficulties of testing code that uses `HttpClient` and similarly tricky-to-fake types, but that's nothing new—if you have dependencies that are hard to use in tests, you'll always face problems.

Suppose you want to test the "magic ordering" code from the previous section. You want to be able to create tasks that'll complete in a specified order, and (in at least some tests) make sure you can perform assertions in between task completions. Additionally, you'd like to do all of this without any other threads getting involved—you want as much control and predictability as possible. In essence, you want to be able to control time.

My solution to this is to essentially fake out time by using a TimeMachine class that provides a way of advancing time programmatically with scheduled tasks that complete in particular ways at specific times. Combine this with a Synchronization-Context that's effectively a manually pumped version of the familiar Windows Forms message pump, and you get a pretty reasonable test harness. I won't show all of the framework code used to host this, as it's a little too long and relatively dull, but it's all in the sample code. I'll show a couple of tests though.

Let's start off with the overall success case: if you program three tasks to complete at times 1, 2, and 3, and call InCompletionOrder with those tasks in a different order, you should still get the *results* in order:

```
[TestMethod]
public void TasksCompleteInOrder()
{
    var tardis = new TimeMachine();
    var task1 = tardis.ScheduleSuccess(1, "t1");
    var task2 = tardis.ScheduleSuccess(2, "t2");
    var task3 = tardis.ScheduleSuccess(3, "t3");

    var tasksOutOfOrder = new[] { task2, task3, task1 };

    tardis.ExecuteInContext(advancer =>
    {
        var inOrder = tasksOutOfOrder.InCompletionOrder().ToList();
        advancer.AdvanceTo(3);
        Assert.AreEqual("t1", inOrder[0].Result);
        Assert.AreEqual("t2", inOrder[1].Result);
        Assert.AreEqual("t3", inOrder[2].Result);
    });
}
```

The ExecuteInContext method temporarily replaces the current thread's SynchronizationContext with a ManuallyPumpedSynchronizationContext (also in the sample code) and then provides an advancer to the delegate specified by the method argument. That advancer can be used to advance time by specific amounts, with tasks completing (and executing continuations) at the appropriate times. In this test you just fast-forward until they've all completed.

Here's a second test that demonstrates that you can control time in a more fine-grained way:

```
// Omitted setup steps, which are the same as the previous test.
tardis.ExecuteInContext(advancer =>
{
    var inOrder = tasksOutOfOrder.InCompletionOrder().ToList();

    Assert.AreEqual(TaskStatus.WaitingForActivation, inOrder[0].Status);
    Assert.AreEqual(TaskStatus.WaitingForActivation, inOrder[1].Status);
```

```
Assert.AreEqual(TaskStatus.WaitingForActivation, inOrder[2].Status);

advancer.Advance();
Assert.AreEqual(TaskStatus.RanToCompletion, inOrder[0].Status);
Assert.AreEqual(TaskStatus.WaitingForActivation, inOrder[1].Status);
Assert.AreEqual(TaskStatus.WaitingForActivation, inOrder[2].Status);

advancer.Advance();
Assert.AreEqual(TaskStatus.RanToCompletion, inOrder[1].Status);
Assert.AreEqual(TaskStatus.WaitingForActivation, inOrder[2].Status);

advancer.Advance();
Assert.AreEqual(TaskStatus.RanToCompletion, inOrder[2].Status);
});
```

Here you can see the output tasks completing in the right order.

You may be wondering why the times here are just integers—you may have expected DateTime and TimeSpan to get involved. This is deliberate—the only timeline you really have is the artificial one set up by the time machine, and the only interesting points in time are the ones where tasks complete.

Of course, the method you're testing is slightly unusual here in two ways:

- It's not actually implemented with async.
- It's given tasks directly as arguments.

If you were testing a more business-focused async method, you'd quite possibly schedule all the results for your dependencies, advance time to complete them all, and then check the result of the returned task. You'd have to be able to provide your production code with fakes in the normal way—the only difference that asynchrony makes here is that instead of using stubs or mocks to return the direct results of calls, you'd ask them to return the tasks produced by the TimeMachine. All the normal benefits of inversion of control still apply—you just need a way of creating appropriate tasks.

This single idea clearly isn't going to be a panacea, but I hope it's at least persuaded you of the *possibility* of unit testing asynchronous code without arbitrary calls to Thread.Sleep and the constant risk of test flakiness.

RUNNING ASYNCHRONOUS TESTS

The tests in the previous section are entirely synchronous. You don't use async or await within the tests themselves at all. When you're using the TimeMachine class for all your tests, that's fairly reasonable, but in other cases you may want to write test methods decorated with async.

You can do so easily:

```
[Test] // NUnit TestAttribute
public async void BadTestMethod()
{
    // Code using await
}
```

This will *compile* against any normal test framework...but it may not do what you expect. In particular, you may end up with all your tests being started in parallel, and quite possibly "finishing" before they get around to asserting anything.

As it happens, NUnit supports asynchronous tests as of version 2.6.2, and the preceding method would work due to some cleverness in the implementation, but if you tried to run it against earlier versions, the test would start and then complete, as far as the test runner was concerned, as soon as it hit the first "slow" await. Any failures later in the method would end up being reported to the test's SynchronizationContext, which may not be expecting it.

For test frameworks that support asynchronous tests, a much better approach is to make those tests return Task, like this:

```
[Test]
public async Task GoodTestMethod()
{
    // Code using await
}
```

Now it's much easier for the test framework to know when your tests have completed, and to check for failure. It has the additional benefit that test frameworks that *don't* support asynchronous tests may not even try to run them, instead reporting a warning, which is far better than running the tests incorrectly. As I write this, the latest versions of NUnit, xUnit, and Visual Studio Unit Testing Framework (also known informally as MS Test) all support asynchronous tests—other frameworks may do so too. Please check the specific framework and version you want to use before starting to write such tests.

You should also be careful of the possibility of deadlocks. Unlike with the time machine tests in the previous section, you probably *don't* want all the continuations executing on a single thread, unless that thread is also pumping as a UI thread would. Sometimes you control all the tasks involved and can reason your way into using a single-threaded context...other times you need to be rather more careful and may well *want* multiple threads able to fire continuations, as long as your test code doesn't execute in parallel with itself. I'd be nervous of this for *unit* tests, but if you're using the same sort of framework for functional tests, integration tests, or even production probing, you'll typically want your tests to be running against real tasks rather than the fakes provided by the time machine.

I'm confident that over time the community will develop some great tools to help us test more and more of our code. I'm convinced that a significant proportion of future code will be naturally asynchronous, and I'm utterly certain that I don't want to be writing such code without tests. We're nearly finished with asynchrony now, but I did promise earlier that I'd come back to that interesting AwaitUnsafeOnCompleted method call in the generated code.

15.6.4 *The awaitable pattern redux*

In section 15.3.3 I showed some imaginary interfaces that give the right basic idea about the awaitable pattern. Even when I explained that this wasn't quite reality, I fudged it a little bit. Unless you're implementing the awaitable pattern itself or looking closely at the decompiled code, you don't really need to know about the fudging, but if you've gotten this far, you probably want to know everything.

The genuine interface I mentioned earlier was `INotifyCompletion`, which looks like this:

```
public interface INotifyCompletion
{
    void OnCompleted(Action continuation);
}
```

There's another interface that extends this, however—still in the `System.Runtime.CompilerServices` namespace:

```
public interface ICriticalNotifyCompletion : INotifyCompletion
{
    void UnsafeOnCompleted(Action continuation);
}
```

All the reasoning behind these two interfaces has *context* at its heart. I've mentioned `SynchronizationContext` a number of times already in this chapter, and you may well have come across it before; it's a synchronization context that allows calls to be marshaled onto an appropriate thread, whether that's a specific thread pool, or a single UI thread, or whatever is required. It's not the only context involved though. There are plenty of them—`SecurityContext`, `LogicalCallContext`, and `HostExecution-Context`, for example. The granddaddy of them all, however, is `ExecutionContext`. It acts as a container for all the other contexts, and it's what we'll focus on in this section.

It's very important that the `ExecutionContext` *flows* across await points; you don't want to come back to your asynchronous method when a task has completed, only to find that you've forgotten which user you're impersonating, for example. In order to flow the context, it needs to be *captured* when you attach the continuation, and then *restored* when the continuation is executed. This is achieved through the `Execution-Context.Capture` and `ExecutionContext.Run` methods, respectively.

There are two pieces of code that can perform this capture/restore pair: the awaiter, and the `AsyncTaskMethodBuilder<T>` class (along with its siblings). You might expect that you could just decide one way or the other, and leave it at that. But various other trade-offs come into play. It's easy to forget to flow the execution context in the awaiter, so it makes sense to implement it *once* in the method-builder code. On the other hand, your awaiter will be directly accessible to any code using it, so you wouldn't want to expose a possible security flaw by relying on all callers using the compiler-generated code…suggesting that it should be in the awaiter code. But equally, you wouldn't want to capture and restore the context twice, redundantly. How can we resolve this dichotomy?

We've already seen the answer: use two different interfaces with subtly different meanings. If you implement the awaitable pattern, your OnCompleted method (which is mandatory) *should* flow the execution context. If you choose to implement ICriticalNotifyCompletion, your UnsafeOnCompleted method should *not* flow the execution context...and should be decorated with the [SecurityCritical] attribute to prevent untrusted code from calling it. The method builders are trusted, of course, and they flow the context, so all is well—partially trusted callers can still use your awaiter efficiently, but would-be attackers won't be able to sidestep context flow.

I've deliberately kept this section fairly brief; I find the whole topic of contexts somewhat confusing, and there are even more complexities I haven't touched on. If you're implementing your own awaiter without delegating to an existing one (and you *probably* won't need to), you should definitely read Stephen Toub's "ExecutionContext vs SynchronizationContext" blog post (http://mng.bz/Ye65) for more details.

15.6.5   *Asynchronous operations in WinRT*

Windows 8 has introduced the Windows Store to the application ecosystem—and alongside it, WinRT. I go into a little more detail about WinRT in appendix C, but it's designed to be a modern, object-oriented, unmanaged environment. In many ways, it's the new Win32. Some of the familiar .NET types aren't available in WinRT, and even those that are available have mostly been stripped of blocking calls related to IO.

Types that still live in the CLR generally expose asynchronous operations via Task<T> as you've already seen, but that type doesn't exist within WinRT itself. Instead, there are a bunch of interfaces, all of which extend one core IAsyncInfo interface:

- IAsyncAction
- IAsyncActionWithProgress<TProgress>
- IAsyncOperation<TResult>
- IAsyncOperationWithProgress<TResult, TProgress>

You can think of the difference between the Action types and the Operation types as being similar to the difference between Task and Task<T>, or between Action and Func: an Action has no return value, whereas an Operation does. The WithProgress versions build progress reporting into the single type, rather than requiring method overloads with IProgress<T> as per the TAP.

The details of these interfaces are beyond the scope of this book, but there are plenty of resources available explaining them. I suggest you start with Stephen Toub's Windows 8 "Diving deep with WinRT and await" blog post (http://mng.bz/F1TF).

In terms of handling these interfaces from C# 5, there are a few important points:

- The `GetAwaiter` extension methods allow you to await actions and operations directly.
- The `AsTask` extension methods allow you to view an action or operation as a task, with support for cancellation tokens and progress reporting via `IProgress<T>`.
- The `AsAsyncOperation` and `AsAsyncAction` extension methods go in the opposite direction, taking a task and returning a WinRT-friendly wrapper.

All of these are provided by the `System.WindowsRuntimeSystemExtensions` class, in the `System.Runtime.WindowsRuntime.dll` assembly.

Once again you've seen the value of the awaitable pattern. The C# compiler really doesn't care that it's calling an extension method in order to await the asynchronous operation. It's just another awaitable type. Most of the time you're likely to be able to leave an asynchronous operation in its native type and await it as normal. It's nice to have the flexibility to treat a WinRT asynchronous operation as a more familiar `Task<T>` for more complex scenarios though.

Another option for running code in the WinRT model of asynchrony is to use the `Run` method in the `System.Runtime.InteropServices.WindowsRuntime.AsyncInfo` class. Using this is cleaner than calling `Task.Run(...).AsAsyncOperation` if you need to hand an `IAsyncOperation` (or `IAsyncAction`) to some other code.

Asynchrony really isn't optional when writing WinRT applications. A lot of the time, the platform won't give you the option of writing synchronous code for IO. Of course, you *can* do all the work yourself, but using the features of C# 5 makes WinRT significantly simpler to use. I'm sure it's no coincidence that the language gained asynchrony at roughly the same time WinRT was released. Microsoft isn't just dipping its toe in the water here; this is how you *will* write Windows Store applications in C#.

15.7 Summary

I hope that the more complicated, deep-dive sections of this chapter haven't obscured the elegance of the asynchronous features of C# 5. The ability to write efficient asynchronous code in a more familiar execution model is a huge step forward, and I believe it will be transformative—once it's well understood. It's been my experience when giving presentations about async that many developers get easily confused by the feature the first time they see and use it. That's entirely understandable, but please don't let that put you off. Hopefully this chapter will help to answer at least some of your questions as you go along, but there's a wealth of documentation out there, and plenty of people ready to help on Stack Overflow, of course.

Speaking of other resources, I should emphasize that I've mostly tried to cover the *language* aspects of asynchrony here, in keeping with the rest of the book. There's much more to asynchronous development than just knowing those language features, though, and I urge you to read everything you can about TPL. Even if you can't use C# 5 yet, if you're using .NET 4 you can start using `Task<T>` as a clean model for asynchronous operations. Whenever you're tempted to reach for a raw `Thread` method, think about whether TPL might provide a higher abstraction to let you achieve the same goal more simply.

To sum up: async functions in C# 5 *rock*. That's not quite all there is to look at though. There are a couple of tiny features that I really ought to cover before wrapping up this edition…

C# 5 bonus features and closing thoughts

This chapter covers

- Changes to captured variables
- Caller information attributes
- Closing thoughts

C# 2 had a bunch of small but disparate features, along with the major ones. C# 3 had several minor features building up to LINQ. Even C# 4 had relatively small features worth going into some detail about.

C# 5 has almost no features beyond asynchrony. It has just two little extras, both tiny. The C# design team always weighs the cost of a feature (in terms of design, implementation, testing, documentation, and developer education) against its benefits. I'm sure there are plenty of outstanding feature requests the team would *like* to satisfy, so presumably the costs of these bite-sized features were just small enough to allow them to make the cut.

The first change isn't so much a *feature* as a correction to an earlier mistake in the language design...

16.1   *Changes to captured variables in foreach loops*

Back in section 5.5.5 I gave a warning about code that used an anonymous function (typically a lambda expression) within a `foreach` loop, capturing the loop variable. The following listing shows a simple example of such code, which *looks* as if it will output x, then y, and then z.

Listing 16.1   Using captured iteration variables

```
string[] values = { "x", "y", "z" };
var actions = new List<Action>();

foreach (string value in values)
{
    actions.Add(() => Console.WriteLine(value));
}

foreach (Action action in actions)
{
    action();
}
```

In C# 3 and C# 4, this would *actually* print z three times—the loop variable (value) would be captured by the lambda expression, and there was notionally just one variable "instance" that changed value on each iteration of the loop. All three delegates would refer to the same variable, and by the time they were executed at the end, the value of that variable would be z. This wasn't an implementation mistake in the compiler; it was how the language was *specified* to behave.

In C# 5, the language works as you'd probably have expected it to in the first place: each iteration of the loop effectively introduces a separate variable. Each of the delegates will refer to a different variable, with the value from that iteration of the loop.

There's not a lot more to say about this feature—it's really just correcting an area of the language that caused problems for a lot of developers. (You'd probably be amazed at how many Stack Overflow questions this caused.)

I want to give one word of warning, though: if you're in the fairly unusual position of writing code that needs to be compiled with various different versions of the C# compiler, you need to be aware that the behavior will vary. The code from listing 16.1 doesn't produce any warnings in any versions of C#—*the behavior just changes silently for C# 5*. Be careful, and make sure you have unit tests to fall back on!

On to the final feature…

16.2   *Caller information attributes*

Some features are very general—lambda expressions, implicitly typed local variables, generics, and the like. Others are more specific—LINQ is really meant to be about querying data of some form or other, even though it's aimed to generalize over many different data sources. The final C# 5 feature is extremely targeted: there are two significant use cases (one obvious, one slightly less so), and I really don't expect it to be used much outside those situations.

16.2.1 *Basic behavior*

.NET 4.5 introduces three new attributes: `CallerFilePathAttribute`, `CallerLine-NumberAttribute`, and `CallerMemberNameAttribute`, all in the `System.Runtime.CompilerServices` namespace. Just as with other attributes, when you apply any of these, you can omit the *Attribute* suffix, and as that's the most common way of using attributes, I'll abbreviate the names appropriately for the rest of the book.

All three attributes can only be applied to parameters, and they're only useful when they're applied to *optional* parameters. The idea is simple: if the call site doesn't provide the argument, the compiler will use the current file, line number, or member name to fill in the argument, instead of taking the normal default value. If the caller *does* supply an argument, the compiler will leave it alone.

The following listing shows an example of both cases.

> **Listing 16.2 Using caller information attributes properly, and abusing them**

```
static void ShowInfo([CallerFilePath] string file = null,
                     [CallerLineNumber] int line = 0,
                     [CallerMemberName] string member = null)
{
    Console.WriteLine("{0}:{1} - {2}", file, line, member);
}
...
ShowInfo();                                    Compiler fills
                                               in everything
ShowInfo("LiesAndDamnedLies.java", -10);                     Compiler only
                                                             fills in name
```

The output from listing 16.2 would be something like this:

```
c:\Users\Jon\Code\Chapter16\CallerIntoDemo.cs:21 - Main
LiesAndDamnedLies.java:-10 - Main
```

Of course, you wouldn't usually give a fake value for any of these arguments, but it's useful to be able to pass the value explicitly, particularly if you want to log the *current* method's caller, using the same attributes.

The member name works for all members, normally in the obvious way, with the following reasonably predictable special names:

- Static constructor: `.cctor`
- Constructor: `.ctor`
- Finalizer: `Finalize`

The name used as part of a method call during a field initializer is the name of the field.

There are two situations in which caller member information *isn't* populated. The first is attribute initialization; listing 16.3 provides an example of an attribute that you might *expect* to be given the name of the member it was applied to, but unfortunately the compiler doesn't fill anything in automatically in this case.

Listing 16.3   Attempting to use caller information attributes in an attribute declaration

```
[AttributeUsage(AttributeTargets.All)]
public class MemberDescriptionAttribute : Attribute
{
    public MemberDescriptionAttribute([CallerMemberName] string member = null)
    {
    Member = member;
    }

    public string Member { get; set; }
}
```

This could definitely be useful. I've seen situations where developers have found attributes via reflection, but had to populate their own data structure to maintain a mapping between the member name and the attribute, which could be done automatically by the compiler.

The dynamic typing omission is more easily forgivable. The following listing demonstrates the kind of usage that unfortunately doesn't work.

Listing 16.4   Attempting to use caller information attributes with dynamic invocation

```
class TypeUsedDynamically
{
    internal void ShowCaller([CallerMemberName] string caller = "Unknown")
    {
        Console.WriteLine("Called by: {0}", caller);
    }
}
...
dynamic x = new TypeUsedDynamically();
x.ShowCaller();
```

Listing 16.3 just prints `Called by: Unknown` as if the attribute weren't present. Although this may seem disappointing, consider the alternative: in order to work, the compiler would need to embed the member name, filename, and line number into every dynamic call that could *possibly* end up requiring the information. Overall, I think the costs would outweigh the benefits for most developers.

16.2.2   Logging

The most obvious case where caller information is useful is when writing to a log file. Previously when logging, you would usually construct a stack trace (using `System` `.Diagnostics.StackTrace`, for example) to find out where the log information came from. This is normally hidden from view in logging frameworks, but it's still there—and ugly. It's potentially an issue in terms of performance, and it's brittle in the face of JIT compiler inlining.

It's easy to see how a logging framework could make use of the new feature to allow caller-only information to be logged very cheaply, even preserving line numbers and member names in the face of a build that had debug information stripped, and even after obfuscation. This doesn't help in cases where you want to log a full stack trace, of course, but it doesn't take away your ability to do that either.

As I write, I'm not aware of any logging frameworks that have taken advantage of this; it would require a build specifically targeting .NET 4.5, to start with, or a framework with the attributes declared explicitly, as you'll see in section 16.2.4. But it should be easy to write your own wrapper classes that make use of whichever logging framework you prefer and provide caller information. Over time, I'm sure the frameworks will catch up and provide this functionality out of the box.

16.2.3 Implementing INotifyPropertyChanged

The less obvious use of just one of these attributes, [CallerMemberName], may be *very* obvious to you if you happen to implement INotifyPropertyChanged frequently.

The interface is very simple—it's a single event of type PropertyChangedEvent-Handler. This is a delegate type with the following signature:

```
public delegate void PropertyChangedEventHandler(Object sender,
                                      PropertyChangedEventArgs e)
```

PropertyChangedEventArgs, in turn, has a single constructor:

```
public PropertyChangedEventArgs(string propertyName)
```

A typical implementation of INotifyPropertyChanged before C# 5 might look something like the following.

Listing 16.5 Implementing INotifyPropertyChanged the old way

```
class OldPropertyNotifier : INotifyPropertyChanged
{
    public event PropertyChangedEventHandler PropertyChanged;

    private int firstValue;
    public int FirstValue
    {
        get { return firstValue; }
        set
        {
            if (value != firstValue)
            {
                firstValue = value;
                NotifyPropertyChanged("FirstValue");
            }
        }
    }

     // Other properties with the same pattern

    private void NotifyPropertyChanged(string propertyName)
    {
        PropertyChangedEventHandler handler = PropertyChanged;
        if (handler != null)
```

```
        {
            handler(this, new PropertyChangedEventArgs(propertyName));
        }
    }
}
```

The purpose of the helper method is to avoid having to put the nullity check in each property. You could easily make it an extension method to avoid repeating it on each implementation, of course.

This isn't just long-winded (which hasn't changed)—it's brittle. The problem is that the name of the property (FirstValue) is specified as a string literal, and if you refactor the property name to something else, you could easily forget to change the string literal. If you're lucky, your tools and tests will help you spot the mistake, but it's still very ugly.

With C# 5, the majority of the code stays the same, but you can make the compiler fill in the property name by using CallerMemberName in the helper method, as follows.

Listing 16.6   Implementing INotifyPropertyChanged using caller information

```
// Within the setter
if (value != firstValue)
{
    firstValue = value;
    NotifyPropertyChanged();
}

...

void NotifyPropertyChanged([CallerMemberName] string propertyName = null)
{
    // Exactly the same code as before
}
```

I've only shown the sections of the code that have changed—it's that simple. Now when you change the name of the property, the compiler will use the new name instead. It's not an earth-shattering improvement, but it's nicer nonetheless.

16.2.4   *Using caller information attributes without .NET 4.5*

Like extension methods, caller information attributes just let you ask the compiler to mess with your code very slightly during the compilation process. They don't use any information you couldn't provide yourself—you'd just need to be careful as you did so. Just like extension methods, it's possible to use them when targeting an earlier version of .NET than the one that *really* contains the attributes—you just have to declare the attributes yourself. This is as simple as copying the declaration from MSDN. The attributes themselves don't have any parameters, so you just need to provide an empty body for the class declaration, which still has to be in the System.Runtime.Compiler-Services namespace.

The C# compiler will treat your user-provided attributes in exactly the same way as it would treat the real ones in .NET 4.5. The downside of this approach is that you'll run into problems if you ever build the same code against .NET 4.5. You'll need to remove your hand-crafted attributes at that point, to avoid confusing the compiler.

If you're using .NET 4, Silverlight 4 or 5, or Windows Phone 7.5, another option is to use the `Microsoft.Bcl` NuGet package. This provides these attributes along with several other handy types you might otherwise be pining for.

And that's it—C# 5 all wrapped up.

16.3   *Closing thoughts*

The first two editions of *C# in Depth* closed with a chapter dedicated to the future as I perceived it at the time of writing. If you own either (or both!) of those editions, you may want to look back and have a quiet chuckle to yourself. I don't think I said anything outrageously wrong, but I clearly had little idea of how much things could change in just a couple of years.

I'd also like to point out that I had no clue what would be coming in either C# 4 or C# 5 until they were announced by Microsoft. Both dynamic typing and asynchronous functions came as big surprises to me. I had the good fortune of presenting my ideas for C# 5 at a conference, with a few members of the C# team in attendance, and I'm *hugely* pleased that they went their own way instead. In case I haven't made myself clear yet, async/await *rocks* as a feature, and it's far beyond anything I could have come up with.

What's in store for the industry? More mobile, more touch input, more distributed cloud services, possibly augmented reality—these are all reasonably safe bets by now. But if those are the most disruptive forces in the industry by the end of 2014, I'll be very disappointed. The best things in computing seem to come out of nowhere—after many years of hard effort by the people involved, of course—and surprise everyone.

The same sort of thing can be said for C#. I still have my wish-list of minor features, and maybe C# 6 will be a tidy-up release, with many minor features instead of the huge ones we've seen in the past. Maybe the language will be expanded in an extendable way, allowing other developers to create those minor features themselves. Or maybe the new killer feature will be something that I didn't even know I needed—yet again.

The C# and .NET teams have certainly not been idle. Even leaving aside C# 5 and all the work required integrating .NET into the Windows 8 UI, we do know *one* project they've been working hard on: Roslyn. Named as a pun on the orientation of Eric Lippert's office when he worked on the project, Roslyn is another name for the "compiler as a service" idea that's been talked about for so long. Roslyn will provide an API that developers can use to analyze C# (or VB) code, modify it programmatically, compile it into IL, and so on. I suspect *relatively* few developers will have any need for this, but those who do will be immensely glad of it, and they'll create wonderful things for the rest of us. Imagine being able to write your own refactoring tools, more sophisticated code convention analysis, code generation, and more—all with an API designed to be powerful and performant enough to be the engine for future releases of Visual

Studio. Perhaps more important for most of us, Roslyn gives the C# team a playground in which it's relatively easy to implement new features. Maybe they'll become even more adventurous and ambitious in the future!

I can state one thing with a fair degree of certainty, though: I'll continue to enjoy writing about, talking about, and using C# for quite some time, whether or not the language evolves any further. I find it hard to believe that programming will become *less* interesting in the next decade.

As in previous editions, I urge you to do awesome things. Write fabulously clear code that your colleagues will love to work with. Develop the Next Big Thing in the open source world. Help other developers on Stack Overflow. Talk to user groups, conferences, friends, and anyone who will listen about whatever your passion may be. I wish you the very best of luck in however many of these you undertake, and I hope this book has provided some small measure of help in achieving your ambitions.

appendix A
LINQ standard
query operators

There are many standard query operators in LINQ, only some of which are supported directly in C# query expressions—the others have to be called manually as normal methods. Some of the standard query operators are demonstrated in the main text of the book, but they're all listed in this appendix.

Most of the examples use the following two sample sequences:

```
string[] words = {"zero", "one", "two", "three", "four"};
int[] numbers = {0, 1, 2, 3, 4};
```

For completeness, I've included the operators we've already looked at, although in most cases chapter 11 contains more detail on them than I've provided here.

The behavior specified here is that of LINQ to Objects; other providers may work differently. For each operator, I've specified whether it uses deferred or immediate execution. If an operator uses deferred execution, I've also indicated whether it streams or buffers its data.

A while ago, I reimplemented LINQ to Objects from scratch in a project called Edulinq, blogging details about every single operator and considering possibilities for optimization, lazy evaluation, and so on. For more detail than you're ever likely to want to know about LINQ to Objects, visit the Edulinq project home page at http://edulinq.googlecode.com.

A.1   Aggregation

The aggregation operators (see table A.1) all result in a single value rather than a sequence. Average and Sum operate either on a sequence of numbers (any of the built-in numeric types) or on a sequence of elements with a delegate to convert from each element to one of the built-in numeric types. Min and Max have overloads for numeric types but can also operate on any sequence either using the default comparer for the element type or using a conversion delegate. Count and Long-Count are equivalent to each other, just with different return types. Both of these have two overloads—one that just counts the length of the sequence, and one that takes a predicate, and only elements matching the predicate are counted.

Table A.1   Examples of aggregation operators

Expression	Result
`numbers.Sum()`	10
`numbers.Count()`	5
`numbers.Average()`	2
`numbers.LongCount(x => x % 2 == 0)`	3 (as a `long`; there are three even numbers)
`words.Min(word => word.Length)`	3 (`"one"` and `"two"`)
`words.Max(word => word.Length)`	5 (`"three"`)

`numbers.Aggregate("seed",`
`  (current, item) => current + item,`
`  result=> result.ToUpper())`
	`"SEED01234"`

The most generalized aggregation operator (shown in the bottom row of table A.1) is just called `Aggregate`. All the other aggregation operators could be expressed as calls to `Aggregate`, although it'd be relatively painful to do so. The basic idea is that there's always a "result so far," starting with an initial seed. An aggregation delegate is applied for each element of the input sequence; the delegate takes the result so far and the input element, and produces the next result. As a final optional step, a conversion is applied from the aggregation result to the return value of the method. This conversion may result in a different type, if necessary. It's not quite as complicated as it sounds, but still you're unlikely to use it often.

All of the aggregation operators use immediate execution. The overload for `Count` that doesn't use a predicate is optimized for implementations of `ICollection` and `ICollection<T>`; in that situation, it'll use the `Count` property of the collection without reading any data.[1]

A.2   *Concatenation*

There's a single concatenation operator: `Concat` (see table A.2). As you might expect, this operates on two sequences and returns a single sequence consisting of all the elements of the first sequence followed by all the elements of the second. The two input sequences must be of the same type, execution is deferred, and all data is streamed.

Table A.2   `Concat` example

Expression	Result
`numbers.Concat(new[] {2, 3, 4, 5, 6})`	0, 1, 2, 3, 4, 2, 3, 4, 5, 6

---

[1] There's no such shortcut for `LongCount`. I've personally never seen this method used in LINQ to Objects.

A.3 Conversion

The conversion operators cover a fair range of uses, but they all come in pairs.

The examples in table A.3 use two additional sequences to demonstrate `Cast` and `OfType`:

```
object[] allStrings = {"These", "are", "all", "strings"};
object[] notAllStrings = {"Number", "at", "the", "end", 5};
```

Table A.3 Conversion examples

Expression	Result
`allStrings.Cast<string>()`	`"These"`, `"are"`, `"all"`, `"strings"` (as `IEnumerable<string>`)
`allStrings.OfType<string>()`	`"These"`, `"are"`, `"all"`, `"strings"` (as `IEnumerable<string>`)
`notAllStrings.Cast<string>()`	Exception is thrown while iterating, at point of failing conversion
`notAllStrings.OfType<string>()`	`"Number"`, `"at"`, `"the"`, `"end"` (as `IEnumerable<string>`)
`numbers.ToArray()`	`0`, `1`, `2`, `3`, `4` (as `int[]`)
`numbers.ToList()`	`0`, `1`, `2`, `3`, `4` (as `List<int>`)

`words.ToDictionary(w => w.Substring(0, 2))`	Dictionary contents:
	`"ze"`: `"zero"`
	`"on"`: `"one"`
	`"tw"`: `"two"`
	`"th"`: `"three"`
	`"fo"`: `"four"`

`// Key is first character of word`
`words.ToLookup(word => word[0])`
	Lookup contents:
	`'z'`: `"zero"`
	`'o'`: `"one"`
	`'t'`: `"two"`, `"three"`
	`'f'`: `"four"`

`words.ToDictionary(word => word[0])`	Exception: can only have one entry per key, so fails on `'t'`

`ToArray` and `ToList` are fairly self-explanatory: they read the whole sequence into memory, returning it either as an array or as a `List<T>`. Both use immediate execution.

`Cast` and `OfType` convert an untyped sequence into a typed one, either throwing an exception (for `Cast`) or ignoring (for `OfType`) elements of the input sequence that aren't implicitly convertible to the output sequence element type using an unboxing or reference conversion. This may also be used to convert typed sequences into more specifically typed sequences, such as converting `IEnumerable<object>` to `IEnumerable<string>`. These use deferred execution and stream their input data.

ToDictionary and ToLookup both take delegates to obtain the key for any particular element. ToDictionary returns a dictionary mapping the key to the element type, whereas ToLookup returns an appropriately typed ILookup<,>. A lookup is like a dictionary where the value associated with a key isn't one element but a sequence of elements. Lookups are generally used when duplicate keys are expected as part of normal operation, whereas a duplicate key will cause ToDictionary to throw an exception. More complicated overloads of both methods allow a custom IEquality-Comparer<T> to be used to compare keys, and a conversion delegate to be applied to each element before it's put into the dictionary or lookup. Both of these methods use immediate execution.

There are two additional operators that I haven't provided examples for: AsEnumerable and AsQueryable. They don't affect the results in an immediately obvious way, so they can't really be demonstrated here. Instead, they affect the manner in which the query is executed. Queryable.AsQueryable is an extension method on IEnumerable that returns an IQueryable (both types being generic or nongeneric, depending on which overload you pick). If the IEnumerable you call it on is already an IQueryable, it returns the same reference; otherwise it creates a wrapper around the original sequence. The wrapper allows you to use all the normal Queryable extension methods, passing in expression trees, but when the query is executed the expression tree is compiled into normal IL and executed directly, using the LambdaExpression.Compile method shown in section 9.3.2.

Enumerable.AsEnumerable is an extension method on IEnumerable<T> and has a trivial implementation, simply returning the reference it was called on. No wrappers are involved—it just returns the same reference. This forces the Enumerable extension methods to be used in subsequent LINQ operators. Consider the following query expressions:

```
// Filter the users in the database with LIKE
from user in context.Users
where user.Name.StartsWith("Tim")
select user;

// Filter the users in memory
from user in context.Users.AsEnumerable()
where user.Name.StartsWith("Tim")
select user;
```

The second query expression forces the compile-time type of the source to be IEnumerable<User> instead of IQueryable<User>, so all the processing is done in memory instead of at the database. The compiler will use the Enumerable extension methods (taking delegate parameters) instead of the Queryable extension methods (taking expression tree parameters). Normally you want to do as much processing as possible in SQL, but when there are transformations that require local code, you sometimes have to force LINQ to use the appropriate Enumerable extension methods. Of course, this isn't specific to databases; the theme of forcing the tail of a query to use `Enumerable` is applicable for other providers too, if they're based on `IQueryable` or something similar.

A.4 *Element operators*

This is another selection of query operators that are grouped in pairs (see table A.4). This time, the pairs all work the same way. There's a simple version that picks a single element if it can or throws an exception if the specified element doesn't exist, and a version with `OrDefault` at the end of the name. All of these operators use immediate execution.

Table A.4 Single element selection examples

Expression	Result
`words.ElementAt(2)`	`"two"`
`words.ElementAtOrDefault(10)`	`null`
`words.First()`	`"zero"`
`words.First(w => w.Length == 3)`	`"one"`
`words.First(w => w.Length == 10)`	Exception: no matching elements
`words.FirstOrDefault` `(w =>w.Length == 10)`	`null`
`words.Last()`	`"four"`
`words.Single()`	Exception: more than one element
`words.SingleOrDefault()`	Exception: more than one element
`words.Single(word => word.Length == 5)`	`"three"`
`words.Single(word => word.Length == 10)`	Exception: no matching elements
`words.SingleOrDefault` `(w =>w.Length == 10)`	`null`

The operator names are easily understood: `First` and `Last` return the first and last elements of the sequence, respectively, throwing an `InvalidOperationException` if the sequence is empty. `Single` returns the only element in a sequence, throwing an exception if the sequence is empty or has more than one element. `ElementAt` returns a specific element by index—the fifth element, for example. An `ArgumentOutOfRangeException` is thrown if the index is negative or too large for the actual number of elements in the collection. In addition, there's an overload for all of the operators other than `ElementAt` to filter the sequence first—for example, `First` can return the first element that matches a given condition.

The `OrDefault` versions of these methods suppress the exceptions I've just described (returning the default value for the element type instead) except in one case: `SingleOrDefault` will return a default value if the sequence is empty, but if there's more than one element, it'll still throw an exception, just like `Single`. This is designed for situations where if everything's correct, the sequence will have zero or one element. If you want to cope with sequences that may have more elements, use `FirstOrDefault` instead.

All of the overloads that don't have a predicate parameter are optimized for instances of `IList<T>`, as they can access the correct element without iterating. There's no optimization when a predicate is involved—it wouldn't make sense for most calls, although it could make a big difference when finding the *last* matching element in a list, by moving backward from the end. At the time of writing, that case isn't optimized, but it could change in a future version.

A.5   *Equality*

There's only one standard equality operator: `SequenceEqual` (see table A.5). This just compares two sequences for element-by-element equality, including order. For instance, the sequence 0, 1, 2, 3, 4 isn't equal to 4, 3, 2, 1, 0. An overload allows a specific `IEqualityComparer<T>` to be used when comparing elements. The return value is a Boolean, and it's computed with immediate execution.

Table A.5   Sequence equality examples

Expression	Result
`words.SequenceEqual` `(new[]{"zero","one","two","three","four"})`	True
`words.SequenceEqual` `(new[]{"ZERO","ONE","TWO","THREE","FOUR"})`	False

`words.SequenceEqual`
`(new[]{"ZERO","ONE","TWO","THREE","FOUR"},`
`StringComparer.OrdinalIgnoreCase)`
	True

Again, LINQ to Objects misses a trick here in terms of optimization: if both sequences have an efficient way of retrieving their counts, it would make sense to check whether those are equal before comparing the elements themselves. As it is, the implementation just walks through both sequences until it reaches the end or finds an inequality.

A.6   *Generation*

Of all the generation operators (see table A.6), only one acts on an existing sequence: `DefaultIfEmpty`. This returns either the original sequence if it's not empty, or a sequence with a single element otherwise. The element is normally the default value for the sequence type, but an overload allows you to specify which value to use.

There are three other generation operators that are just static methods in `Enumerable`:

- `Range` generates a sequence of integers, with the parameters specifying the first value and how many values to generate.
- `Repeat` generates a sequence of any type by repeating a specified single value for a specified number of times.
- `Empty` generates an empty sequence of any type.

All of the generation operators use deferred execution and stream their output—in other words, they don't just prepopulate a collection and return that. The exception is `Empty`, which returns an empty array of the correct type. An empty array is completely immutable, so the same array can be returned for every call for the same element type.

Table A.6 Generation examples

Expression	Result
`numbers.DefaultIfEmpty()`	`0, 1, 2, 3, 4`
`new int[0].DefaultIfEmpty()`	0 (within an `IEnumerable<int>`)
`new int[0].DefaultIfEmpty(10)`	10 (within an `IEnumerable<int>`)
`Enumerable.Range(15, 2)`	`15, 16`
`Enumerable.Repeat(25, 2)`	`25, 25`
`Enumerable.Empty<int>()`	An empty `IEnumerable<int>`

A.7 *Grouping*

There are two grouping operators, but one of them is `ToLookup`, which you've already seen in section A.3 as a conversion operator. That just leaves `GroupBy`, which we examined in section 11.6.1 in the form of the `group ... by` clause in query expressions. It uses deferred execution but buffers its results: when you start iterating over the resulting sequence of groups, the whole of the input is consumed.

The result of `GroupBy` is a sequence of appropriately typed `IGrouping<,>` elements. Each element has a key and a sequence of elements that match that key. In many ways, this is just a different way of looking at a lookup—instead of having random access to the groups by key, the groups are enumerated in turn. The order in which the groups are returned is the order in which their respective keys are discovered. Within a group, the order is the same as in the original sequence.

`GroupBy` has a daunting number of overloads, allowing you to specify not only how a key is derived from an element (which is always required) but also optionally the following:

- How to compare keys.
- A projection from an original element to the element within a group.

- A projection that takes both a key and a sequence of matching elements. The overall result in this case is a sequence of elements of the result type of the projection.

Table A.7 contains examples of the second and third options, as well as the simplest form. Custom key comparisons are slightly more long-winded to demonstrate, but they work in the obvious way.

Table A.7 `GroupBy` examples

Expression	Result
`words.GroupBy(word => word.Length)`	Key: 4; Sequence: `"zero"`, `"four"` Key: 3; Sequence: `"one"`, `"two"` Key: 5; Sequence: `"three"`

`words.GroupBy`
`  (word => word.Length,    // Key`
`   word => word.ToUpper() // Group element`
`  )`
	Key: 4; Sequence: `"zero"`, `"four"`
	Key: 3; Sequence: `"one"`, `"two"`
	Key: 5; Sequence: `"three"`

`// Project each (key, group) pair to string`
`words.GroupBy`
`  (word => word.Length,`
`   (key, g) => key + ": " + g.Count())`
	`"4: 2"`, `"3: 2"`, `"5: 1"`

The option specified by the last bullet point is rarely used, in my experience.

A.8 Joins

Two operators are specified as join operators, `Join` and `GroupJoin`, both of which you saw in section 11.5 using the `join` and `join ... into` query expression clauses, respectively. Each method takes several parameters: two sequences, a key selector for each sequence, a projection to apply to each matching pair of elements, and optionally a key comparison.

For `Join` the projection takes one element from each sequence and produces a result; for `GroupJoin` the projection takes an element from the left sequence and a sequence of matching elements from the right sequence. Both use deferred execution and stream the left sequence but read the right sequence in its entirety when the first result is requested.

For the join examples in table A.8, we'll match a sequence of names (Robin, Ruth, Bob, Emma) against a sequence of colors (Red, Blue, Beige, Green) by looking at the first character of both the name and the color, so Robin will join with Red and Bob will join with both Blue and Beige, for example.

Note that Emma doesn't match any of the colors—the name doesn't appear at all in the results of the first example, but it *does* appear in the second, with an empty sequence of colors.

Table A.8   Join examples

Expression	Result

`names.Join // Left sequence`
`  (colors, // Right sequence`
`   name => name[0], // Left key selector`
`   color=>  color[0], // Right key selector`
`   // Projection for result pairs`
`   (name, color) => name + " - " + color`
`  )`
	`"Robin - Red",`
	`"Ruth - Red",`
	`"Bob - Blue",`
	`"Bob - Beige"`

`names.GroupJoin`
`  (colors,`
`   name => name[0],`
`   color => color[0],`
`   // Projection for key/sequence pairs`
`   (name, matches) => name + ": " +`
`      string.Join("/", matches.ToArray())`
`  )`
	`"Robin: Red",`
	`"Ruth: Red",`
	`"Bob: Blue/Beige",`
	`"Emma: "`

A.9   *Partitioning*

The partitioning operators either *skip* an initial part of the sequence, returning only the rest, or *take* only the initial part of a sequence, ignoring the rest. In each case, you can either specify how many elements are in the first part of the sequence or specify a condition—the first part of the sequence continues until the condition fails. After the condition fails for the first time, it isn't tested again—it doesn't matter whether later elements in the sequence match. All of the partitioning operators use deferred execution and stream their data.

Partitioning effectively divides the sequence into two distinct parts, either by position or by predicate. In each case, if you concatenate the results of `Take` or `TakeWhile` with the results of the corresponding `Skip` or `SkipWhile`, providing the same argument to both calls, you'll end up with the original sequence: each element will occur exactly once, in the original order. This is demonstrated by the calls in table A.9.

Table A.9   Partitioning examples

Expression	Result
`words.Take(2)`	`"zero", "one"`
`words.Skip(2)`	`"two", "three", "four"`
`words.TakeWhile(word => word.Length <= 4)`	`"zero", "one", "two"`
`words.SkipWhile(word => word.Length <= 4)`	`"three", "four"`

A.10   *Projection*

You've seen two projection operators (`Select` and `SelectMany`) in chapter 11. `Select` is a simple one-to-one projection from a source element to a result element. `Select-Many` is used when there are multiple `from` clauses in a query expression; each element in the original sequence is used to generate a new sequence. Both projection operators (see table A.10) use deferred execution.

Table A.10   Projection examples

Expression	Result
`words.Select(word => word.Length)`	`4, 3, 3, 5, 4`

`words.Select`
`  ((word, index) =>`
`    index.ToString() + ": " +word)`
	`"0: zero", "1: one", "2: two",`
	`"3: three", "4: four"`

`words.SelectMany`
`  (word => word.ToCharArray())`
	`'z', 'e', 'r', 'o', 'o', 'n', 'e', 't',`
	`'w', 'o', 't', 'h', 'r', 'e', 'e', 'f',`
	`'o', 'u', 'r'`

`words.SelectMany`
`  ((word, index) =>`
`    Enumerable.Repeat(word, index))`
	`"one", "two", "two",`
	`"three", "three", "three",`
	`"four", "four", "four", "four"`

There are additional overloads you didn't see in chapter 11. Both methods have overloads that allow the index within the original sequence to be used in the projection, and `SelectMany` either flattens all of the generated sequences into a single sequence without including the original element at all, or it uses a projection to generate a result element for each pair of elements. Multiple `from` clauses always use the overload that takes a projection. (Examples of this are long-winded and not included here. See chapter 11 for more details.)

.NET 4 introduced a new operator called `Zip`. This isn't officially a standard query operator according to MSDN, but it's worth knowing about anyway. It takes two sequences and applies the specified projection to each pair: the first element from each sequence, then the second element from each sequence, and so on. The resulting sequence finishes when *either* of the source sequences does. Table A.11 shows two examples of `Zip`, using the names and colors from section A.8. `Zip` uses deferred execution and streams its data.

Table A.11   `Zip` examples

Expression	Result

`names.Zip(colors, (x, y) => x + "-" + y)`	`"Robin-Red",`
	`"Ruth-Blue",`
	`"Bob-Beige",`
	`"Emma-Green"`

Table A.11 Zip examples (continued)

Expression	Result

`// Second sequence stops early`
`names.Zip(colors.Take(3),`
`    (x, y) => x + "-" + y)`
	`"Robin-Red"`,
	`"Ruth-Blue"`,
	`"Bob-Beige"`

A.11 Quantifiers

The quantifier operators shown in table A.12 all return a Boolean value, using immediate execution:

- `All` checks whether all the elements in the sequence satisfy the given predicate.
- `Any` checks whether any of the elements in the sequence satisfy the given predicate, or whether there are any elements at all for the parameterless overload.
- `Contains` checks whether the sequence contains a particular element, optionally specifying a comparison to use.

Table A.12 Quantifier examples

Expression	Result
`words.All(word => word.Length > 3)`	`false` (`"one"` and `"two"` have exactly three letters)
`words.All(word => word.Length > 2)`	`true`
`words.Any()`	`true` (the sequence isn't empty)
`words.Any(word => word.Length == 6)`	`false` (no six-letter words)
`words.Any(word => word.Length == 5)`	`true` (`"three"` satisfies the condition)
`words.Contains("FOUR")`	`false`
`words.Contains("FOUR",` `    StringComparer.OrdinalIgnoreCase)`	`true`

`Any` is a particularly useful operator that's often forgotten. If you're trying to find out whether a sequence contains any items (or any items matching a predicate), it's much better to use `source.Any(...)` than `source.Count(...) > 0`. They should give the same results, but `Any` can stop as soon as it's found the first item, whereas `Count` has to count *all* the items, even though you only need to know whether the result is nonzero.

The overload for `Contains` that doesn't specify a custom comparison is optimized if the source implements `ICollection<T>` by delegating to the interface implementation. This means `Enumerable.Contains()` will still be fast when called on a Hash-Set<T>, for example.

A.12   *Filtering*

The two filtering operators are OfType and Where. For details and examples of the OfType operator, see section A.3. The Where operator returns a sequence containing all the elements matching the given predicate. It has an overload to allow the predicate to take account of the element's index. It's unusual to require the index, and the where clause in query expressions doesn't use this overload. Where always uses deferred execution and streams its data. Table A.13 demonstrates both overloads.

Table A.13   Filtering examples

Expression	Result
words.Where(word => word.Length > 3)	"zero", "three", "four"
words.Where ((word, index) => index < word.Length)	"zero", // index=0, length=4 "one", // index=1, length=3 "two", // index=2, length=2 "three", // index=3, length=5 // Not "four", index=4, length=4

A.13   *Set-based operators*

It's natural to be able to consider two sequences as sets of elements. The four set-based operators all have two overloads, one using the default equality comparison for the element type, and one where the comparison is specified in an extra parameter. All of them use deferred execution.

The Distinct operator is the simplest—it acts on a single sequence and just returns a new sequence of all the distinct elements, discarding duplicates. The other operators also make sure they only return distinct values, but they act on two sequences:

- Intersect returns elements that appear in both sequences.
- Union returns the elements that are in either sequence.
- Except returns elements that are in the first sequence but not in the second. (Elements that are in the second sequence but not the first are *not* returned.)

The examples of these operators in table A.14 use two new sequences: abbc ("a", "b", "b", "c") and cd ("c", "d").

Table A.14   Set-based examples

Expression	Result
abbc.Distinct()	"a", "b", "c"
abbc.Intersect(cd)	"c"
abbc.Union(cd)	"a", "b", "c", "d"
abbc.Except(cd)	"a", "b"
cd.Except(abbc)	"d"

All of these operators use deferred execution, but the buffering/streaming distinction is slightly more complicated. `Distinct` and `Union` both stream their input sequences, whereas `Intersect` and `Except` read the whole of the right input sequence to start with, but then stream the left input sequence in a way similar to the join operators. *All* these operators keep a set of the elements they've already returned so as not to return duplicates. This means that even `Distinct` and `Union` are unsuitable for sequences that are too large to fit into memory, unless you know that there will be a limited set of distinct elements.

A.14 *Sorting*

You've seen all the sorting operators before: `OrderBy` and `OrderByDescending` provide a primary ordering, whereas `ThenBy` and `ThenByDescending` provide subsequent orderings for elements that aren't differentiated by the primary one. In each case a projection is specified from an element to its sorting key, and a comparison (between keys) can also be specified. Unlike some other sorting algorithms in the framework (such as `List<T>.Sort`), the LINQ orderings are *stable*—in other words, if two elements are regarded as equal in terms of their sorting key, they'll be returned in the order they appeared in the original sequence.

The final sorting operator is `Reverse`, which simply reverses the order of the sequence. All of the sorting operators (see table A.15) use deferred execution, but buffer their data.

Table A.15 Sorting examples

Expression	Result
`words.OrderBy(word => word)`	`"four"`, `"one"`, `"three"`, `"two"`, `"zero"`
`// Order words by second character` `words.OrderBy(word => word[1])`	`"zero"`, `"three"`, `"one"`, `"four"`, `"two"`

`// Order words by length;`
`// equal lengths returned in original`
`// order`
`words.OrderBy(word => word.Length)`
	`"one"`, `"two"`, `"zero"`, `"four"`, `"three"`

`words.OrderByDescending` `   (word => word.Length)`	`"three"`, `"zero"`,s `"four"`, `"one"`, `"two"`

`// Order words by length and then`
`// alphabetically`
`words.OrderBy(word => word.Length)`
`    .ThenBy(word => word)`
	`"one"`, `"two"`, `"four"`, `"zero"`, `"three"`

`// Order words by length and then`
`// alphabetically backwards`
`words.OrderBy(word => word.Length)`
`    .ThenByDescending(word => word)`
	`"two"`, `"one"`, `"zero"`, `"four"`, `"three"`

`words.Reverse()`	`"four"`, `"three"`, `"two"`, `"one"`, `"zero"`

appendix B
Generic collections
in .NET

There are many generic collections in .NET, and the list has grown over time. This appendix covers the most important generic collection interfaces and classes you need to know about. There are additional nongeneric collections in System .Collections, System.Collections.Specialized and System.ComponentModel, but I won't cover those here. Likewise, I won't mention the LINQ interfaces, such as ILookup<TKey, TValue>. This appendix is more reference than guidance—think of it as an alternative to navigating around MSDN while you're coding. Obviously MSDN will provide more details in most cases, but the aim here is to allow you to quickly skim over the various interfaces and implementations available when choosing a particular collection to use in your code.

I haven't indicated the thread-safety of each collection, but MSDN can provide more details. None of the normal collections support multiple concurrent writers; some support a single writer with concurrent readers. Section B.6 lists the concurrent collections that were added to .NET 4. Additionally, section B.7 discusses the read-only collection interfaces introduced in .NET 4.5.

B.1   Interfaces

Almost all the interfaces you need to know about are in the System.Collections .Generic namespace. Figure B.1 shows how the major interfaces prior to .NET 4.5 are related; I've included the nongeneric IEnumerable as the interface root as well. This *doesn't* include the read-only interfaces in .NET 4.5, as the diagram would have been too complicated to be useful.

As you've already seen several times, the most fundamental generic collection interface is IEnumerable<T>, representing a sequence of items that can be iterated over. IEnumerable<T> allows you to ask for an iterator of type IEnumerator<T>. The separation between the iterable sequence and the iterator enables multiple iterators to run independently over the same sequence at the same time. If you want to think in database terms, a table is an IEnumerable<T>, whereas a cursor is an IEnumerator<T>. These are the only variant collection interfaces covered in this appendix, becoming IEnumerable<out T> and IEnumerator<out T> in .NET 4; all

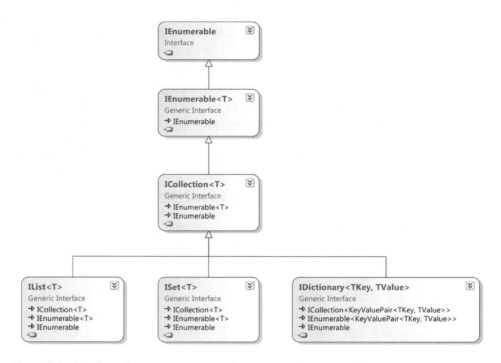

Figure B.1 Interfaces in `System.Collections.Generic`, up to .NET 4

the other interfaces involve values of the element type going both in and out of members, so they have to be invariant.

Next comes `ICollection<T>`—this extends `IEnumerable<T>` but adds two properties (`Count` and `IsReadOnly`), mutation methods (`Add`, `Remove`, and `Clear`), `CopyTo` (which copies the contents to an array), and `Contains` (which determines if the collection contains a particular element). All the standard generic collection implementations implement this interface.

`IList<T>` is all about positioning: it provides an indexer, `InsertAt` and `RemoveAt` (to match `Add`/`Remove` but with positions), and `IndexOf` (to determine the position of an element within the collection). Iterating over an `IList<T>` will generally return the item at index 0, then index 1, and so on. This isn't thoroughly documented, but it's a reasonable assumption to make. Likewise, it's usually expected that random access to an `IList<T>` by index is efficient.

`IDictionary<TKey, TValue>` represents a mapping from a unique key to a value for that key. The values don't have to be unique, and may be null; keys can't be null. Dictionaries can be regarded as collections of key/value pairs, which is why `IDictionary <TKey, TValue>` extends `ICollection<KeyValuePair<TKey, TValue>>`. Values can be retrieved with the indexer or `TryGetValue`; unlike the nongeneric `IDictionary` type, if you attempt to fetch the value for a missing key, the indexer of `IDictionary<TKey, TValue>` throws a `KeyNotFoundException`. The purpose of `TryGetValue` is to allow you to detect missing keys in situations where it's expected in normal operation.

ISet<T> is a new interface in .NET 4, representing a distinct set of values. It's been retroactively applied to HashSet<T> from .NET 3.5, and .NET 4 introduces a new implementation—SortedSet<T>.

Usually it's fairly clear which interface (and even implementation) you want to use when *implementing* functionality. It can be significantly harder to decide how to expose that collection as part of an API; the more specific you are in what you return, the more your callers will be able to rely on additional functionality specified by those types. This may make the caller's life easier, at the expense of future flexibility within your implementation. I usually prefer to use interfaces for the return types of methods and properties, rather than guaranteeing a particular implementation class. You should also think carefully before exposing a mutable collection in an API, particularly if that collection represents part of the state of the object or type. Returning either a copy or a read-only wrapper around the collection is usually preferable, unless the whole purpose of the method is to allow mutation via the returned collection.

B.2   *Lists*

In many ways, lists are the simplest and most natural type of collection. There are many implementations in the framework, with different abilities and performance characteristics. A few big-hitters are used all over the place, and some more esoteric ones are used for specialist situations.

B.2.1   *List<T>*

List<T> is the default choice for lists in most cases. It implements IList<T> and therefore ICollection<T>, IEnumerable<T>, and IEnumerable. Additionally, it implements the nongeneric ICollection and IList interfaces, boxing and unboxing as required, and performing execution-time type checks to make sure that new elements are always of a type that's compatible with T.

Internally List<T> stores an array, and it keeps track of both the logical size of the list and the size of the backing array. Adding an element is either a simple case of setting the next value in the array, or (if the array is already full) copying the existing contents into a new, bigger array and then setting the value. This means the operation has complexity of $O(1)$ or $O(n)$ depending on whether the values need to be copied. The expansion strategy isn't documented—and therefore isn't guaranteed—but in practice the approach has always been to expand to double the newly required size. This results in an *amortized complexity* of $O(1)$ for appending an item to the end of the list; sometimes it'll be more, but that becomes increasingly rare as the list grows larger.

You can explicitly manage the size of the backing array by getting and setting the Capacity property; the TrimExcess method has the effect of making the capacity exactly equal to the current size. In practice, this is rarely necessary, but if you already know the eventual size of the list when you create it, you can pass an initial capacity into the constructor, avoiding unnecessary copying.

Removing an element from a `List<T>` requires all the later elements to be copied down, so its complexity is $O(n - k)$ where k is the index of the element you're removing; trimming the tail of a list is cheaper than removing the head. On the other hand, if you're trying to remove an element by value instead of by index (`Remove` rather than `RemoveAt`), you'll effectively end up with an $O(n)$ operation wherever the element is: each element has to be either checked for equality or shuffled down.

Various methods on `List<T>` act as a sort of precursor to LINQ. `ConvertAll` projects one list into another; `FindAll` filters the original list into a new list containing only the values that match the specified predicate. `Sort` performs a sort using either the default equality comparer for the type or one specified as an argument. There's a big difference between `Sort` and the `OrderBy` of LINQ, though: `Sort` modifies the contents of the original list, rather than yielding an ordered copy. Also, `Sort` is unstable, whereas `OrderBy` is stable; equal elements in the original list may be reordered when using `Sort`. One aspect of `List<T>` that isn't supported by LINQ is binary search: if you have a list that's already sorted in the right way for the value you're looking for, the `BinarySearch` method is more efficient than using the linear `IndexOf` search.[1]

One somewhat controversial aspect of `List<T>` is the `ForEach` method. This does exactly what it sounds like—it iterates over the list and executes a delegate (specified as an argument to the method) for each value. Many developers have requested that this be added as an extension method for `IEnumerable<T>`, but this suggestion has been resisted so far; Eric Lippert makes the case for it being philosophically troubling on his blog (see http://mng.bz/Rur2). Calling `ForEach` using a lambda expression seems overkill to me; on the other hand, if you already have a delegate you want to execute on each element on the list, you might as well get `ForEach` to do that for you, as it's already there.

B.2.2 Arrays

Arrays are in some senses the lowest level of collection in .NET. All arrays derive directly from `System.Array`, and they're the only collections with direct support in the CLR. Single-dimensional arrays implement `IList<T>` (and the interfaces it extends) and the nongeneric `IList` and `ICollection` interfaces; rectangular arrays only support the nongeneric interfaces. Arrays are always mutable in terms of their elements, but always fixed in terms of their size. All the mutating methods of the collection interfaces (such as `Add` and `Remove`) are explicitly implemented and throw `NotSupportedException`.

Arrays of reference types are always covariant; there's an implicit conversion from a `Stream[]` reference to `Object[]`, for example, and an explicit conversion the other way around.[2] This means that changes to the array have to be verified at execution time—the array itself knows what type it is, so if you try to store a non-`Stream`

---

[1] Binary search is $O(\log n)$ complexity; a linear search is $O(n)$.

[2] Somewhat confusingly, this also means there's an implicit conversion from `Stream[]` to `IList<Object>`, even though `IList<T>` itself is invariant.

reference in a `Stream[]` by converting the array reference to an `Object[]` first, an `ArrayTypeMismatchException` will be thrown.

There are two different flavors of array as far as the CLR is concerned. A *vector* is a single-dimensional array with a lower bound of 0; anything else counts as an *array*. Vectors perform better and are what you almost always use in C#. An array of the form `T[][]` is still a vector, but with an element type of `T[]`; only *rectangular arrays* in C#, such as new `string[10, 20]`, end up as arrays in CLR terminology. You can't create an array with a nonzero lower bound directly in C#—you have to use `Array.Create-Instance`, which allows you to specify lower bounds, lengths, and the element type individually. If you create a single-dimensional array with a nonzero lower bound, you can't then successfully cast it to `T[]`—the compiler will allow the cast, but it will fail at execution time.

The C# compiler has built-in support for arrays in a number of ways. Not only does it know about how to create and index them, but it also supports them directly in `foreach` loops; if you iterate using an expression that's known to be an array at compile time, that iteration will use the `Length` property and the array indexer, rather than creating an iterator object. This is more efficient, but the performance difference is usually negligible.

Like `List<T>`, arrays support methods such as `ConvertAll`, `FindAll`, and `Binary-Search`, although in the case of arrays, these are static methods of the `Array` class, taking the array as the first parameter.

To come back to my first point, arrays are pretty low-level data structures. They're important as the building blocks for many other collections, and they're efficient in appropriate situations, but you should think twice before using them too heavily. Again, Eric has blogged on this topic, labeling them "somewhat harmful" (see http://mng.bz/3jd5). I don't want to overstate this point, but it's worth being aware of the shortcomings of arrays when choosing a collection type.

B.2.3   LinkedList<T>

When is a list not a list? When it's a linked list. `LinkedList<T>` is a list in many ways—in particular, it's a collection that maintains the order in which you add items—but it doesn't implement `IList<T>`. This is because it doesn't obey the implied contract of efficient access by index. It's a classical computer science doubly linked list: it maintains a head node and a tail node, and each node has a reference to the next and previous node within the list. Each node is exposed as a `LinkedListNode<T>`, which is handy if you want to maintain an insertion/removal point somewhere in the middle of the list. The list explicitly maintains a size, so accessing the `Count` property is efficient.

Linked lists are inefficient in terms of space compared with array-backed lists, and they don't support indexed operations, but they're fast at inserting or removing elements at arbitrary points in the list, as long as you have a reference to the node at the relevant point. These operations have O(1) complexity, as all that's required is fixing up the next/previous references in the surrounding nodes. Inserting or removing from the head or tail of the list is just a special case of this, where there's always immediate access to the node you need to change. Iterating (either forward or backward) is also efficient, as it's just a matter of following the chain of references.

Although `LinkedList<T>` implements the standard methods, such as `Add` (which adds to the tail of the list), I'd suggest using the explicit `AddFirst` and `AddLast` methods to make it clear exactly what's going on. There are matching `RemoveFirst` and `RemoveLast` methods, and `First` and `Last` properties. All of these return the nodes within the list rather than the values of those nodes; the properties return a null reference if the list is empty.

B.2.4 Collection<T>, BindingList<T>, ObservableCollection<T>, and KeyedCollection<TKey, TItem>

`Collection<T>` is a member of the `System.Collections.ObjectModel` namespace, as are all the remaining lists we'll look at. Like `List<T>`, it implements both the generic and nongeneric collection interfaces.

Though you *can* use `Collection<T>` on its own, it's more commonly used as a base class. It always acts as a wrapper to another list: you either specify one in the constructor, or a new `List<T>` will be created behind the scenes. All mutating actions on the collection go through protected virtual methods (`InsertItem`, `SetItem`, `RemoveItem`, and `ClearItems`); derived classes can intercept these methods, raising events or providing other custom behavior. The wrapped list is accessible to derived classes via the `Items` property. If this list is read-only, the public mutating methods throw an exception rather than calling the virtual methods; you don't need to recheck this when you override them.

`BindingList<T>` and `ObservableCollection<T>` derive from `Collection<T>` in order to provide binding capabilities. `BindingList<T>` has been available since .NET 2.0, but `ObservableCollection<T>` was introduced with Windows Presentation Foundation (WPF). Of course, you don't have to use them for data binding in user interfaces—you may have your own reasons to be interested in changes to a list. In that case, you should see which collection provides notifications in a more useful form when you're deciding which to use. Note that you'll only be notified of changes that occur through the wrapper; if the underlying list is shared with other code that may modify it on its own, that won't raise any events in the wrapper.

`KeyedCollection<TKey, TItem>` is a sort of hybrid between a list and a dictionary, allowing an item to be fetched by key as well as by index. Unlike normal dictionaries, the key should be effectively embedded within the item, rather than being independent. In many cases this is natural; for example, you might have a `Customer` type with a `CustomerID` property. `KeyedCollection<,>` is an abstract class; derived classes implement the `GetKeyForItem` method to provide a way of extracting a key from any item added to the collection. In our customer scenario, the `GetKeyForItem` method would just return the ID for the given customer. Just like a dictionary, the key must be unique within the collection—attempting to add another item with the same key will fail with an exception. Although null keys aren't permitted, GetKeyForItem can return null (if the key type is a reference type), in which case the key will be ignored (and the item won't be fetchable by its key).

B.2.5   *ReadOnlyCollection<T> and ReadOnlyObservableCollection<T>*

Our final two lists are more wrappers, providing read-only access even when the underlying list is mutable. Again, both generic and nongeneric collection interfaces are implemented. A mixture of explicit and implicit interface implementation is used so that callers using a compile-time expression of the concrete type will be discouraged from using mutating operations that will fail.

ReadOnlyObservableCollection<T> derives from ReadOnlyCollection<T> and implements the same INotifyCollectionChanged and INotifyPropertyChanged interfaces as ObservableCollection<T>. A ReadOnlyObservableCollection<T> instance can only be constructed with an ObservableCollection<T> backing list. Even though the collection is still read-only for callers, they can observe changes made elsewhere to the backing list.

Though usually I'd advise using an interface when deciding the return type of methods in an API, it can be useful to deliberately expose ReadOnlyCollection<T> to provide a clear indication to callers that they won't be able to modify the returned collection. But you'll still need to document whether the underlying collection could be changed elsewhere, or whether it's effectively constant.

B.3   *Dictionaries*

The choices for dictionaries in the framework are much more limited than those of lists. There are only three mainstream nonconcurrent implementations of IDictionary <TKey, TValue>, although it's also implemented by ExpandoObject (as you saw in chapter 14), ConcurrentDictionary (which we'll look at along with the other concurrent collections), and RouteValueDictionary (used for routing web requests, particularly in ASP.NET MVC).

Just as a reminder, the primary purpose of a dictionary is to provide an efficient lookup from a key to a value.

B.3.1   *Dictionary<TKey, TValue>*

Unless you have specialist requirements, Dictionary<TKey, TValue> is the default choice of dictionary in much the same way that List<T> is the default list implementation. It uses a hash table to implement an efficient lookup, although this means that the efficiency of the dictionary depends on how good your hashing function is. You can either use the default hashing and equality functions (calls to Equals and Get-HashCode within the key objects themselves) or specify an IEqualityComparer<TKey> as a constructor argument.

The simplest use case is to implement a dictionary with string keys, which uses the keys in a case-insensitive way, as shown in the following code:

```
var comparer = StringComparer.OrdinalIgnoreCase;
var dict = new Dictionary<String, int>(comparer);
dict["TEST"] = 10;
Console.WriteLine(dict["test"]);                    ⟵——— Outputs 10
```

Although the keys within a dictionary have to be unique, the hash codes don't. It's perfectly acceptable for two unequal keys to have the same hash; this is known as a *hash collision*, and although it reduces the efficiency of the dictionary slightly, it'll still function correctly. The dictionary *will* fail if the keys are mutable and change their hash codes after they've been inserted into the dictionary. Mutable dictionary keys are almost always a bad idea, but if you absolutely *have* to use them, make sure you don't change them after insertion.

The exact details of the implementation of the hash table are unspecified and may change over time, but one important aspect can cause confusion: *there's no ordering guarantee within* Dictionary<TKey, TValue>, *even though it might appear that way*. If you add items to a dictionary and then iterate over it, you may see the items come out in the insertion order, but *please don't rely on it*. It's somewhat unfortunate that as a quirk of the implementation, simply adding entries without ever deleting any tends to preserve order—an implementation that happened to scramble the order naturally would probably cause less confusion.

Like List<T>, Dictionary<TKey, TValue> keeps its entries in an array and expands this when it needs to, leading to amortized O(1) expansion. Access by key is also O(1) assuming a reasonable hash; if all the keys have the same hash code, you'll end up with O(n) access because the dictionary has to check each key in turn for equality. In most practical scenarios, this isn't an issue.

B.3.2 *SortedList<TKey, TValue> and SortedDictionary<TKey, TValue>*

A casual observer might imagine that a class named SortedList<,> would be a list... but no. Both of these types are actually dictionaries, and neither implements IList<T> at all. It might be more informative for them to be named ListBacked-SortedDictionary and TreeBackedSortedDictionary, but it's too late to change now.

There's a lot of commonality between these two classes: both use an IComparer <TKey> instead of an IEqualityComparer<TKey> to compare keys, and both maintain the keys in a sorted fashion, based on that comparison. Both have O(log n) performance when finding values, effectively performing a binary search. But their internal data structures are very different: SortedList<,> maintains an array of entries that's kept sorted, whereas SortedDictionary<,> uses a red-black tree structure (see the Wikipedia entry at http://mng.bz/K1S4). This leads to significant differences in insertion and removal times as well as memory efficiency. If you're creating a dictionary from mostly sorted data, a SortedList<,> will populate efficiently; if you imagine the steps involved in keeping a List<T> sorted, you can see that adding a single item to the end of the list is cheap (O(1) if you ignore expansion), whereas adding items randomly is expensive, because it involves copying existing items (O(n) in the worst case). Adding items to the balanced tree in a SortedDictionary<,> is always fairly cheap (O(log n) complexity), but it involves a separate tree node on the heap for each entry, leading to more overhead and memory fragmentation than the array of key/value entry structures in a `SortedList<,>`.

Both collections expose their keys and values as separate collections, and in both cases the returned collection is live in that it'll change as the underlying dictionary changes. But the collections exposed by a `SortedList<,>` implement `IList<T>`, so you can effectively access entries by sorted key index if you really want to.

I don't want to put you off too much with all this talk of complexity. Unless you have a very large amount of data, you probably don't need to worry much about which implementation you use. If you *are* likely to have vast numbers of entries in your dictionary, you should carefully analyze the performance characteristics of both collections to work out which one to use.

B.3.3   *ReadOnlyDictionary<TKey, TValue>*

Once you're familiar with `ReadOnlyCollection<T>`, which we discussed in section B.2.5, `ReadOnlyDictionary<TKey, TValue>` should hold no surprises for you. Again, it's simply a wrapper around an existing collection (an `IDictionary<TKey, TValue>` this time) that hides all mutating operations behind explicit interface implementation and throws a `NotSupportedException` if they're called anyway.

As with the read-only lists, this really is just a wrapper; if the underlying collection (the one passed to the constructor) is modified, those modifications will be visible through the wrapper.

B.4   Sets

Prior to .NET 3.5, there was no public set collection in the framework at all. When developers needed something to represent a set in .NET 2.0, they'd typically use a `Dictionary<,>`, using the set items as keys and providing dummy values. This situation was improved somewhat with `HashSet<T>` in .NET 3.5, and now .NET 4 has added a `SortedSet<T>` and a common `ISet<T>` interface. Although logically a set interface could consist merely of `Add`/`Remove`/`Contains` operations, `ISet<T>` specifies a number of other operations to manipulate the set (`ExceptWith`, `IntersectWith`, `Symmetric-ExceptWith`, and `UnionWith`) and to test for various more complex conditions (`Set-Equals`, `Overlaps`, `IsSubsetOf`, `IsSupersetOf`, `IsProperSubsetOf`, and `IsProper-SupersetOf`). The parameters for all of these methods are expressed in terms of `IEnumerable<T>` rather than `ISet<T>`, which is initially surprising, but it means that sets interact with LINQ in a natural way.

B.4.1   *HashSet<T>*

A `HashSet<T>` is effectively a `Dictionary<,>` without the values. It has the same performance characteristics, and again you can specify an `IEqualityComparer<T>` to customize how items are compared. Again, you must not rely on a `HashSet<T>` maintaining the order in which you add values.

One additional feature supported by HashSet<T> is the RemoveWhere method, which removes any entry that matches a given predicate. This allows you to prune a set without worrying about the normal prohibition against modifying a collection while you iterate over it.

B.4.2 SortedSet<T> (.NET 4)

Just like the previous HashSet<T> comparison with Dictionary<,>, a SortedSet<T> is like a valueless SortedDictionary<,>. It maintains a red-black tree of values, providing $O(\log n)$ complexity for addition, removal, and containment checking. When you iterate over the set, the values will be yielded in a sorted order.

It provides the same RemoveWhere method as HashSet<T> (despite this not being in the interface) and additionally provides properties (Min and Max) to return the minimum and maximum values. A more intriguing method is GetViewBetween, which returns another SortedSet<T> offering a view on the original set between a lower and upper bound, both of which are inclusive. This is a mutable, live view—changes to the view are reflected in the original set, and vice versa. The following example demonstrates this:

```
var baseSet = new SortedSet<int> { 1, 5, 12, 20, 25 };
var view = baseSet.GetViewBetween(10, 20);
view.Add(14);
Console.WriteLine(baseSet.Count);              ◁——— Outputs 6
foreach (int value in view)
{
    Console.WriteLine(value);              ◁      Outputs 12, 14, 20
}
```

Although GetViewBetween is convenient, it's not entirely free: operations on the view may be more expensive than expected, in order to keep internal consistency. In particular, accessing the Count property of a view is an $O(n)$ operation if the underlying set has changed since the last tree walk. Like all powerful tools, this should be used with care.

One final feature of SortedSet<T>: it exposes a Reverse() method that allows you to iterate over it in reverse order. This isn't used by Enumerable.Reverse(), which buffers the contents of the sequence it's called on. If you know you'll want to access a sorted set in reverse order, it may be useful to keep an expression of type Sorted-Set<T> instead of using a more general interface type, so that you can access this more efficient implementation.

B.5 Queue<T> and Stack<T>

Queues and stacks are staples of every computer science course. They're sometimes referred to as FIFO (first in, first out) and LIFO (last in, first out) structures, respectively. The basic idea is the same for both data structures: you add items to the collection, and at some other point you remove them. The difference is the order in which they're removed: a queue acts like a queue in a shop, where the first person to join the queue is the first to be served; a stack acts like a stack of plates where the last plate placed on the top is the first to be taken off it. One common use for queues and stacks is to maintain a list of work items still to be processed.

Just as with LinkedList<T>, although you *can* use the normal collection interface methods to access queues and stacks, I recommend using the class-specific ones to make your code clearer.

B.5.1   *Queue<T>*

Queue<T> is implemented with a circular buffer: essentially it maintains an array, with an index remembering the next slot to add an item into, and another index remembering the next slot to take an item from. If the add index catches up with the remove index, the contents are copied into a larger array.

Queue<T> provides the Enqueue and Dequeue methods to add and remove items; a Peek method allows you to see what item will be dequeued next, without actually removing it. Both Dequeue and Peek throw InvalidOperationException if they're called on an empty queue. Iterating over the queue yields values in the order they'd be dequeued.

B.5.2   *Stack<T>*

The Stack<T> implementation is even simpler than Queue<T>—you can think of it as being just like a List<T>, but with a Push method to add a new item to the end of the list, Pop to remove the final item, and Peek to look at the final item without removing it. Again, Pop and Peek throw InvalidOperationException when called on an empty stack. Iterating over the stack yields values in the order they'd be popped—so the most recently added value is yielded first.

B.6   *Concurrent collections (.NET 4)*

As part of Parallel Extensions in .NET 4, there are several new collections in a new System.Collections.Concurrent namespace. These are designed to be safe in the face of concurrent operations from multiple threads, with relatively little locking. The namespace also contains three classes that are used for partitioning collections for parallel operations, but we won't be looking at those here.

B.6.1   *IProducerConsumerCollection<T> and BlockingCollection<T>*

Three of the new collections implement the new IProducerConsumerCollection<T> interface, which is designed to be used with BlockingCollection<T>. When describing queues and stacks, I mentioned that they're often used to store work items for later processing; the producer/consumer pattern is a way of executing these work items concurrently. Sometimes there's a single producer thread creating work and multiple consumer threads executing the work items. In other cases, the consumers can also be producers; for example, a web crawler may process a web page and discover more links to be crawled later.

IProducerConsumerCollection<T> acts as an abstraction for the data storage of the producer/consumer pattern, and BlockingCollection<T> wraps this in an easy-to-use form and also provides the ability to limit how many items can be buffered at any one time. BlockingCollection<T> assumes that nothing else will be adding to the wrapped collection directly; all the interested parties should use the wrapper for both adding and removing work items. The constructor overloads that don't take an IProducerConsumerCollection<T> parameter use a ConcurrentQueue<T> for backing storage.

The IProducerConsumerCollection<T> only provides three particularly interesting methods: ToArray, TryAdd, and TryTake. ToArray copies the current contents of the collection to a new array; this is a snapshot of the collection at the point when the method is called. TryAdd and TryTake both follow the normal TryXXX pattern, returning a Boolean value to indicate success or failure, and they do what you'd expect: attempt to add an item to the collection, or attempt to remove one from the collection. Allowing an efficient failure mode reduces the need for locking. In a Queue<T>, for example, you'd want to hold a lock in order to combine the operations of "test whether there are any items in the queue" and "dequeue an item if there is one"— otherwise Dequeue could throw an exception.

BlockingCollection<T> layers blocking behavior on top of these nonblocking methods, with a host of overloads to allow timeouts and cancellation tokens to be specified. Usually you won't need to use BlockingCollection<T> or IProducer-ConsumerCollection<T> directly; you'll call other parts of Parallel Extensions that'll use them for you. It's worth knowing they're there, though, in case you need your own custom behavior.

B.6.2 ConcurrentBag<T>, ConcurrentQueue<T>, and ConcurrentStack<T>

The framework comes with three implementations of IProducerConsumer-Collection<T>. Essentially, they differ in terms of the order in which items are retrieved; the queue and stack act as you'd expect them to from their nonconcurrent equivalents, whereas ConcurrentBag<T> doesn't guarantee any ordering.

All three implement IEnumerable<T> in a thread-safe way. The iterator returned by GetEnumerator() will iterate over a snapshot of the collection; you can modify the collection while you're iterating, and the changes won't be seen within the iterator. All three also offer a TryPeek method that's similar to TryTake, but that doesn't remove a value from the collection. Unlike TryTake, this method isn't specified in IProducer-ConsumerCollection<T>.

B.6.3 ConcurrentDictionary<TKey, TValue>

ConcurrentDictionary<TKey, TValue> implements the standard IDictionary <TKey, TValue> interface (whereas none of the concurrent collections implements IList<T>) and is essentially a thread-safe hash-based dictionary. It supports multiple threads reading and writing concurrently, and also allows thread-safe iteration, although unlike the three collections from the previous section, modifications made to the dictionary while iterating may or may not be reflected in the iterator.

There's more to it than just thread-safe access. Whereas normal dictionary implementations basically offer add-or-update via the indexer, and add-or-throw via the Add method, ConcurrentDictionary<TKey, TValue> offers a veritable smorgasbord of options. You can update the value associated with a key based on its previous value, get a value based on a key or add it if the key wasn't present beforehand, conditionally update a value only if it was what you expected it to be before, and many other possibilities, all of which act atomically. It's all bewildering to start with, but Stephen Toub of the Parallel Extensions team has a blog post giving details of when you should use which method (see http://mng.bz/WMdW).

B.7   Read-only interfaces (.NET 4.5)

.NET 4.5 introduced three new collection interfaces: IReadOnlyCollection<T>, IReadOnlyList<T>, and IReadOnlyDictionary<TKey, TValue>. As I write this, they're not widely used—but it's worth being aware of them, mostly so you know what they're *not*. Figure B.2 shows how they relate to each other and to the IEnumerable interfaces.

If you thought that ReadOnlyCollection<T> was stretching the truth with its name, these interfaces are even more sneaky. They don't just allow for mutations to be made

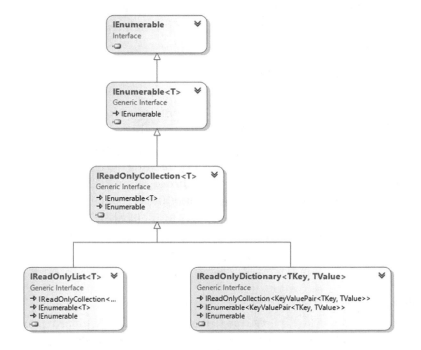

Figure B.2   Read-only interfaces in .NET 4.5

by other code; they even allow mutations through the very same object, if that happens to be a mutable collection. For example, `List<T>` implements `IReadOnlyList<T>` even though it's clearly not a read-only collection.

That's not to say the interfaces aren't useful, of course. In particular, both `IReadOnlyCollection<T>` and `IReadOnlyList<T>` are covariant in `T`, just like `IEnumerable<T>` but exposing more operations. Unfortunately `IReadOnlyDictionary<TKey, TValue>` is invariant in both type parameters, partly due to it implementing `IEnumerable<KeyValuePair<TKey, TValue>>`—which is invariant because `KeyValuePair<TKey, TValue>` is a struct, which is therefore invariant in itself. Additionally, the covariance of `IReadOnlyList<T>` means that it can't expose any methods accepting a `T`, such as `Contains` and `IndexOf`. The big benefit is that it *does* expose an indexer to fetch items by index.

I can't see myself using these interfaces much right now, but in the future I think they'll be very important. In late 2012, Microsoft released their first preview of a NuGet package of immutable collections, called `Microsoft.Bcl.Immutable`. A BCL team blog post (http://mng.bz/Xlqd) gives more details, but fundamentally it does what it says on the tin: fully immutable collections, along with freezable (mutable until they're frozen) collections. Of course, if the element type is mutable (such as `StringBuilder`), then this only gets you so far, but I'm still excited about it, for all the normal reasons that immutability is helpful.

B.8   *Summary*

The .NET Framework contains a rich set of collections (although not a particularly rich collection of sets). These have been gradually growing, along with the rest of the framework, although the most commonly used collections are likely to be `List<T>` and `Dictionary<TKey, TValue>` for some time to come.

There are certainly data structures that could be added in the future, but the benefit always has to be weighed against the cost of adding something to the core framework. Maybe we'll see explicitly tree-based APIs in the future, rather than them being an implementation detail of existing collections. Maybe we'll see Fibonacci heaps, weak-reference caches, and the like—but as you've seen, there's already a lot for developers to take in, and there's a risk of information overload.

If there's a particular data structure you need for your project, it's worth looking online for an open source implementation; Wintellect's Power Collections have a particularly strong history as an alternative to the built-in collections (http://powercollections.codeplex.com). But in most cases, the framework is likely to be adequate for your needs. Hopefully this appendix has expanded your horizons slightly in terms of what's available out of the box.

appendix C
Version summaries

The version numbers in .NET can be confusing sometimes. The framework, runtime, Visual Studio, and C# are all numbered separately. This appendix is a quick guide to how they fit together and the major features in each release. In each case, I've described the features from releases 2.0 and upward; listing all the features of .NET 1.0 and 1.1 would be fairly pointless.

C.1 *Desktop framework major releases*

When developers refer to releases of .NET, they usually mean the major releases of the desktop framework. In most cases, a framework release has been accompanied by a release of Visual Studio (or Visual Studio .NET, as it was named for the 2002 and 2003 releases). The exception to this was .NET 3.0, which was essentially only a set of libraries (although those libraries were pretty significant). A set of Visual Studio 2005 extensions was made available for the new features, but Visual Studio 2008 contained more support. Table C.1 shows which version of which aspect of the framework was released when.

When .NET 3.5 was released, .NET 2.0 SP1 and .NET 3.0 SP1 were also released; these contained the 2.0 SP1 CLR and BCL. Similarly, .NET 3.5 SP1's release coincided with .NET 2.0 SP2 and .NET 3.0 SP2.

Table C.1 Desktop framework releases and their components

Date	Framework	Visual Studio	C#	CLR
February 2002	1.0	2002	1.0	1.0
April 2003	1.1	2003	1.2	1.1
November 2005	2.0	2005	2.0	2.0
November 2006	3.0	(Extensions to 2005)	n/a	2.0
November 2007	3.5	2008	3.0	2.0 SP1
April 2010	4	2010	4.0	4.0 (there was no version 3.0)
August 2012	4.5	2012	5.0	4.0 or 4.5[a]

a. This depends on your point of view. You'll find out more later.

Visual Studio 2008 was the first release to support *multitargeting*, allowing you to choose which version of the framework you want to build for. In many cases, you can use new features of C# while targeting an earlier release—this is basically the case if the feature is implemented solely by compiler magic, without any support from the CLR or libraries. More information on how to do this is available on the book's website (see http://mng.bz/YpRB)—in some cases there are workarounds if a feature doesn't quite work out of the box. It's worth noting that if you target .NET 2.0 (you can't target 1.0 or 1.1) from Visual Studio 2008 or 2010, you'll actually be targeting the relevant service pack (2.0 SP1 or 2.0 SP2); this means it's possible to build code that uses new features from a service pack (one notable introduction was `System.DateTimeOffset` in 2.0 SP1) and then find it fails if you try to run it on a machine that genuinely has the original release of .NET 2.0. Personally, I'd try to update machines to at least run the latest service pack, and ideally a more recent full framework release.

C.2   C# language features

If you've read the whole book, you should be able to write this section yourself. (It's tempting to leave a bunch of blank lines for you to fill in, but I'm not *quite* that lazy.) One trivial fact: the version number of 1.2 in table C.1 isn't a typo; looking at the specifications, Microsoft really did skip 1.1 in order to release a C# 1.2 compiler with .NET 1.1. The changes in version 1.2 were mostly minor, but there was one significant change in the long term: it's only from C# 1.2 and onward that the translated code for a `foreach` loop tests whether the iterator implements `IDisposable` and disposes of it accordingly. As you've seen, this change is crucial for iterator blocks that have resources to clean up.

Anyway, for the sake of completeness, here are the language features, along with the chapter references for more details.

C.2.1   C# 2.0

The major features of C# 2 were generics (see chapter 3), nullable types (chapter 4), anonymous methods and other delegate-related enhancements (chapter 5), and iterator blocks (chapter 6). Additionally, several smaller features were introduced: partial types, static classes, properties with different access modifiers for getters and setters, namespace aliases, pragma directives, and fixed-sized buffers. See chapter 7 for more details.

C.2.2   C# 3.0

C# 3 primarily built toward LINQ, although many features are useful elsewhere. Automatic properties, implicit typing of arrays and local variables, object and collection initializers, and anonymous types are all covered in chapter 8. Lambda expressions and expression trees (chapter 9) extended the delegate-related progress made in version 2.0, and extension methods (chapter 10) provided the last ingredient for query expressions (chapter 11). Partial methods were only added in C# 3, but are covered with the inclusion of partial types in chapter 7.

C.2.3 *C# 4.0*

C# 4.0 has some features aimed at interoperability but doesn't have the same single-mindedness of C# 3.0. Again, there's a reasonably clear divide between the small features shown in chapter 13 (named arguments, optional parameters, better COM interop, generic variance) and the huge feature of dynamic typing (chapter 14).

C.2.4 *C# 5.0*

C# 5.0 is all about the asynchrony we saw in chapter 15, with two other very small features (changes to `foreach` variable capture, and caller info attributes) sneaking into chapter 16. Even though asynchrony only introduces a single new kind of expression (`await`, within an `async` function), it changes the execution model enormously. I'd argue that even if the C# team had been ready to deliver other large new language features (and for all I know, they were), holding them back for a while would be a sensible option. It's important that the C# community really looks at async/await carefully, and that will take time.

C.3 *Framework library features*

It'd be impossible to list all of the new features in the framework in a sensible fashion here. In particular, each area of the framework (Windows Forms, ASP.NET, and so on) gets extra features in each release—not just the core base class library. I've included the features I believe are the most important highlights. MSDN has a far more comprehensive list at http://mng.bz/6tiZ.

C.3.1 *.NET 2.0*

The biggest features in the 2.0 libraries supported features of the CLR and languages: generics and nullable types. Whereas nullable types didn't require many changes, several of the generic collections you're used to now have been present since .NET 2.0, and the reflection API had to be updated accordingly.

Many areas received relatively minor updates, such as support for compression, multiple active result sets (MARS) over a single connection to SQL Server, and many static helper I/O methods such as `File.ReadAllText`. It's probably fair to say that these weren't as significant as the changes to user interface frameworks.

ASP.NET gained master pages, precompilation abilities, and various new controls. Windows Forms took a big leap in terms of layout abilities with `TableLayoutPanel` and similar classes, as well as gaining better support for performance enhancements such as double buffering, a new data binding model, and ClickOnce deployment. `BackgroundWorker` was introduced in .NET 2.0 to make it easier to update a UI safely in multithreaded applications; it's not strictly part of Windows Forms, although that was its primary use case until Windows Presentation Foundation arrived in .NET 3.0. Speaking of which...

C.3.2 .NET 3.0

.NET 3.0 was somewhat curious as a major release with no CLR changes, no language changes, and no changes to existing libraries. Instead, it consisted of four new libraries:

- Windows Presentation Foundation (WPF) is the next-generation user interface framework; this was a revolution rather than an evolution of Windows Forms, although the two can live side by side. It has a very different model from Windows Forms, being much more compositional in nature. Silverlight's user interface is based on WPF.

- Windows Communication Foundation (WCF) is an architecture for building service-oriented applications; it's extensible rather than being limited to a single protocol and aims to unify the existing RPC-like communication channels, such as remoting.

- Windows Workflow Foundation (WF) is a system for building workflow applications.

- Windows CardSpace is a secure identity system.

Of these four areas, WPF and WCF have flourished, whereas WF and CardSpace appear not to have taken off so well. That's not to say that the latter technologies aren't being used, or that they won't become more important in the future, but they're not nearly as widespread as I write this.

C.3.3 .NET 3.5

The big new feature in .NET 3.5 was LINQ, supported by C# 3.0 and VB 9. This included LINQ to Objects, LINQ to SQL, LINQ to XML, and expression tree support underlying it.

Other areas also gained important features: it became a lot easier to use AJAX in ASP.NET, WCF and WPF each gained a whole host of improvements, an add-in framework (System.AddIn) was introduced, various new cryptography algorithms were included, and much more. As a developer interested in both concurrency and time-related APIs, I feel obliged to draw your attention to the introduction of Reader-WriterLockSlim and the much-needed TimeZoneInfo and DateTimeOffset types. If you're using .NET 3.5 or higher but are still relying on DateTime everywhere, you should be aware that there are better options available.[1]

.NET 3.5 SP1's most notable library features were the Entity Framework and related ADO.NET technologies, but other technologies had minor improvements as well. Also importantly, .NET 3.5 SP1 introduced the Client Profile—a smaller version of the desktop .NET Framework that doesn't include a lot of the libraries aimed at server-side development. This allows a smaller deployment footprint for client-only applications.

---

[1] My personal feeling is that this still isn't enough support for the complex and intriguing world of dates and times, which is why I started the Noda Time project (see https://code.google.com/p/noda-time/), but at least with TimeZoneInfo there's finally a clean way of representing a time zone other than the local one.

C.3.4   .NET 4

A lot of work went into the .NET 4 libraries for a long time, in various guises. The DLR is a huge addition, and you've also seen (very briefly) Parallel Extensions in other chapters. As usual, the user interface technologies have a raft of improvements, although notably the focus for rich client changes is WPF rather than Windows Forms. A lot of tweaks have been made to existing core APIs to make them that much easier to use, such as `String.Join` accepting an `IEnumerable<T>` instead of insisting on a string array. These aren't earth-shattering improvements, but if they make every developer's life just a little bit simpler, that can have a large cumulative impact. You've already seen how some of the existing generic interfaces and delegates have become covariant or contravariant (`IEnumerable<T>` becoming `IEnumerable<out  T>` and `Action<T>` becoming `Action<in T>`, for example) but there are new types to explore as well.

There's a new namespace for numerical calculations, `System.Numeric`. At the time of this writing, it only contains the `BigInteger` and `Complex` types, but I wouldn't be surprised to see `BigDecimal` join them in the future. There are other new types within the `System` namespace, such as `Lazy<T>` for lazily initialized values and a `Tuple` family of generic classes that provide the same sort of functionality as the `Pair<T1, T2>` class from chapter 3, but for up to eight type parameters. `Tuple` also supports *structural comparisons*, as represented by the new `IStructuralEquatable` and `IStructural-Comparable` interfaces in the `System.Collections` namespace. Although the full Reactive Extensions classes you saw in chapter 12 aren't in .NET 4, the core interfaces `IObserver<T>` and `IObservable<T>` are in the `System` namespace. I've brought up these specific items because although new areas like the Managed Extensibility Framework (MEF) get a lot of attention, it's easy to overlook simple types like these. It's good to see that time is being spent on the whole framework, not just on shiny new cool stuff.

C.3.5   .NET 4.5

Again, the biggest driver in .NET 4.5's changes is almost certainly asynchrony. There are asynchronous versions of just about every API you could want one for: if it could take a while, you should be able to do it asynchronously. The Task Parallel Library from .NET 4 has been expanded (and optimized) to help with this too.

There are lots of other changes within .NET 4.5, and it would be foolish to try to describe all of them. Even the MSDN page listing the highlights (http://mng.bz/6tiZ) is longer than I'd want to include here. But most of those changes will depend on the project you're building, whereas the sweep of asynchrony across the whole platform is likely to impact everyone, over time.

C.4   Runtime (CLR) features

CLR changes are often less visible to many developers than new library and language features. Obviously there are some particularly shiny features such as generics that'll catch everyone's attention, but others are less obvious. The CLR has also changed less frequently than either the language or the framework libraries, at least in terms of major releases.

C.4.1 CLR 2.0

In addition to generics, the CLR required one extra change to support the new language features of C# 2: the behavior of boxing and unboxing nullable value types that we explored in chapter 4.

CLR 2.0 had other major changes. The most significant ones were support for 64-bit processors (both x64 and IA64) and the ability to host the CLR within SQL Server 2005. The SQL Server integration required new hosting APIs to be designed, so that the host could have a lot more control over the CLR, including how it allocates memory and threads. This allows a diligent host to make sure that code running in the CLR won't compromise other aspects of a critical process, such as a database.

.NET 3.5 included CLR 2.0 SP1, and .NET 3.5 SP1 included CLR 2.0 SP2; these had relatively minor changes, such as tweaks to the access that code in a `DynamicMethod` has to private members of another type. The CLR team is always looking for ways to improve performance as well, with improvements in garbage collection, the JIT, startup times, and so on.

C.4.2 CLR 4.0

Although the CLR didn't need to change in order to accommodate the DLR, the team has still been hard at work. These are some of the highlights:

- Interop marshaling performance and consistency improvements with IL stubs everywhere (see this .NET Framework Blog post for details: http://mng.bz/ 56H6)
- A background garbage collector to replace the concurrent collector in CLR 2.0
- An improved security model based on the concept of transparency, which is the successor to Code Access Security (CAS)
- Type equivalence, used to support the embedded PIA feature of C# 4
- Side-by-side execution of different CLRs within the same process

The CLR in .NET 4.5 includes a number of improvements, mostly around garbage collection. You can think of it as a minor release, effectively. Alongside pure performance benefits, the 64-bit CLR also supports the `<gcAllowVeryLargeObjects>` configuration option, which allows for the creation of enormous arrays, even when the elements are large structures...assuming you have the memory, of course. In terms of the version number, the picture is slightly complicated. In documentation, you may well see this version of the CLR referred to as CLR 4.5. However, it still advertises itself as 4.0 if you consult the `Environment.Version` property. For example, at the time of writing the CLR I'm running reports version 4.0.30319.18033. The build and revision numbers may potentially change over time due to service packs.

More details of all of the new features are available on the .NET Framework Blog (http://blogs.msdn.com/b/dotnet).

C.5   Related frameworks

It's rare for anything in computing to do well with a one-size-fits-all model, and .NET is no exception. Even the desktop framework isn't really a single version: there's the client profile, the 32-bit and 64-bit JITs, and the server and workstation CLRs tuned for different tasks. Beyond that, there are separate frameworks that have their own version histories, tailored to different environments.

C.5.1   Compact Framework

The Compact Framework was originally aimed at mobile devices running Windows Mobile. Since then, it's been retargeted for Xbox 360, Windows Phone 7, and Symbian S60.

The Compact Framework major release schedule has traditionally mirrored that of the desktop framework, although there's no release corresponding to .NET 3.0. Just to keep things interesting, the most up-to-date release (used by some Windows Mobile devices and WP7) is version 3.7.

Early versions of the Compact Framework were missing some fairly core functionality, which was largely filled by community efforts; later releases have plugged many of the more significant gaps, although obviously it's still a subset of the desktop framework. The GUI layer depends on the exact platform; for example, on the Xbox 360 you'd use XNA, Windows Mobile supports Windows Forms, and WP7 supports both XNA and Silverlight. Code running on the Compact Framework is JIT-compiled and garbage-collected, although the Compact Framework collector isn't generational like the ones in the desktop framework.

C.5.2   Silverlight

Silverlight (http://silverlight.net/) is aimed at running applications either within browsers, or (as of Silverlight 3) in a sandboxed environment, usually originally installed from a browser. As such, it's a natural competitor to Flash; it has the obvious advantage of allowing C# developers to write applications in a familiar language against a familiar library. Silverlight installs a streamlined CLR (called CoreCLR—see http://mng.bz/G32M) and class library—for example, the nongeneric collections aren't supported, and neither is Windows Forms. The presentation layer of Silverlight is based on WPF, but they're not identical. It has particularly strong support for media, with features such as deep zoom and adaptive video streaming.

Silverlight 1 was released in September 2007, although it was restricted to a mixture of XAML to construct the UI and JavaScript for logic. It wasn't until Silverlight 2 was released in October 2008 that the full experience of delivering Silverlight applications built with C# became a reality. Some of the features from CoreCLR (side-by-side CLR hosting within a single process, and the declarative transparency security model) are now features in the desktop CLR for version 4.0. It also included an early version of the Dynamic Language Runtime.

Progress continued unabated, with Silverlight 3 being released in July 2009 with more controls, more video codecs, as well as offline and out-of-browser applications. The Silverlight team repeated the nine-month release cycle, releasing Silverlight 4 in the same week as .NET 4 with another long list of new features. Windows Phone 7 supported Silverlight 3 and some features of Silverlight 4, and then when the Windows Phone 7.1 SDK was released (to support the phone with a consumer-branded version of 7.5, just to add confusion), that supported more of Silverlight 4 again. Both Windows Phone 7.x versions used an evolution of the Compact Framework CLR.

Windows Phone 8 supports the Silverlight API for backward compatibility, but also supports the new Windows Phone Runtime API which is closer to the WinRT API used for Windows Store applications. Additionally, Windows Phone 8 uses a version of CoreCLR rather than the one from the Compact Framework.

Silverlight itself is now dead in terms of further development. While I'm sure many developers are still using it, there will be no new versions released. However, WinRT should feel very familiar to Silverlight developers. Microsoft has attempted to make the transition from Silverlight applications to Windows Store applications pretty smooth.

C.5.3 *Micro Framework*

The Micro Framework (see http://mng.bz/D9qy) is a tiny implementation of .NET, designed to run on very constrained devices. It doesn't support generics, it's interpreted rather than JIT-compiled, and it ships with a limited set of classes, but it *does* include a presentation layer, built around WPF. In order to save space, you only need to deploy the parts of the framework you actually need—at its smallest, it can take up a mere 390 KB. Obviously, this is a somewhat niche area, but the ability to write managed code for embedded devices has great appeal. It won't be suitable for all situations—it's not a real-time system, for example—but where it's applicable, it's likely to dramatically improve developer productivity.

The release history hasn't followed that of the desktop framework at all: it was first seen in the SPOT watch in 2004, but version 1.0 was released in 2006. Since then it has iterated several times in rapid succession. Version 4.0 of the Micro Framework shipped on November 19, 2009—and in a move that still delights and surprises me, the majority of this version was released open source under the Apache 2.0 license. Some libraries, such as the TCP/IP stack and cryptography implementations, are still closed for various reasons; these companion libraries can be downloaded in binary form for specific architectures.

C.5.4 *Windows Runtime (WinRT)*

WinRT isn't another version of .NET—it's a whole new Windows platform, introduced in Windows 8. It aims to provide a sandboxed environment on both x86 and ARM processor architectures, and supports multiple languages—primarily C# and VB via .NET, C++/CX (a new flavor of C++ specifically targeting WinRT), and JavaScript. It's an unmanaged API, but it's designed to integrate very closely with .NET, so that C# and VB.NET developers can really use the same APIs as C++/CX and JavaScript developers. There's no need for a wrapper API to be built around it, as was the case for Win32 with Windows Forms. The API has been designed with asynchrony in mind right from the start; using asynchrony is the *natural* way of developing apps targeting WinRT.

As Windows 8 is a young operating system, we have yet to see how well this will pan out in the long run, and developers wanting to create apps to run on Windows 8 can still target the traditional desktop, but it's clear that Microsoft believes that WinRT is an important way forward for client-side development. In particular, the Windows Phone API and the Windows Store API are likely to converge more and more closely in the future.

C.6 *Summary*

With so many versions of so many different components, it's easy to get confused—and even easier to confuse someone else. As a final piece of advice (and I mean final—it's hard to sneak anything deep and meaningful into an index), I recommend that you try to be as clear as possible on this topic when communicating with others. If you're using anything other than the desktop framework, say so. If you're going to quote a version number, specify exactly what you mean—"3.0" could mean using C# 2.0 and .NET 3.0, or it could mean using C# 3.0 and .NET 3.5. Aside from anything else, after you've read this book, you have *absolutely no excuse* for claiming you're using "C# 3.5" or "C# 4.5" unless you're deliberately trying to wind me up.

index

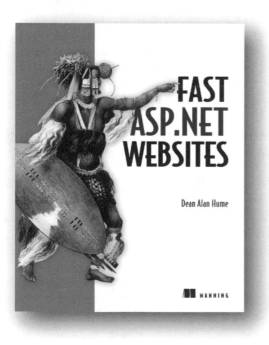